The Final Triumph of God

# The Final Triumph of God

*Jesus, the Eyewitnesses,
and the Resurrection of the Body
in 1 Corinthians 15*

James P. Ware

William B. Eerdmans Publishing Company
Grand Rapids, Michigan

Wm. B. Eerdmans Publishing Co.
2006 44th Street SE, Grand Rapids, MI 49508
www.eerdmans.com

© 2025 James P. Ware
All rights reserved
Published 2025

Book design by Lydia Hall

Printed in the United States of America

31  30  29  28  27  26  25     1  2  3  4  5  6  7

ISBN 978-0-8028-7947-9

**Library of Congress Cataloging-in-Publication Data**

A catalog record for this book is available from the Library of Congress.

*Contents*

| | | |
|---|---|---|
| | *Foreword* by A. Andrew Das | vii |
| | *List of Abbreviations* | xii |
| | *Bibliography* | xxix |
| | *Introduction:* The Unique Importance and Untapped Riches of Paul's Resurrection Chapter | 1 |
| 1. | Chapter 15 as the Culmination of 1 Corinthians | 11 |
| 2. | A Deepened Revelation of the Gospel (15:1–2) | 55 |
| 3. | The Cross and the Resurrection in the Apostolic Formula (15:3–4) | 66 |
| | *Excursus 1:* Purported Ancient Parallels to the Resurrection of Jesus | 98 |
| 4. | The Eyewitnesses in the Apostolic Formula (15:5–7) | 105 |
| 5. | Paul the Final Eyewitness in the Apostolic Formula (15:8–11) | 123 |
| | *Excursus 2:* The Implications of the Apostolic Formula for History and Faith | 143 |
| 6. | The Futility of Faith Apart from the Resurrection (15:12–19) | 154 |
| 7. | The Last Adam's Triumph over Death (15:20–23) | 190 |
| | *Excursus 3:* The Good News of the Resurrection in the World into Which It Came | 204 |

CONTENTS

| 8. | The Eternal Reign of the Father and the Son (15:24–28) | 211 |
| 9. | The Futility of Taking Up the Cross without the Resurrection (15:29–34) | 245 |
| 10. | The Philosophical Challenge to the Resurrection (15:35) | 267 |
| 11. | Testimonies within Creation to the Glorification of the Flesh (15:36–41) | 275 |
| | *Excursus 4:* Two False Trails Regarding Paul's Analogy of the Seed | 305 |
| 12. | The Glorified Body of the Resurrection (15:42–44a) | 310 |
| 13. | The Bestowal of the Holy Spirit by the Risen Son of God (15:44b–49) | 333 |
| 14. | The Mystery of the Glorification of the Flesh (15:50–53) | 367 |
| 15. | The Resurrection of the Body as the Final Triumph of God (15:54–58) | 392 |
| | *Acknowledgments* | 413 |
| | *Index of Authors* | 415 |
| | *Index of Subjects* | 423 |
| | *Index of Scripture and Other Ancient Texts* | 429 |

*Foreword*

James P. Ware's groundbreaking commentary on 1 Corinthians 15 is perhaps the most comprehensive to date. Not a page goes by without fresh, satisfying interpretations building on the best recent scholarly work. This rich volume remains accessible to the pastor, Bible study leader, or interested lay reader. While it is well researched, Ware cites only what is relevant to the text at hand and does not catalogue every ancient or modern source. This text-based approach models the wisdom of the late Abraham Malherbe, who admonished his Yale students to interpret texts from the inside out. One must never lose sight of the meanings of words, the grammatical features of a text, genre, similar features and parallels among contemporaries, and how the ideas fit together into a larger, cohesive whole.[1] So absorbed is Ware with the text—in the very best sense—that he does not offer concluding reflections. Perhaps I may indulge a friend by highlighting some of the treasures the reader will encounter in these pages.

Ware's text-based approach raises substantial questions for a new paradigm in Pauline studies. Historic Christianity interpreted the resurrected Jesus in 1 Cor 15 as endowed with an improved version of his earthly body but still flesh and bones, just as in the Gospels and Acts. As early as 1872, however, Hermann Lüdemann described the πνεῦμα ("spirit") of the resurrected "spiritual body" (σῶμα πνευματικόν) in 1 Cor 15:44 as consisting of "heavenly light substance" in agreement with Stoic patterns of thought.[2] Otto Pfleiderer likewise denied a fleshly resurrection, whether Jesus's or the believer's at the Last Day, favoring a "spiritual corporeity,"

---

1. E.g., Abraham J. Malherbe, "The Task and Method of Exegesis," *ResQ* 5 (1961): 169–78.
2. Hermann Lüdemann, *Die Anthropologie des Apostels Paulus und ihre Stellung innerhalb seiner Heilslehre: Nach den vier Hauptbriefen* (Kiel: Universitäts-Buchhandlung, 1872), 147–50.

a "heavenly light-substance."[3] Ernst Teichmann's 1896 book claimed a non-fleshly spiritual resurrection consisting of fine, pneumatic stuff.[4] By the mid-twentieth century, Rudolf Bultmann summarily claimed, "The accounts of the empty grave, of which Paul still knows nothing, are legends."[5]

Dale Martin's influential *The Corinthian Body* (1995) breathed new life into the claim, and Christ's "spiritual body" was quickly affirmed by Jeffrey Asher (2000), Peter Lampe (2002), and Troels Engberg-Pedersen (2009).[6] Even before Martin, Paula Fredriksen in 1991 had reached similar conclusions.[7] The resurrection will consist not of a body of flesh and bones, but of a light, ethereal "spiritual body." What has been emerging in the last few decades, then, has been a new paradigm for understanding the resurrection that would overturn historic Christian claims. The early Christian creeds would have drawn rightly on the Gospels and Acts but misunderstood the apostle Paul. "Flesh and blood cannot inherit the kingdom of God" (1 Cor 15:50).

Prominent voices have dissented: Richard B. Hays, Martin Hengel, N. T. Wright, and Volker Rabens.[8] Missing has been a careful, text-based study of 1 Cor 15. Enter James P. Ware. Ware points early on to vv. 5–8, a pre-Pauline confession of

---

3. Otto Pfleiderer, *Paulinism: A Contribution to the History of Primitive Christian Theology* (vol. 1, *Exposition of Paul's Doctrine*; trans. E. Peters; London: Williams & Norgate, 1877), 260; cf. 128, 201.

4. Ernst Teichmann, *Die paulinische Vorstellungen von Auferstehung und Gericht und ihre Beziehungen zur jüdischen Apokalyptik* (Freiburg: Mohr, 1896).

5. Rudolf Bultmann, *Theology of the New Testament* (trans. Kendrick Grobel; New York: Charles Scribner's Sons, 1951), 45; orig., *Theologie des Neuen Testaments* (9th ed.; Tübingen: Mohr Siebeck, 1984), 48: "Legende sind die Geschichten vom leeren Grabe, von dem Paulus noch nichts weiss."

6. Dale B. Martin, *The Corinthian Body* (New Haven: Yale University Press, 1995); Jeffrey R. Asher, *Polarity and Change in 1 Corinthians 15: A Study of Metaphysics, Rhetoric, and Resurrection* (HUT 42; Tübingen: Mohr Siebeck, 2000); Peter Lampe, "Paul's Concept of a Spiritual Body," in *Resurrection: Theological and Scientific Assessments* (ed. Ted Peters, Robert John Russell, and Michael Welker; Grand Rapids: Eerdmans, 2002), 103–14; Troels Engberg-Pedersen, "Complete and Incomplete Transformation in Paul—a Philosophical Reading of Paul on Body and Spirit," in *Metamorphoses: Resurrection, Body and Transformative Practices in Early Christianity* (ed. Turid Karlsen Seim and Jorum Okland; Berlin: de Gruyter, 2009), 123–46.

7. Paula Fredriksen, "Vile Bodies: Paul and Augustine on the Resurrection of the Flesh," in *Biblical Hermeneutics in Historical Perspective* (ed. Mark S. Burrows and Paul Rorem; Grand Rapids: Eerdmans, 1991), 75–87.

8. Richard B. Hays, *First Corinthians* (Interpretation; Louisville: Westminster John Knox, 1997), 270–75; Martin Hengel, "Das Begräbnis Jesu bei Paulus und die leibliche Auferstehung aus dem Grabe," in *Auferstehung—Resurrection* (ed. Friedrich Avemarie and Hermann Lichtenberger; WUNT 135; Tübingen: Mohr Siebeck, 2001), 119–83; N. T. Wright, *The Resurrection of the Son of God*, vol. 3 of *Christian Origins and the Question of God* (Minneapolis: Fortress, 2003),

*Foreword*

resurrection appearances that Ware dates to within two to five years of Jesus's death and resurrection (!), and as Ware demonstrates, 1 Cor 15 is the climax of the letter. From the very first chapters, Paul has been targeting the wisdom of the world that had made its way into the Corinthian congregation, a wisdom that categorically dismissed that flesh and bone will one day rise from the dead. Not even the Greek and Roman gods possessed such power. Whether in Greek antiquity (Homer, Hesiod, Aeschylus, Sophocles, Herodotus), the philosophical schools, or the mystery cults, corpses will remain just that, garbage according to the second-century Celsus. Paul draws attention in v. 35 to the mockery of the resurrection by "some" at Corinth (15:12, 34). This philosophy threatens to render the proclamation of Christ's death and resurrection "in vain" (15:2, 14, 17, 58).

A Stoic approach to the bodies of 1 Cor 15, Ware shows, just does not work. The verb "raise" (ἐγείρω) never means an assumption into heaven or transubstantiation into an ethereal state. Further, the Stoics defined *pneuma*/πνεῦμα in terms of the *sublunar*, airy heavens and *not* the celestial sphere. *No* ancient text identifies πνεῦμα with that sphere. For the Stoics, the planets and heavenly bodies were not made of pneumatic "stuff" but rather *divine fire*. Paul does not refer to "spirit-matter" elsewhere in his letters. The key, for Paul, is his innovative contrast of πνεῦμα with ψυχή, and the πνεῦμα remains *God's* Spirit. In vv. 42–44 a σῶμα ψυχικόν is changed into a σῶμα πνευματικόν. The *same subject* governs vv. 42–44; it is the *same* body. Body *x* does not metamorphosize to body *y*, but a perishable body *x* is changed to an imperishable body *x* in what is not a subtraction but an *addition*, an enhancement. A body enlivened or determined by its soul will enjoy an enlivening *also* by the Spirit in its return to life (contra Fredriksen). Paul therefore uses σάρξ to refer to a whole person apart from God's Spirit. For *x* to "change" (according to Paul's mystery), it must continue to exist. Similarly, the use of ψυχικός rules out a future ethereal body without flesh and bones. Even as the ψυχικός person of 1 Cor 2:14 *has* flesh and bones and is not just soul, the πνευματικός would have to be similarly endowed. The Spirit, enjoyed as a down payment (2 Cor 1:22; 5:5) or firstfruits (Rom 8:23) "in" the body, will be given directly "*to*" the resurrected body! The "life-giving Spirit" in v. 45 is not, then, astral stuff. As for "flesh and blood" not inheriting the kingdom of God in v. 50, one must consider the chiastic structure connecting this to v. 53, as Paul identifies "corruptibility" as the defining feature of "flesh and blood" (cf. Sir 14:17–18; 17:30–32; Matt 16:27; Gal 1:16; 1 En. 15.4; T. Ab. 13.7; cf. the *positive* "flesh and bones"). The mortal, corruptible body will be rendered

---

340–61; Volker Rabens, *The Holy Spirit and Ethics in Paul: Transformation and Empowering for Religious-Ethical Life* (WUNT 2.283; Tübingen: Mohr Siebeck, 2010).

incorruptible and immortal. In denying a fleshly resurrection, modern scholars have, ironically, joined the very ranks of those Paul opposed at Corinth.

Since this volume is a *commentary*, Ware is not just responding to the new Stoic paradigm in Pauline studies. He is also resolving perennial interpretive issues along the way, including the untimely birth of Paul, the baptism for the dead, and the supposed subordinationist Christology of the chapter. As for Paul's untimely birth (1 Cor 15:8), Ware dispenses with the notion that Paul received only a visionary experience of the risen Christ, against David Friedrich Strauss of old (*The Christ of Faith and the Jesus of History*, 1835) and Adela Yarbro Collins and Dale Allison of late.[9] Christ appeared to Paul as an ἐκτρώμα, prematurely cut short in the birthing process and *not* a late birth. Paul's birth had failed in the womb, and so he did not see Jesus in the same way as the others *before the ascension*. Even as they had *seen* the risen Jesus, so also had Paul, but lastly. He saw the *crucified* (1:23) one arisen!

In vv. 20–28 Paul looks forward to the moment when the Son submits to the Father, leading many to affirm a sort of modern Arianism, a nondivine, nonincarnational Christology (with James D. G. Dunn and Wayne Meeks), or even the eternal functional subordinationist Christologies of some modern evangelicals (e.g., Wayne Grudem).[10] Second Temple Judaism, however, never anticipated a temporary, interim reign of the coming Messiah but one that would last forever. "Until" (ἄχρι) does not necessarily point to the *end* of an action but an action's *goal*, in this case to deliver the kingdom to the Father. Paul never says the Son ceases to rule, nor do early Christian sources. The Father reigns *in* and *through* the Son! Paul ascribes descriptions, actions, and functions of the Father to the Son, often with both as subjects, and sometimes including also the "life-giving Spirit"— an early trinitarian theology on display. Ware documents the many biblical texts

---

9. Adela Yarbro Collins, "The Empty Tomb in the Gospel according to Mark," in *Hermes and Athena: Biblical Exegesis and Philosophical Theology* (ed. Eleonore Stump and Thomas P. Flint; Notre Dame: University of Notre Dame Press, 1993), 107–48, here 115–31; Adela Yarbro Collins, "Ancient Notions of Transferal and Apotheosis in Relation to the Empty Tomb Story in Mark," in *Metamorphoses: Resurrection, Body and Transformative Practices in Early Christianity* (ed. Turid Karlsen Seim and Jorunn Okland; Berlin: de Gruyter, 2009), 41–57; Dale C. Allison Jr., *The Resurrection of Jesus: Apologetics, Criticism, History* (New York: T&T Clark, 2021).

10. James D. G. Dunn, "1 Corinthians 15:45—Last Adam, Life-Giving Spirit," in *Christ and Spirit in the New Testament* (ed. Barnabas Lindars and Stephen S. Smalley; Cambridge: Cambridge University Press, 1973), 127–42; James D. G. Dunn, *The Theology of Paul the Apostle* (Grand Rapids: Eerdmans, 1998), 254–55, 261–65; Wayne A. Meeks, *Christ Is the Question* (Louisville: John Knox, 2006), 130–32; Wayne A. Grudem, *Systematic Theology* (2nd ed.; Grand Rapids: Zondervan, 2020), 301–18.

alluded to in the chapter, referring to Yahweh in the original, which Paul reapplies to Christ (e.g., Jer 9:23–24 in 1 Cor 15:31).

Paul asks in v. 29 about those "baptized for the sake of (ὑπέρ) the dead." The most common view, proxy baptism, is unattested in antiquity, except for Marcion's use of this verse. Nor is this a reference to Christians' being baptized in general, since Paul is identifying a *subset* of the faithful. Ultimately, Ware interprets this verse in its immediate context: Paul's own suffering and struggle with wild beasts at Ephesus (vv. 30–32) should be taken literally (anticlimactic if not) as Paul employs a word limited to arena combat (with which even Roman citizens sometimes had to contend). Thus Paul is pointing in v. 29 to people baptized in view of the dangers the martyrs faced. Whereas scholars such as Candida Moss have contended that early Christian martyrdom is largely a myth, if he is correct Ware is identifying the earliest reference to it, and even to arena combat.[11] At the end of the day, at the end of the age, as Augustine put it: "[Christ] came from heaven to be clothed with a body of earthly mortality, that He might clothe it with heavenly immortality" (*Civ.* 13.23; trans. Marcus Dods, *NPNF*[1] 2:258).

*A. Andrew Das*
*Niebuhr Distinguished Chair and Professor of Religious Studies*
*Elmhurst University*

---

11. Candida Moss, *The Myth of Persecution: How Early Christians Invented a Story of Martyrdom* (New York: HarperCollins, 2013).

# Abbreviations

Ancient Sources

Abbreviations of biblical books follow *The SBL Handbook of Style* (2d ed.) and (deuterocanonical books excepted) are not provided below.

    For text-critical symbols of New Testament manuscripts employed in this commentary see the introduction to E. Nestle and K. Aland, *Novum Testamentum Graece* (28th ed.).

*Deuterocanonical Books of the Old Testament*

| | |
|---|---|
| Ep Jer | Epistle of Jeremiah |
| 1 Esd | 1 Esdras |
| Jdt | Judith |
| 2 Macc | 2 Maccabees |
| Sir | Sirach |
| Tob | Tobit |
| Wis | Wisdom of Solomon |

*Pseudepigrapha and Other Ancient Jewish Sources*

| | |
|---|---|
| 2 Bar. | 2 Baruch |
| 1 En. | 1 Enoch |
| 2 En. | 2 Enoch |
| Jos. Asen. | Joseph and Aseneth |
| Josephus | |
|   *A.J.* | *Antiquitates judaicae* |

|              |                                          |
|--------------|------------------------------------------|
| *B.J.*       | *Bellum judaicum*                        |
| *Vita*       | *Vita*                                   |
| Jub.         | Jubilees                                 |
| 4 Macc.      | 4 Maccabees                              |
| Mart. Ascen. Isa. | Martyrdom and Ascension of Isaiah   |
| Philo        |                                          |
|   *Abr.*    | *De Abrahamo*                   |
|   *Agr.*    | *De agricultura*                |
|   *Conf.*   | *De confusione linguarum*       |
|   *Congr.*  | *De congressu eruditionis gratia* |
|   *Det.*    | *Quod deterius potiori insidari soleat* |
|   *Ebr.*    | *De ebrietate*                  |
|   *Gig.*    | *De gigantibus*                 |
|   *Ios.*    | *De Iosepho*                    |
|   *Leg.*    | *Legum allegoriae*              |
|   *Migr.*   | *De migratione Abrahami*        |
|   *Mos.*    | *De vita Mosis*                 |
|   *Mut.*    | *De mutatione nominum*          |
|   *Plant.*  | *De plantatione*                |
|   *Post.*   | *De posteritate Caini*          |
|   *Somn.*   | *De somniis*                    |
|   *Spec.*   | *De specialibus legibus*        |
|   *Virt.*   | *De virtutibus*                 |
| Pss. Sol.    | Psalms of Solomon                        |
| 1QH          | Thanksgiving Hymns                       |
| 4QMessAp     | Messianic Apocalypse                     |
| Sib. Or.     | Sibylline Oracles                        |
| T. Ab.       | Testament of Abraham                     |
| T. Benj.     | Testament of Benjamin                    |
| T. Job       | Testament of Job                         |
| T. Levi      | Testament of Levi                        |

*Greco-Roman Sources*

Achilles Tatius
  *Leuc. Clit.*    *Leucippe et Clitophon*
Aeschines
  *Tim.*    *In Timarchum*

## ABBREVIATIONS

Aeschylus
   *Cho.*          *Choephori*
   *Eum.*         *Eumenides*
Anth. pal.       Anthologia palatina
Appian
   *Bell. civ.*      *Bella civilia*
Apuleius
   *De deo Socr.*   *De deo Socratico*
   *Metam.*      *Metamorphoses*
Aretaeus
   *Sign. diut.*    *De causis et signis diuturnorum morborum*
Aristophanes
   *Eccl.*         *Ecclesiazusae*
   *Lys.*          *Lysistrata*
   *Nub.*         *Nubes*
   *Ran.*         *Ranae*
Aristotle
   *Cael.*         *De caelo*
   *Cat.*          *Categoriae*
   *De an.*        *De anima*
   *Eth. eud.*     *Ethica eudemia*
   *Eth. nic.*     *Ethica nicomachea*
   *Frag.*         *Fragmenta*
   *Gen. an.*      *De generatione animalium*
   *Gen. corr.*    *De generatione et corruptione*
   *Mag. mor.*    *Magna moralia*
   *Metaph.*      *Metaphysica*
   *Oec.*         *Oeconomica*
   *Part. an.*      *De partibus animalium*
   *Phys.*         *Physica*
   *Pol.*          *Politica*
Callimachus
   *Epigr.*        *Epigrammata*
   *Hymn Cer.*    *Hymnus in Cererem*
Catullus
   *Carm.*       *Carmina*
Cicero
   *Div.*          *De divinatione*
   *Fam.*         *Epistulae ad familiares*

|   |   |
|---|---|
| *Fin.* | *De finibus* |
| *Leg.* | *De legibus* |
| *Nat. d.* | *De natura deorum* |
| *Off.* | *De officiis* |
| *Rep.* | *De republica* |
| *Tusc.* | *Tusculanae disputationes* |

Cornutus
|   |   |
|---|---|
| *Nat. d.* | *De natura deorum* |

Demosthenes
|   |   |
|---|---|
| *Cor.* | *De corona* |
| *Timocr.* | *In Timocratem* |

Dio Cassius
|   |   |
|---|---|
| *Hist. rom.* | *Historiae romanae* |

Dio Chrysostom
|   |   |
|---|---|
| *4 Regn.* | *De regno iv* |
| *Socr.* | *De Socrate* |
| *Tumult.* | *De tumultu* |

Diodorus Siculus
|   |   |
|---|---|
| *Bib. hist.* | *Bibliotheca historica* |

Diogenes Laertius
|   |   |
|---|---|
| *Vit. phil.* | *Vitae philosophorum* |

Dionysius of Halicarnassus
|   |   |
|---|---|
| *Ant. rom.* | *Antiquitates romanae* |
| *Rhet.* | *Ars rhetorica* |

Epictetus
|   |   |
|---|---|
| *Diatr.* | *Diatribai* |
| *Ench.* | *Enchiridion* |

Epicurus
|   |   |
|---|---|
| *Ep. Her.* | *Epistula ad Herodotum* |

Euripides
|   |   |
|---|---|
| *Alc.* | *Alcestis* |
| *Andr.* | *Andromache* |
| *Bacch.* | *Bacchae* |
| *Frag.* | *Fragmenta* |
| *Hec.* | *Hecuba* |
| *Hel.* | *Helena* |
| *Iph. taur.* | *Iphigenia taurica* |

Galen
|   |   |
|---|---|
| *Const. art.* | *De constitutione artis medicae* |

## ABBREVIATIONS

Herodotus
   *Hist.*          *Historiae*
Hesiod
   *Op.*           *Opera et dies*
   *Theog.*       *Theogonia*
Hesychius
   *Lex.*          *Lexicon*
Hippocrates
   *Coac.*        *Praenotiones coacae*
   *Mul.*         *De morbis mulierum*
   *Nat. mul.*    *De natura muliebri*
   *Nat. puer.*   *De natura pueri*
   *Oct.*         *De octimestri partu*
*Hom. Aph.*     *Homeric Hymn to Aphrodite*
*Hom. Dem.*    *Homeric Hymn to Demeter*
*Hom. Dion.*    *Homeric Hymn to Dionysus*
Homer
   *Il.*           *Ilias*
   *Od.*          *Odyssea*
Hyginus
   *Fab.*          *Fabulae*
Isocrates
   *Antid.*       *Antidosis*
   *Archid.*      *Archidamus*
   *Ep.*           *Epistulae*
   *Evag.*        *Evagoras*
   *Hel. enc.*    *Helenae encomium*
   *Nic.*          *Nicocles*
   *Paneg.*      *Panegyricus*
   *Phil.*         *Philippus*
   *Plat.*         *Plataicus*
Lucian
   *Abdic.*       *Abdicatus*
   *Anach.*      *Anacharsis*
   *Dial. meretr.*  *Dialogi meretricii*
   *Dial. mort.*   *Dialogi mortuorum*
   *Fug.*         *Fugitivi*
   *Hermot.*     *Hermotimus*
   *Luct.*         *De luctu*

|   |   |
|---|---|
| *Peregr.* | *De morte Peregrini* |
| *Philops.* | *Philopseudes* |
| *Pisc.* | *Piscator* |
| *Pro imag.* | *Pro imaginibus* |
| *Rhet. praec.* | *Rhetorum praeceptor* |
| *Tyr.* | *Tyrannicida* |

Lucretius
|   |   |
|---|---|
| *Nat.* | *De rerum natura* |

Lysias
|   |   |
|---|---|
| *Caede Erat.* | *De caede Eratosthenis* |
| *C. Sim.* | *Contra Simonem* |
| *Epitaph.* | *Epitaphius* |
| *Erat.* | *In Eratosthenem* |
| *Or.* | *Orationes* |

Megasthenes
|   |   |
|---|---|
| *Frag.* | *Fragmenta* |

Ovid
|   |   |
|---|---|
| *Metam.* | *Metamorphoses* |

Pausanius
|   |   |
|---|---|
| *Descr.* | *Graeciae descriptio* |

Petronius
|   |   |
|---|---|
| *Satyr.* | *Satyricon* |

Philodemus
|   |   |
|---|---|
| *Mort.* | *De morte* |

Philostratus
|   |   |
|---|---|
| *Her.* | *Heroicus* |
| *Vit. Apoll.* | *Vita Apollonii* |

Pindar
|   |   |
|---|---|
| *Isthm.* | *Isthmionikai* |
| *Nem.* | *Nemeonikai* |
| *Ol.* | *Olympionikai* |
| *Pyth.* | *Pythionikai* |

Plato
|   |   |
|---|---|
| *Alc. maj.* | *Alcibiades major* |
| *Apol.* | *Apologia* |
| *Crit.* | *Crito* |
| *Euthyphr.* | *Euthyphro* |
| *Gorg.* | *Gorgias* |
| *Leg.* | *Leges* |

## ABBREVIATIONS

| | |
|---|---|
| *Parm.* | *Parmenides* |
| *Phaed.* | *Phaedo* |
| *Phaedr.* | *Phaedrus* |
| *Pol.* | *Politicus* |
| *Prot.* | *Protagoras* |
| *Resp.* | *Respublica* |
| *Theaet.* | *Theaetetus* |
| *Tim.* | *Timaeus* |

Pliny the Elder

| | |
|---|---|
| *Nat.* | *Naturalis historia* |

Plutarch

| | |
|---|---|
| *Cat. Min.* | *Cato Minor* |
| *Cons. ux.* | *Consolatio ad uxorem* |
| *Def. orac.* | *De defectu oraculorum* |
| *Dem.* | *Demosthenes* |
| *Fac.* | *De facie in orbe lunae* |
| *Fat.* | *De fato* |
| *Frag.* | *Fragmenta* |
| *Gen. Socr.* | *De genio Socratis* |
| *Is. Os.* | *De Iside et Osiride* |
| *Plac. philos.* | *De placita philosophorum* |
| *Pomp.* | *Pompeius* |
| *Quaest. conv.* | *Quaestionum convivialum* |
| *Rom.* | *Romulus* |
| *Sull.* | *Sulla* |
| *Vit. pud.* | *De vitioso pudore* |
| *Vit. X orat.* | *Vitae decem oratorum* |

Polybius

| | |
|---|---|
| *Hist.* | *Historiae* |

Pseudo-Apollodorus

| | |
|---|---|
| *Bibl.* | *Bibliotheca* |
| *Ep.* | *Epitome* |

Pseudo-Hippocrates

| | |
|---|---|
| *Ep.* | *Epistulae* |

Pseudo-Plato

| | |
|---|---|
| *Def.* | *Definitiones* |

Seneca

| | |
|---|---|
| *Ep.* | *Epistulae morales* |
| *Marc.* | *Ad Marciam de consolatione* |

|  |  |  |
|---|---|---|
| | *Polyb.* | *Ad Polybium de consolatione* |
| | *Prov.* | *De providentia* |
| Sextus Empiricus | | |
| | *Math.* | *Adversus mathematicos* |
| | *Pyr.* | *Pyrrhoniae hypotyposes* |
| Sophocles | | |
| | *El.* | *Elektra* |
| | *Trach.* | *Trachiniae* |
| Soranus | | |
| | *Gyn.* | *Gynaecia* |
| Strabo | | |
| | *Geogr.* | *Geographica* |
| Theognis | | |
| | *Eleg.* | *Elegiae* |
| Theophrastus | | |
| | *Caus. plant.* | *De causis plantarum* |
| | *Hist. plant.* | *Historia plantarum* |
| Thucydides | | |
| | *Hist.* | *Historiae* |
| Vergil | | |
| | *Aen.* | *Aeneid* |
| Xenophon | | |
| | *Cyn.* | *Cynegeticus* |
| | *Cyr.* | *Cyropaedia* |
| | *Mem.* | *Memorabilia* |
| | *Oec.* | *Oeconomicus* |

*Ancient Christian Sources*

|  |  |  |
|---|---|---|
| Ambrose | | |
| | *Ep.* | *Epistulae* |
| | *Spir.* | *De Spiritu Sancto* |
| Aristides | | |
| | *Apol.* | *Apologia* |
| Athanasius | | |
| | *C. Ar.* | *Orationes contra Arianos* |
| | *Inc.* | *De incarnatione* |
| Athenagoras | | |
| | *Leg.* | *Legatio pro Christianis* |
| | *Res.* | *De resurrectione* |

## ABBREVIATIONS

Augustine
- *Civ.* — *De civitate Dei*
- *Doctr. chr.* — *De doctrina christiana*
- *Faust.* — *Contra Faustum Manichaeum*
- *Tract. Ev. Jo.* — *In Evangelium Johannis tractatus*
- *Trin.* — *De Trinitate*

Barn. — Epistle of Barnabas

Basil of Caesarea
- *Ep.* — *Epistulae*
- *Spir.* — *De Spiritu Sancto*

Chrysostom
- *Hom. 1 Cor.* — *Homiliae in epistulam i ad Corinthios*

1 Clem. — 1 Clement
2 Clem. — 2 Clement

Clement of Alexandria
- *Paed.* — *Paedagogus*
- *Protr.* — *Protrepticus*
- *Strom.* — *Stromateis*

Const. ap. — Constitutiones apostolorum

Cyprian
- *Ep.* — *Epistulae*
- *Laps.* — *De lapsis*
- *Unit. eccl.* — *De catholicae ecclesiae unitate*

Cyril of Alexandria
- *Ador.* — *De adoratione*
- *Quod un.* — *Quod unus sit Christus*
- *Thes.* — *Thesaurus*

Cyril of Jerusalem
- *Cat.* — *Catecheses*

Did. Apost. — Didascalia Apostolorum
Diogn. — Epistle to Diognetus

Epiphanius
- *Ancor.* — *Ancoratus*

Eusebius
- *Dem. ev.* — *Demonstratio evangelica*
- *Hist. eccl.* — *Historia ecclesiastica*

Eustathius
- *Comm. Il.* — *Commentarii ad Homeri Iliadem*

| | |
|---|---|
| Gos. Phil. | Gospel of Philip |
| Gregory the Great | |
| *Moral.* | *Moralia in Job* |
| Gregory of Nazianzus | |
| *Ep.* | *Epistulae* |
| *Or.* | *Orationes* |
| Gregory of Nyssa | |
| *In illud* | *In illud: Tunc et ipse filius* |
| *Quod non* | *Quod non sint tres dei* |
| *Spir.* | *De Spiritu Sancto* |
| Herm. Mand. | Shepherd of Hermas, Mandates |
| Herm. Sim. | Shepherd of Hermas, Similitudes |
| Herm. Vis. | Shepherd of Hermas, Visions |
| Hilary | |
| *Trin.* | *De Trinitate* |
| Hippolytus | |
| *Noet.* | *Contra haeresin Noeti* |
| *Trad. ap.* | *Traditio apostolica* |
| Ign. *Eph.* | Ignatius, *To the Ephesians* |
| Ign. *Rom.* | Ignatius, *To the Romans* |
| Ign. *Smyrn.* | Ignatius, *To the Smyrnaeans* |
| Ign. *Trall.* | Ignatius, *To the Trallians* |
| Irenaeus | |
| *Epid.* | *Epideixis* |
| *Haer.* | *Adversus haereses* |
| Jerome | |
| *Comm. Isa.* | *Commentariorum in Isaiam libri XVIII* |
| *Epist.* | *Epistulae* |
| *Jo. Hier.* | *Adversus Joannem Hierosolymitanum liber* |
| *Jov.* | *Adversus Jovinianum libri II* |
| John of Damascus | |
| *Fid. orth.* | *De fide orthodoxa* |
| Justin Martyr | |
| *1 Apol.* | *Apologia i* |
| *Dial.* | *Dialogus cum Tryphone* |
| Mart. Pol. | Martyrdom of Polycarp |
| Methodius | |
| *Res.* | *De resurrectione* |

## ABBREVIATIONS

Minucius Felix
    Oct. — *Octavius*
Olympiodorus
    Comm. Job — *Commentarii in Job*
Origen
    Cels. — *Contra Celsum*
    Comm. Matt. — *Commentarium in evangelium Matthaei*
    Hom. Exod. — *Homiliae in Exodum*
    Princ. — *De principiis*
    Sel. Ps. — *Selecta in Psalmos*
Ps.-Clem. *Hom.* — Pseudo-Clementines, *Homilies*
Rufinus
    Symb. — *Commentarius in symbolum apostolorum*
Severian of Gabala
    Frag. 1 Cor. — *Fragmenta in epistulam i ad Corinthios*
Tatian
    Or. Graec. — *Oratio ad Graecos*
Tertullian
    An. — *De anima*
    Apol. — *Apologeticus*
    Bapt. — *De baptismo*
    Carn. Chr. — *De carne Christi*
    Marc. — *Adversus Marcionem*
    Mon. — *De monogamia*
    Praescr. — *De praescriptione haereticorum*
    Prax. — *Adversus Praxean*
    Pud. — *De pudicitia*
    Res. — *De resurrectione carnis*
    Virg. — *De virginibus velandis*
Theodoret
    Comm. 1 Cor. — *Interpretatio epistulae i ad Corinthios*
Theophilus of Antioch
    Autol. — *Ad Autolycum*
Zosimus of Panopolis
    Cheir. — *Cheirokmeta*

## Secondary Literature

| | |
|---|---|
| AB | Anchor Bible |
| Aquinas, *1 Cor.* | Aquinas, Thomas. *Super primam epistolam ad Corinthios*. In *Super epistolas S. Pauli lectura*. Edited by Cai Raffaele. 8th rev. ed. 2 vols. Turin, 1953 |
| Aquinas, *ST* | Aquinas, Thomas. *Summa Theologiae*. Edited by Petrus Caramello. 3 vols. Turin and Rome, 1952–1956 |
| *AUSS* | *Andrews University Seminary Studies* |
| BA | Bauer, W., K. Aland, and B. Aland. *Griechisch-deutsches Wörterbuch zu den Schriften des Neuen Testaments und der frühchristlichen Literatur*. 6th ed. Berlin, 1988 |
| *BBR* | *Bulletin for Biblical Research* |
| BDAG | Bauer, W., F. W. Danker, W. F. Arndt, and F. W. Gingrich. *A Greek-English Lexicon of the New Testament and other Early Christian Literature*. 3d ed. Chicago, 1999 |
| BDF | Blass, F., A. Debrunner, and R. W. Funk. *A Greek Grammar of the New Testament and Other Early Christian Literature*. Chicago, 1961 |
| BDR | Blass, F., A. Debrunner, and F. Rehkopf. *Grammatik des neutestamentlichen Griechisch*. 18th ed. Göttingen, 2001 |
| BECNT | Baker Exegetical Commentary on the New Testament |
| BECS | Brill Exegetical Commentary Series |
| BETL | Bibliotheca Ephemeridum Theologicarum Lovaniensium |
| BGBE | Beiträge zur Geschichte der biblischen Exegese |
| *Bib* | *Biblica* |
| *BibAn* | *The Biblical Annals* |
| *Bijdr* | *Bijdragen: Tijdschrift voor filosofie en theologie* |
| *BLE* | *Bulletin de littérature ecclésiastique* |
| *BSac* | *Bibliotheca Sacra* |
| BTCB | Brazos Theological Commentary on the Bible |
| *BZ* | *Biblische Zeitschrift* |
| BZNW | Beihefte zur Zeitschrift für die neutestamentliche Wissenschaft |
| *CBQ* | *Catholic Biblical Quarterly* |
| Calvin, *Inst.* | Calvin, John. *Institutio christianae religionis*. Vols. 3–5 of *Joannis Calvini opera selecta*. Edited by Peter Barth and Wilhelm Niesel. Munich, 1926–1952 |
| ConBNT | Coniectanea Biblica: New Testament Series |

ABBREVIATIONS

| | |
|---|---|
| Cremer | Cremer, H. *Biblico-Theological Lexicon of New Testament Greek*. 4th ed. Edinburgh, 1954 |
| *CTJ* | *Calvin Theological Journal* |
| *CTR* | *Criswell Theological Review* |
| *CurBR* | *Currents in Biblical Research* |
| *CurTM* | *Currents in Theology and Mission* |
| *DRev* | *Downside Review* |
| Dssm, *BS* | Deissmann, A. *Bible Studies*. Translated by A. Grieve. London, 1923 |
| EDNT | *Exegetical Dictionary of the New Testament*. Edited by H. Balz and G. Schneider. Grand Rapids, 1990–1993 |
| EKKNT | Evangelisch-Katholischer Kommentar zum Neuen Testament |
| ER | *The Encyclopedia of Religion*. Edited by L. Jones. 15 vols. 2d ed. New York, 2004 |
| ERT | *Evangelical Review of Theology* |
| ESEC | Emory Studies in Early Christianity |
| *EvQ* | *Evangelical Quarterly* |
| Frisk | Frisk, H. *Griechisches Etymologisches Wörterbuch*. 2 vols. Heidelberg, 1973 |
| GRBS | *Greek, Roman, and Byzantine Studies* |
| Greg | *Gregorianum* |
| HBT | *Horizons in Biblical Theology* |
| HNT | Handbuch zum Neuen Testament |
| HNTC | Harper's New Testament Commentaries |
| HTR | *Harvard Theological Review* |
| HUT | Hermeneutische Untersuchungen zur Theologie |
| *HvTSt* | *Hervormde teologiese studies* |
| IBC | Interpretation: A Bible Commentary for Teaching and Preaching |
| ICC | International Critical Commentary |
| *IDS* | *In die Skriflig* |
| IG | *Inscriptiones Graecae* |
| IGUR | *Inscriptiones Graecae Urbis Romae* |
| Int | *Interpretation* |
| *ITQ* | *Irish Theological Quarterly* |
| JAC | *Jahrbuch für Antike und Christentum* |
| JBL | *Journal of Biblical Literature* |
| JBQ | *Jewish Bible Quarterly* |
| JETS | *Journal of the Evangelical Theological Society* |
| JSHJ | *Journal for the Study of the Historical Jesus* |
| JSJ | *Journal for the Study of Judaism in the Persian, Hellenistic, and Roman Periods* |

| | |
|---|---|
| JSJSup | Journal for the Study of Judaism Supplements |
| *JSOT* | *Journal for the Study of the Old Testament* |
| *JSNT* | *Journal for the Study of the New Testament* |
| JSNTSup | Journal for the Study of the New Testament Supplement Series |
| *JSPL* | *Journal for the Study of Paul's Letters* |
| *JTS* | *Journal of Theological Studies* |
| KEK | Kritisch-exegetischer Kommentar über das Neue Testament |
| KJV | King James Version |
| Kühner-G. | Kühner, R., and B. Gerth. *Ausführliche Grammatik der Griechischen Sprache*. 3d ed. 2 parts in 4 vols. Hanover, 1892–1904 |
| *LB* | *Linguistica Biblica* |
| L&N | *Greek-English Lexicon of the New Testament: Based on Semantic Domains*. Edited by J. P. Louw and E. A. Nida. 2d ed. New York, 1989 |
| LNTS | Library of New Testament Studies |
| LSJ | Liddell, H. G., R. Scott, with R. S. Jones. *Greek-English Lexicon*. 9th ed. Oxford, 1940 |
| LUT | Lutherbibel (Luther Bible) |
| MM | Moulton, J. H., and G. Milligan. *The Vocabulary of the Greek Testament: Illustrated from the Papyri and Other Non-Literary Sources*. Grand Rapids, 1980 |
| Metzger | Metzger, B. M. *A Textual Commentary on the Greek New Testament*. 3d ed. New York, 1971 |
| *MTZ* | *Münchener theologische Zeitschrift* |
| NA[28] | *Novum Testamentum Graece*, Nestle-Aland, 28th ed. |
| NAB | New American Bible |
| NCBC | New Cambridge Bible Commentary. |
| *Neot* | *Neotestamentica* |
| NIGTC | New International Greek Testament Commentary |
| *NovT* | *Novum Testamentum* |
| NovTSup | Novum Testamentum Supplements |
| *NPNF*[1] | *Nicene and Post-Nicene Fathers*, Series 1 |
| NRSV | New Revised Standard Version |
| *NTS* | *New Testament Studies* |
| OCD | *Oxford Classical Dictionary*. Edited by N. G. L. Hammond and H. H. Scullard. 2d ed. Oxford, 1970 |
| POuT | De Prediking van het Oude Testament |
| *ProEccl* | *Pro Ecclesia* |
| PTMS | Pittsburgh Theological Monograph Series |
| QD | Quaestiones Disputatae |
| *RB* | *Revue biblique* |

## ABBREVIATIONS

| | |
|---|---|
| *ResQ* | *Restoration Quarterly* |
| *RevScRel* | *Revue des sciences religieuses* |
| Rob., *Gram.* | Robertson, A. T. *A Grammar of the Greek New Testament in the Light of Historical Research.* 4th ed. Nashville, 1934 |
| Robinson | Robinson, E. *A Greek-English Lexicon of the New Testament.* London, 1852 |
| *SBET* | *Scottish Bulletin of Evangelical Theology* |
| SBLDS | Society of Biblical Literature Dissertation Series |
| SBLSBS | Society of Biblical Literature Sources for Biblical Study |
| SBLStBL | Society of Biblical Literature Studies in Biblical Literature |
| SBLSymS | Society of Biblical Literature Symposium Series |
| SBR | Studies of the Bible and Its Reception |
| SBT | Studies in Biblical Theology |
| *ScES* | *Science et esprit* |
| Schmidt, *Syn.* | Schmidt, J. H. H. *Synonymik der Griechischen Sprache.* 4 vols. Leipzig, 1876–1886 |
| *SJOT* | *Scandinavian Journal of the Old Testament* |
| *SJT* | *Scottish Journal of Theology* |
| Smyth | Smyth, H. W. *Greek Grammar.* Revised by G. M. Messing. Cambridge, 1956 |
| SNTSMS | Society for New Testament Studies Monograph Series |
| SP | Sacra Pagina |
| *SPhilo* | *Studia Philonica* |
| SPL | *Synopsis of the Pauline Letters in Greek and English.* J. Ware. Grand Rapids, 2010 |
| ST | *Summa Theologiae* |
| StBibAnt | *Studies in the Bible and Antiquity* |
| SVF | *Stoicorum Veterum Fragmenta.* Edited by H. von Arnim. 4 vols. Berlin, 1978 |
| *SwJT* | *Southwestern Journal of Theology* |
| TDNT | *Theological Dictionary of the New Testament.* Edited by G. Kittel and G. Friedrich. Translated by G. W. Bromiley. 10 vols. Grand Rapids, 1964–1976 |
| TGST | Tesi Gregoriana, Serie Teologia |
| Thayer | Thayer, J. H. *A Greek-English Lexicon of the New Testament.* 4th ed. Grand Rapids, 1977 |
| *Them* | *Themelios* |
| ThH | Théologie historique |
| THKNT | Theologischer Handkommentar zum Neuen Testament |

| | |
|---|---|
| *TLNT* | *Theological Lexicon of the New Testament.* C. Spicq. Translated and edited by James D. Ernest. 3 vols. Peabody, 1994 |
| TNTC | Tyndale New Testament Commentaries |
| Trench, *Syn.* | Trench, R. C. *Synonyms of the New Testament.* 9th ed. Grand Rapids, 1953 |
| *TS* | *Theological Studies* |
| *TynBul* | *Tyndale Bulletin* |
| *TZ* | *Theologische Zeitschrift* |
| *VC* | *Vigiliae Christianae* |
| VTSup | Vetus Testamentum Supplements |
| *WTJ* | *Westminster Theological Journal* |
| WUNT | Wissenschaftliche Untersuchungen zum Neuen Testament |
| *WW* | *Word and World* |
| *ZNW* | *Zeitschrift für die neutestamentliche Wissenschaft und die Kunde der älteren Kirche* |
| *ZTK* | *Zeitschrift für Theologie und Kirche* |

# *Bibliography*

Throughout this work, modern commentaries on 1 Corinthians are cited simply by author surname and page number. Several standard works of reference are also cited only by author surname in either full or shortened form. The latter are also included in the list of abbreviations.

## COMMENTARIES ON 1 CORINTHIANS

Aquinas, Thomas. *Super primam epistolam ad Corinthios*. In *Super epistolas S. Pauli lectura*. Edited by Cai Raffaele. 8th rev. ed. 2 vols. Turin: Marietti, 1953.
Barrett, C. K. *A Commentary on the First Epistle to the Corinthians*. HNTC. New York: Harper & Row, 1968.
Bender, Kimlyn J. *1 Corinthians*. BTCB. Grand Rapids: Brazos, 2022.
Ciampa, Roy E., and Brian S. Rosner. *The First Letter to the Corinthians*. Grand Rapids: Eerdmans, 2010.
Collins, Raymond F. *First Corinthians*. SP 7. Collegeville, MN: Liturgical, 1999.
Conzelmann, Hans. *1 Corinthians*. Translated by J. W. Leitch. Hermeneia. Philadelphia: Fortress, 1975.
Ellicott, Charles J. *St. Paul's First Epistle to the Corinthians*. London: Longmans & Green, 1887.
Ellis, E. Earle. *1 Corinthians: A Commentary*. Edited by Terry L. Wilder. London: T&T Clark, 2022.
Fee, Gordon D. *The First Epistle to the Corinthians*. Rev. ed. Grand Rapids: Eerdmans, 2014.
Fitzmyer, Joseph A. *First Corinthians*. AB 32. New Haven: Yale University Press, 2008.
Garland, David E. *1 Corinthians*. BECNT. Grand Rapids: Baker Academic, 2003.

Godet, Frédéric L. *Commentary on the First Epistle to the Corinthians*. Translated by A. Cusin. 2 vols. Edinburgh: T&T Clark, 1886–1887.
Hays, Richard B. *First Corinthians*. IBC. Louisville: Knox, 1997.
Keener, Craig S. *1–2 Corinthians*. NCBC. Cambridge: Cambridge University Press, 2005.
Lang, Friedrich. *Die Briefe an die Korinther*. Göttingen: Vandenhoeck & Ruprecht, 1986.
Lightfoot, J. B. *Notes on the Epistles of St. Paul*. Peabody, MA: Hendrickson, 1993.
Lindemann, Andreas. *Der Erste Korintherbrief*. HNT 9.1. Tübingen: Mohr Siebeck, 2000.
Morris, Leon. *The First Epistle of Paul to the Corinthians*. 2d ed. TNTC. Grand Rapids: Eerdmans, 1985.
Reasoner, Mark. *1 Corinthians*. BECS. Leiden: Brill, forthcoming.
Robertson, Archibald, and Alfred Plummer. *A Critical and Exegetical Commentary on the First Epistle of St Paul to the Corinthians*. ICC. New York: Scribner's, 1911.
Sampley, J. Paul. "The First Letter to the Corinthians." Pages 10:771–1003 in *The New Interpreter's Bible*. Nashville: Abingdon, 2001.
Schrage, Wolfgang. *Der erste Brief an die Korinther (1Kor 15,1–16,24)*. EKKNT 7.4. Zurich: Benziger, 2001.
Schreiner, Thomas R. *1 Corinthians*. TNTC 7. Downers Grove, IL: IVP Academic, 2018.
Senft, Christophe. *La première épître de Saint Paul aux Corinthiens*. 2d ed. Geneva: Labor et Fides, 1990.
Thiselton, Anthony C. *The First Epistle to the Corinthians*. NIGTC. Grand Rapids: Eerdmans, 2000.
Weiss, Johannes. *Der erste Korintherbrief*. 9th ed. KEK. Göttingen: Vandenhoeck & Ruprecht, 1910.
Wolff, Christian. *Der erste Brief des Paulus an die Korinther*. 3d ed. THKNT 7. Leipzig: Evangelische Verlagsanstalt, 2011.

## Other Works

Achtemeier, Paul J. "The Continuing Quest for Coherence in St. Paul: An Experiment in Thought." Pages 132–45 in *Theology and Ethics in Paul and His Interpreters*. Edited by Eugene H. Lovering Jr. and Jerry L. Sumney. Nashville: Abingdon, 1996.
Ackerman, David A. *Lo, I Tell You a Mystery: Cross, Resurrection, and Paraenesis in the Rhetoric of 1 Corinthians*. PTMS 54. Eugene, OR: Pickwick, 2006.
Ahern, Barnabas. "The Indwelling Spirit, Pledge of Our Inheritance (Eph 1:14)." *CBQ* 9 (1947): 179–89.
Allison, Dale C., Jr. *The Resurrection of Jesus: Apologetics, Polemics, History*. New York: Bloomsbury, 2021.
Altermath, François. *Du corps psychique au corps spirituel: Interprétation de 1 Cor. 15,35–*

49 par les auteurs chrétiens des quatre premiers siècles. BGBE 18. Tübingen: Mohr Siebeck, 1977.

Aquinas, Thomas. *Summa Theologiae*. Edited by Peter Caramello. 3 vols. Turin and Rome: Marietti, 1952–1956.

Arnim, Hans von, ed. *Stoicorum Veterum Fragmenta*. 1905–1924. 4 vols. Berlin: de Gruyter, 1978.

Asher, Jeffrey R. *Polarity and Change in 1 Corinthians 15: A Study of Metaphysics, Rhetoric, and Resurrection*. Tübingen: Mohr Siebeck, 2000.

———. "ΣΠΕΙΡΕΤΑΙ: Paul's Anthropogenic Metaphor in 1 Corinthians 15:42–44." *JBL* 120 (2001): 101–22.

Bachmann, Michael. "1Kor 15,12f.: Resurrection of the Dead (= Christians)?" *ZNW* 92 (2001): 295–99.

———. "Zur Gedankenführung in 1. Kor. 15, 12ff." *TZ* 34 (1978): 265–76.

Bailey, J. W. "The Temporary Messianic Reign in the Literature of Early Judaism." *JBL* 53 (1934): 170–87.

Bailey, Kenneth E. "The Structure of 1 Corinthians and Paul's Theological Method with Special Reference to 4:17." *NovT* 25 (1983): 152–81.

Baird, William. "'One against the Other': Intra-Church Conflict in 1 Corinthians." Pages 116–36 in *The Conversation Continues: Studies in Paul and John*. Edited by J. L. Martyn and R. Fortna. Nashville: Abingdon, 1990.

Ballard, C. Andrew. *To Know All Mysteries: The Mystagogue Figure of Classical Antiquity and in Saint Paul's Letters to the Corinthians*. Paul in Critical Contexts. Lanham, MD: Lexington Books/Fortress Academic, 2022.

Barclay, John M. G. "The Resurrection in Contemporary New Testament Scholarship." Pages 13–30 in *Resurrection Reconsidered*. Edited by Gavin D'Costa. Oxford: Oneworld, 1996.

Barth, Karl. *The Resurrection of the Dead*. Translated by H. J. Stenning. 1933. Repr., Eugene, OR: Wipf & Stock, 2003.

Barthélemy, Dominique. *Les devanciers d'Aquila*. VTSup 10. Leiden: Brill, 1963.

Bauckham, Richard. *Jesus and the Eyewitnesses: The Gospels as Eyewitness Testimony*. Grand Rapids: Eerdmans, 2006.

Bauer, Walter, K. Aland, and B. Aland. *Griechisch-deutsches Wörterbuch zu den Schriften des Neuen Testaments und der frühchristlichen Literatur*. 6th ed. Berlin: de Gruyter, 1988.

Bauer, Walter, F. W. Danker, W. F. Arndt, and F. W. Gingrich. *A Greek-English Lexicon of the New Testament and Other Early Christian Literature*. 3d ed. Chicago: University of Chicago, 2000.

Baur, F. C. "Die Christus Partei in der korinthischen Gemeinde." *Tübinger Zeitschrift für Theologie* 5 (1831): 61–206.

Becker, Jürgen. *Die Auferstehung Jesu Christi nach dem Neuen Testament: Ostererfahrung und Osterverständnis im Urchristentum.* Tübingen: Mohr Siebeck, 2007.

BeDuhn, Jason David. "'Because of the Angels': Unveiling Paul's Anthropology in 1 Corinthians 11." *JBL* 118 (1999): 295–320.

Beers, Holly. *The Followers of Jesus as the 'Servant': Luke's Model from Isaiah for the Disciples in Luke-Acts.* LNTS 535. London: Bloomsbury T&T Clark, 2015.

———. "The Servant(s) in Luke-Acts." Pages 189–207 in *Isaiah's Servants in Early Judaism and Christianity: The Isaian Servant and the Exegetical Formation of Community Identity.* Edited by Michael A Lyons and Jacob Stromberg. WUNT 2.554. Tübingen: Mohr Siebeck, 2021.

Bell, Richard H. "The Resurrection Appearances in 1 Corinthians 15." In *Epiphanies of the Divine in the Septuagint and the New Testament.* Edited by Roland Deines and Mark Wreford. Tübingen: Mohr Siebeck, 2024.

Belleville, Linda L. "Continuity or Discontinuity: A Fresh Look at 1 Corinthians in the Light of First-Century Epistolary Forms and Conventions." *EvQ* 59 (1987): 15–37.

———. "Paul's Christological Use of the Exodus-Wilderness Rock Tradition in 1 Corinthians 10:4." Pages 129–39 in *Scripture, Texts, and Tracings in 1 Corinthians.* Edited by Linda L. Belleville and B. J. Oropeza. Lanham, MD: Lexington/Fortress, 2019.

Bergeron, Joseph W., and Gary R. Habermas. "The Resurrection of Jesus: A Clinical Review of Psychiatric Hypotheses for the Biblical Story of Easter." *ITQ* 80 (2015): 157–72.

Beuken, W. A. M. *Jesaja.* 4 vols. POuT. Nijkerk: Callenbach, 1979–1989.

———. "The Main Theme of Trito-Isaiah: 'The Servants of YHWH.'" *JSOT* 47 (1990): 67–87.

Bird, Michael F. "Justified by Christ's Resurrection: A Neglected Aspect of Paul's Doctrine of Justification." *SBET* 22 (2004): 72–91.

Bishop, Eric F. F. "The Risen Christ and the Five Hundred Brethren (1 Cor 15,6)." *CBQ* 18 (1956): 341–44.

Bjerkelund, Carl J. *Parakalô: Form, Funktion und Sinn der Parakalô-Sätze in den paulinischen Briefen.* Oslo: Universitetsforlaget, 1967.

Blass, Friedrich, Albert Debrunner, and Friedrich Rehkopf. *Grammatik des neutestamentlichen Griechisch.* 18th ed. Göttingen: Vandenhoeck & Ruprecht, 2001.

Blenkinsopp, Joseph. "The Servant and the Servants in Isaiah and the Formation of the Book." Pages 1:155–75 in *Writing and Reading the Scroll of Isaiah: Studies of an Interpretive Tradition.* Edited by Craig C. Broyles and Craig A. Evans. 2 vols. Leiden: Brill, 1997.

Bockmuehl, Markus. *Revelation and Mystery in Ancient Judaism and Pauline Christianity.* WUNT 2.36. Tübingen: Mohr Siebeck, 1990.

Boer, Martinus C. de. "The Composition of 1 Corinthians." *NTS* 40 (1994): 229–45.

———. *The Defeat of Death: Apocalyptic Eschatology in 1 Corinthians 15 and Romans 5.* JSNTSup 22. 1988. Repr., London: T&T Clark, 2019.

———. "Paul's Use of a Resurrection Tradition in 1 Cor 15,20–28." Pages 639–51 in *The Corinthian Correspondence*. Edited by R. Bieringer. BETL 75. Leuven: Peeters, 1996.

Bolt, Peter G. "Life, Death, and the Afterlife in the Greco-Roman World." Pages 51–79 in *Life in the Face of Death: The Resurrection Message of the New Testament*. Edited by Richard N. Longenecker. Grand Rapids: Eerdmans, 1998.

Bonneau, Normand. "The Logic of Paul's Argument on the Resurrection Body in 1 Cor 15:35–44a." *ScEs* 45 (1993): 79–92.

Borg, Marcus J. "The Truth of Easter." Pages 129–42 in Marcus J. Borg and N. T. Wright, *The Meaning of Jesus: Two Visions*. San Francisco: HarperSanFrancisco, 1999.

Borland, James A. "The Meaning and Identification of God's Eschatological Trumpets." Pages 63–73 in *Looking into the Future: Evangelical Studies in Eschatology*. Edited by David W. Baker. Grand Rapids: Baker Academic, 2001.

Bostock, D. Gerald. "Osiris and the Resurrection of Christ." *ExpTim* 112 (2001): 265–71.

Bowen, Clayton R. "'I Fought with Beasts at Ephesus.'" *JBL* 42 (1923): 59–68.

Braun, Herbert. "Das 'Stirb und Werde' in der Antike und im Neuen Testament." Pages 136–58 in *Gesammelte Studien zum Neuen Testament und seiner Umwelt*. Tübingen: Mohr Siebeck, 1962.

Bremmer, Jan N. *The Rise and Fall of the Afterlife: The 1995 Reed-Tucker Lectures at the University of Bristol*. London: Routledge, 2002.

Briggman, Anthony. "Spirit-Christology in Irenaeus: A Closer Look." *VC* 66 (2012): 1–19.

Brodeur, Scott. *The Holy Spirit's Agency in the Resurrection of the Dead: An Exegetico-Theological Study of 1 Corinthians 15,44b–49 and Romans 8,9–13*. TGST 14. Rome: Gregorian University Press, 2004.

Brookins, Timothy A. *Corinthian Wisdom, Stoic Philosophy, and the Ancient Economy*. SNTSMS 159. Cambridge: Cambridge University Press, 2014.

———. "Reconsidering the Coherence of 1 Corinthians 1:10–4:21." *NovT* 62 (2020): 139–56.

———. *Rediscovering the Wisdom of the Corinthians: Paul, Stoicism, and Spiritual Hierarchy*. Grand Rapids: Eerdmans, 2024.

Brown, Paul J. *Bodily Resurrection and Ethics in 1 Cor 15: Connecting Faith and Morality in the Context of Greco-Roman Mythology*. WUNT 2.360. Tübingen: Mohr Siebeck, 2014.

Brown, Raymond. *The Semitic Background of the Term "Mystery" in the New Testament*. Philadelphia: Fortress, 1968.

———. *The Virginal Conception and Bodily Resurrection of Jesus*. New York: Paulist, 1973.

Bruce, F. F. *Paul: Apostle of the Heart Set Free*. Grand Rapids: Eerdmans, 2000.

Bryan, Christopher. *The Resurrection of the Messiah*. Oxford: Oxford University Press, 2011.

Bucher, Theodor G. "Auferstehung Christi und Auferstehung der Toten." *MTZ* 27 (1976): 1–32.

———. "Die logische Argumentation in 1. Korinther 15,12–20." *Bib* 55 (1974): 465–86.

———. "Nochmals zur Beweisführung in 1. Korinther 15,12–20." *TZ* 36 (1980): 129–52.

Bultmann, Rudolf. *Theologie des Neuen Testaments*. 9th ed. Tübingen: Mohr Siebeck, 1984.

Bünker, Michael. *Briefformular und rhetorische Disposition im 1 Korintherbrief*. Göttingen: Vandenhoeck & Ruprecht, 1983.

Burchard, C. "1 Korinther 15,39–41." *ZNW* 75 (1984): 235–58.

Burgess, Jonathan S. *The Death and Afterlife of Achilles*. Baltimore: Johns Hopkins University Press, 2009.

Burnett, David A. "A Neglected Deuteronomic Scriptural Matrix for the Nature of the Resurrection Body in 1 Corinthians 15:39–42?" Pages 187–211 in *Scripture, Texts, and Tracings in 1 Corinthians*. Edited by Linda L. Belleville and B. J. Oropeza. Lanham, MD: Lexington/Fortress, 2019.

Bynum, Caroline Walker. *The Resurrection of the Body in Western Christianity, 200–1336*. New York: Columbia University Press, 1999.

Byrne, Brendan. "Eschatologies of Resurrection and Destruction: The Biblical Significance of Paul's Dispute with the Corinthians." *DRev* 104 (1986): 288–98.

Calvin, John. *Institutio christianae religionis*. Vols. 3–5 of *Joannis Calvini opera selecta*. Edited by Peter Barth and Wilhelm Niesel. Munich: Kaiser, 1926–1952.

Campbell, Constantine R. *Paul and the Hope of Glory: An Exegetical and Theological Study*. Grand Rapids: Zondervan Academic, 2020.

Carr, Frederick David. "Beginning at the End: The Kingdom of God in 1 Corinthians." *CBQ* 81 (2019): 449–69.

Cerfaux, L. *Christ in the Theology of St. Paul*. New York: Herder & Herder, 1959.

Chadwick, Henry. "Origen, Celsus, and the Resurrection of the Body." *HTR* 41 (1948): 83–102.

Chilton, Bruce D. *Resurrection Logic: How Jesus' First Followers Believed God Raised Him from the Dead*. Waco: Baylor University Press, 2019.

Ciampa, Roy E., and Brian S. Rosner. "The Structure and Argument of 1 Corinthians: A Biblical/Jewish Approach." *NTS* 52 (2006): 205–18.

Classen, Carl Joachim. *Rhetorical Criticism of the New Testament*. Leiden: Brill, 2002.

Claudel, Gërard. *La confession de Pierre. Trajectoire d'une péricope évangélique*. Paris: Gabalda, 1988.

Conzelmann, Hans. "On the Analysis of the Confessional Formula in 1 Corinthians 15:3–5." *Int* 20 (1966): 15–25.

Cook, John Granger. "1 Cor 15:33: The Status Quaestionis." *NovT* 62 (2020): 375–91.
———. "1 Cor 15,40–41: Paul and the Heavenly Bodies." *ZNW* 113 (2022): 159–79.
———. *Empty Tomb, Resurrection, Apotheosis*. WUNT 410. Tübingen: Mohr Siebeck, 2018.
———. "A Naked Seed: Platonism, Stoicism, or Agriculture in 1 Cor 15,37." *ZNW* 111 (2020): 289–309.
———. "Philo's *Quaestiones et solutiones in Genesin* 4.102 and 1 Cor 10:3: The πνευματικὸν βρῶμα." *NovT* 59 (2017): 384–89.
———. "Philo's *Quaestiones in Genesin* and Paul's σῶμα πνευματικόν." Pages 303–21 in *Alexandria: Hub of the Ancient World*. Edited by Benjamin Schliesser, Jan Rüggemeier, Thomas J. Kraus, and Jörg Frey. Tübingen: Mohr Siebeck, 2021.
———. "Resurrection in Paganism and the Question of an Empty Tomb in 1 Corinthians 15." *NTS* 63 (2017): 56–75.
Coppins, Wayne. "Doing Justice to the Two Perspectives of 1 Corinthians 15,1–11." *Neot* 44 (2010): 282–91.
Cover, Michael Benjamin. "The Divine Comedy at Corinth: Paul, Menander and the Rhetoric of Resurrection." *NTS* 64 (2018): 532–50.
Cremer, Hermann. *Biblico-Theological Lexicon of New Testament Greek*. 4th ed. Edinburgh: T&T Clark, 1954.
Crossan, John Dominic. *Jesus: A Revolutionary Biography*. San Francisco: HarperOne, 2009.
Crouzel, Henri. "La doctrine origènienne du corps réssuscité." *BLE* 31 (1980): 175–200, 241–66.
Cullmann, Oscar. *Peter: Disciple, Apostle, Martyr. A Historical and Theological Essay*. Translated by Floyd V. Filson. Philadelphia: Westminster, 1953.
Dahl, M. E. *The Resurrection of the Body: A Study of 1 Corinthians 15*. SBT 36. London: SCM, 1962.
Dahl, Nils. "Paul and the Church at Corinth according to I Corinthians 1–4." Pages 40–61 in *Studies in Paul: Theology for the Early Christian Mission*. Minneapolis: Augsburg, 1977.
Dale, Jeffrey M. "First Corinthians as an Eschatological Counter to Spiritualizing Tendencies." *Conversations with the Biblical World* 37 (2018): 76–98.
Davis, Stephen T. "'Seeing' the Risen Jesus." Pages 126–47 in *The Resurrection: An Interdisciplinary Symposium on the Resurrection of Jesus*. Edited by Stephen T. Davis, Daniel Kendall, and Gerald O'Collins. Oxford: Oxford University Press, 1997.
Dawes, G. W. "'But If You Can Gain Your Freedom' (1 Corinthians 7:17–24)." *CBQ* 52 (1990): 681–97.
Deissmann, G. Adolf. *Bible Studies*. Translated by Alexander Grieve. London: T&T Clark, 1923.

BIBLIOGRAPHY

DeMaris, Richard E. "Corinthian Religion and Baptism for the Dead (1 Corinthians 15:29): Insights from Archaeology and Anthropology." *JBL* 114 (1995): 661–82.

Dempster, Stephen. "From Slight Peg to Cornerstone to Capstone: The Resurrection of Christ on 'The Third Day' According to the Scriptures." *WTJ* (2014): 371–409.

Derickson, Gary W. "Incarnational Explanation for Jesus' Subjection in the Eschaton." Pages 217–32 in *Looking into the Future: Evangelical Studies in Eschatology*. Edited by David W. Baker. Grand Rapids: Baker Academic, 2001.

Doole, J. Andrew. "'I Have Fought with Wild Beasts . . . But I Will Stay Until Pentecost': What (Else) Can 1 Corinthians Teach Us about Ephesus?" *NovT* 60 (2018): 140–61.

Doty, William G. *Letters in Primitive Christianity*. Philadelphia: Fortress, 1973.

Downing, F. Gerald. *Cynics, Paul, and the Pauline Churches*. London: Routledge, 1998.

Dunn, James D. G. "1 Corinthians 15:45—Last Adam, Life-Giving Spirit." Pages 127–41 in *Christ and Spirit in the New Testament*. Edited by Barnabas Lindars and Stephen S. Smalley. Cambridge: Cambridge University Press, 1973.

———. "How Are the Dead Raised? With What Body Do They Come? Reflections on 1 Corinthians 15." *SwJT* 45 (2002): 4–18.

———. *The Theology of Paul the Apostle*. Grand Rapids: Eerdmans, 1998.

Dunsch, Boris. "Menander bei Paulus: Oralität, Performanz und Zituationstechnik im Corpus Paulinum." *JAC* 53 (2010): 5–19.

Dykstra, William. "1 Corinthians 15:20–28, An Essential Part of Paul's Argument against Those Who Deny the Resurrection." *CTJ* 4 (1969): 195–211.

Eadie, John. *A Commentary on the Greek Text of the Epistle of Paul to the Galatians*. London: Griffin, 1869.

Eckstein, Hans-Joachim. "Die Wirklichkeit der Auferstehung Jesu: Lukas 24,34 als Beispiel früher formelhafter Zeugnisse." Pages 1–29 in *Die Wirklichkeit der Auferstehung*. Edited by Hans-Joachim Eckstein and Michael Welker. Neukirchen-Vluyn: Neukirchener, 2002.

Eijk, A. H. C. van. "Resurrection-Language: Its Various Meanings in Early Christian Literature." *Studia Patristica* 12.1 (1975): 271–76.

Ellis, E. Earle. "*Soma* in 1 Corinthians." *Int* 44 (1990): 132–44.

Endsjø, Dag Øistein. *Greek Resurrection Beliefs and the Success of Christianity*. New York: Macmillan, 2009.

———. "Immortal Bodies, before Christ: Bodily Continuity in Ancient Greece and 1 Corinthians." *JSNT* 30 (2008): 417–36.

Engberg-Pedersen, Troels. "Complete and Incomplete Transformation in Paul—A Philosophical Reading of Paul on Body and Spirit." Pages 123–46 in *Metamorphoses: Resurrection, Body and Transformative Practices in Early Christianity*. Edited by Turid Karlsen Seim and Jorunn Økland. Berlin: de Gruyter, 2009.

———. *Cosmology and Self in the Apostle Paul: The Material Spirit*. Oxford: Oxford University Press, 2010.

———. "The Material Spirit: Cosmology and Ethics in Paul." *NTS* 55 (2009): 179–97.

Eriksson, Anders. "Fear of Eternal Damnation: *Pathos* Appeal in 1 Corinthians 15 and 16." Pages 115–26 in *Paul and Pathos*. Edited by Thomas H. Olbricht and Jerry L. Sumney. SBLSBS 16. Atlanta: Scholars, 2001.

———. *Traditions as Rhetorical Proof: Pauline Argumentation in 1 Corinthians*. ConBNT 29. Stockholm: Almqvist & Wiksell, 1998.

Erlemann, Kurt. "Der Geist als ἀρραβών (2 Kor 5,5) im Kontext der paulinischen Eschatologie." *ZNW* 83 (1992): 202–23.

Evans, Christopher F. *Resurrection and the New Testament*. London: SCM, 1970.

Evans, Craig A. "Jewish Burial Traditions and the Resurrection of Jesus." *JSHJ* 3 (2005): 233–48.

Farmer, William R. "Reflections on Isaiah 53 and Christian Origins." Pages 260–80 in *Jesus and the Suffering Servant: Isaiah 53 and Christian Origins*. Edited by William R. Bellinger and William R. Farmer. Harrisburg, PA: Trinity Press International, 1998.

Farnell, L. R. *Greek Hero Cults and Ideas of Immortality*. Oxford: Clarendon, 1921.

Fee, Gordon D. *Pauline Christology: An Exegetical Theological Study*. Peabody, MA: Hendrickson, 2007.

Fergusson, David. "Barth's *Resurrection of the Dead*: Further Reflections." *SJT* 56 (2003): 65–72.

Finkenzeller, Josef. "Die Auferstehung Christi und unsere Hoffnung." Pages 181–270 in *Frage nach Jesus*. Graz: Styria, 1973.

Frazer, James George. *The Golden Bough: A Study in Magic and Religion*. 3d ed. New York: Macmillan, 1915.

Fredericks, Daniel C. "A Question of First Importance: ἐν πρώτοις in 1 Corinthians 15:3." *BBR* 32 (2022): 165–81.

Fredrickson, David. "God, Christ, and All Things in 1 Corinthians 15:28." *WW* 18 (1998): 254–63.

Fredriksen, Paula. *Paul: The Pagans' Apostle*. New Haven: Yale University Press, 2017.

———. "Vile Bodies: Paul and Augustine on the Resurrection of the Flesh." Pages 75–87 in *Biblical Hermeneutics in Historical Perspective*. Edited by Mark S. Burrows and Paul Rorem. Grand Rapids: Eerdmans, 1991.

Fringer, Rob A. "Dying to Be the Church: 1 Corinthians 15 and Paul's Shocking Revelation about Death and Resurrection." *ERT* 41 (2017): 174–84.

Frisk, Hjalmar. *Griechisches Etymologisches Wörterbuch*. 2 vols. Heidelberg: Winter, 1973.

Gaffin, Richard B. "'Life-Giving Spirit': Probing the Center of Paul's Pneumatology." *JETS* 41 (1998): 573–89.

Gant, Peter. *Seeing Light: A Critical Enquiry into the Origins of Resurrection Faith*. Durham: Sacristy, 2019.

Gerhardsson, Birger. "Evidence for Christ's Resurrection According to Paul: 1 Cor 15:1–11." Pages 73–91 in *Neotestamentica et Philonica: Studies in Honour of Peder Borgen*. Edited by David E. Aune, Torrey Seland, and Jarl Henning Ulrichsen. NovTSup 106. Leiden: Brill, 2003.

Gieniusz, Andrzej. "'As a Miscarriage': The Meaning and Function of the Metaphor in 1 Cor 15:1–11 in Light of Num 12:12 (LXX)." *BibAn* 3 (2013): 93–107.

———. "Jesus' Resurrection Appearances in 1 Cor 15,5–8 in the Light of the Syntagma ὤφθη + Dative." *BibAn* 9 (2019): 481–92.

Gignilliat, Mark S. *Paul and Isaiah's Servants: Paul's Theological Reading of Isaiah 40–66 in 2 Corinthians 5:14–6:10*. LNTS 330. London: T&T Clark, 2007.

———. "Paul and Isaiah's Servants in 2 Corinthians." Pages 243–53 in *Isaiah's Servants in Early Judaism and Christianity: The Isaian Servant and the Exegetical Formation of Community Identity*. Edited by Michael A. Lyons and Jacob Stromberg. WUNT 2.554. Tübingen: Mohr Siebeck, 2021.

Gillman, John. "Transformation in 1 Cor 15,50–53." *ETL* 58 (1982): 309–33.

Gilmour, S. MacLean. "The Christophany to More Than Five Hundred Brethren." *JBL* 80 (1961): 248–52.

———. "Easter and Pentecost." *JBL* 81 (1962): 62–66.

Given, Mark D. "Paul and Writing." Pages 237–60 in *As It Is Written: Studying Paul's Use of Scripture*. Edited by Stanley E. Porter and Christopher D. Stanley. SBLSymS 50. Atlanta: Society of Biblical Literature, 2008.

Gladd, Benjamin J. "The Last Adam as the 'Life-Giving Spirit' Revisited: A Possible Old Testament Background of One of Paul's Most Perplexing Phrases." *WTJ* 71 (2009): 297–309.

Goppelt, Leonhard. *Typos: The Typological Interpretation of the Old Testament in the New*. Translated by Donald E. Madvig. Grand Rapids: Eerdmans, 1982.

Graham, Daryn. "The Placement of Paul's Composition in Troas: A Fresh Approach." *Them* 46 (2021): 592–607.

Grass, Hans. *Ostergeschehen und Osterberichte*. Göttingen: Vandenhoeck & Ruprecht, 1962.

Green, Celia, and Charles McCreery. *Apparitions*. London: Hamilton, 1975.

Grindheim, Sigurd. "A Theology of Glory: Paul's Use of Δόξα Terminology in Romans." *JBL* 136 (2017): 451–65.

———. "Wisdom for the Perfect: Paul's Challenge to the Corinthian Church (1 Corinthians 2:6–16)." *JBL* 121 (2002): 689–709.

Grudem, Wayne. *Systematic Theology*. 2d ed. Grand Rapids: Zondervan Academic, 2020.

Gundry, Robert H. *Sōma in Biblical Theology: With Emphasis on Pauline Anthropology*. SNTSMS 29. New York: Cambridge University Press, 1976.

Habermas, Gary R. *Risen Indeed: A Historical Investigation into the Resurrection of Jesus.* Bellingham, WA: Lexham Academic, 2021.

Hall, David R. "A Disguise for the Wise: ΜΕΤΑΣΧΗΜΑΤΙΣΜΟΣ in 1 Corinthians 4:6." *NTS* 40 (1994): 143–49.

Hamilton, James M. "'That God May Be All in All': The Trinity in 1 Corinthians 15." Pages 95–108 in *One God in Three Persons: Unity of Essence, Distinction of Persons, Implications for Life.* Edited by Bruce A. Ware and John Starke. Wheaton, IL: Crossway, 2015.

Hansen, G. Walter. "Resurrection and the Christian Life in Paul's Letters." Pages 203–24 in *Life in the Face of Death: The Resurrection Message in the New Testament.* Edited by Richard N. Longenecker. Grand Rapids: Eerdmans, 1998.

Harriman, K. R. "A Synthetic Proposal about the Corinthian Resurrection Deniers." *NovT* 62 (2020): 180–200.

Hauger, Martin. "Die Deutung der Auferweckung Jesu Christi durch Paulus." Pages 31–58 in *Die Wirklichkeit der Auferstehung.* Edited by Hans-Joachim Eckstein and Michael Welker. Neukirchen-Vluyn: Neukirchener, 2010.

Hays, Richard. *Echoes of Scripture in the Letters of Paul.* New Haven: Yale University Press, 1989.

Head, Peter M. "Named Letter-Carriers in the Oxyrynchus Papyri." *JSNT* 31 (2009): 279–99.

Heil, John Paul. *The Rhetorical Role of Scripture in 1 Corinthians.* SBLStBL 15. Atlanta: SBL Press, 2005.

Heil, Uta. "Theo-logische Interpretation von 1Kor 15,23–28." *ZNW* 84 (1993): 27–35.

Hengel, Martin. "Das Begräbnis Jesu bei Paulus und die leibliche Auferstehung aus dem Grabe." Pages 119–83 in *Auferstehung—Resurrection.* Edited by Friedrich Avemarie and Hermann Lichtenberger. WUNT 135. Tübingen: Mohr Siebeck, 2001.

Hill, C. E. "Paul's Understanding of Christ's Kingdom in 1 Corinthians 15:20–28." *NovT* 30 (1988): 297–320.

Hill, Wesley. *Paul and the Trinity: Persons, Relations, and the Pauline Letters.* Grand Rapids: Eerdmans, 2015.

Hoffmann, P. *Zur neutestamentliche Überlieferung von der Auferstehung Jesu.* Darmstadt: Wissenschaftliche Buchgesellschaft, 1988.

Hollander, Harm W., and J. Holleman. "The Relationship of Death, Sin, and Law in 1 Cor 15:56." *NovT* 35 (1993): 270–91.

Hollander, Harm W., and Gijsbert E. van der Hort. "The Apostle Paul Calling Himself an Abortion: 1 Cor. 15:8 within the Context of 1 Cor. 15:8–10." *NovT* 28 (1996): 224–36.

Holleman, Joost. "Jesus' Resurrection as the Beginning of the Eschatological Resurrection (1 Cor 15,20)." Pages 653–60 in *The Corinthian Correspondence.* Edited by Reimund Bieringer. BETL 125. Leuven: Peeters, 1996.

———. *Resurrection and Parousia: A Traditio-Historical Study of Paul's Eschatology in 1 Corinthians 15*. NovTSup 84. Leiden: Brill, 1996.
Horn, F. W. "1 Kor 15,56—Ein exegetischer Stachel." *ZNW* 82 (1991): 88–105.
Horsley, Richard. "Wisdom of Words and Words of Wisdom in Corinth." *CBQ* 39 (1977): 224–39.
Hull, Michael F. *Baptism on Account of the Dead (1 Corinthians 15:29): An Act of Faith in the Resurrection*. Atlanta: SBL Press, 2005.
Hultgren, Stephen. "The Origin of Paul's Doctrine of the Two Adams in 1 Corinthians 15.45–49." *JSNT* 25 (2003): 343–70.
Hurd, John Coolidge. *The Origin of 1 Corinthians*. Macon: Mercer University Press, 1983.
Jamieson, R. B. "1 Corinthians 15.28 and the Grammar of Paul's Christology." *NTS* 66 (2020): 187–207.
Jeremias, Joachim. "Artikelloses Χριστός: Zur Ursprache von I Cor 15,3b–5." *ZNW* 57 (1966): 211–15.
———. *The Eucharistic Words of Jesus*. Philadelphia: Fortress, 1966.
———. "'Flesh and Blood Cannot Inherit the Kingdom of God' (I Cor. xv. 50)." *NTS* 2 (1956): 151–59.
———. "Nochmals: Artikelloses Χριστός in I Cor 15,3." *ZNW* 60 (1969): 214–19.
Jobes, Karen H., and Moisés Silva. *Invitation to the Septuagint*. Grand Rapids: Baker Academic, 2000.
Johnson, Andrew. "Firstfruits and Death's Defeat: Metaphor in Paul's Rhetorical Strategy in 1 Cor 15:20–28." *WW* 16 (1996): 456–64.
———. "On Removing a Trump Card: Flesh and Blood and the Reign of God." *BBR* 13 (2003): 175–92.
———. "Turning the World Upside Down in 1 Corinthians 15: Epistemology, the Resurrected Body and the New Creation." *EvQ* 75 (2003): 291–309.
Jones, Peter R. "1 Corinthians 15:8: Paul the Last Apostle." *TynBul* 36 (1985): 3–34.
———. "Paul Confronts Paganism in the Church: A Case Study of First Corinthians 15:45." *JETS* 49 (2006): 713–37.
Jordaan, G. J. C. "The Consummation of the Kingdom of God: A Response to the Paper of P. C. Potgieter." *IDS* 35 (2001): 226–32.
Käsemann, Ernst. *Commentary on Romans*. Translated by Geoffrey W. Bromiley. Grand Rapids: Eerdmans, 1980.
Kató, Szabolcs-Ferencz. "Resurrection on the Day of the Omer? Interpreting 1 Corinthians 15:20 in the Light of Leviticus 23:9–15 and Menaḥot 10:2–3." *Neot* 56 (2022): 71–86.
Kearney, Peter J. "He Appeared to 500 Brothers (I Cor xv 6)." *NovT* 22 (1980): 264–84.
Kelly, J. N. D. *Early Christian Creeds*. 3d ed. New York: Longman, 1972.
———. *The Epistles of Peter and of Jude*. London: Black, 1969.

Kendall, Daniel, and Gerald O'Collins. "Christ's Resurrection and the Aorist Passive of *egeirō*." *Greg* 74 (1993): 725–35.

Kierkegaard, Søren. *Journals and Papers*. Translated by Howard V. Hong and Edna H. Hong. Bloomington: Indiana University Press, 1970.

Kister, Menahem. "'First Adam' and 'Second Adam' in 1 Cor 15:45–49 in the Light of Midrashic Exegesis and Hebrew Usage." Pages 351–65 in *The New Testament and Rabbinic Literature*. Edited by Reimund Bieringer, Florentino García Martínez, Didier Pollefeyt, and Peter Tomson. JSJSup 136. Leiden: Brill, 2010.

———. "'In Adam': 1 Cor 15:21–22; 12:27 in Their Jewish Setting." Pages 685–90 in *Flores Florentino: Dead Sea Scrolls and Other Jewish Studies in Honour of Florentino García Martínez*. Edited by Anthony Hilhorst, Émile Puech, and Eibert Tigchelaar. Leiden: Brill, 2007.

Klappert, Berthold. "Zur Frage des semitischen oder griechischen Urtextes von I. Kor. xv. 3–5." *NTS* 13 (1966–1967): 168–73.

Klauck, H.-J. *Ancient Letters and the New Testament: A Guide to Context and Exegesis*. Waco: Baylor University Press, 2006.

Klinghardt, Matthias. "Himmlische Körper: Hintergrund und argumentative Funktion von 1Kor 15,40f." *ZNW* 106 (2015): 216–44.

Kloppenborg, John. "An Analysis of the Pre-Pauline Formula in 1 Corinthians 15:3b–5 in Light of Some Recent Literature." *CBQ* 18 (1978): 351–67.

Kneale, Martha. "Logic." *OCD*, 616–17.

Koch, Dietrich-Alex. "The Origin, Function and Disappearance of the 'Twelve': Continuity from Jesus to the Post-Easter Community." *HvTSt* 61 (2005): 211–29.

Kotansky, Roy D. "The Resurrection of Jesus in Biblical Theology: From Early Appearances (1 Corinthians 15) to the 'Sindonology' of the Empty Tomb." Pages 83–107 in *Reconsidering the Relationship between Biblical and Systematic Theology in the New Testament*. Edited by Benjamin E. Reynolds, Brian Lugioyo, and Kevin J. Vanhoozer. Tübingen: Mohr Siebeck, 2014.

Kreitzer, L. Joseph. *Jesus and God in Paul's Eschatology*. JSNTSup 19. Sheffield: Sheffield Academic, 1987.

Kremer, J. *Das älteste Zeugnis von der Auferstehung Christi: Eine bibeltheologische Studie zur Aussage und Bedeutung von 1 Kor 15, 1–11*. 3d ed. Stuttgart: Katholisches Bibelwerk, 1970.

Kühner, Raphael, and Bernhard Gerth. *Ausführliche Grammatik der Griechischen Sprache*. 2 parts in 4 vols. 3d ed. Hanover: Hahnsche, 1898.

Kurth, Thomas. *Senecas Trostschrift an Polybius, Dialog 11: Ein Kommentar*. Stuttgart: Teubner, 1994.

Lambrecht, Jan. "Just a Possibility? A Reply to Johan S. Vos on 1 Cor 15,12–20." *ZNW* 91 (2000): 143–45.

———. "Line of Thought in 1 Cor 15,1–11." *Greg* 72 (1991): 655–70.
———. "Paul's Christological Use of Scripture in 1 Corinthians 15:20–28." *NTS* 28 (1982): 502–27.
———. Review of Anders Eriksson, *Traditions as Rhetorical Proof*. *Bib* 80 (1999): 438–41.
———. "Structure and Line of Thought in 1 Cor. 15:23–28." *NovT* 32 (1990): 143–51.
———. "Three Brief Notes on 1 Corinthians 15." *Bijdr* 62 (2001): 28–41.
Lampe, Peter. "Paul's Concept of a Spiritual Body." Pages 103–14 in *Resurrection: Theological and Scientific Assessments*. Edited by Ted Peters, Robert John Russell, and Michael Welker. Grand Rapids: Eerdmans, 2002.
Lapidge, M. "Stoic Cosmology." Pages 169–78 in *The Stoics*. Edited by J. M. Rist. Berkeley: University of California, 1978.
Legarreta-Castillo, Felipe de Jesús. *The Figure of Adam in Romans 5 and 1 Corinthians 15: The New Creation and Its Ethical and Social Reconfiguration*. Minneapolis: Fortress, 2014.
Lehmann, Karl. *Auferweckt am Dritten Tag nach der Schrift: Früheste Christologie, Bekenntnisbildung and Schriftauslegung im Lichte von 1 Kor. 15, 3–5*. 2d ed. QD 38. Freiburg: Herder, 1968.
Lehtipuu, Outi. "'Flesh and Blood Cannot Inherit the Kingdom of God': The Transformation of the Flesh in the Early Christian Debates Concerning Resurrection." Pages 147–68 in *Metamorphoses: Resurrection, Body and Transformative Practices in Early Christianity*. Edited by Turid Karlsen Seim and Jorunn Økland. Berlin: de Gruyter, 2009.
Lessing, Gotthold Ephraim. "On the Proof of the Spirit and of Power." Pages 51–56 in *Lessing's Theological Writings*. Edited and translated by Henry Chadwick. Stanford: Stanford University Press, 1957.
Levison, John R. "Inspiration and the Divine Spirit in the Writings of Philo Judaeus." *JSJ* 26 (1995): 271–323.
———. "The Prophetic Spirit as an Angel According to Philo." *HTR* 88 (1995): 189–207.
Lewis, Scott M. *"So That God May Be All in All": The Apocalyptic Message of 1 Corinthians 15,12–34*. TGST 42. Rome: Gregorian University Press, 1998.
Liddell, H. G., and R. Scott, with R. S. Jones. *Greek-English Lexicon*. 9th ed. Oxford: Clarendon, 1940.
Lienhard, Joseph T. "The Exegesis of 1 Cor 15,24–28 from Marcellus of Ancyra to Theodoret of Cyrus." *VC* 37 (1983): 340–59.
Lightfoot, J. B. *The Epistle of St. Paul to the Galatians*. Grand Rapids: Zondervan, 1957.
Lincoln, Andrew T. *Paradise Now and Not Yet: Studies in the Role of the Heavenly Dimension in Paul's Thought with Special Reference to His Eschatology*. SNTSMS 43. Cambridge: Cambridge University Press, 1981.
Lindemann, Andreas. "Die Auferstehung der Toten: Adam und Christus nach 1 Kor 15."

Pages 155–67 in *Eschatologie und Schöpfung*. Edited by Martin Evang, Helmut Merklein, and Michael Wolter. Berlin: de Gruyter, 1997.

———. "Paulus als Zeuge der Auferstehung Jesu Christi." Pages 55–64 in *Paulus, Apostel Jesu Christi: Festschrift für Günter Klein zum 70. Geburtstag*. Edited by Michael Trowitzsch. Tübingen: Mohr Siebeck, 1988.

Litfin, Duane. *St. Paul's Theology of Proclamation: 1 Corinthians 1–4 and Greco-Roman Rhetoric*. SNTSMS 79. Cambridge: Cambridge University Press, 1994.

Litwa, M. David. *We Are Being Transformed: Deification in Paul's Soteriology*. BZNW 187. Berlin: de Gruyter, 2012.

Longenecker, Richard N. "Is There Development in Paul's Resurrection Thought?" Pages 171–202 in *Life in the Face of Death: The Resurrection Message of the New Testament*. Edited by Richard N. Longenecker. Grand Rapids: Eerdmans, 1998.

Louw, J. P., and E. A. Nida, eds. *Greek-English Lexicon of the New Testament: Based on Semantic Domains*. 2d ed. New York: United Bible Societies, 1989.

Lüdemann, Gerd. *The Resurrection of Jesus: History, Experience, Theology*. London: SCM, 1994.

Lührmann, Dieter. "Freundschaftsbrief trotz Spannungen: Zu Gattung und Aufbau des Ersten Korintherbriefs." Page 298–314 in *Studien zum Text und zur Ethik des Neuen Testaments*. Edited by W. Schrage. Berlin: de Gruyter, 1986.

Lütgert, W. *Freiheitspredigt und Schwarmgeister in Korinth: Ein Beitrag zur Characteristik der Christuspartei*. Gütersloh: Bertelsmann, 1908.

Lyons, Michael A. "Psalm 22 and the 'Servants' of Isaiah 54; 56–66." *CBQ* 77 (2015): 640–56.

MacGregor, Kirk R. "1 Corinthians 15:3B–6A, 7 and the Bodily Resurrection of Jesus." *JETS* 49 (2006): 225–34.

MacMullen, Ramsay. *Christianizing the Roman Empire, AD 100–400*. New Haven: Yale University Press, 1984.

———. *Paganism in the Roman Empire*. New Haven: Yale University Press, 1981.

Malcolm, Matthew R. *Paul and the Rhetoric of Reversal in 1 Corinthians: The Impact of Paul's Gospel on His Macro-Rhetoric*. SNTSMS 155. Cambridge: Cambridge University Press, 2013.

Malherbe, Abraham J. *Ancient Epistolary Theorists*. SBLSBS 19. Atlanta: Scholars, 1988.

———. "The Beasts at Ephesus." *JBL* 87 (1968): 71–80.

———. *The Letters to the Thessalonians*. AB 32B. New York: Doubleday, 2000.

Martin, Dale. *The Corinthian Body*. New Haven: Yale University Press, 1995.

———. "When Did Angels Become Demons?" *JBL* 129 (2010): 657–77.

Martini, Jeromey. "An Examination of Paul's Apocalyptic Narrative in First Corinthians 15:20–28." *CTR* 8 (2011): 57–70.

Maston, Jason. "Anthropological Crisis and Solution in the *Hodayot* and 1 Corinthians 15." *NTS* 62 (2016): 533–48.
McGrath, James F. *The Only True God: Early Christian Monotheism in Its Jewish Context.* Urbana: University of Illinois Press, 2009.
McIver, Robert K. "Eyewitnesses as Guarantors of the Accuracy of the Gospel Traditions in the Light of Psychological Research." *JBL* 131 (2012): 529–46.
Meeks, Wayne A. *Christ Is the Question.* Louisville: Knox, 2006.
———. *The First Urban Christians.* 2d. ed. New Haven: Yale University Press, 2003.
Merklein, Helmut. "Die Einheitlichkeit des ersten Korintherbriefes." *ZNW* 75 (1984): 153–83.
Metzger, Bruce M. "A Suggestion Concerning the Meaning of 1 Cor. xv.4b." *JTS* 8 (1957): 118–23.
———. *A Textual Commentary on the Greek New Testament.* 3d ed. London: United Bible Societies, 1971.
Meyer, Ben F. "Did Paul's View of the Resurrection of the Dead Undergo Development?" *TS* 47 (1986): 363–87.
Milinovich, Timothy. *Beyond What Is Written: The Performative Structure of 1 Corinthians.* Eugene, OR: Pickwick, 2013.
Mitchell, Margaret M. "Concerning ΠΕΡΙ ΔΕ in 1 Corinthians." *NovT* 31 (1989): 229–56.
———. *Paul and the Rhetoric of Reconciliation: An Exegetical Investigation of the Language and Composition of 1 Corinthians.* Louisville: Westminster John Knox, 1991.
Mitchell, Matthew W. "Reexamining the 'Aborted Apostle': An Exploration of Paul's Self-Description in 1 Corinthians 15.8." *JSNT* 25 (2003): 469–85.
Moore, Terri. *The Mysteries, Resurrection, and 1 Corinthians 15: Comparative Methodology and Exegesis.* Lanham, MD: Fortress Academic, 2018.
Morissette, Rodolphe. "L'antithèse entre le 'psychique' et le 'pneumatique' en 1 Corinthiens, xv, 44 à 46." *RevScRel* 46 (1972): 97–103.
———. "La chair et le sang ne peuvent hériter du Règne de Dieu (I Cor., XV, 50)." *ScEs* 26 (1974): 39–67.
———. "La conditione de ressuscité. 1 Corinthiens 15,34–49: Structure littéraire de la péricope." *Bib* 53 (1972): 208–28.
Moritz, Ludwig Alfred. "Corn." *OCD*, 291.
Moule, C. F. D. *The Birth of the New Testament.* HNTC. New York: Harper & Row, 1962.
Moulton, J. H., and G. Milligan. *Vocabulary of the Greek Testament.* London: Hodder & Stoughton, 1930.
Murphy-O'Connor, Jerome. "'Baptized for the Dead' (1 Cor xv, 29): A Corinthian Slogan." *RB* 88 (1981): 532–43.
———. *Paul: A Critical Life.* Oxford: Oxford University Press, 1996.

———. "Tradition and Redaction in 1 Cor 15:3–7." *CBQ* 43 (1981): 582–89.

Murray, John. "Who Raised Up Jesus?" *WTJ* 3 (1941): 113–23.

Nasrallah, Laura Salah. "Grief in Corinth: The Roman City and Paul's Corinthian Correspondence." Pages 109–39 in *Contested Spaces: Houses and Temples in Roman Antiquity and the New Testament*. Edited by David L. Balch and Annette Weissenrieder. WUNT 285. Tübingen: Mohr Siebeck, 2012.

Nickelsburg, George W. E. "An ἔκτρωμα, Though Appointed from the Womb: Paul's Apostolic Self-Description in 1 Corinthians 15 and Galatians 1." *HTR* 79 (1986): 198–205.

Nilsson, Nils, and Johan Croon. "Orphism." *OCD*, 759–60.

Nordgaard, Stefan. "Paul's Appropriation of Philo's Theory of 'Two Men' in 1 Corinthians 15.45–49." *NTS* 57 (2011): 348–65.

O'Collins, Gerald. "Peter as Witness to Easter." *TS* 73 (2012): 263–85.

O'Connell, Jake H. *Jesus' Resurrection and Apparitions: A Bayesian Analysis*. Eugene, OR: Resource, 2016.

O'Donnell, Matthew Brook. "Some New Testament Words for Resurrection and the Company They Keep." Pages 136–63 in *Resurrection*. Edited by Stanley Porter, Michael A. Hayes, and David Tombs. Sheffield: Sheffield Academic, 1999.

O'Reilly, Matt. *Paul and the Resurrected Body: Social Identity and Ethical Practice*. ESEC 22. Atlanta: SBL Press, 2020.

Padgett, Alan G. "The Body in Resurrection: Science and Scripture on the 'Spiritual Body.'" *WW* 22 (2002): 155–63.

Pagels, Elaine E. "'The Mystery of the Resurrection': A Gnostic Reading of 1 Corinthians 15." *JBL* 93 (1974): 276–88.

Paige, Terence. "Who Believes in 'Spirit'? Πνεῦμα in Pagan Usage and Implications for the Gentile Christian Mission." *HTR* 95 (2002): 417–36.

Park, Janghoon. "The Identity of Death in 1 Corinthians 15:20–28: Understanding the Cosmic and Forensic Dimensions of Death in Paul." *Korean Evangelical New Testament Studies* 19 (2020): 194–232.

Pascuzzi, Maria. "Baptism-Based Allegiance and the Divisions in Corinth: A Reexamination of 1 Corinthians 1:13–17." *CBQ* 71 (2009): 813–29.

Patrick, James E. "Living Rewards for Dead Apostles: 'Baptized for the Dead' in 1 Corinthians 15:29." *NTS* 52 (2006): 71–85.

Paulsen, Henning. "Schisma und Häresie: Untersuchungen zu 1 Kor 11:18, 19." *ZTK* 79 (1982): 180–211.

Pearson, Birger. "Hellenistic-Jewish Wisdom Speculation and Paul." Pages 43–66 in *Aspects of Wisdom in Judaism and Early Christianity*. Edited by Robert L. Wilken. Notre Dame: Notre Dame University Press, 1975.

———. "Mystery and Secrecy in Paul." Pages 287–302 in *Mystery and Secrecy in the Nag Hammadi Collection and Other Ancient Literature: Ideas and Practices.* Edited by C. H. Bull, L. I. Lied, and J. D. Turner. Leiden: Brill, 2012.

———. *The Pneumatikos-Psychikos Terminology in 1 Corinthians: A Study in the Theology of the Corinthian Opponents and Its Relation to Gnosticism.* SBLDS 12. Missoula, MT: Scholars, 1973.

Perrin, Nicholas. "On Raising Osiris in 1 Corinthians 15." *TynBul* 58 (2007): 117–28.

Peterson, Jeffrey. "Christ Our Pasch: Shaping Christian Identity in Corinth." Pages 133–44 in *Renewing the Tradition.* Edited by Mark W. Hamilton, Thomas R. Olbricht, and Jeffrey Peterson. Eugene, OR: Wipf & Stock, 2006.

———. "The Extent of Christian Theological Diversity: Pauline Evidence." *ResQ* 47 (2005): 1–12.

Pfleiderer, Otto. *Paulinism: A Contribution to the History of Primitive Christian Theology.* Vol. 1, *Exposition of Paul's Doctrine.* Translated by E. Peters. London: Williams & Norgate, 1877.

Pickup, Martin. "'On the Third Day': The Time Frame of Jesus' Death and Resurrection." *JETS* 56 (2013): 511–42.

Pitts, Andrew W. "Philosophical and Epistolary Contexts for Pauline Paraenesis." Pages 269–336 in *Paul and the Ancient Letter Form.* Edited by S. E. Porter and S. A. Adams. Leiden: Brill, 2010.

Pogoloff, Stephen M. *Logos and Sophia: The Rhetorical Situation of 1 Corinthians.* SBLDS 134. Atlanta: Scholars, 1992.

Poirier, John C. "Psalm 16:10 and the Resurrection of Jesus 'on the Third Day' (1 Corinthians 15:4)." *JSPL* 4 (2014): 149–67.

Popko, Łukasz. "Why Paul Was Not Wrong in Quoting Hosea 13:14." *BibAn* 9 (2019): 493–512.

Porter, Stanley. *The Apostle Paul: His Life, Thought, and Letters.* Grand Rapids: Eerdmans, 2016.

Potgieter, Pieter. "The Consummation of the Kingdom of God: Reflections on the Final Victory of Christ as Portrayed in Paul's First Epistle to the Corinthians." *IDS* 35 (2001): 216–25.

Prince, Deborah Thompson. "The 'Ghost' of Jesus: Luke 24 in Light of Ancient Narratives of Post-Mortem Apparitions." *JSNT* 29 (2007): 287–301.

Proctor, Mark A. "'If Christ Has Not Been Raised': 1 Corinthians 15:17 and the Hamartiological Inefficacy of a Compromised Gospel." *CBQ* 83 (2021): 619–37.

Rabens, Volker. *The Holy Spirit and Ethics in Paul: Transformation and Empowering for Religious-Ethical Life.* WUNT 2.283. Tübingen: Mohr Siebeck, 2010.

Radl, Walter. "Der Sinn von γνωρίζω in 1 Kor 15:1." *BZ* 28 (1984): 243–45.

Raeder, Maria. "Vikariatstaufe in I Cor 15:29?" *ZNW* 46 (1955): 258–61.

Rashkow, Ilona. "'Ones Who Have Fallen Out' (*NEFEL*): Spontaneous, Accidental, and Intentional Miscarriage Laws in Ancient Israel." *JBQ* 50 (2022): 255–63.

Reaume, John D. "Another Look at 1 Corinthians 15:29, 'Baptized for the Dead.'" *BSac* 152 (1995): 457–75.

Redman, Judith C. "How Accurate Are Eyewitnesses? Bauckham and the Eyewitnesses in the Light of Psychological Research." *JBL* 129 (2010): 177–97.

Richards, Larry. "Ὑποταγήσεται in 1 Corinthians 15:28b." *AUSS* 38 (2020): 203–6.

Riesenfeld, Harald. "Das Bildwort vom Weizenkorn bei Paulus (zu I Cor 15)." Pages 43–55 in *Studien zum Neuen Testament und zur Patristik*. Berlin: Akademie, 1961.

Ring, George C. "Christ's Resurrection and the Dying and Rising Gods." *CBQ* 6 (1944): 216–29.

Robertson, A. T. *A Grammar of the Greek New Testament in the Light of Historical Research*. 4th ed. Nashville: Broadman, 1934.

Robinson, Edward. *Greek and English Lexicon of the New Testament*. 2d ed. New York: Harper, 1859.

Robinson, James M. "Jesus—From Easter to Valentinus (or to the Apostles' Creed)." *JBL* 101 (1982): 5–37.

Rose, H. J. "Demeter." *OCD*, 324.

———. *Religion in Greece and Rome*. New York: Harper, 1959.

Rosner, Brian. "Temple and Holiness in 1 Corinthians 15." *TynBul* 42 (1991): 137–45.

Rowe, C. Kavin. "Biblical Pressure and Trinitarian Hermeneutics." *ProEccl* 11 (2002): 295–312.

Sandelin, Karl-Gustav. *Die Auseinandersetzung mit der Weisheit in 1. Korinther 15*. Åbo: Åbo Akademi, 1976.

Sanders, E. P. *Jesus and Judaism*. Minneapolis: Fortress, 1985.

Sandnes, Karl Olav, and Jan-Olav Henriksen. *Resurrection: Text and Interpretation, Experience and Theology*. Eugene, OR: Pickwick, 2020.

Saw, Insawn. *Paul's Rhetoric in 1 Corinthians 15: An Analysis Utilizing the Theories of Classical Rhetoric*. Lewiston, NY: Mellen, 1995.

Schaefer, Markus. "Paulus, 'Fehlgeburt' oder 'unvernunftiges Kind'?: Ein Interpretationsvorschlag zu 1 Kor 15,8." *ZNW* 85 (1994): 207–17.

Schep, J. A. *The Nature of the Resurrection Body: A Study of the Biblical Data*. Grand Rapids: Eerdmans, 1964.

Schlier, Heinrich. "Die Anfänge des christologischen Credo." Pages 13–58 in *Zur Frühgeschichte der Christologie*. Edited by B. Weite. QD 51. Freiburg: Herder, 1970.

Schmidt, J. H. H. *Synonymik der Griechischen Sprache*. 4 vols. Leipzig: Teubner, 1876–1886.

Schmithals, Walter. *Gnosticism in Corinth: An Investigation of the Letters to the Corinthians*. Nashville: Abingdon, 1971.

Schmitt, Joseph. "Le 'Milieu' littéraire de la 'Tradition' citée dans I Cor., XV, 3b–5." Pages 169–

84 in *Resurrexit: Actes du Symposium International sur la Résurrection de Jésus*. Edited by Édouard Dhanis. Rome: Libreria Editrice Vaticana, 1974.

Schneider, Bernardin. "The Corporate Meaning and Background of 1 Cor 15,45b—'O ESCHATOS ADAM EIS PNEUMA ZŌIOPOIOUN." *CBQ* 29 (1967): 144–61.

Schoeps, H. J. *Paul: The Theology of the Apostle in the Light of Jewish Religious History*. Translated by Harold Knight. Philadelphia: Westminster, 1961.

Scholla, Robert. "Into the Image of God: Pauline Eschatology and the Transformation of Believers." *Greg* 78 (1997): 33–54.

Schubert, P. *Form and Function of the Pauline Thanksgivings*. BZNW 30. Berlin: de Gruyter, 1939.

Scott, James M. "Paul's Comparison of Himself with '*the* Abortion' (1 Cor 15:8): A Missing Link between the Qumran Book of Giants and the Manichaean Book of Giants." *JSJ* 50 (2019): 291–318.

Sharp, Daniel B. "Vicarious Baptism for the Dead: 1 Corinthians 15:29." *StBibAnt* 6 (2014): 36–66.

Sider, Ronald. "The Pauline Conception of the Resurrection Body in 1 Corinthians XV.35–54." *NTS* 21 (1975): 428–39.

———. "St. Paul's Understanding of the Nature and Significance of the Resurrection in I Corinthians xv, 1–19." *NovT* 19 (1975): 124–41.

Simon, Marcel. "From Greek Hairesis to Christian Heresy." Pages 101–16 in *Early Christian Literature and the Classical Intellectual Tradition*. Edited by W. Schoedel and R. L. Wilken. ThH 153. Paris: Beauchesne, 1979.

Sleeper, C. Freeman. "Pentecost and Resurrection." *JBL* 84 (1965): 389–99.

Smith, Daniel A. *Revisiting the Empty Tomb: The Early History of Easter*. Minneapolis: Fortress, 2010.

———. "Seeing a Pneuma(tic) Body): The Apologetic Interests of Luke 24:36–43." *CBQ* 72 (2010): 742–72.

Smith, J. Z. "Dying and Rising Gods." *ER* 4:2535–40.

Smith, M. S. "The Death of 'Dying and Rising Gods' in the Biblical World." *SJOT* 12 (1998): 257–313.

Smith, Murray J., and Ian J. Vaillancourt. "Enthroned and Coming to Reign: Jesus' Eschatological Use of Psalm 110:1 in Mark 14:62." *JBL* 141 (2022): 513–31.

Smyth, Herbert Weir. *Greek Grammar*. Revised by Gordon M. Messing. Cambridge: Harvard University Press, 1956.

Söding, Thomas. "'Die Kraft der Sünde ist das Gesetz' (1Kor 15,56): Anmerkungen zum Hintergrund und zur Pointe einer gesetzeskritischen Sentenz des Apostels Paulus." *ZNW* 83 (1992): 74–84.

Spicq, Ceslas. *Theological Lexicon of the New Testament*. Translated and edited by James D. Ernest. 3 vols. Peabody, MA: Hendrickson, 1994.

Spörlein, Bernhard. *Die Leugnung der Auferstehung: Eine historisch-kritische Untersuchung zu I Kor 15*. Regensburg: Pustet, 1971.
Stenger, Werner. "Beobachtungen zur Argumentationsstruktur von 1 Kor 15." *LB* 45 (1979): 71–128.
Sterling, Gregory E. "'Wisdom among the Perfect': Creation Traditions in Alexandrian Judaism and Corinthian Christianity." *NovT* 37 (1995): 355–84.
Strawbridge, Jennifer R. "How the Body of Lazarus Helps to Solve a Pauline Problem." *NTS* 63 (2017): 588–603.
———. *The Pauline Effect: The Use of the Pauline Epistles by Early Christian Writers*. SBR 5. Berlin: de Gruyter, 2015.
Strüder, Christof W. "Preferences Not Parties: The Background of 1 Cor 1,12." *ETL* 79 (2003): 431–55.
Suh, Michael K. W. *Power and Peril: Paul's Use of Temple Discourse in 1 Corinthians*. BZNW 239. Berlin: de Gruyter, 2020.
Sumney, Jerry. "Post-Mortem Existence and Resurrection of the Body in Paul." *HBT* 31 (2009): 12–26.
Sysling, Harry. *Teḥiyyat ha-Metim: The Resurrection of the Dead in the Palestinian Targums of the Pentateuch and Parallel Traditions in Classical Rabbinic Literature*. Tübingen: Mohr Siebeck, 1996.
Szymik, Stefan. "The Corinthian Opponents of the Resurrection in 1 Cor 15:12: The Epicurean Hypothesis Reconsidered." *BibAn* 10 (2020): 437–56.
Talbert, Charles H. "The Concept of Immortals in Mediterranean Antiquity." *JBL* 94 (1975): 419–36.
Tannehill, Robert C. "Participation in Christ: A Central Theme in Pauline Soteriology." Pages 225–39 in *The Shape of the Gospel*. Eugene, OR: Wipf & Stock, 2007.
Teichmann, Ernst. *Die paulinische Vorstellungen von Auferstehung und Gericht und ihre Beziehungen zur jüdischen Apokalyptik*. Freiburg: Mohr, 1896.
Thayer, Joseph Henry. *A Greek-English Lexicon of the New Testament*. 4th ed. Grand Rapids: Baker, 1977.
Thielman, Frank. *Paul and the Law: A Contextual Approach*. Downers Grove, IL: IVP Academic, 1994.
Thiessen, Jacob. "Firstfruits and the Day of Christ's Resurrection: An Examination of the Relationship between the 'Third Day' in 1 Cor 15:4 and the 'Firstfruit' in 1 Cor 15:20." *Neot* 46 (2012): 379–93.
Thiselton, Anthony C. *The Living Paul: An Introduction to the Apostle's Life and Thought*. Downers Grove, IL: InterVarsity, 2009.
———. "Realized Eschatology at Corinth." *NTS* 24 (1978): 510–26.
Thomasen, Einar. "Valentinian Ideas about Salvation as Transformation." Pages 169–86 in *Metamorphoses: Resurrection, Body and Transformative Practices in*

*Early Christianity*. Edited by Turid Karlsen Seim and Jorunn Økland. Berlin: de Gruyter, 2009.

Thüsing, Wilhelm. *Per Christum in Deum: Studien zum Verhältnis von Christozentrik und Theozentrik in den paulinischen Hauptbriefen*. 2d ed. Münster: Aschendorff, 1965.

Toit, A. B. du. "Primitive Christian Belief in the Resurrection of Jesus in the Light of Pauline Resurrection and Appearance Terminology." *Neot* 23 (1989): 309–30.

Tomlin, G. "Christianity and Epicureanism in 1 Corinthians." *JSNT* 68 (1997): 51–72.

Trench, R. C. *Synonyms of the New Testament*. 9th ed. Grand Rapids: Eerdmans, 1953.

Tuckett, Christopher M. "The Corinthians Who Say 'There Is No Resurrection of the Dead' (1 Cor 15,12)." Pages 247–75 in *The Corinthian Correspondence*. Edited by Reimund Bieringer. BETL 125. Leuven: Leuven University Press, 1996.

Turner, Seth. "The Interim, Earthly Messianic Kingdom in Paul." *JSNT* 25 (2003): 323–42.

Twelftree, Graham H. "The Historian and the Miraculous." *BBR* 28 (2018): 199–217.

Vlachos, Chris Alex. "Law, Sin, and Death: An Edenic Triad? An Examination with Reference to 1 Corinthians 15:56." *JETS* 47 (2004): 277–98.

Vorster, J. N. "Resurrection Faith in 1 Corinthians 15." *Neot* 23 (1989): 287–307.

Vos, Johan S. "Argumentation und Situation in 1Kor. 15." *NovT* 41 (1999): 313–33.

———. "Die Logik des Paulus in 1Kor 15,12–20." *ZNW* 90 (1999): 78–97.

Walker, William O., Jr. "1 Corinthians 15:29–34 as a Non-Pauline Interpolation." *CBQ* 69 (2007): 84–103.

Walter, Nikolaus. "Leibliche Auferstehung? Zur Frage der Hellenisierung der Auferweckungshoffnung bei Paulus." Pages 109–28 in *Paulus, Apostel Jesu Christi: Festschrift für Günter Klein zum 70. Geburtstag*. Edited by Michael Trowitzsch. Tübingen: Mohr Siebeck, 1998.

Walton, Francis R. "After-Life." *OCD*, 23–24.

Ware, Bruce, and John Starke, eds. *One God in Three Persons: Unity of Essence, Distinction of Persons, Implications for Life*. Wheaton, IL: Crossway, 2015.

Ware, James P. *Paul and the Mission of the Church: Philippians in Ancient Jewish Context*. Grand Rapids: Baker Academic, 2011.

———. *Paul's Theology in Context: Creation, Incarnation, Covenant, and Kingdom*. Grand Rapids: Eerdmans, 2019.

———. "The Resurrection of Jesus in the Pre-Pauline Formula of 1 Cor 15.3–5." *NTS* 60 (2014): 475–98.

———. "The Servants of the Servant in Isaiah and Philippians." Pages 255–71 in *Isaiah's Servants in Early Judaism and Christianity: The Isaian Servant and the Exegetical Formation of Community Identity*. Edited by Michael A. Lyons and Jacob Stromberg. WUNT 2.554. Tübingen: Mohr Siebeck, 2021.

———. *Synopsis of the Pauline Letters in Greek and English*. Grand Rapids: Baker Academic, 2010.

Wasserman, Emma. "Gentile Gods at the Eschaton: A Reconsideration of Paul's 'Principalities and Powers' in 1 Corinthians 15." *JBL* 136 (2017): 727–46.

Watson, Duane F. "Paul's Rhetorical Strategy in 1 Corinthians 15." Pages 231–49 in *Rhetoric and the New Testament: Essays from the 1992 Heidelberg Conference*. Edited by Stanley E. Porter and Thomas R. Olbricht. JSNTSup 90. Sheffield: JSOT Press, 1993.

Watson, Francis. "The Triune Divine Identity: Reflections on Pauline God-Language, in Disagreement with J. D. G. Dunn." *JSNT* 80 (2000): 99–124.

Webber, Randall C. "A Note on 1 Corinthians 15:3–5." *JETS* 26 (1983): 265–69.

Wedderburn, A. J. M. "The Problem of the Denial of the Resurrection in I Corinthians xv." *NovT* 23 (1981): 229–41.

Wegener, Mark A. "The Rhetorical Strategy of 1 Corinthians 15." *CurTM* 31 (2004): 438–55.

Welborn, Laurence L. "On the Discord in Corinth: 1 Corinthians 1–4 and Ancient Politics." *JBL* 106 (1987): 85–111.

———. *Politics and Rhetoric in the Corinthian Epistles*. Macon: Mercer University Press, 1997.

Wells, Bruce. "Death in the Garden of Eden." *JBL* 139 (2020): 639–60.

Wenham, David. *Paul: Follower of Jesus or Founder of Christianity?* Grand Rapids: Eerdmans, 1995.

Wheelwright, Philip. *The Presocratics*. Indianapolis: Odyssey, 1966.

White, Joel R. "'Baptized on Account of the Dead': The Meaning of 1 Corinthians 15:29 in Its Context." *JBL* 116 (1997): 487–99.

———. "'He Was Raised on the Third Day According to the Scriptures' (1 Corinthians 15:4): A Typological Interpretation Based on the Cultic Calendar in Leviticus 23." *TynBul* 66 (2015): 103–19.

———. "Recent Challenges to the *communis opinio* on 1 Corinthians 15.29." *CurBR* 10 (2012): 379–95.

White, John L. "Ancient Greek Letters." Pages 85–105 in *Graeco-Roman Literature and the New Testament*. Edited by David E. Aune. SBLSBS 21. Atlanta: Scholars, 1988.

———. "The Greek Documentary Letter Tradition Third Century B.C.E. to Third Century C.E." *Semeia* 22 (1981): 89–106.

Wiles, Gordon P. *Paul's Intercessory Prayers: The Significance of the Intercessory Prayer Passages in the Letters of Paul*. SNTSMS 24. Cambridge: Cambridge University Press, 1974.

Williams, David J. *Paul's Metaphors: Their Context and Character*. Peabody, MA: Hendrickson, 1999.

Williams, H. H. Drake. "Encouragement to Persevere: An Exposition of 1 Corinthians 15:58." *ERT* 32 (2008): 74–81.

Wilson, Andrew. "The Strongest Argument for Universalism in 1 Corinthians 15:20–28." *JETS* 59 (2016): 805–12.

Wilson, Jack H. "The Corinthians Who Say There Is No Resurrection of the Dead." *ZNW* 59 (1960): 90–107.

Winter, Bruce. *Philo and Paul among the Sophists: Alexandrian and Corinthian Responses to a Julio-Claudian Movement.* 2d ed. Grand Rapids: Eerdmans, 2002.

Witetschek, Stephan. "Peter in Corinth? A Review of the Evidence from I Corinthians." *JTS* 69 (2018): 66–82.

Wright, N. T. *The Climax of the Covenant: Christ and the Law in Pauline Theology.* Minneapolis: Fortress, 1991.

———. *The Resurrection of the Son of God.* Vol. 3 of *Christian Origins and the Question of God.* Minneapolis: Fortress, 2003.

Yarbro Collins, Adela. "Ancient Notions of Transferal and Apotheosis in Relation to the Empty Tomb Story in Mark." Pages 41–57 in *Metamorphoses: Resurrection, Body and Transformative Practices in Early Christianity.* Edited by T. K. Seim and J. Økland. Berlin: de Gruyter, 2009.

———. "The Empty Tomb in the Gospel according to Mark." Pages 107–48 in *Hermes and Athena: Biblical Exegesis and Philosophical Theology.* Edited by Eleonore Stump and Thomas P. Flint. Notre Dame: University of Notre Dame Press, 1993.

Zeller, Dieter. "Die angebliche enthusiastische oder spiritualistische Front in 1 Kor 15." *SPhilo* 13 (2001): 176–89.

———. "Die Formel εἶναι τὰ πάντα ἐν πᾶσιν (1 Kor 15,28)." *ZNW* 101 (2010): 148–52.

———. "Gibt es religionsgeschichtliche Parallelen zur Taufe für die Toten (1 Kor 15,29)?" *ZNW* 98 (2007): 68–76.

INTRODUCTION

# *The Unique Importance and Untapped Riches of Paul's Resurrection Chapter*

First Corinthians 15 is the fullest treatment of the hope of the resurrection within the entire Bible. The chapter also includes the earliest known Christian confession of Jesus's resurrection. This apostolic formula, preserved in 1 Cor 15:3–8, is older than any book of the New Testament and was formulated within two to five years of the first Good Friday and Easter. The importance of 1 Cor 15 for the New Testament doctrine of the resurrection is thus unsurpassed by any other passage.

The chapter also contains perhaps the fullest exposition of the second coming of Christ within Paul's letters (15:20–28, 51–52), the most dramatic and theologically rich of Paul's so-called hardship catalogues (15:29–34), and a climax whose poetic and theological grandeur renders it one of the most sublime passages within the New Testament (15:54–58). The chapter also contains two major christological statements (15:24–28 and 15:44b–49), which are also widely regarded as among the most difficult and controversial passages within the entire New Testament. First Corinthians 15 is also well known for its numerous other unresolved exegetical puzzles, such as Paul's self-description as an untimely birth in 15:8, his allusion to those baptized for the sake of the dead in 15:29, and his reference to fighting with beasts at Ephesus in 15:32.

Ancient evidence reveals that 1 Cor 15 was among the most studied of all Pauline texts by the first Christians.[1] The use and impact of this chapter within the early church were truly extraordinary. The central importance of this chapter for

---

1. See Jennifer R. Strawbridge, *The Pauline Effect: The Use of the Pauline Epistles by Early Christian Writers* (SBR 5; Berlin: de Gruyter, 2015), 11 n. 38, 97.

INTRODUCTION

Christian theological reflection, teaching, and preaching on the resurrection has continued throughout the history of the church until the present day.

For all these reasons, 1 Cor 15 is worthy of the closest study.

## The Nature of This Book

This book is a verse-by-verse commentary on 1 Cor 15. It aims to provide the most complete and extensive scholarly treatment of this chapter available in any modern language, casting fresh light on each verse of the chapter and on the chapter as a whole. This book offers a new contribution to the scholarly discussion of the nature of Jesus's resurrection, the historicity of Jesus's resurrection, and the nature of the resurrection hope that Paul expounds in this unique chapter. The commentary is written not only for scholars but also for clergy as a resource for preaching and teaching, and for all who wish to enrich their understanding of New Testament theology.

## The Contemporary Debate over Paul's Resurrection Chapter

As the fullest treatment of the resurrection in the Bible, this chapter has traditionally been read as the capstone of the biblical teaching on the resurrection in the Old Testament, the gospels, the book of Acts, and the rest of the New Testament. As this commentary will show, the historic reading of 1 Cor 15 as the most ample exposition of the same hope of resurrection found throughout the Bible fully coheres with Paul's teaching in this chapter. But in recent decades a rival interpretation of this chapter has become widely influential, according to which 1 Cor 15 proclaims a *different* conception of the resurrection than what we find in the four gospels, elsewhere in the New Testament, and in historic Christian teaching. The massive historical and theological claim of this rival interpretation requires unpacking.

In the canonical gospels, as virtually all scholars concur, the resurrection of Christ, and the hope of resurrection for followers of Christ, is a concrete and physical reality involving the body of flesh and bones. In Luke's Gospel, for example, the resurrection narrative begins with the disciples' discovery that Jesus was no longer in the tomb (24:1–12; cf. 24:23–24). At the climax of the narrative, Jesus shows himself alive to the Twelve and the other disciples, inviting them to "touch me and see, because a spirit does not have flesh and bones as you see that I have" (Luke 24:39). In John's Gospel, Jesus invites doubting Thomas to probe the scars in his hands and side (John 20:24–29). The speeches of the apostles in Acts similarly stress that the flesh of Jesus was raised without undergoing decay (2:25–31; 13:34–37), and that the risen Jesus ate and drank with his disciples (10:40–42; cf. 1:3–4). In the gospels and Acts, Jesus's bodily resurrection from the tomb fulfills the creator God's promised conquest of death, bringing the hope of bodily resurrection for all who believe (John 5:24–29; 6:39–40, 44, 54; Acts 4:1–2; 23:7–10; 24:14–15; 26:6–8; 26:22–23).

In the scriptural interpretation of the ancient church from the first century onward, the resurrection hope expounded in 1 Cor 15 was understood, in congruity with the gospels and Acts, in terms of a resurrection of the flesh, identifying the resurrected body of this passage with the earthly, fleshly body raised to life and transformed to be imperishable.[2] To be sure, "Gnostic" interpreters such as the Valentinians and Ophites, who believed that the material world and the physical body were inherently evil, read this chapter in ways that excluded a literal resurrection of the body (Gos. Phil. 56.26–57.22; Irenaeus, *Haer.* 1.30.13).[3] And the Alexandrian exegete Origen, influenced by Gnostic thought, apparently interpreted 1 Cor 15 as involving a resurrection of a heavenly or spiritual body composed of ethereal matter, distinct from the earthly body of flesh (*Sel. Ps.* 11.384 [on Ps 1:5]; *Comm. Matt.* 17.29–30; *Princ.* 2.10–11; *Cels.* 5.18–23).[4] However, Gnostic readings of this chapter were rejected within the ancient church, and Origen's teaching on the resurrection was condemned as heretical by the Fifth Ecumenical Council (Constantinople II).[5] Patristic interpretation, from Clement of Rome in the first

---

2. The fullest discussion is found in François Altermath, *Du corps psychique au corps spirituel: Interprétation de 1 Cor. 15,35–49 par les auteurs chrétiens des quatre premiers siècles* (BGBE 18; Tübingen: Mohr Siebeck, 1977). See also M. E. Dahl, *The Resurrection of the Body: A Study of 1 Corinthians 15* (SBT 36; London: SCM, 1962), 37–50.

3. See further Elaine E. Pagels, "'The Mystery of the Resurrection': A Gnostic Reading of 1 Corinthians 15," *JBL* 93 (1974): 276–88; and Outi Lehtipuu, "'Flesh and Blood Cannot Inherit the Kingdom of God': The Transformation of the Flesh in the Early Christian Debates Concerning Resurrection," in *Metamorphoses: Resurrection, Body and Transformative Practices in Early Christianity* (ed. Turid Karlsen Seim and Jorunn Økland; Berlin: de Gruyter, 2009), 147–68.

4. See Henry Chadwick, "Origen, Celsus, and the Resurrection of the Body," *HTR* 41 (1948): 83–102; and Henri Crouzel, "La doctrine origènienne du corps réssuscité," *BLE* 31 (1980): 175–200, 241–66. The precise nature of Origen's views remains controversial; Crouzel's article is widely considered the authoritative study of the subject.

5. Leading opponents of Origen's exegesis of 1 Cor 15 were Methodius (*Res.* 2–3) and Jerome (*Jo. Hier.* 25–36). However, even among Origen's chief admirers, his interpretation of that chapter as excluding the earthly flesh from salvation was emphatically rejected. Cf. Gregory of Nyssa, *De anima* 1898–1923; *In sanctum pascha* 251–270; Rufinus, *Symb.* 42–45. Origen's views on the nature of the resurrection body were declared heretical at Constantinople II in anathemas 10 and 11 of the so-called Fifteen Anathemas against Origen.

INTRODUCTION

century to Augustine in the fifth, unanimously interpreted 1 Cor 15, in agreement with the canonical gospels, in terms of a physical resurrection of the body of flesh and bones.[6] This reading was in agreement with the generally received ancient Christian doctrine of resurrection as the reconstitution and glorious transformation of the present mortal body, a transformation involving "enhancement of what is, not metamorphosis into what is not."[7] M. E. Dahl described this orthodox conception as involving the claim that "the resurrection body is *this* body restored and improved in a miraculous manner."[8] The church's historic creeds gave expression to this hope in the most striking way by affirming "the resurrection of the *flesh*."[9] Throughout almost two millennia, exegesis of 1 Corinthians 15 was carried out in the context of this conviction—shared alike by Catholic, Orthodox, and Protestant interpreters—that the resurrection hope of the faithful that Paul expounds in this chapter is a resurrection of the flesh.

However, an important shift took place around the turn of the previous century. In an influential monograph published in 1896, Ernst Teichmann argued, in a reading with clear affinities to that of Origen, that Paul in this chapter envisions a "spiritual" resurrection body, that is, a body no longer made up of flesh but composed of spirit or πνεῦμα, the same fine pneumatic "stuff" of which the heavenly bodies are composed.[10] In striking contrast to the historic, ecclesial interpretation, in Teichmann's view Paul in 1 Corinthians 15 explicitly *opposes* a resurrection of the flesh.[11] Teichmann's approach found many imitators, so that by the midpoint

---

6. See 1 Clem. 24–26; Irenaeus, *Haer.* 5.7–14; Tertullian, *Res.* 48–57; Methodius, *Res.* 1.13–14; 3.5–6; Rufinus, *Symb.* 41–47; Jerome, *Epist.* 108.23–24; and Augustine, *Civ.* 20.20; 22.21–24.

7. Caroline Walker Bynum, *The Resurrection of the Body in Western Christianity, 200–1336* (New York: Columbia University Press, 1999), 8.

8. Dahl, *Resurrection of the Body*, 7.

9. Cf. the Old Roman Creed (ca. AD 175): πιστεύω εἰς . . . σαρκὸς ἀνάστασιν ("I believe in . . . the resurrection of the flesh"); Creed of Jerusalem (ca. 350): πιστεύομεν . . . εἰς σαρκὸς ἀνάστασιν ("we believe in . . . the resurrection of the flesh"); Const. ap. 7.41 (fourth century): βαπτίζομαι καὶ . . . εἰς σαρκὸς ἀνάστασιν ("I am baptized also . . . into the resurrection of the flesh"); Creed of the First Council of Toledo (400): *resurrectionem vero humanae credimus carnis* ("we believe indeed in the resurrection of our human flesh"); Apostles' Creed (sixth century): *credo in . . . carnis resurrectionem* ("I believe in . . . the resurrection of the flesh"); Symbol of Faith of Leo IX (1053): *credo etiam veram resurrectionem eiusdem carnis, quam nunc gesto* ("I believe also in the true resurrection of the same flesh which I now have").

10. Ernst Teichmann, *Die paulinische Vorstellungen von Auferstehung und Gericht und ihre Beziehungen zur jüdischen Apokalyptik* (Freiburg: Mohr, 1896), 33–62.

11. Teichmann, *Auferstehung*, 5. An important precursor to Teichmann's study was the work of Otto Pfleiderer, *Paulinism: A Contribution to the History of Primitive Christian Theology* (vol. 1, *Exposition of Paul's Doctrine*; trans. E. Peters; London: Williams & Norgate, 1877). Similarly to Teichmann, Pfleiderer argued that Paul's conception of the resurrection in 1 Cor 15 did not in-

of the previous century M. E. Dahl could describe a reading along these lines as "the accepted exegesis" of the chapter.[12] That was perhaps an overstatement even at the time, and in recent decades a number of studies have appeared by such scholars as N. T. Wright, Richard Hays, and Martin Hengel opposing this revisionist reading and interpreting 1 Cor 15, in continuity with the four gospels and the church's historic teaching, in terms of the resurrection of the flesh and its glorious transformation to imperishability.[13] However, an interpretation of this chapter largely along the lines suggested by Teichmann has in recent years found significant scholarly support. Prominent advocates of this rival interpretation include Dale Martin, Troels Engberg-Pedersen, and Jeffrey R. Asher, but a number of other interpreters maintain this position as well. Despite differences in detail, these scholars all argue that Paul in 1 Cor 15 envisions an ethereal or "spiritual" resurrection body: a body composed of spirit that excludes participation of the earthly body of flesh and bones in the life of the world to come.[14]

---

volve "the old fleshly body," but a new "spiritual corporeity ... analogous to the heavenly body of the risen Christ, which consists ... of heavenly light-substance (δόξα)" (260; cf. 128, 131–32).

12. Dahl, *Resurrection of the Body*, 7–19.

13. N. T. Wright, *The Resurrection of the Son of God* (vol. 3 of *Christian Origins and the Question of God*; Minneapolis: Fortress, 2003), 340–61; Hays, 270–75; Martin Hengel, "Das Begräbnis Jesu bei Paulus und die leibliche Auferstehung aus dem Grabe," in *Auferstehung—Resurrection* (ed. Friedrich Avemarie and Hermann Lichtenberger; WUNT 135; Tübingen: Mohr Siebeck, 2001), 119–83; Thiselton, 1257–1306; E. Earle Ellis, "Soma in 1 Corinthians," *Int* 44 (1990): 132–44; Andrew Johnson, "Turning the World Upside Down in 1 Corinthians 15: Epistemology, the Resurrected Body and the New Creation," *EvQ* 75 (2003): 291–309; Ronald Sider, "St. Paul's Conception of the Resurrection Body in 1 Corinthians XV.35–54," *NTS* 21 (1975): 428–39; Bernhard Spörlein, *Die Leugnung der Auferstehung: Eine historisch-kritische Untersuchung zu I Kor 15* (Regensburg: Pustet, 1971), 109–21; and Ben F. Meyer, "Did Paul's View of the Resurrection of the Dead Undergo Development?" *TS* 47 (1986): 363–87.

14. See, for example, Dale Martin, *The Corinthian Body* (New Haven: Yale University Press, 1995), 108–32; Troels Engberg-Pedersen, *Cosmology and Self in the Apostle Paul: The Material Spirit* (Oxford: Oxford University, 2010), 8–38; Engberg-Pedersen, "Complete and Incomplete Transformation in Paul—A Philosophical Reading of Paul on Body and Spirit," in Seim and Økland, *Metamorphoses*, 123–46; Engberg-Pedersen, "The Material Spirit: Cosmology and Ethics in Paul," *NTS* 55 (2009): 179–97; Jeffrey R. Asher, *Polarity and Change in 1 Corinthians 15: A Study of Metaphysics, Rhetoric, and Resurrection* (Tübingen: Mohr Siebeck, 2000), 153–68; Daniel A. Smith, *Revisiting the Empty Tomb: The Early History of Easter* (Minneapolis: Fortress, 2010), 27–45; Bruce Chilton, *Resurrection Logic: How Jesus' First Followers Believed God Raised Him from the Dead* (Waco: Baylor University Press, 2019), 67–86; Paula Fredriksen, "Vile Bodies: Paul and Augustine on the Resurrection of the Flesh," in *Biblical Hermeneutics in Historical Perspective* (ed. Mark S. Burrows and Paul Rorem; Grand Rapids: Eerdmans, 1991), 75–87; Nikolaus Walter, "Leibliche Auferstehung? Zur Frage der Hellenisierung der Auferweckungshoffnung bei Paulus," in *Paulus, Apostel Jesu Christi: Festschrift für Günter Klein zum 70. Geburtstag* (ed. Michael Trow-

This latter reading of 1 Cor 15 is the basis for a view of Christian origins in which belief in the resurrection of Jesus's crucified body from the tomb, such as we see reflected in the narratives of the four gospels, was a later development, unknown to Paul and the earliest Christ followers. As Rudolf Bultmann famously remarked, "The [gospels'] accounts of an empty tomb are legends, of which Paul as yet knew nothing."[15] These scholars claim to find in the primitive apostolic confession of 1 Cor 15:3–8 an understanding of Jesus's "resurrection" as his translation to heaven in a postmortem disincarnate form discontinuous with his crucified body.[16] In this view, belief in the resurrection of Jesus's crucified body from the tomb was neither primitive nor apostolic but a later conception in discontinuity with the earliest kerygma.

This once novel interpretation of 1 Cor 15 is today widespread and pervasive not only in specialized studies of that chapter or the resurrection in general but also in the wider scholarly literature touching upon Paul's teaching on the resurrection or on 1 Cor 15. In the scholarly literature it is routinely assumed that Paul's teaching in this chapter is incompatible with the doctrine of the resurrection of the flesh that we find in the four gospels and in the church's historic teaching. Close exegesis and argument are commonly considered unnecessary. It is

---

itzsch; Tübingen: Mohr Siebeck, 1998), 59; Lindemann, 324–73 (the "more likely" interpretation); James D. G. Dunn, "How Are the Dead Raised? With What Body Do They Come? Reflections on 1 Corinthians 15," *SwJT* 45 (2002): 4–18; Peter Lampe, "Paul's Concept of a Spiritual Body," in *Resurrection: Theological and Scientific Assessments* (ed. Ted Peters, Robert John Russell, and Michael Welker; Grand Rapids: Eerdmans, 2002), 103–14; Jerry Sumney, "Post-Mortem Existence and Resurrection of the Body in Paul," *HBT* 31 (2009): 12–26. For an influential version of this thesis from the previous generation, see Hans Grass, *Ostergeschehen und Osterberichte* (Göttingen: Vandenhoeck & Ruprecht, 1962), 146–73.

15. Rudolf Bultmann, *Theologie des Neuen Testaments* (9th ed.; Tübingen: Mohr Siebeck, 1984), 48: "Legende sind die Geschichten vom leeren Grabe, von dem Paulus noch nichts weiss."

16. See Smith, *Empty Tomb*, 13–45; Dale C. Allison Jr., *The Resurrection of Jesus: Apologetics, Polemics, History* (New York: Bloomsbury, 2021), 336–56; cf. 42–43, 53–64, 72–80, 83–89, 129–36, 144–45, 249–61; Jürgen Becker, *Die Auferstehung Jesu Christi nach dem Neuen Testament: Ostererfahrung und Osterverständnis im Urchristentum* (Tübingen: Mohr Siebeck, 2007), 149–71; Adela Yarbro Collins, "The Empty Tomb in the Gospel According to Mark," in *Hermes and Athena: Biblical Exegesis and Philosophical Theology* (ed. Eleonore Stump and Thomas P. Flint; Notre Dame: University of Notre Dame Press, 1993), 111–14; Marcus J. Borg, "The Truth of Easter," in Marcus J. Borg and N. T. Wright, *The Meaning of Jesus: Two Visions* (San Francisco: HarperSanFrancisco, 1999), 129–42; James M. Robinson, "Jesus—From Easter to Valentinus (or to the Apostles' Creed)," *JBL* 101 (1982): 5–37; Joost Holleman, *Resurrection and Parousia: A Traditio-Historical Study of Paul's Eschatology in 1 Corinthians 15* (NovTSup 84; Leiden: Brill, 1996), 142–44; Lampe, "Spiritual Body," 103–14; Lindemann, 325–36; Grass, *Ostergeschehen*, 146–73; and Walter, "Auferstehung," 109–27.

## The Unique Importance and Untapped Riches of Paul's Resurrection Chapter

normally considered sufficient to cite (in English translation) Paul's description of the resurrected body as a "spiritual body" in 1 Cor 15:44, or his reference to Christ as a "life-giving Spirit" in 15:45, or (above all) Paul's statement in 15:50 that "flesh and blood cannot inherit the kingdom of God." The latter verse is a widely used "prooftext" that Paul, contrary to the canonical gospels, did not affirm that Jesus rose in the flesh and did not believe in a coming resurrection of the flesh. Thus Dale Martin asserts: "Paul himself believes that the resurrected body will not be composed of flesh (see v. 50)."[17] Paula Fredriksen writes that Christ arose "in a spiritual body, Paul insists, and definitely *not* in a body of flesh and blood (1 Cor 15:44, 50)."[18] Dag Øistein Endsjø speaks of "the fleshless resurrection body of Paul."[19] And Ernst Käsemann can confidently assert: "The idea of . . . the resurrection of the flesh . . . is un-Pauline."[20]

The implications of this interpretation of 1 Cor 15 are massive, going to the heart of the Christian faith. If this reading of 1 Cor 15 is valid, the church's historic doctrine of the resurrection, expressed in her creeds and worship, is a late and inauthentic imposition contrary to the faith of the apostles and the first Christians. Moreover, in this reading the accounts in our canonical gospels of Jesus's bodily resurrection from the tomb do not reflect the message of the earliest eyewitnesses but later legends. In this interpretation of the chapter, the good news of the resurrection proclaimed in 1 Cor 15 and the good news narrated by Matthew, Mark, Luke, and John are different gospels indeed. For (in this reading) they are fundamentally at variance regarding the meaning of the affirmation that Jesus has been raised from the dead on the third day and the nature of the hope that Jesus's resurrection offers those who believe.

We will see in this commentary that this widespread interpretation is founded upon a mistaken exegesis. The resurrection Paul defends and expounds in 1 Cor 15, in continuity with the four gospels and historic Christian teaching, is the resurrection of the flesh. Moreover, we will find that the apostolic formula in 1 Cor 15:3–8 presupposes a narrative of the kind we see in the canonical gospels, involving an empty tomb as well as eyewitness encounters with a Jesus risen in the same body

---

17. Martin, *Body*, 126.
18. Paula Fredriksen, *Paul: The Pagans' Apostle* (New Haven: Yale University Press, 2017), 4.
19. Dag Øistein Endsjø, *Greek Resurrection Beliefs and the Success of Christianity* (New York: Macmillan, 2009), 141–47.
20. Ernst Käsemann, *Commentary on Romans* (trans. Geoffrey W. Bromiley; Grand Rapids: Eerdmans, 1980), 237. See also Chilton, *Resurrection Logic*, 76; Paul J. Achtemeier, "The Continuing Quest for Coherence in St. Paul: An Experiment in Thought," in *Theology and Ethics in Paul and His Interpreters* (ed. Eugene H. Lovering Jr. and Jerry L. Sumney; Nashville: Abingdon, 1996), 138; Keener, 131.

in which he was crucified. In Paul's resurrection chapter we find a robust doctrine of bodily resurrection. The resurrection Paul proclaims in 1 Cor 15 is not the mere transferal to an ethereal or spiritual state supposed by Teichmann and his modern heirs, offering yet one more expectation of spiritual afterlife among many in the ancient world. The resurrection Paul proclaims in this chapter is the conquest of bodily death. It is the final triumph of God.

Although the following pages will reveal the coherence of the historic and ecclesial interpretation of the resurrection in 1 Cor 15 with Paul's teaching in this chapter, this commentary does not simply repeat previous scholarly arguments in support of the historic exegesis. Rather, the commentary breaks fresh ground, offering new evidence and arguments not previously considered, which I believe are decisive in their force. The commentary thus offers a fresh contribution to the scholarly discussion of Paul's teaching regarding both Jesus's resurrection and the future resurrection of those who belong to Christ.

## 1 Corinthians 15 and Christology

Paul's resurrection chapter also plays an important role in contemporary scholarly discussion of the Christology of the New Testament. Of crucial importance in this discussion are the two major christological statements within this chapter, 15:24–28 and 15:44b–49. These passages are often thought to problematize or even preclude a divine Christology within Paul's thought. The latter passage, 15:44b–49, is the main source for James D. G. Dunn's claim that Paul's letters evince a "Spirit-Christology" that identifies Christ with the Spirit and is incompatible with an incarnational Christology.[21] Many scholars regard 15:24–28, in its depiction of the Son's submission to the Father (15:27–28), as evidence of a so-called low Christology in which the Son is not divine but is merely an exalted creature.[22] This passage is also an exegetical centerpiece within a recent proposal by a number of evangelical theologians, the most prominent of whom is Wayne A. Grudem, that the New Testament exhibits a divine but subordinationist Christology involving

---

21. James D. G. Dunn, "1 Corinthians 15:45—Last Adam, Life-Giving Spirit," in *Christ and Spirit in the New Testament* (ed. Barnabas Lindars and Stephen S. Smalley; Cambridge: Cambridge University Press, 1973), 127–42; Dunn, *The Theology of Paul the Apostle* (Grand Rapids: Eerdmans, 1998), 261–65.

22. See, for example, James F. McGrath, *The Only True God: Early Christian Monotheism in Its Jewish Context* (Urbana: University of Illinois Press, 2009), 49–50, 53; Dunn, *Theology of Paul*, 248–49, 254–55.

an eternal functional subordination of the Son in his divine nature to the Father.[23] And almost all modern interpreters, including scholars who recognize a divine Christology in Paul, read 1 Cor 15:24–28 as teaching that the reign and lordship of Christ are temporary and will one day cease.[24] Joseph Fitzmyer reflects the consensus view when he states that this passage "denotes the time when the risen Christ's reign comes to an end."[25]

This volume offers a new contribution to these current christological debates. We will find that each of the widely held positions mentioned above reflect a misreading of Paul's resurrection chapter. The commentary will show that the interpretation of 1 Cor 15:24–28 in terms of a temporary reign of Christ, despite its almost universal acceptance among contemporary interpreters, has its source in a failure to read this passage in its historical and literary context. As we will see, the kingdom and reign of Christ in 1 Cor 15:24–28 is not temporary but everlasting and without end. Moreover, we will see that both 15:24–28 and 15:44b–49 reflect a fully divine and incarnational Christology, in which the identity of the one God includes both the Father and the Son. What is more, these passages do not support a subordinationist Christology but presuppose the eternal coequality of the Father and the Son. Indeed, we will discover that the chapter as a whole, in its reflection on the resurrection as the work of Father, Son, and Holy Spirit, reveals a structure and line of thought for which the only adequate language is the language of the Trinity.

## Uncovering the Riches of Paul's Resurrection Chapter

The widespread but mistaken interpretation of 1 Cor 15 in terms of an ethereal resurrection body not only introduces foreign ideas into the passage but also conceals the rich doctrine of the resurrection within this chapter. The chief aim of this commentary will be to draw out for the reader this rich theology of the

---

23. See Wayne Grudem, *Systematic Theology* (2d ed.; Grand Rapids: Zondervan Academic, 2020), 301–18. For an example of the important role of 1 Cor 15:24–28 among advocates of this view, see James M. Hamilton, "'That God May Be All in All': The Trinity in 1 Corinthians 15," in *One God in Three Persons: Unity of Essence, Distinction of Persons, Implications for Life* (ed. Bruce A. Ware and John Starke; Wheaton, IL: Crossway, 2015), 95–108; see also Keener, 127.

24. E.g., Wesley Hill, *Paul and the Trinity: Persons, Relations, and the Pauline Letters* (Grand Rapids: Eerdmans, 2015), 131–34; C. E. Hill, "Paul's Understanding of Christ's Kingdom in 1 Corinthians 15:20–28," *NovT* 30 (1988): 311–20; R. B. Jamieson, "1 Corinthians 15.28 and the Grammar of Paul's Christology," *NTS* 66 (2020): 201–2; Schrage, 175; Collins, 552–53; Schreiner, 314.

25. Fitzmyer, 571.

resurrection that Paul develops throughout 1 Cor 15 and which illuminates all of Paul's epistles and the entire Bible. Paul's conception of the resurrection in this chapter reveals the inseparable connection—which so many interpreters have failed to grasp—between Paul's emphasis on the sanctifying work of the Spirit, conformity to Christ, and the Christian moral life in 1 Cor 1–14 and the hope of the resurrection in 1 Cor 15. First Corinthians 15 is thus not only doctrinal but also a call to radical discipleship. For in the theology of the resurrection that Paul places at the heart of his exposition in 1 Cor 15, the bodily resurrection is the physical completion of the moral conformity to the image of the incarnate Son of God that is begun in baptism and increased through faith and its fruits in the life of cruciform discipleship to Christ. It is the culmination of the Spirit's salvific work through the gift of the Holy Spirit to the physical body. It is the consummation of union with God.

The first chapter of this commentary also offers a new proposal regarding the until now unresolved enigma of the unity and coherence of 1 Corinthians, demonstrating that chapter 15 is the goal and culmination of the epistle and the climax of Paul's confrontation with the false human wisdom claimed by some at Corinth (1:18–4:21). First Corinthians 15 thus unifies and clarifies the entire letter. This commentary also offers fresh proposals regarding a number of long-standing exegetical enigmas, including Paul's reference to himself as an untimely birth in 15:8, his mention of baptism for the sake of the dead in 15:29, and his allusion to fighting with the beasts at Ephesus in 15:32. Four excurses—on purported ancient parallels to the resurrection of Jesus, the historical and theological implications of the apostolic confession in 15:3–8, the uniqueness of the hope of the resurrection in the context of the pagan world into which it came, and the ancient background to Paul's analogy of the seed in 15:36–38—further enhance the usefulness of the commentary for the reader.[26] In all the ways aforementioned, this commentary aims to contribute to the scholarly discussion and practical use of 1 Cor 15, the great resurrection chapter of the Bible.

---

26. Throughout this work, all translations of biblical passages and other ancient texts are the author's. All translations of medieval texts and modern scholarly literature in languages other than English are the author's unless otherwise noted.

CHAPTER 1

*Chapter 15 as the Culmination of 1 Corinthians*

Sometime in AD 54, in the midst of missionary labors, severe afflictions, and tumultuous persecutions in the city of Ephesus, Paul wrote his first epistle to the church he had founded at Corinth.[1] No modern scholar doubts the authenticity of 1 Corinthians as a genuine letter of the apostle Paul. But there is no consensus regarding the structure, logic, and coherence of the epistle.

THE ENIGMA OF THE UNITY AND COHERENCE OF 1 CORINTHIANS

Many scholars see no inner coherence within the letter or discernible connection between its various parts. The letter seems a haphazard assemblage of miscellaneous topics rather than a unified whole. "The salient feature of 1 Corinthians is the absence of any detectable logic in the arrangement of its contents."[2] This apparent lack of a unified conception underlying the epistle led a number of interpreters in the past to reject the integrity of the letter, theorizing that the letter is a composite document made up of two or more originally independent letters of Paul. The weakness of such theories has been demonstrated by a number of scholars, with the result that such theories have largely fallen out of favor today.[3] However, Martinus de Boer has more recently proposed a variation of the partition

---

1. For Paul's ministry in Ephesus, see 1 Cor 15:32; 2 Cor 1:8–11; Acts 19. That 1 Corinthians was composed at Ephesus, as virtually all interpreters concur, is beyond doubt in light of 1 Cor 16:8–9. The revisionist scenario advocated by Daryn Graham that Paul wrote the letter in Troas (see Acts 16:6–10) before his first visit to Corinth is clearly impossible. See "The Placement of Paul's Composition in Troas: A Fresh Approach," *Them* 46 (2021): 592–607.

2. Jerome Murphy-O'Connor, *Paul: A Critical Life* (Oxford: Oxford University Press, 1996), 253.

3. The classic study is that of Helmut Merklein, "Die Einheitlichkeit des ersten Korinther-

CHAPTER 1

thesis, arguing that the letter is "a composite of Paul's own making," made up of two different letters composed on different occasions.[4] It is revealing regarding the lack of apparent unity within 1 Corinthians that a number of recent commentators regard de Boer's composite-letter thesis as highly plausible.

In disagreement with the general view that 1 Corinthians lacks a global structure, a few scholars have argued for a unified conception underlying the letter. The most influential of these is Margaret Mitchell. Analyzing the letter in light of the canons of ancient deliberative rhetoric, she concludes that "1 Corinthians is a single letter of unitary composition which contains a deliberative argument persuading the Christian community at Corinth to become reunified."[5] The appeal to unity is introduced in 1:10, which Mitchell takes to be the "thesis statement" of the letter, with 1:18–15:57 serving as rhetorical "proofs" or arguments for the desirability of unity and an end to factionalism. This appeal to unity, according to Mitchell, underlies every section of the letter, and unifies the entire epistle.[6] The roots of the problem of disunity at Corinth, she argues, are in Paul's view not doctrinal but ethical and social: Paul "names their problem as factionalism, utilizing very strong terminology derived from ancient politics."[7] The apostle does not take sides in these squabbles, but rather "in his oscillating arguments in 1 Corinthians Paul seeks to conciliate different sides."[8] His purpose is "to urge reconciliation of divided factions."[9]

A number of scholars follow Mitchell in this reading of the letter.[10] However, Mitchell's analysis is not fully convincing. The theme of unity may seem to fit chapters 1–4, but to regard the diverse topics Paul addresses in chapters 5–15 as merely a series of arguments subserving a general call to reconciliation seems forced. "In an effort to show the rhetoric of the letter, a procrustean bed has been made."[11] Moreover, as David A. Ackerman has shown convincingly, Paul in this

---

briefes," *ZNW* 75 (1984): 153–83, a relentless critique of the exegetical fallacies underlying the partition theories.

4. Martinus C. de Boer, "The Composition of 1 Corinthians," *NTS* 40 (1994): 229–45.

5. Margaret M. Mitchell, *Paul and the Rhetoric of Reconciliation: An Exegetical Investigation of the Language and Composition of 1 Corinthians* (Louisville: Westminster John Knox, 1991), 1.

6. Mitchell, *Rhetoric*, 65–295.

7. Mitchell, *Rhetoric*, 302.

8. Mitchell, *Rhetoric*, 302.

9. Mitchell, *Rhetoric*, 303.

10. For example, Matt O'Reilly, *Paul and the Resurrected Body: Social Identity and Ethical Practice* (ESEC 22; Atlanta: SBL Press, 2020), 44–45; Hays, 8–9; Insawn Saw, *Paul's Rhetoric in 1 Corinthians 15: An Analysis Utilizing the Theories of Classical Rhetoric* (Lewiston, NY: Mellen, 1995), 177–93.

11. Fitzmyer, 55.

letter does not merely urge reconciliation of differing factions but strongly endeavors to correct particular behaviors and beliefs of the Corinthians.[12] As Thiselton rightly notes, the inadequacy of Mitchell's argument is that she underemphasizes "the theological basis of the unity" to which Paul calls them in this letter.[13]

The weakness of Mitchell's thesis is particularly evident in her treatment of chapter 15. Mitchell sees 1 Cor 15 as evidence at Corinth of "different views on the resurrection . . . another facet of the church's dissension."[14] She accordingly regards the chapter as the culmination of Paul's exhortation to concord. But what is Paul's response according to Mitchell? In her reading, Paul's counsel to the Corinthians is platitudinous and suspiciously postmodern. She portrays Paul in this chapter as seeking to reconcile those with opposing views of the resurrection, urging that the resurrection "is not earned by individuals or groups, and is thus not to be boasted in or disputed about."[15] But to the contrary, as we will see, Paul in this chapter directly challenges those at Corinth who deny the resurrection, reaffirms the resurrection of the dead in the strongest possible terms, and condemns its denial by some at Corinth as incompatible with the gospel and as destructive of life in Christ.

In a more recent proposal, Roy E. Ciampa and Brian S. Rosner find an underlying "global structure" within the epistle not (as Mitchell) in a call to congregational concord but in the theme of "the sanctification of gentile believers that they may glorify God."[16] Ciampa and Rosner offer a persuasive critique of Mitchell's thesis for its failure to factor in Paul's concern within the letter for sexual purity (chapters 5–7), avoidance of idolatry (8:1–11:1), and worship that glorifies God (11:2–14:40). Ciampa and Rosner's understanding of the letter's purpose is more robust and recognizably Pauline than the thesis of Mitchell. However, Ciampa and Rosner's thesis, on their own admission, fails to explain the function of chapters 1–4 within the epistle. According to Ciampa and Rosner, the theme of sanctification, which they propose as the "overall logic" of the epistle, is not found in chapters 1–4: "In 1 Corinthians Paul deals with Corinthian factionalism first in order to clear the way for this more important matter."[17] Moreover, although correctly recognizing that chapter 15 is the "climax" of the epistle, Ciampa and

---

12. David A. Ackerman, *Lo, I Tell You a Mystery: Cross, Resurrection, and Paraenesis in the Rhetoric of 1 Corinthians* (PTMS 54; Eugene, OR: Pickwick, 2006).

13. Thiselton, 39.

14. Mitchell, *Rhetoric*, 176.

15. Mitchell, *Rhetoric*, 177.

16. Roy E. Ciampa and Brian S. Rosner, "The Structure and Argument of 1 Corinthians: A Biblical/Jewish Approach," *NTS* 52 (2006): 205–18.

17. Ciampa and Rosner, "Structure and Argument," 214.

Rosner nonetheless fail to explain how this chapter, with its doctrinal focus on the resurrection, relates to the theme of gentile sanctification.

Karl Barth famously argued that chapter 15 is "the very peak and crown" of the letter.[18] According to Barth, chapter 15 "forms not only the close and crown of the whole Epistle, but also provides the clue to its meaning."[19] Yet he did not regard the letter as possessing a literary, rhetorical, or even thematic unity. Rather, the unity that Barth proposed was one of theological conception, in which "the secret theme of the Epistle," the "red thread which runs through the whole," receives its crowning expression in the doctrine of the resurrection expounded in chapter 15.[20] Barth's proposal has been followed by some scholars.[21] But the majority of scholars have judged it inadequate.[22] There are two difficulties with Barth's proposal. The first problem is that Barth's obscure discussion never clarifies what the "secret theme" of the letter is, and his commentators are not entirely agreed on the point.[23] The second problem with Barth's proposal is that the conception that he claims comes to unique fullness of expression in 1 Cor 15 is, according to Barth, central to *every* Pauline letter.[24] Barth's proposal thus does not provide an explanation of this *particular* Pauline letter. Barth's thesis may provide helpful insights into the unity of Paul's theology and into the importance of 1 Cor 15 as a key expression of that theology, but it does not provide a persuasive case for the unity of 1 Corinthians. The strength of Barth's thesis is its correspondence with the *sense* of many scholars that chapter 15 in some way provides the climax and key to the letter. But Barth's thesis does not provide a *ground* for this sense in Paul's literary and rhetorical structuring of the letter.

Two additional proposals regarding the unity of the letter should be mentioned. Kenneth E. Bailey argues that 1 Corinthians is a scrupulously arranged collection of "five carefully constructed essays" that share a common structure and are closely interconnected with one another.[25] Timothy Milinovich argues

18. Karl Barth, *The Resurrection of the Dead* (trans. H. J. Stenning; 1933; repr., Eugene, OR: Wipf & Stock, 2003), 101. On this work, see David Fergusson, "Barth's *Resurrection of the Dead*: Further Reflections," *SJT* 56 (2003): 65–72.

19. Barth, *Resurrection*, 5.

20. Barth, *Resurrection*, 73, 97.

21. Barth's thesis is followed by Thiselton, 39, 1169; Ackerman, *Mystery*, 77; Schrage, 7–8.

22. See Gordon P. Wiles, *Paul's Intercessory Prayers: The Significance of the Intercessory Prayer Passages in the Letters of Paul* (SNTSMS 24; Cambridge: Cambridge University Press, 1974), 137.

23. Barth, *Resurrection*, 13–124. On Barth's "reticence" regarding the subject matter of chapter 15, the resurrection of the dead, see Ferguson, "Barth's *Resurrection*," 70–72.

24. Barth, *Resurrection*, 5.

25. Kenneth E. Bailey, "The Structure of 1 Corinthians and Paul's Theological Method with Special Reference to 4:17," *NovT* 25 (1983): 152–81.

that the letter has not a linear arrangement but an elaborate concentric structure consisting of three major chiastic ring compositions that are further subdivided into three inner ring sets each, making nine ring sets in all.[26] Space precludes discussion of either proposal here. Suffice to say that, despite a number of good exegetical insights, the complex network of connections within the letter claimed by Bailey and Milinovich are overall strained and unconvincing.

There is, then, no current consensus whether 1 Corinthians has a detectable structure or arrangement, and, if so, what that structure or arrangement might be. Three issues in particular remain unresolved enigmas.

(1) The first of these is the relationship of chapters 1–4 to the rest of the epistle. Martinus de Boer calls this "the crucial interpretive difficulty of 1 Corinthians."[27] Paul's focus in chapters 1–4 on his gospel, Corinthian factionalism, and the foolishness of the kerygma in contrast with human wisdom appears to have little or no connection to the behavioral and practical issues addressed in the remainder of the epistle. Neither the proposal of Mitchell (chapters 5–15 consist merely of further arguments bolstering the call to unity in chapters 1–4) nor the proposal of Ciampa and Rosner (chapters 1–4 are merely preliminary to the call to sanctification in chapters 5–15) provides a convincing resolution of the problem.

(2) Another unresolved question is the nature of the Corinthian claims to wisdom and partisan strife opposed by Paul in chapters 1–4. The folly of the gospel in contrast with human wisdom, the dominant theme of chapters 1–4, is seemingly not taken up elsewhere in the letter, and the varied attempts to correlate the topics taken up in chapters 5–16 with the Corinthian factions of chapters 1–4 have not won wide acceptance.[28] How are the Corinthian claim to wisdom in chapters 1–4 and the divisions and problems in chapters 5–16 related?

(3) A third question is the function of chapter 15 within the epistle. Many scholars can find no discernible relation of chapter 15 to the rest of the letter.[29] As one scholar puts it, the chapter is "a discrete, stand-alone item that can be

---

26. Timothy Milinovich, *Beyond What Is Written: The Performative Structure of 1 Corinthians* (Eugene, OR: Pickwick, 2013).

27. De Boer, "Composition," 243. On this issue, see further Nils Dahl, "Paul and the Church at Corinth according to I Corinthians 1–4," in *Studies in Paul: Theology for the Early Christian Mission* (Minneapolis: Augsburg, 1977), 40–61; Duane Litfin, *St. Paul's Theology of Proclamation: 1 Corinthians 1–4 and Greco-Roman Rhetoric* (SNTSMS 79; Cambridge: Cambridge University Press, 1994), 150.

28. See the comments of de Boer, "Composition," 243–44.

29. According to Hans Conzelmann, 1 Cor 15 "is a self-contained treatise on the resurrection of the dead" (Conzelmann, 249). In a similar vein, Stephen M. Pogoloff regards the chapter as a recycled sermon that Paul tagged on to the end of the letter. See *Logos and Sophia: The Rhetorical Situation of 1 Corinthians* (SBLDS 134; Atlanta: Scholars, 1992), 280.

CHAPTER 1

considered independent of its immediate context in the epistle."[30] A number of other interpreters, following Barth, regard chapter 15 as the climax of the letter.[31] But Barth's argument has also been widely criticized.[32] And, as we have seen, Barth's argument is not persuasive. And yet many interpreters express, alongside and even in spite of their theories as to the letter's structure, their strong sense that chapter 15 is in some way the capstone of the whole epistle. So Richard Hays can write of chapter 15: "Clearly, Paul has saved the weightiest matter for last—as any good preacher would do. This eloquent chapter, coming at the end of the body of Paul's long letter, anchors the whole discussion."[33] But this contradicts his own verdict regarding the structure of the letter, which follows Margaret Mitchell in considering chapter 15 as merely the last of a series of arguments subserving a general exhortation to unity.[34] The question of the function of chapter 15 within the letter has previously not received a convincing answer.

## The Way Forward: Epistolary Analysis, Rhetorical Criticism, and the Epistolary Situation

I believe that each of these enigmas can be resolved through more precise exegesis of the letter. In considering the structure of the letter, I will make primary use of epistolary analysis, employ a limited and cautious use of rhetorical criticism, and apply judicious attention to the epistolary situation. A brief discussion of each is necessary before we begin.

The value of epistolary analysis, which is the investigation of Paul's epistles in light of the structural features and conventions of ancient letters, is universally recognized. Scholarly study has illumined both the ancient letter form and Paul's distinctive adaptation of that form.[35] But the fruits of this study have not yet been fully exploited in the study of this particular Pauline letter. Epistolary analysis

---

30. Mark A. Wegener, "The Rhetorical Strategy of 1 Corinthians 15," *CurTM* 31 (2004): 439.

31. Thiselton, 39, 1169; Ackerman, *Mystery*, 77; Frederick David Carr, "Beginning at the End: The Kingdom of God in 1 Corinthians," *CBQ* 81 (2019): 452–53.

32. Carl J. Bjerkelund, *Parakalô: Form, Funktion und Sinn der Parakalô-Sätze in den paulinischen Briefen* (Oslo: Universitetsforlaget, 1967), 145; Wiles, *Intercessory Prayers*, 137.

33. Hays, 252.

34. Hays, 8–9.

35. On the ancient letter and epistolary analysis of Paul, see William G. Doty, *Letters in Primitive Christianity* (Philadelphia: Fortress, 1973); John L. White, "Ancient Greek Letters," in *Graeco-Roman Literature and the New Testament* (ed. David E. Aune; SBLSBS 21; Atlanta: Scholars, 1988); John L. White, "The Greek Documentary Letter Tradition Third Century B.C.E. to Third Century C.E.," *Semeia* 22 (1981): 89–106; Abraham J. Malherbe, *Ancient Epistolary Theorists*

will provide our primary foundation as we investigate the structure of Paul's first letter to the Corinthians.

The value of rhetorical criticism in the interpretation of Paul is more controversial. Here scholars are often sharply divided. According to Dale Martin, "Paul's letters follow common rhetorical conventions, contain rhetorical topoi, figures, and techniques, and are readily analyzable as pieces of Greco-Roman rhetoric."[36] Margaret Mitchell's influential study of 1 Corinthians discussed above similarly argues that the letter is a "hybrid" document merging a deliberative rhetorical argument within an epistolary framework.[37] Thomas R. Schreiner, by contrast, rejects the claim "that Paul's letters are structured by the canons of Greek rhetoric."[38] And, as we saw, Joseph Fitzmyer regards Mitchell's rhetorical analysis of 1 Corinthians as forcing Paul's thought into an untenable "procrustean bed."[39]

Rhetorical analysis can, in my view, be a helpful tool for the study of Paul. After all, Augustine, prior to his conversion a leading teacher of rhetoric, considered Paul "our great orator" (*Doctr. chr.* 4.15). But Augustine also considered the idea that Paul followed the canons of rhetoric to be risible (4.11). Rather, his eloquence flowed spontaneously from the wisdom given to him by God (4.11–12). Augustine's observations suggest that a nuanced approach to rhetorical analysis of Paul is necessary, one that respects the individuality, spontaneity, and creativity of Paul's rhetorical genius. A judicious approach is especially important when investigating the rhetorical structure or *dispositio* of Paul's argument. Here, as Carl Joachim Classen notes, "extreme caution" is called for.[40] We will therefore make only a limited and cautious use of rhetorical analysis as we unlock the logic of Paul's letter.

Finally, a penetrating exegesis of Paul must include attention to the epistolary situation. Andrew W. Pitts has helpfully noted the difference between the ancient philosophical letter-essays (such as, for example, the letters of Epicurus) and Paul's epistles. These letter-essays, Pitts points out, are "philosophical treatises on moral topics with epistolary framing."[41] Paul in his letters, by contrast, addressed concrete "situational and contextual factors within the communities to which he

---

(SBLSBS 19; Atlanta: Scholars, 1988); and H.-J. Klauck, *Ancient Letters and the New Testament: A Guide to Context and Exegesis* (Waco: Baylor University Press, 2006).

36. Dale Martin, *The Corinthian Body* (New Haven: Yale University Press, 1995), 52.
37. Mitchell, *Rhetoric*, 20–64, 186–88, 296.
38. Schreiner, 18; similarly skeptical is Ellis, 47–54.
39. Fitzmyer, 55.
40. Carl Joachim Classen, *Rhetorical Criticism of the New Testament* (Leiden: Brill, 2002), 27.
41. Andrew W. Pitts, "Philosophical and Epistolary Contexts for Pauline Paraenesis," in *Paul and the Ancient Letter Form* (ed. S. E. Porter and S. A. Adams; Leiden: Brill, 2010), 269–336.

CHAPTER 1

was writing," and writes "with a constant sense of the audience in mind."[42] The interpreter of 1 Corinthians must therefore address the situation that called forth the letter, including the nature of the division at Corinth (1:10–11) and the character of the wisdom claimed by some but regarded by Paul as incompatible with the gospel (1:17–31). At the same time, the interpreter must avoid an undisciplined mirror reading that interprets every statement of Paul in the letter as necessarily countering its mirror opposite at Corinth. We will therefore endeavor to pursue a responsible approach that explores the epistolary situation as an integral element of the letter but focuses on Paul's own direct statements regarding the situation at Corinth, avoiding all speculative hypotheses and reconstructions.

## The Structure of the Letter as a Whole

### Identifying the Main Body of the Epistle

Let us, then, begin our investigation of the logic and structure of this epistle. Epistolary analysis allows us to readily identify the constituent parts and main body of the letter:

I. Letter Opening (1:1–9)
    A. Salutation (1:1–3)
    B. Thanksgiving (1:4–9)
II. Body of the Letter (1:10–16:14)
    A. Body Opening (1:10–17)
    B. Main Body (1:18–15:58)
    C. Body Closing (16:1–14)
III. Letter Closing (16:15–24)
    A. Commendation (16:15–18)
    B. Greetings (16:19–20)
    C. Signature (16:21–22)
    D. Closing Benediction (16:23–24)

On this basic outline only a few remarks are needed. That 1:1–3 constitutes the salutation or prescript of the letter, 1:4–9 the epistolary thanksgiving, and 1:10 the opening of the body of the letter is universally recognized. It is thus universally acknowledged that the main argument of the epistle begins in 1:10. Epistolary

---

42. Pitts, "Epistolary Contexts," 287.

*Chapter 15 as the Culmination of 1 Corinthians*

analysis also permits us to identify 1:10–17 as the "body opening" of the letter, establishing 1:18 as the beginning of the central body of the epistle.[43] Having identified where the main body of the letter begins, we can work backward from the end of the letter to identify where the main body of the epistle reaches its culmination. The commendation (16:15–18), greetings (16:19–20), signature (16:21–22), and closing benediction (16:23–24) are all familiar features of the Pauline letter closing.[44] This would indicate that 16:15–24 functions as the letter closing. The letter closing is normally preceded in Paul's letters by a body closing. The body closing in Paul's letters frequently functions as a transition between the main body of the letter and the letter closing, often referring to Paul's travel plans, an upcoming visit, or the travel plans of coworkers. Since the body closing has this transitional character, the main argument of a Pauline letter, which begins with the body opening, thus frequently concludes at the close of the main body.[45] The body closing in 1 Corinthians occurs in 16:1–14 and evinces each of these transitional features. This would indicate that the main body and argument of 1 Corinthians, which begins in 1:10, comes to a conclusion in 15:58.

Some scholars, to be sure, place the conclusion of the main body of the epistle at 16:4. However, this is based on a misapprehension. These interpreters assume that Paul's mention of the collection for the saints in 16:1–4 introduces a new topic within the body of the letter. But Paul discusses the collection in 16:1–4 in connection with the larger discussion of his travel plans within the body closing of 16:1–14 (cf. 16:2, ἵνα μὴ ὅταν ἔλθω τότε λογεῖαι γένωνται; 16:3, ὅταν δὲ παραγένωμαι; 16:4, ἐὰν δὲ ἄξιον ᾖ τοῦ κἀμὲ πορεύεσθαι). This would indicate that the main argument of the letter concludes at 15:58.

That the main argument of the epistle concludes with chapter 15, rather than 16:1–4, is also evident from the contents and tone of the two sections. Here rhetorical and stylistic criticism helpfully confirm the results of our epistolary analysis. Chapter 15 begins by identifying its subject as the gospel (15:1–2), continues

---

43. See *SPL* §4 (see esp. p. 8); Doty, *Letters*, 43 (although Doty closes the body opening at 1:16).

44. For these elements elsewhere in Paul's letters, see *SPL* §6–9. The appeal regarding Stephanus's household in 16:15–18 is classed here as a commendation because, as Fee notes, "the language implies that they are now the bearers of Paul's letter back to the church" (Fee, 920). Cf. Linda L. Belleville, "Continuity or Discontinuity: A Fresh Look at 1 Corinthians in the Light of First-Century Epistolary Forms and Conventions," *EvQ* 59 (1987): 15–37, who observes that 16:15–18 is "a note of commendation . . . designating Stephanus, Fortunatus, and Achaicus as the official letter bearers of 1 Corinthians" (34). On the role of the letter bearer in antiquity, see Peter M. Head, "Named Letter-Carriers in the Oxyrynchus Papyri," *JSNT* 31 (2009): 279–99.

45. See, for example, Romans, where the body closing (15:14–33) functions as a transition between the main body of the letter (1:13–15:13) and the letter closing (16:1–27), with the main argument of the letter concluding in 15:13.

CHAPTER 1

with a lengthy defense and exposition of the resurrection hope (15:3–52), builds to a climactic affirmation of the resurrection (15:53–57), and concludes with an exhortation to stand firm in this hope (15:58). The style and tone throughout is earnest and exalted, swelling to a ringing climax and final exhortation. In 16:1–4, by contrast, the subject matter is the collection for the saints and Paul's upcoming visit, and there is a marked shift to a more practical, prosaic, and subdued tone and style. The reason for this shift is that 16:1–4, as we have seen, begins the transitional body closing segment of the letter. From both an epistolary and rhetorical standpoint, the main substance of the epistle comes to a conclusion at the close of chapter 15.[46] The main body of the letter occurs in 1:18–15:58.

*The Structure of the Main Body of the Letter*

Within the framework of 1:18–15:58, scholars agree that Paul addresses the following ten topics, all apparently relating to issues that had arisen in the church at Corinth: (1) factions and false wisdom (1:18–4:21); (2) a case of incest (5:1–13); (3) lawsuits (6:1–11); (4) sexual immorality (6:12–20); (5) marriage and celibacy (chapter 7); (6) meat sacrificed to idols (8:1–11:1); (7) head coverings in worship (11:2–16); (8) conduct at the Lord's Supper (11:17–34); (9) spiritual gifts (12:1–14:40); and (10) the resurrection (chapter 15). Virtually all scholars consider 1:10–4:21 (topic 1) to form a single, coherent unit. All who hold to the integrity of the epistle also regard 8:1–11:1 (topic 6) as making up a single unit. Most scholars believe Paul has deliberately grouped topics 7 (11:2–16), 8 (11:17–34), and 9 (12:1–14:40) together and regard 11:2–14:40 as a coherent section of the epistle focused on conduct in worship.[47] The precise relationship of topics 2–5 (chapters 5–7) is controverted. However, Ciampa and Rosner have made a strong argument for also regarding chapters 5–7 as forming a coherent block within the structure of the letter. The unity of chapters 5–7 is held by a number of other scholars as well. If we accept this suggestion, we have the following overall structure of the main body of the letter (1:18–15:58):

---

46. Margaret Mitchell has been, to a degree, rightly criticized for her claim that the body of the epistle concludes at 15:58 (*Rhetoric*, 290–92). Epistolary analysis clearly reveals, as we have seen, that 16:1–14 is the body closing of the letter. However, epistolary analysis also reveals the transitional character of the body closing in Paul's letters and that 15:58 concludes the *main* body of the letter. And Mitchell is surely correct in sensing that, from a rhetorical standpoint, the main substance of the epistle comes to a conclusion at the close of chapter 15.

47. E.g., Bailey, "Structure," 170–73; Wolff, 243–348; Ciampa and Rosner, "Structure and Argument."

1. Division and False Wisdom (1:18–4:21)
2. Sexual Morality and Community Discipline (5–7)
   a. Incest (5:1–13)
   b. Lawsuits (6:1–11)
   c. Sexual Immorality (6:12–20)
   d. Marriage and Celibacy (7:1–40)
3. Meat Sacrificed to Idols (8:1–11:1)
4. Conduct in Worship (11:2–14:40)
   a. Head Coverings in Worship (11:2–16)
   b. Conduct at the Lord's Supper (11:17–34)
   c. Spiritual Gifts (12:1–14:40)
5. The Resurrection (15)

In light of this outline of the main body of the letter, two observations can be made. First, Paul in this letter addresses not one topic but a variety of topics. Margaret Mitchell's claim that the epistle has a single theme, of which the various parts of the letter offer only examples or proofs, cannot be sustained. Paul is clearly concerned about each of these issues for their own sake, not merely as proofs or examples of something else. Theories arguing for a single theme in 1 Corinthians are not consistent with the makeup of the letter.

Second, the sequence in which Paul addresses these topics does not appear to be random or haphazard. It is clear that Paul had become aware of the issues he raises in the letter through oral reports (1:11; 5:1; cf. 16:15–18) and a letter from the Corinthians (7:1; possibly 8:1; 12:1; 16:1; 16:12).[48] Many scholars believe the order of topics in 1 Corinthians simply follows the sequence in which these topics occurred in the letter and in the oral reports. However, it is more plausible, in light of Paul's evident grouping of related topics in chapters 5–7 and 11–14, that Paul determined the order of topics in the letter. From the chaos of the oral and written reports, the apostle skillfully crafted a letter readily divisible into great blocks (1:18–4:21; chapters 5–7; 8:1–11:1; 11:2–14:40; and chapter 15), each with its own recognizable structure and argument.

But is there an overall or global structure to the letter that connects these varied parts of the letter into a whole? Further literary and rhetorical analysis will reveal that there is.

---

48. Interpreters often regard the occurrences of περὶ δέ within the letter subsequent to 7:1 (8:1; 12:1; 16:1, 12) as further references to this letter from the Corinthians. However, as Margaret Mitchell has shown, this assumption is questionable. See "Concerning ΠΕΡΙ ΔΕ in 1 Corinthians," *NovT* 31 (1989): 229–56.

CHAPTER 1

## Keys to the Plan of the Epistle in the Salutation and Thanksgiving

As is well known, the salutation and thanksgiving in Paul's epistles serve to foreshadow the primary themes to be developed in the body of the letter.[49] This is certainly the case in 1 Corinthians, where virtually every important topic or theme within the letter is foreshadowed in the epistolary salutation and thanksgiving. The themes distinctive to Paul's salutation and thanksgiving in this letter are: (1) the *calling* of the Corinthians (1:2, "called to be saints"; 1:9, "called into fellowship with his Son") and their initial *sanctification* at baptism (1:2, "sanctified in Christ Jesus"; cf. 1:2, "called to be saints"); (2) their unity as a *church of God* with all who call on the Lord (1:2, "the church of God in Corinth ... together with all those who call on the name of our Lord Jesus Christ in every place, their Lord and ours"); (3) their enrichment in *speech and knowledge* (1:5, "in everything you were enriched in him, in all speech and in all knowledge"); (4) their lacking in no charism or *spiritual gift* (1:7); and, the most expansively stated of all the themes, (5) their eager expectation of *the day of the Lord Jesus Christ* (1:7, "eagerly awaiting the revelation of our Lord Jesus Christ"; 1:8, "until the consummation ... in the day of our Lord Jesus Christ"), portrayed as the perfection of their union with Christ (1:9, "God is faithful, through whom you were called into fellowship with his Son").

The accent on the Corinthians as a body of believers within *the church of God everywhere* (theme 2 above) is found throughout the letter and is distinctive to 1 Corinthians. Of the eight occurrences of "the church of God" (ἡ ἐκκλησία τοῦ θεοῦ) or "the churches of God" (αἱ ἐκκλησίαι τοῦ θεοῦ) in Paul, five are found in 1 Corinthians (1:2; 10:32; 11:16, 22; 15:9). Moreover, Paul's use of "the church of God" progresses in the letter from a purely local sense in 1:2 ("the church of God at Corinth"), to a somewhat wider usage (10:32; 11:22), to a sense encompassing the church universal (15:9, "I persecuted the church of God"). This theme of the church universal is also found in Paul's references to "all the churches everywhere" in 4:17, "all the churches" in 7:17 and 14:33, and "all those who call on the name of the Lord Jesus Christ in every place" (an expression unique among the Pauline letters) in 1:2. What is especially striking, in considering the unity of the letter, is that this theme of the unity of the Corinthians with the church of God everywhere is found in *each* of the five major divisions of the main body of the letter identified above: 1:18–4:21 (4:17, "all the churches everywhere"), chapters 5–7 (7:17, "all the churches"), 8:1–11:1 (10:32, "the church of God"), 11:2–14:40 (11:16, "the churches of

---

49. P. Schubert, *Form and Function of the Pauline Thanksgivings* (BZNW 30; Berlin: de Gruyter, 1939), 27; Doty, *Letters*, 32–33; Belleville, "Continuity," 19; Wolff, 19.

God"; 11:22, "the church of God"; 14:33, "all the churches"), and chapter 15 (15:9, "the church of God").

More striking still, the other four elements within 1 Cor 1:1–9 appear to correspond to the *individual* major divisions of the letter we have identified above. Paul's mention of the Corinthians' enrichment in *speech* (λόγος) and *knowledge* (γνῶσις) in 1:5 foreshadows a theme found throughout the letter, but which is especially prominent in the apostle's focus on speech, wisdom, and knowledge in 1:18–4:21 (see especially 1:18–2:16; 3:18–23; 4:14–15, 19–20) and 8:1–11:1 (see especially 8:1–13). Paul's focus on the *calling* of the Corinthians (1:2, 9) and their initial *sanctification* in baptism (1:2) adumbrates themes prominent in both chapters 1–4 (calling: 1:24, 26; sanctification: 1:30; 3:17) and chapters 5–7 (calling: 7:15, 17–18, 20–22, 24; sanctification: 6:11, 7:14, 34). The theme of *spiritual gifts* (1:7, χάρισμα) foreshadows Paul's full discussion of the topic in 11:2–14:40 (cf. χαρίσματα, 12:4, 9, 28, 30–31). And Paul's stress on *the consummation of the kingdom* and the perfection of union with Christ in 1:7–9 looks ahead to Paul's treatment of the resurrection in chapter 15. These topics of the salutation and thanksgiving correspond to all five of the major divisions of the letter: 1:18–4:21, chapters 5–7, 8:1–11:1, 11:2–14:40, and chapter 15. The correspondences of the five themes of the salutation and thanksgiving to the larger letter may be summarized as follows:

| Salutation and Thanksgiving | Body of Letter |
| --- | --- |
| church of God everywhere (1:2) | whole letter |
| calling and sanctification (1:2, 9) | chapters 1–4, 5–7 |
| speech and knowledge (1:5) | chapters 1–4, 8:1–11:1 |
| spiritual gifts (1:7) | chapters 11–14 |
| consummation of the kingdom (1:7–9) | chapter 15 |

Paul thus in the salutation and thanksgiving foreshadows themes found within each of the five major divisions of the epistle identified by modern scholarship.[50] From this fact several important conclusions follow.

---

50. Linda Belleville has likewise seen that the key themes of the salutation and thanksgiving adumbrate the major divisions of the letter, although with a slightly different construal of the correspondences than that proposed here. She argues that Paul in the thanksgiving introduces the topic of each major division of the letter in the same sequential order of these divisions within the body of the epistle, namely: speech (1:5 = chapters 1–4), knowledge (1:5 = chapters 5–7, 8–11), spiritual gifts (1:7 = chapters 12–14), parousia of Christ (1:7–9 = chapter 15). See Belleville, "Continuity," 16–21; similarly Wolff, 7, 19–20. This is an attractive hypothesis but falls short of definite proof. My argument is more minimal, and I think inescapable: that the key themes of the salutation and thanksgiving foreshadow themes within each of the letter's five major divisions.

First, Paul clearly conceived of 1 Corinthians as a unity and executed it in accord with a definite plan. The partition theories, including de Boer's proposal that 1 Corinthians is Paul's own combination of two originally independent letters (chapters 1–4 and chapters 5–16), are thus ruled out.

Second, Paul did not envision the letter as having a single theme (such as unity) but as addressing multiple issues. Single-topic proposals, such as Margaret Mitchell's, are not consistent with the evidence of 1 Cor 1:1–9. Nonetheless, Paul clearly conceived the letter as a unified whole.

A third conclusion may also be drawn: chapter 15 seems to have a climactic and culminating place in Paul's plan for the letter. This is already strongly suggested by Paul's placement of the chapter, as we have seen, as the final element of the main body of the epistle. And now we find that the element foreshadowing chapter 15 within the thanksgiving (1:7–9, the consummation of salvation at the advent of Christ) is also the final and climactic element within the thanksgiving period.[51] Thus, strikingly, the final major theme within the thanksgiving—the perfection of union with Christ in the day of the Lord (1:7–9)—corresponds to the final major division of the main body of the epistle (chapter 15). Paul, it seems, conceived of the letter to the Corinthians as a unity and carried it out according to a plan, with chapter 15 as the final piece within that structure.

Another feature of the thanksgiving, although ignored in previous discussion of the letter's structure, also foreshadows chapter 15 and points to its culminating force within the letter. This element is Paul's reference to "the testimony to Christ" (τὸ μαρτύριον τοῦ Χριστοῦ) in 1:6. As the vast majority of commentators have recognized, the genitive τοῦ Χριστοῦ is objective and the expression τὸ μαρτύριον τοῦ Χριστοῦ denotes the apostolic testimony to Christ.[52] This reference in 1:6 to "the testimony to Christ" is the only place within the thanksgiving where Paul refers directly to the gospel he brought to the Corinthians. Moreover, Paul's choice of the word μαρτύριον "testimony" shows he is thinking primarily of the apostolic witness to the *resurrection* (see Acts 4:33, ἀπεδίδουν τὸ μαρτύριον οἱ ἀπόστολοι τῆς ἀναστά-

---

51. References to the parousia of Christ also occur at or near the close of Paul's thanksgivings in Phil 1:10–11; 1 Thess 1:10; 3:11–13; 2 Thess 1:7–10. This has led some scholars to regard such an "eschatological climax" as a constituent feature of the Pauline thanksgiving (e.g., Doty, *Letters*, 33). However, this is a mistaken inference. Such an eschatological climax is not found in Paul's thanksgivings outside 1 Corinthians, Philippians, and 1–2 Thessalonians, and in each of these epistles the parousia and the resurrection are a key topic within the letter (1 Cor 15; Phil 3:7–11, 20–21; 1 Thess 4:13–5:11; 2 Thess 2:1–12). The eschatological climax of the thanksgiving period in 1 Cor 1:7–9 foreshadows the eschatological climax with which Paul will close the main body of the epistle in 1 Cor 15 (cf. Belleville, "Continuity," 36).

52. See Fitzmyer, 132; Fee, 38–39; Wolff, 21; Barrett, 37–38; Godet, 1:54; Schreiner, 55.

σεως τοῦ κυρίου Ἰησοῦ). These themes of 1:6 will be developed, in their totality, only in chapter 15. To be sure, Paul will focus on his initial proclamation at Corinth in 1:17–18, 2:1–5, 3:1–2, and 3:5–11. But only in chapter 15 will Paul summarize the gospel he brought to the Corinthians (15:1–2) and recount the apostolic testimony to the resurrection (15:3–8).[53] In addition, the vocabulary of witness or testimony, introduced here in v. 6 of the thanksgiving, will be used again in the letter only in chapter 15.[54] And in chapter 15 this vocabulary of testimony will refer explicitly to the eyewitness apostolic testimony to the resurrection of Jesus (εὑρισκόμεθα δὲ καὶ ψευδομάρτυρες τοῦ θεοῦ, ὅτι ἐμαρτυρήσαμεν κατὰ τοῦ θεοῦ ὅτι ἤγειρεν τὸν Χριστόν, 15:15). Paul's thanksgiving for the Corinthians' reception of the testimony to Christ in 1:6 thus clearly has a companion and a sequel—chapter 15. We now see not only that 1 Corinthians has a global structure, which includes chapter 15, but also that chapter 15 is the culminating element in that structure.

As expositors concur, Paul depicts the testimony to Christ of 1:6 as the source or cause of the Corinthians' enrichment with speech and knowledge in 1:5 and of their enrichment with spiritual gifts in 1:7.[55] The sequel to 1:6 in chapter 15 therefore lends a subtly ironic force to Paul's thanksgiving for the Corinthians. For Paul in 1:5–7 portrays the very gifts of which they boast (1:5, 7) as the outworking and proof of the apostolic testimony to Christ's resurrection (1:6)—which (as Paul will explicitly charge in chapter 15) some at Corinth deny by saying "there is no resurrection of the dead" (15:12–19).

As we now turn to the body opening of the letter (1:10–17), we will find that the evidence of this portion of the letter will confirm, and in spades at that, the climactic place of chapter 15 within the plan and structure of 1 Corinthians.

## The Body Opening as the Key to the Epistle

The body opening of 1 Corinthians is 1:10–17.[56] From the standpoint of epistolary analysis, the body opening in Paul's epistles always serves to introduce the central subject matter of the letter previously anticipated in the introductory

---

53. Rightly Bailey: "the testimony in Paul's mind [in 1:6] is the creed he quotes in 15:3–7" ("Structure," 157). As Wolff notes, the testimony of 1:6 is "the apostle's church-founding message of the crucified and risen Christ (15,3–5), the witness to which is Paul himself (15,8–15)" (Wolff, 21).

54. With NA[28] and most expositors, I regard τὸ μυστήριον τοῦ θεοῦ (P[46] ℵ A C) as original in 2:1, and the variant reading τὸ μαρτύριον τοῦ θεοῦ (ℵ[2] B D) as secondary.

55. See Fitzmyer, 132; Wolff, 21–22; Fee, 38–39; Schreiner, 55; Ellis, 35.

56. *SPL* §4 (see esp. p. 8).

thanksgiving.[57] The rhetorical analysis of Margaret Mitchell similarly identifies 1:10 as the thesis statement of the epistle and 1:11–17 as its narrative elaboration introducing the main argument of the letter in 1:18–15:58.[58] Carl J. Bjerkelund, in his exhaustive study of παρακαλῶ clauses in Paul, reaches similar conclusions regarding the fundamental place of 1 Cor 1:10–17 within the letter as a whole. According to Bjerkelund, "*Parakalō*-clauses with prepositional expressions play a central role in the structure of Paul's letters, and indicate a transition to a new section."[59] Paul employs just such an expression at the beginning of the body opening in 1:10–17 (1:10, παρακαλῶ δὲ ὑμᾶς, ἀδελφοί, διὰ τοῦ ὀνόματος τοῦ κυρίου ἡμῶν Ἰησοῦ Χριστοῦ). Bjerkelund also concludes that "the first *parakalō*-clause of a letter contains the real concern of the apostle."[60] If the first παρακαλῶ clause occurs "strikingly early" in the letter (as it does here in 1 Corinthians), this has its cause in "definite circumstances in the community which are unsettling the apostle."[61] Epistolary, rhetorical, and formal analysis thus all converge to indicate that 1:10–17 introduces Paul's major concern within the letter.

This brings us to the most striking and mysterious fact about this epistle. The themes introduced in 1:10–17—the call to unity (1:10), Corinthian factionalism (1:10–12), the apostle and his gospel (1:17), speech (λόγος, 1:17), wisdom (σοφία, 1:17), and the gospel made vain through human wisdom (1:17)—form a fitting introduction to chapters 1–4, but they seem entirely absent from the remainder of the letter. Paul's concern with factionalism at Corinth is an important theme within chapters 1:18–4:21 (see especially 3:1–4, 18, 21; 4:18–20) but "appears absent from the rest of 1 Corinthians."[62] The same problem, as Martinus de Boer notes, is apparent in regard to the themes of gospel, speech, and wisdom: "In chapters 1–4, the crucial issue is the preaching of the apostle, the how as well as the what. Everything revolves around the terms λόγος and σοφία and the relation between the two. In chapters 5–16, on the other hand, the issues are fundamentally practical and behavioural."[63] De Boer calls this "the crucial interpretive difficulty of 1 Corinthians, the relationship between chapters 1–4 and chapters 5–16."[64]

---

57. Doty, *Letters*, 34–35. Cf. Belleville, "Continuity," 22: "The function of the opening formula is to give the primary reason for writing."
58. Mitchell, *Rhetoric*, 198–202. So also O'Reilly, *Resurrected Body*, 44–45 (1:10 and 1:11–17 form the *propositio* and *narratio* respectively).
59. Bjerkelund, *Parakalô*, 189. Cf. 142.
60. Bjerkelund, *Parakalô*, 189.
61. Bjerkelund, *Parakalô*, 189. Cf. 138, 141.
62. John Coolidge Hurd, *The Origin of 1 Corinthians* (Macon: Mercer University Press, 1983), 45.
63. De Boer, "Composition," 241.
64. De Boer, "Composition," 243. Cf. Litfin, *Proclamation*, 150: "one matter which has found little agreement is the relationship of chapters 1–4 to the remainder of the epistle."

How are chapters 1–4 related to the rest of the letter? This brings us also to the much-vexed question of the nature of the factionalism at Corinth and of the "Corinthian wisdom" with which Paul engages in chapters 1–4. A close analysis of the body opening of the epistle (1:10–17) will reveal the answer to each of these questions.

## 1 Corinthians 1:10: Paul's Chief Concern in the Epistle

As we have seen, epistolary, formal, and rhetorical analysis all converge to indicate that in 1 Cor 1:10 we find, in the words of Carl Bjerkelund, "the real concern of the apostle" in the letter. And there is no question what that concern of the apostle is. That concern is the discord and dissension at Corinth.

> And I exhort you, brothers and sisters, by the name of our Lord Jesus Christ, that you all speak the same thing, and that there be no divisions among you, but that you be made complete in the same mind and in the same judgment. (1:10)

What does this crucial passage tell us regarding how Paul understood the source and nature of the dissension at Corinth? It is considered axiomatic in modern scholarship that the dissension that concerned Paul at Corinth was not doctrinal, but ethical and sociological in nature. Stephen Pogoloff states categorically that "Paul is addressing an exigence of the ethical dimensions of division, not doctrinal divergence."[65] Using a little plainer English, Laurence L. Welborn can assert confidently that "it is a power struggle, not a theological controversy, which motivates the writing of 1 Corinthians 1–4."[66] Welborn can even claim: "It is no longer necessary to argue against the position that the conflict which evoked 1 Corinthians 1–4 was essentially theological in character."[67] As widespread and as confidently stated as this view may be, a close exegesis of 1 Cor 1:10 alone is sufficient to demolish it.

In this passage, Paul urges the Corinthians to rectify the situation by agreement in *speech* (ἵνα τὸ αὐτὸ λέγητε πάντες), in *way of thinking* (ὁ αὐτὸς νοῦς), and in *judgment* (ἡ αὐτὴ γνώμη). Paul thereby exhorts them to have a common *understanding* and a common *doctrine*. This would indicate that in Paul's understanding the discord had a doctrinal or theological component. However, Margaret Mitchell denies that Paul's language in 1 Cor 1:10 reveals a concern for doctrinal divergence at Corinth. Mitchell claims that Paul in 1:10 is using "political vocabulary," with

---

65. Pogoloff, *Logos and Sophia*, 104.
66. Laurence L. Welborn, "On the Discord in Corinth: 1 Corinthians 1–4 and Ancient Politics," *JBL* 106 (1987): 89.
67. Welborn, "Discord," 88.

each of the key phrases in the verse being "a stock phrase in Greek literature for political order and peace."[68] She holds that "1 Corinthians 1:10 contains technical language derived from political oratory and treatises concerning political unity."[69] These texts, she says, concern political factions and squabbles, and the expression τὸ αὐτὸ λέγειν (the key phrase used by Paul in 1 Cor 1:10) denotes within these texts "persons in a state of political or social unity" as "allies, compatriots, even co-partisans."[70] Paul's use of these political terms in 1 Cor 1:10 reveals that his concern is not heresy but "factionalism," and that the remedy is "the political unity which he urges on the Corinthian Christians."[71] Laurence L. Welborn similarly argues that Paul's political language in 1 Cor 1:10 shows that the apostle is not concerned with "a religious heresy" but with "factions engaged in a struggle for power."[72] According to these scholars, the unity to which Paul calls the Corinthians in 1:10 has no specific content, theological or otherwise. This assertion has acquired the status of a scholarly commonplace. But it is founded upon two fallacies and a falsehood.

The first fallacy is the claim that the meaning of these expressions in these *political* texts determines *Paul's* meaning in 1 Corinthians. The second fallacy is the assumption that because these terms are used in political contexts, they must solely seek to redress personal "partisanship," "squabbles," and "power struggles," denoting a merely personal, practical, and social unity. But in these political contexts, these terms invariably express agreement in political *viewpoint, doctrine,* or *policy*.[73] Presumably in philosophical, legal, or religious contexts, they would denote agreement in these spheres. And we don't need to presume. This brings us to the falsehood. For the claim of Mitchell, Welborn, and others that the language of 1 Cor 1:10 is technical political vocabulary (which has seemed so convincing to a generation of scholars) is founded upon a rather outrageous selectivity and cherry-picking of the evidence. Let us take Paul's expressions in 1:10 one by one. The phrase ὁ αὐτὸς νοῦς is rare prior to Paul and is *never* used of

68. Mitchell, *Rhetoric*, 68, 182.
69. Mitchell, *Rhetoric*, 65. Mitchell here follows the work of Laurence L. Welborn, who argues that "Paul describes the situation in the church in terms like those used to characterize conflicts within city-states by Greco-Roman historians" ("Discord," 86).
70. Mitchell, *Rhetoric*, 68–70.
71. Mitchell, *Rhetoric*, 68–80.
72. Welborn, "Discord," 87. Cf. 89–90: "Paul's goal in 1 Corinthians 1–4 is not the refutation of heresy but what Plutarch describes as the object of the art of politics—the preservation of στάσις."
73. For τὸ αὐτὸ λέγειν, see Thucydides, *Hist.* 5.31.6; Polybius, *Hist.* 2.62.4; 5.104.1; Josephus, *A.J.* 18.375, 378. For ἡ αὐτὴ γνώμη, see Thucydides, *Hist.* 1.113.2; 3.70.6; 5.46.4; Lysias, *Erat.* 58; *Epitaph.* 67; *Or.* 25.3, 15, 21, 29; 26.18; Isocrates, *De pace* 122; *Phil.* 58; *Plat.* 32; *Evag.* 53; *Archid.* 37; Polybius, *Hist.* 38.10.8; Dionysius of Halicarnassus, *Ant. rom.* 4.70.4; Appian, *Bell. civ.* 4.12.97.

political agreement. It is always used elsewhere of *agreement in thought*, as for example by Strabo to refer to the agreement in content between the Greek and Persian versions of an inscription (*Geogr.* 15.3.7–8). The expression ἡ αὐτὴ γνώμη occurs thirty times in ancient Greek literature (outside 1 Cor 1:10) for agreement between persons or groups. Of these, eighteen occur within political texts or contexts, but twelve occur within other contexts. This phrase ἡ αὐτὴ γνώμη expresses an *agreement in intellectual judgment*. The sphere of agreement is determined by the context.[74] The phrase τὸ αὐτὸ λέγειν occurs twelve times (outside Paul) to denote the verbal agreement of persons or groups. Of these, only five are used of political agreement, and seven are used in other contexts. Josephus, for instance, uses the phrase of the agreement of Jeremiah's and Ezekiel's prophecies (*A.J.* 10.107). Xenophon uses it of the agreement of multiple messengers in the content of their report (*Cyr.* 2.1.4, πάντες ταὐτὸ λέγουσιν). Aristotle employs the expression for the agreement of two philosophical schools on a point of doctrine regarding the soul (*De an.* 409a31).[75] The synonymous expression τὰ αὐτὰ λέγειν occurs nine times in ancient Greek literature to denote verbal agreement of persons or groups. Margaret Mitchell cites one of these from a political context.[76] But she fails to mention the other eight instances, all of which occur in nonpolitical contexts. Plato, for example, uses the expression for agreement in philosophical teaching (*Theaet.* 178b, Πρωταγόραν ἢ ἄλλον τινὰ τῶν ἐκείνῳ τὰ αὐτὰ λεγόντων).[77] Simply put, the expressions τὸ αὐτὸ λέγειν and τὰ αὐτὰ λέγειν denote agreement in λόγος, truth claims expressed in speech. The precise nature of the λόγος is determined by the context.

The claim, then, that Paul in 1 Cor 1:10 employs technical political terms denoting a merely pragmatic unity is not consistent with the function of these terms in ancient Greek literature.[78] The agreement denoted by these terms always has, as

---

74. Instances in legal or forensic contexts: Philo, *Spec.* 3.73; Josephus, *A.J.* 16.369; Lysias, *Caede Erat.* 36, 47; *C. Sim.* 21; Antiphon, *De choreuta* 7. Instances of other types of agreement: Isocrates, *Hel. enc.* 39.4; *Nic.* 50; *Evag.* 27; *Ep.* 7.13; Plutarch, *Cat. Min.* 62.3; *Vit. X orat.* 846e. For the instances of ἡ αὐτὴ γνώμη within political texts and contexts, see the preceding note.

75. Cf. Dio Chrysostom, *4 Regn.* 135 (agreement in moral philosophy); Dionysius of Halicarnassus, *Ant. rom.* 1.67.3; Ps.-Clem. *Hom.* 16.4.3 (religious agreement); and Josephus, *A.J.* 17.35 (agreement in counsel). For the instances denoting agreement on political policy, see note 73 above.

76. Thucydides, *Hist.* 4.20, cited in Mitchell, *Rhetoric*, 69.

77. For other instances in nonpolitical contexts, see Justin, *1 Apol.* 20.4; Plato, *Gorg.* 449c2; Strabo, *Geogr.* 12.8.7; 15.1.57; Dionysius of Halicarnassus, *Rhet.* 8.12; 9.6; Megasthenes, *Frag.* 30.

78. I have cited only instances in which these phrases express agreement between individuals or groups. I have not included the frequent instances in which these expressions denote agreement with what one has *previously* believed or said. But this usage also provides further

we have seen, a specific *content*. These expressions, as we have seen, denote agreement in *thought* (ὁ αὐτὸς νοῦς), *intellectual judgment* (ἡ αὐτὴ γνώμη), and public *speech* or *doctrine* (τὸ αὐτὸ λέγειν). The unity that Paul urges in 1:10 thus involves a specific content. What is the nature of this content? In the παρακαλῶ clause near the close of chapter 4, which corresponds to the opening παρακαλῶ clause in 1:10, Paul exhorts the Corinthians to "be imitators of me" (4:16). This suggests that the unity to which Paul calls the Corinthians in 1:10 is a unity in conformity with the teaching and practice of *Paul*. First Corinthians 4:17 would seem to confirm that the issue is one of following both Paul's *practice* and *teaching* (τὰς ὁδούς μου ... διδάσκω). Paul is not (contra Mitchell) merely seeking to "conciliate different sides" but to recall the divided church at Corinth to his gospel. The phrase τὸ αὐτὸ λέγειν, as we have seen, means to agree in λόγος, the specific λόγος in mind made clear by the context. Paul will shortly name this λόγος as "the *word* of the cross" (ὁ λόγος ὁ τοῦ σταυροῦ, 1:18). But only at a later point in the letter will Paul fully define and summarize this λόγος. He will do so in chapter 15:

> And I make known to you, brothers and sisters, the gospel which I gospel-proclaimed to you, which you also received, in which you also stand, through which you are also being saved, through the very *word* which I gospel-proclaimed to you [τίνι λόγῳ εὐηγγελισάμην ὑμῖν], if you hold it fast—unless you believed in vain. (15:1–2)

Paul's language in 1:10 can thus be seen as a pointer to Paul's own summary of his gospel in 15:1–2 and thus to chapter 15. But this is only the tip of the iceberg.

Paul's exhortation in 1:10 that "all" (πάντες) speak the same thing implies "some" (τινές) who do not. This is not mirror reading, for in the next verse Paul is explicit on the point: "For it was reported to me concerning you, my brothers and sisters, by the household of Chloe, that there are divisions among you" (1:11). We find the plural indefinite pronoun used of persons and connected with divisiveness in only three places within this letter.[79] In 4:18–20 it describes "some" as being self-inflated in their human wisdom and speech (λόγος, 4:19, 20) and opposed to Paul. The other two occurrences, both found in chapter 15, describe those who deny the resurrection:

15:12  πῶς λέγουσιν ἐν ὑμῖν τινες ὅτι ἀνάστασις νεκρῶν οὐκ ἔστιν;

---

evidence that these terms express agreement in the *content* of what is thought or said and not friendly relations, as Mitchell and Welborn would have it.

79. The other uses of the plural indefinite pronoun with reference to persons are not connected with divisiveness or factions (6:11; 8:7; 9:22; 10:7–9; 15:6).

15:34  ἀγνωσίαν γὰρ θεοῦ <u>τινες</u> ἔχουσιν.

Once again, we find Paul's language leading us to chapter 15. In addition, Paul in 1:10 qualifies the schisms as "among you" (ἐν ὑμῖν), and he adds this qualifier consistently in his references to schism throughout chapters 1–3 and 11:18–19:

1:10   ἵνα... μὴ ᾖ <u>ἐν ὑμῖν</u> σχίσματα
1:11   ἔριδες <u>ἐν ὑμῖν</u> εἰσιν
3:3    ὅπου γὰρ <u>ἐν ὑμῖν</u> ζῆλος καὶ ἔρις
3:18   εἴ τις δοκεῖ σοφὸς εἶναι <u>ἐν ὑμῖν</u>
11:18  ἀκούω σχίσματα <u>ἐν ὑμῖν</u> ὑπάρχειν
11:19  αἱρέσεις <u>ἐν ὑμῖν</u> εἶναι ... οἱ δόκιμοι ... <u>ἐν ὑμῖν</u>[80]

We find this qualifier elsewhere in the letter regarding division in only one place, in chapter 15 regarding those who deny the resurrection:

15:12  πῶς λέγουσιν <u>ἐν ὑμῖν</u> τινες ὅτι ἀνάστασις νεκρῶν οὐκ ἔστιν;

Moreover, Paul's concern that all at Corinth *say* the same thing (ἵνα τὸ αὐτὸ λέγητε πάντες) implies the existence of some who *say* something different. The verb "say" indicates that this difference involves, in some way, doctrine, confession, and belief. Although Paul deals with many issues in chapters 5–14, they are all practical and moral problems, not doctrinal ones. Where in the letter do we find some who *say* something different? Only in one place within the entire epistle— those who deny the resurrection in chapter 15:

15:12  πῶς <u>λέγουσιν</u> ἐν ὑμῖν τινες ὅτι ἀνάστασις νεκρῶν οὐκ ἔστιν;
15:35  Ἀλλ' <u>ἐρεῖ</u> τις· πῶς ἐγείρονται οἱ νεκροί;[81]

In the opening παρακαλῶ clause of 1:10 we find, as Carl Bjerkelund has shown, "the real concern of the apostle." It is thus striking that, again and again, we find Paul's language in 1:10 leading us to chapter 15. And the apostle's exhortation in 1:10 that *all* at Corinth *say* the same thing, and that there be no divisions *among them*,

---

80. The only other instances of ἐν ὑμῖν in the letter, none of which are directly tied to factionalism, are 1:6; 2:2; 3:16; 5:1; 6:2, 5, 19; 11:13, 30; and 14:25.

81. Cf. 15:33, φθείρουσιν ἤθη χρηστὰ <u>ὁμιλίαι κακαί</u>. On the ὁμιλίαι κακαί of 15:33 as referring to the speech of those at Corinth who deny the resurrection, see the discussion of 15:33 in the commentary below.

indicates that this concern involves *some* who *say* something different *among them*. This is precisely what we find in chapter 15. First Corinthians 1:10 finds its only counterpart and full explanation within that chapter:

1:10   ἵνα τὸ αὐτὸ λέγητε πάντες καὶ μὴ ᾖ ἐν ὑμῖν σχίσματα
15:12  πῶς λέγουσιν ἐν ὑμῖν τινες ὅτι ἀνάστασις νεκρῶν οὐκ ἔστιν;

I am not arguing for the resurrection as the sole topic or theme within the letter. As we have seen, single-topic proposals are not consistent with the makeup of this epistle, which addresses multiple topics. And it is evident that a major concern of the letter is the call to sanctification and moral conformity to Christ. But the elements within the epistolary thanksgiving (1:4–9) and the opening παρακαλῶ clause (1:10) pointing forward to chapter 15 are unmistakable, and they reveal that the foremost concern on the apostle's mind is the denial of the resurrection at Corinth. Moreover, in chapter 15 we will learn that the Christian moral life and the resurrection are inseparably connected, for there Paul will portray his model of cruciform discipleship to Christ as grounded in the hope of the resurrection (15:19, 30–32, 58; cf. 6:12–20) and undermined by its denial (15:32–34). The language and thought of 1:10 reveals that the apostle's concern is above all a doctrinal and theological one. In chapter 15 we learn the doctrine about which Paul is chiefly concerned: the resurrection of the dead.

*1 Corinthians 1:11–16: Corinthian Factionalism*

After divulging that he has learned of factionalism at Corinth from those of Chloe (1:11), Paul writes in 1:12: "And I say this, that each of you says, 'I am of Paul,' and 'I am of Apollos,' and 'I am of Cephas,' and 'I am of Christ.'" On a superficial reading of 1:12, Paul would seem to identify four distinct factions at Corinth. A few scholars do indeed presume four factions corresponding to the fourfold division within 1:12: the Paul party, an Apollos party, a Cephas party, and a Christ party.[82] But most interpreters agree that although Paul chooses to frame the situation in this way, no such four divisions actually existed at Corinth. F. C. Baur in the nineteenth century argued that behind Paul's description in 1:12 there were not four but two factions: a Paul-Apollos party and a Cephas-Christ party.[83] Walter Schmithals in the twentieth century claimed that Paul in 1 Corinthians addresses a single group

---

82. So Welborn, "Discord," 90–93, 98 n. 64.
83. F. C. Baur, "Die Christus Partei in der korinthischen Gemeinde," *Tübinger Zeitschrift für Theologie* 5 (1831): 61–206.

*Chapter 15 as the Culmination of 1 Corinthians*

of opponents—the Christ party of 1:12.[84] Birger Pearson argues that behind the ostensible four factions of 1:12 "there are essentially two factions: Paul people and Apollos people."[85] According to Pearson, Paul's opponents at Corinth were this "Apollos party." Many interpreters take a similar approach in identifying two groups out of the ostensible four factions of 1:12: a Paul party loyal to the apostle and an Apollos party favoring Apollos over Paul.[86] Others envision three parties: a Paul faction, an Apollos faction, and a Cephas faction.[87] Still others hypothesize these same three factions, but with the most important division at Corinth being between the adherents of Paul and those of Apollos.[88] The sheer variety of suggestions would suggest that the observation of William Baird is correct: "The attempt to find three or four groups on the basis of 1:12 is mistaken."[89]

However, other scholars have taken an altogether different approach. These interpreters suggest that the Corinthian factionalism involves adherence not to Paul, Apollos, or Cephas but to divisive factions among the Corinthians. In this view, Paul in 1:12 employs a rhetorical device whereby the names of Paul, Apollos, and Peter serve as stand-ins or surrogates for internal divisions within the church at Corinth.[90] Paul's consistent practice elsewhere of never naming opponents (cf. 2 Cor 2:5–7; Gal 5:10) supports this view. And further evidence for this view is overwhelming in 1 Cor 1–4. First, Paul tells us so himself both at the beginning (1:12) and the conclusion (4:6) of the discussion. For he introduces 1:12 with the qualifier λέγω δὲ τοῦτο ("And I say this")—indicating that what follows is not a rehearsal of the situation but Paul's own analysis and interpretation of it.[91] And in 4:6, summing up

---

84. Walter Schmithals, *Gnosticism in Corinth: An Investigation of the Letters to the Corinthians* (Nashville: Abingdon, 1971), 113–14.

85. Birger Pearson, "Mystery and Secrecy in Paul," in *Mystery and Secrecy in the Nag Hammadi Collection and Other Ancient Literature: Ideas and Practices* (ed. C. H. Bull, L. I. Lied, and J. D. Turner; Leiden: Brill, 2012), 290.

86. So Pogoloff, *Logos and Sophia*, 173–96; Bruce Winter, *Philo and Paul among the Sophists: Alexandrian and Corinthian Responses to a Julio-Claudian Movement* (2d ed.; Grand Rapids: Eerdmans, 2002), 172–202; Maria Pascuzzi, "Baptism-Based Allegiance and the Divisions in Corinth: A Reexamination of 1 Corinthians 1:13–17," *CBQ* 71 (2009): 813–29.

87. Mitchell, *Rhetoric*, 81–99.

88. So Schreiner, 62–63; Fitzmyer, 142–45.

89. William Baird, "'One against the Other': Intra-Church Conflict in 1 Corinthians," in *The Conversation Continues: Studies in Paul and John* (ed. J. L. Martyn and R. Fortna; Nashville: Abingdon, 1990), 131.

90. So Timothy Brookins, "Reconsidering the Coherence of 1 Corinthians 1:10–4:21," *NovT* 62 (2020): 141–43, 149–52; similarly Martin, *Body*, 58, 69–70.

91. Here Mitchell is correct: "Paul does not quote Corinthian slogans in 1:12, because the four phrases there are preceded by λέγω δὲ τοῦτο, which introduces Paul's commentary on the

his entire treatment of factionalism at Corinth in 1:12–4:5, he tells the Corinthians explicitly that "I have transferred these things, brothers and sisters, to myself and Apollos for your sake" (ταῦτα δὲ, ἀδελφοί, μετεσχημάτισα εἰς ἐμαυτὸν καὶ Ἀπολλῶν δι' ὑμᾶς). To fit the assumption of an "Apollos party" at Corinth, many scholars have taken the verb μετασχηματίζω here to mean "speak figuratively" or "speak metaphorically," often with reference to the images of agriculture (3:5–9), construction (3:10–18), and stewardship (4:1–5) that Paul has just used for himself and Apollos.[92] But such a usage of this verb is not found elsewhere. The verb μετασχηματίζω in its normal usage means to "transform" (Phil 3:21) or "disguise" (2 Cor 11:13–15). Here in 4:6, as David Hall has shown convincingly, this verb must refer to a covert allusion or disguise, whereby Paul makes statements about something or someone else in the guise of statements about Apollos and himself.[93] "In other words, when Paul describes the relationship between himself and Apollos, what he is really concerned about is certain unnamed teachers who were at work in the church at Corinth."[94] This is the way 4:6 was read in antiquity by John Chrysostom. This rhetorical device, says Chrysostom, in which the persons in question are "hidden under the names of Paul and Apollos," allows Paul to address the problem without naming names (*Hom. 1 Cor.* 12.1). Paul in 1 Cor 1:12–4:6 thus develops a very effective argument from the lesser to the greater: if it would be wrong to form factions around even the great apostles and evangelists Paul, Apollos, and Peter, how much more wrong is it to foment divisions around certain self-inflated and self-authorized figures at Corinth?[95] The self-importance and self-inflation of these persons is subjected to withering scorn in the verse that follows: "For who considers you superior? And what do you have that you did not receive? And if you received it,

---

report of Chloe's people" (*Rhetoric*, 86); see also Christof W. Strüder, "Preferences Not Parties: The Background of 1 Cor 1,12," *ETL* 79 (2003): 448–49.

92. E.g., Fee, 181–82; Ciampa & Rosner, 175.

93. David R. Hall, "A Disguise for the Wise: ΜΕΤΑΣΧΗΜΑΤΙΣΜΟΣ in 1 Corinthians 4:6," *NTS* 40 (1994): 144.

94. Hall, "Disguise," 144. So also Robertson & Plummer, 80–81; Fitzmyer, 214–15; Brookins, "Coherence," 151.

95. So Chrysostom, commenting on 1:12: "Paul [in chapters 1–4] does not speak concerning himself, nor concerning Peter, nor concerning Apollos. Rather, he shows that if one must not rely on these, how much less on others? For he shows that he is not speaking of them, when further on he says: 'But these things I have transferred to myself and Apollos, that in our persons you may learn not to surpass what is written.' For if it was wrong to call themselves by the names of Paul and Apollos and Cephas, how much more by the names of others? For if it was wrong to be partisans of their teacher [i.e., Paul], and of the first of the apostles [i.e., Peter], and one who had instructed so many [i.e., Apollos], how much more to be partisans of those who are nothing?" (*Hom. 1 Cor.* 3.1).

why boast as if you did not receive it?" (4:7). This verse is normally taken as a general admonition of the Corinthians.[96] But this ignores the fact that the pronoun, verbs, and participle in this verse are in the singular. Paul here addresses a *single individual* who boasts in his superiority. This can be neither Apollos, who was no longer in Corinth, nor the Corinthians as a whole. As Chrysostom notes, Paul in 4:7 "turns from addressing those led to addressing their leaders."[97] Paul almost certainly addresses here an individual (or individuals) causing division at Corinth.

The nature of Paul's exhortation in 1 Cor 1–4 offers further evidence. Paul in chapters 1–4, and throughout the letter, portrays Apollos positively as his fellow laborer (3:5–9), as being among the gifts of God to the church (3:21–23), and as one with whom Paul pleaded that he return to Corinth (16:12). But he portrays the divisive wisdom at Corinth as destructive of the Christian community (3:17). In 3:18 Paul writes: "If anyone thinks he is wise among you in this age, let him become a fool, that he may become wise." Paul is here explicit that the source of the division is not Apollos (who was no longer at Corinth), but an individual who boasts in his wisdom *among the Corinthians* (ἐν ὑμῖν, 3:18).[98] Moreover, Paul throughout chapters 1–4 contrasts human λόγος and σοφία with the power of God: "And my word and my proclamation was not in persuasive words of wisdom, but in demonstration of the Spirit and of power, that your faith may not be in the wisdom of human beings, but in the power of God" (2:4–5). Therefore it is striking that when he returns to this theme at the conclusion of chapter four, the human λόγος in question is not that of Apollos but of some who have become self-inflated at Corinth: "But I will come quickly to you if the Lord wills, and I will learn, not the word of those who are inflated, but the power; for the kingdom of God is not in word, but in power" (4:19–20). It is *their* λόγος, not that of Apollos.

A careful reading of 1 Cor 1:11–16, together with chapters 1–4, thus indicates that the source of the wisdom dividing the church at Corinth is not Apollos but certain individual teachers among the Corinthians, whom Paul in 1 Corinthians publicly castigates but does not name.

*1 Corinthians 1:17: The Corinthian Wisdom*

As the climax and thesis statement of the body opening, 1:17 introduces the key themes of the epistle. In the first clause of 1:17 Paul recalls his apostolic commis-

---

96. E.g., Garland, 136–37; Fee, 186–87.
97. John Chrysostom, *Hom. 1 Cor.* 12.1: Λοιπὸν ἀφεὶς τοὺς ἀρχομένους, πρὸς τοὺς ἄρχοντας τρέπεται.
98. Rightly Brookins, "Coherence," 149.

CHAPTER 1

sioning by Christ to proclaim the gospel: οὐ γὰρ ἀπέστειλέν με Χριστὸς βαπτίζειν ἀλλ' εὐαγγελίζεσθαι. Within the context of 1:13–16, with its focus on Paul's ministry among the Corinthians (cf. also the reference to the initiatory rite of baptism in 1:17), this clause also recalls Paul founding proclamation at Corinth. We thus find here three elements: (1) Paul's apostolic commissioning by the risen Christ; (2) the proclamation of the gospel; and (3) Paul's foundational preaching among the Corinthians. Within 1 Corinthians, the first element recurs in 9:1–2, the second element in 4:15 and 9:12–23, and the third element in 2:15, 3:1–10, 4:15, and 9:1–2. Both the first and third elements recur in 9:1–2, and both the second and third elements appear in 4:15. But all three elements do not converge again within the letter until 1 Cor 15:1–11:

> And I make known to you, brothers and sisters, the *gospel* which I *gospel-proclaimed* [τὸ εὐαγγέλιον ὃ εὐηγγελισάμην] to you . . . by which you are also being saved, through the very word I *gospel-proclaimed* [εὐηγγελισάμην] to you . . . and last of all . . . he appeared also to me. For I am the least of *the apostles* [τῶν ἀποστόλων], and am unfit to be called an *apostle* [ἀπόστολος] . . . Whether, then, it is I or they, so we proclaim, and so you believed. (15:1–2, 8–9, 11)

All these three themes of the letter that are introduced in 1:17—Paul's commissioning by the risen Lord, the good news, and Paul's founding proclamation at Corinth—find their climactic statement in 15:1–11. Not only that but Paul's proclamation of the good news introduced in 1:17 (ἀπέστειλέν με Χριστὸς . . . εὐαγγελίζεσθαι) receives its definitive statement and summary in 15:1–11, where Paul specifically rehearses the content of his gospel (γνωρίζω δὲ . . . τὸ εὐαγγέλιον ὃ εὐηγγελισάμην, 15:1). Paul will recall his founding proclamation to the Corinthians throughout chapters 1–4, but only in chapter 15 will he proclaim it afresh.

Through the phrase οὐκ ἐν σοφίᾳ λόγου (1:17), placed immediately after the verb εὐαγγελίζομαι, Paul introduces the theme of a wisdom (σοφία) and speech (λόγος) incompatible with his gospel. Throughout 1 Cor 1–4, as all interpreters concur, Paul will contrast this "wisdom of the world" embraced by some at Corinth with the word and wisdom of God.[99] In 1 Cor 1–4, "everything revolves around the terms λόγος and σοφία and the relation between the two."[100] What was the nature of this Corinthian claim to wisdom introduced in 1:17 by the phrase σοφία λόγου? In the nineteenth century F. C. Baur identified this wisdom with the teaching of Judaizers at Corinth,

---

99. Baird, "Conflict," 129. Within 1 Cor 1–4, the word σοφία occurs sixteen times, σοφός ten times, and λόγος nine times.
100. De Boer, "Composition," 241.

*Chapter 15 as the Culmination of 1 Corinthians*

who allied themselves with Peter and opposed Paul's law-free gospel.[101] Walter Schmithals in the mid-twentieth century identified it as a form of Gnostic teaching.[102] Neither Baur's "Judaizing" thesis nor Schmithals's "Gnostic" thesis has stood the test of time.[103] According to Birger Pearson, this teaching opposed by Paul was a Philo-like "Alexandrian Jewish wisdom" introduced at Corinth by Apollos.[104] But in recent decades a general consensus has emerged that the wisdom Paul opposed at Corinth was an overemphasis on rhetorical art, the sophisticated oratory prized by the educated elite.[105] On this reading, the Corinthian wisdom was a matter not of *content* but of *form* or *method*—the powerful and persuasive speech of the cultured rhetor or sophist. "The σοφία that Paul fears will undermine the community is nothing other than rhetoric."[106] According to a wide consensus of scholars, the σοφία λόγου of 1:17 is "clever rhetoric" or "rhetorically sophisticated speech." The phrase has no reference to the *content* of the message but to the *method* of presentation employed—the sophisticated oratory of the upper-class rhetor or sophist.[107]

However, as Timothy A. Brookins has now shown convincingly, evidence for this widespread view is lacking. Rather, as Brookins demonstrates, σοφία in the first century AD predominantly refers not to rhetoric but to *philosophy*, and λόγος regularly refers not to eloquence but to reasoned *discourse*.[108] Thus in the phrase σοφία λόγου in 1:17, Brookins argues, the σοφία is "philosophical wisdom,"

---

101. Baur, "Christus Partei."

102. Schmithals, *Gnosticism in Corinth*, 117–301. W. Lütgert had previously identified Paul's chief opponents at Corinth with the "Christuspartei" of 1:12, and as "antinomistische Gnostiker" in his study *Freiheitspredigt und Schwarmgeister in Korinth: Ein Beitrag zur Charakteristik der Christuspartei* (Gütersloh: Bertelsmann, 1908).

103. See Timothy A. Brookins, *Corinthian Wisdom, Stoic Philosophy, and the Ancient Economy* (SNTSMS 159; Cambridge: Cambridge University Press, 2014), 3.

104. Pearson, "Mystery," 290–93. See also his earlier and fuller discussion in "Hellenistic-Jewish Wisdom Speculation and Paul," in *Aspects of Wisdom in Judaism and Early Christianity* (ed. Robert L. Wilken; Notre Dame: Notre Dame University Press, 1975), 43–66. For a very similar reconstruction, see Richard Horsley, "Wisdom of Words and Words of Wisdom in Corinth," *CBQ* 39 (1977): 224–39. For cogent criticism of this view, see Dieter Zeller, "Die angebliche enthusiastische oder spiritualistische Front in 1 Kor 15," *SPhilo* 13 (2001): 176–89.

105. E.g., Pogoloff, *Logos and Sophia*, 108–27, 173–96; Winter, *Philo and Paul*, 141–202; Litfin, *Proclamation*, 160–262; Thiselton, 142–47, 205, 218–21, 265–66; Martin, *Body*, 38–68; Ciampa & Rosner, 87–88; Sigurd Grindheim, "Wisdom for the Perfect: Paul's Challenge to the Corinthian Church (1 Corinthians 2:6–16)," *JBL* 121 (2002): 689–709.

106. Laurence L. Welborn, *Politics and Rhetoric in the Corinthian Epistles* (Macon: Mercer University Press, 1997), 30.

107. See, for example, Pogoloff, *Logos and Sophia*, 108–27; Thiselton, 142–47, 205, 218–21, 265–66.

108. Brookins, *Corinthian Wisdom*, 30–44, 58–61.

and λόγος refers to "wisdom's content."[109] Was the specific form of philosophical wisdom advocated by some at Corinth, as Brookins goes on to argue, a Christian development of Stoic philosophy?[110] Or was the philosophical basis of this wisdom, as others have argued, drawn from other particular philosophical schools or movements?[111] Or was this wisdom an eclectic mix of ideas and maxims drawn from popular philosophy? This is a debatable question. We will consider what we can know regarding the nature of the philosophical wisdom boasted by some at Corinth more fully in chapters 6 and 10 of this commentary.

However, what our ancient sources, in my view, place beyond question is that the predominant default referent of σοφία in the first century was not rhetoric but philosophy. Sextus Empiricus tells us that the philosophers "say that philosophy is the pursuit of wisdom, and that wisdom is the knowledge of matters divine and human" (*Math.* 9.13: τὴν φιλοσοφίαν φασὶν ἐπιτήδευσιν εἶναι σοφίας, τὴν δὲ σοφίαν ἐπιστήμην θείων τε καὶ ἀνθρωπίνων πραγμάτων). Cicero defines *philosophia* as *studium sapientiae* or "the study of wisdom" (*Tusc.* 1.1). He also defines the philosopher as *sapientiae studiosus* or "the student of wisdom" (5.9) and uses *philosophia* and *sapientia* ("wisdom") interchangeably (*Fin.* 1.3).[112] According to Seneca's definition, "philosophy is the love of and seeking after wisdom" (*Ep.* 89.4: *philosophia sapientiae amor est et adfectatio*). Seneca's definition reminds us of Paul's words in 1 Cor 1:23: "Ἕλληνες σοφίαν ζητοῦσιν ("the gentiles seek after wisdom"). Philo similarly defines philosophy: "For philosophy is the pursuit of wisdom, and wisdom is the knowledge of matters divine and human, and their causes" (*Congr.* 79: ἔστι γὰρ φιλοσοφία ἐπιτήδευσις σοφίας, σοφία δὲ ἐπιστήμη θείων καὶ ἀνθρωπίνων καὶ τῶν τούτων αἰτίων). The regular term for rhetoric, by contrast, was ἡ ῥητορική and, for the one skilled in rhetoric, ῥήτωρ. Lucian, for example, in his lampoon of the Second Sophistic, entitled Ῥητόρων Διδάσκαλος, refers to this art as ἡ ῥητορική (*Rhet. praec.* 3, 6, 9–10, 14, 16, 23–24, 26), and to its practitioners as ῥήτορες (4, 6–7, 11–15, 24–25), never once using the terms σοφία or σοφός.

---

109. Brookins, *Corinthian Wisdom*, 39–44.

110. Brookins, *Corinthian Wisdom*, 153–229. Brookins argues this thesis at length in *Rediscovering the Wisdom of the Corinthians: Paul, Stoicism, and Spiritual Hierarchy* (Grand Rapids: Eerdmans, 2024). Brookins concludes that the worldview of the wise at Corinth may be helpfully described as a kind of Christian "sub-Stoicism" (*Wisdom of the Corinthians*, 206–35).

111. For the argument that it was Epicureanism, see G. Tomlin, "Christianity and Epicureanism in 1 Corinthians," *JSNT* 68 (1997): 51–72; for the case that it was Cynicism, see F. Gerald Downing, *Cynics, Paul, and the Pauline Churches* (London: Routledge, 1998).

112. See also Cicero, *Off.* 2.43 (*illa sapientia quam σοφίαν Graeci vocant... rerum est divinarum atque humanarum scientia*) and *Tusc.* 4.26 (*sapientiam esse rerum divinarum et humanarum scientiam*).

Therefore, when Paul in 1 Cor 1:17 (and throughout chapters 1–4) speaks of a human wisdom or σοφία incompatible with the gospel, he refers not to rhetoric but to philosophy. This means that what Paul found objectionable in the Corinthian wisdom was not its *method* of presentation but its *content*.

Two factors within the immediate context confirm that the σοφία λόγου that Paul opposes to the gospel in 1:17 is not a matter of form but of content. First, the reference to "word" or "speech" (λόγος) in 1:17 looks backward to Paul's exhortation that all at Corinth "speak" (λέγω) the same thing in 1:10. As we saw, the expression τὸ αὐτὸ λέγειν ("speak the same thing") denotes agreement in the *content* of what is spoken. Second, the reference to "word" or "speech" (λόγος) in 1:17 looks immediately forward to the contrasting "word of the cross" (ὁ λόγος ὁ τοῦ σταυροῦ) in 1:18. As Timothy A. Brookins notes helpfully, the precise syntax of ὁ λόγος ὁ τοῦ σταυροῦ is important here. "The article preceding the qualifying genitive is unnecessary and serves discursively to distinguish between two *types* of λόγος. . . . In short, λόγος carries the same semantic force in vv. 17 and 18 and Paul draws a distinction between two 'words' or 'accounts' of things."[113]

But what is the specific content of this word or message that Paul opposes to the word of the cross? The answer is provided in the closing words of 1:17, which serve to climax the body opening as a whole: the gospel must not be corrupted with σοφία λόγου, "so that the cross of Christ might not be made vain" (ἵνα μὴ κενωθῇ ὁ σταυρὸς τοῦ Χριστοῦ). Paul here uses the verbal form κενόω, derived from the adjective κενός "vain." Paul will repeat this charge in 3:20, where he quotes a passage from Job describing the reasoning of the "wise" (σοφοί) as "futile" (μάταιος). This theme that corrupting the gospel with human wisdom renders the gospel vain (κενός) or futile (μάταιος) is introduced in 1:17 at the climax of the body opening, leading the reader to expect it will be a key theme of the epistle. However, this theme is found only in chapters 1–3, and it is not found in chapters 4–14. Moreover, this theme is not explained or resolved within either chapters 1–3 or anywhere else in the letter—until chapter 15. A major theme of this chapter is that when the hope of the bodily resurrection is denied, the gospel and faith are made vain (κενός), without purpose (εἰκῇ), and futile (μάταιος):

15:2   "unless you believed *in vain* [εἰκῇ]"
15:14   "*vain* [κενὸν] then is our proclamation, *vain* [κενὴ] also is your faith"
15:17   "*futile* [ματαία] is your faith, you are still in your sins"
15:58   "knowing that your labor is not *in vain* [κενός] in the Lord"

---

113. Brookins, "Coherence," 145.

CHAPTER 1

Although generally ignored by previous expositors, the evidence is overwhelming. The theme of the vanity of the gospel when corrupted by human wisdom, which is introduced at the climax of the body opening in 1:17 as a key theme of the epistle, finds its resolution and completion in chapter 15.

Paul in 1:17–18 sets this vain (κενωθῇ, 1:17) word of human wisdom (σοφία λόγου, 1:17) in contrast with the word of the cross (ὁ λόγος ὁ τοῦ σταυροῦ, 1:18). This contrast, too, finds its completion and resolution in chapter 15, where these two words or messages, for the first time in the letter, are explicitly defined. For in chapter 15 we learn that the message that makes the gospel vain is the denial of the resurrection (15:2, 14, 17, 58), and here Paul, for the only time in the letter, explicitly defines "the word which I gospel-proclaimed to you" (τίνι λόγῳ εὐηγγελισάμην ὑμῖν, 15:2). Just as we saw how "the word of the cross" in 1:18 specified the true word (ὁ λόγος ὁ τοῦ σταυροῦ) while having in view the false word (σοφία λόγου, 1:17), so too in 15:2 the phrase τίνι λόγῳ ("the very word") specifies the true word (the gospel of the risen Christ in 15:3–11) while having in view the false word (the denial of the resurrection in 15:12).

*Conclusion Regarding the Body Opening in 1:10–17*

Our study of the body opening of 1 Corinthians reveals that chapter 15 is the goal and culmination of this epistle. As all Pauline scholars concur, the language and themes of the body opening of Paul's epistles function to introduce the key themes of the letter. Time and time again we found the language and themes of 1 Cor 1:10–17—the call to unity in teaching, Paul's apostolic commissioning by the risen Lord, the proclamation of the gospel, Paul's founding preaching at Corinth, Corinthian factionalism, the Corinthian wisdom, and the danger of the gospel made vain through human wisdom—have their resolution and climactic affirmation in the fifteenth chapter of the letter. Our study has also revealed that Paul's concern with the Corinthian wisdom, which he opposes throughout chapters 1–4, was not its form but its content, and that his chief concern was the denial of the resurrection. In addition, Paul's model in chapters 1–4 of lowly self-sacrifice for the sake of Christ (4:9–17), in contrast with the inflated self-seeking of the self-professed wise at Corinth (4:7, 18–21), receives its capstone in chapter 15, which reveals that hope in the resurrection is the foundation of the cruciform life of discipleship modeled by the apostle (15:19, 30–34, 58). This has, in turn, enabled us to unlock a long-standing mystery of the letter: why (according to the dominant scholarly exegesis of the epistle) the themes introduced in 1:10–17 seem to pertain only to chapters 1–4 and not to the rest of the letter. Through a more penetrating exegesis, we have seen that each of these themes introduced in 1:10–17 and developed in

*Chapter 15 as the Culmination of 1 Corinthians*

chapters 1–4 receive their climactic statement in chapter 15, which is the goal and climax of the entire epistle.

## CHAPTER 15 AS THE CULMINATION OF 1:18–4:21

German New Testament scholars employ a helpful term and concept: the *Folgetext*. The *Folgetext* is a passage that forms the necessary follow-up or complement to a preceding passage. The passage that precedes it is not complete in itself but presupposes and requires a later passage in the document to complete its meaning: the *Folgetext*. Our study of the thanksgiving (1:4–9) and body opening (1:10–17) of the letter has already provided strong evidence that chapter 15 is the culmination of the epistle, and that the foremost among Paul's concerns with the Corinthian wisdom was its denial of the resurrection. We will now see that 1:18–4:21 requires and presupposes Paul's exposition regarding the resurrection in chapter 15. We will see that 1:18–4:21 has a *Folgetext*: chapter 15. Standing as they do at the beginning and ending of the main body of the letter, 1:18–4:21 and 15:1–58 thus form an *inclusio* or frame for the content of the letter as a whole.

*1 Corinthians 1:18–2:5: The Gospel versus Human Wisdom*

The focus of 1:18–2:5 is the gospel Paul proclaimed at Corinth and its reception among the Corinthians. The section contains a rich variety of terms for preaching and for the reception of the message (λόγος, κήρυγμα, κηρύσσω, πίστις, πιστεύω, ἀπόλλυμι, σῴζω), terms that are found rarely, if at all, elsewhere in chapters 1–14 and nowhere in combination with one another, as they are in 1:18–2:5. The term λόγος with reference to Paul's initial preaching at Corinth (1:18; 2:1, 4) and the key term κήρυγμα (1:21; 2:4) are entirely absent elsewhere in chapters 1–14. The terms πίστις, πιστεύω, ἀπόλλυμι, and σῴζω are found elsewhere in chapters 1–14, but nowhere in the extraordinary combination with words for Paul's initial preaching we find in 1:18–2:5. In the short space of 2:4–5 we find κήρυγμα (2:4), λόγος (2:4), and πίστις (2:5). In 1:18–21 we see combined λόγος (1:18), κήρυγμα (1:21), ἀπόλλυμι (1:18–19), σῴζω (1:18, 21), and πιστεύω (1:21). This striking combination of terms for Paul's preaching and its reception at Corinth is a unique feature of 1:18–2:5 that is not found anywhere else in the first fourteen chapters of the letter.

However, we find this dense concentration of terms for Paul's preaching and its reception strikingly present again, and in even denser concentration, in chapter 15. Within the space of 15:1–19 we find all these key terms of 1:18–2:5: λόγος with reference to Paul's preaching (15:2), κηρύσσω (15:11–12), κήρυγμα (15:14), πίστις (15:14),

CHAPTER 1

πιστεύω (15:2), ἀπόλλυμι (15:18), and σώζω (15:2). We also find the same notable combinations, such as κήρυγμα and πίστις in 15:14 (cf. 2:4–5), κηρύσσω and πιστεύω in 15:11 (cf. 1:21, 23), and λόγος, πιστεύω, and σώζω in 15:2 (cf. 1:18–21). Clearly, Paul in chapter 15 has returned to the theme of the beginning of the letter in 1:18–2:5: his gospel and its reception by the Corinthians.[114] However, chapter 15 does not merely complement 1:18–2:5 but has a climactic force. For the aforementioned combination of terms in 15:1–19 is joined by *other* key terms for the apostolic preaching *absent* from 1:18–2:5—εὐαγγέλιον (15:1), εὐαγγελίζομαι (15:1–2), and μαρτυρέω (15:15). The result is an even *more* dense and rich concentration of terms for the gospel and its reception in 15:1–19 than in 1:18–2:5. Moreover, 15:1–19 excels 1:18–2:5 in providing Paul's own explicit restatement and definition of the gospel he proclaimed to the Corinthians (15:1–11).

In 1:18–2:5, Paul contrasts the gospel with the wisdom of this world (cf. 2:6–16; 3:18–20). An important theme of chapters 1–2 is that the world through its wisdom cannot know (γινώσκω) God (1:21, 2:16), the wisdom of God (2:6, 8), or the things of God (2:11, 14). In exposing the incapacity of the world's wisdom, Paul expresses, in an indirect way, the defective nature of the wisdom boasted by some at Corinth—its incapacity to lead to the knowledge of God. But why does the Corinthian wisdom lack knowledge of God? This is not explained in 1:18–4:21, and the theme is not found in chapters 5–14. However, this theme emphatically recurs, and receives its full resolution and explanation, in chapter 15. In 15:34, Paul affirms that "some" (τινές)—clearly the same "some" of 15:12 who say that there is no resurrection—"have *lack of knowledge* of God" (ἀγνωσίαν γὰρ θεοῦ τινες ἔχουσιν, 15:34). Here Paul confronts the Corinthian claim to wisdom directly and brings to a climax the theme of the incapacity of the world's wisdom to know God. To reject the hope of the resurrection is to be without knowledge of God.

A further theme of 1:18–2:5 is that the purpose of the gospel's reversal of human wisdom is that all boasting may be in the Lord (1:26–31; cf. 3:18–23). Its introductory statement is in 1:31: "let the one who boasts, boast in the Lord" (ὁ καυχώμενος ἐν κυρίῳ καυχάσθω). This theme recurs in various ways throughout the letter (4:7; 5:6; 9:15–16; 13:3), and Paul skillfully interweaves this theme with the theme of the "self-inflation" (φυσιόω) of the self-professed wise at Corinth (4:6, 18–19; 5:2; 8:1; 13:4). However, the final statement of this theme within the letter is 15:31: "I say this on oath, brothers and sisters, by my boasting in you which I have in Christ Jesus our

---

114. Cf. Dieter Lührmann, "Freundschaftsbrief trotz Spannungen: Zu Gattung und Aufbau des Ersten Korintherbriefs," in *Studien zum Text und zur Ethik des Neuen Testaments* (ed. W. Schrage; Berlin: de Gruyter, 1986), 298–314: chapter 15 is "a return to the beginning of the letter" in 1:18–4:21 (306).

Lord" (νὴ τὴν ὑμετέραν καύχησιν, ἀδελφοί, ἣν ἔχω ἐν Χριστῷ Ἰησοῦ τῷ κυρίῳ ἡμῶν). First Corinthians 1:31 and 15:31 thus form an *inclusio*. They are linked together not only as the first and last statements of the theme of boasting within the letter but also as the only explicit reference in the letter to boasting *in the Lord* (1:31, ἐν κυρίῳ; 15:31, ἐν Χριστῷ Ἰησοῦ τῷ κυρίῳ ἡμῶν). And this theme receives its climactic expression in 15:54–57, where Paul performatively enacts the boasting in the Lord enjoined in 1:31, exalting in the triumph of God over death through the resurrection of the dead.

*1 Corinthians 2:6–16: The Mysterious Wisdom Foreordained for Our Glory*

Paul throughout 1:18–2:5 contrasts the word of the cross with the wisdom of the world. However, we learn in 2:6–16 that Paul does speak a form of wisdom (σοφία) among the mature. Yet it is not a wisdom of this age (2:6), but "God's wisdom which has been concealed in a mystery" (2:7, θεοῦ σοφίαν ἐν μυστηρίῳ τὴν ἀποκεκρυμμένην). Paul in 2:1 (according to the most likely reading) similarly refers to the gospel as "the mystery of God" (τὸ μυστήριον τοῦ θεοῦ). What is the content of this mystery?

Paul in 4:1 refers to the apostles as stewards of "the mysteries of God" (μυστήρια θεοῦ). The use of the plural here (as well as in 13:2 and 14:2) suggests that the mystery is multifaceted. The multidimensional nature of the mystery is also suggested by the use of the plural relative pronoun ἅ twice to describe the content of this mystery in 2:9 (cf. the plural in 2:12: τὰ ὑπὸ τοῦ θεοῦ χαρισθέντα ἡμῖν). A few interpreters have imagined this wisdom to be an esoteric theosophy different from Paul's gospel of the crucified and risen Christ. But this conflicts with 2:8 and ignores the fundamental identity of this mystery with the wisdom of God that Paul proclaims in 1:18–31. In understandable overreaction to this mistaken view, the great majority of scholars insist that this wisdom is indistinguishable from Paul's founding missionary message he brought to the Corinthians. But this view conflicts frontally with 2:6 and 3:1–4, where Paul specifically distinguishes the two. The answer would seem to be that the hidden wisdom of which Paul speaks in 2:6–16, accessible only to the mature (2:6) and the spiritual (2:14–16; 3:1), involves nothing other than a deepened and enriched comprehension of the mystery of Christ and his saving work.[115]

Scholars also debate whether this mystery involves the past saving acts of Christ and the present life of believers in him or the eschatological inheritance of the faithful at the second coming of Christ.[116] On the one hand, the identity of this

---

115. For parallels to this conception elsewhere in the New Testament, see Rom 1:11, 15; Eph 1:15–23; 3:14–19; 4:11–16; Col 1:28–2:3; Heb 5:11–6:3.

116. Arguing that this mystery refers to the present life in Christ is Grindheim, "Wisdom for

CHAPTER 1

wisdom as a deeper unfolding of 1:18-31 would seem to preclude a strictly future understanding. On the other hand, the foreordination of this mysterious wisdom "for our glory" (2:7) would seem to include, and even highlight, the future aspect of the salvation plan of God. This is also suggested by the statement that God has "prepared" (ἡτοίμασεν) these things for those who love him.[117] The interpretation of this passage within the primitive church also emphasizes the future aspect of the mystery (1 Clem. 34; Mart. Pol. 2; Theophilus of Antioch, *Autol.* 1.14; Tertullian, *Res.* 27). It is probably best to conclude, therefore, with Markus Bockmuehl, that this wisdom has a comprehensive content, involving "the overall plan of salvation" but including and even highlighting "a deeper knowledge of the inheritance which is in store for those who love God."[118]

Several factors indicate that Paul's discussion of the mysterious wisdom of God in 1 Cor 2:6-16 does not stand alone in the letter but finds its deeper unfolding and intended completion in Paul's exposition of the resurrection in chapter 15:

(1) In 2:6 the wisdom of God is hidden from "the rulers of this age, who are being abolished" (τῶν ἀρχόντων τοῦ αἰῶνος τούτου τῶν καταργουμένων).[119] In only one other place within the letter does Paul speak of *rulers* (ἄρχοντες) being *abolished* (καταργέω)—in chapter 15, where Christ *abolishes* all *rule* opposed to him (15:24, ὅταν καταργήσῃ πᾶσαν ἀρχήν). In 2:6, the abolition of the rulers is portrayed as being *underway*; in 15:24 it is portrayed as *completed* at Christ's second coming.

(2) In 2:7 the wisdom of God concealed in a mystery was foreordained before the ages "for our glory" (εἰς δόξαν ἡμῶν), and Jesus is described as "the Lord of glory" (ὁ κύριος τῆς δόξης). Here δόξα "glory" is used in its specialized sense, attested throughout the New Testament and of crucial importance within Paul's theology, to refer to the radiant splendor that belongs to God's own nature, and which he imparts to the faithful in partial measure now but in its fullness at the resurrection.[120] The word δόξα in this sense is not found again within the letter until chapter 15. Here the theme does not merely return but reaches a true climax. For

---

the Perfect," 696-97. For the view that this mystery refers to the eschatological inheritance of the faithful, see Birger A. Pearson, *The Pneumatikos-Psychikos Terminology in 1 Corinthians: A Study in the Theology of the Corinthian Opponents and Its Relation to Gnosticism* (SBLDS 12; Missoula, MT: Scholars, 1973), 34-35; Fitzmyer, 176-79.

117. For the use of the verb ἑτοιμάζω in future eschatological contexts, see Matt 20:23 // Mark 10:40, οἷς ἡτοίμασται; Matt 25:34, τὴν ἡτοιμασμένην ὑμῖν βασιλείαν; John 14:2, ἑτοιμάσαι τόπον ὑμῖν; and Heb 11:16, ἡτοίμασεν γὰρ αὐτοῖς πόλιν.

118. Markus Bockmuehl, *Revelation and Mystery in Ancient Judaism and Pauline Christianity* (WUNT 2.36; Tübingen: Mohr Siebeck, 1990), 160-66.

119. On the identity of the rulers in 2:6-8, which is controversial, see the commentary on 15:24 in chapter 8.

120. E.g., Rom 5:2; 8:18, 21, 30; 9:23; 2 Cor 3:18; Eph 3:16; Col 1:11, 27; 1 Thess 2:12; 2 Thess 2:14; 1 Pet 1:8; 4:13-14; 5:10. Cf. Wolff, 55; Fitzmyer, 176.

in chapter 15, δόξα with reference to the divine glory is found *six* times (15:40–41, 43) and, as we will see, forms a major theme within the chapter. In chapter 15, as in 2:6–8, the glory imparted to the faithful (εἰς δόξαν ἡμῶν, 2:7) is the divine glory of the risen Christ (ὁ κύριος τῆς δόξης, 2:8).

(3) In 2:13 Paul introduces the term πνευματικός, and in 2:14–15 he introduces the contrasting pair ψυχικός and πνευματικός. This contrasting pair will not be found again in the letter until chapter 15 (15:44, 46). The term πνευματικός will play an important role throughout the epistle (2:13; 3:1; 10:2, 4; 12:1; 14:1, 37), but its final usage is in 15:44 and 46, where the combination of ψυχικός and πνευματικός also recurs. First Corinthians 15:44–46 thus forms an *inclusio* with 2:13–15 and a climactic application of the πνευματικός terminology employed by Paul throughout the letter.

(4) In 2:6–16 Paul describes the divine wisdom that he imparts as a mystery (μυστήριον, 2:7), and in 4:1 he portrays this as a complex of interlocking mysteries (μυστήρια) that embrace the whole salvation plan of God, including the consummation of the kingdom. As a number of scholars have noted, Paul's treatment of the mysteries of divine wisdom in 2:6–16 and 4:1 finds a striking resolution and completion in chapter 15, where Paul divulges one of these mysteries (15:51, ἰδού, μυστήριον ὑμῖν λέγω).[121] The revelatory character of Paul's pronouncement in 15:51 is made emphatic by the particle ἰδού, which occurs only here within the letter. What Paul describes in 2:6–16—the apostolic revelation of divine mysteries—he performatively enacts in 15:51–52. In fact, in light of the connections with 2:6–16 we have traced throughout chapter 15, it becomes clear that chapter 15 as a whole, from its introductory words γνωρίζω δὲ ὑμῖν ("I *make known* to you") in 15:1 to the climactic ἰδού, μυστήριον ὑμῖν λέγω ("Behold, I tell you a *mystery*!") in 15:51, is best understood as enacting and embodying what Paul describes in 2:6–16—an authoritative apostolic pronouncement, in words taught by the Spirit, of one facet of the manifold wisdom of God.

## *1 Corinthians 3:17–20: The Corrupting Wisdom without Knowledge of God*

Throughout much of 1:18–4:21, as we have noted, Paul addresses the Corinthian claim to wisdom only indirectly, through his focus on the vain character of the wisdom of this world. However, in 3:10–16 he turns to address the situation at Corinth more directly, and in 3:17–20 he confronts the self-professed wise at Corinth head-on:

> If someone corrupts the temple of God, God will corrupt him. For the temple of God is holy, and this is what you are. Let no one deceive himself; if someone

---

121. So, rightly, Bailey, "Structure," 176, 179–80; Bockmuehl, *Revelation and Mystery*, 172–73; cf. Lührmann, "Freundschaftsbrief," 306.

thinks he is wise among you in this age, let him become a fool, that he may become wise. For the wisdom of this world is foolishness in the sight of God. For it is written, "the one who catches the wise in their cunning," and "The Lord knows the reasonings of the wise, that they are futile." (3:17–20)

Paul here clearly regards the error of the wise at Corinth as a fundamental one, corrupting the church and bringing divine judgment of everlasting destruction on its purveyors. This passage alone, in its intensity and fervor, is sufficient to show the weak character of the widely held thesis that the Corinthian wisdom involved nothing more than an overemphasis on rhetorical display. But the intensity and fervor of this passage are fully explained if Paul's chief concern with the Corinthian wisdom is its denial of the resurrection. We have already found a mass of evidence that this is the case. This passage itself provides further evidence, for Paul's reproof of the self-professed wise at Corinth in 3:17–19 has striking parallels, in both tone and content, to his warning to the Corinthians in 15:33–34 regarding the evil influence of those who deny the resurrection:

| | |
|---|---|
| If *someone* [τις] *corrupts* [φθείρει] the temple of God, God *will corrupt* [φθερεῖ] him ... Let no one *deceive* [ἐξαπατάτω] himself; if *someone* [τις] thinks he is wise among you in this age, let him become a fool, that he may become wise. For the wisdom of this world is *foolishness* [μωρία] in the sight of *God*. (3:17–19a) | Do not *be deceived* [πλανᾶσθε]— "evil communications *corrupt* [φθείρουσιν] good morals." Wake up from your stupor, as is right, and stop sinning; for *some* [τινες] have *lack of knowledge* [ἀγνωσίαν] of *God*. (15:33–34) |

Moreover, in 3:20 Paul quotes a passage from Job that describes the reasonings (διαλογισμοί) of the wise (σοφοί) as "futile" (μάταιος). This recalls the theme introduced in 1:17 that corrupting the gospel with human wisdom renders the cross of Christ vain (οὐκ ἐν σοφίᾳ λόγου, ἵνα μὴ κενωθῇ ὁ σταυρὸς τοῦ Χριστοῦ). And it looks ahead to chapter 15, where (as we have seen) a major theme of the chapter is that the denial of the resurrection makes the gospel vain (15:2, 14, 17, 58). The specific adjective μάταιος "futile," which Paul introduces for the first time in the letter here in 3:20, has its only other occurrence in the epistle in 15:17 (<u>ματαία</u> ἡ πίστις ὑμῶν).

*1 Corinthians 4:9–13: Paul's Cruciform Model of Radical Discipleship*

There is a striking relationship between 1 Cor 4:9–13 and 15:30–32. These two passages are both hardship catalogues.[122] They are the only two hardship catalogues

---

122. For further examples in Paul's letters, see *SPL* §17, "Hardship Catalogue."

*Chapter 15 as the Culmination of 1 Corinthians*

found within the letter. Paul's description of the apostles in 4:9 as ἐπιθανάτιοι ("ones condemned to death") finds its only parallel in the letter in 15:31: καθ' ἡμέραν ἀποθνῄσκω ("daily I die"). Likewise, the apostolic afflictions are portrayed in 4:11 as taking place ἄχρι τῆς ἄρτι ὥρας ("until the present *hour*"), and Paul's afflictions in 15:30 are depicted as taking place πᾶσαν ὥραν ("throughout every *hour*"). In 4:9–13, Paul sets forth his apostolic model of cruciform discipleship, taking up the cross for the sake of Christ and the gospel, which he contrasts with the lifestyle of the inflated self-professed wise at Corinth (4:6–8, 18–20). In chapter 15, Paul brings this portrayal to a culmination in his depiction of his example of radical devotion to Christ as motivated by the hope of the resurrection (15:30–32), and in his portrayal of the denial of the resurrection as undermining Christian morality and discipleship (15:32–34).

*Summary of 1 Corinthians 1:18–4:21 as Culminating in Chapter 15*

To sum up our discussion of Paul's engagement with the Corinthian claim to philosophical wisdom in 1:18–4:21, we have seen that these chapters anticipate and require Paul's exposition regarding the resurrection in chapter 15. In 1:18–4:21, Paul's twin focus is on his gospel and the corruption of that gospel through the wisdom claimed by some at Corinth. This twin focus finds its resolution and culmination in chapter 15, in Paul's restatement of his gospel (15:1–11) and his direct refutation of the denial of the resurrection by the self-proclaimed wise at Corinth (15:12–58). Paul's model of radical discipleship in 4:9–13, in contrast with the conduct of the self-proclaimed wise at Corinth (4:6–8, 18–20), finds its counterpart and completion in 15:30–32, where we find this cruciform discipleship is founded in the hope of the resurrection and undermined by the denial of the resurrection. First Corinthians 1:18–4:21 has a necessary *Folgetext* within the letter, and it is chapter 15. Forming the beginning and close of the main body of the letter, 1:18–4:21 and 15:1–58 thus form an *inclusio* that frames the epistle as a whole.

## Anticipations of Chapter 15 in 1 Corinthians 5–14

Chapters 5–14 have a different character than 1:18–4:21. Chapters 1–4 have a unified focus, on the gospel Paul brought to Corinth and the danger of the corruption of that gospel by human wisdom. Chapters 1–4 find their counterpart and resolution in chapter 15, where Paul summarizes his gospel and refutes the false wisdom of those at Corinth who deny the resurrection. In chapters 5–14, by contrast, Paul deals with a diversity of topics, called forth by specific needs perceived by Paul among the Corinthians. These topics cannot be reduced to a single theme, nor do

CHAPTER 1

all of them relate directly to chapter 15. However, we will now see something striking within these chapters. We will find within these chapters a number of passages that point forward to chapter 15—passages that, indeed, require and presuppose chapter 15 as their *Folgetext*. I do not claim that the evidence in each of the cases below is equally conclusive. But, taken cumulatively, the passages provide strong evidence that throughout what many have considered the aimless wanderings of chapters 5–14, the apostle has chapter 15 as the climax and culmination of the epistle firmly in his sights.

*1 Corinthians 6:12–20: A Puzzling Rhetorical Strategy Explained by Chapter 15*

In 1 Cor 6:12–20 Paul exhorts the Corinthians to avoid sexual immorality. In 6:13b–14 he grounds this moral exhortation in the resurrection of the body to come: "But the body is not for sexual immorality but for the Lord, and the Lord is for the body. And God both raised the Lord, and will raise us, through his power." As Matt O'Reilly has shown persuasively, Paul's argument here anticipates and requires his exposition of the resurrection in chapter 15.[123] For the cogency of Paul's argument in 6:12–20 depends upon the reality of the bodily resurrection (6:13–14). But, as we know, some at Corinth denied the resurrection (15:12). Apart from chapter 15, O'Reilly notes, Paul's introduction in 6:13–14 of this "contested topic" would be "puzzling" and "a peculiar rhetorical strategy."[124] The answer to the puzzle is that Paul employs an argument here that he will fully ground only later in chapter 15.[125] "In this way, the effectiveness of 6:12–20 depends on the success of the argument in chapter 15."[126] O'Reilly also observes that Paul's language in 6:19 regarding the body (σῶμα) as a temple of the Holy Spirit (τὸ ἅγιον πνεῦμα) "may anticipate the language of σῶμα πνευματικόν in 15:44."[127] Moreover, Paul's assertion in 6:13 that "the Lord is for the body" (the meaning of which has puzzled scholars) finds its full explanation in chapter 15, where (as we will see in our exposition of the chapter) in the resurrection the bodies of the faithful are transformed to imperishability through participation in the glory of the risen Christ.

---

123. O'Reilly, *Resurrected Body*, 97–109.
124. O'Reilly, *Resurrected Body*, 102.
125. The verb ἐγείρω is used for the first time in the letter in 6:14, and nowhere thereafter outside chapter 15—but in that chapter the verb ἐγείρω is used nineteen times.
126. O'Reilly, *Resurrected Body*, 108. Lührmann also notes the way in which 6:13–14 anticipates the argument of chapter 15 ("Freundschaftsbrief," 306).
127. O'Reilly, *Resurrected Body*, 105.

*1 Corinthians 7:39 and 11:30: The Language of "Sleep" Foreshadowing Chapter 15*

The verb κοιμάω is an important component within the New Testament vocabulary of the resurrection. The verb is used metaphorically to describe the bodies of believers who have died as being only "asleep," awaiting their awakening to eternal life at the resurrection (cf. Matt 27:52; Acts 7:60; 2 Pet 3:4). However, this verb is relatively rare in Paul and is used outside of 1 Corinthians only in Paul's teaching on the resurrection in 1 Thess 4:13–18 (see 4:13, 15). It is therefore striking that this verb denoting the resurrection hope occurs *twice* in 1 Cor 1–14 and, in both cases, in connection with *other* topics (7:39; 11:30), a phenomenon that occurs nowhere else in Paul. In chapter 15 this verb occurs *four* times, forming a key component of the vocabulary of that chapter (15:6, 18, 20, 51). Like Paul's introduction of the topic of resurrection in 6:13–14, his use of the resurrection term κοιμάω in 7:39 and 11:30 seems to anticipate and prepare for his teaching on the resurrection in chapter 15.

*1 Corinthians 9:1–5: An Anticipation of the List of Apostolic Witnesses in 15:5–11*

Paul writes in 1 Cor 9:1:

> Am I not free? Am I not an apostle? Have I not seen Jesus our Lord? Are you not my work in the Lord?

Two elements are present here that have been found previously within the letter: (1) Paul's apostolic *commission* (ἀπόστολος, 9:1), already introduced within the body opening as a theme of the epistle (1:17, ἀπέστειλέν με Χριστός; cf. 4:9); and (2) Paul's apostolic *work* or labor (9:1, ἔργον), a theme found also in 3:8 (κόπος). But a third element is introduced here for the first time in the letter: Paul's *seeing* of the risen Lord (ὁράω, 9:1). Paul's seeing of the risen Lord is found in only one other place within the letter: 1 Cor 15:8–10. In 1 Cor 15:8–10, in fact, we find all three elements of 9:1 closely conjoined—Paul's apostolic commission, his apostolic work, and his eyewitness encounter with the risen Christ:

> And last of all . . . he *appeared* [ὤφθη] to me as well. . . . I am the least of the apostles, and am unfit to be called an *apostle* [ἀπόστολος] . . . but more abundantly than all of them I have *labored* [ἐκοπίασα]. (15:8–10)

In 9:5 we find Paul grouped among other apostolic figures: "the rest of the apostles, the brothers of the Lord, and Cephas." We find the same list of figures in

CHAPTER 1

only one other place within the epistle—in Paul's list of apostolic eyewitnesses of the risen Lord in 15:5–8. But here we find the list in precisely the *reverse* order:

| | |
|---|---|
| Do not *we* have authority to lead about a sister as wife, as also the rest of *the apostles* and *the brothers of the Lord* and *Cephas*? (9:5) | He appeared to *Cephas* ... then he appeared to *James*, then to all *the apostles*. And last of all ... he appeared to *me*. (15:5–8) |

The key themes and vocabulary of 9:1 (Paul's apostleship, apostolic work, and eyewitness encounter with the risen Christ) and the nearly identical list of apostolic figures given in 9:5 all reappear in 15:5–11. This suggests that 1 Cor 9:1–5 serves an anticipatory or preparatory function, anticipating the list of apostolic eyewitnesses to the risen Christ in 15:5–11.

*1 Corinthians 9:25: The Incorruptible Wreath as an Anticipation of Chapter 15*

In 9:25 Paul contrasts the "corruptible" (φθαρτός) wreath of victory of the athletic competitor with the "incorruptible" (ἄφθαρτος) wreath for which the Corinthians should strive.[128] The adjectives φθαρτός and ἄφθαρτος, and their cognate nouns φθορά "corruption" and ἀφθαρσία "incorruptibility," do not occur elsewhere in the letter prior to chapter 15. But in chapter 15 there is a veritable explosion of such language (φθαρτός, 15:53–54; φθορά, 15:42, 50; ἄφθαρτος, 15:52; ἀφθαρσία, 15:42, 50, 52, 54). Moreover, the incorruptible wreath of victory (στέφανος) in 9:25 looks ahead to the victory (νῖκος) over death in 15:54–57.[129] This would suggest that 1 Cor 9:25 is another element within the letter serving to anticipate the climactic fifteenth chapter.

*1 Corinthians 11:18–19: Defection from the Faith Unaddressed until Chapter 15*

At the outset of his discussion of conduct at the Lord's Supper, Paul tells the Corinthians, "For, first, on the one hand, when you come together as a church, I hear that there are schisms among you" (11:18). The term Paul uses here, σχίσματα "divisions," is the same term Paul used in 1:10 with reference to the factionalism at Corinth. Moreover, when Paul says in 11:18 ἀκούω σχίσματα ἐν ὑμῖν ὑπάρχειν ("I hear that there are divisions among you"), this recalls his wording in 1:11: ἐδηλώθη γάρ μοι ...

---

128. On the image of the wreath of victory in Paul, see David J. Williams, *Paul's Metaphors: Their Context and Character* (Peabody, MA: Hendrickson, 1999), 273.

129. I am indebted for this insight to Ernst Wendland in private communication.

*Chapter 15 as the Culmination of 1 Corinthians*

ὅτι ἔριδες ἐν ὑμῖν εἰσιν ("for it was reported to me ... that there are disputes among you"). The most natural reading would seem to be to identify the divisions here with the schisms mentioned earlier in the epistle. However, the great majority of scholars hold that the divisions here are entirely unrelated to those in 1:10–11.[130] The divisions Paul mentions in 11:18, it is said, involve merely the inappropriate conduct at the eucharistic table that Paul describes in 11:21–22 and 11:33–34. However, such an interpretation is unlikely for several reasons:

(1) Paul in 11:19 further defines the σχίσματα of 11:18 with the word αἵρεσις (11:19, δεῖ γὰρ καὶ αἱρέσεις ἐν ὑμῖν εἶναι). The word αἵρεσις in antiquity refers to "a group that holds tenets distinctive to it, *sect, party, school, faction*" or to "that which distinguishes a group's thinking, *opinion, dogma*."[131] The word thus seems always to include the idea of shared *tenets*, *views*, or *doctrine*. It was a neutral term in Hellenistic usage, regularly denoting one of the various philosophical schools and viewpoints such as the Stoics, Epicureans, Peripatetics, and so forth (Epictetus, *Diatr.* 2.19.20; Philo, *Plant.* 151; Diodorus Siculus, *Bib. hist.* 2.29).[132] The word is found in Josephus in this neutral sense with reference to the three major sects within Jewish religious life: the Pharisees, Sadducees, and Essenes (Josephus, *Vita* 10, 12; 191, 197; *A.J.* 18.288, 293; 20.199). The word is used in this sense within the book of Acts with reference to Sadducees, Pharisees, and Christ followers (Acts 5:17; 15:5; 24:5, 14; 26:5; 28:22). We find the word used for the first time in an unambiguously *negative* sense within early Christian documents, yet still with reference to tenets or doctrines and thus to false *teaching* (2 Pet 2:1; Ign. *Eph.* 6.2; *Trall.* 6.1; Justin, *Dial.* 35.3; Origen, *Cels.* 3.12).

Although all scholars are in agreement with the general picture drawn here, some scholars argue that the use of αἵρεσις in some of our very earliest Christian texts, including 1 Cor 11:19, is an exception to its universal use elsewhere as denoting view or doctrine.[133] However, this consistent usage of αἵρεσις elsewhere in Hel-

---

130. So Matthew R. Malcolm, *Paul and the Rhetoric of Reversal in 1 Corinthians: The Impact of Paul's Gospel on His Macro-Rhetoric* (SNTSMS 155; Cambridge: Cambridge University Press, 2013), 91–92; de Boer, "Composition," 239 n. 32; Belleville, "Continuity," 28; Fitzmyer, 433.

131. BDAG, s.v. "αἵρεσις." These are the only two senses BDAG supplies for the word.

132. The notion of shared *doctrine* inherent in the word is clear from Diogenes Laertius's remark that, in the view of the majority, Scepticism cannot be a αἵρεσις since it has no doctrines (*Vit. phil.* 1.120). It is also reflected in the Sceptic philosopher Sextus Empiricus's own hesitation on the matter (*Pyr.* 1.16). He decides that Pyrrhonism can be classed as a αἵρεσις, since it is "a way of life following a certain form of rational argumentation" (λόγος, 1.17). Cf. the similar conclusion of Diogenes Laertius (*Vit. phil.* 1.20). The term can also be used of a group with shared political tenets (Appian, *Bell. civ.* 5.1.2; 5.8.70).

133. E.g., Marcel Simon, "From Greek Hairesis to Christian Heresy," in *Early Christian Literature and the Classical Intellectual Tradition* (ed. W. Schoedel and R. L. Wilken; ThH 153; Paris:

CHAPTER 1

lenistic, Jewish, and early Christian literature to denote a group with distinctive tenets or beliefs would strongly suggest that also in the case of 1 Cor 11:19—our earliest occurrence of the term in early Christian sources—the word αἵρεσις retains its normal connotation of view or teaching.[134] The word clearly has a negative connotation in v. 19 and thus refers to *heretical factions*.

(2) There is a second reason why the divisions of 11:18–19 cannot be, as so many claim, merely behavioral and social. For what this reading cannot explain is why Paul *contrasts* these divisive groups with those who are approved among the Corinthians: "for it is necessary there also be *heretical factions* [αἱρέσεις] among you, in order that *those who are approved* [οἱ δόκιμοι] may be revealed among you" (11:19). The δεῖ ("it is necessary") here has in mind the eschatological necessity of the divinely ordained salvation plan (cf. Mark 8:31; 13:7, 10; 1 Cor 15:25, 53), and the approval envisioned is that of Christ and God. Clearly, the stakes are high in the view of the apostle, no less than salvation versus judgment (cf. 9:27, ἀδόκιμος). Moreover, Henning Paulsen has shown that a saying not found in the gospels but attributed in the primitive church to Jesus, foretelling the rise of schisms and heretical factions, most likely underlies Paul's statement.[135] If so, the inapplicability of the social interpretation is obvious. In any case, the seriousness of the matter and of Paul's statement is striking indeed. Scholars who assume these αἱρέσεις are merely social are generally forced to conclude that Paul is speaking ironically or is even sarcastically repeating a Corinthian slogan![136] These interpreters find themselves entirely unable to explain the obvious gravity of the situation in the eyes of Paul. But if these divisions, as Paul's use of the term αἵρεσις suggests, involved false teaching—a serious defection from the faith—then everything in the passage falls into place.

Paul introduces his reference to the divisions with the phrase πρῶτον μέν (11:18), indicating that this is the first of at least two issues with which he will deal regard-

---

Beauchesne, 1979), 109; following Simon is Pogoloff, *Logos and Sophia*, 101. Simon, in addition to 1 Cor 11:19, also cites Gal 5:20; Titus 3:10; Herm. Sim. 9.23.5.

134. BDAG, s.v. "αἵρεσις" includes 1 Cor 11:19 under meaning 1, "a group that holds tenets distinctive to it, *sect, party, school, faction*." According to Robinson, αἵρεσις in 1 Cor 11:19 denotes "*discord, dissension*, arising from difference of views" (Robinson, s.v. "αἵρεσις"). See also Tertullian, *Praescr.* 5.

135. Henning Paulsen, "Schisma und Häresie: Untersuchungen zu 1 Kor 11:18, 19," *ZTK* 79 (1982): 180–211. For the tradition, see Justin, *Dial.* 35.3 (ἔσονται σχίσματα καὶ αἱρέσεις); Ps.-Clem. *Hom.* 16.21.4 (ἔσονται γάρ, ὡς ὁ κύριος εἶπεν, ψευδαπόστολοι, ψευδεῖς προφῆται, αἱρέσεις, φιλαρχίαι); Did. Apost. 23.

136. So Fitzmyer, 433 (Paul is speaking "ironically"); Thiselton, 858–60 (Paul repeats a Corinthian maxim in order to criticize it).

ing the Lord's Supper (11:17). The second issue emerges in 11:20.[137] He addresses this second issue—the conduct of the Corinthians at the fellowship meal—in 11:20–32, and he brings this to a fitting conclusion in 11:33–34. However, the first issue—Corinthian factionalism—is not further addressed by Paul within the chapter. These factions with false views, introduced by Paul in 11:18–19 as a grave danger undermining the faith of the church at Corinth, are abruptly laid aside. Rhetorically, 11:18–19 requires a *Folgetext*, a follow-up passage in which this issue is fully addressed and resolved. Do we find such a *Folgetext* within the letter, in which Paul deals directly with some at Corinth holding beliefs he considered incompatible with the gospel? Yes, we do, 1 Cor 15:12: "How do some among you say that there is no resurrection of the dead?" Only in chapter 15 do we find Paul's language of αἵρεσις in 11:18–19, and the life or death gravity of these divisive teachings in the mind of Paul, fully explained. In 11:18–19 we appear to find yet another passage within the letter requiring chapter 15 as its resolution and climax.

Space does not permit the discussion of other elements within chapters 5–14 that anticipate chapter 15 (6:3; 7:29–31; 8:6; 10:1–4; 13:8–13). However, we will touch upon these over the course of the commentary.

Conclusion

The unity and coherence of 1 Corinthians is a hitherto unresolved enigma. There is no consensus whether the letter has a detectable logic and structure, and if so, what that logic might be. The relationship of chapters 1–4, with their focus on the foolishness of the gospel in contrast with the vanity of human wisdom, to the rest of the letter, where these themes are reputedly absent, has remained an unresolved question. The nature of the Corinthian claim to wisdom opposed by Paul in chapters 1–4, and Paul's apparent failure to engage these issues elsewhere in the letter, have also remained unexplained. The lack of any discernible relation of chapter 15 to the rest of the letter has been a further difficulty.

In this chapter we have seen how a more precise exegesis of the letter reveals the crucial role of chapter 15 as the true climax of the letter and resolves each of these questions. Epistolary analysis of the salutation (1:1–3), thanksgiving (1:4–9), and macrostructure of the letter reveals that the epistle does not address a single theme—rendering single-topic hypotheses unsustainable—but that the letter

---

137. As A. T. Robertson notes: "In 1 Cor. 11:18, πρῶτον μὲν γάρ, the contrast is implied in 11:20 ff." (Rob., *Gram.*, 1152). With πρῶτον μέν, contrast with a second or more points is always implied; see Kühner-G., 2.2:272, who cite Thucydides, *Hist.* 2.74, where the contrast first follows in 2.75.

does have a unified structure and plan, which reaches its climax and resolution in chapter 15. The body opening (1:10–17) of the letter reveals that Paul's call to unity is not a generic exhortation to a pragmatic unity, but one calling for conformity in teaching and doctrine. Paul's language in this body opening indicates that the chief theme of the epistle is the divisive Corinthian wisdom he opposes in 1:10–4:21, and that the wisdom in question was not rhetorical art but philosophical wisdom. Again and again, the language of the body opening points forward to chapter 15, revealing that the chief of Paul's concerns with the self-professed wise at Corinth was their denial of the resurrection. This explains—in a way that the reigning identification of the Corinthian wisdom with rhetorical skill entirely fails to do—why Paul portrays this wisdom as incompatible with the gospel and destructive of the church at Corinth. Paul's example in chapters 1–4 of cruciform discipleship (4:9–16), in contrast with the self-professed wise at Corinth (4:6–8, 18–20), finds its completion and interpretive key in chapter 15, where Paul portrays the resurrection hope as the foundation of his apostolic model of radical devotion to Christ (15:30–32, 58) and depicts the denial of the resurrection as overturning Christian morality and discipleship (15:19, 32–34). In chapter 15 Paul will thus disclose the inseparable connection between the resurrection and the Christian moral life and affirm that the source of the failure of the wise at Corinth to walk in moral conformity to Christ is their denial of the resurrection. Paul's engagement with this human wisdom that renders the gospel vain—the focus of 1:18–4:21—thus reaches its resolution and climax in chapter 15, where Paul takes the denial of the resurrection by the self-professed wise at Corinth head-on. Throughout the varied topics addressed in chapters 5–14, Paul continues to prepare his readers for this chapter. Chapter 15 is thus the goal and culmination of the epistle, unifying and clarifying the entire letter.

In chapter 15, we come to Paul's chief concern within the letter, and to the climax and resolution of Paul's interaction with the self-professed wise at Corinth begun in chapters 1–4. Only in chapter 15 do we discover the precise nature of this human wisdom that renders the gospel vain—the denial of the resurrection—and receive Paul's full response. Chapter 15, which so many interpreters have regarded as having no discernible relation to the rest of the letter, is in fact the culmination and interpretive key of the entire epistle.

CHAPTER 2

## *A Deepened Revelation of the Gospel*

15:1–2

Hans Lietzmann wrote of 1 Corinthians 15: "Without internal or external connection with what has been said before, the treatment of a new theme now follows."[1] Scholars have generally acquiesced in this judgment, but with a sense, ever since Barth, that Lietzmann could not be completely right. The exegesis offered in the previous chapter has shown that Lietzmann was completely wrong. The thanksgiving (1:4–9) and body opening (1:10–17) of the letter point to chapter 15 as embodying the culminating theme of the epistle. The topic of this chapter is the chief issue at stake in Paul's battle with the divisive Corinthian wisdom in chapters 1–4; and throughout the varied topics addressed throughout chapters 5–14, Paul prepares his readers for this chapter. Chapter 15 is not separable from the rest of the letter, as Lietzmann thought. It is the culmination of the epistle, which unifies and clarifies the entire letter.

Although not separable from the rest of the letter, chapter fifteen does form a discrete literary unit within the epistle (15:1–58). Here all scholars are agreed on very good grounds, as we will see. There is also widespread scholarly agreement that 1 Cor 15 is composed of six major divisions or segments: vv. 1–11, 12–19, 20–28, 29–34, 35–49, and 50–58.[2] For all their differences and disagreements, the various rhetorical treatments of 1 Cor 15 are also in remarkable agreement regarding

---

1. As cited in Karl Barth, *The Resurrection of the Dead* (trans. H. J. Stenning; 1933; repr., Eugene, OR: Wipf & Stock, 2003), 6.
2. See, for example, Martinus de Boer, *The Defeat of Death: Apocalyptic Eschatology in 1 Corinthians 15 and Romans 5* (JSNTSup 22; 1988; repr., London: T&T Clark, 2019), 93–95; Felipe de Jesús Legarreta-Castillo, *The Figure of Adam in Romans 5 and 1 Corinthians 15: The New Creation and Its Ethical and Social Reconfiguration* (Minneapolis: Fortress, 2014), 120–25.

CHAPTER 2

these basic divisions of the chapter.[3] These major divisions may be further subdivided into twelve distinct units: vv. 1–2, 3–11, 12–19, 20–23, 24–28, 29–34, 35, 36–41, 42–44a, 44b–49, 50–53, and 54–58. These units, as the commentary will show, reflect Paul's own structuring of the chapter, and the chapters that follow in the commentary will correspond to each of these twelve segments of the chapter (with three chapters devoted to the all-important apostolic confession in vv. 3–11). We begin, then, with the first major segment of the letter, 1 Cor 15:1–11, and Paul's introduction to that segment in 15:1–2. As we will see, vv. 1–2 also form the introduction to the entire chapter.

## VERSES 1–2

*¹ And I make known to you, brothers and sisters, the gospel which I gospel-proclaimed to you, which you also received, in which you also stand, ² through which you are also being saved, through the very word which I gospel-proclaimed to you, if you indeed hold it fast—unless you believed in vain.*

The transitional δέ, the disclosure formula employing the verb γνωρίζω, and the insertion of the vocative address ἀδελφοί, together function to demarcate the transition to a new topic in 15:1.[4] The final word of v. 2, ἐπιστεύσατε, corresponds to the final word of v. 11, ἐπιστεύσατε, thus forming an *inclusio* that marks off 15:1–11 as a literary unit.[5] Verses 1–2 form Paul's introduction to this unit (15:1–11).[6] How-

---

3. See Duane F. Watson, "Paul's Rhetorical Strategy in 1 Corinthians 15," in *Rhetoric and the New Testament: Essays from the 1992 Heidelberg Conference* (ed. Stanley E. Porter and Thomas R. Olbricht; JSNTSup 90; Sheffield: JSOT Press, 1993), 231–49; Werner Stenger, "Beobachtungen zur Argumentationsstruktur von 1 Kor 15," *LB* 45 (1979): 71–128; Mark I. Wegener, "The Rhetorical Strategy of 1 Corinthians 15," *CurTM* 31 (2004): 438–55; David A. Ackerman, *Lo, I Tell You a Mystery: Cross, Resurrection, and Paraenesis in the Rhetoric of 1 Corinthians* (PTMS 54; Eugene, OR: Pickwick, 2006), 85–98; Anders Eriksson, *Traditions as Rhetorical Proof: Pauline Argumentation in 1 Corinthians* (ConBNT 29; Stockholm: Almqvist & Wiksell, 1998), 232–78; and Insawn Saw, *Paul's Rhetoric in 1 Corinthians 15: An Analysis Utilizing the Theories of Classical Rhetoric* (Lewiston, NY: Mellen, 1995), 221–26.

4. Rightly Linda L. Belleville, "Continuity or Discontinuity: A Fresh Look at 1 Corinthians in the Light of First-Century Epistolary Forms and Conventions," *EvQ* 59 (1987): 24–26; Wayne Coppins, "Doing Justice to the Two Perspectives of 1 Corinthians 15,1–11," *Neot* 44 (2010): 283; Fitzmyer, 540.

5. Fitzmyer, 545.

6. Theories of an elaborate concentric or ring structure within 15:1–11 are not persuasive; contra Timothy Milinovich, *Beyond What Is Written: The Performative Structure of 1 Corinthians*

*A Deepened Revelation of the Gospel*

ever, 15:1–2 has a broader function as well. For the key themes of vv. 1–2—*knowledge* of the gospel, *standing firm* in it, and *vanity*—all recur at the conclusion of the chapter:

| | |
|---|---|
| And I *make known* to you, *brothers and sisters*, the gospel . . . in which you stand . . . if you *hold it fast* . . . unless you believed *in vain*. (15:1–2) | So then, my beloved *brothers and sisters*, be *firm, immovable* . . . *knowing* that your labor is not *in vain* in the Lord. (15:58) |

Through this dense recurrence of themes, 15:1–2 and 15:58 form an *inclusio* that encompasses all of chapter fifteen and marks off 15:1–58 as a distinct literary unit within the letter. Verses 1–2 thus form Paul's introduction not only to 15:1–11 but to the entire chapter. And, as we will see, it is a powerful introduction indeed.

*15:1. And I make known to you, brothers and sisters.* Paul's opening words γνωρίζω δὲ ὑμῖν, ἀδελφοί constitute a major "disclosure formula" (cf. 10:1; 11:3; 12:1, 3; see also 2 Cor 8:1; Gal 1:11).[7] This formula indicates the introduction of a new topic in 15:1.[8] According to J. B. Lightfoot, an epistolary disclosure in Paul that employs γνωρίζω "introduces some statement on which the apostle lays special emphasis."[9] The verb here thus provides, as Conzelmann points out, "a ceremonious introduction" to this climactic chapter.[10] The topic introduced here, Paul wants the Corinthians to know, is of the utmost importance.

But Paul's choice of the verb γνωρίζω here is also quite arresting. The verb γνωρίζω means to make known something previously unknown.[11] But the direct object of the verb is τὸ εὐαγγέλιον ὃ εὐηγγελισάμην ὑμῖν "the gospel which I gospel-proclaimed to you"—something the Corinthians already knew (or should have known) quite well. Many commentators take the expedient of construing the verb here in the sense "remind."[12] But this is ruled out by the semantic range of the verb, which is cognate with other terms of knowledge in the letter such

---

(Eugene, OR: Pickwick, 2013), 188–93, and Rob A. Fringer, "Dying to Be the Church: 1 Corinthians 15 and Paul's Shocking Revelation about Death and Resurrection," *ERT* 41 (2017): 180.

7. See Belleville, "Continuity," 24–26.
8. Cf. Coppins, "Two Perspectives," 283.
9. J. B. Lightfoot, *The Epistle of St. Paul to the Galatians* (Grand Rapids: Zondervan, 1957), 79.
10. Conzelmann, 250 n. 16.
11. See Walter Radl, "Der Sinn von γνωρίζω in 1 Kor 15:1," *BZ* 28 (1984): 243–45; cf. BDAG, s.v. "γνωρίζω"; Frisk, 1:308–9; Schmidt, *Syn.*, 1:287.
12. So Barth, *Resurrection*, 125–26; Jan Lambrecht, "Three Brief Notes on 1 Corinthians 15," *Bijdr* 62 (2001): 29–30; Weiss, 345.

CHAPTER 2

as γινώσκω, γνῶσις, and ἀγνωσία, and always involves the introduction of new or further knowledge.[13]

What is the answer to the dilemma? Paul's choice of the verb γνωρίζω here no doubt has "a critical undertone."[14] As Joseph Fitzmyer observes, "Paul is politely chiding the Corinthians."[15] Paul here already has in mind the presence of some at Corinth who deny the resurrection (15:12). Later in the chapter, Paul will criticize this lack of knowledge of the gospel among some at Corinth more directly: "For some [τινες] have lack of knowledge [ἀγνωσίαν] of God; I speak to your shame!" (15:34).

But the formal and ceremonious tone of this verb elsewhere in Paul would suggest that the element of critique does not exhaust its meaning here. Two factors point in the right direction. First, as we have seen, 15:1–2 forms an *inclusio* with 15:58. This would indicate that the verb γνωρίζω serves to introduce not just 15:1–11 but the entire chapter as well. Second, the verb γνωρίζω, although always involving further knowledge, can be used not only of *initial* knowledge but also of a further *deepening* of knowledge (cf. John 17:26, ἐγνώρισα αὐτοῖς τὸ ὄνομά σου καὶ γνωρίσω "I *made known* to them your name, and *will make* it *known*"). This suggests that Paul is making the gospel known to the Corinthians not only by rehearsing it to them, as he will do in 15:3–11, but also by making it more fully known to them through the exposition of the rest of the chapter (15:12–58). The verb γνωρίζω at the beginning of the chapter corresponds to the verb οἶδα at its close: by making the gospel more fully known to the Corinthians (γνωρίζω, 15:1), the Corinthians will know (οἶδα, 15:58) that their labor is not in vain in the Lord.

The terms of knowledge Paul employs in chapter 15 (15:1, γνωρίζω; 15:34, ἀγνωσία; 15:58, οἶδα) recall Paul's discussion of the claims to wisdom among some at Corinth in chapters 1–4. There Paul, as we saw in the previous chapter, contrasted the wisdom of the world with the knowledge of the gospel (1:18–2:16; 3:18–20) and portrayed himself and his fellow apostles as stewards of the knowledge and mysteries of God, as revealed to them by the Spirit (2:6–16; 4:1). In the LXX, and especially in Daniel, the verb γνωρίζω "ranks among the terms expressive of *divine revelation*."[16] Through the use of this verb in 15:1, Paul solemnly conveys to the Corinthians his intention to *enact* this apostolic function in the instruction that follows.[17] Paul's instruction in the chapter will culminate in the revelation of a

---

13. Radl, "Sinn," 243. On the derivation of γνωρίζω, see Frisk, 1:308–9.
14. Wolff, 354 n. 22.
15. Fitzmyer, 544. Cf. Godet, 2:326; Coppins, "Two Perspectives," 283.
16. Cremer, 678.
17. "Paul begins this section by setting his argument in the form of a revelatory proclamation." See Fringer, "Church," 179.

*A Deepened Revelation of the Gospel*

divine mystery (15:51, ἰδού, μυστήριον ὑμῖν λέγω).[18] In this way, Paul's portrayal in 2:6–16 of the divine wisdom mediated through the apostles, in words taught by the Spirit, finds its resolution and completion within the letter through his authoritative apostolic teaching regarding the resurrection in chapter 15. In 2:6–16 Paul described this wisdom not as an esoteric theosophy different from the message of the crucified and risen Christ but as a deepened comprehension of the mystery of Christ and of his saving work. Thus in 1 Cor 15, what Paul makes known to the Corinthians is but a fuller revelation and disclosure of the gospel he first proclaimed to them (15:1, τὸ εὐαγγέλιον ὃ εὐηγγελισάμην ὑμῖν).

*the gospel which I gospel-proclaimed to you.* What Paul makes known to the Corinthians is "the gospel" (τὸ εὐαγγέλιον). Paul's favored term for the message he proclaimed to the gentiles differs from other terms for the missionary proclamation in its stress on the *joyfulness* of its content. It is the "good news" or "joyful announcement." Most interpreters assume that this gospel will form the subject matter of only vv. 1–11. However, we have seen that γνωρίζω introduces not only vv. 1–11 but the entire chapter as well. This would indicate that Paul understands the entire chapter, which will be devoted to the proclamation and defense of the resurrection, as an exposition of the gospel. Paul will begin that exposition in 15:3. But in 15:1–2 Paul will first further identify that gospel through no less than five relative clauses.

As the first relative clause expresses, this gospel is the one "which I gospel-proclaimed to you" (ὃ εὐηγγελισάμην ὑμῖν, 15:1). Like its cognate noun, εὐαγγέλιον, the verb εὐαγγελίζομαι means "*to preach*, including always the idea of *glad tidings.*"[19] The use of verb and noun in tandem, with εὐαγγέλιον as the object of εὐαγγελίζομαι, occurs elsewhere in the New Testament only in 2 Cor 11:7 and Gal 1:11. It adds extraordinary emphasis and focus upon the gospel, and it also recalls to the minds of the Corinthians Paul's initial proclamation to them.

*which you also received.* This gospel is also, as the second relative clause states, the gospel "which you also received" (ὃ καὶ παρελάβετε, 15:1). The verb παραλαμβάνω is commonly used in early Christianity for the *reception* or *acceptance* of the apostolic testimony to Jesus (see, for example, 1 Cor 11:23; Gal 1:9; Phil 4:9; 1 Thess 2:13). In such contexts, the stress of the verb lies in the concrete, objective act of recep-

---

18. 15:51 is the climax of a series of revelatory disclosures directed to the Corinthians in the latter part of the letter: 12:3, διὸ γνωρίζω ὑμῖν; 12:31, ὑμῖν δείκνυμι; 15:1, γνωρίζω δὲ ὑμῖν; 15:51, μυστήριον ὑμῖν λέγω.

19. Robinson, s.v. "εὐαγγελίζω."

CHAPTER 2

tion and thus on the content of the message (cf. 1 Cor 15:3; Gal 1:12; 2 Thess 3:6). The verb also includes the personal involvement of the subject not only in the acts of welcome and assent but also in a binding commitment to safeguard what has been received.[20] Paul here recalls this binding commitment to the minds of the Corinthians.

*in which you also stand.* Paul's third relative clause further describes the good news he brought to the Corinthians as the gospel "in which you also stand" (ἐν ᾧ καὶ ἑστήκατε, 15:1). Here as elsewhere, Paul employs the perfect tense of ἵστημι to denote standing firm in grace or in the faith (cf. Rom 5:2; 11:20; 1 Cor 10:12; 2 Cor 1:24). Uniquely here, Paul speaks of standing firm in the *gospel*, continuing his striking emphasis in the passage on the gospel and its content.

*15:2. through which you are also being saved.* Paul now describes the glad tidings he proclaimed, which the Corinthians had also received and in which they also stand, with yet a fourth relative clause: "through which you are also being saved" (δι' οὗ καὶ σῴζεσθε, 15:2). The adjunctive καί inserted before each of the verbs following εὐηγγελισάμην ὑμῖν lends to each verb an ascending force, culminating in σῴζεσθε in 15:2.[21] In its regular Hellenistic usage, the verb means to "save from an immediate threat," not merely of harm or loss but of complete destruction.[22] In the LXX, however, the verb has a wider usage, denoting deliverance not only from destruction but also from bondage, oppression, and affliction (cf. Judg 2:16; 6:14; 1 Kgdms 10:1; Pss 33:6; 105:8, 10, 21). In the New Testament, the predominant conception of the verb is, as in the Hellenistic usage, deliverance from complete destruction, as attested by the regular pairing of the verb with the antonym ἀπόλλυμι "destroy" (cf. Matt 8:25, 39; 16:25; Mark 8:35; Luke 6:9; 9:24; Jas 4:12; see also Phil 1:28; 3:19–20). We find this sense of the verb in 1 Cor 1:18, where Paul contrasts "those who are being saved" (οἱ σῳζόμενοι) with "those are who are on the way to destruction" (οἱ ἀπολλύμενοι). As his use of the present tense in both 1:18 and 15:2 shows, salvation in Paul's thought has a present as well as a future dimension. Through the present tense σῴζεσθε in 15:2, Paul portrays the Corinthians as on the way to final salvation. This final salvation, as the chapter will make abundantly clear, is the resurrection of the body. Thus, already with σῴζεσθε in v. 2, Paul has the resurrection in view.

First Peter 1:23–25 describes the gospel message (τὸ ῥῆμα τὸ εὐαγγελισθέν, 1:25) as the seed of imperishable life (σπορᾶς ... ἀφθάρτου), and 2 Tim 1:10 speaks of life

20. Cf. John Chrysostom, *Hom. 1 Cor.* 38.2; Barth, *Resurrection*, 126.
21. Cf. Godet, 2:327.
22. *TLNT* 3:344. See the examples collected in *TLNT* 3:345–49; LSJ, s.v. "σῴζω"; Cremer, 532.

and imperishability coming about "through the gospel" (ζωὴν καὶ ἀφθαρσίαν διὰ τοῦ εὐαγγελίου). So also here in 1 Cor 15:2, Paul, by means of the prepositional phrase δι' οὗ, portrays the gospel as the source and means of a life that is imperishable. And in the chapter that follows, Paul will unpack how the present union of the faithful with Christ (15:20, 45–49) is the beginning and source of the imperishable life of the resurrection to come (15:42–44, 52, 53–54). This portrayal of the Corinthians as on the way to final salvation, through the present tense σῴζεσθε, also packs a powerful exhortation and warning—attaining to the resurrection requires continuing in the faith, persevering in radical discipleship, and enduring suffering and affliction for the sake of Christ. Paul will flesh out this theme as the chapter proceeds (15:19, 29–34, 48–49, 58).

*through the very word which I gospel-proclaimed to you.* A fifth relative clause now follows with τίνι λόγῳ εὐηγγελισάμην ὑμῖν ("through the very word which I gospel-proclaimed to you"). The term λόγος "word," here, as in 1:18 (ὁ λόγος ὁ τοῦ σταυροῦ) and 2:4 (ὁ λόγος μου), is a synonym for the gospel (τὸ εὐαγγέλιον) and denotes the content or substance of Paul's message—it is the word or message "which I gospel-proclaimed to you" (εὐηγγελισάμην ὑμῖν).[23] Through εὐηγγελισάμην ὑμῖν Paul skillfully recalls the first of the series of relative clauses in 15:1, ὃ εὐηγγελισάμην ὑμῖν ("which I gospel-proclaimed to you"). The interrogative τίς functions here as a relative, a Hellenistic usage found in both the LXX and the New Testament.[24] The dative τίνι λόγῳ is dative of means, modifying σῴζεσθε, and serves as a light parenthesis, clarifying and reinforcing the preceding δι' οὗ—"through which you are being saved, that is, through that very word which I gospel-proclaimed to you."[25] The shift to τίς after four straight instances of ὅς is striking.[26] The word τίς when used as a relative is specific and emphatic: "the *very* word which I gospel-proclaimed." The clause τίνι λόγῳ εὐηγγελισάμην ὑμῖν thus conveys a condition and a warning. It is *this* message, the precise word and gospel Paul proclaimed to them, that saves and no other.

---

23. Rightly Garland, 682; Collins, 533; Thiselton, 1185.

24. E.g., Mark 14:36, οὐ τί ἐγὼ θέλω ἀλλὰ τί σύ; Gen 38:25; Lev 21:17; Deut 29:17; Luke 17:8; 1 Tim 1:7. See BDR §298.4; Rob., *Gram.*, 737–38; BDAG, s.v. "τίς," (section 1.b); Robinson, s.v. "τίς." As MM notes, the usage is also "fairly common in the papyri" (636).

25. Rightly BDR §478 n. 1 (correcting earlier editions and BDF §478); Rob., *Gram.*, 425; cf. Fee, 799–80. The clause is not to be taken with κατέχετε, as suggested by Fitzmyer, 545; Godet, 2:326–27; and Weiss, 346. The verb κατέχω takes an accusative complement, never a dative; cf. BDAG, s.v. "κατέχω."

26. Cf. Rob., *Gram.*, 738.

CHAPTER 2

*if you indeed hold it fast.* According to Ceslas Spicq, the verb κατέχω is a "technical term" of "NT kerygma and catechesis."[27] In such contexts it denotes to *hold fast* or *hold faithfully* to the teaching (cf. Luke 8:15; 1 Cor 11:2; 1 Thess 5:21; Heb 3:6, 14; 10:23). The clause εἰ κατέχετε forms the protasis to the apodosis σῴζεσθε: the Corinthians are in the process of being saved through the apostolic kerygma—but only if they hold firm to it.[28] The use of εἰ with the indicative κατέχετε (rather than ἐάν with the subjunctive) expresses Paul's confidence that the Corinthians will remain steadfast in the gospel: "if you indeed (as I am confident you will) hold it fast."[29] Nonetheless, the condition adds to the warning tone of the previous clause. The Corinthians must hold fast to the gospel Paul proclaimed to them—their salvation depends upon it.

*unless you believed in vain.* The majority of commentators take the final clause of v. 2, introduced by ἐκτὸς εἰ μή, as the negation of κατέχετε "hold fast," as in the NIV: "Otherwise, you have believed in vain."[30] However, this suggested reading is not possible; it is founded upon an ignorance of ancient Greek syntax. The adverbial expression ἐκτὸς εἰ μή (a postclassical melding of ἐκτὸς εἰ and εἰ μή) always indicates a *qualification* or an *exception* to a preceding statement, never the negation of a condition.[31] In all its occurrences in antiquity the phrase uniformly means "except, unless," never "otherwise."[32] In 15:2 it introduces a qualification to the affirmation σῴζεσθε: "you are being saved ... *unless* you believed in vain."

What does this mean? Through the aorist ἐπιστεύσατε "you believed," Paul again recalls to the minds of the Corinthians their first acceptance of the message (cf. 15:1, παρελάβετε). The words πιστεύω and πίστις, found throughout the letter, are especially prominent in chapter 15 (πιστεύω, 15:2, 11; πίστις, 15:14, 17). For the adverb εἰκῇ, the lexica suggest two possible senses: (1) "in vain," "to no purpose," or "to no avail"; and (2) "haphazardly," "without due consideration," or "without cause."[33] Underlying these two senses is apparently a core meaning of *without purpose*, in which "purpose" can have the sense of (1) *end* or *result* ("in vain,"

---

27. *TLNT* 2:288.
28. The reading ὀφείλετε κατέχειν "you ought to hold it fast" of D F G is clearly secondary.
29. See BDR §§371–73; Rob., *Gram.*, 1007–12.
30. So Schrage, 29; Wolff, 355; Collins, 533–34; Ciampa & Rosner, 744; Fitzmyer, 545; Barrett, 337.
31. See Kühner-G., 2.2:219; BDR §376; LSJ, s.v. "ἐκτός" ("unless"); BDAG, s.v. "ἐκτός" ("marker of an exception, *except*"); Robinson, s.v. "ἐκτός" ("except, unless"); Dssm, *BS*, 118.
32. See 1 Cor 14:5; 1 Tim 5:19; Dio Chrysostom, *Tumult.* 2; Plutarch, *Dem.* 9.6; Lucian, *Pisc.* 6; *Philops.* 17; *Luct.* 19; *Pro imag.* 23, 28; *Tyr.* 12–13; *Dial. mort.* 11.4; *Dial. meretr.* 1.2.
33. Frisk, 1:453; Thayer, s.v. "εἰκῇ"; Robinson, s.v. "εἰκῇ." BDAG, s.v. "εἰκῇ," divides these two senses into four: (1) "without cause," (2) "to no avail," (3) "to no purpose," and (4) "without due consideration, in a haphazard manner" (281).

*A Deepened Revelation of the Gospel*

"to no purpose," "to no avail"); or (2) *rationale* or *cause* ("haphazardly," "without cause," "without due consideration"). Sense 2 is apparently the meaning in force in Col 2:18 and Matt 5:22 (as a variant reading attested in ℵ² D K L W among others). Thiselton suggests that this is the intended sense in 15:2, denoting a superficial or incoherent response to the gospel.[34] But Paul himself tells us that the Corinthians "believed" (ἐπιστεύσατε, 15:11), "received" (παρελάβετε, 15:1), and "stand" (ἑστήκατε, 15:1) in the gospel he proclaimed. As the great majority of interpreters have recognized, sense 2 (i.e., "without due consideration") can hardly be the meaning in force here. This leaves sense 1 (i.e., "in vain"), which is common in texts of the first and second centuries AD.[35] It is clearly the meaning in force in Rom 13:4, Gal 3:4, and Gal 4:11. Moreover, in Gal 3:4 and 4:11, where the meaning of εἰκῇ is doubtless "in vain," the context is very similar to 1 Cor 15:2 (involving the gospel, preaching, and faith). In 15:2, the adverb εἰκῇ means "in vain."

Why does Paul introduce the qualification "unless you believed in vain"? The key is that 15:2, which raises the possibility that the Corinthians have *believed* (πιστεύω) *in vain* (εἰκῇ), anticipates 15:14 ("your *faith* is *in vain*, and our proclamation is *in vain*") and 15:17 ("your *faith* is *futile*"). In 15:12–19 Paul will drive home the point that if there is no resurrection of the dead, as some at Corinth claim, faith in the gospel is in vain. Paul's qualification in 15:2, "unless you believed in vain," is thus, as Richard Hays notes, "a deft foreshadowing of verses 12–19."[36] Without the resurrection, the gospel and faith are in vain. The theme of the vanity of the gospel apart from the resurrection, the focus of 15:12–19, will continue in 15:29–34 and culminate in 15:58. Thus, in foreshadowing 15:12–19, v. 2 anticipates the entire chapter.

First Corinthians 15:1–2 provides an introduction to the chapter of great rhetorical power. Paul's skilled use of asyndeton (clauses unjoined by syntactic connectors) throughout these verses adds urgency and emphasis to this opening.[37] This effect is heightened by Paul's striking use of assonance in these verses (παρελάβετε ... ἑστήκατε ... σῴζεσθε ... κατέχετε ... ἐπιστεύσατε). The repeated use of adjunctive καί in vv. 1–2 has a ladder effect, culminating with σῴζεσθε ("you are also being saved"). Up to that point, Paul's introduction stresses his common agreement with the Corinthians in the saving gospel. Then, very effectively, Paul introduces

---

34. Thiselton, 1186.

35. Epictetus, *Diatr.* 1.4.21; 2.23.3–4; 3.24.112; 4.3.3; 4.11.27; Lucian, *Anach.* 35, 38. See also the Greek translation of Aquila (Ps 126:2; Jer 6:29) and Symmachus (Jer 6:29).

36. Hays, 255. Cf. Lindemann, 328 and Fee, 801, the latter writing that it is "meant to anticipate what he will say in the next phase of the argument [vv. 14–19]."

37. Rob., *Gram.*, 427. The repeated instances of καί in this passage are all adjunctive, not connective.

the note of condition, contingency, and qualification. "Paul's introduction of new elements ... of contingency ('if you hold on') and possible futility ('unless you believed in vain') add a sting to this opening."[38] Paul, in fact, in 15:2 expresses *three* conditions on which the salvation of the Corinthians through the gospel depends: (1) "through the very word which I gospel-proclaimed to you" (i.e., it is *this* gospel that saves); (2) "if you hold it fast" (i.e., the Corinthians must continue in it); and (3) "unless you believed in vain" (i.e., this gospel is saving only if the promise of the resurrection is true).[39] The heart of Paul's concern comes to expression in the final condition, punctuated by a series of powerful alliterations: ἐκτὸς εἰ μὴ εἰκῇ ἐπιστεύσατε. This is the rhetorical climax of Paul's introduction and the heart of the matter in the mind of the apostle. Apart from the hope of the bodily resurrection, the gospel and faith are to no purpose and in vain.

In 1 Cor 15:1–2, we have reached the beginning of the resolution and climax of 1 Corinthians. For Paul's introduction to the chapter in 15:1–2 forms a striking multilevel *inclusio* with the opening of the letter in 1:17–18:

(1) The twofold use of εὐαγγελίζομαι in 15:1 and 15:2 forms an *inclusio* with the first use of εὐαγγελίζομαι within the letter in 1:17. (2) The occurrences of the verb σῴζω in 15:2 and 1:18 are linked as the first and last uses of σῴζω within the letter, and as the only occurrences of this verb within the epistle in the present tense, describing salvation as in progress but not yet fully accomplished. (3) The word λόγος, used of Paul's gospel in 15:2, recalls the identical word used to describe Paul's message in 1:18. In both 1:18 and 15:2 it is this word (λόγος) through which the Corinthians are being saved (1:18, τοῖς σῳζομένοις; 15:2, σῴζεσθε). Moreover, both 1:18 and 15:1–2 share a focus on the specific content and identity of this λόγος (15:2, τίνι λόγῳ εὐηγγελισάμην ὑμῖν, "through *the very* word I gospel-proclaimed to you"; 1:18, ὁ λόγος ὁ τοῦ σταυροῦ, "the word *which is* of the cross"). (4) In 15:1–2 the language of word or speech is combined with the language of knowledge and wisdom (15:1, γνωρίζω; 15:2, λόγος), recalling the same combination in 1:17–18 (1:17, ἐν λόγῳ σοφίας; 1:18, ὁ λόγος). (5) Finally, ἐκτὸς εἰ μὴ εἰκῇ ἐπιστεύσατε ("unless you believed in *vain*") in 15:2 recalls ἵνα μὴ κενωθῇ ὁ σταυρὸς τοῦ Χριστοῦ ("that the cross of Christ not be made *vain*") in 1:17.

Previous scholarship has failed to appreciate the connections between 1:17–18 and 15:1–2, and the massive implications of these links. As we saw in the previous

---

38. Reasoner, on 15:2 (here and throughout this book Reasoner's forthcoming commentary is cited not by page but by chapter and verse of 1 Corinthians).

39. For the presence in 15:1–2 of both an "agreement-perspective," highlighting Paul and the Corinthians' common agreement in the gospel, and also an "uncertainty perspective," highlighting Paul's concern regarding the Corinthians, see Coppins, "Two Perspectives."

*A Deepened Revelation of the Gospel*

chapter, 1:17 forms the final verse of the epistle's body opening, which in Paul's letters always introduces an epistle's key themes, and 1:18 forms the opening verse of the main body of the epistle. The reappearance in 15:1–2 of this entire cluster of themes from 1:17–18, for the very first time within the letter, reveals that we have now come to the climax of the epistle. As we go through the chapter, we will find again and again that the chief themes of the thanksgiving (1:4–9), body opening (1:10–17), and first four chapters of the letter (1:18–4:21) find their climactic affirmation in 1 Cor 15, revealing that, within Paul's structure and plan for the epistle, chapter 15 is the capstone.

It is a fact insufficiently noted by interpreters that Paul begins this chapter on the hope of the resurrection with an introduction concerning the *gospel*. The commentators tell us that the subject of 1 Cor 15 is the resurrection of the body. And so it is. But, in the apostle's mind, the subject of 1 Cor 15 is the gospel. Paul is clear that his dispute with those at Corinth who deny the resurrection involves the very faith itself. If there is no resurrection, faith in the gospel is in vain. For Paul, then, the point at issue in 1 Cor 15, as Chrysostom saw, is nothing less than "the faith as a whole."[40] "What is involved is the *substance*, the *whole* of the Christian revelation."[41] In Paul's defense and exposition of the resurrection in 1 Cor 15, as his introduction in 15:1–2 makes clear, we have reached not only the capstone of 1 Corinthians but the very heart of Paul's gospel.

---

40. John Chrysostom, *Hom. 1 Cor.* 38.2.
41. Barth, *Resurrection*, 112.

CHAPTER 3

# *The Cross and the Resurrection in the Apostolic Formula*

## 15:3-4

There is almost universal scholarly consensus that 1 Corinthians 15:3-7 (or at a minimum 15:3-5) contains a carefully preserved tradition predating Paul's apostolic activity and received by him within two to five years of the founding events of Jesus's passion, death, and resurrection.[1] Several lines of evidence converge to reveal the presence of a pre-Pauline apostolic formula within these verses. Paul's main object in recounting what he proclaimed to the Corinthians, as the rest of the chapter will make clear, is to confirm the truth of the resurrection. But the content of 15:3-7 includes not only Christ's resurrection but also his substitutionary death for our sins.[2] In addition, these verses contain a striking amount of vocabulary and expressions that are unusual or uncommon in Paul.[3] Moreover, in employing the words "transmit" (15:3, παραδίδωμι) and "receive" (15:1, 3, παραλαμβάνω), Paul uses the ancient Christian technical terms that describe the transmission and reception of the apostolic testimony to Jesus.[4] Finally, in 15:11 Paul is

---

1. Cf. Hans Conzelmann, "On the Analysis of the Confessional Formula in 1 Corinthians 15:3-5," *Int* 20 (1966): 15-25; Heinrich Schlier, "Die Anfänge des christologischen Credo," in *Zur Frühgeschichte der Christologie* (ed. B. Weite; Freiburg: Herder, 1970), 27-28, 56; J. Kloppenborg, "An Analysis of the Pre-Pauline Formula in 1 Corinthians 15:3b-5 in Light of Some Recent Literature," *CBQ* 18 (1978): 351-67; Gerd Lüdemann, *The Resurrection of Jesus: History, Experience, Theology* (London: SCM, 1994), 33-38; and Birger Gerhardsson, "Evidence for Christ's Resurrection According to Paul: 1 Cor 15:1-11," in *Neotestamentica et Philonica: Studies in Honour of Peder Borgen* (ed. David E. Aune, Torrey Seland, and Jarl Henning Ulrichsen; NovTSup 106; Leiden: Brill, 2003), 75-91; Hays, 255.

2. Kloppenborg, "Pre-Pauline Formula," 351.

3. Kloppenborg, "Pre-Pauline Formula," 351-52; Conzelmann, 251-52; Wolff, 355-56.

4. Παραδίδωμι: Luke 1:2; Rom 6:17; 1 Cor 11:23; 2 Thess 2:15; Jude 3; παραλαμβάνω: 1 Cor 11:23;

explicit that what he transmitted to the Corinthians was not his teaching alone but the common proclamation of Peter, James, and all the apostolic eyewitnesses enumerated in 15:3–7 (15:11, "Whether, then, it is I or they, so we proclaim, and so you believed").[5] The presence within 15:3–7 (or 15:3–5) of an apostolic formula predating Paul's mission is beyond a reasonable doubt.

At the same time, a number of facets of this primitive confession continue to be matters of dispute, including the precise parameters of the formula within 1 Cor 15:1–11, the original language of its composition, and its function within the life of the early church.[6] Let us take each of these issues in turn.

GENRE OF THE FORMULA

What, precisely, *is* this statement?[7] Scholars often refer to it as a "creed," a "creedal form," or a "creedal confession."[8] However, although 15:3–7 has a definite, fixed content, there is no indication that it is a "creed" in the sense of a statement of faith with a fixed, unalterable wording. As almost universally recognized by scholars of ancient Christianity, full, fixed-wording creeds did not develop until the second century.[9] This absence of fixed-wording creeds is evident in the fact that the ancient summaries of the faith found elsewhere in Paul's letters, although in agreement with 15:3–7 in their content, do not match it in their structure and vocabulary (cf. Rom 1:3–4; 4:24–25; 1 Cor 8:6; 11:23–25; 1 Thess 1:9–10). The statement in 15:3–7, then, had a fixed content but not necessarily a fully fixed vocabulary and wording. At the same time, 15:3–7 seems to fall somewhere between a freely worded statement and a full, fixed-wording creed. For (as we will see) it has a definite, fixed structure, and its wording appears to have had a semi-fixed, semi-stereotyped character, as revealed by the recurrence of identical ex-

---

Gal 1:9; Phil 4:9; 1 Thess 2:13; 4:1; 2 Thess 3:6. Cf. Schrage, 18; Wolff, 355–56; Kloppenborg, "Pre-Pauline Formula," 351; Conzelmann, 251.

5. Kloppenborg, "Pre-Pauline Formula," 357.

6. For full discussion and the relevant literature, see Karl Lehmann, *Auferweckt am Dritten Tag nach der Schrift: Früheste Christologie, Bekenntnisbildung und Schriftauslegung im Lichte von 1 Kor. 15, 3–5* (2d ed.; QD 38; Freiburg: Herder, 1968), 17–157; Schrage, 14–26.

7. The fullest discussion of the form and function of the confession is found in Lehmann, *Auferweckt*, 43–67; see also Joseph Schmitt, "Le 'Milieu' littéraire de la 'Tradition' citée dans I Cor., XV, 3b–5," in *Resurrexit: Actes du Symposium International sur la Résurrection de Jésus* (ed. Édouard Dhanis; Rome: Libreria Editrice Vaticana, 1974), 169–84.

8. Cf. Collins, 530 ("creed"); Garland, 689 ("creedal form"); Thiselton, 1189 ("creedal confession").

9. The classic treatment of the subject is J. N. D. Kelly, *Early Christian Creeds* (3d ed.; New York: Longman, 1972), 1–130.

pressions in confessional summaries found elsewhere in the New Testament (cf. Rom 14:9, Χριστὸς ἀπέθανεν καὶ ἔζησεν; Gal 1:4, τοῦ δόντος ἑαυτὸν ὑπὲρ τῶν ἁμαρτιῶν ἡμῶν; Luke 24:34, ἠγέρθη ὁ κύριος καὶ ὤφθη Σίμωνι). As a summary fixed in content, fixed in its structure, and partially fixed in wording, 15:3–7 is "a confessional statement, containing the essential elements of the kerygma in an extremely compressed form."[10]

## Function of the Formula

But what was the context, setting, and function of this confession within the kerygmatic proclamation of the early church? Some scholars seem to assume that in his preaching Paul simply transmitted this bare and terse formula without further elaboration. But Birger Gerhardsson has argued persuasively that this brief formulaic statement presupposes a narrative of these events.[11] As Jeffrey Peterson notes: "The passage summarizes a fuller account previously related to Paul's converts."[12] From 1 Corinthians alone, we can reconstruct the following elements within the narrative Paul related to the Corinthians, the knowledge of which he assumes within the letter:

1. Jesus's teaching and gathering of disciples (7:10–11; 11:23–25)
2. Jesus's betrayal (11:23)
3. The Last Supper and institution of the Lord's Supper (10:16–17; 11:23–25)
4. Jesus's crucifixion (1:17, 18, 23; 15:3) on Passover (5:7)
5. Jesus's burial (15:4)
6. Jesus's resurrection (15:4) on Sunday (16:2), the third day after his burial (15:4)
7. The appearances of the risen Christ to apostolic eyewitnesses (9:1; 15:5–8; 15:15)
8. The apostolic proclamation of the resurrection (15:9, 11, 15)
9. The birth of the church (1:1–2; 15:9)

---

10. Kloppenborg, "Pre-Pauline Formula," 365.
11. Gerhardsson, "Evidence," 89–91; cf. Karl Olav Sandnes and Jan-Olav Henriksen, *Resurrection: Text and Interpretation, Experience and Theology* (Eugene, OR: Pickwick, 2020), 91–92; Dale C. Allison Jr., *The Resurrection of Jesus: Apologetics, Polemics, History* (New York: Bloomsbury, 2021), 40–41; Jeffrey Peterson, "Christ Our Pasch: Shaping Christian Identity in Corinth," in *Renewing the Tradition* (ed. Mark W. Hamilton, Thomas R. Olbricht, and Jeffrey Peterson; Eugene, OR: Wipf & Stock, 2006), 133–44.
12. Jeffrey R. Peterson, "The Extent of Christian Theological Diversity: Pauline Evidence," *ResQ* 47 (2005): 5 n. 15. Cf. Christopher Bryan, *The Resurrection of the Messiah* (Oxford: Oxford University Press, 2011), 48: "what we have here *implies* a narrative and is meaningless without one."

*The Cross and the Resurrection in the Apostolic Formula*

The evidence of another early formula confirms the setting of such formulas within and alongside a larger narrative that they summarize and presuppose. Hans-Joachim Eckstein, in an examination of the pre-Lukan traditional formula in Luke 24:34 ("the Lord has truly risen, and he appeared to Simon"), points out that this formula is placed by Luke precisely within a narrative setting that begins with an empty tomb (24:1–11) and climaxes with Jesus showing himself to the Twelve and those with them (24:33–40), eating and drinking with them (24:41–43), and inviting them to "touch me and see, because a spirit does not have flesh and bones, as you see that I have" (24:39). The narrative that unfolds in Luke 24, and the kind of narrative presupposed by the pre-Lukan formula embedded within it, reveal a striking coherence.[13]

The confession of 15:3–7, then, functioned as a highly condensed summary of a larger narrative focused on the saving events of Jesus's passion, death, burial, resurrection, and postresurrection appearances to the disciples.

### Parameters of the Confession

What is the precise extent within 1 Cor 15:1–11 of the confession that Paul "received" and "transmitted" (15:3) to the Corinthians? Let us take first the formula that Paul "transmitted." Isolating this is quite straightforward. 15:1–2 is clearly an introduction to the formula, 15:9–10 is Paul's commentary on v. 8, and 15:11 is Paul's summary comment on the formula as a whole. This leaves the whole of 15:3–8 as the tradition that Paul, as virtually all scholars concur, transmitted to the Corinthians.

But what are the parameters of the formula that Paul "received"? The mention of Paul as the last witness in 15:8 was most likely not in place in the tradition when Paul first received it. Moreover, Paul's witness is introduced very differently than the previous witnesses (ἔσχατον δέ) and seems to form a kind of appendix to the list. Likewise 15:6b, in light of its time reference contemporary to the time of writing (ἕως ἄρτι), appears to be a Pauline comment on 15:6a of the original formula. If v. 6b and v. 8 may be confidently identified as Pauline expansions, this leaves us with 15:3–6a, 7. Regarding the extent of the original pre-Pauline confession within these verses, there is virtual scholarly unanimity that the pre-Pauline confession comprises at the very least vv. 3–5. But some interpreters argue that the tradition received by Paul

---

13. Hans-Joachim Eckstein, "Die Wirklichkeit der Auferstehung Jesu: Lukas 24,34 als Beispiel früher formelhafter Zeugnisse," in *Die Wirklichkeit der Auferstehung* (ed. Hans-Joachim Eckstein and Michael Welker; Neukirchen-Vluyn: Neukirchener, 2002), 1–29.

CHAPTER 3

comprises 15:3–6a and 7, regarding only 5:6b and 15:8 as Pauline expansions of the original formula.[14] Other scholars limit the tradition received by Paul to 15:3–5.[15]

The evidence is, in fact, overwhelming in favor of the former view. First, it is hardly probable that Paul would switch from recitation of the formula "which I also received" (15:3) in 15:3–5 to another tradition or traditions altogether in 15:6–7, with no indication that he was doing so. Second, 15:6a is noteworthy not only for its non-Pauline vocabulary but also for its marked assonance conducive to committing these core facts to memory: ἔπειτα ὤφθη ἐπάνω πεντακοσίοις ἀδελφοῖς ἐφάπαξ. Paul's commentary in 15:6b, by contrast, exhibits no such assonance and reflects Paul's normal vocabulary.

But, I would argue, what is in decisive favor of vv. 6a and 7 being part of the original formula is that this confession has a carefully structured, formulaic character that does not cease at v. 5 but continues through v. 7. These verses have a fourfold structure delineated by the fourfold occurrence of the word ὅτι "that": (1) Christ died for our sins; (2) he was buried; (3) he rose again; (4) he appeared to eyewitnesses (15:3–7).[16] The fourth component of the structure has its own internal three-part structure marked out by the threefold repetition of the word ὤφθη (15:5–7). In this way the different witnesses are carefully enumerated in three divisions: (1) Peter, then the Twelve; (2) over five hundred brothers and sisters at the same time; and (3) James, then all the apostles. In the first and third instances of ὤφθη, the witnesses are further subdivided into an individual and a group, in each case delineated by the word εἶτα (15:5, 7). The corresponding structure of v. 5 and v. 7 can hardly be accidental. And the structure of vv. 6–7, in which ἔπειτα ὤφθη connects the clauses and εἶτα serves as an internal connector within clauses, seems to only make sense as part of a larger structure that includes v. 5:

---

14. So Richard Bauckham, *Jesus and the Eyewitnesses: The Gospels as Eyewitness Testimony* (Grand Rapids: Eerdmans, 2006), 307; Richard H. Bell, "The Resurrection Appearances in 1 Corinthians 15," in *Epiphanies of the Divine in the Septuagint and the New Testament* (ed. Roland Deines and Mark Wreford; Tübingen: Mohr Siebeck, 2024); Kirk R. MacGregor, "1 Corinthians 15:3B–6A, 7 and the Bodily Resurrection of Jesus," *JETS* 49 (2006): 225–34; Bruce D. Chilton, *Resurrection Logic* (Waco: Baylor University Press, 2019), 80–81. Chilton also includes 15:6b within the original pre-Pauline confession.

15. So Jerome Murphy-O'Connor, "Tradition and Redaction in 1 Cor 15:3–7," *CBQ* 43 (1981): 582–89; Randall C. Webber, "A Note on 1 Corinthians 15:3–5," *JETS* 26 (1983): 265–69; Jürgen Becker, *Die Auferstehung Jesu Christi nach dem Neuen Testament: Ostererfahrung und Osterverständnis im Urchristentum* (Tübingen: Mohr Siebeck, 2007), 103–4; C. F. Evans, *Resurrection and the New Testament* (London: SCM, 1970), 41–46; Schrage, 19–21; Wolff, 356–58; Conzelmann, 251.

16. The ὅτι discourse markers here doubtless were added by Paul, but reflect the confession's original structure; Paul thereby "itemizes or emphasizes each component" of the original formula. See Kloppenborg, "Pre-Pauline Formula," 361.

| | | | |
|---|---|---|---|
| 15:5 | ὤφθη | (individual) | εἶτα (associated group) |
| 15:6 | ἔπειτα ὤφθη | (group) | |
| 15:7 | ἔπειτα ὤφθη | (individual) | εἶτα (associated group) |

This would indicate that the original confession continued beyond 15:5 and through 15:7. Moreover, the movement from the initial mention of "Cephas," the chief of the apostles, in 15:5 to the climactic reference to "all the apostles" in 15:7 provides a sense of symmetry and closure to vv. 5–7, which also suggests these verses functioned as a whole within the original confession.

Finally, that the original non-Pauline formula extends through the close of v. 7 is strongly suggested by its closing words εἶτα τοῖς ἀποστόλοις πᾶσιν ("then to all the apostles"). This is striking, for it might seem to exclude Paul from the number of the apostles. Verse 8 will correct this possible wrong impression. But if Paul were expressing this in his own preferred manner, we should expect something like εἶτα τοῖς πρὸ ἐμοῦ ἀποστόλοις πᾶσιν ("then to all those who were apostles before me"; cf. Gal 1:17). It is difficult to conceive, if v. 7 is Paul's own addition to the original confession, that he would choose to express himself in this way, open to misunderstanding on a point so vital to him. But this wording makes perfect sense if it is not from Paul but from the original apostolic confession that Paul received.

For these reasons, I believe the evidence is decisive that the original pre-Pauline, apostolic confession that Paul received consisted of 15:3–7, with the exception of the Pauline comment in 15:6b. The original confession (with Paul's comment set off in italics) may be set out as follows:

> ³ Christ died for our sins in fulfillment of the Scriptures, ⁴ and he was buried, and he was raised on the third day in fulfillment of the Scriptures, ⁵ and he appeared to Cephas, then to the Twelve. ⁶ Then he appeared to more than five hundred brothers and sisters at the same time, *of whom the majority remain until now, but some have fallen asleep.* ⁷ Then he appeared to James, then to all the apostles.

## Date, Original Language, and Provenance of the Formula

Concerning the approximate date of the original formula there is general agreement. In stating that he "transmitted" (15:3) these core beliefs to the Corinthians, Paul refers to his founding of the church at Corinth in (as all historians are agreed) AD 50 or 51. In stating that he "received" (15:3) this confessional formula, Paul is almost certainly referring to his fifteen-day conference that occurred three years after

CHAPTER 3

his conversion with Peter and James in Jerusalem (Gal 1:18–19).[17] Paul's visit to Jerusalem occurred at the latest in AD 37 or 38.[18] Since this formula was already a fixed and stable tradition when Paul received it, its origin must be traced to several years prior to Paul's visit. This formula can thus hardly be dated later than AD 34 or 35.

Regarding the original language of the formula there has been great debate. Joachim Jeremias famously argued that the confession bears unmistakable traces of a Semitic original, and this view has been championed by a number of scholars, most notably Berthold Klappert.[19] Others have argued that the evidence supports a Greek original.[20] The linguistic evidence in my judgment is not decisive either way.[21] Debate regarding the confession's original language has raged so intensely because this issue gets at the question whether this formula originated in the Aramaic-speaking apostolic community in Jerusalem or had its origins elsewhere. But, as a number of scholars have pointed out, we have much more direct evidence for answering this question. For, as we have seen, Paul received this tradition during his fifteen-day conference with the apostles Peter and James in Jerusalem (Gal 1:18–19). That the apostolic community in Jerusalem was the source of the tradition recounted in 15:3–7 is confirmed by 15:11: "Whether, then, it is I or they, thus we proclaim, and thus you believed." In 15:11, the "they" (ἐκεῖνοι) refers to the list of apostolic eyewitnesses to the resurrection in 15:5–7, and the present tense "we proclaim" (κηρύσσομεν) affirms their ongoing activity not only as eyewitnesses but also as proclaimers of the tradition recounted in 15:3–7.[22] So then, although our linguistic evidence is not decisive, our evidence from Paul's letters is. Taken together, 1 Cor 15:3–11 and Gal 1:18–19 reveal quite unambiguously that the formula Paul recounts in 15:3–7 had its origins in the apostolic community at Jerusalem led by Peter, James, and the Twelve.

The implications of this astoundingly early apostolic confession for our knowledge of the earliest apostolic preaching and for the historicity of Jesus's resur-

---

17. Chilton, *Resurrection Logic*, 81; Bell, "Resurrection Appearances."

18. See, conveniently, Stanley Porter, "The Chronology of Paul's Ministry and His Imprisonments," in *The Apostle Paul: His Life, Thought, and Letters* (Grand Rapids: Eerdmans, 2016), 50 (he places the event in AD 37); Chilton, *Resurrection Logic*, 79 (AD 35).

19. See Joachim Jeremias, *The Eucharistic Words of Jesus* (Philadelphia: Fortress, 1966), 101–5; Jeremias, "Artikelloses Χριστός: Zur Ursprache von I Cor 15,3b–5," *ZNW* 57 (1966): 211–15; Jeremias, "Nochmals: Artikelloses Χριστός in I Cor 15,3," *ZNW* 60 (1969): 214–19; Berthold Klappert, "Zur Frage des semitischen oder griechischen Urtextes von I. Kor. xv. 3–5," *NTS* 13 (1966–1967): 168–73; Chilton, *Resurrection Logic*, 82.

20. So Conzelmann, 252–54.

21. So (in my view rightly) Schrage, 23–24; Wolff, 359; Fitzmyer, 542.

22. Cf. Kloppenborg, "Pre-Pauline Formula," 357; Bauckham, *Eyewitnesses*, 265–66; Jan Lambrecht, review of Anders Eriksson, *Traditions as Rhetorical Proof*, *Bib* 80 (1999): 438–41.

rection are enormous. We will consider these in excursus 2 following chapter five once we have carefully unpacked the content of this formula in this and the following two chapters in the commentary below.

## Verse 3

*For I transmitted to you in the beginning, what I also received, that Christ died for our sins in fulfillment of the Scriptures,*

*For I transmitted to you in the beginning.* Many scholars think that the explanatory γάρ here refers specifically to τίνι λόγῳ in 15:2.[23] However, Paul's striking use of rhythmic assonance and homoioteleuton in 15:1–2 unites these verses into a rounded whole, and brings them to a rounded close (παρελάβετε ... ἑστήκατε ... σῴζεσθε ... κατέχετε ... ἐπιστεύσατε). The explanatory γάρ in 15:3 thus most likely enlarges upon Paul's full description of τὸ εὐαγγέλιον ("the gospel"), and the Corinthians' reception of it, in 15:1–2. In the word "transmit" (παραδίδωμι), Paul employs the ancient church's technical term for the transmission of the apostolic testimony to Jesus (cf. 11:23; see also Luke 1:2; Rom 6:17; 2 Thess 2:15; Jude 3).[24] These are the core teachings that Paul passed on to the Corinthians when he founded the church at Corinth in AD 50 or 51.

Paul transmitted these core teachings to the Corinthians "in the beginning" (ἐν πρώτοις). The expression ἐν πρώτοις here is taken by the great majority of modern commentators as referring to preeminence or importance, often rendered as "as of first importance" or the like.[25] But this is not a possible meaning of ἐν πρώτοις in 15:3. To be sure, in a handful of instances in ancient Greek literature ἐν πρώτοις does denote preeminence in rank, dignity, or value. But in all such instances, πρώτοις is *masculine*, referring to persons, and the phrase ἐν πρώτοις in these instances means "among the foremost persons" or "among those preeminent" (Homer, *Il.* 15.643; *Od.* 8.180; Herodotus, *Hist.* 8.69, 94; 9.86; 1 Kgdms 9:22 LXX). But in all other instances in ancient Greek literature, πρώτοις is *neuter*, and the expression ἐν πρώτοις functions adverbially, denoting precedence in either space

---

23. E.g., Schrage, 32; Fitzmyer, 545; Fee, 801; Robertson & Plummer, 332.
24. See Kloppenborg, "Pre-Pauline Formula," 351; Schrage, 18; Bauckham, *Eyewitnesses*, 264–65; James P. Ware, *Paul's Theology in Context: Creation, Incarnation, Covenant, and Kingdom* (Grand Rapids: Eerdmans, 2019), 207–8.
25. E.g., Schrage, 32; Garland, 683; Fitzmyer, 545 ("as of prime importance"); Collins, 534; Ciampa & Rosner, 745; Fee, 801–2; along with many others. So likewise BA, s.v. "πρῶτος" (1.c); BDAG, s.v. "πρῶτος" (2.a.α).

(i.e., "at the head") or time (i.e., "from the beginning"). The spatial sense is well attested but relatively infrequent (cf. Gen 33:2 LXX, where it is opposed to ὀπίσω; Homer, *Il.* 9.424). The temporal sense is the normal and by far most frequent meaning of the phrase (e.g., Plato, *Resp.* 522c; Aeschines, *Tim.* 4; 3 Kgdms 21:9 LXX; Epictetus, *Ench.* 20; Theophilus of Antioch, *Autol.* 1.10; 2.6–7). In the temporal use, the plural has no force; rather the expression has an absolute sense (e.g., "from the beginning," "first," "from the outset"). Illustrative examples are T. Benj. 10.8–9, κρινεῖ κύριος ἐν πρώτοις τὸν Ἰσραήλ . . . καὶ τότε κρινεῖ πάντα τὰ ἔθνη ("the Lord will judge Israel *first* . . . and then he will judge all the nations") and Theophilus of Antioch, *Autol.* 2.10, ταῦτα ἐν πρώτοις διδάσκει ἡ θεία γραφή ("the divine Scripture teaches these things *in the beginning*").

In 1 Cor 15:3 ἐν πρώτοις is neuter, not masculine, and thus the rare sense of prominence is excluded. The spatial sense is also excluded. Therefore the temporal sense, the overwhelmingly most common sense of the phrase in ancient literature, is also the only possible sense of the term in 15:3.[26] Some scholars have asked, if ἐν πρώτοις is temporal, why Paul does not use the more common expression ἐν ἀρχῇ? The answer may lie in the pleasing alliterative quality that the expression contributes to the passage (<u>π</u>αρέδωκα γὰρ ὑμῖν ἐν <u>π</u>ρώτοις, ὃ καὶ <u>π</u>αρέλαβον).

Why does Paul add that he transmitted these core teachings "in the beginning"? Throughout the New Testament, and especially in Paul's letters, we find a "back to the beginning" motif—the exhortation to hold fast to the gospel as it was received in the beginning (Rom 16:17; Gal 1:8–9; 2 Thess 2:15; 1 John 2:24; Jude 3). Throughout 1 Corinthians, Paul recalls to the Corinthians their first reception of the gospel (1:6, 13–17, 26–31; 2:1–5; 3:1–2, 10; 4:14–15; 6:11; 10:1–4; 11:2, 23; 12:2–3; 14:36). In 15:1–2, with its intense focus on Paul's founding proclamation and the Corinthians' initial reception of the gospel, Paul brought this theme of the letter to its climax. Here in 15:3, through ἐν πρώτοις "in the beginning," Paul continues and bolsters this theme. What is at stake, Paul once again reminds the Corinthians, is the very message that founded the Christian community at Corinth and gives it its identity.

*what I also received.* The verb "received" (παραλαμβάνω) forms the counterpart to "transmitted" (παραδίδωμι), in that, as the latter is the early Christian term for the transmission of the apostolic testimony to Jesus, the former is the ancient Christian technical term for the *reception* of the apostolic testimony to Jesus (1 Cor 11:23; cf. Gal 1:9; Phil 4:9; 1 Thess 2:13; 4:1; 2 Thess 3:6). The καί "also" connects παρέλα-

---

26. So, rightly, Robinson, s.v. "πρῶτος" (1.a, "first of all"); Daniel C. Fredericks, "A Question of First Importance: ἐν πρώτοις in 1 Corinthians 15:3," *BBR* 32 (2022): 165–81.

βον to the preceding παρέδωκα and expresses, as Godet points out, "the exact conformity" of what Paul transmitted to the Corinthians with what he himself received.[27] Paul received these core teachings from the apostolic witnesses he will enumerate in 15:5–7: Cephas, James, and the Twelve (cf. Gal 1:18–19; 2:1–10), who are also the "they" of 15:11. Verse 3a (the introduction to the formula) thus forms an *inclusio* with v. 11 (the conclusion to the formula), each focusing on the common apostolic proclamation.[28] Here in 15:3, Paul stresses the origin of the tradition he passed on to the Corinthians in the testimony of Peter, James, and the Twelve (cf. 9:5). In 15:11 he will stress his and their common preaching of this same tradition. And as 11:23 makes clear, the tradition Paul received had its source, through the eyewitness testimony of the apostles, in Jesus himself (11:23, ἐγὼ γὰρ παρέλαβον ἀπὸ τοῦ κυρίου).

Paul states in 1 Cor 15:3 that he himself "received" (παρέλαβον) the gospel he transmitted to the Corinthians, but in Gal 1:12 he states that he did not "receive" the gospel from a human being (οὐδὲ γὰρ ἐγὼ παρὰ ἀνθρώπου παρέλαβον) but through Christ himself (ἀλλὰ δι' ἀποκαλύψεως Ἰησοῦ Χριστοῦ). Is this a contradiction? Interpreters are virtually unanimous that it is not, but the usual explanations are not entirely convincing. One common explanation is that what Paul received (1 Cor 15:3) was "the facts," and what came by revelation from Christ (Gal 1:12) was "the import of the facts."[29] Another common view is that Paul in 1 Cor 15:3 is thinking of "the formulation," in Gal 1:12 he is thinking of "the content of the gospel as a whole."[30] But the distinction between the gospel and the formulation is untenable in light of 1 Cor 15:1 (γνωρίζω δὲ ὑμῖν, ἀδελφοί, τὸ εὐαγγέλιον), and the apostolic tradition Paul received included both the facts and the theological import of the facts (cf. 15:3, Χριστὸς ἀπέθανεν ὑπὲρ τῶν ἁμαρτιῶν ἡμῶν; 15:3, 4: κατὰ τὰς γραφάς).

What, then, is the explanation? Paul's point in Galatians appears to be that, like the apostles before him, he had seen, heard, and been commissioned by the Lord Jesus himself (Gal 1:11–12, 15–16; cf. 1:1).[31] At the same time, Galatians and 1 Corinthians together make clear that Paul was dependent on the earlier apostolic eyewitnesses for the gospel narrative of Jesus's deeds, teaching, passion, and

---

27. Godet, 2:330.
28. Cf. Lambrecht, review of Eriksson, *Traditions*, 440–41.
29. Robertson & Plummer, 333; similarly Garland, 683–84.
30. Fitzmyer, 345; similarly Ciampa & Rosner, 745.
31. In Gal 1:12, the οὐδέ modifies ἐγώ (cf. Smyth §§2690, 2814–15; Kühner-G., 2.2:338 [§545]), and thus includes implicit reference to the other apostles: "for neither I (i.e., any more than the apostles before me) received it or was taught it from a human being, but through revelation of Jesus Christ" (Gal 1:12). Rightly John Eadie, *A Commentary on the Greek Text of the Epistle of Paul to the Galatians* (London: Griffin, 1869), 35–36.

CHAPTER 3

resurrection (Gal 1:18–19; 2:2, 7–9; 1 Cor 7:10–11; 11:23–26), core formulations of the gospel (1 Cor 15:3–7), and practices such as baptism and the Eucharist (1 Cor 6:11; 10:1–4; 11:23–26). First Corinthians 15:3 and Gal 1:11–12 make two different, but ultimately harmonious, points.

*that Christ.* The subject of every finite verb within 15:3b–8 (with the exception of 15:6b) is Χριστός "Christ." The title Χριστός refers to the anointed messianic king from the lineage of David foretold in the Scriptures as coming to deliver Israel and reign over all nations (Isa 8:23–9:6[9:1–7]; 11:1–10; Ps 2; Amos 9:7–15; Mic 5:1–5; Zech 9:9–10). Many scholars hold that its anarthrous usage here indicates that the title "Christ" has lost its messianic meaning and become no more than a proper name or, as Joseph Fitzmyer puts it, "Jesus' second name."[32] But as popular as this view is, I believe it fails to adequately grasp the formula's Jewish context. That a first-century Jew could apply the epithet "Christ" without full consciousness of the messianic claim involved is simply not credible historically. This messianic sense is also demanded by the formula's twofold reference to the works of Christ as the fulfillment of *Scripture*.[33] It is also suggested by Paul's occasional use, in his reflections on the formula within the chapter, of *articular* Χριστός (15:15, 22, 23).

And Paul's predominant use of anarthrous Χριστός is not inconsistent with a messianic sense of the term. As Joachim Jeremias has in my view shown convincingly, the use of the messianic title without the article was common in Palestinian Judaism.[34] A key bit of evidence is John 4:25, where Μεσσίας occurs without the article. Used anarthrously, Μεσσίας or Χριστός can function much like a proper name without losing its core meaning as the title of the messianic deliverer. In this way, anarthrous Χριστός identifies Jesus as the promised messianic deliverer, familiar to the community of those who belong to him. This explains why "Χριστός (without the article) frequently appears as subject in kerygmatic statements in which Jesus is presented as the perfecter of the work of salvation."[35] Thus Χριστός without the article is Paul's preferred epithet for Jesus throughout the chapter (15:12, 13, 16, 17, 18, 19, 20, 23; cf. 15:31, 57).

But one more thing—the most vital of all—must be said about the epithet Χριστός within this formula. Although it is not explicit in this brief summary, Paul transmitted these core beliefs in the context of a gospel whose epicenter is the incarnation—the mystery of the eternal Son of God come in human flesh (Rom 1:3–

---

32. Fitzmyer, 546; similarly Fee, 803; Lindemann, 330.
33. Wolff, 361.
34. Jeremias, "Artikelloses Χριστός," 211–12; Jeremias, "Nochmals: Artikelloses Χριστός," 214–19.
35. Conzelmann, 254–55.

*The Cross and the Resurrection in the Apostolic Formula*

4; 8:3–4; 9:5; Gal 4:4–6; Phil 2:5–11). He is not only the long-awaited messianic king but also the divine Son of God (1 Cor 1:9). This Christ is also the creator: he is the "one Lord, Jesus Christ, through whom are all things" (8:6). Within this confessional formula, the one called "Christ" is God come in the flesh. As we will see, the incarnation will be at the center of the thought of the chapter we are studying.

*died for our sins.* Christ's death for us is a key theme throughout the epistle:

| 1:13  | ἐσταυρώθη ὑπὲρ ὑμῶν |
| 5:7   | τὸ πάσχα ἡμῶν ἐτύθη Χριστός |
| 8:11  | δι' ὃν Χριστὸς ἀπέθανεν |
| 11:24 | τὸ σῶμα τὸ ὑπὲρ ὑμῶν |

The fullest expression of this theme in the letter now comes in 15:3: Χριστὸς ἀπέθανεν ὑπὲρ τῶν ἁμαρτιῶν ἡμῶν ("Christ died for our sins"). Moreover, the formula's statement that "Christ died for our sins" recalls and brings to a climax "the word of the cross" in 1:18. We saw in the previous chapter how the climactic role of 1 Cor 15 within the letter is made clear by the repetition of the key themes and vocabulary of the thesis statement of the letter found in 1:17–18 (gospel, word, salvation, vanity) in only one other place within the letter—15:1–2. Now the central theme of that thesis statement—"the word of the cross" (1:18)—finds its climax in the confessional statement "Christ died for our sins" (15:3).

What does this first pillar of the confessional statement mean? The preposition ὑπέρ with the genitive is used everywhere else in the New Testament (except Gal 1:4) of *persons*. But here it is used in regard to *sins*. Therefore the preposition here "may convey a hint of a double meaning—Christ died on our behalf, that is, to deal with our sins."[36] The phrase "for our sins" seems therefore to express, in a condensed form, two distinct conceptions: (1) "Christ died for us" (Rom 5:8, Χριστὸς ὑπὲρ ἡμῶν ἀπέθανεν; cf. 1 Thess 5:10, τοῦ ἀποθανόντος ὑπὲρ ἡμῶν); and (2) Christ died "as a sacrifice for sin" (Rom 8:3, περὶ ἁμαρτίας; cf. Rom 4:25, παρεδόθη διὰ τὰ παραπτώματα ἡμῶν). This clause "presumes that the sins of humankind made Christ's death necessary."[37]

In the preposition ὑπέρ, the idea of vicarious substitution is present (cf. 1:13, ἐσταυρώθη ὑπὲρ ὑμῶν).[38] The vicarious and substitutionary force of the language

---

36. Barrett, 338.
37. Garland, 685.
38. The preposition ἀντί is not necessary to express the idea of substitution, as some have claimed. In Euripides's *Alcestis*, ὑπέρ is used frequently as a preposition or prefix (*Alc.* 155, 284,

here is also indicated by the fact that the source of this language is almost certainly the Suffering Servant Song of Isa 52:13–53:12 (see especially 53:5, 12).[39] Christ gives his life as a vicarious satisfaction for our sins (cf. Rom 4:25, "who was *delivered up* because of our transgressions"; Rom 8:32, "he [God] *delivered him up* on behalf of us all"). As Gordon Fee observes, the presence of this conception in this apostolic formula reveals that "the concept of substitution is woven into the very earliest of the Christian creeds."[40] In the crucifixion, in which the Son of God freely offered himself as a sacrifice, he bore the punishment we deserved for our sins so that we might be reconciled to God. The theology of God incarnate is at the center of this theology of the atonement. *This* sin offering is of *infinite* value, because it is the self-offering of the eternal Son of God made flesh.

We thus find in this apostolic confession a clear expression of the concept of vicarious satisfaction, or what is often called "penal substitutionary atonement." It is often claimed that this is a nonbiblical, non-Pauline, late Western conception, which often has been traced to Anselm in the eleventh century. This is mistaken. The concept is evident in Galatians, where the curse that lies on every human being due to sin is borne and taken away by the Son of God enduring the curse of God: "Christ redeemed us from the curse of the law by becoming a curse for us" (Gal 3:13). It is evident in 2 Cor 5:21: "The one who knew no sin, God made sin on our behalf, that we might become the righteousness of God in him" (cf. Rom 3:24–26). It is found throughout the New Testament: "He bore our sins in his body upon the tree" (1 Pet 2:24; cf. Mark 10:45; Matt 20:28). Moreover, this conception is found throughout ancient Christian writings, both in the East and the West, from the second century onward.[41] At the same time, it would be wrong to think of this atonement as only a forensic or legal transaction that takes away the guilt of sin. As Paul will unpack as the chapter proceeds, the cross and resurrection bring union with God (15:47–48), the gift of the Holy Spirit (15:45, 48), and divine sanctifying power (15:10, 30–32, 45, 48). Moreover, these saving acts of Christ bring

---

682, 690, 701) alongside ἀντί as a preposition or prefix (*Alc.* 282, 340, 461, 524, 716, 956) to denote Alcestis's substitutionary death in the place of her husband Admetus.

39. William Farmer, "Reflections on Isaiah 53 and Christian Origins," in *Jesus and the Suffering Servant: Isaiah 53 and Christian Origins* (ed. William R. Bellinger and William R. Farmer; Harrisburg, PA: Trinity Press International, 1998), 263; Wolff, 362; Jeremias, "Artikelloses Χριστός," 215; Fee, 803–4; Schreiner, 303. For the debate regarding the literary echo of Isaiah 53 within the formula, see Schrage, 24–25.

40. Fee, 804.

41. E.g., Diogn. 5; Justin, *Dial.* 95; Athanasius, *Inc.* 6–9; *C. Ar.* 2.55; Cyril of Jerusalem, *Cat.* 13.33; Cyprian, *Laps.* 17; Eusebius, *Dem. ev.* 4.12; Ambrose, *Ep.* 41.7; Jerome, *Comm. Isa.* 14.53.5; Augustine, *Trin.* 14.18; 16.21; Gregory the Great, *Moral.* 17.30.46

renewal of the divine image (15:22, 45–49), the defeat of the demonic powers (15:24–25), the conquest of death (15:18, 20–26, 52–57), and a share, body and soul, in the divine glory of the risen Son of God (15:42–49). But these dimensions of the atonement are only made possible through this substitutionary sacrifice, the Son of God's supreme act of love in identification with sinful humanity.[42]

*in fulfillment of the Scriptures.* The expression κατὰ τὰς γραφάς, which will be repeated again in 15:4, is not found in the LXX or elsewhere in the New Testament. However, we do find κατὰ τὴν γραφήν, likewise used of the Scriptures, in 1 Chr 15:15 LXX and 2 Chr 30:5 LXX. The literal sense of the expression is "in conformity with the Scriptures," but as used here it means specifically "in fulfillment of the Scriptures." As Robertson and Plummer note, "The double appeal to Scripture in so brief a statement is deliberate and important."[43]

In this phrase, Scripture is contemplated as a unified whole.[44] Because of this, some have thought that the formula's assertion "Christ died for our sins in fulfillment of the Scriptures" has no particular scriptural passages in view.[45] But this is impossible. As Jeffrey Peterson has shown, Paul in 1 Corinthians presumes the Corinthians' knowledge, as a result of his prior proclamation, of a whole series of Old Testament passages and of a specific reading of these passages as finding their fulfillment in Christ (e.g., Exod 12 in 1 Cor 5:7, τὸ πάσχα ἡμῶν ἐτύθη Χριστός).[46] The expression "in fulfillment of the Scriptures" thus presupposes a whole Christological exegesis of the Old Testament, including specific passages (cf. Rom 1:2).

The expression here in v. 3 refers to the clause "Christ died for our sins." What passages might be in view here? Certainly the fourth Servant Song of Isaiah (52:13–53:12), which is echoed in the words of institution tradition in 1 Cor 11:23–25, and which we have argued is reflected in the very wording of the formula itself in 15:3. Doubtless also the Passover narrative of Exod 12, which Paul understands (and presumes the Corinthians understand) as a type of Christ's passion and the Eucharist (1 Cor 5:7–8).[47] And the narrative of the words of institution in 1 Cor 11:23–25, which Paul received and transmitted to the Corinthians, portrays the crucifixion

---

42. For illuminating discussion, see Robert C. Tannehill, "Participation in Christ: A Central Theme in Pauline Soteriology," in *The Shape of the Gospel* (Eugene, OR: Wipf & Stock, 2007), 225–39.
43. Robertson & Plummer, 333.
44. Conzelmann, 255.
45. E.g., Barrett, 339.
46. Peterson, "Christ Our Pasch," 133–44.
47. Peterson, "Christ Our Pasch," 135–42.

of Christ as bringing to fulfillment the new covenant prophesied by Jeremiah (Jer 31:31–34).

The formula's conception of Christ's death as the fulfillment of the Scriptures doubtless also included an understanding of the cross as typologically foreshadowed in the sacrifices of the Old Testament and as bringing to pass the Old Testament expectation of a new and ultimate divine work of atonement, forgiveness, and renewal.[48] In this coming divine work of atonement, the Lord would "redeem Israel from all their iniquities" (Ps 130:8), "wash away" the sins of Jacob (Isa 4:4; cf. 44:22–23), and "purify the house of David and the people of Jerusalem from sin and from impurity" (Zech 13:1). Thus in Rom 8:3, Paul denotes Jesus's crucifixion with the expression περὶ ἁμαρτίας, the term in constant use in the LXX for the "sin offering" prescribed in the law of Moses (e.g., Lev 5:7; 9:2; 16:3, 5; Num 8:8; Ps 39:7), in order to describe Christ as the true "sin offering" or "sacrifice for sin" to which the Old Testament sacrifices looked forward. And in Rom 8:32 Paul echoes Gen 22:16 in order to portray the lamb provided by God to Abraham at the (near) sacrifice of Isaac as but a foreshadowing of the sacrifice of Christ.

In light of all the above, we can see that the expression "in fulfillment of the Scriptures" in 15:3 presupposes a christological reading of the Old Testament narrative as a whole, and specific passages within it, as fulfilled in Christ crucified.

## Verse 4

*and that he was buried, and that he was raised on the third day in fulfillment of the Scriptures,*

*and that he was buried.* The verb θάπτω used here denotes proper burial in a tomb, grave, or sepulcher. Craig Evans in his study of ancient burial customs concludes that "θάπτω ('to bury') can only refer to being properly buried, not left hanging on a cross or thrown into a ditch."[49] Evans also points out that the reference to burial in the ancient Jewish context also involved "a known place of burial."[50] This ancient formula is thus in full agreement with the gospel narratives of Jesus's burial in a known tomb (Matt 27:57–61; Mark 15:42–47; Luke 23:50–56; John 19:38–42).

---

48. E.g., Isa 4:4–5; 44:22–23; Jer 33:8; 50:20; Ezek 36:22–38 (esp. 25–27, 33); Hos 2:14–23 (esp. 19–20, 23); Zech 13:1; cf. Ps 130:7–8; Isa 43:25; 54:8–10; 55:3; 59:15–21.
49. Craig A. Evans, "Jewish Burial Traditions and the Resurrection of Jesus," *JSHJ* 3 (2005): 246.
50. Evans, "Jewish Burial Traditions," 248. Following Evans, Sandnes and Henriksen provide further arguments and evidence (*Resurrection*, 94–96).

The important place of the burial of Jesus within the earliest kerygma is evident not only here but also in Rom 6:4, where believers are said in their baptism to be *buried* with Christ (συνετάφημεν οὖν αὐτῷ; cf. Col 2:12, συνταφέντες αὐτῷ). Strikingly, Paul's exposition of baptism in Rom 6:3–4, to a church he had never visited, reflects the same narrative of death-burial-resurrection that we find in 1 Cor 15:3–4, revealing the unity of Christian teaching in the apostolic era.[51]

How does the reference to Jesus's burial function within this ancient apostolic formula? Some scholars see the assertion ἐτάφη "he was buried" as simply confirming the reality of Jesus's death and possessing no independent significance.[52] But this is disproven by the preceding καὶ ὅτι "and that," which marks this out as an independent clause and assertion within the formula.[53] Rather than merely confirming Christ's death, the reference to the burial anticipates the reference to the resurrection in the following clause. "Mentioning the burial prepares for the resurrection."[54] Moreover, the mention of the burial makes clear the *bodily* character of the resurrection spoken of in the clause that follows—it is the rising to life of Jesus's crucified and buried body.[55] This fact will be affirmed by every word of the formula that now follows in v. 4.

*and that he was raised.* We now come to the affirmation of this apostolic confession on which Paul will focus throughout the chapter: Christ is risen. It is therefore essential to grasp precisely what this means. To do so, we must fully understand the meaning of the word that the formula uses to describe this event.

### Resurrection Language in Antiquity

A number of scholars hold that the biblical language of "resurrection" was elastic, denoting some form of ascension to heavenly life after death but not necessarily a revival of the earthly, mortal body. As Marcus Borg puts it, "resurrection could involve something happening to a corpse, namely the transformation of a corpse, but it need not."[56] Along similar lines, Engberg-Pedersen argues that Paul uses

---

51. Peterson, "Diversity," 9–10.
52. So Lindemann, 331; Conzelmann, 255.
53. Rightly Wolff, 362.
54. Sandnes and Henriksen, *Resurrection*, 93; likewise Wolff, 362–63; Ronald J. Sider, "St. Paul's Understanding of the Nature and Significance of the Resurrection in I Corinthians xv, 1–19," *NovT* 19 (1975): 134–36.
55. N. T. Wright, *The Resurrection of the Son of God* (vol. 3 of *Christian Origins and the Question of God*; Minneapolis: Fortress, 2003), 321; Fitzmyer, 547; Ciampa & Rosner, 748; Fee, 805.
56. Marcus J. Borg, "The Truth of Easter," in Marcus J. Borg and N. T. Wright, *The Meaning of*

the language of resurrection to denote the "passing-away" of the flesh-and-bones body, the "coming-to-be" of a body composed of corporeal *pneuma*, and its ascension to astral immortality.[57] He is followed, among others, by Dale Allison.[58] Scholars who take either of these approaches generally interpret the formula's affirmation that Jesus "has been raised" to mean that Jesus has been taken up into heaven in a celestial form or body discontinuous with the earthly body of flesh and bones. On this understanding of resurrection language in antiquity, the formula's confession that Jesus is "raised" is entirely consistent with the crucified body of Jesus either (on Borg's view) moldering in the grave or (on Engberg-Pedersen and Allison's view) ceasing to exist and being replaced by a body of ethereally material substance. A similar understanding of the verb underlies Adela Yarbro Collins's claim that in this earliest formula, unlike the Synoptic Gospels and John, "the resurrection of Jesus did not involve the revival of his corpse."[59]

However, as has been shown by a number of scholars, most notably Martin Hengel and N. T. Wright, such approaches reflect a misunderstanding of the function of resurrection language in its ancient Jewish context. In that context, the language of "resurrection" denoted not a general hope of life after death but the specific hope of the reversal of death through the mortal body's restoration to life and its transformation to be imperishable.[60] The argument of Hengel and Wright is persuasive. The terms that express the resurrection hope within ancient Jewish texts consistently denote the restoration of the mortal body to immortal life (e.g., Dan 12:2–3; Isa 26:19; Job 19:25–27; 42:17 LXX; 2 Macc 7; Sib. Or. 4.179–192). The very few

---

*Jesus: Two Visions* (San Francisco: HarperSanFrancisco, 1999), 31. Similarly John M. G. Barclay, "The Resurrection in Contemporary New Testament Scholarship," in *Resurrection Reconsidered* (ed. Gavin D'Costa; Oxford: Oneworld, 1996), 17–18; Chilton, *Resurrection Logic*, 57–64; P. Lampe, "Paul's Concept of a Spiritual Body," in *Resurrection: Theological and Scientific Assessments* (ed. T. Peters, R. J. Russell, M. Welker; Grand Rapids: Eerdmans, 2002), 103–14; Daniel A. Smith, *Revisiting the Empty Tomb: The Early History of Easter* (Minneapolis: Fortress, 2010), 13–45; J. Holleman, *Resurrection and Parousia: A Traditio-Historical Study of Paul's Eschatology in 1 Corinthians 15* (NovTSup 84; Leiden: Brill, 1996), 142–44; Peter Gant, *Seeing Light: A Critical Enquiry into the Origins of Resurrection Faith* (Durham: Sacristy, 2019), 191–200.

57. Troels Engberg-Pedersen, *Cosmology and Self in the Apostle Paul: The Material Spirit* (Oxford: Oxford University Press, 2010), 27–28, 37–38.

58. Allison, *Resurrection*, 135–36, esp. 136 n. 109.

59. Adela Yarbro Collins, "The Empty Tomb in the Gospel According to Mark," in *Hermes and Athena: Biblical Exegesis and Philosophical Theology* (ed. E Stump and T. P. Flint; Notre Dame: University of Notre Dame Press, 1993), 111.

60. See Martin Hengel, "Das Begräbnis Jesu bei Paulus und die leibliche Auferstehung aus dem Grabe," *Auferstehung—Resurrection* (ed. F. Avemarie and H. Lichtenberger; WUNT 135; Tübingen: Mohr Siebeck, 2001), 150–83; and Wright, *Resurrection*, 85–206.

counterexamples that have been adduced are, in my judgment, not convincing.[61] Given the function of resurrection language in antiquity, it is impossible to escape the conclusion that the formula's proclamation that Jesus has been "raised" denotes an event involving the revival of Jesus's crucified body of flesh and bones.

But there is much more to be said. For this argument of Wright, Hengel, and others is strongly corroborated by striking and conclusive further evidence. This evidence involves the verb ἐγείρω, the specific verb used in the formula for the resurrection event itself (καὶ ὅτι ἐγήγερται, 15:4). To see this evidence, we must now turn to a study of this verb.

### The Semantic Meaning of the Verb ἐγείρω

Surprisingly, given its importance in this early formula and its central place in early Christian language for the resurrection, the verb ἐγείρω generally receives little attention from commentators. And yet the semantics of this key term offers important additional evidence regarding the nature of Jesus's resurrection in this ancient confessional formula. Although space precludes a full discussion here, in what follows I will offer the results of comprehensive analysis of this verb in summary form. The following analysis offers explosive and previously unexplored evidence that I believe is decisive in its force.[62]

---

61. 1 En. 103.4, which is occasionally cited in this regard, does not employ resurrection language. Similarly in Jub. 23.30–31, the term "rise up" does not denote resurrection but the exaltation of the people of God who "see great peace" and "drive out their enemies." The reinterpretation of the resurrection language of the New Testament by so-called "Gnostic" interpreters such as the Valentinians and Ophites, within the framework of an anti-Jewish and docetic Christology that excluded a literal resurrection of the earthly body (cf. Gos. Phil. 56.26–57.22; Irenaeus, *Haer.* 1.30.13), was a later development.

62. What follows here draws on my earlier study, "The Resurrection of Jesus in the Pre-Pauline Formula of 1 Cor 15.3–5," *NTS* 60 (2014): 475–98. The conclusions of this study are followed by Sandnes and Henriksen, *Resurrection*, 96–98, 105–6, and by John Granger Cook in "Resurrection in Paganism and the Question of an Empty Tomb in 1 Corinthians 15," *NTS* 63 (2017): 57–60, and Cook, *Empty Tomb, Resurrection, Apotheosis* (WUNT 410; Tübingen: Mohr Siebeck, 2018), 13–21. Cook helpfully provides further discussion and textual evidence. Dale Allison concurs that the argument of this study is persuasive (*Resurrection*, 144) but strangely fails to grasp the implications of the argument (*Resurrection*, 136 n. 109; 248–61). The most extensive previous treatments of the verb ἐγείρω are the analyses of A. Oepke in *TDNT* 2:333–37, and J. Kremer in *EDNT* 1:372–76. Kremer also provides a brief but perceptive treatment in *Das älteste Zeugnis von der Auferstehung Christi: Eine bibeltheologische Studie zur Aussage und Bedeutung von 1 Kor 15, 1–11* (3d ed.; Stuttgart: Katholisches Bibelwerk, 1970), 40–47. Individual aspects of the semantics of the verb are discussed in A. H. C. van Eijk, "Resurrection-Language: Its Various Meanings in Early Christian Literature," *Studia Patristica* 12.1 (1975): 271–76. The word is also

CHAPTER 3

Within the New Testament, ἐγείρω is the predominant verbal form used to refer to the resurrection event (whether of Christ or of the faithful).[63] However, the verb was also a common term of everyday ancient life, and its specialized function as resurrection language grew out of that wider usage. And it is that wider nonresurrection usage that provides the key to understanding the meaning of ἐγείρω when it is used to denote resurrection. Two basic senses of the word may be distinguished. Perhaps the earliest meaning of the verb (sense 1) is *to awaken, raise from sleep* (transitive) or *to wake up, rise from sleep* (intransitive). This meaning is widely attested across all periods.[64] A number of related senses grow out of this first basic meaning of the verb.[65]

In a usage (sense 2) that appears first in the fourth century BC but is very common thereafter, ἐγείρω is used apart from the concept of previous sleep or quietude to mean *to raise up, set upright* (transitive), or *to rise up, stand upright* (intransitive).[66] This second major sense of the verb (i.e., rising to stand) is closely connected

---

discussed briefly in Josef Finkenzeller, "Die Auferstehung Christi und unsere Hoffnung," in *Frage nach Jesus* (Graz: Styria, 1973), 203–5; and Bernhard Spörlein, *Die Leugnung der Auferstehung: Eine historisch-kritische Untersuchung zu 1 Kor 15* (Regensburg: Pustet, 1971), 36–37. The first comprehensive analysis of the semantics of this ancient Greek verb is my 2014 essay.

63. The verb ἐγείρω denoting resurrection occurs eight-four times in the New Testament. Compounds of ἐγείρω are also used in the same sense: ἐξεγείρω (once) and συνεγείρω (three occurrences). Other terms used with reference to resurrection include ἀνίστημι (thirty-three occurrences), ἀνάστασις (thirty-eight occurrences), ἐξανάστασις (once), and ἔγερσις (once).

64. See, for example, Homer, *Il.* 5.413; 24.344; *Od.* 5.48; 15.46; Aristophanes, *Nub.* 9; *Lys.* 18; Plato, *Apol.* 31a; *Tim.* 46a; Herodotus, *Hist.* 4.9.1; Aristotle, *Oec.* 1345a; Epictetus, *Diatr.* 1.5.6; 4.1.47; Diodorus Siculus, *Bib. hist.* 10.29.1; Philo, *Somn.* 1.174; *Ios.* 126; Gen 41:4 LXX; Prov 6:9 LXX; Matt 1:24; 8:25–26; Acts 12:7; Rom 13:11. Cf. Kremer, in *EDNT* 1:372; Van Eijk, "Resurrection-Language," 273–74; Frankenzeller, "Auferstehung," 203. On the roots of this meaning within the verb's etymology, see Frisk, 1:437–38.

65. A related sense that appears from the earliest period is *to rouse up, stir up* (transitive) or *be roused up* (intransitive) from quietude or inactivity (cf. Homer, *Il.* 5.208; *Od.* 24.164; Hesiod, *Theog.* 666; Aristophanes, *Lys.* 306; *Eccl.* 71; Plato, *Apol.* 30a; *Resp.* 440c; Herodotus, *Hist.* 7.49.6; Aristotle, *Eth. nic.* 1116b; Sib. Or. 4.137; Prov 10:12 LXX; 15:1 LXX; Dan 11:25 LXX; Matt 24:7; Justin, *Dial.* 52.2). Perhaps connected with this sense is the use of the verb with reference to figures or persons *rising up, coming into prominence*, or *coming into existence* (cf. Matt 11:11; 24:11; John 7:52). This usage also occurs in the LXX, other Jewish literature, and the New Testament in the active, transitive sense of God *arousing* or *raising up* prophets, deliverers, or kings (cf. Judg 2:16 LXX; 3:9 LXX; T. Levi 18.2; Luke 1:69; Acts 13:22). The verb is also used in this sense frequently of armies or nations *stirring up* or *being roused up* to battle or war (cf. Homer, *Il.* 2.440; 4.352; 1 Esd 1:23; Matt 24:7).

66. Of persons being *raised upright*: 2 Kgdms 12:17 LXX; Eccl 4:10 LXX; Jer 28:12 LXX; Acts 3:7; 10:26; Jas 5:15. Of persons *standing up*: Exod 5:8 LXX; Ps 126:2 LXX; Tob 6:18; Matt 26:46; Luke 11:8; Rev 11:1. Related to this meaning is the use of the verb to describe the *erecting* of various types

to the first (i.e., waking from sleep). For the verb in this first sense does not mean (as can the English verb *waken*) to rise from sleep merely in the sense of gaining consciousness but rather *to rise from the position of sleep*.[67] In other words, "ἐγείρω does not make a distinction between *awaken* and *stand up*."[68] The verb means *to rise to a standing position*, with the presence or absence of the additional idea of sleep being determined by contextual factors. Our verbal compound *to get up*, in its general denotation of rising to a standing position with the capacity for specific reference to rising from the posture of sleep, is perhaps the nearest English equivalent.

Here we must highlight a feature of the verb's semantic range that has emerged from our study and that is crucial for its use as resurrection language. Although often translated by the English verbs *to raise* or *rise*, the semantic range of ἐγείρω is quite different. Like ἐγείρω, these English verbs can be used of *rising* to stand from a reclining position or from the posture of sleep. However, the English verbs also frequently express the wider concept of *ascension* or *elevation*. We speak, for instance, of a spark that *rises* from the flames, of the moon *rising* into the night sky, or of a balloon that *rises* into the air. The Greek verb ἐγείρω, however, has a more restricted semantic range and cannot mean *to raise* or *rise* in this wider sense of elevation or ascension. Rather, ἐγείρω means *to get up* or *stand up*, that is, *to raise from a supine to a standing position*. Thus the Greek verb is regularly used to denote the *raising* or *rising up* of one who has *fallen* (Exod 23:5; 1 Kgdms 5:3; Eccl 4:10; Jdt 10:23; Philo, *Agr.* 122; *Mut.* 56; *Migr.* 122; Matt 12:11; Mark 9:27; Acts 9:8; 1 Clem. 59.4). It is also used of one *kneeling* or *prostrate* being *raised back to a standing position* (1 Kgdms 2:8; 2 Kgdms 12:17; Ps 112:7; Dan 10:10; Philo, *Ebr.* 156; *Post.* 149; Matt 17:7; Luke 11:8; Acts 10:26; Herm. Vis. 2.1.3; 3.2.4). The verb is used of one *lying down*—very frequently one who is *lying sick*—who is *restored to a standing posture* (Matt 8:15; 9:5–7; Mark 1:31; 2:9, 11–12; Luke 5:23–24; John 5:8; Acts 3:6–7; Jas 5:15). The verb is also frequently used of one *sitting* who *rises to stand* (Ps 126:2; Isa 14:9; Matt 26:46; Mark 3:3; 10:49; 14:42; Luke 6:8; John 11:29; 13:4; 14:31; Herm. Vis. 1.4.1). In no instance within ancient Greek literature does ἐγείρω denote the concept of ascension, elevation, or assumption. Rather, it denotes the action whereby one who is prone, sitting, prostrate, or lying down is *restored to a standing position*.

The analogical use of ἐγείρω as resurrection language grows out of the semantic map of the verb sketched above. Whether the sensory metaphor employed for

---

of physical structures: e.g., 1 Esd 5:44 (temple); Sir 49:13 (walls); Sib. Or. 3.290 (temple); Philo, *Conf.* 133 (tower); *Post.* 54 (cities); John 2:19–20 (temple).

67. Evident in such passages as Aristotle, *Oec.* 1345a; Xenophon, *Oec.* 5.4; Plutarch, *Pomp.* 36.4; Matt 2:13–14; 2:20–21; 8:26; 26:46; Mark 14:42.

68. Kremer, in *EDNT* 1:372.

CHAPTER 3

denoting resurrection involves simply the arising of one *supine* or *fallen* (sense 2) or involves the additional idea of the arising of one supine in *sleep* (sense 1) may be debated.[69] But in either case, the verb's basic semantic meaning of *getting up* or *arising to stand* is present. The verb ἐγείρω does not mean *to rise* in the sense that a balloon rises into the air but in the sense of *arising to stand*. In resurrection contexts the verb does not therefore denote that the dead *ascend* or are *assumed* somewhere; rather, the verb signifies that the corpse, lying supine in the grave, *gets up* or *arises to stand* from the tomb. When used with reference to the dead, therefore, the term refers unambiguously to the reanimation or revivification of the corpse.

An inscription from Rome provides additional evidence.[70] The final line of this burial inscription reads ἐντεῦθεν οὐθὶς ἀποθανὼν ἐγ[ε]ίρετ[αι] ("no one who has died arise[s] from here"). In this inscription, the use of the adverb ἐντεῦθεν "from here," together with ἐγείρω unambiguously indicates the concept of getting up or arising *from the tomb*.[71] The very frequent addition of the prepositional phrase ἐκ νεκρῶν to the verb likewise suggests an implicit notion of arising *from among the dead* or *from the grave*.[72] So in 1 Cor 15, where the simple Χριστὸς ... ἐγήγερται ("Christ ... has been raised") within the confessional formula in 15:3–4 is more fully expressed in 15:12 as Χριστὸς ... ἐκ νεκρῶν ἐγήγερται ("Christ ... has been raised from the dead").

Why have we devoted such close attention to this verb? The reason is that the semantic range of the verb ἐγείρω sketched above is of crucial significance for the debate regarding the meaning of this verb within the confessional formula of 1 Cor 15. As we have seen, those scholars who argue that this formula describes an event that did not involve the revival of Jesus's corpse commonly interpret the formula's affirmation that Jesus "has been raised" (ἐγήγερται) to mean that Jesus has been *assumed* or *taken up* into heaven in a celestial or ethereal body discontinuous with his earthly, physical body. So for Joost Holleman, the formula's use of ἐγείρω for the Easter event indicates that "Jesus was believed to have been *raised into heaven*."[73] The claim of

---

69. On the question see Kremer, *Zeugnis*, 45; Oepke, in *TDNT* 2:333–34.
70. *IGUR* 3.1406 (date uncertain).
71. A tomb inscription from Thessaly of uncertain date (*IG* 9.2.640) appears to reflect the same conception: θανόντα γὰρ οὐδὲν ἐγείρει ("for nothing raises up one who has died").
72. See especially John 12:17, ὅτε τὸν Λάζαρον ἐφώνησεν ἐκ τοῦ μνημείου καὶ ἤγειρεν αὐτὸν ἐκ νεκρῶν, where the two clauses appear to function epexegetically. Cf. Matt 17:9; Mark 6:14; Luke 9:7; John 2:22; 12:1, 9, 17; 21:14; Acts 3:15; 4:10; 13:31; Rom 4:24; 6:4, 9; 7:4; 8:11; 10:9; 1 Cor 15:20; Gal 1:1; Eph 1:20; Phil 3:11; Col 2:12; 2 Tim 2:8; Heb 11:19; 1 Pet 1:21. Cf. also the addition to the verb of the articular ἐκ τῶν νεκρῶν in Eph 5:14; 1 Thess 1:10 and ἀπὸ τῶν νεκρῶν in Matt 14:2; 27:64; 28:7.
73. Holleman, *Resurrection* 143 (italics mine).

this ancient confession is thus that "God vindicated Jesus by *lifting* him out of the realm of death and into his heavenly realm; there Jesus received a new and immortal body."[74] Einar Thomasen similarly argues that for the very earliest Christ followers Jesus's resurrection involved "a spiritual body that *rises* from the present one as a new and transformed being."[75] Gerd Lüdemann likewise maintains that, for Paul, the confession that Jesus has been "raised" means that "Jesus was *exalted* from the cross directly to God."[76] Andreas Lindemann puts this view succinctly: in this pre-Pauline formula "ἐγήγερται denotes not restoration to life, but exaltation to heaven."[77]

However, in view of the evidence provided above regarding the verb's semantic range, the assumption that ἐγείρω can mean "raise" in this sense is excluded. Indeed, such an interpretation is profoundly unhistorical, for it is founded upon associations arising from English or other modern language translations, not the actual language of the formula itself. The verb ἐγείρω, when applied to the dead, does not denote ascension or elevation but restoration from a recumbent position to a standing posture. The very semantics of this ancient Greek verb involves the concept of the mortal body's restoration to life. Of course, within early Christian proclamation of Jesus's resurrection the verb denoted much more than the mere reanimation of Jesus's corpse, including also the idea of transformation, from weakness and mortality to glory, power, and imperishability (cf. Rom 6:9–10; 2 Cor 13:4; Phil 3:21). "Christ, having been raised from the dead never dies again; death no longer has power over him" (Rom 6:9). But, as our study of the semantics of ἐγείρω has shown, the subject of this glorious transformation is understood within the formula as Jesus's crucified body, which in being "raised" does not *ascend* to heaven but *gets up* from the tomb. It is thus beyond doubt that the apostolic formula of 1 Cor 15 affirms that Jesus arose on the third day in his crucified body, leaving behind an empty tomb.

The linguistic meaning of the verb ἐγείρω is of decisive significance for the debate regarding the nature of Jesus's resurrection within the formula. The semantics of this key term, when used to denote resurrection, necessarily entails the revivification of the body in the tomb. This verb within the pre-Pauline formula thus denotes the revivification of the crucified and entombed body of Jesus. The assumption that the formula's affirmation that Jesus has been "raised" denotes a postmortem ascension to heaven that left his body in the grave may be an infer-

---

74. Holleman, *Resurrection* 144 (italics mine); similarly Smith, *Empty Tomb*, 27–45.

75. Einar Thomasen, "Valentinian Ideas about Salvation as Transformation," in *Metamorphoses: Resurrection, Body and Transformative Practices in Early Christianity* (ed. Turid Karlsen Seim and Jorunn Økland; Berlin: de Gruyter, 2009), 169 (italics mine).

76. Lüdemann, *Resurrection of Jesus*, 71.

77. Lindemann, 332: "das ἐγήγερται nicht Wiederbelebung, sondern Erhöhung meint."

ence possible from English or other modern language translations, but it is not a possible inference from the Greek wording of this ancient formula. Neither Marcus Borg's contention that the verb ἐγείρω is used within the formula without reference to the corpse of Jesus nor the assumption of Troels Engberg-Pedersen and Dale Allison that it refers to a transubstantiation of the corpse into a disincarnate, ethereal state is consistent with the actual meaning of this ancient Greek verb. In affirming that Jesus has been "raised," this pre-Pauline confession affirmed the resurrection of Jesus's crucified body from the tomb.

*The Voice and Tense of the Verb ἐγείρω in the Formula*

The perfect passive ἐγήγερται may be purely passive in sense (i.e., "he was raised") with God the Father as the understood agent (cf. 15:15; Rom 6:4, ἠγέρθη Χριστὸς ἐκ νεκρῶν διὰ τῆς δόξης τοῦ πατρός).[78] However, as A. B. du Toit has argued, passive forms of ἐγείρω in the LXX are overwhelmingly middle intransitive in sense, including in the key resurrection passages.[79] This may suggest such a sense here in the formula (i.e., "he rose"). Either the passive or middle sense is possible.[80]

It is striking that in a sequence of four verbs in which the other three verbs are all aorists (15:3, ἀπέθανεν; 15:4, ἐτάφη; 15:5, ὤφθη), the formula here uses the perfect (15:4, ἐγήγερται). This is all the more striking given the verb's modification by a past-time indicator (τῇ ἡμέρᾳ τῇ τρίτῃ). In this way, the formula strongly emphasizes the present and continuing reality of Jesus's resurrection.[81] "Christ, having been raised from the dead, can no longer die; death no longer has dominion over him" (Rom 6:9). Even as throughout the New Testament, so too in this astoundingly early confession Jesus's physical body, now risen from the dead, is immortal, imperishable, and everlasting. "Thus, the confessional formula does not just narrate past events: it proclaims Christ as risen Lord."[82]

---

78. So Schrage, 38; Wolff, 363; Fitzmyer, 547; Garland, 686; Fee, 806 n. 65.
79. A. B. du Toit, "Primitive Christian Belief in the Resurrection of Jesus in the Light of Pauline Resurrection and Appearance Terminology," *Neot* 23 (1989): 326–27.
80. On this question of the transitivity of the passive form of the verb ἐγείρω, see Matthew Brook O'Donnell, "Some New Testament Words for Resurrection and the Company They Keep," in *Resurrection* (ed. Stanley Porter, Michael A. Hayes, and David Tombs; Sheffield: Sheffield Academic, 1999), 136–63; Daniel Kendall and Gerald O'Collins, "Christ's Resurrection and the Aorist Passive of *egeirō*," *Greg* 74 (1993): 725–35; and John Murray, "Who Raised Up Jesus?" *WTJ* 3 (1941): 113–23.
81. BDR §342.1; Rob., *Gram.*, 896; cf. Kühner-G., 2.1:167–69 (§386.13); Ellicott, 288–89.
82. Hays, 257.

## The Lack of Explicit Mention of an Empty Tomb in the Formula

We must pause here to consider another objection to the physical and bodily character of the resurrection of Jesus confessed in this formula. A frequent argument of those scholars who hold that the resurrection of Jesus is understood within the confessional formula as an event unrelated to Jesus's corpse is the absence of any mention within the formula of an empty tomb. In the view of these interpreters, the empty tomb is *conspicuous by its absence* within this early confession. If an empty tomb had been known from the beginning, they maintain, it seems unlikely that it would have been omitted from this primitive formula. The fact that the formula speaks only of Jesus's death, burial, resurrection, and appearances to the disciples, with no mention whatsoever of an empty tomb, suggests to these scholars that belief in an empty tomb, such as we see reflected in the four gospels, was a later development unknown to Paul and the earliest Christ followers.[83] Rudolf Bultmann's terse apothegm remains the classic statement of the thesis: "The accounts of an empty tomb are legends, of which Paul as yet knew nothing."[84]

However, this argument is entirely unconvincing. Two lines of evidence are of extraordinary importance, although until recently neither has been previously brought to bear on the question.[85] The first involves the source we know as Luke-Acts. This document, although significantly later than the pre-Pauline formula in 1 Cor 15, nevertheless provides relevant evidence. As a result of its distinctive two-part composition, Luke-Acts is unique within ancient Christianity in containing both a *narrative* of the resurrection (Luke 24), and *confessional summaries* of this event (within the apostolic speeches in Acts). This permits us to see a striking feature of early Christian traditions regarding the resurrection: whereas the empty tomb has a prominent place within the full resurrection *narrative* in Luke's Gospel (Luke 24:1–12; cf. 24:23–24), it is never mentioned explicitly in the *narrative summaries* within Acts. These summaries, like the formula in 1 Cor 15:3–7, instead focus exclusively on Jesus's *death*, his *burial*, his *resurrection*, and his *appearances* to the apostles (Acts 13:26–37), or, more narrowly, on his *death, resurrection*, and

---

83. For the argument, see H. Grass, *Ostergeschehen und Osterberichte* (Göttingen: Vandenhoeck & Ruprecht, 1962), 146–47; James M. Robinson, "Jesus—From Easter to Valentinus (or to the Apostles' Creed)," *JBL* 101 (1982): 12; Lindemann, 331–32; Borg, "Truth," 132; and many others.

84. Rudolf Bultmann, *Theologie des Neuen Testaments* (9th ed.; Tübingen: Mohr Siebeck, 1984), 48: "Legende sind die Geschichten vom leeren Grabe, von dem Paulus noch nichts weiss."

85. What follows is adapted from Ware, "Pre-Pauline Formula," 480–82, which proposes a resolution of the question through an examination of previously unexplored form-critical evidence. The conclusions of this study are followed by Allison, *Resurrection*, 130 and Sandnes and Henriksen, *Resurrection*, 105–6.

CHAPTER 3

*appearances* (10:36–41), or, more narrowly still, on his *death* and *resurrection* (2:22–32; 3:13–15; 4:10; 17:31). The empty tomb, although implicit within the confessional summaries in the kerygmatic claim that Jesus's body did not undergo decay (2:25–31; 13:34–37), is never itself an explicit theme within these summaries. This would suggest that, for the author of Luke-Acts and most likely also for his readers, the empty tomb had its proper home within narratives of the resurrection event, but it was not to be expected within shorter formulae, or even narrative summaries, concerning this event.

This is confirmed by a further striking fact: the phenomenon we see at work in Luke-Acts is consistent with early Christian formulae and creeds as a whole. Despite their great variety, none of the confessional formulae or creedal fragments known to us from the first two centuries contains any reference to the empty tomb. These formulas make explicit mention only of Jesus's death and resurrection or, more rarely, of Jesus's death, burial, and resurrection.[86] This situation remains the same even after the rise of full creeds in the latter half of the second century: all the creedal statements of the ancient church known to us from this period onward focus exclusively on Jesus's death, burial, and resurrection (or, less frequently, only on Jesus's death and resurrection), omitting any reference to a vacant tomb.[87] And yet these creeds had their *Sitz im Leben* within a theological milieu in which the empty tomb narratives of the canonical gospels were widely known and received as authoritative, and in which the understanding of the future resurrection as a resurrection of the flesh was a theological given regularly

---

86. Cf. Rom 1:3–4; 4:24–25; 8:34; 10:8–10; 1 Thess 4:14; 1 Pet 3:18–22; Ign. *Smyrn.* 1.1–2; *Trall.* 9; Justin, *1 Apol.* 21.1; 31.7; 42.4; 46.5; *Dial.* 63.1; 85.2; 132.1; Irenaeus, *Haer.* 1.10.1; 3.4.2; 3.16.6; Tertullian, *Prax.* 2; *Praescr.* 13; *Virg.* 1.

87. Cf. the Old Roman Creed (ca. AD 175): τὸν ἐπὶ Ποντίου Πιλάτου σταυρωθέντα καὶ ταφέντα, καὶ τῇ τρίτῃ ἡμέρᾳ ἀναστάντα ἐκ τῶν νεκρῶν ("who was crucified under Pontius Pilate and was buried, and on the third day rose from the dead"); Creed of Jerusalem (ca. 350): τὸν σταυρωθέντα καὶ ταφέντα καὶ ἀναστάντα ἐκ νεκρῶν τῇ τρίτῃ ἡμέρᾳ ("who was crucified and buried and rose from the dead on the third day"); Const. ap. 7.41 (fourth-century): σταυρωθέντα ἐπὶ Ποντίου Πιλάτου καὶ ἀποθανόντα ὑπὲρ ἡμῶν, καὶ ἀναστάντα ἐκ νεκρῶν μετὰ τὸ παθεῖν τῇ τρίτῃ ἡμέρᾳ ("crucified under Pontius Pilate and died for us, and risen from the dead after his suffering on the third day"); Creed of Milan (ca. 375): *passus, et sepultus, et tertia die resurrexit a mortuis* ("suffered death, was buried, and on the third day he rose from the dead"); Creed of Hippo (ca. 400): *crucifixum sub Pontio Pilato, mortuum, et sepultum, tertia die resurrexit* ("crucified under Pontius Pilate, died, was buried, on the third day he rose again"); Creed of Ravenna (ca. 400): *crucifixus est et sepultus, tertia die resurrexit* ("was crucified and buried, on the third day he rose again"); Creed of the First Council of Toledo (400): *crucifixum, mortuum et sepultum, et tertia die resurrexisse* ("crucified, died, and buried, on the third day he rose again"); Apostles' Creed (sixth century): *crucifixus, mortuus et sepultus, descendit ad inferna, tertia die resurrexit a mortuis* ("was crucified, died, and was buried; he descended into hell; on the third day he rose from the dead").

*The Cross and the Resurrection in the Apostolic Formula*

expressed explicitly within these creeds themselves.[88] This situation (in which the empty tomb is assumed, but not creedally expressed) coheres with our evidence from Luke-Acts, and leads to an important form-critical conclusion: for all ancient Christians for whom we have evidence, reference to the empty tomb was confined to full *narratives* of the resurrection event (such as we see in the canonical gospels) and was not considered appropriate or expected within *confessional formulae* regarding that event (such as we see in 1 Cor 15:3–7).

The claim that the empty tomb is conspicuous by its absence in 1 Cor 15:3–7 is thus based on a misapprehension regarding the form and limits of such summaries. As we have seen, *no formula, creedal fragment, or creed known to us from the ancient church contains any reference to the empty tomb*. The absence of the empty tomb from the confessional formula in 1 Cor 15:3–7 thus provides no evidence for a nonbodily or ethereal understanding of Jesus's resurrection within that formula.

A further factor provides corroborating evidence that the apostolic formula assumes an empty tomb. As Craig Evans has shown, reference to burial within an ancient Jewish context always involves "a known place of burial."[89] The formula's claim that Jesus was "buried" and then "raised" (15:4) is therefore inconceivable unless the tomb, at that known place of burial, was found to be empty. The wording of the formula thus involves an implicit claim to eyewitness testimony to an empty tomb. The confession's claim to eyewitness testimony thus involves both the (implicit) claim to have seen the empty tomb (15:4), and the (explicit) claim to have seen the risen Lord (15:5–8). In this twin claim, the formula is in striking coherence with the resurrection narratives of the gospels (Matt 28; Mark 16; Luke 24; John 20–21).

*on the third day.* The quantity, diversity, and breadth of the evidence within the New Testament for the time reference to Jesus's resurrection "on the third day" are

---

88. Cf. the Old Roman Creed: πιστεύω εἰς ... σαρκὸς ἀνάστασιν ("I believe in ... the resurrection of the flesh"); Creed of Jerusalem: πιστεύομεν ... εἰς σαρκὸς ἀνάστασιν ("we believe ... in the resurrection of the flesh"); Const. ap. 7.41: βαπτίζομαι καὶ ... εἰς σαρκὸς ἀνάστασιν ("I am baptized also ... into the resurrection of the flesh"); Creed of Milan: *credo in ... carnis resurrectionem* ("I believe in ... the resurrection of the flesh"); Creed of Hippo: *credimus in ... resurrectionem carnis* ("we believe in ... the resurrection of the flesh"); Creed of Ravenna: *credo in ... carnis resurrectionem* ("I believe in ... the resurrection of the flesh"); Creed of the First Council of Toledo: *resurrectionem vero humanae credimus carnis* ("we truly believe in the resurrection of our human flesh"); Apostles' Creed: *credo in ... carnis resurrectionem* ("I believe in ... the resurrection of the flesh").

89. Evans, "Jewish Burial Traditions," 248.

truly remarkable.[90] No less than *seven* different expressions are used in the New Testament to locate Jesus's resurrection chronologically as occurring on the third day after his death and burial. Such expressions occur an astonishing *twenty-eight* times in the New Testament. Of these, ten occur within Matthew (expressed in six different ways), six within Mark (four different expressions), eight within Luke (three different expressions), four in John (two different expressions), one in Acts, and one in Paul's letters (the apostolic confession in 1 Cor 15). The evidence may be summarized as follows:

| | |
|---|---|
| 1. τῇ ἡμέρᾳ τῇ τρίτῃ | Luke 18:33; 1 Cor 15:4 |
| 2. τῇ τρίτῃ ἡμέρᾳ | Matt 16:21; 17:23; 20:19; Luke 9:22; 13:32; 24:7, 46; Acts 10:40 |
| 3. μετὰ τρεῖς ἡμέρας | Matt 27:63; Mark 8:31; 9:31; 10:34 |
| 4. ἐν τρισὶν ἡμέραις | Matt 27:40; Mark 15:29; John 2:19, 20 |
| 5. διὰ τριῶν ἡμερῶν | Matt 26:61; Mark 14:58 |
| 6. τρεῖς ἡμέρας καὶ τρεῖς νύκτας | Matt 12:40 |
| 7. τῇ μιᾷ τῶν σαββάτων | Mark 16:2; Luke 24:1; John 20:1, 19 |

cf. Matt 27:64, ἕως τῆς τρίτης ἡμέρας; 28:1, εἰς μίαν σαββάτων; Luke 24:21, τρίτην ταύτην ἡμέραν ἄγει.

These references to the third day occur within the New Testament in five different contexts. (1) Jesus's passion predictions in the gospels (Matt 16:21; 17:23; 20:19; 27:63–64; Mark 8:31; 9:31; 10:34; Luke 9:22; 18:33; cf. Matt 27:64; Luke 13:12); (2) Jesus's prophecy of his rebuilding of the temple (Matt 26:61; 27:40; Mark 14:58; 15:29; John 2:19–20); (3) Jesus's saying regarding the sign of Jonah (Matt 12:40); (4) the resurrection narratives within the gospels (Matt 28:1; Mark 16:2; Luke 24:1, 7, 21, 46); and (5) the confessional summaries in Acts and in Paul's letters (Acts 10:40; 1 Cor 15:4). It is an amusing feature of modern scholarship that many interpreters regard these varied expressions for "the third day" as involving serious discrepancies or even as incompatible with one another.[91] But the New Testament authors clearly regarded them as compatible. Matthew, for instance, uses the following *interchangeably*: τῇ τρίτῃ ἡμέρᾳ (Matt 16:21; 17:23; 20:19), μετὰ τρεῖς ἡμέρας (Matt 27:63),

---

90. Cf. Schrage, 39. For discussion, see Wolff, 364–67; Lehmann, *Auferweckt*, 159–241, 262–350; Grass, *Ostergeschehen*, 127–35; Becker, *Auferstehung*, 107–9; Sandnes and Henriksen, *Resurrection*, 98–99.

91. E.g., Allison, *Resurrection*, 28–31.

τρεῖς ἡμέρας καὶ τρεῖς νύκτας (Matt 12:40), διὰ τριῶν ἡμερῶν (Matt 26:61), ἐν τρισὶν ἡμέραις (Matt 27:40), and εἰς μίαν σαββάτων (Matt 28:1).

All four gospels recall Jesus's prophetic foretelling of his resurrection on the third day (e.g., Matt 16:21; 17:23; 20:19; Mark 8:31; 9:31; 10:34; Luke 9:22; 18:33; John 2:19–20) and narrate its fulfillment through his death and burial on Friday and his resurrection on Sunday, "the first day of the week" (Matt 28:1; Mark 16:2; Luke 24:1; John 20:1, 19). Luke within his resurrection narrative, in addition to narrating Jesus's resurrection on the first day of the week (Luke 24:1), specifically recalls Jesus's prediction of his resurrection on the third day (24:7–8) and uses third-day language twice more within his narrative of the resurrection appearances (24:21, 46). To an astounding degree (twenty-six occurrences within the gospels alone), the specific chronological indication that Jesus rose to life "on the third day" is woven into the very warp and woof of the narrative of all four gospels.

We find this identical chronological notice of Jesus's resurrection "on the third day" within our confessional formula in 1 Cor 15:4. Given the virtual scholarly unanimity regarding the primitive origin of this formula, dating to the very beginning of the Christian movement, this confession provides crucial evidence regarding this aspect of the ancient kerygma. The formula reveals that the proclamation of Jesus's resurrection "on the third day" goes back to the very beginnings of Christianity and to the earliest apostolic preaching. It is one more way in which this astoundingly early formula presupposes the narratives we find in the four gospels and thus confirms their historicity.

The qualification that Christ was raised "on the third day" also provides further confirmation of the bodily and physical character of Jesus's resurrection. This datum is not consistent with the claim of some scholars that Jesus's resurrection is understood within the formula as a spiritual exaltation to heaven from the cross without connection to his physical body placed in the tomb.[92] For in this confession's claim that Jesus died, was buried, and was raised on the third day, the qualifier "on the third day" indicates that, three days after his burial, something happened to Jesus's body. And, as we have seen, the verb ἐγήγερται "he was raised" indicates precisely what that was—his body rose again from the tomb.

The majority of interpreters rightly take the words "on the third day" within the formula as a historical and chronological indicator, consistent with the usage of this and equivalent phrases within the gospels. These scholars regard "on the third day" within the confession as denoting the day on which the tomb was found empty, the day on which Jesus's first resurrection appearances took place, or

---

92. For scholars who make this and similar claims, see notes 56–59 above.

CHAPTER 3

both.[93] However, some scholars interpret these words in the formula not chronologically but as a metaphorical and theological expression associating Jesus's resurrection with divine deliverance and salvation.[94] This is not a historically valid interpretation of the formula for several reasons:

1. This interpretation reads "on the third day" within the formula in isolation from the massive evidence for this expression elsewhere in the New Testament (on which see above). This proposed reading of this expression in the formula is contrary to the uncontested meaning of this phrase in its twenty-seven instances elsewhere in the New Testament.
2. This reading requires a complex and unlikely scenario in which an originally chronological expression was given (in the formula) a metaphorical and theological meaning, which was then later in the gospels misunderstood as historical and chronological. This is far-fetched and gratuitous.
3. Acts 10:40, the only other instance within the New Testament of this expression within a confessional summary, provides an important test case as to how it is to be understood in the summary of 1 Cor 15:4. In Acts 10:40, as all interpreters are agreed, τῇ τρίτῃ ἡμέρᾳ ("on the third day") is chronological and historical.
4. The closest parallel in the New Testament to 1 Cor 15:3–4 is Luke 24:46: "Thus it is written, that the Christ would suffer, and rise from the dead on the third day." In both 1 Cor 15:3–4 and Luke 24:46 (a) Christ (b) suffers death and (c) rises from the dead (d) on the third day (e) in fulfillment of the Scriptures. In Luke 24:46, "on the third day" is beyond dispute a chronological and historical reference. The close correspondence of Luke 24:46 and 1 Cor 15:3–4 on all other points strongly suggests that in 1 Cor 15:3–4, as in Luke 24:46, the words "on the third day" are a chronological indicator.

Those scholars who deny a literal and chronological meaning of the phrase "on the third day" within the formula raise an important objection. As we have seen, the majority view takes "on the third day" within the confession as a chronological reference to the day on which the tomb was discovered empty, to the day on which Jesus's first resurrection appearances took place, or to both. But scholars who argue for a metaphorical meaning of the expression point out that the for-

---

93. For the view that "on the third day" refers to the day on which the tomb was found empty, see Sider, "Understanding," 136–39; Sandnes and Henriksen, *Resurrection*, 99; Wolff, 364–67; Garland, 686; Bryan, *Resurrection*, 49. For the claim that this phrase refers to the day of Jesus's first resurrection appearances, see Gerhardson, "Evidence," 83. For the view that "on the third day" refers to both of these, see Fee, 806.

94. So Evans, *Resurrection*, 48–49 ("not intended as a chronological but as a theological statement"); Lehman, *Auferweckt*, 159–241, 262–350; Conzelmann, 256; Schrage, 39–43.

mula neither asserts that the tomb was found empty on the third day nor that the risen Jesus first appeared to the apostles on the third day, but that Jesus *rose* on the third day. How, these scholars ask, could the apostles know the precise day of the resurrection itself? How could they know Jesus rose on the third day and not on the first or second?[95] This is a valid question, for in the formula, as everywhere else in the New Testament, the expression "on the third day" refers to the resurrection itself.

But the answer is not far to seek. In Luke's resurrection narrative, the angels at the tomb recall to the women Jesus's prediction of his resurrection "on the third day" (Luke 24:7), and Luke tells us, "they remembered his words" (24:8). The apostles and first eyewitnesses had not only experienced the empty tomb "on the first day of the week" and Jesus's first resurrection appearances on the third day after his death and burial, but they also recalled Jesus's words that he would rise to life after three days.[96] Luke also indicates further communication from Jesus on the matter following the resurrection (24:46). For the first disciples, the recollection of the words of Jesus, the empty tomb, the resurrection appearances, and Jesus's words following the resurrection were all mutually interpretive and the foundation of the primitive apostolic proclamation of Jesus's resurrection "on the third day."[97]

*in fulfillment of the Scriptures.* The twofold reference to the fulfillment of the Scriptures (15:3, 4) within this brief confession is striking. That the saving events proclaimed within the formula bring the Old Testament Scriptures to their fulfillment belongs to the very heart of this early confession. The phrase κατὰ τὰς γραφάς, unique within the New Testament but with analogous expressions in the LXX, refers to the Scriptures as a unified whole. At the same time, as we saw in discussion of 15:3, this expression presupposes a christological exegesis of the Old Testament, including specific passages, transmitted to the first believers as an integral component of the apostolic preaching.

---

95. For the argument, see for example Evans, *Resurrection*, 48–49.

96. On the persuasive evidence for the historicity of Jesus's predictions of his passion and resurrection, see Wright, *Resurrection*, 408–11; Allison, *Resurrection*, 187–92.

97. Similarly Fee, 806. Another view recognizes the literal and chronological nature of the expression "on the third day" within the formula and its direct reference to the resurrection itself, but argues that its source was a chain of reasoning based on Ps 16:10; so John C. Poirier, "Psalm 16:10 and the Resurrection of Jesus 'on the Third Day' (1 Corinthians 15:4)," *JSPL* 4 (2014): 149–67; Martin Pickup, "'On the Third Day': The Time Frame of Jesus' Death and Resurrection," *JETS* 56 (2013): 511–42. However, such a process of exegetical reasoning hardly explains the remarkable centrality and breadth of the tradition of Jesus's third-day resurrection in primitive Christianity (twenty-eight occurrences within the New Testament). The datum gave rise to the exegesis; the exegesis cannot account for the datum.

CHAPTER 3

A few interpreters have suggested that "in fulfillment of the Scriptures" in 15:4 refers only to "he was raised," and not also to "on the third day."[98] However, this would not be consistent with the structure of the formula. For in this structure, the first (15:3) and third (15:4b) clauses are parallel, and in the first clause the expression κατὰ τὰς γραφάς refers to that whole clause. The word order of 15:4b, in which the phrase "on the third day" immediately precedes "in fulfillment of the Scriptures," confirms this. As most interpreters have recognized, the claim of scriptural fulfillment has reference both to "he was raised" and "on the third day."[99]

In the christological exegesis of the Old Testament that accompanied the transmission of this ancient confession, what specific passages would have been proclaimed as fulfilled in Christ's resurrection? The formula itself provides no specifics. However, the apostolic speeches in the book of Acts, whose primitive character is widely recognized, provide a rich historical resource. Here we find, in addition to a number of global statements regarding Jesus's fulfillment of "all the prophets" (Acts 3:18, 21, 24; 10:43; 26:22–23), the following individual passages adduced in the apostolic proclamation as fulfilled in Jesus's resurrection: Ps 16:8–11 (Acts 2:24–32; 13:34–37); Isa 52:13 (Acts 3:13); Ps 118:22 (Acts 4:10–11); Ps 2:7 (Acts 13:30–33); Isa 55:3 (Acts 13:34); and a combination of Isa 49:6 and 53:11 (Acts 26:22–23).

What specific passages lie behind the formula's claim regarding the fulfillment of the Scriptures through Jesus's resurrection specifically "on the third day"? A common view is that the reference is to Hos 6:2.[100] However, there are no quotations or allusions to this text anywhere else in the New Testament. What is most likely in view here is a remarkably consistent motif within the Old Testament, expressed in numerous passages, that "link 'the third day' with the day of salvation and divine manifestation."[101] This motif is present, among other passages, in:

Gen 22:4: Abraham raises his eyes to Mount Moriah "on the third day"
Gen 42:18: Joseph releases his brothers "on the third day"
Exod 19:11, 16: The Lord manifests himself on Mount Sinai "on the third day"

---

98. Bruce M. Metzger, "A Suggestion Concerning the Meaning of 1 Cor. xv.4b," *JTS* 8 (1957): 118–23; J. A. Schep, *The Nature of the Resurrection Body: A Study of the Biblical Data* (Grand Rapids: Eerdmans, 1964), 122 n. 77. This is considered as a possibility by Fitzmyer, 548–49; Ciampa & Rosner, 748.

99. So Fee, 807; Lindemann, 331; Garland, 686–87.

100. E.g. Kloppenborg, "Pre-Pauline Formula," 363.

101. Garland, 687. So also Lehmann, *Auferweckt*, 159–241, 262–90; Stephen Dempster, "From Slight Peg to Cornerstone to Capstone: The Resurrection of Christ on 'the Third Day' According to the Scriptures," *WTJ* (2014): 371–409 (with Hos 6:1–3 forming the scriptural capstone of this theme); Fee, 807; Bryan, *Resurrection*, 50; Schrage, 39–43; Lindemann, 331–32.

*The Cross and the Resurrection in the Apostolic Formula*

2 Kgs 2:17: Search for the assumed Elijah "for three days"
2 Kgs 20:1–11: Hezekiah's healing from mortal illness "on the third day"
Jonah 1:17: Jonah in the belly of the fish "three days and three nights"
Hos 6:2: The Lord will raise up Israel "on the third day"
Esth 5:1: Esther comes before the king for the salvation of her people "on the third day"

Among these, certain passages doubtless played a larger role than others, such as Jonah 1:17 (cf. Matt 12:38–40; 16:4; Luke 11:29–30) and perhaps Hos 6:1–2. But it is most likely the entire scriptural pattern that was in view. This pattern, as we have seen, was not the source of the confession that Jesus's resurrection took place "on the third day." Rather, the chronological fact of Jesus's resurrection on the third day after his death and burial led the first Christians to read these Old Testament passages in an entirely new way.[102]

There is another passage that most likely figured in the christological exegesis of the Old Testament as pointing forward to Jesus's resurrection "on the third day." All four gospels state that Jesus was crucified on a Friday (Matt 27:62; Mark 15:42; Luke 23:54; John 19:31). John's Gospel specifically states that the eve of Passover, Nisan 14, took place on Friday, the day of Jesus's crucifixion (John 18:28; 19:14). The Synoptic Gospels are usually thought to follow a different chronology, placing that Friday on Nisan 15, the day after Passover. However, a historically informed reading of the Synoptics reveals this is mistaken, for the events they narrate as occurring on Friday, including the activity of the Sanhedrin and Jewish officials (cf. Luke 22:47–23:23), the execution of criminals (cf. Acts 12:3–4), and the activities of burial (cf. Mark 16:1; Luke 23:56; John 19:42), were not possible after the feast had begun on the evening of Nisan 14. The "first day of the week" (Matt 28:1; Mark 16:2; Luke 24:1; John 20:1, 19), the day after the Sabbath, thus fell on Nisan 16. The Feast of Firstfruits, in which the first sheaf of the harvest portending the full harvest to come was offered to God, took place on Nisan 16 (Lev 23:9–14). As will be shown in the commentary on 15:20, we can conclude with a high degree of confidence that, in the christological exegesis assumed in this ancient confession, just as the Passover was understood as typically foreshadowing the crucifixion (1 Cor 5:7–8), so too the Feast of Firstfruits of Lev 23:19–24, which took place on the third day after Passover, was understood as a prophetic type foreshadowing the resurrection of Christ "on the third day."

---

102. See Wolff, 367–68.

EXCURSUS 1

# Purported Ancient Parallels to the Resurrection of Jesus

In recent decades, a number of New Testament scholars, most notably Dag Øistein Endsjø and Charles H. Talbert, have claimed to find an ancient parallel to the early Christian proclamation of the resurrection of Christ in the Greco-Roman tradition of the immortalization of divine-human heroes and their translation to heaven or the Elysian Fields. In the view of these scholars, this was a bodily and physical translation and immortalization. Thus, according to Endsjø, the "Christian dogma that Christ had gained bodily incorruptibility and immortality could therefore be seen by the Greek contemporaries ... as a repetition of what many mythical and historical men and women had already gone through."[1] Further: "That Jesus died, was resurrected, and became immortal, after which he disappeared from the ordinary world, was in complete agreement with a pattern we repeatedly find in the more general Greek tradition."[2] For, according to these scholars, among the ancient heroes we find "many mythical and historical examples of people who were resurrected from the dead and made physically immortal."[3]

However, this claim is founded on a radical misunderstanding of the nature of hero cults in antiquity. In the ancient understanding, the translation of heroes

---

1. Dag Øistein Endsjø, "Immortal Bodies, before Christ: Bodily Continuity in Ancient Greece and 1 Corinthians," *JSNT* 30 (2008): 431. See further Endsjø, *Greek Resurrection Beliefs and the Success of Christianity* (New York: Macmillan, 2009), 54–104; Charles H. Talbert, "The Concept of Immortals in Mediterranean Antiquity," *JBL* 94 (1975): 419–36; cf. Paul J. Brown, *Bodily Resurrection and Ethics in 1 Cor 15: Connecting Faith and Morality in the Context of Greco-Roman Mythology* (WUNT 2.360; Tübingen: Mohr Siebeck, 2014), 43–49, 89–94.

2. Endsjø, "Immortal Bodies," 423. Talbert similarly claims that Luke-Acts's account of Jesus's resurrection and ascension is "a portrayal of Jesus in the mythology of the immortals" ("Immortals," 435).

3. Endsjø, "Immortal Bodies," 425.

involved the divinization and immortalization of their soul or divine portion after its release from their mortal human body. These figures therefore do not provide a parallel to the resurrection of Christ.

We begin with the heroes of the so-called Heroic Age. Endsjø assumes that semi-divine figures such as Achilles, Menelaus, Castor, and Ino were, through translation, "made physically immortal."[4] But this was not the ancient conception. In fact, the tomb of each of these heroes was well known in antiquity, and their tomb and physical remains were centers of their cult. Let us take each of these four heroes in turn. According to the dominant myth in antiquity, Achilles's goddess mother Thetis snatched him from the pyre and translated him to the White Island, identified in antiquity with the paradisical Elysian Fields of Homer and with Hesiod's Isles of the Blessed. But in the myth, Achilles's translation to dwell immortally in the White Island of the Euxine Sea (Ps.-Apollodorus, *Ep.* 5.5; Pindar, *Ol.* 2.78–80; *Nem.* 4.49–50; Euripides, *Andr.* 1259–1262; *Iph. taur.* 435–438) was followed by the burning of his body to ashes (Pindar, *Pyth.* 3.100–103; *Isthm.* 8.54–67) and the burial of his bones (Ps.-Apollodorus, *Ep.* 5.5). The tomb of Achilles at Troy was widely known and venerated in antiquity (Philostratus, *Her.* 52.3–54.1; cf. Euripides, *Hec.* 35–44).[5] How was it believed that Achilles was translated, and yet his bones lay entombed at Troy? As Jonathan S. Burgess has shown, our texts presuppose "that Achilles was *both* buried and translated, and that this was possible through separation of the mortal from the immortal in Achilles."[6] A Thessalian hymn to Thetis regarding the translation, preserved in Philostratus's *Heroicus*, makes this explicit:

> Dark-eyed Thetis, Thetis, spouse of Peleus, you gave birth to your great son Achilles. As much of him as his mortal nature bore, Troy obtained, but as much as the child drew from your immortal lineage, the Euxine Sea holds. (*Her.* 53.10)[7]

According to the *Heroicus*, Achilles's human body perished and lies buried at Troy, but the divine portion of Achilles lives on immortally in the White Island. Achilles's immortality in the Isles of the Blessed does not include his human body but requires his release from it.

---

4. Endsjø, "Immortal Bodies," 423–25; cf. Endsjø, *Resurrection Beliefs*, 54–70.

5. On the tomb of Achilles, see Jonathan S. Burgess, *The Death and Afterlife of Achilles* (Baltimore: Johns Hopkins University Press, 2009), 111–31.

6. Burgess, *Afterlife of Achilles*, 101.

7. The Greek reads Θέτι κυανέε, Θέτι Πηλεία / τὸν μέγαν ἃ τέκες υἱὸν Ἀχιλλέα, τοῦ / θνατὰ μὲν ὅσον φύσις ἤνεγκε, / Τροία λάχε· σᾶς δ' ὅσον ἀθανάτου / γενεᾶς παῖς ἔσπασε, Πόντος ἔχει. For further discussion of this passage, see Burgess, *Afterlife of Achilles*, 101–2.

EXCURSUS 1

Menelaus and his wife Helen (the daughter of Zeus and Leda) were believed to have been translated to dwell together immortally in the Elysian Fields (Homer, *Od.* 4.561–569; Euripides, *Hel.* 1666–1669; Ps.-Apollodorus, *Ep.* 6.30). But the tomb of Menelaus and Helen at Therapne in Sparta was an important center of their cult (Pausanias, *Descr.* 3.19.9–10).[8] Likewise, belief in Castor's translation to Mount Olympus (Homer, *Od.* 11.298–304; Pindar, *Nem.* 10.55–90; Ps.-Apollodorus, *Bibl.* 3.137 [3.11]; Hyginus, *Fab.* 80) went hand in hand with the veneration of his remains at Sparta (Pausanias, *Descr.* 3.13.1; cf. Hyginus, *Fab.* 80). Ino, the daughter of Cadmus and the goddess Harmonia, was believed to have been translated and made immortal as the goddess Leucothea (Homer, *Od.* 5.333–338; Pindar, *Ol.* 2.28–30; Hyginus, *Fab.* 2, 4, 224). But her tomb and remains at Megara were widely known and revered (Pausanias, *Descr.* 1.42.7). Such is the case with the translation of all the other semi-divine beings of the Heroic Age to Elysium, such as Peleus (Pindar, *Ol.* 2.78; Euripides, *Andr.* 1254–1262), Cadmus (Pindar, *Ol.* 2.78; Euripides, *Bacch.* 1330–1339), and Rhadamanthys (Homer, *Od.* 4.563–565; Pindar, *Ol.* 2.71–76; *Pyth.* 2.73–74). The translation of these heroes was not thought to include their human bodies; these were left behind in their tombs.[9]

This was also the ancient understanding in the case of those heroes whose translation involved the disappearance of their bodies. The great model for these translation and disappearance narratives was the apotheosis of Heracles, who by translation from the burning pyre "ascended to immortality" (Hyginus, *Fab.* 36). Afterward his bones could not be found, for he had been translated from the human realm to join the gods (Diodorus Siculus, *Bib. hist.* 4.38.5, ἐξ ἀνθρώπων εἰς θεοὺς μεθεστάσθαι; cf. Ps.-Apollodorus, *Bibl.* 2.160 [2.7]). Endsjø assumes that the ancient conception was that Heracles was "translated, body and soul, to heaven."[10] But the understanding in antiquity was that Heracles had, through translation, shed or discarded his human body. Hyginus tells us that Heracles "discarded his human body and was translated to immortality" (*Fab.* 102). Philostratus asserts that, through translation, Heracles "left behind his human nature" (*Her.* 28.1, ἀπίων τῆς ἀνθρωπείας φύσεως). In Artemon's description, "Hercules, his mortal nature burned away, goes into heaven from Mt. Oeta in Thessaly, with the approval of the gods" (Pliny, *Nat.* 35.51). So also in Ovid's retelling of the myth, in his translation "the hero of Tiryns discarded his mortal limbs [*mortalis Tirynthius exuit artus*],

---

8. On the tomb of Menelaus, see L. R. Farnell, *Greek Hero Cults and Ideas of Immortality* (Oxford: Clarendon, 1921), 322–24.

9. Cf. John Granger Cook, *Empty Tomb, Resurrection, Apotheosis* (WUNT 410; Tübingen: Mohr Siebeck, 2018), 291–302 (on Protesilaus the hero).

10. Endsjø, "Immortal Bodies," 426; cf. Endsjø, *Resurrection Beliefs*, 58–60.

the human nature received from his mother Alcmene, so that not a trace of them remained. But in his divine nature, received from his father Zeus, he was received among the stars" (Ovid, *Metam.* 9.251–272; cf. Lucian, *Hermot.* 7).

This is also the sense in which the translation and disappearance of other legendary and historic hero figures were understood. Endsjø asserts that the hero Aristeas of Proconnesus was "most clearly resurrected" and became "physically immortal."[11] However, Aristeas, when he appeared after his translation and disappearance, did not appear bodily but as a ghost (φάσμα; Herodotus, *Hist.* 4.15.3) and as a raven (4.15.2).[12] Romulus, the legendary founder of Rome, is often cited by New Testament scholars as a figure believed to have been translated to bodily immortality.[13] Cicero in his *Republic* narrates the story of his disappearance and later appearance to Julius Proculus, announcing his new status as the god Quirinus (Cicero, *Rep.* 2.17–20; cf. *Leg.* 1.3–5). But later in the same work, Cicero says of Heracles and Romulus that "their bodies were not translated to heaven" (frag. of *Rep.* 3.32, preserved in Augustine, *Civ.* 22.4). According to Ovid, in the course of his translation to heaven Romulus's mortal body was dissolved (Ovid, *Metam.* 14.824–425, *corpus mortale per auras dilapsum tenues*). And the Stoic Balbus in Cicero's *De natura deorum* counts Romulus among the divine heroes whose souls (*animi*) are immortal (*Nat. d.* 2.62). It is presumably the same conception at work in the translations of the fifth-century heroes Empedocles (Diogenes Laertius, *Vit. phil.* 8.67–69) and Cleomedes (Pausanias, *Descr.* 6.9.6–8; Plutarch, *Rom.* 28.5–6).

Peregrinus (second century AD) is often cited as an example of one believed to be a bodily translated hero.[14] But Lucian, our source, is explicit that the body of Peregrinus perished in the flames of the pyre, and the stories of his apparitions afterward are understood as entirely consistent with this fact (Lucian, *Peregr.* 36–42). The situation is the same in the case of Apollonius of Tyana (first-century AD), to whom the emperor Caracalla consecrated a hero's shrine (ἡρῷον) in AD 215 (Dio Cassius, *Hist. rom.* 77.18.4). In Philostratus's *Life of Apollonius* (published shortly after the emperor's dedication of the shrine), the purpose of Apollonius's apparition is to reveal that his soul is immortal, confirming his Neopythagorean doctrine of the transmigration of the soul and of the body as its confining prison (*Vit. Apoll.* 8.31; cf. 5.42). As John Granger Cook observes, "Philostratus' narrative

11. Endsjø, "Immortal Bodies," 425; cf. Endsjø, *Resurrection Beliefs*, 62–63.
12. Similarly the hero Astrabacus, whose hero shrine or ἡρῷον is noted by Pausanias (*Descr.* 3.16.6), appeared after his death as a ghost (φάσμα; Herodotus, *Hist.* 6.69).
13. So Deborah Thompson Prince, "The 'Ghost' of Jesus: Luke 24 in Light of Ancient Narratives of Post-Mortem Apparitions," *JSNT* 29 (2007): 294–95; Talbert, "Immortals," 423; Endsjø, "Immortal Bodies," 426.
14. So Talbert, "Immortals," 425, 428–29; Endsjø, *Resurrection Beliefs*, 98–99.

shows that the disappearance of Apollonius' body was thoroughly compatible with the view that it was only the immortal soul which survived."[15]

The heroes, then, were understood as disincarnate souls freed from their human bodies, whether through death or translation. According to Philostratus's *Heroicus*, all the heroes are disembodied souls who, if they appear, appear as ghosts (*Her.* 18.1–2; 20.4–21.1; 33.47; 43.3). Dionysius of Halicarnassus explains the way the translation of heroes was understood in antiquity as follows: "the souls of all those who become demigods are said to have gone up to heaven, having left behind their mortal bodies" (*Ant. rom.* 7.72.13, ὅσων ἡμιθέων γενομένων αἱ ψυχαὶ τὰ θνητὰ ἀπολιποῦσαι σώματα εἰς οὐρανὸν ἀνελθεῖν λέγονται). Diogenes Laertius describes the Stoic teaching that "heroes are the departed souls of the good" (*Vit. phil.* 7.151, ἥρωας τὰς ὑπολελειμμένας τῶν σπουδαίων ψυχάς). Aetius informs us that Pythagoras, Plato, and the Stoics alike taught that "heroes are souls separated from their bodies" (*SVF* 2.1101, εἶναι δὲ καὶ ἥρωας τὰς κεχωρισμένας ψυχὰς τῶν σωμάτων). Philostratus in the *Heroicus* writes of the heroes: "You see, for souls so divine and blessed, the beginning of their life is their purification from the body" (*Her.* 7.3, ψυχαῖς γὰρ θείαις οὕτω καὶ μακαρίαις ἀρχὴ βίου τὸ καθαρεῦσαι τοῦ σώματος). The souls of heroes were universally conceived as a special class of disembodied souls, divine even prior to death and after death fully divinized. Thus the need to appease the hero through cult and sacrifice, for in the case of the hero, "his spirit after death is regarded as of supernormal power."[16]

In short, all the heroes whom Endsjø and others assume received bodily immortalization were, in the ancient conception, understood as disembodied souls, freed once for all from their physical human bodies. The translation of heroes therefore does not provide a parallel to the resurrection of Christ. Tellingly, the ancients, who (as we will see in chapter 6) knew the language of resurrection, never applied this language to these figures and only used the language of resurrection to deny its possibility. Far from providing a parallel to the resurrection, in the translation of heroes we find yet another expression of the universal ancient pagan belief that it is impossible for the human body to partake of immortality. Even these semi-divine heroes, in order to be divinized and immortalized, had to leave their physical human bodies behind.

Another claimed parallel to the resurrection of Jesus in antiquity is the purported widespread worship, in the mysteries and elsewhere, of "dying and rising gods" believed to have returned bodily from the dead. J. G. Frazer popularized

---

15. Cook, "Empty Tomb," 393.
16. Farnell, *Greek Hero Cults*, 343.

*Purported Ancient Parallels to the Resurrection of Jesus*

this thesis of dying and rising gods in antiquity over a century ago.[17] However, the majority of historians of religion today argue that such a conception of dying and rising deities did not exist in pagan antiquity, at least prior to the second century AD.[18] But recently John Granger Cook, in a thorough review of the relevant sources, has sought to rehabilitate Frazer's thesis in a modified form, arguing that the evidence "thoroughly justifies the continued use of the category of dying and rising gods."[19] Cook finds the evidence most clear in the cases of two gods in particular: the god Osiris in the mysteries of Isis and the god Dionysus in the mysteries devoted to him in conjunction with the worship of Apollo at Delphi.[20]

However, the evidence in our texts strongly supports the majority scholarly position. The ancient sources do not conceive of the gods in question as risen from the dead. Cook argues that, among these gods, "The resurrection of Osiris is the closest analogy to the resurrection of Jesus."[21] But in Plutarch's *Isis and Osiris*, our fullest account of the myths and rituals of the Isis cult, the body of Osiris remains in the tomb (Plutarch, *Is. Os.* 358a–b; 359a–d; 364f–365a), and Osiris remains in Hades, where he reigns as ruler of the underworld (382a–f; cf. 358b).[22] Osiris was the god of the dead, not of the living, and thus within the Greco-Roman world he was widely identified with the god Hades or Pluto (382e–f).[23] Cook claims that, next to Osiris, "The rebirth or resurrection of Dionysus also provides a fairly close analogy to the resurrection of Jesus."[24] Here again the information provided by Plutarch, who was priest of Apollo at Delphi and initiated into the mysteries of Dionysus, is decisive.[25] According to Plutarch, "the people of Delphi believe that

---

17. James George Frazer, *The Golden Bough: A Study in Magic and Religion* (New York: Macmillan, 1915).

18. See J. Z. Smith, "Dying and Rising Gods," *ER* 4:2535–40; M. S. Smith, "The Death of 'Dying and Rising Gods' in the Biblical World," *SJOT* 12 (1998): 257–313; and Terri Moore, *The Mysteries, Resurrection, and 1 Corinthians 15* (Lanham, MD: Lexington, 2018), 69–72. Jan N. Bremmer concurs that this conception emerged only in late antiquity and suggests that one factor was the influence of Christianity; see *The Rise and Fall of the Afterlife: The 1995 Read-Tucker Lectures at the University of Bristol* (London: Routledge, 2002), 52–55.

19. Cook, *Empty Tomb*, 56–143 (quote on 143). See also Cook, "Resurrection in Paganism," 65–73.

20. Cook, *Empty Tomb*, 74–87, 132–40.

21. Cook, *Empty Tomb*, 143.

22. Cf. Moore, *Mysteries*, 69–70; George C. Ring, "Christ's Resurrection and the Dying and Rising Gods," *CBQ* 6 (1944): 218–19. The key term for Osiris's postmortem renewal in Plutarch, *Is. Os.* 377b (ἀναβιόω) is used in Philostratus's *Heroicus* for the revival of the hero Protesilaus's soul apart from his body (*Her.* 58.2; cf. 2.9–11; 7.3).

23. On Osiris's role as god of the underworld within Egyptian thought, see Nicholas Perrin, "On Raising Osiris in 1 Corinthians 15," *TynBul* 58 (2007): 117–28.

24. Cook, *Empty Tomb*, 143.

25. For Plutarch's initiation into "the mystic symbols of the rites of Dionysus," see Plutarch,

the remains of Dionysus [τὰ τοῦ Διονύσου λείψανα] lie in state with them, beside the oracle" (365a).

Neither Osiris nor Dionysus, then, was understood by their worshipers to be resurrected from the dead. These gods died, but they did not rise from the dead. We similarly lack evidence for such claims regarding Persephone, Adonis, Attis, Mithras, and other deities. The postmortem experiences of the gods within these myths certainly suggest their continued survival and even flourishing within the underworld (Plutarch, *Is. Os.* 364f–365a; 377b), which corresponds to the promise within the mysteries of a blessed afterlife of the soul for their initiates. But, just as neither the mysteries nor the traditional rites offered the worshiper a hope of rising bodily from the dead, so too these gods were never portrayed as being resurrected to bodily life.

Thus, neither in the case of the translation of semi-divine heroes nor in the purported "dying and rising" gods of the mysteries do we find a conception of bodily resurrection. In neither case do we find a parallel to the resurrection of Jesus. In the ancient world into which it came, the early Christian proclamation of Jesus's resurrection from the dead was absolutely unique.

---

*Cons. ux.* 10. Cook questions whether Plutarch was an initiate (*Empty Tomb*, 137), but he is apparently unaware of this passage. In light of *Cons. ux.* 10, that Plutarch was an initiate of the mysteries of Dionysus is beyond dispute.

CHAPTER 4

## The Eyewitnesses in the Apostolic Formula

15:5–7

As we have seen, the primitive confession of 15:3–8 has a fourfold structure, delineated by the fourfold occurrence of the word ὅτι "that": (1) Christ died for our sins, (2) he was buried, (3) he rose again, and (4) he appeared to eyewitnesses. The fourth component of this structure, the appearances to eyewitnesses (15:5–8), has its own internal four-part structure marked out by the fourfold repetition of the verbal form ὤφθη "he appeared." In this way the different witnesses are carefully delineated into four groups: (1) Peter, then the Twelve (15:5); (2) over five hundred brothers and sisters at the same time (15:6); (3) James, then all the apostles (15:7); and (4) Paul last of all (15:8).

As we saw in the previous chapter, 15:3–7 is the pre-Pauline portion of the formula that Paul himself received in the 30s. First Corinthians 15:8 provides the addition of the appearance to Paul, with 15:3–8 thus forming the confession Paul transmitted to the Corinthians in AD 50. In this chapter we will consider the list of witnesses in 15:5–8 as a whole, explore the meaning of the key verb related to their eyewitness testimony, and then provide commentary on each verse up through v. 7. We will reserve the commentary on the appearance to Paul in v. 8 and Paul's remarks on the formula in vv. 9–11 for the following chapter.

THE LIST OF WITNESSES WITHIN THE FORMULA

The previous chapters of the letter have carefully prepared the way for this climactic list of apostolic eyewitnesses in 15:5–8. Paul has referred within the epistle (more than in any other letter) to the *apostolic body*: 4:9 (οἱ ἀπόστολοι), 9:5 (οἱ λοιποὶ

CHAPTER 4

ἀπόστολοι), and 12:28–29 (ἀπόστολοι). He has referenced *Cephas* in 1:12, 3:22, and 9:5. He has mentioned *the brothers of the Lord* in 9:5. And he has referred to *his own apostleship* in 1:1, 9:1–2, and 9:5 (all ἀπόστολος) and in 1:17 (ἀποστέλλω). Thus the only members of the list in 15:5–8 not mentioned previously in the epistle are the Twelve (15:5b) and the five hundred brothers and sisters (15:6). Strikingly, all four of those common to the prior portions of the letter and to 15:5–8 (Paul, the apostolic body, the brothers of the Lord, and Cephas) occur in 9:5, and there in the precise *reverse* of the order we find in the formula, forming a sort of chiasm with 15:5–8:

9:5       (a) Paul (i.e., "we") (b) "the rest of the apostles" (c) "the brothers of the Lord" (d) "Cephas"
15:5–8   (d') "Cephas" (c') "James" (b') "all the apostles" (a') Paul (i.e., "me")

Within the list of apostles and eyewitnesses in 15:5–8, only three apostles are named: Cephas, James, and Paul. This is extremely significant. In all four gospels and in Acts, Peter, James, and John form a core inner circle of apostolic pillars within the larger college of the twelve apostles. A shift within this core group took place when James, the brother of John, was martyred in 44 AD (Acts 12:2). Thereafter we see James, the brother (or cousin) of Jesus, although not a member of the Twelve, functioning among the inner circle of the apostles (Acts 12:17; 15:1–35; Gal 1:18–19; 2:9). And (as I have shown elsewhere) at the latest by the time of the apostolic council in AD 48/49, where Paul was given the right hand of fellowship by Peter, James, and John (Gal 2:6–9), Paul was included with Peter, James, and John among the core body of apostolic pillars (cf. 1 Clem. 5–6; Ign. *Rom.* 4.3; Irenaeus, *Haer.* 3.3.2).[1] Thus we see that the three apostles given special prominence among the list of witnesses in 15:5–8 are each members of this core body of apostolic pillars: Cephas, James, and Paul.

This fact illumines a hitherto perplexing question: the supposed contrast between the four gospels, where we learn that the first eyewitnesses of the resurrection were women, and the list of eyewitnesses in 15:5–8, where only male disciples are named. The consensus of scholars is that the names of women were omitted from the list of eyewitnesses in the apostolic formula for missionary purposes, to increase the credibility of the list within its ancient context, in which the validity of testimony by women was widely questioned. Scholars usually divide only on whether this was a commendable attempt at cross-cultural communication or a devious and cowardly acquiescence to sexism. But, as our discussion above has

---

1. For fuller discussion, see James P. Ware, *Paul's Theology in Context: Creation, Incarnation, Covenant, and Kingdom* (Grand Rapids: Eerdmans, 2019), 217–33.

shown, this analysis simply misses the point. None of the eyewitnesses, whether male or female, including the Twelve, are individually identified or named except Peter, James, and Paul. Their special prominence within the list reflects their function as the core or pillar apostles within the apostolic body.

There is also a further fascinating feature shared by the three named figures in this list, which we will explore more fully in excursus 2: each of the named apostles in this list of eyewitnesses would die as martyrs for their proclamation of the resurrection.

The appearances of Christ in 15:5–8 function to confirm the historical reality of 15:4b: Christ is risen from the dead. The argument is an empirical one based on eyewitness testimony and the evidence of the senses. This was famously denied by Karl Barth and has been routinely denied by many scholars since.[2] In our consideration of the historical and theological implications of the formula in excursus 2, we will discuss the mistaken nature of the theological misgivings that lead so many interpreters to deny the appeal to empirical evidence in this apostolic confession. But it is an unmistakable part of this early formula and of the way Paul uses it here.[3] This is the reason for the mention of *multiple* eyewitnesses: "the resurrection appearances to so many have a cumulative effect."[4] The eyewitnesses to the resurrected Jesus confirm the historical reality of his resurrection. The apostolic proclamation summarized in the formula was received by the Corinthians through faith (15:2; cf. 1:18–31), but its content was confirmed by empirical evidence and historical fact. This ancient confession proclaimed the physical resurrection of Jesus's crucified body from the tomb on the third day, an event in space and time verified by eyewitness testimony.

## The Meaning of ὤφθη in the Apostolic Formula

The verbal form ὀφθῆναι—the aorist passive of the verb ὁρᾶν "to see"—is a passive with middle intransitive meaning (i.e., "to appear").[5] Thus the recipients of the

---

2. Cf. Karl Barth, *The Resurrection of the Dead* (trans. H. J. Stenning; 1933; repr., Eugene, OR: Wipf & Stock, 2003), 130–45; similarly Lindemann, 336; Barrett, 341; Fee, 817; Andrzej Gieniusz, "Jesus' Resurrection Appearances in 1 Cor 15,5–8 in the Light of the Syntagma ὤφθη + Dative," *BibAn* 9 (2019): 481–92.

3. Rightly Jan Lambrecht, "Line of Thought in 1 Cor 15,1–11," *Greg* 72 (1991): 665–69; Lambrecht, "Three Brief Notes on 1 Corinthians 15," *Bijdr* 62 (2001): 29; Ciampa & Rosner, 748–49, 752; Schreiner, 304; Garland, 687; Hays, 256.

4. Schreiner, 304.

5. BDR §313; cf. Karl Olav Sandnes and Jan-Olav Henriksen, *Resurrection: Text and Interpre-*

CHAPTER 4

appearances are expressed not by means of ὑπό with the genitive but by a dative of indirect object. This construction of ὀφθῆναι with the dative is infrequent in pagan literature but quite common in the LXX and ancient Jewish writings.[6] The construction is used most frequently in the LXX as a virtual technical term for God's self-manifestation.[7] It is also used, in both the LXX and the New Testament, of the appearances of angels (Tob 12:22; Luke 1:11; 22:43). The construction ὤφθη plus the dative thus includes the idea of the revelatory action and initiative of the subject.[8] This is evident in Philo's exegesis of Gen 12:7, where he notes that this text says "not that the wise man saw God, but that God appeared to the wise man" (οὐχ ὅτι ὁ σοφὸς εἶδε θεόν, ἀλλ' ὅτι ὁ θεὸς ὤφθη τῷ σοφῷ), because Abraham could not see God unless God first chose to reveal and manifest himself to him (*Abr.* 79–80). The use of ὤφθη with the dative for each of the appearances of Jesus within the ancient formula thus portrays them not as haphazard events but rather as ones taking place by the sovereign revelatory will and initiative of Jesus himself. This verb within the formula fits with the other verbs used for Jesus's resurrection appearances in the New Testament, all of which in one way or another stress Jesus's own initiative in these encounters.[9] In these encounters, this ancient confession claims, the disciples did not catch sight of Jesus by circumstance or contrary to his will; rather, Jesus revealed himself to chosen apostles and eyewitnesses.

Some scholars hold that this intransitive and revelatory function of ὀφθῆναι plus the dative indicates that ὤφθη within the formula refers only to an unspecified revelatory event and does not necessarily include the idea of Jesus being seen

---

*tation, Experience and Theology* (Eugene, OR: Pickwick, 2020), 100; Hans-Joachim Eckstein, "Die Wirklichkeit der Auferstehung Jesu: Lukas 24,34 als Beispiel früher formelhafter Zeugnisse," in *Die Wirklichkeit der Auferstehung* (ed. Hans-Joachim Eckstein and Michael Welker; Neukirchen-Vluyn: Neukirchener, 2010), 14; Wolff, 368.

6. Gieniusz, "Resurrection Appearances," 483–87; Wolff, 368.

7. In the LXX, see Gen 12:7; 17:1; 18:1; 26:2, 24; 31:13; 35:1, 9; 48:3; Exod 3:2; Lev 9:23; Num 16:19; Judg 6:12; 3 Kgdms 3:5; 9:2; 11:9; 2 Chr 1:7; 3:1; 7:12; cf. without dative in Exod 16:10; Num 14:10; 20:6; Isa 40:5; 2 Macc 2:8. See Gieniusz, "Resurrection Appearances," 484–87; Sandnes and Henriksen, *Resurrection*, 100; Collins, 531–32; Wolff, 368; Eckstein, "Wirklichkeit," 15–16.

8. So Stephen T. Davis, "'Seeing' the Risen Jesus," in *The Resurrection: An Interdisciplinary Symposium on the Resurrection of Jesus* (ed. Stephen T. Davis, Daniel Kendall, and Gerald O'Collins; Oxford: Oxford University Press, 1997), 134: the verb ὤφθη "emphasizes the revelatory initiative of the one who appears." Likewise Gieniusz, "Resurrection Appearances," 484–87; Garland, 687–88; Wolff, 368; Fitzmyer, 549.

9. E.g., John 21:1, ἐφανέρωσεν ἑαυτόν; Acts 1:3, παρέστησεν ἑαυτὸν ζῶντα; John 20:19, 24, ἦλθεν ὁ Ἰησοῦς; John 20:26 and 21:13, ἔρχεται ὁ Ἰησοῦς; Matt 28:9, Ἰησοῦς ὑπήντησεν αὐταῖς; Luke 24:36, ἔστη ἐν μέσῳ; John 20:19, 26, ἔστη εἰς τὸ μέσον.

*The Eyewitnesses in the Apostolic Formula*

by the disciples.[10] But this is mistaken. Although primarily intransitive in force and emphasizing the initiative of the subject (i.e., "he appeared"), ὤφθη nonetheless also retained for ancient speakers its passive force as well (i.e., "he was seen"). This is evident from passages, in both the LXX and New Testament, where the passive ὤφθη is followed and explained by *active* forms of ὁράω with an accusative direct object identical to the subject of ὤφθη.[11] This phenomenon is found in the use of ὤφθη in the accounts of Jesus's resurrection appearances in Luke and Acts (cf. Luke 24:34, ὤφθη Σίμωνι, with 24:39, ἴδετε τὰς χεῖράς μου καὶ τοὺς πόδας μου; Acts 9:17, ὁ ὀφθείς σοι, with 9:27, εἶδεν τὸν κύριον). So here in the list of witnesses Paul will say ὤφθη κἀμοί (15:8, "he *appeared* also to me"), but earlier in the letter he says οὐχὶ Ἰησοῦν τὸν κύριον ἡμῶν ἑόρακα (9:1, "have I not *seen* Jesus our Lord?"). Clearly ὤφθη in these passages includes the passive idea of the subject being seen. The verbal form ὤφθη within the formula appears to have been carefully chosen, expressing both that Jesus, as an act of divine self-manifestation, *appeared* to the disciples, and that he *was seen* by them.

According to this ancient confession, then, the persons and groups enumerated in 15:5-8 saw the risen Lord. But in what way did they see him? Some scholars rather vaguely suggest that ὤφθη within the formula denotes something less than objective sight of a bodily risen Jesus. John M. G. Barclay, for instance, claims that while it is "not entirely clear" what the verb means here, "it seems to imply something rather less physical than the risen Jesus in Luke, who has a tangible body and eats fish."[12] Scholars who interpret ὤφθη within the confession in this way often hold that the appearances of Jesus enumerated in the formula are visions of a celestial Lord ascended to heaven in an ethereal or nonphysical mode, no longer in his crucified body.[13] Such a meaning of ὤφθη within vv. 5-8 of the

---

10. E.g., Gërard Claudel, *La confession de Pierre. Trajectoire d'une péricope évangélique* (Paris: Gabalda, 1988), 153-57.

11. Cf. Num 14:10, ἡ δόξα κυρίου ὤφθη ἐν νεφέλῃ, with 14:22, οἱ ἄνδρες οἱ ὁρῶντες τὴν δόξαν μου; Luke 1:11, ὤφθη δὲ αὐτῷ ἄγγελος κυρίου, with 1:12, καὶ ἐταράχθη Ζαχαρίας ἰδών; Luke 9:31, οἱ ὀφθέντες ἐν δόξῃ, with 9:32, εἶδον ... τοὺς δύο ἄνδρας.

12. John M. G. Barclay, "The Resurrection in Contemporary New Testament Scholarship," in *Resurrection Reconsidered* (ed. Gavin D'Costa; Oxford: Oneworld, 1996), 24.

13. E.g., Roy D. Kotansky, "The Resurrection of Jesus in Biblical Theology: From Early Appearances (1 Corinthians 15) to the 'Sindonology' of the Empty Tomb," in *Reconsidering the Relationship between Biblical and Systematic Theology in the New Testament* (ed. Benjamin E. Reynolds, Brian Lugioyo, and Kevin J. Vanhoozer; Tübingen: Mohr Siebeck, 2014), 83-107; H. Grass, *Ostergeschehen und Osterberichte* (Göttingen: Vandenhoeck & Ruprecht, 1962), 146-47; Daniel A. Smith, *Revisiting the Empty Tomb: The Early History of Easter* (Minneapolis: Fortress, 2010), 27-45; J. Holleman, *Resurrection and Parousia: A Traditio-Historical Study of Paul's Eschatology in 1 Corinthians 15* (NovTSup 84; Leiden: Brill, 1996), 143-44; Weiss, 349-50; Lindemann, 332.

CHAPTER 4

formula would directly contradict vv. 3–4, where, as we have seen, the language of this confession, through its choice of the verb ἐγείρω, is unambiguous that Jesus is physically risen from the tomb in the same body in which he was crucified. Such a contradiction would reduce the formula to unintelligibility.

But there is no conflict between vv. 3–4 and vv. 5–8 of the formula. The claim that ὤφθη refers within this confession to nonocular or visionary sight is simply mistaken. In fact, the verb ὁράω is the regular term in ancient Greek for what one sees with the eyes with ordinary ocular sight.[14] To be sure, this meaning is cancelable in certain contexts, and thus the verb is also frequently used of visionary sight or perception. In its passive form, the verb can be used of visionary experiences (Acts 16:9–10) and the sighting of the ghosts (εἴδωλα) of divinized demigods or heroes (Dionysius of Halicarnassus, *Ant. rom.* 6.13.4; Philostratus, *Her.* 18.1–2; 21.1; Ps.-Hippocrates, *Ep.* 27.130–131). But the passive can also refer to the normal ocular observation of persons in their physical bodies (e.g., Gen 46:29 LXX; 3 Kgdms 18:2 LXX; Acts 7:26). The verb ὤφθη does not in itself determine what kinds of seeing and objects are in view.[15] The context must determine this. And the context of this apostolic confession indicates that ὤφθη in 15:5–8 must refer, as many interpreters have recognized, to ordinary ocular sight of Jesus's physical body.[16] The following considerations are decisive:

(1) The sequence of verbs within 15:3–5 is critical. The verbs have a single subject: "Christ died . . . *he* was buried . . . *he* was raised . . . *he* appeared." According to the syntax of this ancient formula, the same crucified body of Christ that died (15:3) and was buried (15:4), rose again (15:4) and was seen (15:5) by the disciples. In this context, where the subject of ὤφθη is the crucified, buried, and risen *body* of Christ, this verb must refer to normal ocular sight of that body.

(2) Within the fourfold sequence of verbs in 15:3–5, the verb that immediately precedes ὤφθη in 15:5 is ἐγήγερται "he was raised," in 15:4. As we have seen, the evidence is decisive that this verb within the pre-Pauline confession denotes the revivification of the crucified and entombed body of Jesus. Since the subject of ἐγήγερται is the physical body of Jesus, the subject of the immediately following verb ὤφθη must be the body of Jesus now risen. The object of sight is Jesus's risen body of flesh and bone, and the verb ὤφθη must refer to ordinary physical vision.

14. See Schmidt, *Syn.*, 1:244–70.
15. Gieniusz, "Resurrection Appearances," 490; Davis, "Risen Jesus," 134–35; Jürgen Becker, *Die Auferstehung Jesu Christi nach dem Neuen Testament: Ostererfahrung und Osterverständnis im Urchristentum* (Tübingen: Mohr Siebeck, 2007), 110–11.
16. Rightly Ronald J. Sider, "St. Paul's Understanding of the Nature and Significance of the Resurrection in I Corinthians xv, 1–19," *NovT* 19 (1975): 139–40; J. A. Schep, *The Nature of the Resurrection Body* (Grand Rapids: Eerdmans, 1964), 124–27; Davis, "Risen Jesus," 134–35; Wolff, 369.

(3) Within 15:5-8, Paul's emphatically placed "last of all" (15:8) sharply distinguishes the appearances of the risen Lord to the apostles in vv. 5-8 from all later visions and ecstatic experiences, including Paul's own later "visions and revelations of the Lord" (2 Cor 12:1).[17] Visionary experiences of Jesus were widespread in the ancient church. But according to this ancient formula, the appearances of the risen Jesus to the apostles were the unique and unrepeatable foundation of the church. Throughout the New Testament, having seen the risen Jesus is the indispensable basis of apostleship (Luke 24:48; Acts 1:8, 21-22; 13:30-31; 1 Cor 9:1; 1 John 1:1-4). None of this is explicable if the appearances in 15:5-8 were regarded as mere visions. Rather, the appearances within the formula must refer, as in the gospels and Acts, to objective eyewitness encounters with Jesus in his physical and tangible risen body.

(4) The appearance to more than five hundred at the same time (15:6) is of decisive importance. For, as we will see in our commentary on this verse, apparitions or visions normally occur to a single individual, and there is no evidence (ancient or modern) for apparitions of the dead occurring to more than a few individuals at the same time. The verb ὤφθη in 15:6 cannot, therefore, refer to an apparition or to a vision but must refer to normal ocular and objective observation of Jesus in his physical body. The same is true of the appearances to the Twelve (15:5) and to all the apostles (15:7). And if this is the case in these instances, it must be the case throughout 15:5-8 as well. Therefore, the claim of so many scholars that ὤφθη in this confession can refer to apparitions or visions of a celestial Christ, ascended to heaven in a nonbodily form, is shown by this crucial clause within the formula to be impossible.

(5) Finally, that ὤφθη in 15:5-8 refers to regular ocular sight of Jesus in his risen flesh-and-bones body is evident in Paul's commentary on the formula in 15:15. Here Paul describes the implications if, as some at Corinth claim, there is no resurrection (15:12) and thus Christ has not been raised (15:13), as the apostles proclaim (15:14). If so, says Paul, "we are even found to be false witnesses [ψευδομάρτυρες] of God, for we have testified [ἐμαρτυρήσαμεν] against God that he raised the Christ, whom he did not raise, if indeed the dead are not raised" (15:15). Here, Paul describes the apostolic accounts of the appearances of Jesus with the legal language of *witness* (μάρτυς) and *bearing testimony* (μαρτυρέω). The apostles "have borne testimony" (ἐμαρτυρήσαμεν) that God raised Jesus from the dead; if this is not true, they are "false witnesses" (ψευδομάρτυρες). Similarly in 1:6, the apostolic proclamation of the resurrection is their "testimony to Christ" (τὸ μαρτύριον τοῦ Χριστοῦ). This is highly significant. In the ancient world, "testimony" is the lan-

---

17. Lang, 213-14, 216; Sandnes and Henriksen, *Resurrection*, 101-2; Schrage, 49.

CHAPTER 4

guage not of religious vision or myth but of facts and history (Cicero, *Leg.* 1.3–5).[18] In the Third Gospel and Acts, Luke uses the language of testimony to describe the claim of the apostles that they saw, touched, and ate and drank with the resurrected Lord (μάρτυς: Luke 24:48; Acts 1:8, 22; 2:32; 3:15; 5:32; 10:41; 13:31; 22:15; 26:16; μαρτύριον: Acts 4:13). In similarly describing the apostolic claim to have seen the Lord as witness and testimony (cf. 1 John 1:2, ἑωράκαμεν καὶ μαρτυροῦμεν), the formula makes clear that this is a claim involving objective physical observation, an empirical and historical claim regarding Jesus's crucified and risen body.

We will discover further evidence that ὤφθη within the formula refers to ordinary ocular sight of Jesus's fleshly body as we discuss each of the witnesses in turn below.

VERSE 5

*and that he appeared to Cephas, then to the Twelve.*

Verse 5 forms a highly compressed narrative in remarkable agreement with the fuller narratives within the four gospels. The confession's reference to Simon as "Cephas" is highly significant. According to all four gospels, Jesus himself bestowed on Peter, whose given name was Simon son of John, the new name of Cephas or "Rock" (Κηφᾶς or Πέτρος, Matt 10:2; 16:18; Mark 3:16; Luke 6:14; John 1:42). According to Matthew, Jesus gave to Peter the keys of the kingdom of God (Matt 16:16–19). In Luke, it was Peter for whom Jesus prayed that he might "strengthen his brothers" (Luke 22:31–32). And according to John, it was Peter whom Jesus commissioned to "shepherd my sheep" (21:15–19; cf. John 1:41–42). Peter is always first on the evangelists' lists of the apostles (Matt 10:2; Mark 3:16; Luke 6:14; Acts 1:13). These lists always use the name betokening Simon's primacy, Πέτρος or "Rock"; Matthew's list specifically designates Peter as the "first" (πρῶτος). Peter's name is likewise always first in the lists of the apostolic inner circle or pillars, Peter, James, and John (Matt 17:1; 26:37; Mark 5:37; 9:2; 14:33; Luke 8:51; 9:28). Peter's priority among the apostles is conspicuous in the narrative of Acts (Acts 1:15–26; 2:14–41; 3:1–4:31; 5:1–42; 8:14–25; 9:32–42; 10–12; 15:6–21) and was considered axiomatic within the ancient church (see Tertullian, *Mon.* 8; *Pud.* 21; Origen, *Hom. Exod.* 5.4; Cyprian, *Unit. eccl.* 4; *Ep.* 33.1; 43.5; Jerome, *Jov.* 1.26). Through the formula's designation of Simon as "Cephas," the name given to him by Jesus and signifying his primacy,

---

18. See the excellent discussion of this passage of Cicero's *De legibus* in John Granger Cook, *Empty Tomb, Resurrection, Apotheosis* (WUNT 410; Tübingen: Mohr Siebeck, 2018), 256–58.

the unique position of Simon among the apostles in the four gospels and Acts is reflected in this ancient confession as well.

In the formula, Jesus appears to Peter first among the apostles. That Jesus appeared first to Peter before the Twelve is also explicit in Luke's Gospel (24:34) and perhaps implicit in Mark (16:7). The formula's use of "Cephas" here in this list of resurrection witnesses may connect Peter's identity as the "Rock" specifically with his role as the first and chief apostolic witness to the resurrection.[19] It is noteworthy that neither the formula nor the gospels affirm that Jesus appeared first to Peter in an absolute sense, but only that he appeared first to Peter among the apostles (cf. Matt 28:9–10; Luke 24:13–35; John 20:11–18).[20] It was Mary Magdalene and the other women at the tomb to whom Jesus first appeared according to the gospels (Matt 28:9–10; John 20:11–18). As we saw above, these women are not absent from the formula for apologetic reasons, as often supposed, but because this ancient confession focuses on Jesus's appearances to the core pillars of the apostolic body: Peter, James, and Paul.

Next in the formula's list of eyewitnesses are the Twelve. The ancient formula's brief reference to the Twelve coheres with the much more detailed picture we get in the four gospels and Acts, which tell us that the Twelve were chosen by Jesus at the beginning of his ministry, were with him throughout his ministry in Galilee, and were eyewitnesses of the events in Jerusalem culminating in his passion, death, and resurrection (see conveniently Acts 1:21–22; 10:37–42; 13:31). As witnesses of Jesus from the time of his baptism by John until his ascension, who were authoritatively commissioned by the risen Lord, the Twelve formed the authoritative core of the apostolic body (Acts 1:2; 1:21–26; 2:14). Their unique foundational role is strikingly expressed in the climactic vision of the book of Revelation, where the gates of the new Jerusalem are inscribed with "the twelve names of the twelve apostles of the Lamb" (Rev 21:14). The Twelve, according to all our chief New Testament documents, formed the nucleus of the apostolic body.[21]

It was subsequent to his appearance to Peter, the formula affirms, that Jesus appeared to the Twelve. Likewise in Luke's narrative, after his appearance to Peter on the first day of the week (Luke 24:1, 34), Jesus appeared to "the eleven and those with them" on the evening of that same day (24:33–43). John's Gospel likewise records a resurrection appearance of Jesus to the Twelve on that evening

---

19. See Gerald O'Collins, "Peter as Witness to Easter," *TS* 73 (2012): 271–72.
20. Cf. Robertson & Plummer, 335.
21. For fuller but often uneven discussion, see Dietrich-Alex Koch, "The Origin, Function and Disappearance of the 'Twelve': Continuity from Jesus to the Post-Easter Community," *HvTSt* 61 (2005): 211–29.

CHAPTER 4

(John 20:19–23), and another appearance to them in Jerusalem eight days later (20:24–29). Matthew narrates a resurrection appearance of Jesus to the eleven in Galilee (Matt 28:16–20). It is likely that the words εἶτα τοῖς δώδεκα ("then to the Twelve") function within the formula to summarize a number of resurrection appearances to the Twelve, just as the confessional summaries in the book of Acts do (Acts 10:40–41; 13:30–31). In any case, that this striking chronological detail—Jesus's appearance first to Peter among the apostles, then to the Twelve—is shared by both this early confession and by the gospels is quite remarkable.[22]

The formula's designation "the Twelve" is, of course, not problematic despite the fact that the group numbered only eleven at the time of the appearances, for "the Twelve" served as their collective title.[23] John uses the identical designation (John 20:24, οἱ δώδεκα) in his resurrection narrative despite the defection of Judas. Thus the confession's language of "the Twelve," rather than posing a difficulty, reveals yet another connection of this early formula to the resurrection narratives in the gospels.

What was the time frame of the appearances to Peter and the Twelve? Luke and Acts tell us that the discovery of the empty tomb and appearances to Peter and the Twelve began on the third day after Jesus's death and burial and continued throughout a forty-day period closed by Jesus's ascension into heaven (Luke 24; Acts 1). Verse 5 of the formula says nothing explicit about the timing of the appearances to Peter and the other eleven apostles, except that they were sequential. But the formula's confession of Jesus's resurrection as "on the third day" (15:4) implies that the resurrection appearances began on that day. If so, this is in striking agreement with the claim of Luke's Gospel that the discovery of the empty tomb, the appearance to Peter, and an appearance to the Twelve all took place on the third day after Jesus's crucifixion (Luke 24:1–8, 21, 34, 36–43). Regarding the time frame of the appearances, the formula seems to presuppose a narrative such as we see in Luke's Gospel.

The resurrection narratives of the gospels and the confessional summaries in Acts indicate that the resurrection appearances of Jesus were extended encounters in which the disciples saw, heard, touched, and ate and drank with Jesus, demonstrating that he had risen from the tomb in his body of flesh and bones (Matt 28:8–20; Luke 24:36–43; John 20:11–29; Acts 1:3–4; 10:40–41; 13:30–31). How does the ancient formula in 1 Cor 15 match up on this score with the gospels and

---

22. The correspondences between 1 Cor 15:5 and the resurrection narratives in the four gospels are insufficiently recognized by Becker, *Auferstehung*, 111–13; Barclay, "Resurrection," 24; and C. F. Evans, *Resurrection and the New Testament* (London: SCM, 1970), 52–56.

23. Fee, 809; Ciampa & Rosner, 749; Thiselton, 1205; Keener, 124.

Acts? Let us take first the claim of the gospels that the apostles saw Jesus not in visions but with ordinary physical sight. As we have seen, in using the verbal form ὤφθη to describe the appearances of the risen Jesus to Peter and to the Twelve, the ancient formula likewise affirms that the disciples, with objective, ocular sight (15:5), looked upon the real and solid body of the risen Jesus (15:3–4), making them eyewitnesses to the historical fact of his resurrection (cf. 15:15). The appearance to all eleven apostles is extremely significant, for it is yet another way in which this ancient formula excludes the possibility that these resurrection appearances were mere apparitions or visions. For, as we will see in our discussion of 15:6, apparitions of the dead, whether in antiquity or modernity, normally occur to a single individual or, at most, a handful of individuals at the same time. The appearances, not only to Peter but also to all eleven apostles at once, thus confirm the unique bodily character of these appearances. In the claim that Peter and the Twelve were physical eyewitnesses of Jesus's bodily resurrection, this ancient confession and the gospels are one.

The other features of the gospel resurrection narratives and of Acts—the touching, eating with, and drinking with the risen Jesus—are not included in this bare summary. However, we have solid evidence that these elements were included in the fuller narrative that accompanied and expanded upon this terse formula. Verse 5 of the formula has a striking parallel in Luke 24:34: ὄντως ἠγέρθη ὁ κύριος καὶ ὤφθη Σίμωνι ("the Lord has truly risen, and he appeared to Simon"). As Hans-Joachim Eckstein has shown, this is an ancient, pre-Lukan confession that perhaps even predates our astonishingly early confession in 1 Cor 15:3–7.[24] In this pre-Lukan formula we find the identical verb and grammatical construction as in 1 Cor 15:5 (Luke 24:34, ὤφθη Σίμωνι; 1 Cor 15:5, ὤφθη Κηφᾷ). In Luke 24:34, the verb ὤφθη functions within a narrative in which the disciples not only physically see but also touch and eat with the risen Lord (Luke 24:33–43). Likewise in Acts 13:31, the verb ὤφθη—the same verb used in the formula—is not only explicitly used of ocular observation of Jesus's body of flesh and bones, risen without seeing corruption (Acts 13:30–31), but also recalls the disciples' experience of eating and drinking with the risen Lord (10:41). It seems impossible not to conclude that we are to understand ὤφθη within v. 5 of the formula in the same way as in this ancient confessional material embedded in Luke 24:34, Acts 10:41, and Acts 13:31, as involving touch and commensality (i.e., eating together) as well as physical sight.

According to the gospels and Acts, the risen Lord commissioned Peter and the Twelve as eyewitnesses able to testify to the truth of Jesus's resurrection from the dead (Luke 1:2; 24:48; John 21:24; Acts 1:8, 22; 2:32; 3:15; 5:32; 10:41; 13:31; cf. 1 John 1:2).

---

24. Eckstein, "Wirklichkeit," 9–16, 22–23.

CHAPTER 4

Here we find another feature held in common by both the gospel narratives and the ancient formula in 1 Cor 15. It is widely recognized that in the LXX and the New Testament, ὤφθη is always accompanied by *verbal revelation* of some sort.[25] This coheres with the gospels' portrayal of the risen Jesus's appearances to the disciples as involving not only the apostles seeing Jesus but also their commissioning by him to be his witnesses (Matt 26:16–20; Luke 24:44–49; John 20:19–23; 21:15–23; Acts 1:3–8; 10:40–42).

VERSE 6

*Then he appeared to more than five hundred brothers and sisters at the same time, of whom the majority remain until now, but some have fallen asleep.*

As we saw in our introduction to the formula in the previous chapter, although many scholars regard 15:6–7 as Paul's own addition, these verses (with the exception of Paul's comment in 15:6b) continue the original apostolic confession as Paul received it.

*Then he appeared to more than five hundred brothers and sisters at the same time.* Now in v. 6 we reach the second component within the fourfold structure of 15:5–8 and come to a new group of witnesses. The formula's direct linking of v. 6 to v. 5 with the simple conjunction ἔπειτα and the repetition of the verb ὤφθη indicate that the appearance of the risen Jesus to the five hundred was of the same character as those to Peter and to the Twelve, involving ocular sight of the physically risen Lord. But the former differs from the latter in the remarkable number involved: "he appeared to more than five hundred."[26] The great majority of these must have been non-apostles, for otherwise, as Jeffrey Peterson points out astutely,

---

25. See Wolff, 368; Garland, 688; Eckstein, "Wirklichkeit," 18–19.
26. The "improper" preposition ἐπάνω ("upon, over, above") normally takes a genitive (e.g., Matt 21:7; 28:2; John 3:31), but when used as here with numbers (in the sense "more than") there is no effect on the case (see BDR §§185 n. 7, 215.2; Rob., *Gram.*, 511, 642, 674). The dative here, as in 15:5, 7, and 8, denotes the recipients of the appearance. For the meaning "more than" as the sense of ἐπάνω in force in 1 Cor 15:6, see BDAG, s.v. "ἐπάνω" (2, "more than"); LSJ, s.v. "ἐπάνω" (VI, "above, more than"); Thayer, s.v. "ἐπάνω" (1.b, "beyond, more than"). For this sense, cf. Mark 14:5; Exod 30:14 LXX; Lev 27:7 LXX; Num 4:3 LXX. Robertson and many lexica refer to ἐπάνω when used with numerals as an adverb of number (e.g., Rob., *Gram.*, 674), but BDR is correct that it is more appropriately designated an improper preposition, for it modifies the number and not the verb (§215).

"the climactic, inclusive reference to 'all the apostles' in v. 7 must depict a second mass Christophany... and the first would lose the uniqueness that the mention of five hundred in v. 6 would suggest."[27] At the same time, it is virtually certain, as many scholars have surmised, that apostles were included in their number.[28] We can also assume that the designation ἀδελφοί is here used in its inclusive sense of both men and women.[29]

When and where did this appearance of the risen Jesus take place, and does it correspond to any of the appearances we know of from the gospels? As Luke-Acts indicates and (as we will see) Paul's language in 15:8 confirms, all of the appearances of the risen Lord (with the single exception of the extraordinary postascension appearance to Paul) took place within the forty-day period between Jesus's resurrection and his ascension (Luke 24:1–53; Acts 1:1–11). This appearance, too, must therefore have taken place among the many others that took place during this forty-day period leading up to the ascension.[30] As to place, some scholars suggest Jerusalem while others suggest Galilee. A number of interpreters suggest an identification of this event with the appearance of Jesus to the eleven in Galilee, recorded in Matt 26:16–20.[31] This is certainly possible, but the formula does not give us anything to go on here.

The ancient confession affirms that the risen Christ appeared to these more than five hundred disciples "all at once" (ἐφάπαξ). Placed last in the clause for emphasis, this adverb powerfully underscores the real, physical, objective character of this appearance.[32] Why is this so? The reason is that it rules out the possibility that this was a subjective vision, a hallucination, or even an "objective vision" sent by God. For in that case we would have a "synchronized ecstasy," that is, the same mental vision occurring to hundreds of individuals at the very same time, which is absurd.[33]

---

27. Jeffrey R. Peterson, "The Extent of Christian Theological Diversity: Pauline Evidence," *ResQ* 47 (2005): 6 n. 16. Cf. Becker, *Auferstehung*, 114.

28. See, e.g., Ciampa & Rosner, 749; Robertson & Plummer, 337; Godet, 2:334–35.

29. So Becker, *Auferstehung*, 117; Schrage, 57 n. 205; Wolff, 370 n. 118; Godet, 2:334; Thiselton, 1206.

30. For this and many other reasons, the identification of this event with the day of Pentecost, as narrated by Luke in Acts 2, is therefore excluded. For this thesis, see S. MacLean Gilmour, "The Christophany to More Than Five Hundred Brethren," *JBL* 80 (1961): 248–52; Gilmour, "Easter and Pentecost," *JBL* 81 (1962): 62–66. Critique of this thesis may be found in C. Freeman Sleeper, "Pentecost and Resurrection," *JBL* 84 (1965): 389–99; Wolff, 370.

31. Eric F. F. Bishop, "The Risen Christ and the Five Hundred Brethren (1 Cor 15,6)," *CBQ* 18 (1956): 341–44; Schreiner, 305 ("perhaps"); Thiselton, 1206 ("plausible"); Robertson & Plummer, 337 ("probably"); Godet, 2:334–35.

32. Cf. Fee, 810; Garland, 689.

33. Gieniusz, "Resurrection Appearances," 490, citing Raymond Brown, *The Virginal Conception and Bodily Resurrection of Jesus* (New York: Paulist, 1973), 91. Joseph W. Bergeron and Gary R. Habermas ask pertinently: "What are the odds that separate individuals in a group could

CHAPTER 4

It also rules out a real or imagined apparition of the dead, for there is no evidence, ancient or modern, of these occurring to more than a few individuals at the same time.[34] These facts serve to explain why this appearance to the five hundred was included in this brief formula. If Jesus's appearance to such an extraordinary number of witnesses cannot be explained as a vision, ghost, or apparition, the only plausible conclusion is that they saw Jesus in his risen body. This clause of the formula is thus of decisive importance regarding the repeated claim of so many scholars that ὤφθη in the formula refers to apparitions or visions of a celestial Lord, ascended to heaven in a nonbodily mode.[35] For this claim is ruled out by v. 6 of the formula.

Another possibility, however, has been suggested by Dale Allison.[36] Allison revives an earlier suggestion of Peter J. Kearney that ἐπάνω in 15:6 be taken not with the numeral but as an adverb of place "above," with the verb ὤφθη "appeared," and that the clause refers to a vision of Jesus in the sky.[37] Allison believes it is "a good bet" that this involved a natural phenomenon, specifically a cluster of clouds in the sky that these disciples mistakenly believed was Jesus.[38]

Allison's thesis is not a plausible interpretation of this clause of the formula for several reasons: (1) The verbal form ὤφθη nowhere in the LXX, ancient Jewish literature, or New Testament refers to a vision in the sky.[39] (2) The claim that ἐπάνω can function as an adverb of place in 15:6 is baseless. As all modern lexica and reference grammars concur, ἐπάνω in 15:6 must be construed with the numeral πεντακοσίοις "five hundred," and means "more than."[40] (3) Within the ancient Jewish context, as we have seen, an appearance denoted by ὤφθη always included a verbal, auditory component, which would not be possible in the case of a cloud vision in the sky. (4) The first Christians, who reported this appearance

---

experience simultaneous and identical psychological phenomena mixed with hallucinations?" See "The Resurrection of Jesus: A Clinical Review of Psychiatric Hypotheses for the Biblical Story of Easter," *ITQ* 80 (2015): 161.

34. See Jake H. O'Connell, *Jesus' Resurrection and Apparitions: A Bayesian Analysis* (Eugene, OR: Resource, 2016), 224–25; Celia Green and Charles McCreery, *Apparitions* (London: Hamilton, 1975), 41.

35. E.g., Kotansky, "Sindonology," 83–107; Grass, *Ostergeschehen*, 146–47; Holleman, *Resurrection and Parousia*, 143–44; Lindemann, 332; Smith, *Empty Tomb*, 27–45.

36. Dale C. Allison Jr., *The Resurrection of Jesus: Apologetics, Polemics, History* (New York: Bloomsbury, 2021), 72–76, 249–51.

37. See Peter J. Kearney, "He Appeared to 500 Brothers (I Cor xv 6)," *NovT* 22 (1980): 264–84 (esp. 265–67).

38. Allison, *Resurrection*, 249–50.

39. Wolff, 370 n. 115.

40. See BDR §§185 n. 7, 215.2; Rob., *Gram.*, 511, 642, 674; BDAG, s.v. "ἐπάνω" (2); LSJ, s.v. "ἐπάνω" (VI); Thayer, s.v. "ἐπάνω," (1.b).

and included it in this ancient formula, were not utter fools, so as to consider a cloud formation in the sky to be evidence that Jesus had been raised from the dead (15:4). (5) The apostle Paul was not an utter fool; yet it would be difficult to escape the conclusion that he was, if he encouraged the Corinthians to verify this information with individuals from among the five hundred (15:6b), when they could testify to nothing more than cloud shapes in the sky.

Allison argues that it is impossible that such a large crowd could see, hear, or identify an "earthbound" Jesus. "There were no concert projection screens back then."[41] This argument is without historical basis. Large crowds saw, heard, and were taught by Jesus in the course of his itinerant teaching ministry (Matt 5:1–2 with 7:28–29; 13:12, 34–36; 14:13–23; Mark 4:1–2; Luke 6:17–20 with 7:1; 11:27–28). At the trial of Socrates in 399 BC, the jury of five hundred (πεντακόσιοι) saw Socrates, heard his defense, verbally interacted with him, and each individually rendered their verdict (Plato, *Apol.* 17a1–18a6; 20d4–21a8; 30a7–30d5; 33c7–34b5; 35e1–36b2; 37e3–38b9; 39e1–42a5). Epictetus informs us that it was not unheard of for philosophers to lecture in outdoor settings to audiences numbering five hundred (πεντακόσιοι) or even up to a thousand (χίλιοι) persons (*Diatr.* 3.23.19; 3.23.35). The ancient evidence reveals the utter fallacy of Allison's argument.

*of whom the majority remain until now.* Paul adds an explanatory comment to the formula in 15:6b. Here οἱ πλείονες denotes "the majority."[42] They "remain" (μένουσιν) in the sense that they are still living (cf. John 21:22–23; Phil 1:25). As the great majority of scholars have recognized, Paul's addition in 15:6b has an evidential purpose— the Corinthians are invited to interrogate individuals among the five hundred for themselves.[43] A few scholars have denied that the clause here has an evidential function.[44] Paul gives neither the names nor addresses of these witnesses, they argue, and so the idea that they could be questioned makes little sense.[45] For the same reason Dale Allison, who agrees with the majority that the clause is evidential in purpose, nonetheless considers Paul's implicit invitation as nothing more than an empty rhetorical ploy.[46] Jürgen Becker has pointed out the miscalculation in this argument. Paul is envisioning the opportunity for cross-examination as taking place

---

41. Allison, *Resurrection*, 250.
42. BDR §244.3.
43. So Becker, *Auferstehung*, 115; Lambrecht, "Three Brief Notes," 29; Schrage, 57–58; Ciampa & Rosner, 749–50; Fee, 810; Godet, 2:335; Weiss, 350; Hays, 257; Wolff, 371–72; Thiselton, 1205; Robertson & Plummer, 337; Schreiner, 305.
44. So Lindemann, 333; Garland, 689–90.
45. Garland, 689; Lindemann, 333.
46. Allison, *Resurrection*, 74.

CHAPTER 4

when members of the five hundred, many of whom were most likely missionaries and evangelists, visited the congregation at Corinth. Paul mentions this possibility only in connection with the five hundred and not the other witnesses in the list, Becker suggests, because out of such a large group the likelihood of regular visits by individuals among them to Corinth was quite high.[47]

Dale Allison imagines that Paul himself knew very few of the five hundred.[48] But this is clearly mistaken. Paul's note that most of them remained alive to the present presumes his knowledge of who among them were alive and who had died, and thus indicates that he had recent contact with a great many of them or with others in direct contact with them. Paul's personal knowledge of many among the five hundred adds further force to their testimony and to this clause of the formula.

The more one considers the appearance to more than five hundred, the more one appreciates the reasons for its inclusion in this terse formula. To a striking degree, it is stubbornly resistive to the reductive theories—whether vision, hallucination, or apparition—whereby ancient (or modern) skeptics might seek to dismiss it. In six Greek words, this clause of the formula excludes the historical possibility that the appearance it reports was an apparition or vision. It bears witness to a historical event explicable only by Jesus's bodily resurrection from the dead. It is a crucial piece of this early confession.

*but some have fallen asleep.* The primary purpose of Paul's comment on the formula in 15:6b is, as we have seen, an evidential one—it is an implicit invitation to verify the testimony of the five hundred through the interrogation of individuals within that body. But in this final clause of Paul's comment we discover a secondary function that prepares for the larger argument of the chapter to follow.[49] For the verb κοιμάω, used with reference to believers who have died, will occur three more times within the chapter (15:18, 20, 51). As we will see in our fuller discussion of 15:18, this verb, derived from the verb κεῖμαι "to lie" and meaning "to *lie down* in sleep," depicts the bodies of the faithful departed as *lying* asleep in death, waiting to be *roused up* (ἐγείρω) at the resurrection (2 Macc 12:44–45; 1 En. 92.3; Matt 27:52; John 11:11; 1 Thess 4:13–15).[50] As such, the verb κοιμάω, as we will see, will form a key part of the language of *bodily* resurrection within the argument of the chapter, in which

---

47. Becker, *Auferstehung*, 114–15. Cf. Richard Bauckham, *Jesus and the Eyewitnesses: The Gospels as Eyewitness Testimony* (Grand Rapids: Eerdmans, 2006), 37, 308.

48. Allison, *Resurrection*, 73: He writes: "one? two? three?"

49. Rightly Schrage, 57–58.

50. The contrast in 15:6b between those who remain and those who have fallen asleep is amplified by the addition of an adjunctive καί before ἐκοιμήθησαν in the textual witnesses A, 33, 1175, 2464, and the correctors of ℵ and D. The omission, however, has far superior manuscript support (P[46] B 1739 1881 and the original hands of ℵ and D) and is to be preferred.

*The Eyewitnesses in the Apostolic Formula*

"Christ has been raised from the dead, the firstfruits of *those who sleep*" (15:20, τῶν κεκοιμημένων). Paul is here already preparing the ground for 15:18, 20 and 51 and the major theme of the chapter: the resurrection of Christ is his triumph over death, entailing the final victory over death for all who belong to Christ.

Verse 7

*Then he appeared to James, then to all the apostles.*

*Then he appeared to James.* Because 15:7 follows the identical structure as 15:5 (a representative individual, then the conjunction εἶτα followed by an associated group), a few exegetes in the past have speculated that 15:7 was originally an alternative or competing tradition to 15:5. But clearly the more natural explanation is that 15:7 continues the set pattern and structure of 15:5 because it formed an integral part of the original apostolic confession. The James to which the formula refers is James of Jerusalem, whom Paul in Galatians calls "the brother of the Lord" (Gal 1:19). He was most prominent among "the brothers of the Lord" mentioned earlier in the epistle (1 Cor 9:5). Present among the first disciples at Jerusalem prior to Pentecost (Acts 1:14), he became in Peter's absence the preeminent leader of the church at Jerusalem (Acts 12:17; 15:13; 21:18; Gal 2:13). Paul not only includes him among the apostles (Gal 1:19; 1 Cor 9:5) but also among the core group of apostolic pillars consisting of Peter, James, and John (Gal 2:9).

As late as a few months before the crucifixion, James was not a follower of Jesus (John 7:2–9). It is therefore likely, although not certain, that this appearance was the means of his conversion. The appearance to James is mentioned nowhere else in the New Testament. But it formed an important part of the apostolic confession that Paul "received" (1 Cor 15:3), doubtless at his fifteen-day conference with Peter and James at Jerusalem (Gal 1:18–19). Paul had multiple contacts with James and thus had multiple opportunities to hear the account of this appearance from James's own lips (Gal 1:19; 2:1–10; cf. Acts 15:4–31; 21:18). The delegates from Corinth to be chosen to take the collection for the saints to Jerusalem would also themselves shortly have opportunity for direct contact with James (1 Cor 16:1–4).[51]

*then to all the apostles.* Paul's letters and Acts make clear that although the Twelve formed the nucleus of the apostolic body, this body was *wider* than the Twelve. The Twelve were at the center of a larger confraternity of apostles, all of whom were (like the Twelve) eyewitnesses of the risen Lord and commissioned by him. This

---

51. As pointed out by Becker, *Auferstehung*, 114–15.

CHAPTER 4

latter group included James (Gal 1:19, 2:9), Barnabas (Acts 14:4, 14; cf. 1 Cor 9:6), Barsabbas (Acts 1:21–26), and others whose names have not come down to us. It is this wider college of apostles to which the ancient confession refers to here.[52] As with the Twelve in 15:5, it is unclear whether the formula refers here to a single appearance or summarizes multiple appearances to the whole body of apostles. In any case, Jesus's appearance to the wider group of "all the apostles" is striking evidence for the physical and bodily character of Jesus's resurrection appearances. For, as we saw in the commentary on v. 6, apparitions of the dead normally occur only to a single individual, and there is no evidence (ancient or modern) that apparitions or visions are experienced by more than two, three, or four persons at a time. The appearance to "all the apostles," a group numbering at the very least in the middle teens, therefore confirms the unique, bodily character of the appearances of the risen Lord to the apostles.

As we have seen, this reference to "*all* the apostles" (τοῖς ἀποστόλοις πᾶσιν) is another piece of evidence that 15:6–7 is not Paul's expansion but belonged to the original apostolic confession he "received" (15:3). For Paul would hardly coin such an expression, which might seem to exclude him from the body of the apostles. The expression also provides further evidence for the astounding antiquity of this confession, for it must go back to a time before the appearance to Paul, when the number of apostles appeared to be closed. But why would the body of apostles be considered definitively closed at such a remarkable early date? The only adequate historical explanation is that the wider narrative context of this apostolic confession corresponded to the narrative we find in Luke-Acts of resurrection appearances commencing on the first Easter Sunday, continuing over a forty-day period, and coming to a close at Jesus's ascension into heaven (Luke 24; Acts 1:1–3, 21–22; 10:37–42; 13:31). That the resurrection appearances recounted in 15:5–7 all occurred prior to the ascension provides further evidence that these appearances correspond to the kind recorded in the four gospels and Acts—extended encounters in which the disciples saw, heard, touched, and ate and drank with the risen Jesus (Matt 28:8–20; Luke 24:39–43; John 20:11–29; Acts 1:3–4; 10:40–42).

---

52. Rightly Fee, 811–12; Ciampa & Rosner, 750; Collins, 537; Thiselton, 1207–8. The placement of πᾶς in predicate position after its substantive puts the stress on the noun and thus here on the apostolic body (BDR §275 n. 5).

CHAPTER 5

## Paul the Final Eyewitness in the Apostolic Formula

15:8–11

In this chapter we conclude our analysis of the apostolic confession in 15:3–8 with commentary on the final verse of the formula in 15:8 and Paul's closing remarks on the confession in 15:9–11. The chapter is followed by an excursus on the massive historical and theological ramifications of this astonishingly early apostolic formula.

VERSE 8

*And last of all, as if to one whose birth had previously failed, he appeared also to me.*

Verse 8 is clearly an addition to the confession that Paul received at his conference with Peter and James in Jerusalem in AD 37 or 38, within four to five years of the founding events of Jesus's crucifixion and resurrection. But, just as clearly, it was part of the confession he transmitted to the Corinthians in AD 50, approximately seventeen years after the first Good Friday and Easter (15:3).

*And last of all.* A few interpreters deny that ἔσχατον here is chronological (i.e., "last"), maintaining that it refers to Paul as the "least" of the apostles (cf. 15:9).[1] But this interpretation is not grammatically tenable. First, ἔσχατον is an adverb modifying ὤφθη, not an adjective referring to Paul; the latter would require ἐσχάτῳ.[2]

---

1. Collins, 537; apparently Fitzmyer, 552.
2. Peter R. Jones, "1 Corinthians 15:8: Paul the Last Apostle," *TynBul* 36 (1985): 17.

CHAPTER 5

Second, ἔσχατον δὲ πάντων ("and last of all") occurs as the last in a series, preceded by ἔπειτα "then," in both 15:6 and 15:7 (cf. 1 Cor 15:23–26; Mark 12:20–22). The great majority of interpreters have recognized ἔσχατον here as chronological, meaning "last."[3] It describes the appearance to Paul as the last in a series of appearances to eyewitnesses tabulated in 15:5–8: Peter, the Twelve, the more than five hundred, James, and all the apostles.[4] Moreover, the word ἔσχατος does not merely denote the last in a series but that which is final and conclusive.[5] Paul's emphatically placed "and last of all" (ἔσχατον δὲ πάντων) thus sharply distinguishes the appearances in the list, including the appearance to Paul, from all later visions and ecstatic experiences, including Paul's own subsequent "visions and revelations of the Lord" that he reports in 2 Cor 12:1–7. The resurrection appearances of Christ to the apostles and other eyewitnesses are unique and unrepeatable—the foundation of the church.[6]

*as if to one whose birth had previously failed.* The noun ἐκτρώματι is in apposition to the pronoun κἀμοί ("also to me"); the formula hereby provides a further description of the apostle. The unusual and strongly cautionary ὡσπερεί "just as if," a *hapax legomenon* in the New Testament, serves notice that this designation is only a metaphor or analogy.[7] The placement of the apposition prior to the pronoun adds further emphasis and indicates that this description of the apostle is of great importance.[8]

The apostle refers to himself as an ἔκτρωμα, an "untimely birth" or "miscarriage." What is the sense of this term, as Paul uses it here? What is the point of the analogy? How does this analogy relate to the context of 15:8 and to Paul's identity as the last of all to whom the risen Christ appeared? Despite extensive study, these

---

3. Schrage, 61; Jones, "Paul the Last," 11–16; Barrett, 344; Garland, 690.

4. The genitive plural πάντων is masculine, not neuter (cf. Robertson & Plummer, 339), and refers to the whole previous list of witnesses, not to the apostles alone. Fuller discussion may be found in Schrage, 61 n. 226.

5. See Schmidt, *Syn.*, 4:527 (§194.3); Cremer, 268.

6. Rightly Martin Hauger, "Die Deutung der Auferweckung Jesu Christi durch Paulus," in *Die Wirklichkeit der Auferstehung* (ed. Hans-Joachim Eckstein and Michael Welker; Neukirchen-Vluyn: Neukirchener, 2010), 38; Schrage, 60–62; Jones, "Paul the Last," 3–34; Wolff, 373; Hays, 257; Garland, 690–91; Schreiner, 306. Paul's use of the perfect tense in 1 Cor 9:1 (οὐχὶ Ἰησοῦν τὸν κύριον ἡμῶν ἑόρακα) expresses the same conception of the foundational and unrepeatable character of these resurrection appearances; see J. A. Schep, *The Nature of the Resurrection Body: A Study of the Biblical Data* (Grand Rapids: Eerdmans, 1964), 126.

7. The adverb is a "statement of comparison, with component of caution, *like, although, as it were*" (BDAG, s.v. "ὡσπερεί"); cf. Thayer, s.v. "ὡσπερεί" ("as, as it were"); LSJ, s.v. "ὡσπερεί" ("just as if").

8. See BDR §453 n. 6; Kühner-G., 2.1:282 (§406.2).

remain highly vexed questions. The answers proposed have proven unconvincing, either because they are not in agreement with the known lexical meaning of the term Paul employs, or because they fail to explain how Paul's use of this term relates to the context. First Corinthians 15:8 is a true *crux interpretum*, for it raises a number of seemingly insoluble problems, to which a satisfactory solution has yet to be offered. However, I believe a close examination of the verse will resolve these questions and reveal the intention of this clause within the formula.

*The Word ἔκτρωμα in Ancient Greek Literature*

Let us begin with the ancient lexical evidence for the meaning of the word ἔκτρωμα outside its use in 1 Cor 15:8. Here the evidence is quite clear and not generally contested. Our evidence includes not only instances of the word ἔκτρωμα but also cognate terms such as ἐκτιτρώσκω, ἔκτρωσις, ἐκτρωσμός, and τρωσμός. A number of ancient writers also provide a definition of the term.

All of the terms mentioned above denote a miscarriage or failed birth. The verb ἐκτιτρώσκω "miscarry" describes this failure of the birth process, and the nouns ἔκτρωσις, ἐκτρωσμός, and τρωσμός (each translated as "miscarriage") name it, with ἔκτρωσις being the noun most commonly used. The latter is the favored term of the medical author Soranus (e.g., *Gyn.* 1.44, 52; 3.17), and τρωσμός the term favored by the medical writer Hippocrates (e.g., *Coac.* 532; *Nat. mul.* 2; *Oct.* 9). Hippocrates tells us that the term τρωσμός is normally used of pregnancies that are cut short later than the first forty days of gestation (*Oct.* 9). Soranus apparently follows the same or a similar time frame when he tells us that the word ἔκτρωσις is properly used of pregnancy loss that occurs in the second month or later (*Gyn.* 3.47).

The word ἔκτρωμα refers to a child brought forth prematurely before it has developed and is capable of life (Aristotle, *Gen. an.* 773b; Num 12:12 LXX; Job 3:16 LXX; Eccl 6:3 LXX; Zosimus of Panopolis, *Cheir.* 2.203). Thus, according to Severian of Gabala, the ἔκτρωμα is a fetus "cast forth before it is fully formed and has received its fitting time in the womb, and is unable to live" (*Frag. 1 Cor.* 272).[9] This meaning of the term is also evident in the use of ἔκτρωμα within the LXX and other Greek versions of the Hebrew Bible to translate the word *nēpel* or "miscarried child" (Job 3:16 LXX; Eccl 6:3 LXX; Ps 58:9 Theodotion [= Ps 57:9 LXX]).[10] There

---

9. Cf. the definitions of the term in Hesychius, *Lex.* ε 1770 ("a child lifeless and untimely, expelled from its mother") and in *Etymologicum Gudianum* ε 448 ("a miscarriage coming forth from the womb untimely and undeveloped").

10. Cf. Matthew W. Mitchell, "Reexamining the 'Aborted Apostle': An Exploration of Paul's Self-Description in 1 Corinthians 15.8," *JSNT* 25 (2003): 473–75. On miscarriage in the ancient

is virtual unanimity within the scholarly literature regarding this meaning of the word in antiquity.[11]

The ἔκτρωμα is untimely (cf. Hesychius, *Lex.* ε 1770, παιδίον νεκρὸν ἄωρον) in that the child is expelled from the uterus before it can properly develop (Zosimus of Panopolis, *Cheir.* 2.203). But ancient medical writers sharply distinguish ἔκτρωσις from premature birth (ὠμοτοκία). Soranus writes that "miscarriage [ἔκτρωσις] is the perishing of the fetus after the second or third month of pregnancy, but premature birth [ὠμοτοκία] is the bearing of a child very near its perfected development but prior to the allotted time" (Soranus, *Gyn.* 3.47; cf. 3.26, 40). In premature birth, the child is endangered and often dies, but sometimes is viable and lives (Soranus, *Gyn.* 3.47; Hippocrates, *Oct.* 1–13). But in ἔκτρωσις, the child does not properly develop (Eustathius, *Comm. Il.* 4.298; Olympiodorus, *Comm. Job* 44) and is incapable of life (Aristotle, *Gen. an.* 773b; cf. Job 3:16 LXX; Eccl 6:3 LXX). The medical writers and others thus normally *contrast* miscarriage (τρωσμός or ἔκτρωσις) with birth or τόκος.[12] The miscarriage is thought of as a failed or frustrated birth process. The child fails to develop properly and is expelled from the womb, nonviable and incapable of life. The ἔκτρωμα is a miscarriage or failed birth.

*The Problem of Paul's Analogy and the Proposed Solutions*

There is, then, little or no controversy regarding the lexical meaning of ἔκτρωμα outside 1 Cor 15:8. But there is, by contrast, much perplexity among interpreters regarding Paul's application of the metaphor in 1 Cor 15:8. The problem is that the known lexical meaning of this word, and the context in which Paul uses it in this verse, seem to involve an impossible contradiction. The preceding context of the chronological list of apostolic witnesses to the resurrection (15:5–7) followed by the appearance to Paul "last of all" (15:8a) would seem to require that the words ὡσπερεὶ τῷ ἐκτρώματι refer to late or delayed birth. A number of modern translations express or accommodate this sense, including the KJV ("as to one born out of due time"), Phillips ("as if to one born abnormally late"), LUT ("als einer unzeitigen Geburt"), NRSV ("as to one untimely born"), and NAB ("as one born out of the nor-

---

Jewish context, see Ilona Rashkow, "'Ones Who Have Fallen Out' (*NEFEL*): Spontaneous, Accidental, and Intentional Miscarriage Laws in Ancient Israel," *JBQ* 50 (2022): 255–63.

11. See, for example, *TLNT* 1:464–66; David J. Williams, *Paul's Metaphors: Their Context and Character* (Peabody, MA: Hendrickson, 1999), 57–58; Harm W. Hollander and Gijsbert E. van der Hort, "The Apostle Paul Calling Himself an Abortion: 1 Cor. 15:8 within the Context of 1 Cor. 15:8–10," *NovT* 28 (1996): 227–28; M. W. Mitchell, "Reexamining," 470–73.

12. E.g., Hippocrates, *Nat. mul.* 1.63; *Mul.* 1.64; 2.1, 13; Aretaeus, *Sign. diut.* 2.11.10; Soranus, *Gyn.* 3.26, 40, 47; cf. Leontius, *Contra Nestorianos* 3.1605: ἔκτρωσις contrasted with γέννησις.

mal course"). However, as much as the context might seem to demand it, very few contemporary interpreters have taken this line.[13] The difficulty with it is the lexical meaning of the word Paul employs. This interpretation, as Garland notes, "is ruled out because an ἔκτρωμα is always born prematurely, never late."[14] More precisely, the word denotes a child whose process of birth is cut short by miscarriage. Markus Schaefer has sought a way out of the difficulty, arguing that Paul in 15:8 alludes to Hos 13:13 MT, where Ephraim is depicted as an unwise child who refuses to be born, and that this allusion determines the meaning of ἔκτρωμα in 1 Cor 15:8 as "Spätgeburt" (late birth).[15] But such a meaning, as we have seen, lies outside the semantic range of the term. Moreover, the word ἔκτρωμα does not occur in Hos 13:13 LXX, and its Hebrew equivalent (*nēpel*) does not appear in Hos 13:13 MT. There is no indication in 1 Cor 15:8 that Paul is echoing or alluding to Hos 13:13.[16]

Another line of interpretation hypothesizes that Paul here takes up a slur used against him by his opponents.[17] The most prominent recent advocate of this view, Gordon Fee, bases this claim largely on Paul's use of the definite article.[18] However, a noun in apposition to a pronoun, as in 15:8, requires a definite article, and thus the article here adds no particular force.[19] Furthermore, there is no ancient evidence for the use of this word as an insult or slur. The claim is gratuitous and fails to illumine Paul's self-description in this ancient formula.

Yet another interpretation claims that Paul's metaphor views the ἔκτρωμα as lifeless and endangering the life of its mother. Paul likewise was without life apart from Christ and deadly to others through his persecution of the church.[20] This

---

13. Among recent interpreters, only Ciampa & Rosner, 751 ("birth beyond term") and Jones, "Paul the Last," 16. Cf. also Robinson, s.v. "ἔκτρωμα."

14. Garland, 692; cf. Schrage, 63.

15. Markus Schaefer, "Paulus, 'Fehlgeburt' oder 'unvernunftiges Kind'?: Ein Interpretationsvorschlag zu 1 Kor 15,8," *ZNW* 85 (1994): 207–17.

16. Another attempt to explain the passage by means of an ingenious but far-fetched claim to a literary echo is found in James M. Scott, "Paul's Comparison of Himself with 'the Abortion' (1 Cor 15:8): A Missing Link between the Qumran Book of Giants and the Manichaean Book of Giants," *JSJ* 50 (2019): 291–318. Scott argues that Paul's self-description is an allusion to Ohyah, a giant who has a dream-vision portending divine judgment within the Qumran Book of Giants (4Q530 2 ii 3–22).

17. H. J. Schoeps, *Paul: The Theology of the Apostle in the Light of Jewish Religious History* (trans. Harold Knight; Philadelphia: Westminster, 1961), 81–82; F. F. Bruce, *Paul: Apostle of the Heart Set Free* (Grand Rapids: Eerdmans, 2000), 86 n. 8; Fee, 812–14; Barrett, 344 ("probable"); cf. BA, s.v. "ἔκτρωμα."

18. Fee, 812–14.

19. BDR §268.3 and n. 6.

20. Andrzej Gieniusz, "'As a Miscarriage': The Meaning and Function of the Metaphor in 1 Cor 15:1–11 in Light of Num 12:12 (LXX)," *BibAn* 3 (2013): 93–107.

interpretation is impossible, for ἔκτρωμα (as we have seen) denotes the nonviable child already separated from the body of its mother. Moreover, ancient medical writers do not discuss life-threatening complications within pregnancy in connection with ἔκτρωσις, where these were rare, but only in connection with δυστοκία or "difficult birth" (Soranus, *Gyn.* 4.1–13).

Another suggestion is that Paul's metaphor concerns "his current status among the apostles" and depicts Paul as "cast off and rejected" from the apostolic body like a miscarried child.[21] But the metaphor applies to Paul's condition at the time the Lord appeared to him, not a state of affairs that ensued some time afterward.[22] And why use a metaphor relating to pregnancy and birth simply to express the idea of rejection and exclusion?

Still another interpretation links Paul's simile to his appointment from the womb in Gal 1:15–16. Like an undeveloped embryo or fetus, through his persecution of the church Paul's call to apostleship remained unrealized, until the risen Christ revealed himself to him and Paul's apostolic call was realized and brought to birth.[23] This reading, while initially attractive, fails on two counts. First, it fails to explain how this sense of ἔκτρωμα fits within the context of the preceding description of Paul as the "last of all" to see the risen Christ. Second, it depends on a meaning of ἔκτρωμα that does not fit within the semantic range of the word. An ἔκτρωμα is not an unborn child that has yet to develop, but a child that fails to develop and is nonviable.

A final approach, perhaps the most popular with recent interpreters, is to understand the term as denoting Paul's unworthiness and unfitness for the task of apostle, his human insufficiency revealing and magnifying God's sufficiency.[24] This thesis, too, has several insurmountable problems. This interpretation does not explain how the ἔκτρωμα relates to the preceding description of Paul as the *last* of the eyewitnesses. And it depends on taking ἔκτρωμα in the sense of a premature and deficient yet viable birth; but we have seen that this term denotes a nonviable child who fails to come to birth.

With one exception, none of the varied proposals show how ὡσπερεὶ τῷ ἐκτρώματι relates to its context—Christ's appearance to Paul as the "last of all." The one

---

21. M. W. Mitchell, "Reexamining," 469–85.
22. Rightly Gieniusz, "Miscarriage," 104.
23. George W. E. Nickelsburg, "An ἔκτρωμα, Though Appointed from the Womb: Paul's Apostolic Self-Description in 1 Corinthians 15 and Galatians 1," *HTR* 79 (1986): 198–205.
24. Hollander and van der Hort, "Calling Himself," 224–36 ("the most worthless man on earth, but in spite of his insufficiency . . . appointed by God to be his apostle"); Garland, 691–93 ("unfit for the task"); Collins, 537 ("ill-prepared for the role that was his"); similarly Schrage, 62–65; Bender, 248–49; Godet, 2:339; *TLNT* 1:464–66; BDAG, s.v. "ἔκτρωμα"; Thayer, s.v. "ἔκτρωμα."

*Paul the Final Eyewitness in the Apostolic Formula*

exception, of course, is the interpretation of ἔκτρωμα as a child born abnormally late. But this interpretation is not consistent with the known semantic meaning in antiquity of the word Paul employs. All of the proposals surveyed are inconsistent either with the metaphor's context in 15:5–8 or with the meaning of its key term. Is there an interpretation of Paul's analogy that is consistent with both? I believe there is.

*A New Solution to the Problem*

The way forward, I would propose, is to begin with the recognition of a fact often ignored by interpreters: Paul's analogy is a *comparative* analogy. The introductory "last of all" (ἔσχατον δὲ πάντων) relates Paul in 15:8 to the Twelve and to the apostolic body in 15:5–7.[25] Logically and syntactically, ὡσπερεὶ τῷ ἐκτρώματι provides a further explication of ἔσχατον δὲ πάντων and thus continues the comparison between Paul and the other apostles. The subjects of the comparison are therefore all the other apostles, on the one hand (15:7, τοῖς ἀποστόλοις πᾶσιν; 15:8, πάντων), and Paul, on the other (15:8, ἔσχατον . . . κἀμοί). The analogy must therefore concern some way in which all the rest of the apostles are *alike*, but in which Paul is *different* from all of them. What way is this?

The semantic domain of Paul's metaphor or simile is that of gestation and birth.[26] Within Paul's comparative analogy, if Paul is a miscarriage, the other apostles must be children brought to birth. At the same time, as Markus Schaefer has shown, Paul's syntax links ἔσχατον δὲ πάντων ("last of all") and ὡσπερεὶ τῷ ἐκτρώματι indissolubly. Both phrases modify ὤφθη "he appeared" adverbially, and ὡσπερεὶ τῷ ἐκτρώματι stands *between* ἔσχατον and its verb.[27] Paul's comparison must therefore include the idea of *time* and *sequence*.[28] The preceding context makes plain that this time and sequence involve the salvation history of Jesus's death, resurrection, and resurrection appearances to his apostles (15:3–7). Is there a conception that unites these seemingly incongruous elements of time, sequence, Jesus's resurrection, his resurrection appearances, and the apostles as children brought to birth? Yes, there is. This requires unpacking.

Throughout the New Testament, believers in Christ, through the gift of the Holy Spirit, enter into a new relationship with the Father and are given new birth as children of God. This theme is especially prominent within the Johannine liter-

---

25. M. W. Mitchell, "Reexamining," 476; Hays, 257; Thiselton, 1210; Schrage, 60–61; Schreiner, 306.
26. L&N places the analogy within the semantic domain of "Birth, Procreation" (§23.55).
27. Schaefer, "Kind," 208–9.
28. Schaefer, "Kind," 209.

CHAPTER 5

ature (John 1:12–13; 3:3–8; 1 John 3:1, 9–10; 5:1–2, 4, 18) and Paul's epistles (Rom 8:14–16; 2 Cor 6:16–18; Gal 3:26–27; 4:6; Phlm 10), including 1 Corinthians (3:1–4; 4:15). It is also present in Luke-Acts through Acts's emphasis on the faithful as brothers and sisters (ἀδελφοί) within the family of God and as sharers through the Spirit in a new divine life (Acts 5:20; 11:18; 13:46, 48).[29]

Within Luke-Acts and John's Gospel, the apostles are the first to receive this new birth in the Spirit (Luke 24:49; Acts 1:4–5, 7–8; 2:1–4; John 20:22), and they do so as the culmination of their participation, as eyewitnesses, in the salvation-historical events of Jesus's passion, death, resurrection, and ascension (Luke 24:48–49; Acts 1:21–22; 10:37–42; 13:31). During the time between Jesus's resurrection and ascension, which Acts specifies was a period of forty days, the apostles on multiple occasions saw, heard, touched, and ate and drank with the risen Jesus (Luke 24:39–43; Acts 1:3–4; 10:40–42; John 20:11–29; 21:1–23; cf. Matt 28:8–20). Shortly after Jesus's ascension, the Holy Spirit was given to the apostles (Luke 24:49; Acts 1:4–5; John 20:17; cf. John 7:39; 14:15–26; 15:26–27; 16:12–15 [John 20:22 is proleptic]). This event, according to Acts, took place on Pentecost (Acts 2:1–4). At Pentecost, the apostles were baptized with the Holy Spirit (Acts 1:5) and given rebirth as children of God by receiving the Spirit of the Father.[30] In this rebirth through the Holy Spirit they are paradigmatic for all believers to come (Acts 2:38; 8:14–17; 10:44–47; 11:15–18; 19:1–7; cf. 1 Cor 12:13). But the apostles' rebirth through the Spirit is also unique, for its purpose is to empower them to give their eyewitness testimony to the unique, unrepeatable events culminating in Jesus's ascension (Luke 24:48–49; Acts 1:7–8; cf. 1:22; 2:32–33; 3:15; 4:33; 10:39–41; 13:31).

Paul, in contrast to the other apostles, was not an eyewitness of Jesus's ministry, crucifixion, or resurrection appearances during the forty days between his resurrection and ascension. He did not participate in these events foundational to the apostolate. When Jesus's ascension seemingly brought the period of his resurrection appearances to a close and thereby established the final membership of the apostolic body, Paul was not among that number. When at Pentecost the apostles received rebirth through the Holy Spirit and were empowered to be eyewitnesses of what they had seen and heard, Paul was not among them. It was as if (ὡσπερεί) his birth had failed. Although called from the womb to be an apostle of Christ (Gal 1:15), he was akin to a failed birth or miscarriage (ἔκτρωμα). It was

---

29. For the faithful as ἀδελφοί, see Acts 1:15; 6:3; 9:30; 10:23; 11:1, 12, 29; 12:17; 14:2; 15:1, 3, 7, 13, 22–23, 32–33, 36, 40; 16:2, 40; 17:6, 10, 14; 18:18, 27; 21:7, 17, 20; 28:14–15.

30. See Luke 24:49, ἡ ἐπαγγελία τοῦ πατρός μου; Acts 1:4, ἡ ἐπαγγελία τοῦ πατρός; 2:33, τήν τε ἐπαγγελίαν τοῦ πνεύματος τοῦ ἁγίου λαβὼν παρὰ τοῦ πατρός; cf. John 20:17, ἀναβαίνω πρὸς τὸν πατέρα μου καὶ πατέρα ὑμῶν.

as such that Christ appeared to him. But through that extraordinary event, Paul would himself be born anew in Christ (Gal 1:16), become an eyewitness of the risen Lord (1 Cor 9:1), and be empowered by the Holy Spirit to become an apostle of Christ (1 Cor 1:1, 17; 4:9; 9:1; 15:9–10).

Paul's metaphor thus refers to the unique postascension appearance of the risen Lord to him and his unique postascension inclusion in the apostolic body. The objection may be raised that this reading assumes the Corinthians possess background knowledge relevant to Paul's metaphor that is not explicitly present in 1 Cor 15:8. But this is true of all proposed interpretations of this verse. The strength of this proposed reading is that its assumed background is the core events of the salvation history at the heart of the New Testament, and of which we can reasonably infer that the Corinthians were aware. In contrast with other proposals, which are inconsistent with either the metaphor's context in 15:5–8 or the lexical meaning of its key term, this interpretation is consistent with both elements and alone resolves all the riddles of this *crux interpretum*. It coheres with the known lexical meaning of ἔκτρωμα within ancient usage. It explains how Paul's metaphor relates to the preceding description of Paul as the "last of all." And it shows how Paul's analogy not only coheres with this context but also deepens and enlarges upon Paul's unique place as the last of the apostles to whom the risen Christ appeared.

*he appeared also to me.* Although under such different circumstances, Paul, like the other apostles, saw the risen Lord.

## Paul among the Apostolic Eyewitnesses

In exploring the appearance of the risen Christ to Paul, we must first address a common but calamitous scholarly blunder. We have seen that the appearances of Christ to the other apostles in 15:5–7 involved their objective ocular observation of Jesus's once crucified and now risen body. But one common scholarly argument maintains that the resurrection appearance to Paul overturns this conclusion. The argument has four steps: (1) Paul in 15:8, it is claimed, indicates that the postascension appearance of the risen Christ to him was exactly the same in character and kind as his resurrection appearances to Peter, the Twelve, James, and the other apostles. (2) But, the argument goes, Christ's appearance to Paul was a visionary or theophanic event not involving normal physical sight of Jesus's flesh-and-bones body. (3) Consequently, the appearances to the other apostles were likewise events involving mental vision or perhaps an "objective vision" sent by God, not ordinary ocular sight. (4) Therefore, the argument concludes, the formula's confession that

CHAPTER 5

Jesus has been raised does not refer to the revival of his corpse but to his nonphysical elevation or assumption of some kind into heavenly glory.[31]

This argument is founded upon a fallacy. We are dependent on Luke-Acts for our knowledge that the resurrection appearance to Paul took place after the ascension. This is explicit nowhere in Paul's letters or elsewhere in the New Testament (although, as we have seen above, it is implicit in Paul's metaphor within this verse). The postascension appearance to Paul is the starting point of these scholars' argument that the resurrection of Christ was nonbodily. But Luke-Acts also informs us that Christ rose from the dead in his physical body and that the apostles saw, heard, touched, and ate and drank with him for a period of forty days before his ascension. These scholars accept the postascension appearance to Paul recorded in Luke-Acts as historical and make this fact the cornerstone of their argument. But they reject the information Luke-Acts provides regarding the empty tomb, Jesus's bodily resurrection, and the preascension appearances to the Twelve. This is the fallacy of selective use of evidence. It renders this argument null and void.

Not only is the argument as a whole a fallacy, but every step in this widely held but misleading argument is false. The concluding third and fourth steps of the argument—that the appearances recounted in the formula were mere apparitions or visions, and therefore Jesus was not bodily raised—are founded on the claims of the first two premises that (1) the postascension resurrection appearance of the risen Lord to Paul was exactly the same in character and kind as Jesus's resurrection appearances to the other apostles, and that (2) the appearance to Paul was not an objective event involving normal ocular sight of Jesus's physical body but an ecstasy or vision. Let us take each of these two claims in order.

(1) First, it is simply not the case that the formula describes the appearance to Paul in exactly the same way as the appearances to the other apostles. To be sure, the formula uses the same verb of seeing (ὤφθη) of both the appearances to the other apostles (15:5–7) and the appearance to Paul (15:8). But here the evidence of Luke-Acts is decisive. In Luke-Acts, the appearances to the apostles within

---

31. For different versions of this argument, see Andreas Lindemann, "Paulus als Zeuge der Auferstehung Jesu Christi," in *Paulus, Apostel Jesu Christi* (ed. Günter Klein and Michael Trowitzsch; Tübingen: Mohr Siebeck, 1988), 55–64; James M. Robinson, "Jesus—From Easter to Valentinus (or to the Apostles' Creed)," *JBL* 101 (1982): 7–17; D. A. Smith, *Revisiting the Empty Tomb: The Early History of Easter* (Minneapolis: Fortress, 2010), 13–16, 27–45, 113; Marcus J. Borg, "The Truth of Easter," in Marcus J. Borg and N. T. Wright, *The Meaning of Jesus: Two Visions* (San Francisco: HarperSanFrancisco, 1999), 132–33; Adela Yarbro Collins, "Ancient Notions of Transferal and Apotheosis in Relation to the Empty Tomb Story in Mark," in *Metamorphoses: Resurrection, Body and Transformative Practices in Early Christianity* (ed. T. K. Seim and J. Økland; Berlin: de Gruyter, 2009), 47; Becker, *Auferstehung*, 159.

the forty-day period between Jesus's resurrection and ascension (Luke 24:19–43; Acts 1:3–4; 10:40–42; 13:31) and the postascension appearance to Paul (Acts 9:1–9; 22:3–11; 26:9–23) are, as all scholars are agreed, portrayed as having a very different nature. As Daniel A. Smith notes, "reading Luke and Acts together makes it clear that Luke did not view the appearances to Peter and to Paul as the same in character."[32] And yet in Luke-Acts, precisely as in the confessional formula in 1 Cor 15:5–8, *the same verb of seeing* (ὁράω in both active and passive forms) is used for both the preascension appearances of Jesus to Peter and the Twelve and for his postascension appearance to Paul.[33] In light of the evidence of Luke-Acts, it is hardly possible to argue that the formula's use of identical verbs for both the earlier appearances and the appearance to Paul *must* indicate that the appearances to the Twelve and to Paul were of an identical kind. In Luke-Acts, they are identical in some respects but different in others.

Moreover, the formula itself (like Luke-Acts) carefully distinguishes the appearance to Paul from the earlier appearances to the other apostles. The appearances to Peter, the Twelve, the more than five hundred brethren, James, and all the apostles are each described in precisely the same way, featuring a repetitive pattern (15:5, ὤφθη; 15:6, ἔπειτα ὤφθη; 15:7, ἔπειτα ὤφθη). But in 15:8, the pattern is broken. In place of ἔπειτα (15:6, 7), we find ἔσχατον δὲ πάντων (15:8). In an enumeration such as the formula, the use of δέ is striking. The conjunction δέ always introduces something that is new and different in some way from what precedes it.[34] Next we find, in emphatic position prior to the verb, the modifier ὡσπερεὶ τῷ ἐκτρώματι. As we have seen, the most plausible reading of this metaphor specifically contrasts the preascension encounters of the apostles with the risen Lord with the postascension appearance to Paul. Moreover, the reference to "all the apostles" (τοῖς ἀποστόλοις πᾶσιν) in 15:7, which is exclusive of Paul, acknowledges that Paul's later, postascension seeing of the risen Lord puts him in a different category than the other apostles. Finally, the superfluous καί in κἀμοί "also to me," also reflects the late and extraordinary nature of Christ's appearance to Paul. The formula itself indicates important differences between the appearances to the other apostles and the appearance to Paul.

(2) The second plank in the argument claims that the appearance to Paul was a nonbodily or visionary event, not involving objective sight of Jesus's risen body.

---

32. Smith, *Empty Tomb*, 113.

33. Cf. Luke 24:34, ἠγέρθη ὁ κύριος καὶ <u>ὤφθη</u> Σίμωνι; 24:39, <u>ἴδετε</u> τὰς χεῖράς μου καὶ τοὺς πόδας μου; Acts 9:17, Ἰησοῦς ὁ <u>ὀφθείς</u> σοι; 9:27, <u>εἶδεν</u> τὸν κύριον; 13:31, <u>ὤφθη</u> ἐπὶ ἡμέρας πλείους τοῖς συναναβᾶσιν αὐτῷ ἀπὸ τῆς Γαλιλαίας εἰς Ἰερουσαλήμ; 26:16, <u>ὤφθην</u> σοι.

34. BDR §447; Kühner-G., 2.2:261–63.

However, this is not the case. To be sure, the appearance of the risen Lord to Paul, as we have seen, differed in important ways from the appearances to the other apostles. Nonetheless, like the other apostles Paul saw with his physical eyes the once crucified and now risen body of Jesus. The evidence for this is multiple and overwhelming. It is as follows.[35]

(a) The sequence of verbs within 15:3–8 has a single subject: "*Christ* died . . . *he* was buried . . . *he* was raised . . . *he* appeared." The subject of the verbs "died," "buried," and "raised" in 15:3–4 is the physical *body* of Christ. Thus the subject of "appeared" in 15:5–8, including the appearance to Paul in 15:8, must likewise be the material body of Christ.

(b) As we saw earlier in the commentary, the verb ἐγείρω in 15:4, which directly precedes the fourfold use of the verb ὁράω in 15:5–8, unambiguously denotes the resurrection of Jesus's physical body from the tomb. The verb ὁράω that directly follows in the succeeding verses, including 15:8, must therefore refer to normal objective sight of that same body.

(c) The emphatically placed "last of all" (ἔσχατον δὲ πάντων) sharply distinguishes the appearances in the list, including the appearance to Paul, from all later visions and revelatory experiences, including Paul's own later "visions and revelations of the Lord" (2 Cor 12:1–7). In the early church, visions and ecstatic experiences were widespread. Yet the formula identifies the appearances it lists as the unique and unrepeatable marks of apostleship. Likewise, in 1 Cor 9:1 Paul's claim to apostleship is grounded in his assertion "I have seen the Lord." This is only explicable if these appearances, including the appearance to Paul, refer to unique eyewitness encounters with Jesus in his once crucified but now risen body.[36]

(d) In Paul's commentary on the formula in the following verses and elsewhere in 1 Corinthians, he repeatedly describes his own apostolic claim to have seen the risen Lord as "witness" and "testimony" (15:15, ἐμαρτυρήσαμεν . . . ψευδομάρτυρες; 1:6, μαρτύριον). This is enormously significant. As noted in the prior chapter, within the ancient world "testimony" was the language of facts and history, specifically delineated from the language of religious vision (Cicero, *Leg.* 1.3–5). The language of "witness" and "testimony" in antiquity always denoted physical sight of objective realities in the real world. This language makes clear that Paul claimed to have seen the risen Lord in his physical body.

---

35. For fuller discussion of points (a) through (d) below, see the previous chapter and its discussion of the significance of the verb ὤφθη throughout vv. 5–8.

36. Rightly Lang, 213–14, 216; Ronald J. Sider, "St. Paul's Understanding of the Nature and Significance of the Resurrection in I Corinthians xv, 1–19," *NovT* 19 (1975): 140; N. T. Wright, *The Resurrection of the Son of God* (vol. 3 of *Christian Origins and the Question of God*; Minneapolis: Fortress, 2003), 326–27; Wolff, 373.

(e) The construction found in 15:8, ὤφθη with the dative, is found once in the gospels, and there refers to ordinary ocular observation of the bodily risen Jesus (Luke 24:34). In their accounts of the resurrection appearances, the gospels make frequent use of active and middle deponent forms of ὁράω to denote objective sight of Jesus's flesh-and-bones body (Matt 28:7, 10, 17; Mark 16:7; Luke 24:39; John 20:18, 20, 25, 27, 29). To argue that Paul in 15:8 is referring to a visionary event or ecstatic experience, one would need to argue that Paul is using the very same language we find throughout the New Testament for the apostles' physical observation of the bodily risen Lord but inexplicably employing this language in an entirely different and contrary way. Such an argument is gratuitous and highly unlikely.

(f) Elsewhere in 1 Corinthians Paul describes Jesus, as proclaimed in the apostolic witness and preaching, as "Christ crucified" (1:23, Χριστὸς ἐσταυρωμένος; cf. 2:2). The perfect participle ἐσταυρωμένος describes a state or condition contemporaneous with Paul's proclamation—the one whom Paul saw and now proclaims is the Crucified One. But if after his resurrection Jesus had assumed some other body or form different from the body that was crucified and laid in the tomb, Paul could not describe the one whom he saw as "Christ crucified." This description assumes that Paul saw Christ in his crucified and now risen body.[37]

(g) Luke-Acts, although later than this formula, provides crucial corroborating evidence. There is a widespread scholarly assumption that Luke-Acts portrays the appearance to Paul not as involving normal ocular sight but as an objective vision.[38] But this is simply a failure to read the text. When Jesus appears to Paul, the bystanders see the radiant light surrounding Jesus (Acts 22:9) and fall to the ground (26:14), although they do not (as Paul does) see Jesus himself (9:7). Paul's companions hear the sound of Jesus's voice (9:7) without (as Paul does) comprehending what he says (22:9).[39] Paul's eyes are physically and (apart from later divine intervention) permanently blinded by the glory emanating from Jesus's body, his sight only restored through a miracle (9:8–9, 17–18; 22:11–13). In Acts, Paul with his physical eyes sees the once crucified, now risen, and glorified body of Christ (9:27; 22:14–15). As a result, Paul, like Peter and the Twelve, is an apostle (14:4, 14).

And yet in Luke-Acts, as in the formula, the appearance to Paul is different in character from the appearances to the other apostles. In Luke-Acts, the ap-

---

37. See Schep, *Resurrection Body*, 127.
38. For example, Evans, *Resurrection*, 55–56; Sandnes and Henriksen, *Resurrection*, 102.
39. On Luke's careful distinction of case in complements of ἀκούω as explaining the claimed contradiction between Acts 9:7 and 22:9, see Rob., *Gram.*, 506.

pearances of Jesus to the Twelve, which take place in the forty-day period between Jesus's resurrection and his ascension, are extended encounters involving sight, sound, and touch (Luke 24:39–43; Acts 1:3–4; 10:40–42; 13:31). By contrast, Paul's mysterious postascension encounter with Jesus in Acts, although equally an objective and physical event, involves only the senses of sight and sound, as the glorified Lord appears to him in an overwhelming and debilitating blaze of light (Acts 9:3–8; 22:6–11; 26:12–18). This matches fully with the portrayal of the appearance to Paul within the formula, as being different from those experienced by the other apostles but nonetheless a true eyewitness encounter with the Lord in his risen body.

But how did Paul see the risen Lord *after* his ascension into heaven? In Acts it is clear that when he speaks to Paul, Jesus is in near proximity to him and the bystanders (9:4–7, 17; 22:7–10; 26:14–15). Paul's response and the ensuing dialogue also assume Jesus's immediate physical presence (9:5–6; 22:8, 10; 26:15–18). Yet that immediate presence involves a radiant glory forbidding all but momentary sight (9:3–4; 22:6–7; 26:13–14) that leaves Paul physically blind (9:8–9, 12, 17–18; 22:11, 13). What appears to be assumed, in both the formula and Luke-Acts, is a unique and ineffable divine miracle, in which the risen Lord came from heaven to reveal himself to Paul in his crucified and now glorified body. As Thomas Aquinas put it, "Christ descended bodily to earth" (*Christus corporaliter ad terram descendat*) to encounter Paul in his "bodily presence" (*corporaliter praesente*).[40] The staggeringly miraculous character of the appearance to Paul is encapsulated in Paul's prefatory ὡσπερεὶ τῷ ἐκτρώματι ("as if to one whose birth has previously failed"), which we have seen refers to Paul's seemingly impossible postascension inclusion, out of due time, among the apostles.

This postascension appearance of the risen Lord to Paul involves a number of mysteries not further clarified within the New Testament. However, the physical reality and yet unique circumstances of the appearance of the risen Christ to Paul illumines the seemingly contradictory evidence in Paul's own letters and in Acts regarding whether he was dependent upon or independent of the Twelve. The evidence is not in fact contradictory but reflects the unique character of Paul's apostleship implicit in the formula "As if one whose birth had previously failed" (15:8). Paul was an eyewitness of neither Jesus's ministry and the culminating events in Jerusalem nor the resurrection appearances of the Lord during the

---

40. Thomas Aquinas, *ST* III, Q. 57, Art. 6, ad 3. Cf. Ellicott: "corporaliter, atque oculis corporeis videndum" (292, citing Estius). The suggestion of Calvin that Christ was not present to Paul, but that Paul was miraculously given a power of sight that could penetrate the heavens (*Inst.* 4.17.29), is not exegetically defensible.

forty days between his resurrection and ascension. Paul therefore was, on the one hand, dependent upon and subordinate to the Twelve (cf. Acts 1:21–22; 10:39–42; 13:30–31). This explains Paul's conference with Peter in Jerusalem in AD 37 to meet with him regarding Peter's eyewitness testimony to the Jesus events (Gal 1:18–19). And it explains why Paul, although himself an apostle, laid his gospel before the apostles in Jerusalem for their consideration at the apostolic council in AD 49 (Gal 2:1–10; Acts 15). But Paul was, on the other hand, truly an apostle, having seen and been commissioned by the risen Lord. This explains his joint partnership on an equal footing with Peter, James, and John in the apostolic mission (Gal 2:9). The formula's portrayal of Paul as an eyewitness of Jesus in his crucified and risen body, albeit in a postascension encounter unique among the apostles, not only matches perfectly with the data in Acts but is also the only scenario that resolves and explains the complex data in Acts and in Paul's own letters regarding his relation to Peter, the Twelve, and the other apostles.

Verse 8 concludes the apostolic formula. Verses 9–11 now provide Paul's own apostolic commentary on that formula.

## Verse 9

*For, you see, I am the least of the apostles, and am unfit to be called an apostle, because I persecuted the church of God.*

It is often held that v. 9 provides the explanation for Paul's reference to himself as an ἔκτρωμα in the previous verse and indicates that this metaphor expresses merely Paul's utter inadequacy for the apostolic task.[41] But as we have seen, Paul's simile in v. 8 does not concern his inadequacy but the unique circumstances of the appearance of the risen Lord to him, which took place after the Lord's ascension and the apparent closure of the apostolic body. The γάρ in v. 9 is thus not causal but a marker of clarification, introducing further comment on the unique circumstances of Paul's apostolic commissioning.[42] Paul's reflection on his apostleship here forms an *inclusio* framing the entire letter (1:17, ἀποστέλλω; 15:9, ἀπόστολος [2×])—yet another indication that chapter 15 forms the goal and climax of the entire epistle. In Paul's lowly self-description, he is "the least of the apostles" (cf. Eph 3:8, "the very least of all saints") and "unfit [οὐκ ἱκανός] to be called an apostle"

---

41. So Schrage, 65; Lindemann, 335; Ciampa & Rosner, 751; Robertson & Plummer, 341.
42. On this function of γάρ, see BDAG, s.v. "γάρ" (2); BA, s.v. "γάρ" (4, "Anknüpfend und fortführend").

CHAPTER 5

(for ἱκανός, as here, in a moral sense, cf. Matt 8:8; Luke 7:6). His lowly status is expressed as a present reality (εἰμί [2×]) but has its basis in Paul's past: "I persecuted the church of God" (cf. Gal 1:13, 23; Phil 3:6). The expression "the church of God" (ἡ ἐκκλησία τοῦ θεοῦ) is a distinctive mark of this letter (1:2, 10:32, 11:22, 15:9, four of its seven instances in the New Testament). Moreover, Paul's use of "the church of God" progresses in the letter from a purely local sense in 1:2, to a somewhat wider usage in 10:32 and 11:22, to a sense here encompassing the church universal. It is sometimes claimed that Paul's theology envisions only local churches and lacks a conception of the universal church. Our text here belies this claim. As Anthony Thiselton notes, "The post-Pauline creedal formula that the Church is one, holy, universal and apostolic is implicit in Paul's earlier writings and becomes explicit in his later ones."[43] The expression also reveals that Paul understands his unworthiness as unworthiness before *God* (ἐδίωξα τὴν ἐκκλησίαν τοῦ θεοῦ).[44]

Paul's unworthiness and unfitness here in 15:9 function to prepare for and highlight the transforming power of the grace of God described in the verse that follows.

VERSE 10

*But by the grace of God I am what I am, and his grace toward me did not prove vain. To the contrary, I have labored more abundantly than them all—yet it is not I, but the grace of God which is with me.*

The focus and concentration of this verse, in a quite striking way, is the grace of God. The word χάρις "grace," together with a noun or pronoun denoting God as the giver, occurs three times within this short verse. The grace of God, here as elsewhere in Paul, is the supernatural divine life of the risen Christ given freely to the unworthy and bringing forgiveness and transforming power. This new life in the risen Christ given to the faithful will be a key theme of the chapter (15:3, 17, 30–31, 45, 48, 56–57). And the chapter will climax with the acclamation τῷ δὲ θεῷ χάρις ("But thanks be to God"), an expression that uses the word χάρις in the sense of "thanksgiving," but which in Paul is always thanksgiving specifically in response to God's unfathomable grace and mercy to the unworthy.

---

43. Anthony C. Thiselton, *The Living Paul: An Introduction to the Apostle's Life and Thought* (Downers Grove, IL: InterVarsity, 2009), 108.

44. Cf. Lindemann, 335.

*But by the grace of God I am what I am.* By the grace of God Paul is a Christian and an apostle.[45] This grace includes Paul's entire life in Christ. But the grace on which Paul here especially focuses is his divine empowerment as an apostolic witness to the risen Christ: "the grace of apostleship" (Rom 1:5, χάρις καὶ ἀποστολή; cf. 1 Cor 3:10, ἡ χάρις τοῦ θεοῦ ἡ δοθεῖσά μοι; Rom 12:3; 15:15; Gal 2:9; Eph 3:2, 7). Apart from God's grace, Paul is unfit (1 Cor 15:9, οὐκ εἰμὶ ἱκανός) to be an apostle; but as in 2 Cor 3:5–6, his fitness (2 Cor 3:5, ἱκανότης) comes from God.

*and his grace toward me did not prove vain.* The adjective κενός "vain" connects to the language of vanity so prominent elsewhere in the letter and chapter (κενός, 15:14 [2×], 58; εἰκῇ, 15:2; κενόω, 1:17; μάταιος, 3:20, 15:17). But the usage here is different. Elsewhere in the letter, this language of vanity expresses the theme that, apart from the resurrection hope, the gospel and faith are in vain (1:17; 3:20; 15:2, 14, 17, 58). But here the thought is that the grace of God, the divine life of the risen Christ, is not fruitless but powerfully at work in Paul's labor for the gospel (cf. Col 1:29). And yet the thought here is related to the larger theme, for the divine power at work in Paul, the most unlikely and least of apostles, reveals the truth that Christ has been raised. It is, like the appearances of the risen Christ in 15:5–8, yet another proof of Christ's resurrection and of the truth of the apostolic proclamation.[46]

*To the contrary, I have labored more abundantly than them all.* In describing his response to the grace of Christ, Paul here presents himself, as he has throughout the letter, as a model for the Corinthians. Here he is a model of that abundant labor for the gospel to which he will exhort the Corinthians in 15:58 (cf. 15:10, περισσότερον ... ἐκοπίασα; 15:58, περισσεύοντες ἐν τῷ ἔργῳ τοῦ κυρίου). We also encounter here an important element of Paul's theology and reading of Scripture, which we will discuss more fully in the commentary on v. 58. Here as elsewhere in Paul (Gal 4:11; Phil 2:16; 1 Thess 3:5; cf. Gal 2:2; 1 Thess 2:1), the collocation of the language of labor and vanity recalls a specific passage of Scripture, the self-description of the Servant of Isaiah in Isa 49:4. In the book of Isaiah, the seed or children promised to the suffering and exalted Servant in 53:10 are identified as the "servants" of chapters 56–66. Early Christian exegesis saw the promise of the Servant of Isaiah fulfilled in Jesus, and the promise of "the servants of the Servant" of Isaiah fulfilled in believers in Christ supernaturally united to him by the power of the Holy Spirit.[47] Paul is here a model "servant of the Servant."

---

45. Schrage, 69 ("Christ und Apostel").
46. Cf. Schrage, 67; Robertson & Plummer, 342.
47. See the essays collected in Michael A. Lyons and Jacob Stromberg, eds., *Isaiah's Servants*

CHAPTER 5

*yet it is not I, but the grace of God which is with me.* The article before the prepositional phrase (included in P⁴⁶ ℵ² A D¹ 33) is lacking in our best manuscripts (ℵ B D* 1739), leaving σὺν ἐμοί ("with me") in what is, for a prepositional phrase, an ambiguous position.[48] Some interpreters take the phrase as predicate (i.e., "but the grace of God [labors] with me"), as if God's grace were working alongside Paul.[49] But Paul does not say *yet it is not I alone* but rather *yet it is not I*. The prepositional phrase must be taken attributively (i.e., "but the grace of God which is with me [labors]"). It is not Paul but solely the grace of God with Paul that is at work. When Paul labors, the true situation is just as Paul explains to the Philippians is the case in their own labors for the gospel: "for it is God who is at work in you, both to will and to work, for his good pleasure" (Phil 2:13). In ascribing everything to God's grace, Paul here models boasting in the Lord, an important theme of the letter introduced in 1:31 and culminating (as we will see) in 15:31.[50]

VERSE 11

*Whether, then, it is I or they, this is what we proclaim, and this is what you believed.*

Verse 11, in its focus on proclamation and belief, corresponds to vv. 1–2.[51] Moreover, the final word of v. 11, ἐπιστεύσατε, corresponds to the final word of v. 2, ἐπιστεύσατε. Verse 11 thus forms an *inclusio* with vv. 1–2, marking off 15:1–11 as a literary unit.[52] Within the larger letter, the combination of κηρύσσω and πιστεύω recalls 1:21 and 23 (the only other place in the letter where this combination occurs), thus once again revealing chapter 15 as the culmination of Paul's exposition in 1:18–2:5 of the foolishness of the kerygma in contrast with human wisdom (cf. κήρυγμα and πίστις in 2:4–5, 15:14).

*Whether, then, it is I or they.* The οὖν "then" is not resumptive, referring back to v. 8.[53] Paul never uses the conjunction in that way. Here, it has a summarizing

---

*in Early Judaism and Christianity: The Isaian Servant and the Exegetical Formation of Community Identity* (WUNT 2.554; Tübingen: Mohr Siebeck, 2021), especially Holly Beers, "The Servant(s) in Luke-Acts," 189–207; Mark S. Gignilliat, "Paul and Isaiah's Servants in 2 Corinthians," 243–53; and James P. Ware, "The Servants of the Servant in Isaiah and Philippians," 255–71.

48. Rob., *Gram.*, 782–83.
49. Robertson & Plummer, 342; Godet, 2:341–42.
50. So Wolff, 375.
51. Collins, 538–39.
52. Fitzmyer, 545.
53. Contra Ellicott, 293; Robertson & Plummer, 342.

function, drawing together the entire unit 15:1–11. The pronoun ἐκεῖνοι "they" is anaphoric, referring back to the apostles mentioned in the preceding list of eyewitnesses in 15:5–7 and in 15:9 –10.[54] The construction εἴτε ... εἴτε, as used by Paul, always presents the differences between contrasted items as without ultimate significance.[55] It is irrelevant which member of the apostolic body brings the message, for the apostolic message is one. Paul's assertion of the unanimity of the apostles reveals the unhistorical character of theories claiming a diversity of conflicting messages within primitive Christianity. As Martin Hengel notes: "If we give 15:11 its due weight, it follows that there existed at the very beginning of earliest Christianity, not an unlimited diversity of conflicting Christologies and confesssions, but instead this *one* gospel of Jesus Christ."[56]

*this is what we proclaim.* The adverb οὕτως (lit. "in this way") refers to the content of vv. 3–8. The term Paul chooses to describe the apostolic messaging is significant, for the verb κηρύσσω "to proclaim," connotes a message with intrinsic authority.[57] The apostolic gospel's intrinsic authority derives from its basis in eyewitness testimony. Verse 11 stresses that the content of this gospel is the testimony of *all* the apostles. This verse thus brings to a powerful climax Paul's proof or demonstration of the historical reality of the resurrection of Christ in 15:1–11.[58]

*and this is what you believed.* The repeated οὕτως again stresses agreement with the precise content of vv. 3–8 (cf. τίνι λόγῳ, "the very word," 15:2). The aorist tense of ἐπιστεύσατε "you believed," coming after the present tense of the preceding κηρύσσομεν, is striking indeed. Some interpreters believe the aorist tense here simply recalls to the minds of the Corinthians their initial reception of the gospel, without any implication of criticism or apprehension about their present state of belief.[59] But J. N. Vorster is more likely correct that the shift in tense is rhetorically significant, subtly raising the question of the Corinthians' present loyalty to the apostolic proclamation. "The urgent question is: 'what about the present?'"[60] This

---

54. The anaphoric use is the most common function of ἐκεῖνος; see Rob., *Gram.*, 707.
55. Lindemann, 335–36.
56. Martin Hengel, "Das Begräbnis Jesu bei Paulus und die leibliche Auferstehung aus dem Grabe," in *Auferstehung—Resurrection* (ed. F. Avemarie and H. Lichtenberger; WUNT 135; Tübingen: Mohr Siebeck, 2001), 122.
57. See Thayer, s.v. "κηρύσσω": "always with a suggestion of formality, gravity, and an authority which must be listened to and obeyed"; cf. Weiss, 353.
58. Ciampa & Rosner, 752.
59. So Robertson & Plummer, 342; Godet, 2:342–43; Thiselton, 1213.
60. J. N. Vorster, "Resurrection Faith in 1 Corinthians 15," *Neot* 23 (1989): 290.

CHAPTER 5

subtle challenge at the close of 15:1–11 prepares the ground for Paul's direct confrontation with the denial of the resurrection at Corinth in the very next verse.

But before we consider Paul's head-on confrontation with the denial of the resurrection by the self-professed wise at Corinth in 15:12–19, we must take a few moments to reflect on the astounding historical and theological implications of the ancient apostolic confession preserved in 1 Cor 15:1–11. This now follows in excursus 2.

EXCURSUS 2

# The Implications of the Apostolic Formula for History and Faith

In our exploration over the previous three chapters of the apostolic formula preserved in 1 Cor 15:3–8, we have seen that this ancient confession proclaims Jesus's resurrection from the tomb on the third day in his crucified body. This result of our study of this astonishingly early apostolic confession has enormous ramifications for the historicity of Jesus's resurrection, the meaning of Jesus's resurrection, and the nature of Christian faith. We must explore each of these in turn.

## The Implications of the Formula for the Historicity of Jesus's Resurrection

The implications of our findings regarding the content of this ancient formula are of the greatest importance for the contemporary debate regarding the historicity of Jesus's resurrection. As this debate has progressed over more than two centuries, issues have been clarified and unworkable hypotheses eliminated, so that today among serious scholars two main positions hold the field. A number of scholars argue that our historical evidence leads inescapably to the conclusion that, three days after his burial, Jesus of Nazareth rose again from the tomb in his crucified body, as the resurrection narratives of all four gospels attest.[1] A num-

---

1. N. T. Wright, *The Resurrection of the Son of God* (vol. 3 of *Christian Origins and the Question of God*; Minneapolis: Fortress, 2003); Martin Hengel, "Das Begräbnis Jesu bei Paulus und die leibliche Auferstehung aus dem Grabe," in *Auferstehung—Resurrection* (ed. F. Avemarie and

ber of alternative explanations proposed in the past—the "conspiracy" theory of Hermann Samuel Reimarus, the "swoon" or "apparent death" theory of H. E. G. Paulus, and the "wrong tomb" theory of Kirsopp Lake—have proven unviable and have been discounted. However, another alternative explanation of the first Easter has had more staying power—that of David Friedrich Strauss in his monumentally influential *The Christ of Faith and the Jesus of History* (1835). Strauss's theory, unlike the others, was a *composite* one. Strauss postulated an earlier stage where apparitions or visions of a postmortem Jesus led to belief in his nonbodily "resurrection" in an ethereal or heavenly form (a stage evident, Strauss claimed, in Paul's letters), and a later stage where legends of an empty tomb and physical resurrection appearances were developed (the stage we see in the gospels). This theory might be called, reflecting its two-stage or composite character, the "apparitions/legends" theory. Today, all historians who reject the claim that Jesus rose from the dead hold, in one form or another, to this theory.

A classic formulation of this theory was provided by Hans Grass's study *Ostergeschehen und Osterberichte*.[2] According to Grass, in the resurrection faith of Paul and the earliest apostles, Jesus's fleshly body lay moldering in the tomb, yet in a new, heavenly body he was now "raised" or exalted to the right hand of God.[3] Mark's legend of the empty tomb first introduced the concept of a physical resurrection of Jesus, which was later augmented in Matthew, Luke, and John by further legendary accounts of Jesus's bodily appearances to the disciples.[4] More recently, Adela Yarbro Collins has proposed a somewhat different version of this same hypothesis. In her view, as in that of Grass, "for Paul, and presumably for many other early Christians, the resurrection of Jesus did not imply that his tomb was empty."[5] Rather, the earliest conception of Jesus being "raised on the third day" involved the bestowal of a new, heavenly body discontinuous with the earthly, physical body.[6] At a later period, Mark composed a fictional story

---

H. Lichtenberger; WUNT 135; Tübingen: Mohr Siebeck, 2001), 119–83; Christopher Bryan, *The Resurrection of the Messiah* (Oxford: Oxford University Press, 2011); John Granger Cook, *Empty Tomb, Resurrection, Apotheosis* (WUNT 410; Tübingen: Mohr Siebeck, 2018); Jake H. O'Connell, *Jesus' Resurrection and Apparitions: A Bayesian Analysis* (Eugene, OR: Resource, 2016); A. B. du Toit, "Primitive Christian Belief in the Resurrection of Jesus in the Light of Pauline Resurrection and Appearance Terminology," *Neot* 23 (1989): 309–30.

2. Grass, *Ostergeschehen und Osterberichte* (Göttingen: Vandenhoeck & Ruprecht, 1962).
3. Grass, *Ostergeschehen*, 146–73.
4. Grass, *Ostergeschehen*, 173–248.
5. Adela Yarbro Collins, "The Empty Tomb in the Gospel According to Mark," in *Hermes and Athena: Biblical Exegesis and Philosophical Theology* (ed. Eleonore Stump and Thomas P. Flint; Notre Dame: University of Notre Dame Press, 1993), 114.
6. Yarbro Collins, "Empty Tomb," 111–14.

## The Implications of the Apostolic Formula for History and Faith

about Jesus being "raised" from an empty tomb to express his belief that, after his death and burial, Jesus's body had been immediately translated from the grave to heaven, divested of his flesh along the way.[7] Only at a still later stage, Yarbro Collins argues, do we encounter Matthew, Luke, John, and Acts transmitting accounts of the physically risen Jesus walking the earth and meeting with his disciples, reflecting their relatively new belief that "Jesus' resurrection entailed the revival of his earthly body."[8]

The historical scenarios offered by Yarbro Collins and Grass, although differing on a number of points, are agreed that the earliest Christ followers regarded Jesus's resurrection as a spiritual event unrelated to the corpse laid in the tomb. Belief in the resurrection of Jesus's crucified body was a later development accompanied by legendary accounts of an empty tomb and of the disciples encountering, touching, and eating with the risen Jesus. On this reconstruction, belief in Jesus's bodily resurrection from the tomb was neither primitive nor apostolic but rather a later conception in discontinuity with the earliest kerygma. In holding to a composite theory postulating original nonbodily apparitions followed by later legends, Grass and Yarbro Collins are representative. Among those scholars who hold to an alternative explanation of the first Easter, the "apparitions/legends" theory is virtually universal. It has no rival.[9]

In a recent work, Dale Allison has offered a distinctive variation on this theory.[10] Allison differs from other proponents in arguing that historically Jesus's tomb was most likely found empty.[11] However, Allison agrees with them that what the first disciples experienced were nonbodily apparitions of Jesus that only later would be transformed into the mythical narratives of a bodily risen Jesus that we

---

7. Yarbro Collins, "Empty Tomb," 115–31; likewise Adela Yarbro Collins, "Ancient Notions of Transferal and Apotheosis in Relation to the Empty Tomb Story in Mark," in *Metamorphoses: Resurrection, Body and Transformative Practices in Early Christianity* (ed. Turid Karlsen Seim and Jorunn Økland; Berlin: de Gruyter, 2009), 41–57.

8. Yarbro Collins, "Empty Tomb," 131; cf. Yarbro Collins, "Transferal," 147.

9. For further versions of this theory, see John Dominic Crossan, *Jesus: A Revolutionary Biography* (San Francisco: HarperOne, 2009); E. P. Sanders, *Jesus and Judaism* (Minneapolis: Fortress, 1985); Bruce D. Chilton, *Resurrection Logic: How Jesus' First Followers Believed God Raised Him from the Dead* (Waco: Baylor University Press, 2019); Peter R. Gant, *Seeing Light: An Enquiry into the Origins of Resurrection Faith* (Durham: Sacristy, 2019); P. Hoffmann, *Zur neutestamentliche Überlieferung von der Auferstehung Jesu* (Darmstadt: Wissenschaftliche Buchgesellschaft, 1988); Daniel A. Smith, *Revisiting the Empty Tomb: The Early History of Easter* (Minneapolis: Fortress, 2010).

10. Dale C. Allison Jr., *The Resurrection of Jesus: Apologetics, Polemics, History* (New York: T&T Clark, 2021). For discussion and reviews of this work, see the special issue of *BBR* 32 (2022): 270–312.

11. Allison, *Resurrection*, 116–66.

find in the gospels.[12] Like the many other advocates of what I am calling the "apparitions/legends" theory, Allison is convinced that this theory provides a satisfying explanatory alternative to the historical claim that Jesus rose from the dead.

However, our findings regarding the apostolic formula in 1 Cor 15:3–8 reveal that it does not. For the apparitions/legends theory, whether in its traditional form as espoused by Grass and Yarbro Collins or the amended form proposed by Allison, depends for its validity on a reading of this ancient formula as bearing witness to nothing more than visions or apparitions of a postmortem, disincarnate Jesus.[13] But this is not an exegetically competent or tenable reading of 1 Cor 15:3–8. For we have seen that this ancient apostolic confession affirms the physical resurrection of Jesus's crucified body from the tomb and claims that eyewitnesses saw him with ordinary physical sight in his risen body. The linguistic meaning of the verb used within the formula to describe Jesus's resurrection is of decisive significance. In chapter 3 of this commentary, we discovered previously unexplored but conclusive evidence that this ancient Greek verb necessarily involves the concept of the physical body's restoration to life. Moreover, we saw in chapters 4 and 5 that the resurrection appearances of Jesus recounted in the formula do not describe visionary encounters but objective events involving normal ocular sight of Jesus's physical body. It is thus beyond doubt that the apostolic formula in 1 Cor 15:3–8 affirms that Jesus arose on the third day in his crucified body, leaving behind an empty tomb. The formula thus reveals the historical impossibility of both postulates of the composite apparitions/legends theory—both the claim of original nonbodily apparitions and the claim of legendary development. For the language of the formula rules out the possibility that the resurrection appearances it describes were nonbodily apparitions. The formula, like the gospels, affirms that Jesus rose bodily from the dead, and describes resurrection appearances of Jesus in his crucified and now risen body. And the astoundingly early date of this confession—in use probably within eighteen months of the first Easter—means that belief in Jesus's bodily resurrection is not a product of later legend, but the testimony of the earliest apostles and eyewitnesses.[14]

Dale Allison seeks to minimize the evidential value of this confession, characterizing it as "meager data," "at best second-hand," and providing "no direct access"

---

12. Allison, *Resurrection*, 336–56; cf. 229, 258–61.

13. Grass, *Ostergeschehen*, 146–73; Yarbro Collins, "Empty Tomb," 111–14; Allison, *Resurrection*, 42–43, 53–64, 72–80, 83–89, 129–36, 144–45, 249–57, 258 n. 118.

14. On the historical value of eyewitness testimony, see Robert K. McIver, "Eyewitnesses as Guarantors of the Accuracy of the Gospel Traditions in the Light of Psychological Research," *JBL* 131 (2012): 529–46, in response to Judith C. Redman, "How Accurate Are Eyewitnesses? Bauckham and the Eyewitnesses in the Light of Psychological Research," *JBL* 129 (2010): 177–97.

to the events it describes.[15] This is historically misleading in the extreme. The eyewitnesses Paul lists are Peter, the Twelve, the more than five hundred brothers and sisters, James, all the apostles, and himself (15:5–8). Paul had multiple contacts with Peter, including a fifteen-day conference with him in Jerusalem (Gal 1:18–19; 2:9). Of the Twelve, Paul had, besides Peter, also met with John the son of Zebedee (Gal 2:9) and almost certainly others as well. Paul also had multiple contacts with James (Gal 1:19; 2:9). It is thus beyond historical controversy that Paul had heard the content of the apostolic testimony that he transmits to the Corinthians in 15:3–7 from the lips of the apostles themselves. Of the more than five hundred brothers and sisters, Paul's statement that "the majority remain until now, but some have fallen asleep" (15:6) presumes his knowledge of who among them were alive and who had died, and thus suggests that he was personally acquainted with at least the majority of them. What is crucial for the historian is that when Paul in 1 Cor 15:3–7 informs us of the testimony to the resurrection by the earliest apostles and eyewitnesses, he was in a position to know.

Moreover, the Corinthians were in a position to interrogate these eyewitnesses for themselves. As many scholars have argued (in my view convincingly), Peter himself had visited and taught the church at Corinth.[16] In addition, Paul's note in regard to the more than five hundred that "the majority remain until now" (15:6) has an evidential function, implying, as we have seen, the regular visits of individuals among their number to Corinth. Regarding James (15:7), several members of the church at Corinth would shortly travel to Jerusalem and meet with James directly (16:3–4). In light of Paul's personal contacts with the eyewitnesses, and the opportunity on the part of the Corinthians of personal contact and interrogation of these same witnesses, the conclusion is inescapable that the confession transmitted to the Corinthians accurately reflects the eyewitness testimony of Peter, the Twelve, the more than five hundred brothers and sisters, James, and Paul himself.

---

15. Allison, *Resurrection*, 336, 357, 358.

16. For the evidence in the primary sources, see 1 Cor 1:12; 3:22; 9:5; and the second-century testimony of Dionysius, bishop of Corinth, in Eusebius, *Hist. eccl.* 2.25.8. The level of confidence we may have in Peter's visit to Corinth is a point of dispute among scholars. Oscar Cullmann considers such a visit a strong possibility but uncertain in *Peter: Disciple, Apostle, Martyr. A Historical and Theological Essay* (trans. Floyd V. Filson; Philadelphia: Westminster, 1953), 53–55. N. T. Wright, however, assumes (on my view rightly) that Peter had visited Corinth (*Resurrection*, 318–19). And recently, in a ground-breaking study, Stephan Witetschek has shown that 1 Cor 1:12, 3:22, and 9:5 lose much of their force in context unless a visit of Peter to Corinth is assumed; see his "Peter in Corinth? A Review of the Evidence from I Corinthians," *JTS* 69 (2018): 66–82. While the evidence is not ironclad, it is extremely strong.

EXCURSUS 2

There is another factor that adds further weight to the historical value of this formula: each of the named apostles in this list of eyewitnesses—Peter, James, and Paul—would die as martyrs for their proclamation of the resurrection. Their martyrdoms are recorded nowhere in the New Testament, but we know of them from reliable primary source evidence from outside the Bible. Josephus, the Jewish historian, provides us with a precious account of the martyrdom of James in Jerusalem in AD 62 (*A.J.* 20.200). At some point in the 60s (the precise dates are disputed), both Peter and Paul would come to Rome, teach and confirm the church there, and become martyrs in Rome for their proclamation of the gospel.[17]

Allison acknowledges that the canonical gospel narratives that describe the disciples' encounters with a physically risen Jesus, if true, are incompatible with any other historical conclusion other than that Jesus was raised bodily from the dead. "If all the relevant texts [i.e., the four gospels] are literally true down to their details, the orthodox conclusion would seem to be inevitable."[18] However, Allison rejects this conclusion, for he believes these narratives are based on later legends, which took decades to develop. Here we see the explosive nature of the evidence provided by the ancient confession in 1 Cor 15. For as we have seen, the primitive confession in 1 Cor 15:3–7, which took shape within months of the founding events, presupposes a narrative of the kind we see in the Synoptics and John, involving an empty tomb and encounters with a Jesus risen in flesh and bones. The apparitions/legends theory championed by Grass, Yarbro Collins, Allison, and so many others is not historically plausible, for it fails to account for this most crucial piece of evidence, the apostolic confession of 1 Cor 15:3–8, and what the ancient Greek of this formula, in its historical context, actually says.

N. T. Wright has asserted that "the proposal that Jesus was bodily raised from the dead possesses unrivaled power to explain the historical data at the heart of early Christianity."[19] Our findings substantiate Wright's claim.[20] The only alternative proposal, the "apparitions/legends" theory, as we have seen, is not a possible explanation of the data. The only historical hypothesis consistent with the evi-

---

17. See 1 Clem. 5–6; Ign. *Rom.* 4.3; Irenaeus, *Haer.* 3.1–3; Dionysius of Corinth *apud* Eusebius, *Hist. eccl.* 2.25.8; the Roman presbyter Gaius *apud* Eusebius, *Hist. eccl.* 2.25.6–7; Tertullian, *Praes.* 36; *Marc* 4.5.

18. Allison, *Resurrection*, 352.

19. Wright, *Resurrection*, 718.

20. The miraculous nature of the resurrection does not impede the possibility of establishing it historically; see Graham H. Twelftree, "The Historian and the Miraculous," *BBR* 28 (2018): 199–217. On the fallacy that modern scientific knowledge has shown the impossibility of miracles, and thus of the resurrection of Christ, see Gary R. Habermas, *Risen Indeed: A Historical Investigation into the Resurrection of Jesus* (Bellingham, WA: Lexham Academic, 2021).

*The Implications of the Apostolic Formula for History and Faith*

dence of the astonishingly early confession preserved in 1 Cor 15:3–8 is that Jesus of Nazareth rose from the dead.

## THE IMPLICATIONS OF JESUS'S RESURRECTION FROM THE DEAD

It is, then, in light of 1 Cor 15:3–8, beyond a reasonable historical doubt that Jesus rose again from the dead. What are the implications of this fact? According to a great chorus of learned voices, there are none at all. A contemporary and influential example is Dale Allison. According to Allison, Jesus's resurrection means nothing, for it is impossible to derive "a theological proposition from history as such."[21] To be sure, Allison does maintain that the implications are massive if the resurrection did *not* happen. In that case, historic Christianity "falls to the ground."[22] But Allison assures us: "It does not, however, work the other way around."[23] Clearly, we must have here a lapse in logic. It is a "heads I win, tails you lose" situation. It can hardly mean everything if Jesus's resurrection did not happen, but nothing if it did.

At the same time, the claim that, if Christ has not been raised, historic Christianity falls to the ground, is clearly cogent. The apostle himself will write to the Corinthians in 1 Cor 15:14: "And if Christ has not been raised, our proclamation is vain, your faith is also in vain." And the claim that a historical fact as such entails no particular theological or existential ramifications, is founded upon a principle of undeniable logical validity. This principle is that facts always need to be interpreted, and this requires a prior framework of understanding within which they are interpreted. Therefore a historical fact in isolation means nothing. Here Allison and others make a valid and significant point.

And yet they are wrong. And their logical blunder comes in their application of this principle to the apostolic witness to Jesus's resurrection. This requires unpacking. According to Allison, Jesus's resurrection from the dead, even if true, has no implications whatsoever for the truth of the Christian faith. This is so, he argues, because Jesus's resurrection as a historical fact "has meaning only within this or that wider religious or philosophical framework, and one cannot unfold its implications except, to recall Quine, within some web of belief."[24] Allison's thought here calls to mind the famed dictum of Gotthold Ephraim Lessing (1729–1781) re-

---

21. Allison, *Resurrection*, 360.
22. Allison, *Resurrection*, 361.
23. Allison, *Resurrection*, 361.
24. Allison, *Resurrection*, 362.

garding the "ugly ditch" between the apostolic witness to Jesus's resurrection and the truth of Christianity: "Accidental truths of history can never become the proof of necessary truths of reason.... That, then, is the ugly, broad ditch which I cannot get across, no matter however often and however earnestly I have tried to make the leap."[25] Here even N. T. Wright concurs. "It has too often been assumed," he avers, "that if Jesus was raised from the dead this automatically 'proves' the entire Christian worldview—including the belief that he was and is ... the Son of God."[26] This is mistaken, Wright claims, for the resurrection as a historical event does not entail its own meaning. "There seems then to be no necessary compulsion, either for those who believe in Jesus' resurrection or for those who disbelieve it, to interpret it within the framework of thought employed by the early Christians themselves."[27] Likewise Allison: "'God raised Jesus from the dead' is a frame-specific Christian doctrine, not a free-floating, historical-critical conclusion. Even if we can, as I believe, muster stout arguments for this or that worldview, the evidence for Jesus' resurrection does not in itself constitute such an argument."[28] The resurrection of Jesus "does not even tell us what religion we should adopt."[29]

But this argument, however many scholars make it and however confidently they do so, is a fallacy. The reason is this. The apostles did not give testimony to a fact in isolation. They did not bear witness to a bare fact apart from its meaning. They did not say, "we have witnessed a miraculous event, make of it what you will." Rather, their testimony included both the fact *and* its meaning. They bore witness not only to a fact but to a "web of belief" unfolding the implications of that fact. They said, "Christ has been raised on the third day in fulfillment of the Scriptures" (15:4). What N. T. Wright calls "the framework of thought employed by the early Christians," which he somehow considers separable from the apostolic witness to the resurrection, was in actuality the very form and content of that witness. Paul can say of the same identical apostolic message "we bore witness" (15:15, ἐμαρτυρήσαμεν) and "we proclaim" (15:11, κηρύσσομεν; cf. 15:14, τὸ κήρυγμα ἡμῶν). He can call the identical apostolic message "our testimony to Christ" (1 Cor 1:6, τὸ μαρτύριον τοῦ Χριστοῦ), and "the good news of Christ" (1 Cor 9:12, τὸ εὐαγγέλιον τοῦ Χριστοῦ; cf. 15:1). The apostolic testimony to the resurrection was given in the context of a narrative of Jesus's deeds, teaching, and saving acts. This included, on the evidence of 1 Corinthians alone: Jesus's teaching (7:10–11), his gathering

---

25. Gotthold Ephraim Lessing, "On the Proof of the Spirit and of Power," in *Lessing's Theological Writings* (ed. and trans. Henry Chadwick; Stanford: Stanford University Press, 1957), 53, 55.
26. Wright, *Resurrection*, 720.
27. Wright, *Resurrection*, 723.
28. Allison, *Resurrection*, 360.
29. Allison, *Resurrection*, 362.

of disciples (11:23–25), betrayal (11:23), Last Supper and institution of the Lord's Supper (11:23–25), crucifixion (1:17, 18, 23; 5:7; 15:3), burial (15:4), resurrection on the third day (15:4; cf. 6:14), and appearances to apostolic eyewitnesses (15:5–8). The testimony of the apostles was given in the context of "the word of the cross" (1:18), which proclaimed Christ as "our wisdom from God, our righteousness, sanctification, and redemption" (1:30). The response to the apostolic testimony involved entry into the believing community, the church (1:2; 2:1–5; 4:17; 6:4; 15:9), and participation in communal practices such as baptism (1:13–17; 6:11; 12:13) and the Eucharist (10:1–4, 16–17; 11:17–34). In short, the apostles' eyewitness testimony to the resurrection was inseparable from their proclamation of the Christian faith. This is why the claim of Lessing in the eighteenth century, and of Allison in the twenty-first, is an unfounded fallacy. It fails to take into account the unique character of the apostles' testimony to Jesus's resurrection, in which fact and meaning are inseparable. *This* fact comes with its own meaning.

The implications of Jesus's resurrection, then, are extraordinary. The one raised is thereby "revealed as the Son of God with power by the Holy Spirit through the resurrection of the dead, Jesus Christ our Lord" (Rom 1:4). Jesus's resurrection warrants belief in him as the incarnate Son of God. And it warrants belief in the teaching of the apostles about him, given in conjunction with their eyewitness testimony to his resurrection. That Jesus's resurrection from the dead verifies the truth of the Christian faith is implicit in the apostolic formula in 1 Cor 15:3–8, in which the apostles' testimony to the resurrection is given in the context of the proclamation of the gospel. And it reflects Paul's own thought within 1 Cor 15, who argues that since "Christ has been raised from the dead" (15:20), "your labor is not in vain in the Lord" (15:58).

## The Relationship of Faith and Reason Assumed in the Confession

The relation between faith and historical evidence assumed within the apostolic formula of 1 Cor 15:3–8 is quite striking. The confession is not consistent with a vacuous and circular Barthian fideism, in which faith is the warrant for faith.[30] Nor is it consistent with an understanding of Jesus's resurrection as "incapable alike of observation and demonstration."[31] Within the formula, by contrast, the truth

---

30. See Karl Barth *The Resurrection of the Dead* (trans. H. J. Stenning; 1933; repr., Eugene, OR: Wipf and Stock, 2003), 130–45.
31. Barrett, 341; similarly Lindemann, 336; Fee, 817.

of Christ's resurrection—and thus the truth of the apostolic proclamation—is grounded in *empirical* evidence: the evidence of the five senses and the testimony of eyewitnesses (15:5–8, 15). In listing the eyewitnesses to Jesus's resurrection, enumerating multiple resurrection appearances, and identifying multiple witnesses, this ancient formula forms not only a confession but also an *argument*—an argument that is fully empirical, reasonable, and rational.

This raises a question. Since historical facts can only be known with a high degree of probability, how can the formula's historical and empirical argument from eyewitness testimony establish the certainty required of faith? This is another aspect of the "ugly, broad ditch" between historical fact and faith contemplated by Lessing. Many have considered this question unanswerable. However, there is an answer to this question, and it lies in the unique character of the formula we have already observed. For this apostolic confession is not only a witness to historical events. It is also the divinely revealed "gospel" or "good news" (1 Cor 15:1), the historical events to which it bears witness are the acts of God in history (15:15), and it mediates "the knowledge of God" (15:34). The faith for which it calls (15:1, 2, 11, 14, 17) is thus faith in God, who cannot lie (e.g., Rom 3:4; 1 John 1:10, 5:10), and is therefore certain. Moreover, this faith is a gift of divine grace worked by the Holy Spirit (1 Cor 1:2, 9, 30–31; 2:14–16; 12:3; 15:10), thus bestowing a divinely given certainty. In both ways, then, as faith in the revelation of God and as faith given by God, this faith is not merely probable but certain. The conception of faith within this ancient confession coheres strikingly with Thomas Aquinas's definition of faith: "an act of the intellect assenting to the truth of God at the command of the will, moved by God through grace."[32]

Thomas's definition brings out a further aspect of faith assumed within the formula and explicit elsewhere in Paul's letters: the role of the will in the act of believing (1 Cor 1:30; 6:9–11; 9:24–10:22; cf. Rom 2:4–5; 2 Cor 7:9–10; 12:21). This nature of faith—as operative not only in the intellect but also in the will—explains why the historical evidence for Jesus's resurrection within this ancient formula, although rendering rival explanations unviable, is persuasive to some but not to others. Given this disparity, Dale Allison asks incredulously whether scholars who have stressed the conclusive nature of the historical evidence for Jesus's resurrection "mean to imply that Christians of conventional conviction are, once all the arguments are sorted out, of greater cerebral endowment than everyone else, or at least better at using the brains they have."[33] But this misses the point, for it fails to grasp the nature of faith presupposed within this ancient confession. Faith does

---

32. Thomas Aquinas, *ST* II-II, Q. 2, Art. 9.
33. Allison, *Resurrection*, 355.

## The Implications of the Apostolic Formula for History and Faith

indeed involve the intellect, but it is not only a matter of the intellect but also of the heart and will. The intellect can only see what the heart and will permit it to see. The formula presumes an understanding of faith in which the intellect assents on the basis of convincing evidence (15:5–8, 11), but only as the whole person is moved by God's grace (15:10). The difference between faith and unbelief, according to this apostolic confession, lies not in the mind but in the heart and the will.

CHAPTER 6

## *The Futility of Faith Apart from the Resurrection*

15:12–19

In v. 12 we learn the reason why Paul has felt it necessary to restate the gospel he brought to the Corinthians (15:1–11) and to make it more fully known to them (cf. γνωρίζω, 15:1) through the exposition of this chapter (15:12–58). The reason is that some at Corinth are saying that "there is no resurrection of the dead" (15:12).

Moreover, vv. 12–19 confirm what we saw in chapter 1 of this commentary: namely, that in coming to chapter 15 and to the topic of the resurrection of the dead, we have come to the climax of the letter as well as the climax and resolution of Paul's interaction with the Corinthian wisdom begun in 1:18–4:21. Let us first take the evidence for this in v. 12. In 1:10, as we saw, Paul begins the body opening of the letter and lays the thematic ground plan of the epistle. This παρακαλῶ clause in 1:10 reveals, as Carl Bjerkelund argued, "the real concern of the apostle."[1] There Paul exhorts that *all* (πάντες) at Corinth *say* (λέγητε) the same thing, and that there be no divisions *among them* (ἐν ὑμῖν). Paul's wording in 1:10 implies that he is concerned that *some* who are *among* the Corinthians are *saying* something different and not in agreement with the apostolic gospel. The striking reverse parallelism between 1:10 and 15:12 reveals that in 15:12 we learn what that something is:

1:10   ἵνα τὸ αὐτὸ <u>λέγητε</u> <u>πάντες</u> καὶ μὴ ᾖ <u>ἐν ὑμῖν</u> σχίσματα
15:12  πῶς <u>λέγουσιν</u> <u>ἐν ὑμῖν</u> <u>τινες</u> ὅτι ἀνάστασις νεκρῶν οὐκ ἔστιν;

---

1. Carl J. Bjerkelund, *Parakalô: Form, Funktion und Sinn der Parakalô-Sätze in den paulinischen Briefen* (Oslo: Universitetsforlaget, 1967), 189.

*The Futility of Faith Apart from the Resurrection*

With 1 Cor 15:12, we have reached the concern that was clearly uppermost in Paul's mind when he penned 1 Cor 1:10.

Let us next consider the vocabulary of 15:12, 14, and 17. In 1:18–2:5, Paul contrasted human wisdom with the foolishness of the gospel, a distinctive feature of that passage being the clustering of the terms κηρύσσω (1:23), κήρυγμα (1:21, 2:4), and πίστις (2:5). Not including chapter 15, these terms are rare in 1 Corinthians, with κηρύσσω occurring elsewhere only in 9:27, πίστις only in 13:13 and 16:13, and κήρυγμα nowhere else. Besides 1:18–2:5, the *combination* of all three terms recurs nowhere else in 1 Cor 1–14 and 16. But all three terms recur again in profusion within 15:12–19 (κηρύσσω, 15:12; κήρυγμα, 15:14; πίστις, 15:14, 17). As we saw in chapter 1 of this commentary, a key theme of 1 Cor 1–4 is that the apostolic kerygma must not be corrupted by human wisdom, lest the gospel be made "vain" (κενόω, 1:17; μάταιος, 3:20). This theme recurs nowhere else in chapters 5–14. But it is a key and central theme within 15:12–19 (κενός, 15:14 [2×]; μάταιος, 15:17). We find here not only the same *words* but also the same *theme*—the *gospel* made *vain*. Thus here we learn the nature of the human wisdom whereby some at Corinth are rendering the gospel vain—the denial of the resurrection of the dead.

Finally, let us observe the vocabulary of 15:15. In 1:6, Paul refers to the gospel as the apostolic "testimony to Christ" (τὸ μαρτύριον τοῦ Χριστοῦ). The elements within Pauline thanksgivings regularly presage key themes within the epistle. It is thus a striking fact that the language of witness or testimony that is introduced in 1:6 does not recur again in the letter (with the possible exception of the variant reading in 2:1) until 15:15. In this verse the vocabulary of testimony abounds and refers, as in 1:6, to the eyewitness testimony of the apostles to Jesus's resurrection (ψευδομάρτυρες ... ἐμαρτυρήσαμεν ... ὅτι ἤγειρεν τὸν Χριστόν).

All these connections within 15:12–19 to the thanksgiving, the body opening, and the first four chapters of the letter (as well as others that we will note in the course of our commentary on vv. 12–19) confirm that in 15:12–19 we have found the chief characteristic of the human wisdom opposed by Paul in 1:18–4:21 and the interpretive key to the entire letter. In 15:12–19, Paul will begin to take the Corinthian wisdom head-on: "How do some among you say that there is no resurrection of the dead?"

## THE BELIEFS OF THOSE WHO DENIED THE RESURRECTION

Scholarship has focused on three interrelated questions regarding the faction at Corinth who denied the resurrection of the dead: (1) What doctrine of the afterlife, if any, did they hold in the place of the resurrection? (2) Did they also deny the

CHAPTER 6

resurrection of Christ? (3) Why did they object to the hope of the resurrection, and what was the source of their objection?[2]

Let us take up each of these questions in turn. First, what were the positive beliefs of those who denied the resurrection regarding the afterlife? A minority of scholars have argued that the opponents of the resurrection at Corinth denied any kind of life after death, believing either that the soul perished together with the body or existed postmortem only in the shadowy underworld of the dead.[3] These scholars generally urge two main arguments in support of this view. First, they point out that belief in an immortal afterlife of the soul was not widespread in antiquity, as belief in the finality of death was much more common and thus the more likely view at Corinth.[4] Second, they claim that Paul's response is fitting for those who believe death brings extinction, but not for those who believe in the immortality of the soul.[5] For Paul argues that if what the objectors say is true, then "those who have died in Christ have perished" (15:18), "we have set our hope in Christ for this life only" (15:19), and all Christian moral struggle, endurance of persecution, and sufferings are in vain (15:29–32). "Let us eat and drink, for tomorrow we die" (15:32). As Paul J. Brown asks: "How does an immortality of the soul encourage one to live a life of dissipation?"[6] Paul's argument only works, it is claimed, if it is directed toward those who believe that the soul perishes with the body or exists postmortem only in the netherworld among the dead. If directed toward those who deny the resurrection of the body but believe in a blessed immortality of the soul, Paul's argument, it is claimed, utterly fails.

Another minority view is that the opponents of the resurrection at Corinth were "pneumatics" or "enthusiasts" with an "over-realized" eschatology, believing in a present spiritual "resurrection" (or present eschatological blessings) rendering a future bodily resurrection unnecessary.[7] Once widely held, this view has in recent years been strongly criticized and has few supporters today.

---

2. The best recent summary of scholarly views on these questions is Matt O'Reilly, *Paul and the Resurrected Body: Social Identity and Ethical Practice* (ESEC 22; Atlanta: SBL Press, 2020), 49–55.

3. So Johan S. Vos, "Argumentation und Situation in 1Kor. 15," *NovT* 41 (1999): 313–33; Stefan Szymik, "The Corinthian Opponents of the Resurrection in 1 Cor 15:12: The Epicurean Hypothesis Reconsidered," *BibAn* 10 (2020): 437–56; Jan Lambrecht, "Three Brief Notes on 1 Corinthians 15," *Bijdr* 62 (2001): 31–35; Paul J. Brown, *Bodily Resurrection and Ethics in 1 Cor 15: Connecting Faith and Morality in the Context of Greco-Roman Mythology* (WUNT 2.360; Tübingen: Mohr Siebeck, 2014), 66–107.

4. E.g. O'Reilly, *Resurrected Body*, 51–52.

5. Vos, "Argumentation und Situation," 317–20, 324–27; Lambrecht, "Three Brief Notes," 33–34.

6. Brown, *Bodily Resurrection*, 74.

7. So Christopher M. Tuckett, "The Corinthians Who Say 'There Is No Resurrection of the

## The Futility of Faith Apart from the Resurrection

The great majority of interpreters today hold that the objectors to the resurrection at Corinth were anthropological dualists, rejecting a bodily resurrection but embracing a heavenly afterlife and the immortality of the soul.[8] During the past heyday of the "over-realized eschatology" thesis, a number of scholars adopted a kind of combination of this view with that thesis, holding that the Corinthian opponents of the resurrection believed in a present spiritual fullness followed by a spiritual but nonbodily afterlife.[9] The major argument brought forward by advocates of this view is the evidence for the practice of baptism for the dead at Corinth (1 Cor 15:29), which clearly seems to presuppose belief in some kind of afterlife. But the seeming incongruence of Paul's argument, as a response to those who hoped for a blessed immortality of the soul, is usually considered a major difficulty with this view.[10]

How should we evaluate these scholarly claims? Of the three hypotheses outlined above, we may dismiss the second one (spiritual "resurrection" in the present). There is no evidence in antiquity before the date of 1 Corinthians for such a belief. The case for the existence of this belief at Corinth relies entirely on a particular interpretation of 1 Corinthians that places an enormous amount of weight on a highly questionable reading of one particular verse, 1 Cor 4:8.[11] Moreover, Paul does not report the opponents at Corinth of the resurrection as saying, like Hymenaeus and Philetus in 2 Tim 2:17–18, τὴν ἀνάστασιν ἤδη γεγονέναι ("the resurrection has already taken place") but ἀνάστασις νεκρῶν οὐκ ἔστιν ("there

---

Dead' (1 Cor 15,12)," in *The Corinthian Correspondence* (ed. Reimund Bieringer; BETL 125; Leuven: Leuven University Press, 1996), 247–75; Andrew T. Lincoln, *Paradise Now and Not Yet: Studies in the Role of the Heavenly Dimension in Paul's Thought with Special Reference to His Eschatology* (SNTSMS 43; Cambridge: Cambridge University Press, 1981), 33–37; Anthony C. Thiselton, "Realized Eschatology at Corinth," *NTS* 24 (1978): 510–26; Collins, 541; and (in the main) Matthew R. Malcolm, *Paul and the Rhetoric of Reversal in 1 Corinthians: The Impact of Paul's Gospel on His Macro-Rhetoric* (SNTSMS 155; Cambridge: Cambridge University Press, 2013), 231–66.

8. See, for example, Dale Martin, *The Corinthian Body* (New Haven: Yale University Press, 1995), 104–8, 120–23; Martinus de Boer, *The Defeat of Death: Apocalyptic Eschatology in 1 Corinthians 15 and Romans 5* (JSNTSup 22; 1988; repr., London: T&T Clark, 2019), 96–105; K. R. Harriman, "A Synthetic Proposal about the Corinthian Resurrection Deniers," *NovT* 62 (2020): 180–200; J. A. Schep, *The Nature of the Resurrection Body: A Study of the Biblical Data* (Grand Rapids: Eerdmans, 1964), 186–88; Schreiner, 308; Timothy A. Brookins, *Corinthian Wisdom, Stoic Philosophy, and the Ancient Economy* (SNTSMS 159; Cambridge: Cambridge University Press, 2014), 192–96.

9. So A. J. M. Wedderburn, "The Problem of the Denial of the Resurrection in I Corinthians xv," *NovT* 23 (1981): 229–41; Jack H. Wilson, "The Corinthians Who Say There Is No Resurrection of the Dead," *ZNW* 59 (1960): 90–107.

10. Cf. the discussion in Wedderburn, "Denial," 230–31, 240–41.

11. Cf. O'Reilly, *Resurrected Body*, 50–51.

CHAPTER 6

is no resurrection of the dead").[12] Christopher Tuckett's attempt to evade this difficulty by the suggestion that vv. 12–19 are in fact an extended quotation of the Corinthians (!) only serves to confirm the untenability of this hypothesis.[13]

But what of the two remaining scholarly hypotheses regarding the afterlife beliefs of the opponents of the resurrection at Corinth—complete annihilation at death or a dualistic concept of the afterlife of the soul? Both of these were common coin in antiquity.[14] They were therefore live options at Corinth. Is there clear evidence for a choice between them? As we have seen, those who advocate the latter option believe they find irrefutable evidence for this view in the practice of baptism on behalf of the dead (15:29). But this argument does not hold up under scrutiny, for it conflates or identifies the "certain ones among you" (ἐν ὑμῖν τινες, 15:12) who deny the resurrection with the Corinthians as a whole. But as J. N. Vorster has convincingly shown, "the deniers of the resurrection should not be identified with the implicit readers."[15] As Vorster observes, Paul's argument throughout the chapter, especially in 15:12 and 15:33–34, "serves to distance 'them' (the deniers) from them (the implied readers)."[16] The opponents of the resurrection, as Matt O'Reilly notes, "are a subgroup of the larger community."[17] There is thus no reason to believe that baptism for the sake of the dead was a practice connected with or congenial to those who denied the resurrection. Moreover, v. 29 does not indicate that the individuals baptized for the dead, of whom Paul speaks to the Corinthians in the third person, necessarily existed *at Corinth*. Finally, the logic of Paul's argument in v. 29 (as we will see in the commentary on that verse) requires that those baptized for the sake of the dead were motivated not by a generic belief in life after death but by a specific belief in bodily resurrection. For all these reasons, therefore, 1 Cor 15:29 offers no direct evidence for a belief in soul survival among the opponents of the resurrection at Corinth.[18]

What, then, of the chief argument of those who advocate that the opponents of the resurrection denied an afterlife of any kind—which is also the chief perplexity of those who advocate they believed in an afterlife of the soul—that Paul's response seems to demand such a view? Paul portrays the position of the opponents of the resurrection as denying any hope beyond this life (15:19) and as

---

12. Wedderburn, "Denial," 231–32; O'Reilly, *Resurrected Body*, 60–61; Harriman, "Synthetic Proposal," 187.
13. See Tuckett, "Corinthians Who Say," 264–74.
14. For beliefs regarding the afterlife in antiquity, see excursus 3 following chapter 7.
15. J. N. Vorster, "Resurrection Faith in 1 Corinthians 15," *Neot* 23 (1989): 290.
16. Vorster, "Resurrection Faith," 289.
17. O'Reilly, *Resurrected Body*, 58. Cf. Szymik, "Opponents," 442–43.
18. So also Vos, "Argumentation und Situation," 324; Lambrecht, "Three Brief Notes," 34.

*The Futility of Faith Apart from the Resurrection*

leading to an ethical nihilism that renders sufferings for Christ in this present life meaningless (15:30–32). This would hardly be an accurate portrayal, or so it is thought, if these opponents embraced belief in the afterlife existence and judgments of an immortal soul. However, as self-evident as this argument may appear to many modern scholars, it fails to grasp the thought of Paul within its Jewish and biblical context. For the apostle, as we will see more fully as his argument proceeds in chapter 15, the human being is a union of body and soul, and salvation can only be the redemption of the whole person (Rom 1:9; 1 Cor 2:11; 1 Thess 5:23). For him, therefore, the prospect of an immortal soul permanently separated from the body is *not a coherent conception* of the human being, let alone a hope of life and salvation to be cherished. Therefore, for Paul a Platonic-like immortality of the soul offers no more hope beyond death than an Epicurean-like belief in extinction.[19] Paul, to be sure, teaches a blessed intermediate state of the soul apart from the body before the resurrection (2 Cor 5:6–8; Phil 1:23); but for Paul such a state is only blessed in light of its fulfillment in the resurrection (2 Cor 5:1–5; Phil 3:7–11, 20–21). Paul's argument in 15:12–19 and 15:29–34, therefore, offers no basis for deciding whether the Corinthian opponents of the resurrection believed in the extinction of the soul at death or in a dualistic conception of the soul's immortality. For Paul, the difference was not worth discussing.

We find, then, that evidence is lacking for *any* of the standard scholarly options for reconstructing the positive beliefs regarding the afterlife of the opponents of the resurrection at Corinth. Whether they believed in the soul's immortality or in its extinction at death is simply not ascertainable from our sources. We do not know whether they even *had* a coherent doctrine of the afterlife to offer. What is clear from our sources is that their denial of the resurrection was a *reaction* to one particular teaching of the apostle—the resurrection. People acting out of reaction, as both ancient and modern examples attest, often have no positive doctrine of their own or must take some time to develop one. There is no way to know whether those among the Corinthians who denied the resurrection had or had not taken this step.

Did the opponents at Corinth of the future resurrection also deny or doubt the resurrection of Christ? A small minority of interpreters have argued that such was the case.[20] These scholars argue that Paul's careful rehearsal of the gospel in 15:1–11, the list of eyewitnesses to Christ's resurrection he provides in 15:5–8, and his indications of uncertainty regarding the present state of the Corinthians' faith

---

19. See the perceptive treatment of this aspect of Paul's thought in Thomas Aquinas, *1 Cor.* 924.
20. So Lambrecht, "Three Brief Notes," 28–31; Wilson, "Corinthians Who Say," 90–107; de Boer, *Defeat*, 103, 105.

CHAPTER 6

in 15:1–2 and 15:11, all indicate that some at Corinth discounted or doubted the resurrection of Jesus from the dead.[21] However, the vast majority of interpreters hold that those at Corinth who denied the resurrection nonetheless believed in the resurrection of Christ.[22] They point to Paul's affirmation that the Corinthians have believed and stand firm in the gospel (15:1, 11) and argue that the logic of Paul's argument in 15:12–19 depends upon the Corinthians' belief in Christ's resurrection. On this majority view, those at Corinth who denied the resurrection did not deny the past resurrection of Christ but the future resurrection of believers. Paul J. Brown advocates a distinctive version of this view, finding the origin of this Corinthian belief in ancient popular mythology, which Brown claims combined belief in the finality of death for all mortals with belief in a few bodily immortalized heroes. This explains, claims Brown, how some at Corinth could believe in the resurrection of Jesus and yet deny any hope beyond death for themselves.[23]

How should we evaluate these arguments? First, Brown's argument, as we saw in excursus 1, is based upon a massive misunderstanding of the nature of hero cults in antiquity. These semi-divine figures were not understood as bodily immortalized but rather as divinized souls who had shed their human bodies. Second, and more crucially, a fallacy is involved in the arguments on both sides in the debate over whether the deniers of the resurrection accepted or rejected the resurrection of Christ. For these arguments are founded upon Paul's statements and assumptions regarding faith at Corinth in 15:1–11 and 15:12–19. But these passages are directed to the Corinthians as a whole, whom Paul distinguishes from those who deny the resurrection ("some among you," 15:12), and whom he seeks to dissuade from the resurrection deniers' influence (15:33–34). Just as we have no direct evidence for the positive beliefs regarding the afterlife of those who denied the resurrection at Corinth (if they had any), so likewise whether they accepted or rejected the resurrection of Christ is not recoverable from the letter.

Why did some at Corinth deny the hope of resurrection, and what was the source of their objections? Most scholars have traced the source of their beliefs to popular philosophy.[24] However, Jack H. Wilson suggests that the source of influence was the mystery cults, and Paul J. Brown argues that it was the afterlife expectations of the traditional mythology.[25] And K. R. Harriman suggests that

21. Cf. de Boer, *Defeat*, 103; Lambrecht, "Three Brief Notes," 29–30.
22. A small sampling include Collins, 543; Sampley, 980; John Coolidge Hurd, *The Origin of 1 Corinthians* (Macon: Mercer University Press, 1983), 200; Scott M. Lewis, *"So That God May Be All in All": The Apocalyptic Message of 1 Corinthians 15,12–34* (TGST 42; Rome: Gregorian University Press, 1998), 42.
23. Brown, *Bodily Resurrection*, 28–107, 138.
24. So, for example, Martin, *Body*, 104–8, 120; Szymik, "Corinthian Opponents."
25. Wilson, "Corinthians Who Say," 103; Brown, *Resurrection and Ethics*, 66–107.

those at Corinth who rejected the resurrection were a mixed group, some of them denying the resurrection due to the influence of popular philosophy and others due to the influence of popular mythology.[26] Here is one place where the evidence of 1 Corinthians permits us to reach positive results regarding those who denied the resurrection at Corinth. The results of our investigation in chapter 1 of this commentary allow us to settle this question. For there we saw that Paul's treatment of the Corinthian wisdom in 1 Cor 1:10–4:21 looked ahead to chapter 15, and that Paul's chief concern with the self-professed wise at Corinth was their denial of the resurrection of the dead. We also saw that the Corinthian claim to wisdom did not involve rhetoric, as usually supposed, but a claim to philosophical knowledge. We thus see that the objection at Corinth to the resurrection was a *philosophical* one based on purported knowledge and wisdom. We therefore find only one solid fact regarding the beliefs of the dissenters from Paul's gospel at Corinth: they claimed, on philosophical grounds, that there is no resurrection of the dead. And yet this simple fact opens up, as we shall discover, a whole new window on Paul's teaching on the resurrection in 1 Cor 15.

## The Denial of the Resurrection at Corinth

We have seen that although much scholarly ink has been spilled on the positive beliefs of the opponents of the resurrection at Corinth regarding the afterlife, we can know little or nothing on this topic. Such results might seem disappointing. However, we do have one solid and crucial piece of information. We know what some at Corinth *denied*. We know, by Paul's own report (15:12–13), that they claimed ἀνάστασις νεκρῶν οὐκ ἔστιν ("there is no resurrection of the dead"). What they denied, then, was ἀνάστασις νεκρῶν. What does this mean?

### What Some at Corinth Denied

The etymology and semantic range of the noun ἀνάστασις are fortunately quite clear. It is derived from the compound verb ἀνίστημι, which is composed of the

---

26. Harriman, "Synthetic Proposal," 180–200. Laura Salah Nasrallah argues that anxiety over death was more heightened at Corinth than elsewhere in the ancient world but fails to provide convincing evidence for this thesis. See her "Grief in Corinth: The Roman City and Paul's Corinthian Correspondence," in *Contested Spaces: Houses and Temples in Roman Antiquity and the New Testament* (ed. David L. Balch and Annette Weissenrieder; WUNT 285; Tübingen: Mohr Siebeck, 2012), 109–39. Moreover, it is not clear how such findings, even if true, would illumine the epistolary situation. The situation at Corinth addressed by Paul in 15:12 is not heightened concern over death but the denial of the resurrection.

CHAPTER 6

prefix ἀνά "up" and the verb ἵστημι "to stand, cause to stand." The verb ἀνίστημι is thus used regularly of one fallen, sitting, or lying down who is *raised to stand* or *rises to stand* (Matt 9:9; Mark 9:27; 14:57; Luke 4:16; 6:8; 11:7–8; 22:45; John 11:31; Acts 9:26, 34, 41; 14:10; 26:16, 30). Correspondingly, its derived noun ἀνάστασις signifies (when used transitively) a "making to stand or rise up" and (when used intransitively) a "standing or rising up."[27] The noun is found, for example, in inscriptions for the *setting up* of a statue or monument.[28] The word ἀνάστασις never denotes the idea of rising up in the sense of elevation or ascension but has, in agreement with its etymology, the more restricted semantic range of *rising or being raised to stand upright*.

The noun ἀνάστασις thus has the core semantic sense of "arising to stand." When used with reference to the dead, ἀνάστασις therefore denotes *the return of the dead body to physical life*. In classical texts, its cognate verb ἀνίστημι is used quite frequently to describe the miraculous return of the dead body to life, a fact always deemed impossible outside the world of myth (Homer, *Il.* 21.55–56; 24.551, 756; Sophocles, *El.* 927; Xenophon, *Cyn.* 1.6; Euripides, *Alc.* 127; Herodotus, *Hist.* 3.62.3–4). The noun, although found less frequently, is likewise used in classical sources to denote the restoration of the dead body to life with the same proviso or assumption of impossibility. In a drama composed by Aeschylus, Apollo declares that "when once the dust has received a man's blood... there is no resurrection" (οὔτις ἔστ' ἀνάστασις, *Eum.* 648). Within the Jewish context, ἀνίστημι is the verb of choice within the LXX in virtually all the key texts that express the hope of bodily resurrection (Isa 26:19; Dan 12:2, 13; Job 42:17; 2 Macc 7:9, 14; 12:44). Second Maccabees, which contains perhaps the fullest and strongest statements of any ancient Jewish document regarding the bodily and fleshly nature of the resurrection, employs the noun ἀνάστασις to denote the resurrection (2 Macc 7:14; 12:43). We see, then, that the word ἀνάστασις was used, in both pagan and Jewish contexts, to denote the miraculous return to life of a once-dead body.

In the construction ἀνάστασις νεκρῶν, the noun ἀνάστασις is paired with the substantive νεκρός. First Corinthians 15:12 is the first occurrence of the word νεκρός within the letter, but it appears with great frequency throughout the remainder of the chapter (15:12, 13, 15, 16, 20, 21, 29, 32, 35, 42, 52). In LSJ, two core meanings are given for νεκρός as a substantive: (1) "*corpse*" and (2) "in pl., *the dead*, as dwellers in the netherworld."[29] The plural νεκροί can be used with reference to the dead conceived as shades or spirits apart from their bodies. However, the use of νεκρός

27. LSJ, s.v. "ἀνάστασις."
28. MM, s.v. "ἀνάστασις."
29. LSJ, s.v. "νεκρός" (I.1, 4).

with reference to the physical corpse is by far the more frequent and normal usage.[30] We see this in the frequent references in the LXX and New Testament to the burial of the νεκροί, that is, the bodies of the dead (Gen 23:4, 6, 8, 11, 13, 15; Tob 2:8; 12:12; Matt 8:22; Luke 9:60; 24:5). We see this also in the term νεκρία within ancient Greek papyri as a designation for the place where corpses were embalmed.[31] That νεκρός denotes the corpse becomes overwhelmingly clear in those passages in the gospels that refer to those restored to physical and bodily life by Jesus as ὁ νεκρός or οἱ νεκροί (Matt 10:8; 11:5; Luke 7:14–15, 22; John 12:1, 9, 17). Although used with reference to the bodies of the dead, the word νεκρός differs from the terms σῶμα "body" and πτῶμα "corpse." For these latter terms refer only to the body, whereas νεκρός denotes the dead as whole persons, body and soul.[32] The definition offered in BDAG captures the normal use of the word: "one who is no longer physically alive, dead person, a dead body, a corpse."[33]

When used in combination with ἀνάστασις, the normal but cancelable meaning of νεκρός with reference to the physical body or corpse becomes explicit and noncancelable.[34] In the construction ἀνάστασις νεκρῶν, the noun ἀνάστασις bears an intransitive sense with the genitive νεκρῶν expressing the subject of the action of the noun. The construction thus functions as the nominal equivalent of verbal phrases employing ἀνίστημι, such as ἀναστήσονται οἱ νεκροί ("the dead shall rise") in Isa 26:19 LXX. The verbal action of *arising to stand* inherent in the noun ἀνάστασις, paired with the substantive νεκρός denoting the *physical corpse*, forcefully expresses the conception of *the resurrection of the dead*, that is, the miraculous return of the dead body to life. The fleshly and bodily character of the resurrection, already inherent in the noun ἀνάστασις, is thus further accentuated by the fuller expression ἀνάστασις νεκρῶν.

In 1 Cor 15:12–13, Paul states the position of some at Corinth who deny the resurrection as ἀνάστασις νεκρῶν οὐκ ἔστιν ("there is no resurrection of the dead"). However, in 15:15–16 (cf. 15:29, 32) he states their view using the expression νεκροὶ οὐκ ἐγείρονται ("the dead are not raised"). Paul clearly regards the two expressions

---

30. See Frisk, 2:299–300.
31. Dssm, *BS*, 142; MM, s.v. "νεκρός."
32. Cf. Homer, *Od.* 11.147, and see Schmidt, *Syn.*, 4:54 (§156.2).
33. BDAG, s.v. "νεκρός."
34. Two main constructions may be distinguished. The first employs ἀνάστασις with the prepositional phrase ἐκ νεκρῶν ("from among the dead"); see, for example, ἀνάστασις ἡ ἐκ νεκρῶν in Luke 20:35 and ἡ ἀνάστασις ἡ ἐκ νεκρῶν in Acts 4:2; cf. Phil 3:11, ἡ ἐξανάστασις ἡ ἐκ νεκρῶν. In the second, ἀνάστασις is paired with the genitive νεκρῶν (ἀνάστασις νεκρῶν, Acts 17:32; 23:6; 24:21; 25:23; Rom 1:4; 1 Cor 15:12, 13, 21; Heb 6:2) or τῶν νεκρῶν (ἡ ἀνάστασις τῶν νεκρῶν, Matt 22:30; 1 Cor 15:42).

CHAPTER 6

as synonymous and equivalent. In our study of the verb ἐγείρω in chapter 3 of the commentary, we saw that the semantics of that verb, when used with reference to the dead, clearly expresses the conception of the dead body's physical resurrection from the grave. This coheres with the same conception of the body's return to physical life that we have now seen is present in the phrase ἀνάστασις νεκρῶν.

For all ancient Greek speakers, then, the expression ἀνάστασις νεκρῶν denoted the concept of resurrection, that is, the physical return to life of the dead body. Within Paul's Jewish context, the phrase ἀνάστασις νεκρῶν and its variants are even more precise, denoting not the mere concept of resurrection but the specific Jewish hope of a coming future resurrection of the bodies of the faithful in the time of the God of Israel's coming reign (Matt 22:30; Acts 23:6; 24:21; 25:23; Heb 6:2; cf. Luke 20:35; Acts 4:2). When he came to Corinth, Paul had proclaimed to the Corinthians that this promise of the God of Israel's conquest of death was now fulfilled in the resurrection of Jesus of Nazareth, the firstfruits of a coming resurrection of all who belong to Christ: "God both raised the Lord to life, and will raise us to life, through his power" (1 Cor 6:14). It is this hope of future bodily resurrection that some at Corinth were now denying: "How can some among you say that there is no resurrection of the dead?" (1 Cor 15:12).

*What Paul Affirms in 1 Corinthians 15*

Our findings regarding the meaning of the "resurrection of the dead" (ἀνάστασις νεκρῶν) denied by some at Corinth is a crucial datum for grasping Paul's teaching in this chapter. For what some at Corinth *deny* is what Paul will *affirm* in 1 Cor 15. Paul, who introduces the expression ἀνάστασις νεκρῶν for the first time in the letter in 15:12–13 to express its denial (ἀνάστασις νεκρῶν οὐκ ἔστιν), will repeat the term again in 15:21, and climactically so in 15:42 (οὕτως καὶ ἡ ἀνάστασις τῶν νεκρῶν), to affirm its reality. Likewise, the negative formulation νεκροὶ οὐκ ἐγείρονται ("the dead are not raised") in 15:15–16, 29, and 32 is powerfully reversed in the affirmation οἱ νεκροὶ ἐγερθήσονται ("the dead will be raised") in 15:52. Paul thus structures the chapter in such a way that the final instances of both ἀνάστασις νεκρῶν and of the verb ἐγείρω are triumphant reaffirmations of what some at Corinth deny!

The ramifications of this fact have been far too little recognized. Paul structures the chapter in order to reaffirm, against the denials by some at Corinth, ἡ ἀνάστασις τῶν νεκρῶν ("the resurrection of the dead," 15:42). This is an important interpretive key to 1 Cor 15, and the one point where grasping the position of the deniers at Corinth is crucial for the interpretation of the chapter. For we have now seen that ἡ ἀνάστασις τῶν νεκρῶν and its variants are a formulation that unambiguously expresses the hope of the physical return of the dead body to life, the hope of fleshly and bodily resurrection. The conclusion is inescapable: what Paul is affirming in 1 Cor 15 is the hope of the resurrection of the flesh. The mistaken claim (discussed in the introduction) of such scholars as Ernst Teichmann, Hans Grass, Dale Martin, Troels Engberg-Pedersen, Dale C. Allison, and a host of others—that Paul in this chapter affirms the resurrection of a body composed of spirit rather than of flesh—is thus ruled out from the start.[35] For what some at Corinth *deny*, and what Paul in this chapter explicitly *affirms*, is ἡ ἀνάστασις τῶν νεκρῶν—the physical restoration of the dead to life in their bodies of flesh and bones.

*Why Some at Corinth Denied the Resurrection*

We posited earlier in this chapter that the denial of the resurrection by the self-professed wise at Corinth was grounded in their claim to knowledge and wisdom. We have now seen precisely what they rejected: the miraculous and material restoration and return of the dead body to life. These two factors enable us to grasp their likely motive for rejecting the resurrection. For within classical antiquity the impossibility and absurdity of the resurrection of the physical body were considered axiomatic for any wise or educated person. Not only the thought, but even the form of the Corinthian slogan, ἀνάστασις νεκρῶν οὐκ ἔστιν ("there is no resurrection of the dead"), finds striking parallels in ancient Greek literature. In the *Iliad*, Achilles says to Priam concerning Hector, οὐδέ μιν ἀναστήσεις ("you will not resurrect him," *Il.* 24.551). In Herodotus, Prexaspes says to Cambyses as an obvious counterfactual: εἰ μέν νυν οἱ τεθνεῶτες ἀνεστέασι ("if now the dead have

---

35. See, for example, Ernst Teichmann, *Die paulinische Vorstellungen von Auferstehung und Gericht und ihre Beziehungen zur jüdischen Apokalyptik* (Freiburg: Mohr, 1896), 33–62; Hans Grass, *Ostergeschehen und Osterberichte* (Göttingen: Vandenhoeck & Ruprecht, 1962), 146–73; Martin, *Body*, 108–32; Troels Engberg-Pedersen, *Cosmology and Self in the Apostle Paul: The Material Spirit* (Oxford: Oxford University, 2010), 8–38; Engberg-Pedersen, "Complete and Incomplete Transformation in Paul—A Philosophical Reading of Paul on Body and Spirit," in *Metamorphoses: Resurrection, Body and Transformative Practices in Early Christianity* (ed. Turid Karlsen Seim and Jorunn Økland; Berlin: de Gruyter, 2009), 123–46; Engberg-Pedersen, "The Material Spirit: Cosmology and Ethics in Paul," *NTS* 55 (2009): 179–97; Dale C. Allison Jr., *The Resurrection of Jesus: Apologetics, Polemics, History* (New York: Bloomsbury, 2021), 136 n. 109, 248–61; Jeffrey R. Asher, *Polarity and Change in 1 Corinthians 15: A Study of Metaphysics, Rhetoric, and Resurrection* (Tübingen: Mohr Siebeck, 2000), 153–68; Daniel A. Smith, *Revisiting the Empty Tomb: The Early History of Easter* (Minneapolis: Fortress, 2010), 27–45; Bruce Chilton, *Resurrection Logic: How Jesus' First Followers Believed God Raised Him from the Dead* (Waco: Baylor University Press, 2019), 67–86; Paula Fredriksen, "Vile Bodies: Paul and Augustine on the Resurrection of the Flesh," in *Biblical Hermeneutics in Historical Perspective* (ed. Mark S. Burrows and Paul Rorem; Grand Rapids: Eerdmans, 1991), 75–87.

CHAPTER 6

risen," *Hist.* 3.62). The philosopher Celsus explains that, for any thinking mind, the concept of resurrection (ἀνάστασις) is impossible and παραλόγως or "contrary to reason" (as quoted in Origen, *Cels.* 5.14; cf. 8.48–49). Athenagoras describes the common pagan belief "that the resurrection is impossible" (ἀδύνατον τὴν ἀνάστασιν, *Res.* 4.4). And in what is perhaps the most noteworthy parallel to the Corinthian slogan in 1 Cor 15:12, Aeschylus in *Eum.* 648 portrays Apollo as expressing the obvious truth that, once one has died, οὔτις ἔστ' ἀνάστασις ("there is no resurrection"). These ancient parallels illumine why some at Corinth rejected belief in the resurrection. Whatever their precise views (if any) regarding the hope of an afterlife (a question that, we have seen, our sources do not permit us to answer), their motive for rejecting the resurrection of the dead was most likely, as it was for so many others in the ancient world and especially those of a learned or philosophic bent, the seemingly obvious absurdity and impossibility of the restoration of a dead body once it has been corrupted in the earth. By way of confirmation, we will see that the questions Paul puts into the mouth of those who deny the resurrection in 15:35 express precisely this claim of the resurrection's absurdity and impossibility.

## The Logic of 1 Corinthians 15:12–19

First Corinthians 15:12–19 is noteworthy for its logical form and character. The whole passage is a striking expression of ancient formal logic. The passage features seven conditional propositions (15:12, 13, 14, 15, 16, 17, 19) closely nested together, each utilizing εἰ with the indicative, a structure redolent of ancient philosophical discussion. Moreover, Paul here utilizes a number of other elements common among the ancient philosophers, such as the argument form *modus tollens* (15:13–15, 16–17), the conditional polysyllogism or *sorites* (15:13–15, 16–18), and the inferential conjunction ἄρα (15:14, 15, 18), as well as (in the majority view) the argument forms *modus ponens* (15:12) and *reductio ad absurdum* (15:13–15, 16–19). It is a rare passage even among the ancient philosophers that combines as many logical forms and features as 1 Cor 15:12–19.

The logical structure of Paul's argument reveals that he is employing not the Aristotelian categorical logic but the conditional logic preferred by the Stoics.[36] The Aristotelian and Stoic systems did not involve opposing conceptions of truth but rather different methods of expressing logical relations, either quantifica-

---

36. Theodor G. Bucher, "Nochmals zur Beweisführung in 1. Korinther 15,12–20," *TZ* 36 (1980): 129–52.

tionally (e.g., "All $x$ is $y$") or through conditional propositions (e.g., "If $x$, then $y$"). Unlike the quantificational logic of Aristotle, the Stoic logical method was marked by the use of conditional syllogisms (normally expressed with the conjunction εἰ together with an indicative verb), the conditional forms *modus ponens* and *modus tollens*, and the compressed form of conditional syllogism known as the *sorites*.[37] All these standard features of the Stoic logic (which was not employed exclusively by Stoics but was widely known and used by ancient philosophers) are found in Paul's argument in 15:12-19. A diagram of the logical structure of Paul's argument is offered at the close of this chapter.

Why does Paul choose to address the denial of the resurrection at Corinth in this strongly logical and philosophical form? What we have learned from the letter concerning the deniers of the resurrection immediately suggests an answer. We saw in chapter 1 of this commentary how the striking connections of 1 Cor 15 to the first four chapters of the letter identify the Corinthian wisdom opposed by Paul in 1:10–4:21 with the denial of the resurrection opposed by the apostle in chapter 15. We have also seen how this wisdom, in which some boasted at Corinth, involved a claim to philosophical wisdom. In this light, the reason for Paul's choice of an intensely logical and philosophical mode of discourse in 15:12-19 is evident. In 15:12-19, the Corinthian faithful hear the apostle engaging the self-professed wise at Corinth on their own intellectual playing field—and beating them at their own game.

Since the nineteenth century, scholars have debated the nature and validity of Paul's argument in 1 Cor 15:12-19, with a number of New Testament scholars finding fault with Paul's logic. The most learned and consequential of these debates regarding the logic of Paul's argument involved the philosopher and logician Theodor G. Bucher and the New Testament scholars Johan S. Vos, Michael Bachmann, and Jan Lambrecht.[38] In this debate, Bucher strongly urged the logical validity and soundness of Paul's argument.[39] Vos, however, argued that Paul's argument is faulty, replacing logic with rhetoric and psychology. Paul's logic fails,

---

37. On the Stoic logic, see the discussion in Diogenes Laertius (*Vit. phil.* 7.44-45, 65-83), and the texts collected in *SVF* 2:193-287. On the relation and ultimate compatibility of the Aristotelian and the Stoic (or Megarian-Stoic) logical systems, see Martha Kneale, "Logic," *OCD*, 616-17.

38. The main contributions within this debate are (in chronological order): Theodor G. Bucher, "Die logische Argumentation in 1. Korinther 15,12-20," *Bib* 55 (1974): 465-86; Bucher, "Auferstehung Christi und Auferstehung der Toten," *MTZ* 27 (1976): 1-32; Michael Bachmann, "Zur Gedankenführung in 1. Kor. 15, 12ff.," *TZ* 34 (1978): 265-76; Bucher, "Beweisführung" (1980); Jan Lambrecht, "Paul's Christological Use of Scripture in 1 Corinthians 15:20-28," *NTS* 28 (1982): 502-27; Johan S. Vos, "Die Logik des Paulus in 1Kor 15,12-20," *ZNW* 90 (1999): 78-97; Jan Lambrecht, "Just a Possibility? A Reply to Johan S. Vos on 1 Cor 15,12-20," *ZNW* 91 (2000): 143-45; and Michael Bachmann, "1Kor 15,12f.: 'Resurrection of the Dead (= Christians)'?" *ZNW* 92 (2001): 295-99.

39. Bucher, Argumentation," 465-71, 486; Bucher, "Beweisführung," 129-52.

CHAPTER 6

claimed Vos, because his premises "are neither objectively verifiable nor generally accepted."[40] Responding to Vos, Lambrecht defended the rational and logical character of Paul's argument in 1 Cor 15:12–19.[41]

The scant discussion of the topic in the years since this classic debate has shed little new light on the logic of Paul's argument.[42] The discussion has doubtless been impeded, as Bucher insisted, by a general deficiency of logical training and knowledge among New Testament scholars.[43] The commentary that follows will seek to illumine Paul's reasoning and logic in vv. 12–19. As we will see, Bucher is correct regarding Paul's logic: Paul's argument is a powerful one, his reasoning valid, and his conclusion sound. But there is also a crucial element within Paul's argument that previous expositors, including Bucher, have failed to fully grasp. This will offer the key to the logical—and even empirical—character of Paul's argument for the resurrection in 1 Cor 15:12–19.

## VERSE 12

*Now if Christ is proclaimed that he has been raised from the dead, how do some among you say that there is no resurrection of the dead?*

*Now if Christ is proclaimed that he has been raised from the dead.* The verb κηρύσσεται "is proclaimed" recalls the verb κηρύσσομεν "we proclaim" in 15:11, and thus the entire confessional summary in 15:1–11.[44] What is proclaimed is that Christ "has been raised" (ἐγήγερται). The centrality of the resurrection within the apostolic preaching is deftly expressed by the pleasing assonance of Paul's construction: εἰ δὲ Χριστὸς κηρύσσεται ὅτι ἐκ νεκρῶν ἐγήγερται. Paul uses the perfect passive form ἐγήγερται, the precise form used within the formula (ἐγήγερται, 15:4). Paul will repeat this identical form *five* times within the passage (15:12, 13, 14, 16, 17). In this way Paul once again (as with κηρύσσεται) intentionally recalls 15:1–11, and he continues to do so throughout vv. 12–19. As Raymond F. Collins notes: "With his

---

40. Vos, "Logik," 96–97. So also, much earlier, Weiss, 353–55.
41. Lambrecht, "Just a Possibility?," 145.
42. A recent attempt to analyze the logic of vv. 12–19 is Mark A. Proctor, "'If Christ Has Not Been Raised': 1 Corinthians 15:17 and the Hamartiological Inefficacy of a Compromised Gospel," *CBQ* 83 (2021): 619–37.
43. Bucher, "Beweisführung."
44. Hays, 238–39; Schreiner, 308.

constant reference to this creedal formula Paul demonstrates that he intends to draw out the implications of the heart of the Christian kerygma."[45]

When Paul here repeats the verb ἐγήγερται from the confessional summary (15:4), he adds the words ἐκ νεκρῶν. Christ has been raised "from the dead." This is indeed "his regular way of speaking of Christ's resurrection."[46] It was implicit in the formula's proclamation that Christ has been raised. But here ἐκ νεκρῶν ἐγήγερται ("has been raised *from the dead*") prepares for ἀνάστασις νεκρῶν ("resurrection *of the dead*") in the next clause. Emphatic by position, ἐκ νεκρῶν links together the resurrection of Christ proclaimed in the formula with the resurrection of the dead to come and focuses special attention on the contradiction involved in the denial of that coming resurrection—which will be the theme of 15:12–19.[47] Used for the first time here within the entire epistle, the word νεκρός will appear frequently throughout the rest of the chapter (15:13, 15, 16, 20, 21, 29, 32, 35, 42, 52), as Paul defends and expounds the truth that the dead will rise.

*how do some among you say.* Paul's language of proclamation earlier in the verse (Χριστὸς κηρύσσεται, "Christ is proclaimed") recalls not only the confessional formula (15:11), as we have seen, but also his reflection on the kerygma in 1:18–2:5 (κηρύσσομεν Χριστόν, 1:23; cf. κήρυγμα, 1:21, 2:4). There he contrasted the apostolic message with the human philosophical wisdom embraced by the self-professed wise at Corinth. Paul now proceeds to draw out the implications of this apostolic kerygma—by directly challenging the teaching of the wise at Corinth that was in conflict with it. Paul's astonished πῶς "how?" here, as it does in Gal 2:14, "signals a contradiction."[48] It is a contradiction of everything that has preceded it in v. 12: the apostolic proclamation that Christ has been raised from the dead. Paul's anxious concern in the programmatic 1 Cor 1:10 was that "you all [πάντες] speak [λέγητε] the same thing, and there be no divisions among you [ἐν ὑμῖν]." As Paul now addresses the problem of "some" (τινες) who are "among you" (ἐν ὑμῖν) and yet "speak" (λέγουσιν) in contradiction to the apostolic gospel, he here discloses the concern uppermost in his thoughts in 1:10, and thus in the entire epistle.

The authors of the contradiction are not the Corinthians as a whole but "some among you" (ἐν ὑμῖν τινες). Although it is ignored by many interpreters, Paul clearly distinguishes those at Corinth who deny the resurrection from the Corinthians

---

45. Collins, 542; cf. Wolff, 377.
46. Fee, 821. We also see this in Rom 4:24, 6:4, 8:11, 10:9, Gal 1:1, 1 Thess 1:10, and elsewhere.
47. Collins, 540; Lambrecht, "Three Brief Notes," 33; Conzelmann, 264; Bachmann, "Resurrection," 298. In the "Western" reading (P[46] D F G), the position of ἐκ νεκρῶν is even more emphatic, transposed before the ὅτι of indirect statement. However, this reading is secondary.
48. Bachmann, "Resurrection," 296 n. 8.

as a whole. And yet in the very words "some among you" lies the source of Paul's grave concern: it is that the "some" (τινες) of whom he speaks are indeed "among you" (ἐν ὑμῖν, emphatic through its position prior to τινες), that is, in the midst of the church at Corinth. The problem, as J. N. Vorster points out, is that "the readers clearly tolerated and were perhaps even positively inclined toward the group of deniers."[49] This complex situation explains the twin notes of confidence and concern we saw in 15:1–11, expressed nowhere more forcefully than in v. 11. There, as we saw, the contrast of the present tense κηρύσσομεν ("we proclaim") and the aorist tense ἐπιστεύσατε ("you believed") raised the question acutely, as Vorster observes, "What about the present?"[50]

*that there is no resurrection of the dead.* As we have seen earlier in this chapter, what was denied at Corinth was "the resurrection of the dead" (ἀνάστασις νεκρῶν), that is, a future return to physical life of the bodies of those who have died. Through his incredulous πῶς "how?"—indicating a *contradiction* between Christ's resurrection and the denial of the resurrection at Corinth—Paul establishes a logical relation between Christ's resurrection and the future resurrection of the dead, which may be expressed in the form of a *modus ponens* argument (see the diagram at the close of the chapter): "If Christ has been raised, there will be a resurrection of the dead. Christ has been raised, as the apostolic kerygma in 15:3–11 has established. Therefore there will be a resurrection of the dead."[51] This, indeed, will be the core of Paul's argument throughout vv. 12–19. Verse 12 thus plays, as most expositors have agreed, an introductory and essential role within the structure of Paul's argument.[52]

However, there is an important element within Paul's thought in v. 12 that has been generally missed by expositors. For interpreters generally pass over or ignore the main verb within the first clause of this verse—κηρύσσεται. But within Paul's syntax, the verb ἐγήγερται "has been raised" is dependent upon the verb κηρύσσεται "is proclaimed." The denial of the resurrection is thus portrayed as in contradiction not (strictly speaking) to Christ's resurrection but to the *apostolic proclamation* of Christ's resurrection. We thus find implicit, within the compressed form of Paul's argument, not one but two "major" premises that

---

49. Vorster, "Resurrection Faith," 304.
50. Vorster, "Resurrection Faith," 290.
51. So most interpreters; cf. Vos, "Logik," 89–90; Lambrecht, "Just a Possibility?," 143–44. So also Aquinas, *1 Cor.* 912–914.
52. So Vos, "Logik," 80–90; Lambrecht, "Christological Use," 503, 518; Lambrecht, "Just a Possibility?," 143–45; contra Bucher, "Argumentation," 465–66.

*The Futility of Faith Apart from the Resurrection*

may be expressed as a polysyllogism: (1) "If the apostolic testimony and proclamation is true, Christ has risen from the dead"; and (2) "If Christ has risen from the dead, there will be a future resurrection from the dead" (see the diagram). Only *one* "minor" premise is necessary to establish the truth of *both* Christ's resurrection and of the resurrection of the dead to come: that the apostolic proclamation is true.

We see, then, that the apostolic kerygma plays a key role in Paul's argument. The terminology that Paul chooses here for the apostolic preaching (κηρύσσω, 15:11, 12; κήρυγμα, 15:14) is itself significant. For the concept of *proclamation*, whether denoted by verb or noun, occurs, as Thayer notes, "always with a suggestion of formality, gravity, and an authority which must be obeyed."[53] The two verbs Paul employs in 15:12 to denote communication (κηρύσσεται and λέγουσιν) thus introduce a subtle but effective contrast. When Paul describes the apostolic message, he chooses the verb κηρύσσω, denoting a proclamation with intrinsic authority (cf. Luke 4:18–19; Rom 10:15; 1 Pet 3:19; Rev 5:2). When he describes the message of those who deny the resurrection, he uses the verb λέγω, denoting mere affirmation with no intrinsic authority.

But from where does the apostolic message derive this authority? Here we come face to face with the entirely empirical and rational basis of Paul's argument. The apostolic κήρυγμα possesses an intrinsic authority because it is founded upon the eyewitness testimony of the apostles. This is not only Paul's own understanding, but this conception is also implicit in the pre-Pauline apostolic formula that Paul transmits in 15:5–7. That is why this formula, as we saw, identifies multiple eyewitnesses, enumerates multiple resurrection appearances, and identifies those who were eyewitnesses to resurrection appearances on multiple occasions. It is why Paul in 15:6b and 15:11 stresses the unanimity and availability of these eyewitnesses. In this ancient Christian understanding, as C. F. D. Moule notes, "to challenge the Christian message was to doubt a body of living eye-witnesses authorized by the Lord himself."[54] To doubt the kerygma is therefore to call into question the validity of eyewitness testimony (cf. 15:3, 5–8, 11, 15). It is to doubt the evidence of the five senses and reject the cogency of rational proof. This is the foundation of Paul's argument, and he will further develop this as the passage proceeds.

---

53. Thayer, s.v. "κηρύσσω." Cf. Weiss, 353.
54. C. F. D. Moule, *The Birth of the New Testament* (HNTC; New York: Harper & Row, 1962), 181.

CHAPTER 6

## Verse 13

*But if there is no resurrection of the dead, neither has Christ been raised.*

As we saw, the compressed argument of v. 12 implies the premise: "If Christ is risen, there will be a future resurrection of the dead." As almost all expositors are agreed, v. 13 now expresses the logically equivalent "contrapositive" of this in the form of the premise: "But if there is no resurrection of the dead, neither has Christ been raised."[55] The εἰ with the indicative expresses the (false) antecedent proposition with definiteness in the typical style of Stoic conditional logic.[56] But the all-important but unstated "minor" premise, "Christ has been raised," was established in 15:3–11. This produces an impeccable *modus tollens* syllogism, which reveals that the proposition "there is no resurrection of the dead" is false. Verse 13 thus makes explicit what was already implicit in v. 12: the resurrection of Christ entails the resurrection of the dead.

But in what way does the resurrection of Christ entail the resurrection of the dead? This is a strong point of controversy among recent interpreters. This question was also an element in the great debate regarding the logic of Paul's argument between Bucher, Bachmann, Vos, and Lambrecht discussed earlier in this chapter. According to Jan Lambrecht, Jesus's resurrection entails the future resurrection as its source and cause.[57] But according to Michael Bachmann and Johan S. Vos, Jesus's resurrection in Paul's argument entails not a future resurrection of the dead but merely the possibility of resurrection. On this view, the necessary connection the apostle envisions between Christ's resurrection and the resurrection of the dead is not a causal connection but an inferential one. Christ has risen, showing that the general negation the dead do not rise is false and proving the reality (in at least this one case) of resurrection.[58] Bachmann argues that Paul's whole point throughout 15:12–21 is to demonstrate the possibility of resurrection; only in 15:22–58 does he turn to argue for a future resurrection of the dead.[59] Bachmann's

---

55. See Vos, "Logik," 89–90; Lambrecht, "Christological Use," 518 n. 4; Lambrecht, "Just a Possibility?," 144–45.

56. On protases utilizing εἰ with the indicative as expressive of *Wirklichkeit* or actuality, see BDR §372. But as Kühner and Gerth make clear, εἰ with the indicative states the condition with definiteness but does not commit the speaker to its truth, so that it can express what the speaker denies; see Kühner-G., 2.2:466–67 n. 1 (§573). Such is the case here, and in 15:14, 15, 16, 17, and 19.

57. Lambrecht, "Just a Possibility?," 144.

58. Bachmann, "Gedankenführung," 265–76; Bachmann, "Resurrection," 295–99; Vos, "Logik," 91. So also Collins, 543–44 (citing Bachmann); Proctor, "Hamartiological Inefficacy," 624–25. Already in Weiss, 353.

59. Bachmann, "Resurrection," 299.

main argument is Paul's use throughout 15:12–21 of the anarthrous expressions ἀνάστασις νεκρῶν (15:12, 13, 21) and νεκροὶ οὐκ ἐγείρονται (15:15, 16, 29, 32). By these, Bachmann claims, Paul refers merely to the abstract possibility of resurrection, in contrast with his use in 15:22–58 of the articular expressions ἡ ἀνάστασις τῶν νεκρῶν (15:42), ἐγείρονται οἱ νεκροί (15:35), and οἱ νεκροὶ ἐγερθήσονται (15:52), which refer to the eschatological resurrection of the dead.[60]

But this interpretation of Paul's argument is untenable. The reasons are many and conclusive:

(1) On this interpretation, Paul seeks to prove one thing (the abstract possibility of resurrection) in 15:12–21 and then argues for something entirely different (the eschatological resurrection) in 15:22–58. His terms for resurrection (ἀνάστασις, ἐγείρω, etc.) would then also be equivocal, meaning one thing in one part of the chapter and something different in the other. There would be no clear or logical connection between Paul's argument in 15:12–21 and his argument in 15:22–58. The mere abstract possibility of resurrection does not logically entail a future resurrection of the dead. Paul's argument would be a failure.

(2) Bachmann's argument simply ignores vv. 18–19, where the resurrection that follows from Christ's resurrection is (as all interpreters concur) not a mere abstract possibility of resurrection but is rather the future resurrection of the faithful. For in vv. 18–19 Paul declares that if Christ is not risen, "then the dead in Christ have perished" (15:18) and "we have hoped in Christ for this life only" (15:19). On Bachmann's view, one must maintain that Paul argues for the abstract possibility of resurrection in vv. 12–17 but then shifts (with no indication he is doing so) to an argument for a future resurrection in vv. 18–19, then back to an argument for the mere possibility of resurrection in vv. 20–21. On this reading, Paul's argument falls apart.

(3) Finally, Bachmann's main argument—the claimed hard and fast distinction between Paul's anarthrous and articular expressions for resurrection in chapter 15—is impossible to sustain. As BDAG points out, in all the key expressions for resurrection the anarthrous and articular forms of νεκρός are interchangeable.[61] In 15:29 and 15:32, the anarthrous phrase νεκροὶ οὐκ ἐγείρονται clearly refers to the hope of future resurrection, for if it is not true, then both baptism on account of the dead (15:29) and Paul's sufferings (15:32) are pointless. In expressions for resurrection, "The article is often omitted with the genitive; so as a rule in ἀνάστασις νεκρῶν."[62] The same anarthrous phrase ἀνάστασις νεκρῶν, which Paul employs in

---

60. Bachmann, "Gedankenführung," 268–72; Bachmann, "Resurrection," 297–98. Cf. BDR §254 n. 7.
61. BDAG, s.v. "νεκρός" (B.1); cf. BA, s.v. "νεκρός" (2.a).
62. BDAG, s.v. "νεκρός" (B.1).

15:13, 15, and 16, is used in 15:21 with quite evident reference to the future resurrection, as is clear from Paul's parallelism: "For since through a human being came death, also through a human being came *resurrection of the dead* [ἀνάστασις νεκρῶν]; for just as in Adam all die, so also in Christ *all will be made alive*" (15:21–22). This is the actual, future resurrection, not the mere possibility of resurrection.

First Corinthians 15:20–23 not only confirms that ἀνάστασις νεκρῶν throughout the chapter denotes the future resurrection but also offers the key to how Paul can say, "If there is no resurrection of the dead, neither has Christ been raised" (15:13). The necessary connection the apostle envisions between Christ's resurrection and the resurrection of the dead is not an *inferential* one (*pace* Bachmann) but rather a *causal* one. His resurrection is the source and wellspring of the resurrection of the faithful. He has risen to life as "the firstfruits of those who sleep" (15:20), the anticipation of the resurrection of all to come: "just as in Adam all die, so also in Christ all will be made alive" (15:22). Through Jesus's conquest of death on the first Easter, all those united to Christ will rise to everlasting life in the time of his coming and reign (15:51–54). Paul's argument assumes the salvation-historical significance of Christ's resurrection as the fulfillment of the promised victory of YHWH over death (cf. 15:4, κατὰ τὰς γραφάς). As most interpreters have recognized, Christ's resurrection entails the resurrection of the dead as cause to effect.[63] The formulation of Thomas Aquinas is still unsurpassed: the resurrection of Christ is the *causa efficiens et exemplaris*, the "efficient and exemplary cause" of the resurrection of the dead.[64] Christ, himself rising to life, conquers death on behalf of all. But to deny the effect is to deny the cause. To deny the future resurrection of the dead is to deny that Christ through his resurrection has conquered death. That is why Paul can write, "if there is no resurrection of the dead, neither has Christ been raised."

Once it is grasped that Christ's resurrection entails the resurrection of the dead as the *causa efficiens et exemplaris*, Paul's argument in 15:12–19 makes itself fully at home within the chapter as a whole. Paul does not, as Bachmann supposes, seek to prove one thing in 15:12–21 and something entirely different in 15:22–58. Rather, Paul's focus throughout is on the hope of future resurrection. We find, then, that Paul's expressions for resurrection are not equivocal but univocal, denoting the eschatological resurrection (15:12–13, 15–16, 21, 29, 32, 35, 42, 52). And we find (as

---

63. So Lambrecht, "Just a Possibility?," 144; Wolff, 378; Conzelmann, 265; Fee, 821–22; Sampley, 980; Robertson & Plummer, 348; Constantine R. Campbell, *Paul and the Hope of Glory: An Exegetical and Theological Study* (Grand Rapids: Zondervan Academic, 2020), 173–74. For the fullest discussion, see William Dykstra, "1 Corinthians 15:20–28, An Essential Part of Paul's Argument against Those Who Deny the Resurrection," *CTJ* 4 (1969): 195–211.

64. Aquinas, *1 Cor.* 912.

we will see in detail in chapter 7) that 1 Cor 15:20–23 is not unrelated to the denial of the resurrection against which Paul argues in 15:12–19, but it is rather "a passionate affirmation and proclamation of that feature of the kerygma which his opponents denied."[65]

## Verse 14

*And if Christ has not been raised, in vain, then, is our proclamation, in vain also is your faith.*

In v. 14, the combination of τὸ κήρυγμα ἡμῶν ("our proclamation") and ἡ πίστις ὑμῶν ("your faith") recalls the pairing of κηρύσσομεν "we proclaim" and ἐπιστεύσατε "you believed" in 15:11.[66] The clause κενὴ καὶ ἡ πίστις ὑμῶν ("in *vain* also is your *faith*") recalls ἐκτὸς εἰ μὴ εἰκῇ ἐπιστεύσατε ("unless you *believed* in *vain*") in 15:2. In this way Paul reveals that in v. 14 he is continuing to draw out the implications of the apostolic kerygma summarized in 15:1–11. But Paul's language of preaching and faith also echoes his contrast of the foolishness of the kerygma with the wisdom of the world in 1:18–2:5—the only other place in the letter where the terms κήρυγμα and πίστις occur together in combination (κήρυγμα, 1:21, 2:4; πίστις, 2:5). And Paul's twofold use of κενός "in vain" recalls the key theme of the body opening of the letter, that the gospel of Christ must not be "made vain" (1:17, κενωθῇ) through human wisdom. Paul develops this theme, for the first time within the letter, in chapter 15. It is a major theme and leitmotif of the chapter (15:2, 14, 17, 58; cf. 15:10). In this way Paul now clarifies the nature of the false human wisdom of which he writes in chapters 1–4 of the letter, which is in conflict with the kerygma and renders it vain—it is the denial of the resurrection by the self-professed wise at Corinth.

Continuing in the highly logical and philosophical vein of the passage, Paul artfully joins the implicit *modus tollens* syllogisms of 15:14–15 to the conditional premise of v. 13, to form a "polysyllogism" known in logic as a conditional *sorites* (a chain argument in which the consequent of the previous premise provides the

---

65. Dykstra, "Essential Part," 211.

66. The reading ὑμῶν after πίστις is to be preferred (rather than ἡμῶν). The reading ἡμῶν (B D 33 1739 1881) may be due to itacism; see Metzger, 567–68. The καί before τὸ κήρυγμα, bracketed by NA[28] as probable but questionable, is also preferable. The inclusion of the καί possesses stronger manuscript attestation (ℵ* A D 33 81) and functions with the verse's second καί to correlate "our proclamation" and "your faith" (καὶ τὸ κήρυγμα ἡμῶν . . . καὶ ἡ πίστις ὑμῶν). This corresponds to the correlation of "we proclaim" and "you believed" in 15:11 through οὕτως (οὕτως κηρύσσομεν καὶ οὕτως ἐπιστεύσατε).

CHAPTER 6

antecedent of the next). Verses 13–15 together form what logicians call an *indirect proof* or a *reductio ad absurdum*—a chain of deductive reasoning establishing the truth of a proposition by showing that its denial entails what is absurd or impossible (see the diagram).[67]

We have already discussed the first stage of Paul's *reductio ad absurdum* argument, which occurs in v. 13—"If there is no resurrection of the dead, then neither has Christ been raised." As we have seen, the unexpressed "minor" premise in 15:13 is "Christ has been raised." Theodor G. Bucher claims that the resurrection of Christ is not something for which Paul argues, but a basic truth that he simply asserts—an unargued, foundational premise underlying his entire argument in 1:12–19.[68] But this claim ignores the obvious fact that v. 13 is only the first stage of Paul's chain of reasoning in 15:13–15. As is widely acknowledged, Paul in 15:14–15 will go on to undergird the premise that Christ is risen with further arguments.[69] He will offer proofs for the resurrection of Christ.

The first proof is offered in v. 14: if Christ is not risen, then the apostolic preaching is in vain, and the Corinthians' faith is in vain (15:14). The key word is κενός, emphatic by position within its clause in both its occurrences in 15:14.[70] For the adjective κενός, BDAG indicates three main senses: (1) "pertaining to being without something material, *empty*"; (2) "pertaining to being devoid of intellectual, moral, or spiritual value, *empty*"; (3) "pertaining to being without purpose or result, *in vain*."[71] The last sense is the predominant one in the New Testament, especially in Paul (2 Cor 6:1; Gal 2:2; Phil 2:16; 1 Thess 2:1; 3:5). Significantly, in the two other occurrences of the word in chapter 15 outside v. 14, the term beyond controversy has this sense (15:10, 58). The apparent meaning of κενός in 15:14 is thus "fruitless, without result, in vain." If Christ is not risen, Paul argues in 15:14, the kerygma of the apostles is futile, for its promise of salvation is empty and in vain.

But that the kerygma's promise of salvation should be in vain is, within Paul's argument, clearly false, for vv. 1–11 have already established that the apostolic

---

67. Almost all modern interpreters are agreed that Paul's argument in 15:13–15 may be described as a *reductio ad absurdum*: see Vos, "Logik," 89–90; Lambrecht, "Just a Possibility?," 145; Werner Stenger, "Beobachtungen zur Argumentationsstruktur von 1 Kor 15," *LB* 45 (1979): 90. An exception is Bucher, "Argumentation," 465–71. Aquinas describes Paul's argument in 15:13–15 as a series of *argumenta ad inconvenientia* (*1 Cor.* 917–923), which most interpreters of Thomas agree is essentially equivalent to the *argumentum ad absurdum*.

68. See Bucher, "Argumentation," 470–71, 480.

69. Rightly Vos, "Logik," 89–90; Lambrecht, "Just a Possibility?," 145.

70. Fitzmyer, 563.

71. BDAG, s.v. "κενός"; following BA, s.v. "κενός." See also *TLNT* 2:303–10.

proclamation, when received with faith, is saving (cf. 15:1–2, τὸ εὐαγγέλιον... δι' οὗ καὶ σῴζεσθε). The saving power of the apostolic proclamation presumes its truth, and we saw that also in 15:12 the truthfulness of the apostolic witness undergirds the truth of Christ's resurrection. In opposing the gospel, the deniers of the resurrection at Corinth are setting up their own self-described wisdom, which is without authority, in opposition to the authoritative message of the apostles who founded the community. The kerygma has intrinsic authority.

Johan S. Vos regards Paul's appeal to the authority of the apostolic kerygma in 15:14 to be "a replacement of logic with rhetoric and psychology."[72] In fact, Paul's whole argument in 15:12–19, according to Vos, lacks logical rigor despite its undeniable "formal logical character," for Paul's premises "are neither objectively verifiable nor generally accepted, indeed, may not have been self-evident even for a portion of the congregation at Corinth."[73] Paul's argument is not convincing, so Vos charges, because it rests on the authority of the apostolic kerygma. Vos's charge is understandable, for might not one make the same claim for any ideology or belief system? Paul, it is claimed, offers no *basis* for the alleged authority of the kerygma. Is this not an argument in a circle, or a vacuous fideism, or both?

No, it is not. Vos's charge misses a crucial link in the chain of thought within 15:12–19, which is also a crucial dimension within Paul's thought as a whole. It is the thought that Paul now expresses in v. 15.

## Verse 15

*And we are also found to be false witnesses of God, for we bore testimony against God that he raised the Christ, whom he did not raise, if indeed, as they claim, the dead are not raised.*

The nature of Paul's argument here, widely misunderstood by interpreters, provides an extraordinary window into his thought. The "we" of this verse are the "whether I or they" of 15:11, the apostolic eyewitnesses to the resurrection in 15:5–8. The word Paul uses to describe the apostolic activity contemplated here is μαρτυρέω (ἐμαρτυρήσαμεν; cf. ψευδομάρτυρες). The verb μαρτυρέω means "to bear witness, give evidence."[74] More fully, the verb denotes "to provide information about a per-

---

72. Vos, "Logik," 96.
73. Vos, "Logik," 96.
74. LSJ, s.v. "μαρτυρέω"; cf. BA, s.v. "μαρτυρέω," which gives the definition "Zeugnis ablegen, Zeuge sein" ("bear witness, be a witness").

son or an event concerning which the speaker has direct knowledge."[75] It means "to attest anything that one knows, and therefore to make declarations with a certain authority."[76] This sense of *direct knowledge* and consequent *authority* that inheres in the word is present in passage after passage within the New Testament (cf. John 3:11; 4:39; 12:17; 19:35; 21:24; Acts 22:5; Rom 10:2; 2 Cor 8:3; Gal 4:15; Col 4:13; 1 John 1:2). The content of this apostolic witness is that Christ has been raised from the dead (15:14a, 15b). As we see in 15:5–8, this involves the claim to have seen the risen Christ (ὤφθη, 15:5, 6, 7, 8; cf. 9:1, οὐχὶ Ἰησοῦν τὸν κύριον ἡμῶν ἑόρακα;). This is a claim to *eyewitness* testimony. If Christ is not risen, the apostles are liars. They are false witnesses (ψευδομάρτυρες) in what they claim to have seen.[77] Because the apostles bear testimony that God raised Christ, a claim involving God and the work of God, this false testimony is against God (ψευδομάρτυρες τοῦ θεοῦ; ἐμαρτυρήσαμεν κατὰ τοῦ θεοῦ).

But this proposition is the final leg in Paul's *reductio ad absurdum* argument. It states an impossibility. The readers are expected to know that the testimony of the apostles is true and thus by *modus tollens* deduce from the premise ("If Christ is not risen, the apostolic testimony is false") the inference that necessarily follows from the conclusive and empirical nature of that eyewitness testimony ("Since the apostolic testimony is true, Christ is risen"). The logic involved here is crucial. Paul's argument does not, as Bucher claims, treat the resurrection of Christ as a basic premise or self-evident truth, assumed and unargued.[78] Nor does Paul's argument, as Vos claims, lack logical grounding in "objectively verifiable" evidence.[79] To the contrary, Paul's argument for the resurrection is grounded in the objective and verifiable evidence of the eyewitness testimony of the apostles. Paul's argument is based on *empirical* evidence—the evidence of the five senses and the testimony of eyewitnesses.[80] The only prior, unargued assumption of

---

75. L&N §33.262.
76. Cremer, 416.
77. The ψευδόμαρτυς is not one who falsely claims the name of witness (on analogy with ψευδάδελφος, ψευδαπόστολος, etc.), but a witness who gives false testimony. See BDR §219 n. 7, and Conzelmann, 265–66. Cf. L&N §33.273: "one who lies about what he pretends to have seen."
78. Bucher, "Argumentation," 470–71, 480.
79. Vos, "Logik," 96–97.
80. The key error in Vos's analysis is his failure to take 15:15 into account in his treatment of Paul's argument; it is absent from his discussion and even from his structural diagram of the passage ("Logik," 89–90). The analysis of Proctor is also inadequate, for he construes v. 15 as merely an appeal to the apostles' "moral character and dependability" ("Hamartiological Inefficacy," 622, 628–30, 635–37). But Paul's argument, like any appeal to eyewitness testimony, is founded upon not only the trustworthiness of the witnesses but also upon their ability to testify authoritatively to empirical facts.

Paul's argument is that empirical evidence is probative. As such, Paul's argument in 15:13–15 is eminently and undeniably logical.[81] It is not only logical in its form, as all expositors agree, but also, as we have now seen, logical in its content as well.

This conception—that the truth of Christ's resurrection, and thus of the gospel and its hope of resurrection to everlasting life, is attested by the empirical, verifiable eyewitness testimony of the apostles—is not found only in 15:15. It is present throughout 1 Corinthians. It is present in Paul's description of the gospel as "our testimony to Christ" (1:6, τὸ μαρτύριον τοῦ Χριστοῦ). It is present in Paul's definition of the apostle as one who has seen the risen Lord (9:1, οὐχὶ Ἰησοῦν τὸν κύριον ἡμῶν ἑόρακα;). And it is powerfully present in 15:1–11 in the list of the eyewitnesses (15:5–8), the naming of eyewitnesses (15:5, 7), the multiplicity of eyewitnesses (15:5–7), and the references to the availability of eyewitnesses (15:6b, 11). It is extremely significant that Paul's first reference to this conception of the eyewitness testimony of the apostles occurs in the epistolary thanksgiving (1:6, τὸ μαρτύριον τοῦ Χριστοῦ). Paul's thanksgivings always foreshadow the key themes of the letter to follow. Paul's inclusion of this concept in the thanksgiving thus indicates that the apostolic testimony to Christ will be a key theme of the epistle. He now fulfills that expectation in chapter 15. The eyewitness testimony of the apostles to the resurrection of Christ is a central and constitutive feature of Paul's thought within 1 Corinthians and of his thought as a whole.

## VERSES 16–17

*16 For if the dead are not raised, neither has Christ been raised. 17 And if Christ has not been raised, futile is your faith; you are still in your sins.*

*15:16. For if the dead are not raised, neither has Christ been raised.* Verse 16 repeats the thought of v. 13, substituting for ἀνάστασις νεκρῶν οὐκ ἔστιν the equivalent νεκροὶ οὐκ ἐγείρονται. Verses 13–15, as we saw, were an *argumentum ad absurdum*, and vv. 16–17 now form the first of a series of further *reductio ad absurdum* arguments extending through v. 19 (see the diagram).[82] The necessity connecting the resurrection of Christ to the future resurrection of the dead expressed here

---

81. Although disagreeing with some points of Bucher's analysis (see above), our analysis here confirms Bucher's claim that Paul's argument is fully logical; see Bucher, "Argumentation," 465–71; Bucher, "Beweisführung," 129–43. Cf. Lambrecht, "Just a Possibility?," 145.

82. For 15:16–19 as a *reductio ad absurdum*, see Vos, "Logik," 89–90; Stenger, "Beobachtungen," 90; Lambrecht, "Just a Possibility?," 145. *Pace* Bucher, "Argumentation," 465–71.

in 15:16 is, as we saw in 15:13, a *causal* and salvation-historical one: the resurrection of Christ is the firstfruits and anticipation of the resurrection of those united to Christ.[83] Paul's logic is impeccable, for to deny the necessary effect of a cause is to deny the cause as well. If the dead are not raised, then Christ has not conquered death.

*15:17. And if Christ has not been raised, futile is your faith.* The *reductio ad absurdum* argument continues in 15:17, undergirding the truth of Jesus's resurrection with reason and logic, as the apostle did in 15:14–15. If Christ is not risen, then the faith of the Corinthians is futile or in vain (μάταιος). The adjective μάταιος is derived from the adverb μάτην "in vain, for nothing."[84] The adjective may have either a causal (i.e., "groundless") or a final (i.e., "useless") sense.[85] However, the latter sense predominates in antiquity, as reflected in the definition given in BDAG: "pertaining to being of no use, *idle, empty, fruitless, useless, powerless, lacking truth.*"[86] Its cognate noun ματαιότης is the word of choice for the LXX translator of Ecclesiastes to express the key conception within that book, the "vanity" or "purposelessness" of human life (e.g., Eccl 1:2, 14; 2:1, 11, 15, 17, 19, 23, 26; 3:19). The meaning "futile, without purpose, vain" is the only sense of the adjective elsewhere within the New Testament (Acts 14:15; 1 Cor 3:20; Titus 3:9; Jas 1:26; 1 Pet 1:18). It is clearly the meaning here as well.

The adjective μάταιος is a close synonym of the adjective κενός, and v. 17 thus effectively restates v. 14. The adjectives κενός and μάταιος are found paired in the LXX (e.g., Job 20:18; Isa 30:7; Hos 12:2), as they are here in Paul (15:14, 17). Like κενός, the adjective μάταιος recalls Paul's description of the wisdom of the world embraced by some at Corinth as empty and vain (3:20, μάταιος; cf. 1:17, κενόω). Paul thus identifies the denial of the resurrection with the vain thoughts of the wise condemned in 3:20. If, as the denial of the future resurrection by the self-professed wise at Corinth implies, Christ is not risen, then faith in Christ is in vain. But within Paul's *reductio ad absurdum* argument, this proposition is clearly false, for Paul has already established in 15:1–2 that the apostolic kerygma, when received with faith, is not fruitless but powerful to save (cf. 15:1–2, τὸ εὐαγγέλιον ... ὃ καὶ παρελάβετε ... δι' οὗ καὶ σῴζεσθε).

---

83. See the discussion of v. 13 above. The necessary connection between Christ's resurrection and the future resurrection of believers receives enhanced emphasis in v. 16 through the assonance of ἐγείρονται ... ἐγήγερται.

84. Frisk, 2:185.

85. Cremer, 418.

86. BDAG, s.v. "μάταιος"; cf. BA, s.v. "μάταιος."

*The Futility of Faith Apart from the Resurrection*

*you are still in your sins.* Paul explains one way in which, if Christ is not risen, the faith of the Corinthians is in vain: they are still in their sins (ἔτι ἐστὲ ἐν ταῖς ἁμαρτίαις ὑμῶν). Paul's reference to "sins" in the plural, unusual for him, shows that he is continuing to draw out the implications of the confessional formula in 15:3–8, which refers to "sins" in the plural (cf. 15:3, ὑπὲρ τῶν ἁμαρτιῶν ἡμῶν).[87] The apostolic kerygma is saving (σῴζεσθε, 15:2), in that it frees from both the guilt and power of sin (cf. Rom 4:6–8; 6:3–6, 17–18; 8:3–4; Gal 1:4). As we saw in our commentary on 15:3, the apostolic formula's description of the death of Christ for sins as the fulfillment of the Scriptures portrays the cross of Christ as fulfilling the promise in Israel's Scriptures of a new and ultimate divine work of atonement, forgiveness, and redemption, which the law and its sacrifices were unable to provide (Ps 130:7–8; Isa 4:4–5; 44:22–23; Jer 33:8; 50:20; Ezek 36:22–38 [esp. vv. 25–27, 35]; Hos 2:14–23 [esp. vv. 19–20, 23]; Zech 13:1). First Corinthians 15:17 also discloses a further important dimension of Paul's thought, for it reveals that "without the resurrection of Christ, Christ's death alone has no atoning, redemptive, or liberating effect in relation to human sin."[88] The denial of the resurrection by some at Corinth is in conflict with the saving power of the kerygma. It thus opposes the kerygma, which (as Paul has shown in 15:1–11 and 15:14–15) is founded upon the authoritative eyewitness testimony of the apostolic body.

## Verse 18

*Then also those who have fallen asleep in Christ have perished.*

*Then also those who have fallen asleep in Christ.* In v. 18 the inferential conjunction ἄρα "then" together with the adjunctive καί introduces a further counterfactual consequence if Christ is not risen.[89] "Those who have fallen asleep in Christ" are Christ followers who have died. The verb κοιμάω, like other words for sleep in both Greek and Latin, was frequently used as a metaphor for death within the

---

87. Wolff, 379; Conzelmann, 266.
88. Thiselton, 1220. For further discussion of this aspect of Paul's thought, see Michael F. Bird, "Justified by Christ's Resurrection: A Neglected Aspect of Paul's Doctrine of Justification," *SBET* 22 (2004): 72–91; Campbell, *Hope of Glory*, 335–39. For a similar emphasis on the role of the resurrection of Christ in the forgiveness of sins, see Rom 4:25; Heb 7:25–28. Proctor's argument that this is not a feature of Paul's thought ("Hamartiological Inefficacy," 619–37) is not convincing.
89. A few expositors read v. 18 and the inferential ἄρα as developing a further consequence of v. 17b: "you are still in your sins" (so Collins, 545). However, on this interpretation Paul makes a detour from his main argument only to return to it abruptly in v. 19. Such a reading is unlikely.

CHAPTER 6

wider ancient world, and in that pagan context it was always used to express the permanence and eternality of death.[90] Ancient Jewish and Christian texts likewise employ the verb κοιμάω as metaphorical language for death but, strikingly, do so in a contrasting and even opposite sense, to depict the dead as only temporarily sleeping, waiting to be awakened at the resurrection (2 Macc 12:45; 1 En. 92.3; Matt 27:52; John 11:11; Acts 7:60; 13:36; 1 Cor 7:39; 11:30; 15:6, 20, 51; 1 Thess 4:13, 14, 15; 2 Pet 3:4).[91] Of the fourteen instances in which κοιμάω is used in this sense in the New Testament, six occur within 1 Corinthians, and four of these occur within chapter 15 (7:39; 11:30; 15:6, 18, 20, 51). The verb κοιμάω is derived from κεῖμαι "to lie."[92] The primary sense of κοιμάω in the passive (the form found in 1 Corinthians and throughout the New Testament) is therefore "to *lie down* in sleep." This conception of *lying* asleep in death, expressed by the verb κοιμάω, forms a fitting complement to the New Testament's language of being *raised* to life in the resurrection, as expressed by the verbs ἀνίστημι and ἐγείρω. The verb κοιμάω thus forms another facet of the vocabulary of bodily resurrection that pervades 1 Cor 15.

The prepositional phrase ἐν Χριστῷ, ambiguous in position, should be taken attributively with κοιμηθέντες.[93] The formula "in Christ" appears with great frequency in Paul, alongside equivalent formulas such as "in the Lord" and "in the Lord Jesus."[94] These formulas express the key Pauline conception of *union with Christ* or, as it is often called, *participation* in Christ. In Paul's teaching, believers enter into a true miraculous union with Christ, becoming the temples of the Holy Spirit (1 Cor 1:9; 3:16–17; 6:19–20; 2 Cor 6:16; 13:5; Gal 2:19–20; 3:27), in fulfillment of the prophetic promise of YHWH's coming and abiding presence with his people (Lev 26:11–12; Ezek 37:27–28) and of the promise of a new temple (Isa 56:6–7; Jer 3:16–17; Ezek 40–48). This supernatural union of the faithful with Christ is in turn the outworking of a prior act of God—the incarnation of God's Son (Rom 8:3–4; Gal 4:4–6; 2 Cor 8:9). This concept of union with Christ, expressed

---

90. LSJ, s.v. "κοιμάω" (sense 3); MM, s.v. "κοιμάομαι." See, for example, Homer, *Il.* 11.241; Callimachus, *Epigr.* 11.1–2. So also Catullus, *Carm.* 5.5–6: *nobis cum semel occidit brevis lux, nox est perpetua una dormienda* ("when once our brief light has set, there is one unending night through which we must sleep"). For further discussion and ancient references, see Abraham J. Malherbe, *The Letters to the Thessalonians* (AB 32B; New York: Doubleday, 2000), 263.

91. See BA, s.v. "κοιμάω"; BDAG, s.v. "κοιμάω." The verb καθεύδω is used in a similar sense in Dan 12:2 LXX; Matt 9:24; Mark 5:39; Luke 8:52; 1 Thess 5:10.

92. Frisk, 1:809. For further discussion, see Schmidt, *Syn.*, 1:450–52.

93. Rob., *Gram.*, 783.

94. For example, "in Christ" in Rom 6:11, 23; 8:39; 12:5; 1 Cor 1:2; 2 Cor 5:21; Gal 3:26; Phil 1:1, 13, 26; 3:8; 4:19, 21; "in the Lord" in Rom 16:11; 1 Cor 7:22; 2 Cor 10:17; Gal 5:10; Phil 1:14; 2:24, 29; 4:1, 4; "in the Lord Jesus" in Rom 14:14; Phil 2:19; "into Christ" in Rom 6:3; Gal 3:27; Phlm 6 and "with Christ" in Rom 6:4; 2 Cor 4:14.

## The Futility of Faith Apart from the Resurrection

in the formula ἐν Χριστῷ, is introduced in the chapter here for the first time. But it will be an absolutely crucial conception in Paul's exposition of the resurrection within the chapter as a whole (15:22, 45–49, 58; cf. 15:23, 57). For, as we will see, the resurrection is the consummation of union with Christ.

*have perished.* Verse 18 is a further stage in Paul's multistage *reductio ad absurdum* argument in 15:12–19. If Christ be not raised (v. 17a), so runs Paul's argument, those united to Christ who have died will not be raised either but have perished eternally (v. 18). But, it is assumed, this is impossible. To many interpreters, the logic of Paul's argument in v. 18 seems lacking. For Paul's argument merely *assumes* (or so it seems) what the opponents of the resurrection at Corinth *deny*—that the dead in Christ will rise. How, therefore, is v. 18 in any sense an *argument* for the future resurrection rather than a mere assertion? Paul's argument, it would seem, is circular.[95]

But these interpreters have missed a crucial nuance within Paul's argument. Paul's precise choice of verb is important: if Christ has not risen, those who sleep in Christ "have perished" (ἀπώλοντο). The verb ἀπόλλυμι used here by Paul is an intensified derivative of ὄλλυμι.[96] It differs from its close synonym φθείρω "to corrupt" in always denoting the complete destruction of a person or thing.[97] Its usual antonym is the verb σῴζω "to save": the two verbs are frequently paired or contrasted within the New Testament (Matt 8:25, 39; 16:25; Mark 8:35; Luke 6:9; 9:24; 1 Cor 1:18; Jas 4:12; cf. Phil 1:28; 3:19–20). The verb ἀπόλλυμι in 15:18 thus recalls δι' οὗ σῴζεσθε ("through which you are being saved") in 15:2, where Paul affirmed that the apostolic kerygma, when received with faith, is saving. Implicit in the *present* tense of σῴζεσθε in 15:2 is the conception that this salvation is a process culminating in the fullness of salvation to come at the advent of Christ (cf. 1 Cor 1:7–9; 3:14–15; 4:5; 5:5; 13:8–13). Paul's argument is thus not circular but makes the claim that the denial of the resurrection by some at Corinth is in conflict with this foundational claim of the kerygma, which Paul has already established in 15:2, that Christ brings not only present salvation, but also future and everlasting salvation (see the diagram at the close of the chapter).

Moreover, the kerygma is saving because it brings about union with Christ. "Those who have fallen asleep in Christ" in v. 18 are those who have died united

---

95. According to Vos, v. 18 is an appeal to emotion rather than to logic ("Logik," 96). Bucher, in order to argue his thesis that Paul's argument in 15:12–19 is fully logical, finds himself forced to deny that v. 18 forms an implication within that argument ("Argumentation," 466, 472).

96. Frisk, 2:378–79.

97. Schmidt, *Syn.*, 4:83–97.

CHAPTER 6

to him through faith. Although, as noted above, the phrase ἐν Χριστῷ should be taken attributively with οἱ κοιμηθέντες, its placement immediately before ἀπώλοντο is probably not accidental. Juxtaposed with ἀπώλοντο, it expresses an impossible contradiction—that those united to Christ should perish. This adds a further dimension to Paul's argument: the denial of the resurrection is a denial not only of the saving power of the kerygma but also of the saving efficacy of union with Christ.

Verse 18 adds to Paul's argument in another important way. We argued above that in vv. 12–13 and 16 the necessary relation posited by Paul between Christ's resurrection and the future resurrection of the dead should not be understood as an *inferential* but as a *causal* one. Christ's resurrection is the source, cause, and wellspring of the coming resurrection of those who belong to Christ. Now, in v. 18, Paul is *explicit* that the resurrection of Christ is the cause of the resurrection of the faithful. Moreover, the logic of vv. 12–13 and 16 entails only that the resurrection of Christ is the *sufficient* cause of the future resurrection—if Christ is risen, the dead will rise. The logic of vv. 12–13 and 16 does not rule out that the resurrection of the dead might also be brought about by other means. But v. 18 *does* rule this out. The logic of v. 18 demands that Christ's resurrection is also the *necessary* cause of the resurrection of the faithful (see the diagram). If and only if Christ has been raised will those united to him by faith also rise to life. This is an important facet of Paul's argument not made explicit until v. 18.

## Verse 19

*If for this life only we have placed our hope in Christ, we are the most wretched of all human beings.*

With v. 19 we come to the final leg of Paul's series of *reductio ad absurdum* arguments in 15:12–19.

*If for this life only.* The teaching of the self-professed wise at Corinth, which Paul has up to now simply reported (15:12–13: "there is no resurrection of the dead"; 15:15–16: "the dead are not raised"), he now redescribes in a way that brings out its implications. It offers hope only "for this life" (ἐν τῇ ζωῇ ταύτῃ). The noun ζωή in the New Testament is most frequently used of that indestructible supernatural life given to the faithful by Christ, but occasionally in the New Testament ζωή denotes the present natural life shared by all human beings (Luke 16:25; Acts 8:33; 17:25; Rom 8:38; 1 Cor 3:22; Phil 1:20; Heb 7:3; Jas 4:14). This is the sense of ζωή in 15:19. The adverbial μόνον is to be taken with ἐν τῇ ζωῇ ταύτῃ ("for this life only").[98]

*we have placed our hope in Christ.* Paul uses ἐλπίζω with a preposition, a construction unknown to classical Greek but common in the LXX and in the Jewish and Christian circles influenced by it. In the LXX, the preposition ἐν is used to describe the ground of hope, which within religious contexts is always the Lord (4 Kgdms 18:5; Pss 32:21; 35:7). It is therefore striking that here in 1 Cor 15:19 the ground of hope is *Christ* (ἐν Χριστῷ). Paul's syntax reveals his divine, incarnational Christology: Jesus is YHWH incarnate. As we will see, Paul's divine Christology will be the key to Paul's thought within this stunning chapter as a whole.

Paul depicts the fixed place of this hope within the lives of believers through his use of the perfect tense.[99] Hope, within Paul's theology, is a crucial component of life in Christ (Rom 5:1–5; 8:24–25; 12:12). It forms part of the triad of faith, hope, and love so central in Paul's writings (1 Cor 13:7, 13; Gal 5:5–6; 1 Thess 1:3; 5:8). The faithful "rejoice in hope of the glory of God" (Rom 5:2). Paul tells the Romans "in hope we were saved" (Rom 8:24). Paul can even describe God as "the God of hope" (Rom 15:13). Throughout Paul's letters, this hope is fixed on the fullness of salvation to come at the second advent of Christ (Rom 5:1–11; 8:18–25; Gal 5:5; 1 Thess 1:2–10; 4:13–18; 5:8–10).

What an unthinkable contradiction, then, within Paul's theology, and what a travesty of the faith, that believers in Christ should place their hope in Christ "for this life only"! If we read Paul's protasis calmly, with no sense of Paul's baffled amazement that followers of Christ could embrace such a contradiction, we have not grasped his meaning. But it is precisely here where some interpreters have questioned the logic of Paul's argument. Assuming, as most scholars do, that the opponents of the resurrection at Corinth did not deny an afterlife altogether but embraced some form of nonbodily afterlife, some ask how Paul can describe such a teaching as offering hope "for this life only"? Why, they ask, is bodily resurrection necessary? Why does some doctrine of the immortality of the soul not suffice to offer hope for a life to come?

This question fails to grasp Paul's biblical and Jewish anthropology. In Paul's theology, the human person is a *composite being* made up of a body as well as a

---

98. Rightly Fitzmyer, 565; Conzelmann, 267. *Pace* Proctor, "Hamartiological Inefficacy," 632–35.

99. BDR §341 n. 2 classes the perfect of ἐλπίζω as a "present perfect" but as "stronger" than the present tense of ἐλπίζω, by virtue of the perfect tense's stress upon the permanent and fixed character of this act of hope.

CHAPTER 6

spirit or soul (Rom 1:9; 1 Cor 2:11; 1 Thess 5:23). The body, as the good creation of God, is an integral aspect of the human being. Salvation, therefore, can only be the redemption of the whole person, body and soul. For Paul, the conception of an immortal soul permanently separated from its body is incoherent and meaningless. Far from offering hope, such a conception from the Pauline standpoint does not even make sense. The salvation of the human *person* requires the resurrection of the *body*.[100]

*we are the most wretched of all human beings.* The adjective ἐλεεινός means "wretched, miserable, pitiable."[101] In Rev 3:17 it is paired with ταλαίπωρος "miserable." For ancient readers, Paul's words may have recalled the declaration of Zeus in the *Iliad* that, in view of human mortality and the finality of death, "of all the creatures which breathe and move upon the earth, there is none more pitiable than a human being" (Homer, *Il.* 17.446–447). But this wretchedness is compounded for Christ followers. Far from being saved through faith in the kerygma (15:2), their belief in the apostolic preaching has made them the most wretched of all human beings—if there is no resurrection.

In what sense are Christ followers *more* wretched than all the others?[102] Paul's thought here assumes something he has made explicit throughout the letter, and will do so again powerfully and climactically in vv. 29–34, that life in Christ requires renunciation, self-denial, privations, and suffering (4:9–16; 5:9–13; 6:9–11; 9:24–27; 10:1–13; 15:29–34). These momentary, light afflictions are not worth comparing to the weight of glory to be revealed at the resurrection (cf. Rom 8:18; 2 Cor 4:17). But if there is no resurrection of the dead, these sufferings are for nothing and in vain (15:14, 17–18). Nor, in that case, do they have any moral value. For if such be the case, these sufferings are not borne for the sake of the truth, for if there is no resurrection of the dead, then the apostolic kerygma is a lie and a falsehood (15:15). And if the apostolic kerygma is false, these sufferings are not borne for the sake of righteousness, for to suffer for a lie is not noble but morally base and foolhardy. With no hope beyond this life, suffering in this life needlessly and ignobly for the sake of a lie, Christ followers would indeed be uniquely wretched among all human beings. Paul makes this point only briefly and in passing here, but he will fully ground and establish it in vv. 29–34. There he will vividly describe the sufferings of

---

100. On this aspect of Paul's thought, see Aquinas, *1 Cor.* 924, and cf. *ST*, Suppl. Q. 75, Art. 1, ad Obj. 2; Q. 75, Art. 1, ad Obj. 3.
101. Robinson, s.v. "ἐλεεινός." Cf. BA, s.v. "ἐλεεινός"; BDAG, s.v. "ἐλεεινός."
102. Among all commentators, the most insightful treatment of v. 19 remains that of Thomas Aquinas (*1 Cor.* 925), to whose insights the discussion in this paragraph is indebted.

Christ followers, with focus on his own apostolic example of suffering for Christ to the point of combat with the beasts in the arena at Ephesus. In 15:29–34 Paul will show that the Christian life of cruciform discipleship is grounded in the hope of the resurrection, and apart from the resurrection it is meaningless and in vain. Verse 19 therefore serves as a prelude to that passage. The verse thus has not only a doctrinal but also an ethical and hortatory purpose, reminding the Corinthians that genuine faith involves radical commitment to Christ.

Margaret Mitchell claims that Paul regarded those at Corinth who held fast to the apostolic proclamation of the resurrection and those who denied it as unnecessarily divided over mere "different views on the resurrection." She claims that Paul's counsel in this epistle is one of tolerance and compromise regarding the two views.[103] Similarly, Jeffrey R. Asher argues that Paul in this letter treats the Corinthian doubters as students, not heretics, regarding their denial of the resurrection as a foolish mistake in need of correction, but he does not call into question their commitment to Christ and the gospel.[104] First Corinthians 15:12–19 reveals the falsehood of such views. In Paul's judgment, those at Corinth who reject the resurrection "have placed themselves in contradiction to the gospel story."[105] The denial of the resurrection is a contradiction of the entire apostolic witness (15:12, 14–15, 17). It is tantamount to calling the apostles false witnesses (15:15). The Corinthians' embrace of this denial would thus "sever their relationship with the apostolic office."[106] In the doctrine of the resurrection, "What is involved is the *substance*, the *whole* of the Christian revelation."[107]

As Paul makes clear in 15:12–19, to deny the hope of the resurrection is to renounce the apostles and the gospel they proclaim. It is to renounce Christ. It is even to renounce the validity of empirical evidence, reason, and the experience of the five senses. Those at Corinth who deny the resurrection have not only denied the faith; they have in the process also lost their reason. That is the message of the relentless and inescapable logic of vv. 12–19. In 15:12–19, we truly see the apostle beating the self-professed wise at Corinth at their own philosophical and logical game.

---

103. Margaret M. Mitchell, *Paul and the Rhetoric of Reconciliation: An Exegetical Investigation of the Language and Composition of 1 Corinthians* (Louisville: Westminster John Knox, 1991), 176–77.

104. Asher, *Polarity and Change*, 30–90. He is followed by Garland, 696.

105. Hays, 260.

106. Vorster, "Resurrection Faith," 299.

107. Karl Barth, *The Resurrection of the Dead* (trans. H. J. Stenning; 1933; repr., Eugene, OR: Wipf & Stock, 2003), 112.

CHAPTER 6

## The Logical Structure of Paul's Argument in 15:12–19

*The Foundations of Paul's Argument in 15:1–11*

| | |
|---|---|
| n | the argument's only prior, unargued assumption |
| n ⊃ p \ n \ ∴ p | argued and established validly in 15:3, 5–8, 11 |
| p ⊃ q \ p \ ∴ q | argued and established validly in 15:3–11 |
| p ⊃ s \ p \ ∴ s | argued and established validly in 15:1–2 |
| s ⊃ ($s^1$ & $s^2$) \ s \ ∴ $s^1$ & $s^2$ | argued and established validly in 15:2–3 |
| (p & s) ⊃ t \ (p & s) \ ∴ t | argued and established implicitly but validly in 15:1–2 |

*The Argument in 15:12–19*

| | | |
|---|---|---|
| 15:12 | [p ⊃ q] \ q ⊃ r \ p \ ∴ r (MP) | First polysyllogism – (πῶς signals contradiction – q sufficient condition of r) |
| 15:13 | ~ r ⊃ ~ q \ | Second polysyllogism – *reductio ad absurdum* |
| 15:14 | ~ q ⊃ ~ s \ s \ ∴ q & r (MT) | |
| 15:15 | ~ q ⊃ ~ p \ ~ p ⊃ ~ n \ n \ ∴ p & q & r (MT) | |
| 15:16 | ~ r ⊃ ~ q \ | Third polysyllogism – *reductio ad absurdum* |
| 15:17 | ~ q ⊃ (~ s & ~$s^1$) \ (s & $s^1$) \ ∴ q & r (MT) | |
| 15:18 | ~ q ⊃ [~ r] \ | Fourth polysyllogism – *reductio ad absurdum* (new element – q *necessary* condition of r) |
| | [~ r ⊃] ~ $s^2$ \ $s^2$ \ ∴ r (MT) | |
| 15:19 | ~ (p & s) ⊃ ~ t \ t \ ∴ p & s (MT) [p ⊃ q \ q ⊃ r \ (p & s) \ ∴ r] (MP) | Concluding syllogism – *reductio ad absurdum* |

## The Futility of Faith Apart from the Resurrection

*The Propositions within Paul's Argument*

    n = empirical evidence is probative
    p = the eyewitness testimony of the apostles to the resurrection is true
    q = Christ is risen
    r = there will be a future resurrection of the dead
    s = the apostolic kerygma received with faith is not in vain but saving
        $s^1$ = this salvation frees from the guilt and power of sin
        $s^2$ = this salvation is a process culminating at the advent of Christ
    t = suffering for the sake of Christ and the gospel is wise

*Logical Symbols*

| | | |
|---|---|---|
| ⊃ | = | if ... then |
| ~ | = | not |
| & | = | and |
| ∴ | = | therefore |
| ( ) | = | encloses an antecedent, consequent, or minor premise involving multiple propositions |
| [ ] | = | encloses a premise, proposition, or syllogism implicit but not explicit in Paul's argument |
| \ | = | separates a premise from a following premise or conclusion |
| (MP) | = | the argument has the form *modus ponens* |
| (MT) | = | the argument has the form *modus tollens* |

CHAPTER 7

## *The Last Adam's Triumph over Death*

15:20–23

Although interpreters have often found the function of vv. 20–23 within the chapter perplexing, sometimes considering the passage a digression from the main thought, these verses in fact have a central place within the argument of the chapter. The passage has a strongly narrative character.[1] It thus contrasts with the propositional and logical structure of 15:12–19. Verses 20–23, in fact, return to and continue the narrative of vv. 1–11, which narrated the story of Christ's death, burial, and resurrection. Verses 20–23 pick up the narrative again at Christ's resurrection (15:20) and bring the story to its climax at his second coming (15:23) and the resurrection of all who belong to Christ (15:22–23). Indeed, by including the fall (15:21–22), the scope of the narrative in 15:20–23 becomes even more sweeping, moving from creation to the final renewal of all things. The truth that was assumed throughout the logical section of vv. 12–19—that the resurrection of Christ from the dead entails the resurrection of all those united to Christ—is now set forth powerfully and directly in the narrative of vv. 20–23.[2] The function of the narrative of 15:20–23 within the overall argument of the chapter is thus quite central and important.

Verses 24–28 will continue the narrative of vv. 20–23 with Christ's abolition of the cosmic and demonic powers (15:24–27) and the restoration of all things to God (15:28). But whereas 15:24–28 is dominated by theological language such as θεός (15:24, 28), πατήρ (15:24), and υἱός (15:28), 15:20–23 is filled with anthropological

---

1. Jeffrey M. Dale, "First Corinthians as an Eschatological Counter to Spiritualizing Tendencies," *Conversations with the Biblical World* 37 (2018): 86–90.
2. Cf. William Dykstra, "1 Corinthians 15:20–28, an Essential Part of Paul's Argument against Those Who Deny the Resurrection," *CTJ* 4 (1969): 208–9.

*The Last Adam's Triumph over Death*

language and vocabulary such as ἄνθρωπος (15:21 [2×]), Ἀδάμ (15:22), and Χριστός (15:20, 22, 23 [2×]), the latter being the Son's royal title emphasizing his representative role on behalf of humanity. This anthropological language reflects the focus of 15:20–23, which is predominantly on the human plane. The focus of vv. 20–23 is on the human being through whom the resurrection has come (15:21), on the two Adams (15:21–22), and on the bodily resurrection of the messiah's people that is to come (15:20, 23). Lying latent within this language focusing on the human realm, as we will see, is the central mystery of the chapter.

First Corinthians 15:20–23 is carefully structured in the form of a chiasm. The structure of the passage may be illustrated as follows:

20  A   Christ, the Firstfruits of the Resurrection
21      B   The Two Human Beings
22      B'  Adam and Christ
23  A'  Christ, the Firstfruits of the Resurrection

These verses take up the thread of 15:12–19, revealing fully for the first time why the resurrection of Christ entails the resurrection of all the dead. It is so because the resurrection of Christ is not an isolated event but the central act of salvation history. It is the conquest of death, now come through a human being, the Christ (15:21–22). He is therefore the firstfruits of the resurrection of all the dead, which must follow at his advent (15:20, 23).

## Verse 20

*But in fact Christ has been raised from the dead, the firstfruits of those who have fallen asleep.*

*But in fact Christ has been raised from the dead.* Verse 20 begins a new section in the strongest possible contrast to what has come before. As the apostle showed in 15:12–19 with inexorable logic, if there is no coming resurrection of the dead, then Christ has not been raised (15:13, 16), and if Christ has not been raised, the apostolic testimony to his resurrection is false witness and vain (15:14–15), the cross of Christ is futile (15:17–18), and the hard life of Christian discipleship is pointless (15:19). But all of this is false. The transitional νυνὶ δέ is here logical, not temporal, "introducing the real situation after an unreal conditional clause or sentence."[3] The phrase here means "but in actual fact" or "but in reality." The

---

3. BDAG, s.v. "νυνί" (2.b); cf. Wolff, 381; Lindemann, 343; Fitzmyer, 569.

CHAPTER 7

hypotheticals of 15:12–19, which necessarily follow if the Corinthian denial of the resurrection is true, are all untrue. The reality is the opposite. The contrast with what precedes is especially pointed by Paul's use not of the simple νῦν but of the more emphatic νυνί.

The reality νυνὶ δέ introduces is that "Christ has been raised from the dead." The assertion Χριστὸς ἐγήγερται ἐκ νεκρῶν recalls and directly contradicts the inference from the denial of the future resurrection in vv. 13 and 16, οὐδὲ Χριστὸς ἐγήγερται ("neither has Christ been raised"). At the same time, the assertion Χριστὸς ἐγήγερται ἐκ νεκρῶν ("Christ has been raised from the dead") recalls and emphatically reaffirms the truth of the apostolic kerygma expressed in 15:12: Χριστὸς κηρύσσεται ὅτι ἐκ νεκρῶν ἐγήγερται ("*Christ* is proclaimed that he *has been raised from the dead*"). Paul's assertion thus also once again recalls and restates the confessional formula of 15:3–8: Χριστὸς ... ἐγήγερται ("Christ ... has been raised," 15:3–4). As we saw in the discussion of 15:4 in chapter 3, the phrase ἐγήγερται ἐκ νεκρῶν expressly denotes a corporeal and physical event involving the body of flesh and bones. Christ, Paul here once more affirms, has been physically raised from the tomb in his crucified body. The perfect tense of ἐγήγερται stresses the present and ongoing reality of Christ's risen life: he is risen from the dead, never to die again, and death no longer has power over him (Rom 6:9).

*the firstfruits of those who have fallen asleep.* Here we have something new in the argument of the chapter. Up to this point in v. 20, Paul has simply reaffirmed the confessional formula of 15:3–4 and the summary of this apostolic kerygma in 15:12—Christ has been raised from the dead. Now with the further description of the risen Lord as "the firstfruits of those who have fallen asleep" (ἀπαρχὴ τῶν κεκοιμημένων), Paul affirms something that was, to be sure, an important part of the thought in 15:12–19 but was only implicit. Now Paul makes it explicit.[4] The phrase thus bears special weight in Paul's argument, and so we must examine it carefully.

Within 15:20, τῶν κεκοιμημένων stands in apposition to νεκρῶν: Χριστὸς ἐγήγερται ἐκ νεκρῶν, ἀπαρχὴ τῶν κεκοιμημένων ("Christ has been raised from *the dead*, the firstfruits of *those who have fallen asleep*"). "Those who have fallen asleep" (οἱ κεκοιμημένοι) is another way of denoting those who have died. But it bears a different connotation or nuance than "the dead" (οἱ νεκροί). As we saw in our full discussion

---

4. The phrase ἀπαρχὴ τῶν κεκοιμημένων is in predicate apposition to Χριστὸς ἐγήγερται ἐκ νεκρῶν. The Byzantine witnesses and a few other later manuscripts (D² K L) append ἐγένετο to the end of the verse, thus making ἀπαρχὴ the predicate of a second independent clause. This reading is clearly secondary.

of the verb in our commentary on 15:18, the verb κοιμάω is derived from κεῖμαι "to lie," and its primary sense in the passive (the form found here and throughout the New Testament) is thus "to *lie down* in sleep."[5] When used of the dead, as here, the verb depicts their bodies as *lying* asleep in death, waiting to be *roused up* (ἐγείρω) or *raised upright* (ἀνίστημι) at the resurrection (2 Macc 12:44–45; 1 En. 92.3; Matt 27:52; John 11:11; Acts 7:60; 13:36; 1 Thess 4:13–15; 2 Pet 3:4). The verb thus forms yet another facet of the New Testament's language of *bodily* resurrection. Perhaps not surprisingly, therefore, of its fourteen instances in the New Testament, six of them are found in 1 Corinthians, and four of those within chapter 15 (15:6, 18, 20, 51). It is an important part of the vocabulary of bodily, physical resurrection within the chapter. The secret to the temporary character of death implicit in the verb is found in 15:18: those who sleep are asleep *in Christ* (οἱ κοιμηθέντες ἐν Χριστῷ, 15:18). And the reason Christ is the secret is that he is the "firstfruits" (ἀπαρχή). What does this mean?

The "firstfruits" (ἀπαρχή) was the first portion of the harvest, which was offered to God in the sanctuary (Exod 23:19; Lev 2:12; 22:12; Num 15:17–21; 18:11–13; Deut 18:4; 26:1–11). The metaphor, when applied to Christ, is powerful and multivalent, necessarily conveying three distinct ideas concerning the relationship between the resurrection of Christ and the resurrection of all the dead:

(1) Christ's resurrection is *anticipatory*. It is first in order of time. This is implicit in the very conception of the ἀπαρχή, which always preceded the rest of the harvest in order of time (Lev 23:14; Josephus, *A.J.* 3.251; Philo, *Spec.* 2.176, 179–180). It is also implicit in the etymology of ἀπαρχή, which is derived from ἀρχή "beginning."[6] Paul will make this point explicit in 15:23 (ἕκαστος δὲ ἐν τῷ ἰδίῳ τάγματι "but each in his own order").

(2) Christ's resurrection is *representative* or exemplary. That is, it is "representative of the same quality or character."[7] The firstfruits are, after all, a part of the harvest. Thus in Paul's construction, τῶν κεκοιμημένων is a partitive genitive, indicating that Christ's resurrection is a part of the resurrection of all the dead. The resurrection of Christ therefore "reveals the type and quality of the coming resurrection of believers."[8] In the resurrection the faithful will "wear the image of

---

5. For the etymology of the verb, see Frisk, 1:809. For further discussion of the verb, see Schmidt, *Syn.*, 1:450–52.

6. Cf. Col 1:18, ὅς ἐστιν ἀρχή, πρωτότοκος ἐκ τῶν νεκρῶν "who is the *beginning*, the *firstborn* from the dead"; Rev 1:5, πρωτότοκος τῶν νεκρῶν "*firstborn* of the dead"; Acts 26:23, πρῶτος ἐξ ἀναστάσεως νεκρῶν "the *first* from the resurrection of the dead."

7. Ciampa & Rosner, 762.

8. Constantine R. Campbell, *Paul and the Hope of Glory: An Exegetical and Theological Study* (Grand Rapids: Zondervan, 2020), 333.

CHAPTER 7

the one from heaven" (15:49). Their bodies will be transformed so as to be "made like the body of his glory" (Phil 3:21).

(3) The resurrection of Christ is the *assurance* or *guarantee* of the future resurrection.[9] As the firstfruits are inevitably followed by the full harvest, so Christ's resurrection entails the resurrection of all who are in Christ. But here the reality (the resurrection of Christ) surpasses the type or analogy (the first portion of the crops). For the firstfruits of the harvested crops logically entail the full harvest, but they are not its cause. By contrast, the resurrection of Christ is the *cause* of the resurrection to come (15:21, δι' ἀνθρώπου ἀνάστασις νεκρῶν; cf. 15:22, 45, 49). The resurrection of Christ is both the *model* and the *cause* of the resurrection of those who belong to Christ. His resurrection is, as Aquinas says, the *causa efficiens et exemplaris* "the efficient and exemplary cause."[10]

With this single expression ἀπαρχὴ τῶν κεκοιμημένων, then, the apostle masterfully lays bare the mistake at the heart of the denial of the resurrection at Corinth and makes plain the premise underlying his entire argument in 15:12–19. The resurrection of Christ was not an odd singularity but the conquest of death (cf. 15:26, 54–57). It is the first stage of a two-stage event, which will culminate in the resurrection of all the dead. It is the beginning, model, and cause—and thus the guarantee—of the coming resurrection.[11]

It is extremely likely that, in referring to Christ as the firstfruits, Paul has in mind not merely firstfruits in general but specifically the Feast of Firstfruits.[12] This observance, enjoined on Israel in Lev 23:9–14, was celebrated on Nisan 16, the

9. Of the three ideas inherent in ἀπαρχή, this is the one stressed as the primary idea by most expositors; see *TLNT* 1:150, 152; Wolff, 381; Fitzmyer, 569; Collins, 547–48, 551; Fee, 829–30; Barrett, 350–51; Ciampa & Rosner, 761; Weiss, 356; Schreiner, 312.

10. Aquinas, *1 Cor.* 913–914.

11. For further discussion, see Andy Johnson, "Firstfruits and Death's Defeat: Metaphor in Paul's Rhetorical Strategy in 1 Cor 15:20–28," *WW* 16 (1996): 456–64. Joost Holleman argues that Paul's portrayal of Jesus's resurrection as the firstfruits is incoherent in "Jesus' Resurrection as the Beginning of the Eschatological Resurrection (1 Cor 15,20)," in *The Corinthian Correspondence* (ed. Reimund Bieringer; BETL 125; Leuven: Peeters, 1996), 653–60. But that is because Holleman begins with what we have seen is a mistaken view of Jesus's resurrection in Paul as a resurrection "in heaven" that does not involve a resurrection of Jesus's crucified body from the tomb (656). On the bodily nature of Jesus's resurrection in the apostolic teaching, see chapters 3 and 4 of the commentary.

12. See Jacob Thiessen, "Firstfruits and the Day of Christ's Resurrection: An Examination of the Relationship between the 'Third Day' in 1 Cor 15:4 and the 'Firstfruit' in 1 Cor 15:20," *Neot* 46 (2012): 379–93; Joel White, "'He was Raised on the Third Day According to the Scriptures' (1 Corinthians 15:4): A Typological Interpretation Based on the Cultic Calendar in Leviticus 23," *TynBul* 66 (2015): 103–19; Szabolcs-Ferencz Kató, "Resurrection on the Day of the Omer? Interpreting 1 Corinthians 15:20 in the Light of Leviticus 23:9–15 and Menaḥot 10:2–3," *Neot* 56 (2022): 71–86.

third day after the Passover on Nisan 14.[13] The two most prominent occasions on which firstfruits were offered were the Feast of Firstfruits (Lev 23:9–14; Josephus, *A.J.* 3.250–251; Philo, *Spec.* 2.162–175) and Pentecost (Exod 23:16; 34:22; Lev 23:15–21; Num 28:26; Josephus, *A.J.* 3.252; Philo, *Spec.* 2.175–186). It is almost certainly the former that Paul has in mind. The word ἀπαρχή used by Paul in 15:20 is not used in the LXX in connection with Pentecost but only in connection with the Feast of Firstfruits (LXX Lev 23:10). Moreover, the Feast of Firstfruits, more than any other occasion involving the offering of firstfruits in the life of ancient Israel, explicitly coheres with and illustrates Paul's understanding of the ἀπαρχή as anticipatory, representative, and promissory. At this feast, a sheaf of barley ears was taken from the standing fields and offered to God in the temple as firstfruits of the harvest (Josephus, *A.J.* 3.251; Philo, *Spec.* 2.162, 171, 175).[14] Only after this offering could the rest of the crop be harvested (Lev 23:24; Josephus, *A.J.* 3.250–251). At this feast, Philo tells us, the Jewish people understood themselves as offering firstfruits not only on behalf of their own land but on behalf of all the earth (Philo, *Spec.* 2.162–171). The coherence of Paul's multivalent conception of Christ as the firstfruits with the practice and understanding in antiquity of the Feast of Firstfruits is striking. Moreover, if Paul's reference to Christ as the firstfruits in 15:20 is a reference to the Feast of Firstfruits on the third day after Passover, this would form a striking complement within the letter to Paul's references to the Passover, the Feast of Unleavened Bread, and Christ as the Passover lamb in 1 Cor 5:6–8.[15]

One further consideration makes it almost certain that Paul is referring to the Feast of Firstfruits here. As we saw in our discussion of the ancient confessional formula in 1 Cor 15:3–8, Jesus was crucified on a Friday, Nisan 14, the day of Passover, and was raised to life on "the third day" (1 Cor 15:4). The day of Christ's resurrection was therefore Sunday, Nisan 16, the day of the Feast of Firstfruits. Paul's contacts with the eyewitnesses of the events (Gal 1:15–18; 2:1–10), his knowledge of the events of the passion week (1 Cor 11:23–25; 15:3–7), and his identification of Jesus as "Christ our Passover" (5:7) indicate his awareness that Jesus's crucifixion took place on Passover. But Paul was also aware that Jesus's resurrection took place "on the third day" after his crucifixion (15:4). This means that Paul was also

---

13. For discussion of the complex calendrical issues involved, and the persuasive evidence for the celebration of the Feast of Firstfruits on Nisan 16, see Thiessen, "Firstfruits," 380–84.

14. Philo designates this offering as ἀπαρχή, as in the LXX (*Spec.* 2.162, 171, 175); Josephus uses the plural ἀπαρχαί (*A.J.* 3.250–251).

15. Cf. David J. Williams, *Paul's Metaphors: Their Context and Character* (Peabody, MA: Hendrickson, 1999), 48 n. 70: 15:20 "complements Paul's earlier reference to the Passover and to Christ as the Passover lamb in 1 Cor 5:6–8."

necessarily aware that the day on which Christ's resurrection took place was the day on which the Feast of Firstfruits was celebrated.[16]

So then, to summarize, the following reasons strongly suggest an allusion to the Feast of Firstfruits in v. 20: (1) Paul's use of the term ἀπαρχή, a word used of feasts in the LXX only in reference to the Feast of Firstfruits; (2) the coherence of the particulars of this feast with Paul's treatment of Christ as the firstfruits in 15:20; (3) Paul's complementary reference to Christ as the Passover lamb in 1 Cor 5:6–8; (4) the historical fact of Jesus's resurrection on the day of the Feast of Firstfruits; and, finally, (5) Paul's awareness of this fact. All these considerations render it virtually certain that Paul's reference to Christ as the firstfruits in 1 Cor 15:20 involves an understanding of the Feast of Firstfruits of Lev 23:19–24 as a prophetic type or foreshadow fulfilled in the resurrection of Christ. Just as Paul understood the Passover as a type fulfilled in the crucifixion of Christ, so he understood the Feast of Firstfruits as a type of Christ's resurrection. This understanding underlies Paul's reference to Christ as "the firstfruits of those who have fallen asleep" in 1 Cor 15:20.

### VERSE 21

*For since indeed through a human being came death, also through a human being came the resurrection of the dead.*

*For since indeed through a human being came death.* The γάρ is explanatory ("you see"), not causal; Paul now further explains in what way Christ is the firstfruits. Paul here alludes to the narrative of Gen 2–3, in particular 2:17 and 3:19.[17] Paul affirms that death came through Adam but does not specify how. However, several considerations are conclusive that Paul's brief statement assumes a larger narrative, in which death entered the world through *sin*: (1) In the narrative of Gen 2–3 echoed by Paul, the source of death is Adam's sin. (2) The common ancient Jewish reading of Gen 2–3 strongly emphasized the sin of Adam as the source and origin of death.[18] (3) Paul's fuller discussion in Rom 5:12–21 finds the cause of death in the original sin of Adam (cf. Rom 5:12, "through one human being sin entered the

---

16. Cf. Kató, "Day of the Omer," 81: "Paul alludes to a tradition in which Jesus dies on 14 Nisan and is resurrected on the day of the Omer [i.e., the feast of Firstfruits]."

17. For a survey of contemporary scholarly understandings of the origin and nature of death in Gen 2–3, see Bruce Wells, "Death in the Garden of Eden," *JBL* 139 (2020): 642–45.

18. On understandings of Adam and the fall in Second Temple Judaism, see Felipe de Jesús Legarreta-Castillo, *The Figure of Adam in Romans 5 and 1 Corinthians 15: The New Creation and Its Ethical and Social Reconfiguration* (Minneapolis: Fortress, 2014), 12–117, 167–76.

world, and death through sin"; see also Rom 6:20–21; Gal 3:21–22). Paul's statement in 1 Cor 15:21 thus assumes, as the vast majority of scholars have recognized, that the way Adam brought death into the world was through his sin and rebellion against God.[19]

From the statement that death came through a human being, it necessarily follows that humanity was originally created free from death. The full conception underlying 15:21 in the apostle's mind may be gathered from all of his letters and stated as follows. The first human being, Adam, was created with a mortal body (1 Cor 15:45, 47; cf. Gen 3:19) but was immune from death by divine grace (Rom 5:12; cf. Gen 2:17; 3:2–3), a gift that was conditional upon his remaining in communion with God (2 Cor 11:2–3; cf. Gen 2:9; 3:22). This gift of immortality was lost through Adam's disobedience (Rom 5:15–19), bringing all Adam's progeny under the power of death (Rom 5:12).[20] First Corinthians 15:21 has a preparatory function within the chapter, for only in the course of the chapter will Paul fully develop this particular thought. First Corinthians 15:45–49 will clarify and emphasize the mortal nature of Adam's created body, even prior to the fall (15:45, 47). And what is only implicit in 15:21—the source of death in original sin—will be explicitly stated and developed in 15:56 ("the sting of death is sin").[21]

This affirmation of 1 Cor 15:21 that humanity was originally created free from death is of highest importance. In the ancient world into which the gospel came, death was considered an eternal and unchangeable reality of the cosmic order of things, one that even the gods were powerless to alter.[22] But in the biblical and

---

19. E.g. Garland, 706; Schreiner, 312. The contrary claim of Jeromey Martini, "An Examination of Paul's Apocalyptic Narrative in First Corinthians 15:20–28," *CTR* 8 (2011): 57–70, esp. 61, and Andreas Lindemann, "Die Auferstehung der Toten: Adam und Christus nach 1 Kor 15," in *Eschatologie und Schöpfung* (ed. Martin Evang, Helmut Merklein, and Michael Wolter; Berlin: de Gruyter, 1997), 158, 166, is wholly unconvincing.

20. According to the traditional ecclesiastical interpretation, the death that entered the world through Adam's sin was human death; animal predation and death preceded the fall. Cf. Aquinas, *ST* I, Q. 96, Art. 1, ad. 2; Q. 97, Art. 1; II-II, Q. 164, Art. 1, ad. 2; Supp, Q. 9.

21. Martinus C. de Boer distinguishes two understandings of death in ancient Jewish thought, as a cosmic power and as the divine penal judgment for sin, and claims that only the former conception has a significant place in Paul's thought. See *The Defeat of Death: Apocalyptic Eschatology in 1 Corinthians 15 and Romans 5* (JSNTSup 22; 1988; repr., London: T&T Clark, 2019), 93–140. However, 1 Cor 15:21 and 15:56 show that Paul views death not only as a cosmic power but also as a penal or forensic divine judgment on sin. In Paul, it is not an either/or, but a both/and. For cogent criticism of the one-sided character of de Boer's thesis, see Janghoon Park, "The Identity of Death in 1 Corinthians 15:20–28: Understanding the Cosmic and Forensic Dimensions of Death in Paul," *Korean Evangelical New Testament Studies* 19 (2020): 194–232.

22. E.g., Homer, *Od.* 3.229–238; *Il.* 16.433; Aeschylus, *Eum.* 647–49; Cicero, *Div.* 2.25; Lucretius, *Nat.* 1–3; Plato, *Tim.* 41a–42e, 69c–73d; Seneca, *Prov.* 6.5–8; Epictetus, *Diatr.* 1.1.10–12.

## CHAPTER 7

Pauline doctrine reflected here in 15:21, human beings were created immune from death for the purpose of everlasting life in communion with their creator. Human beings, together with their bodies, are the good creation of a good creator.[23] Death is an inversion of creation, not the original purpose of its divine design. It is, as Paul will shortly reaffirm, an intruder into the good creation, an "enemy" (15:26). And the second half of v. 21 will affirm the conquest of death by Christ.

*also through a human being came the resurrection of the dead.* As we saw in the full discussion of the term in the commentary on 15:12, the expression ἀνάστασις νεκρῶν ("the resurrection of the dead") unambiguously expresses the hope of the physical return to life of the dead body or corpse, that is, the hope of fleshly and bodily resurrection. The reciprocal καί connects this clause to the preceding one: like death, which came "through a human being," the resurrection of the dead also (καί) comes "through a human being" (δι' ἀνθρώπου). But what is the timing of this latter event? Verse 21 lacks any verbs. Blass, Debrunner, and Rehkopf along with A. T. Robertson assume that the future tense ἔσται is understood—"also through a human being *will be* the resurrection of the dead."[24] But this is surely mistaken. For in Paul's theology, the promised resurrection of the dead has already come true in the resurrection of Christ. He has even now been "revealed as the Son of God, according to the Spirit of holiness, by the resurrection of the dead" (Rom 1:4, ἐξ ἀναστάσεως νεκρῶν). He is not only the cause of the resurrection but also its firstfruits. In Christ's resurrection, the resurrection of the dead has come. Thus a past tense verb such as ἐγένετο is to be understood in the second clause of 15:21: "also through a human being *came* the resurrection of the dead."

The two clauses, 15:21a and 15:21b, are not coordinate. Rather, as the conjunction ἐπειδή indicates, 15:21a ("for since indeed through a human being came death") is the *reason* or *cause* for 15:21b ("also through a human being came the resurrection of the dead"). The captivity of humanity to sin and death is the reason for the incarnation, passion, and resurrection of the Son of God. Behind v. 21 thus lies the whole Pauline gospel of the love of Christ (2 Cor 5:14), God sending his Son (Rom 8:3; Gal 4:4–6), and the Son of God undoing the curse of Adam by becoming a curse for us (Gal 3:10–14). God's unlimited and unalterable power could

---

23. See James P. Ware, *Paul's Theology in Context: Creation, Incarnation, Covenant, and Kingdom* (Grand Rapids: Eerdmans, 2019), 7–23. The idiosyncratic claim of Jason David BeDuhn that Paul had a "demiurgical" anthropology, in which the created order was brought into being by mediation of angels and not directly by God, is in flat contradiction to Paul's epistles (cf. 1 Cor 8:6, πάντα δι' αὐτοῦ καὶ ἡμεῖς δι' αὐτοῦ). See BeDuhn, "'Because of the Angels': Unveiling Paul's Anthropology in 1 Corinthians 11," *JBL* 118 (1999): 295–320.

24. BDR §128 n. 5; Rob., *Gram.*, 395. So also Wolff, 381.

*The Last Adam's Triumph over Death*

not alone bring about the resurrection of the dead, for humanity was *justly* under the power of death (cf. 15:56). Only Christ crucified (1:23; cf. 15:3) could satisfy the divine justice and wrath against sin and, by his resurrection, free humanity from the power of death.

The great majority of expositors, apparently mesmerized by the neat parallel between the two human beings drawn in 15:21, fail to grasp the mystery that Paul places at the heart of this verse. How death came through a human being is clear, but how can the resurrection of the dead come "through a human being" (δι' ἀνθρώπου)? For, within ancient Jewish and biblical thought, only *God* has the power to conquer death and bring about the resurrection of the dead. He is the living God (Dan 12:7 LXX; 2 Cor 3:3; 6:16; 1 Thess 1:9), who alone gives life (Deut 32:39; 1 Sam 2:6; 2 Kgs 5:7; Ps 68:20; 1 Tim 6:13). He is the God "who gives life to the dead" (Rom 4:17; Jos. Asen. 20.7; 4QMessAp 5 and 7; m. Ber. 5:2). It is God who "raises the dead" (Acts 26:8; 2 Cor 1:9). He alone "raises the dead and gives life" (John 5:21). How, then, can the resurrection of the dead come "through a *human being*" (δι' ἀνθρώπου)?

The mystery will be resolved in 15:44b–49, where Paul will again take up the Adam typology, the two human beings, and the language of ἄνθρωπος. There we will find that this human being (ἄνθρωπος) is God incarnate, who has come from heaven (15:47, ὁ δεύτερος ἄνθρωπος ἐξ οὐρανοῦ). He is the divine Son of God (15:28), the source and giver, together with the Father, of the Holy Spirit (15:45). The seeming contradiction at the heart of 15:21 will thus be resolved in the course of the chapter—through the mystery of the incarnation. Once again we see that 15:21 has a preparatory function within Paul's exposition, here pointing to a mystery that will form the very heart of the chapter.

VERSE 22

*For just as in Adam all die, so also in Christ all will be made alive.*

*For just as in Adam all die.* The γάρ is explanatory, further explaining v. 21. The present tense ἀποθνῄσκουσιν expresses the present reality of death "in Adam." As most interpreters concur, the ἐν in the expression ἐν τῷ Ἀδάμ is not instrumental ("through Adam"), and thus merely equivalent to δι' ἀνθρώπου in 15:21, but rather is local ("in Adam").[25] The expression "in Adam," which is unique here in Paul, is clearly modeled on the expression "in Christ," which is ubiquitous in Paul and

---

25. See, for example, Fitzmyer, 570.

## CHAPTER 7

will follow immediately in the next clause. To explain how Paul understands all human beings to be "in Adam," there is no need to invoke the rather ambiguous notion of "corporate personality."[26] Human beings are "in Adam" by virtue of their *union* with him as their ancestor, through whom they inherit original sin (Rom 5:19, "through the disobedience of the one human being, the many were made sinners") and through whom they are in the power of death (Rom 5:12, "through one human being sin entered into the world, and through sin, death"). Thus "in Adam all die."

In an analogous way (ὥσπερ ... οὕτως καί) but in striking contrast, "in Christ all will be made alive" (ἐν τῷ Χριστῷ πάντες ζῳοποιηθήσονται). Here the verb ζῳοποιηθήσονται denotes the physical resurrection of the body of flesh and bones. This is evident in its contrast with ἀποθνῄσκουσιν in the first clause of 15:22—for it is the physical, fleshly body that dies. It is also evident in the use of the verb ζῳοποιέω elsewhere in the New Testament, where it regularly refers to the bodily resurrection (e.g., John 5:21; Rom 4:17, θεοῦ τοῦ ζῳοποιοῦντος τοὺς νεκρούς; 8:11, ζῳοποιήσει καὶ τὰ θνητὰ σώματα ὑμῶν). It is also evident in the parallel thought and structure of 15:21-22, in which ζῳοποιηθήσονται in v. 22 is parallel to ἀνάστασις νεκρῶν in v. 21, which we have seen denotes bodily resurrection.

The verb ζῳοποιηθήσονται is a divine passive. The resurrection, by its very nature, is solely the work of God "who gives life to the dead" (Rom 4:17, θεοῦ τοῦ ζῳοποιοῦντος τοὺς νεκρούς; Jos. Asen. 20.7, τῷ θεῷ τῷ ζῳοποιοῦντι τοὺς νεκρούς). It is thus quite striking that Paul here affirms that the dead will be made alive *in Christ*, and in 15:45 he will be explicit that *Christ* is the life giver (ζῳοποιοῦν). As we saw in 15:21, so also here the divine identity of the Son is an unmistakable aspect of the apostle's thought.

In contrast with ἀποθνῄσκουσιν, which is present tense, ζῳοποιηθήσονται is in the future tense. Although, as we saw in v. 21, the resurrection of the dead has come in Christ's resurrection, the resurrection of the rest of the dead is a future event. Who are the "all" (πάντες) who will share in this life? Three different views have been held. (1) A few expositors argue that "all" denotes all human beings without exception and thus betokens a coming universal resurrection to life and salvation for all, irrespective of their response to the gospel.[27] (2) Other interpreters posit that Paul is thinking here of the twofold resurrection of the

---

26. Contra Menahem Kister, "'In Adam': 1 Cor 15:21-22; 12:27 in Their Jewish Setting," in *Flores Florentino: Dead Sea Scrolls and Other Jewish Studies in Honour of Florentino García Martínez* (ed. Anthony Hilhorst, Émile Puech, and Eibert Tigchelaar; Leiden: Brill, 2007), 685-90; Thiselton, 1225-26.

27. So Lindemann, "Auferstehung," 159-61, 166-67; de Boer, *Defeat*, 109-13, 173-76, 187-88.

righteous to life and of the wicked to judgment, as expressed in a number of New Testament texts (e.g., Matt 25:31–46; John 5:24–29; Acts 24:15).[28] (3) However, the great majority of expositors understand the "all" to denote all who are in Christ and the verb ζωοποιηθήσονται to betoken the resurrection of the faithful to life and salvation.[29]

Of the three views, the first is ruled out by the larger evidence of Paul's letters. Paul speaks frequently of the condemnation of those who reject Christ, including in 1 Corinthians (1:18; 3:16–17; 5:4–5, 13; 6:9–11; 7:16; 8:11; 9:22–27; 10:33; 11:32). In regard to the second view, the twofold resurrection both to life and to judgment is certainly a key component of Paul's gospel (Rom 14:10–12; 2 Cor 5:10; cf. Acts 17:30–31; 24:15). However, there are persuasive reasons for concluding that Paul here focuses exclusively on the resurrection to life of those in Christ (i.e., the third view). The key is the expression "in Christ" (ἐν τῷ Χριστῷ). To be sure, both ἐν τῷ Ἀδάμ and ἐν τῷ Χριστῷ function predicatively and modify their respective verbs. But in so doing they express the circumstances under which the action of these verbs takes place. The "all" of 15:22a die by virtue of their *union with Adam* (ἐν τῷ Ἀδάμ); the "all" of 15:22b will be made alive by virtue of their *union with Christ* (ἐν τῷ Χριστῷ). "The two πάντες embrace those only to whom each of the two powers extends."[30] In addition, the phrase ἐν τῷ Χριστῷ was used immediately prior, in 15:18–19, with specific reference to the faithful. Moreover, as Rodolphe Morissette has shown, 15:49 in its structure clearly mirrors and recalls 15:22, and in v. 49 it is beyond controversy that it is solely believers in Christ who are in view.[31] Finally, that the reference in 15:22b is to those in union with Christ is confirmed in 15:23, where those raised to life are explicitly identified as "those who belong to Christ" (οἱ τοῦ Χριστοῦ). An instructive parallel to the thought in 15:22 is found in Rom 5:17, where death reigns over all human beings through Adam, but those who will reign in life through Jesus Christ are only "those who receive the abundance of grace and the free gift of righteousness."[32] Verse 22 thus has in view the resurrection to life of those who belong to Christ (cf. Phil 3:11).

The focus of ζωοποιηθήσονται is on the future resurrection. But the expression ἐν τῷ Χριστῷ ("in Christ") also brings into view the union with Christ in the present, which will culminate in the resurrection to come: the decision to follow

28. Mentioned as a possible reading by Godet, 2:354–55.
29. So Wolff, 385; Garland, 707; Ciampa & Rosner, 764–65; Fitzmyer, 571; Godet, 2:353–54; Conzelmann, 269; Hays, 264.
30. J. C. K. Hofmann, cited in Godet, 2:354.
31. Rodolphe Morissette, "L'antithèse entre le 'psychique' et le 'pneumatique' en 1 Corinthiens, xv, 44 à 46," *RevScRel* 46 (1972): 108.
32. I am indebted for this observation to Schreiner, 313.

CHAPTER 7

Christ, incorporation into Christ, the gift of the Holy Spirit, and the present life of discipleship in Christ. The affirmation in 15:22 that all in Christ will be made alive thus functions not only as a promise of the future resurrection but also as an exhortation to perseverance in following Christ in the present.

## VERSE 23

*But each in his own order: the firstfruits, Christ, then those who belong to Christ at his coming.*

*But each in his own order.* The word τάγμα may mean either (1) "division, group"; or (2) "order, rank."[33] Because the word is often used of military divisions, a few expositors have supposed Paul is employing a military metaphor.[34] But this appears far-fetched.[35] The sense "order, rank" seems to be the meaning in force here.

*the firstfruits, Christ, then those who belong to Christ.* The repetition of the term ἀπαρχή "firstfruits" from 15:20 rounds off the neat chiasm of 15:20–23 (see the diagram at the beginning of the chapter). Paul here makes obvious what we saw was already implicit in v. 22: the promise of resurrection to life is for "those who belong to Christ" (οἱ τοῦ Χριστοῦ). The universalism that we saw a few interpreters wrongly surmise in 15:22 finds its definitive disproof here in 15:23.

By means of the expression "those who belong to Christ," v. 23 includes in its purview the present life of discipleship in Christ. As Wolfgang Schrage comments insightfully, "in light of Rom 7:4, 8:9, Gal 3:17–19, and 5:24, among the marks of belonging to Christ one must reckon possession of the Spirit, baptism, and conduct of life."[36] According to Paul in Romans, belonging to Christ means possessing the Spirit of Christ (Rom 8:9, εἰ δέ τις πνεῦμα Χριστοῦ οὐκ ἔχει, οὗτος οὐκ ἔστιν αὐτοῦ; cf. 1 Cor 6:18; Gal 5:24–25). That Paul has especially in mind here the communion of believers in the Holy Spirit is suggested by 15:45, where he will focus on the present life-giving power of the Spirit of Christ, and by 15:48, where he will describe the faithful as "heavenly" in view of their participation in the Spirit of God. The expression "those who belong to Christ," then, assumes a whole narrative of baptism into Christ, reception of the Holy Spirit, and life under the lordship of Christ

---

33. See BDAD, s.v. "τάγμα."
34. E.g., Hays, 264–65; Robertson & Plummer, 354.
35. Cf. Schrage, 167.
36. Schrage, 168 n. 752.

(Rom 7:4; 8:9; 14:8; 1 Cor 3:23; 6:19; 2 Cor 10:7; Gal 3:29; 5:24–25).[37] The expression thus includes a hortatory dimension, a call to discipleship.

Paul thus here portrays the resurrection not in isolation but as the climax of a narrative that begins with Christ's first advent, and which includes conversion to Christ, the gift of the Holy Spirit, participation in the sacraments, and the life of discipleship to Christ. Paul in this way reveals, in the same verse in which he speaks of the "order" of resurrection as firstfruits and harvest, one reason for this order. Without the gap of time between Christ's resurrection and ours, there would be no place for cruciform conformity to Christ, for sharing in the cross of Christ through suffering and discipleship. Thomas Aquinas captures this element of Pauline thought insightfully:

> The resurrection of Christ is the cause of our resurrection by virtue of his humanity united to the Word [John 1:14]. But this effect of Christ's resurrection operates in conformity with the divine will. And therefore it was not fitting that the effect should follow immediately, but according to the disposition of Christ, the Word of God; so that we first be conformed to the suffering and death of Christ in this suffering and mortal life, and only afterwards come to participation in the likeness of his resurrection.[38]

*at his coming.* Among the various expressions for the second coming of Christ in the New Testament, the word παρουσία that Paul uses here emphasizes Jesus's personal presence. The words ἐν τῇ παρουσίᾳ αὐτοῦ ("at his coming"), which occur at the very close of 15:23, provide a neat transition to 15:24–28, where the focus is entirely on the advent of Christ. Verses 23–28 thus form a climax to the various references to Christ's coming throughout the epistle (1:7–8; 4:5; 5:5; 7:29–31; 11:26; 13:8–13).

---

37. Ciampa & Rosner are no doubt correct that Paul here also includes among those who belong to Christ the righteous prior to Christ's first advent (765).

38. Aquinas, *ST* III, Q. 56, Art. 1, ad 1.

EXCURSUS 3

# The Good News of the Resurrection in the World into Which It Came

The ancient apostolic formula that Paul recounts in 1 Cor 15:3–8 proclaimed that Jesus's resurrection was the fulfillment of the Jewish Scriptures (15:4). And Paul throughout 1 Cor 15 portrays the coming resurrection of those who belong to Christ as the fulfillment of the God of Israel's promised conquest of death foretold by the prophets (Isa 25:6–9; 26:19; Dan 12:2; 2 Macc 7). But what were the beliefs, hopes, and expectations regarding death and the afterlife in the wider ancient world into which this good news of the resurrection came?

## The Most Ancient Worship and Myths

The religious beliefs and practices within the preclassical and early classical world, from the earliest times through the seventh century BC, did not concern or address life after death.[1] There was little or no conception of an afterlife except the shadowy and lifeless Hades we find in the epics of Homer. Through the influence of Homer's works, especially the eleventh book of the *Odyssey*, this conception "became fixed as the popular eschatology of all antiquity."[2]

Homer also reveals the conception of the paradisical Elysium (*Od.* 4.561–569), identified in antiquity with the Isles of the Blessed (ἐν μακάρων νήσοισι) that we find in Hesiod (*Op.* 156–173). But this was not considered an afterlife hope for mere mortals (cf. *Op.* 167, διχ' ἀνθρώπων) but the fate of half divine and half hu-

---

1. H. J. Rose, *Religion in Greece and Rome* (New York: Harper, 1959), 46.
2. Francis R. Walton, "After-Life," *OCD*, 23.

man demigods (called ἥρωες and ἡμίθεοι), born of the intercourse of a god with a human being, such as Achilles (Pindar, *Ol.* 2.78–80; *Nem.* 4.49–50; Euripides, *Andr.* 1259–1262; *Iph. taur.* 435–438), Peleus (Pindar, *Ol.* 2.78; Euripides, *Andr.* 1254–1262), Cadmus (Pindar, *Ol.* 2.78; Euripides, *Bacch.* 1330–1339), and Rhadamanthys (Homer, *Od.* 4.563–565; Pindar, *Ol.* 2.71–76; *Pyth.* 2.73–74). It was occasionally also the fate of favored humans with a special connection to the gods, such as Menelaus, who through his marriage to Helen (the daughter of Zeus and Leda) became a son-in-law of Zeus (Homer, *Od.* 4.561–569; Euripides, *Hel.* 1666–1669; Ps.-Apollodorus, *Ep.* 6.30). In each case, the conception is one of full divinization: the individual taken to the Elysian Fields is now, through immortalization, a ἥρως or divine "hero" worthy of sacrifice, prayer, and worship.

But this did not involve the human body of the hero. In the ancient understanding, the translation of heroes to the Elysian Fields involved the divinization and immortalization of their souls, after their release from their human bodies.[3] Nowhere within the ancient myths of the pre-Homeric and Homeric age do we find, even for divine heroes and favorites of the gods, a hope of *bodily* immortality. This was believed to be impossible, even for the gods. As the goddess Athena explains to Telemachus in the *Odyssey*, "not even the gods can deliver anyone, even one they love, from death, the common fate of all" (Homer, *Od.* 3.236–237).

At the same time, these ancient myths may suggest a longing for the immortality of the body, in their repeated conceptions of a bodily life that, although not everlasting, was of extraordinary length and perdurance. The human beings of Hesiod's golden generation lived long lives of perpetual youth, free from the ills of old age, until a gentle, sleeplike death took them away (*Op.* 108–120). An ancient hymn tells us that the nymphs, because of their extraordinarily long lives, "belong to the class neither of mortals nor immortals" (*Hom. Aph.* 259, αἵ ῥ' οὔτε θνητοῖς οὔτ' ἀθανάτοισιν ἕπονται). Several texts equate their lifetime to that of a great tree (*Hom. Aph.* 256–272; Ovid, *Metam.* 8.741–779). Plutarch narrates a debate on the life span of the nymphs, with opinions ranging from thousands to hundreds of thousands of years (Plutarch, *Def. orac.* 2.415c–416c). The Hyperboreans, the "Dwellers beyond the North Wind" who were favorites of Apollo, were thought to lead lives supremely blessed, filled with music and feasting, free from care, sickness, and old age (Pindar, *Pyth.* 10.29–49). Thus, in Aeschylus a τύχη ὑπερβόρεος ("Hyperborean fortune") is good fortune beyond the lot of mere mortals (*Cho.* 373).[4] But, although leading lives of extraordinary length, they were not immortal

---

3. For the ancient evidence, see the full discussion in excursus 1.
4. For further references to the Hyperboreans, see *Hom. Dion.* 29; Ps.-Apollodorus, *Bibl.* 1.27 [1.4]; 2.113 [2.5], 120 [2.5]; Bacchylides, *Epinicia* 3.23–62.

(Herodotus, *Hist.* 4.32–36). Strabo tells us that they lived to an age of one thousand years (*Geogr.* 15.1.57). This recurrent notion of bodily life of extraordinary length—as seen in the conceptions of the golden generation, the nymphs, and the Hyperboreans—may reveal an inchoate longing for everlasting bodily life. Yet these notions did not involve an actual conception or hope of bodily immortality. We may also find such a longing for bodily salvation in the ancient stories of Asclepius and Heracles raising the dead to life, most notably in the myth of the resurrection of Alcestis by Heracles (Ps.-Apollodorus, *Bibl.* 1.106 [1.9]; Hyginus, *Fab.* 51; Euripides, *Alc.* 1006–1163). But these figures were raised back to a mortal life and would die again. We do not find here a notion of resurrection to everlasting life.

## The Rise of Orphism, the Mysteries, and the Philosophical Movements

In the sixth century BC or perhaps earlier, the so-called Orphic movement arose within the ambit of the traditional worship and myths. But it introduced a constellation of religious ideas very different from what we find in the pre-Homeric and Homeric periods: the divine origin of the soul, the evil nature of the body as the prison of the soul, rewards and punishments in the afterlife based on one's ethical conduct in this life, and reincarnation.[5] These beliefs drew upon a foundational myth in which humans were formed from the ashes of the Titans, who had swallowed Dionysus, the divine child of Zeus and Persephone. Human beings were consequently a mix of divine good and Titanic evil, a divine soul imprisoned in an evil body. Over time, these Orphic ideas and similar conceptions were spread through ancient "mystery" cults, such as those dedicated to Dionysus and to Demeter. "Orpheus," Pseudo-Apollodorus tells us, "also discovered the mysteries of Dionysus" (Ps.-Apollodorus, *Bibl.* 1.15 [1.3]). The Eleusinian mysteries, centered around the underworld goddesses Demeter and Persephone, promised to its initiates a better afterlife in the realm of the dead (*Hom. Dem.* 470–482; Aristophanes, *Ran.* 154–164, 455–459). Pythagoras (sixth century BC) founded, as Plato tells us, a religious "way of life" (Plato, *Resp.* 600d) based on Orphic ideas and accompanied by initiatory mysteries (Herodotus, *Hist.* 2.81), to which he added his own cosmological, mathematical, and philosophical speculations (Diogenes Laertius *Vit. phil.* 8.1–23).[6] In the poet Pindar (fifth century BC) we find the concepts of

---

5. Rose, *Religion*, 92–96; Nils Nilsson and Johan Croon, "Orphism," *OCD*, 759–60.
6. For a survey of Pythagoras's teachings, see Philip Wheelwright, *The Presocratics* (Indianapolis: Odyssey, 1966), 200–234.

rewards and punishments in Hades and of reincarnation or metempsychosis (*Ol.* 2.55–80). And in Pindar we find the "Isle of the Blessed" (μακάρων νᾶσος)—identical with Hesiod's Isles of the Blessed and Homer's Elysium—as a place no longer reserved only for demigods and heroes, as in the Homeric conception, but open to all human beings after three entirely pure lives within the wheel of rebirth (*Ol.* 2.70–71). But in all these expressions of Orphic and related streams of thought, the afterlife in view is that of souls, not bodies. There is no conception in either Orphic thought or in the ancient mystery cults of an imperishable *bodily* life.

Some scholars have claimed to find a conception of resurrection within ancient Egyptian religion, in particular in the worship and rites associated with the Egyptian god Osiris. One writer has even claimed that the early Christian doctrine of the resurrection, in particular Paul's teaching on the resurrection in 1 Cor 15, is an outgrowth of this alleged Osirian concept of resurrection and bodily immortality.[7] But Osiris was the Egyptian god of the dead and of the underworld, and his rites involved no promise of resurrection but only of protection and blessing within the realm of the dead.[8]

The thought of Plato (429–347 BC), the disciple of Socrates, was heavily indebted to the Orphic teachings.[9] We find in Plato several familiar Orphic doctrines: the divine origin of the soul (*Tim.* 41a–43a, 90a–d; *Phaedr.* 245c–249d), the inferior nature of the body as the prison of the soul (*Phaedr.* 250; *Leg.* 828d; *Phaed.* 66; *Tim.* 69c–d, 81d–e), rewards and punishments in the afterlife based on one's ethical conduct in this life (*Tim.* 41c–42d, 44a–c), and reincarnation or the transmigration of souls (*Phaedr.* 248a–249d; *Tim.* 90–92; *Phaed.* 80a–84b). However, unlike his philosophical predecessor Pythagoras, Plato was openly hostile to the Homeric mythological gods and sought to found these beliefs on a solely philosophical basis. Thus Cicero in the *Tusculan Disputations*, although tracing the doctrine of the immortality of the soul back to the Pythagoreans, says Plato was the first to give rational proofs for this doctrine (*Tusc.* 1.38–39). Plato was also distinctive in conceiving of a *celestial* immortality, for whereas the mysteries offered hopes for a more blessed existence of the soul in Hades or the netherworld, Plato's doctrine envisioned the disembodied soul as dwelling not in Hades but among the celestial bodies in the astral heavens (*Phaedr.* 247; *Tim.* 41c–42d). And yet, we do not find in Plato, any more than in the Orphic literature or in the mysteries, a conception of resurrection and everlasting bodily life.

---

7. So D. Gerald Bostock, "Osiris and the Resurrection of Christ," *ExpTim* 112 (2001): 265–71.

8. See Nicholas Perrin, "On Raising Osiris in 1 Corinthians 15," *TynBul* 58 (2007): 117–28; George C. Ring, "Christ's Resurrection and the Dying and Rising Gods," *CBQ* 6 (1944): 217–18.

9. Walton, "After-Life," 23.

EXCURSUS 3

## The Period from Plato to the Coming of the Christian Gospel

Alongside the various mystery rites and the great philosophical schools, the traditional worship of the gods in the ensuing centuries continued to flourish, with its ancient pantheon, rites, and oracles. Just as in the earliest period, the traditional rites were focused on securing the blessings of this life and offered no afterlife hope. Likewise the cult of heroes, just as it had from the most ancient times, continued to serve as a means of securing blessings and averting harm within their worshipers' lifetimes, but it offered no hope beyond death (Philostratus, *Her.* 8–22, 52–57). During this period, as throughout pagan antiquity, hopes for the afterlife were mediated not through the traditional rites and worship but through the mysteries and through philosophy. The mystery cults of Dionysus, of Demeter and Persephone, and of Isis and Osiris were throughout this period major sources of hope concerning the soul's immortality and afterlife blessedness in the underworld (Cicero, *Tusc.* 1.13; Apuleius, *Metam.* 11; Plutarch, *Cons. ux.* 10; *Def. orac.* 417b–c).[10] But these cults did not offer a hope of resurrected bodily life. Hopes for the soul's survival and postmortem flourishing were also inculcated by philosophy. To be sure, the philosophers were not in agreement on the question. Plato's doctrine of the soul's astral immortality continued to be influential. But the possibility of personal survival following the death of the body was rejected by both Plato's disciple Aristotle (*De an.* 407b–408b, 415b, 430a) and, even more emphatically so, by the Epicureans (Lucretius, *Nat.* 3.417–829; Philodemus, *Mort.* 1, 19, 20, 26, 28–32). The Stoics took a kind of intermediate position, holding to the disembodied soul's perdurance through long ages in the sublunar heavens but denying both its reincarnation and its immortality (*SVF* 1.146, 522; 2.814, 817, 1105; Seneca, *Marc.* 24–26; *Ep.* 102.21, 28–29; *Polyb.* 9.3, 8; Diogenes Laertius, *Vit. phil.* 7.156–157). Thus Cicero's summary of the Stoic view: "The Stoics grant us a lavish lease of life, as if we were crows; they claim our souls will continue for a long period, but deny they will do so forever" (*Tusc.* 1.77). But the doctrine of the soul's immortality was a central teaching among the Neopythagoreans and Middle Platonists, and often found expression in the form of an eclectic mix of doctrines drawn from the various schools (see Vergil, *Aen.* 6.730–751; Cicero, *Tusc.* 1.24–76; *Rep.* 6.9–29; Plutarch, *Gen. Socr.* 21–22, 24; *Fac.* 28–30). But no philosopher, regardless of school, envisioned that a deceased human being might live again. This was thought to be impossible. Here popular thought and the philosophers

---

10. Cf. Peter G. Bolt, "Life, Death, and the Afterlife in the Greco-Roman World," in *Life in the Face of Death: The Resurrection Message of the New Testament* (ed. Richard N. Longenecker; Grand Rapids: Eerdmans, 1998), 75–77.

were in agreement.[11] In a drama of Aeschylus, Apollo declares that "when once the dust has received a man's blood . . . there is no resurrection" (*Eum.* 648, οὔτις ἔστ' ἀνάστασις). Nowhere in pagan religion, philosophy, or thought do we find the hope of resurrection—the hope of the body's restoration from death to life and its transformation to imperishability.

## SUMMARY AND CONCLUSION

Within the ancient pagan world, there was a great diversity of beliefs regarding life after death. Although hope for life following death was left unaddressed by the traditional worship of the gods and its rites, and was denied by many philosophers and thinkers, belief in the soul's survival and immortality was widespread, mediated through the mystery rites and the teachings of the philosophers. But neither in the traditional worship nor in the mysteries nor in ancient philosophy do we find a hope of bodily resurrection. This was something new that came with the Christian gospel. This gospel did not provide yet one more variation on the hope we find in the Orphic teachings, the mystery cults, and the philosophers—the survival and immortality of the soul. It replaced all of this with a new doctrine and a new hope—the resurrection of the body.

In such varied conceptions as the translation of heroes in Homer, the Orphic teaching of the body as the prison of the soul, and Plato's doctrine of heavenly immortality, we see a common element that runs throughout ancient pagan thought. Eternal life, if it is conceived, is only possible by the *elimination* of the human body. The human body cannot partake of immortality. It must be shed or discarded. This is not merely a Platonic or Orphic perspective but is the common conception in polytheistic pagan antiquity from the earliest times. Thus, in the most ancient myths, when Thetis seeks to make her baby son Achilles immortal, she casts him into the fire to burn away his human nature received from Peleus (Ps.-Apollodorus, *Bibl.* 3.171 [3.13]). So also Achilles, in order to be translated to immortality in the Elysian Fields, has to leave his mortal body behind at Troy (Philostratus, *Her.* 53.10). Similarly, when the goddess Demeter sought to make the child Demophoön immortal, she "attempted to strip off his mortal flesh" (περιῄρει τὰς θνητὰς σάρκας αὐτοῦ) in the fire (Ps.-Apollodorus, *Bibl.* 1.31 [1.5]; cf. *Hom. Dem.* 223–262; Plutarch, *Is. Os.* 357a–b). Immortality involved a minus, not a plus. It involved a diminution and a lessening of the human being—the loss of the hu-

---

11. See Homer, *Il.* 16.433; Plato, *Tim.* 41a–42e, 69c–73d; Lucretius, *Nat.* 1–3; Cicero, *Div.* 2.25; Seneca, *Prov.* 6.5–8; Epictetus, *Diatr.* 1.1.10–12. Cf. Bolt, "Afterlife," 66–78.

man body. This conception, in one way or another, is virtually universal in ancient pagan thought. But to be human requires a human body. Therefore, by excluding the body from the hope of immortality, "no pagan cult held out promise of afterlife for the worshiper as he knew and felt himself to be."[12]

We find the most striking contrast to this in the Christian doctrine of the resurrection, as found in 1 Cor 15. In 1 Cor 15, eternal life involves not a minus but a plus. It does not involve an immortality of the soul apart from the body. Rather, it involves the whole human being, the body as well as the soul. It entails the enhancement and enrichment of the mortal human body through the miracle of the resurrection, making it immortal and imperishable, partaking in everlasting life, the very life of God. This, in contrast with the pagan notions, is indeed a promise of everlasting life as one knows and feels oneself to be. And yet it is still more. It is a promise of the body's glorification, through the communication to the body of the glory that belongs to God's own nature and being. It is a promise of everlasting union and fellowship with God in both body and soul. This illumines why Paul described his message as "the good news" and expected this to resonate with his pagan hearers. This hope was unique in the ancient pagan world into which it came.

---

12. Ramsay MacMullen, *Paganism in the Roman Empire* (New Haven: Yale University Press, 1981), 136.

CHAPTER 8

## *The Eternal Reign of the Father and the Son*

15:24–28

First Corinthians 15:24–28 is the second of two units—15:20–23 and 15:24–28—which form a larger whole. The narrative of 15:20–23 culminates in the resurrection of the dead at the second advent of Christ, and 15:24–28 continues that narrative. But 15:20–23, as we saw, is anthropological in emphasis: the word ἄνθρωπος occurs twice, the name Ἀδάμ once, and Jesus is repeatedly called Χριστός (4×), his royal title or honorific emphasizing his representative role on behalf of humanity. In vv. 20–23 the focus is on the human plane and on the resurrection of Christ and of those who belong to Christ. But vv. 24–28 are theological in emphasis. In vv. 24–28, the focus is on the divine plane: on God, his reign, and his final victory over death, Satan, and the demonic powers that oppose God and enslave humanity. In 15:24–28, the title Χριστός does not occur at all. Instead, we find (in order) ὁ θεός (15:24), [ὁ] πατήρ (15:24), ὁ υἱός (15:28), and ὁ θεός (15:28). The focus in 15:24–28 is on the Father and the Son and on their final triumph and eternal reign. There is a stress throughout the passage on totality and universality. The word πᾶς occurs repeatedly—a total of ten times within vv. 24–28.[1] This striking repetition of the word πᾶς accents the universality of the triumph of God, of the Father and of the Son.

In one of the great ironies of modern scholarship, this passage, with its accent on the eternal triumph and reign of the Father and the Son, is read by virtually all modern interpreters as teaching that the reign and lordship of Christ are tem-

---

1. Scott M. Lewis, *"So That God May Be All in All": The Apocalyptic Message of 1 Corinthians 15,12–34* (TGST 14; Rome: Gregorian University Press, 1998), 50–51.

CHAPTER 8

porary, surpassable, and will one day come to an end.[2] A number of interpreters go even further and assert that the passage's portrayal of the Son's submission to the Father is proof of a low, nondivine, and nonincarnational Christology, in which Jesus is merely God's human vice-regent.[3] Just as chapter 15 as a whole has been repeatedly misused as evidence of a more or less "Gnostic" conception of resurrection in Paul that excludes the redemption of the physical body (on this, see the introduction), so 15:24–28 has been employed as the key prooftext for an essentially "Arian" Christology in Paul that denies the divinity of the Son. But as we will see, the conception of a temporary reign of Christ is foreign to Paul's thought in this passage, and the pericope is a powerful expression of Paul's incarnational and Trinitarian theology.

Verses 24–28 exhibit a concentric structure, which may be illustrated as follows:[4]

| 24 | A | Christ Delivers the Kingdom to the Father and Abolishes All Opposing Rule |
| 25 | B | All Enemies Placed under Christ's Feet |
| 26 | C | The Destruction of Death |
| 27a | B' | All Things Subjected under Christ's Feet |
| 27b–28 | A' | All Things Subject to the Son and the Son to the Father—God is All in All |

---

2. E.g., Wesley Hill, *Paul and the Trinity: Persons, Relations, and the Pauline Letters* (Grand Rapids: Eerdmans, 2015), 131–34; Seth Turner, "The Interim, Earthly Messianic Kingdom in Paul," *JSNT* 25 (2003): 332; C. E. Hill, "Paul's Understanding of Christ's Kingdom in 1 Corinthians 15:20–28," *NovT* 30 (1988): 311–20.

3. E.g., James D. G. Dunn, *The Theology of Paul the Apostle* (Grand Rapids: Eerdmans, 1998), 254–55; Wayne A. Meeks, *Christ Is the Question* (Louisville: Knox, 2006), 130–32.

4. For similar outlines of the structure of 15:24–28, see C. E. Hill, "Christ's Kingdom," 300; W. Hill, *Paul and the Trinity*, 128–29. Wesley Hill and C. E. Hill both (independently) propose, as I do here, that 15:24–28 forms a concentric structure. John Paul Heil follows C. E. Hill, with additional arguments in *The Rhetorical Role of Scripture in 1 Corinthians* (SBLStBL 15; Leiden: Brill, 2005), 212–15. The arguments of Lambrecht against a concentric structuring of the passage are not persuasive; see "Structure and Line of Thought in 1 Cor. 15:23–28," *NovT* 32 (1990): 143–51. Rhetorical treatments of 15:24–28 include Duane F. Watson, "Paul's Rhetorical Strategy in 1 Corinthians 15," in *Rhetoric and the New Testament* (ed. Stanley E. Porter and Thomas H. Olbricht; JSNT 90; Sheffield: JSOT, 1993), 240–42; Margaret M. Mitchell, *Paul and the Rhetoric of Reconciliation: An Exegetical Investigation of the Language and Composition of 1 Corinthians* (Louisville: Westminster John Knox, 1993), 287–89; Michael Bünker, *Briefformular und rhetorische Disposition im 1 Korintherbrief* (Göttingen: Vandenhoeck & Ruprecht, 1983), 69. However, these treatments are relatively unhelpful and lack the insights into the structure of the passage found in the treatments of Wesley Hill, C. E. Hill, and John Paul Heil.

As the structure of the passage shows, at the heart of God's victory is the conquest of the last enemy: death (15:26). Only through the victory over death does God become all in all (15:28). The passage thus reveals the importance of the resurrection for the doctrine of the being and nature of God. "If there is no resurrection of the dead, then death remains unconquered and still holds sway beyond the end as a power set over against God."[5] In 15:24–28, Paul reveals the central place of the resurrection in the final triumph of God.

The passage exhibits a striking movement of thought that we find elsewhere in Paul, which will recur at the climax of the chapter in vv. 54–57. It is a line of thought that begins with contemplation of the bodily resurrection (15:20–23), moves to contemplation of Christ's defeat of the demonic powers (15:24–25), then moves to contemplation of the resurrection as the conquest of death (15:26), and climaxes with celebration of the way in which this reveals the surpassing greatness, glory, and grandeur of God (15:28).

## Verses 24–25

*24 Then will be the consummation, when he delivers the kingdom to him who is God and Father, when he fully abolishes every opposing rule, and every dominion and power; 25 for he must reign as king "until he puts all the enemies under his feet."*

In 15:24–25, Paul shows how the resurrection fits within the consummation of Christ's reign. It is a perplexing fact of modern scholarship that these verses, whose focus is the glorious consummation of Christ's universal reign, are read by the vast majority of contemporary interpreters as a prooftext that Christ's reign is only temporary, and will reach its termination at his second coming. To be sure, a few scholars have recognized the eternal duration of the reign of Christ in 15:24–25.[6] However, the great majority of interpreters consider it axiomatic that these verses teach a limited and temporary reign of Christ. Joseph Fitzmyer writes of v. 24, "*telos* denotes the time when the risen Christ's reign comes to an end."[7] According to Wesley Hill, in these verses "Christ . . . exercises sovereignty that has an eschatological terminus, after which point he surrenders that sovereignty

---

5. Garland, 704.
6. E.g. Wilhelm Thüsing, *Per Christum in Deum: Studien zum Verhältnis von Christozentrik und Theozentrik in den paulinischen Hauptbriefen* (2d ed.; Münster: Aschendorff, 1965), 238–54; Karl-Gustav Sandelin, *Die Auseinandersetzung mit der Weisheit in 1. Korinther 15* (Åbo: Åbo Akademi, 1976), 70; Ciampa & Rosner, 766, 772–73; Robertson & Plummer, 355.
7. Fitzmyer, 571.

CHAPTER 8

back to God."[8] The second advent of Christ, C. E. Hill tells us, will bring about "the closure of the work of his royal dispensation."[9] Many other scholars find in these verses proof of a temporary reign of Christ, which will end at his advent or a time subsequent to his advent.[10]

The main debate has not been over whether Paul in 15:24–25 teaches a temporary reign of Christ, for that is assumed by all but a small number of scholars, but rather the timing of that temporary reign. Of those interpreters who advocate a temporary reign of Christ, a relatively small minority hold that in these verses Paul has in mind an interim earthly reign beginning at Christ's second advent and continuing for a limited period.[11] However, the great majority of those scholars who hold to an interim reign of Christ equate this with the present reign of Christ at the right hand of God, which will continue until its closure at his second coming.[12]

Some scholars who find an end to Christ's reign in 15:24–25, such as Wesley Hill, regard a temporary reign of Christ as fully compatible with an incarnational Christology and a Trinitarian theology.[13] Other interpreters draw a different deduction. James D. G. Dunn concludes from the putative temporary character of his reign that, in the apostle's theology, Christ is not divine but merely an exalted creature who functions as God's plenipotentiary or vice-regent.[14] For Pieter Potgieter, it is an "open question" in light of 15:24–25 whether at his second coming Christ will divest himself not only of his kingdom but also of his human nature.[15] C. K. Barrett concludes from these verses: "For Paul, God is an ultimate term, Christ a penultimate."[16] For Wayne Meeks, the temporary character of Christ's reign in 15:24–25 reveals the invalidity of the historic Christian claim that "Jesus is both the

---

8. W. Hill, *Paul and the Trinity*, 134.
9. C. E. Hill, "Christ's Kingdom," 320.
10. See, for example, Lindemann, 347 ("die zeitliche begrenzte βασιλεία Christi"); Schrage, 175; Weiss, 359; Collins, 552–53; Conzelmann, 272 n. 88; Godet, 2:361; Schreiner, 314.
11. The two main advocates of this position in recent decades are Seth Turner, "The Interim, Earthly Messianic Kingdom in Paul," *JSNT* 25 (2003): 323–42, and L. Joseph Kreitzer, *Jesus and God in Paul's Eschatology* (JSNTSup 19; Sheffield: Sheffield Academic, 1987), 131–64.
12. The fullest and most influential exposition of this view is C. E. Hill, "Christ's Kingdom."
13. W. Hill, *Paul and the Trinity*, 120–34; similarly R. B. Jamieson, "1 Corinthians 15.28 and the Grammar of Paul's Christology," *NTS* 66 (2020): 187–207.
14. James D. G. Dunn, *Theology of Paul*, 248–49, 254–55, 308–10, 529.
15. Pieter Potgieter, "The Consummation of the Kingdom of God: Reflections on the Final Victory of Christ as Portrayed in Paul's First Epistle to the Corinthians," *IDS* 35 (2001): 216–25; similarly G. J. C. Jordaan, "The Consummation of the Kingdom of God: A Response to the Paper of P. C. Potgieter," *IDS* 35 (2001): 229–30.
16. Barrett, 357.

## The Eternal Reign of the Father and the Son

last word and the sufficient word about God's relation to humanity."[17] Meeks, who rejects the validity of Christian conversion and mission, finds his chief argument for this stance in these verses.[18]

But all of this is founded upon a radical misconception. Paul does not teach a temporary reign of Christ in 15:24–25. The notion that he does has its source in an inadequate exegesis that fails to read these verses in their historical and literary context.

To demonstrate this, we must first explore the historical context. That Paul's thought in 15:24–25 belongs to the ancient Jewish context is made evident by his language of God, the consummation, the kingdom, and his allusion to Ps 110:1. Clearly, vv. 24–25 must be read within this ancient Jewish context. But there is no conception in Second Temple Jewish thought of a temporary, interim reign of the messiah. Rather, in ancient Jewish thought the kingdom and reign of the messianic king will endure forever:

> 2 Sam 7:13: "I will establish the throne of his kingdom forever."
> 
> 2 Sam 7:16: "Your kingdom shall endure before me forever; your throne shall be established before me forever."
> 
> Isa 9:7(6): "Of the increase of his reign and of peace there shall be no end, upon the throne of David and over his kingdom... from this time forth and forevermore."
> 
> Ezek 37:24–25: "My servant David will be king over them.... David my servant will be their prince forever."
> 
> Pss. Sol. 17.4: "his kingdom will not cease before you (μὴ ἐκλείπειν ἀπέναντί σου βασίλειον αὐτοῦ)."[19]

Likewise, the reign of the Son of Man of Daniel, who was frequently identified with the messianic king in ancient Jewish thought, is eternal:

> Dan 7:14: "His kingdom is an everlasting kingdom, which will never be destroyed."

The very idea of a temporary reign of the Christ or of the Son of Man is foreign to biblical and ancient Jewish thought. To be sure, a conception of a temporary messianic kingdom occurs in post-Christian Judaism (4 Ezra 7.26–30; 13.39–50; 2 Bar. 29; 73–74). But this concept, which is in strong contrast to the biblical con-

---

17. Meeks, *Christ Is the Question*, 123.
18. Meeks, *Christ Is the Question*, 123–32.
19. Cf. Pss 72:5–7, 17; 89:4(5), 29(30), 36–37(37–38); 132:12; Jer 33:17.

CHAPTER 8

ception, is found only in Jewish texts dated after the Second Temple Period, at least several decades after Paul's writing of 1 Corinthians.[20]

Moreover, in all our New Testament texts outside 1 Cor 15, the kingdom or reign of Christ is eternal. In the New Testament, the concept of a temporary reign of Christ is unknown:

> Luke 1:33: βασιλεύσει ἐπὶ τὸν οἶκον Ἰακὼβ εἰς τοὺς αἰῶνας, καὶ τῆς βασιλείας αὐτοῦ οὐκ ἔσται τέλος "He will reign over the house of Jacob forever, and of his kingdom there will be no end."
> 2 Pet 1:11: εἰς τὴν αἰώνιον βασιλείαν τοῦ κυρίου ἡμῶν καὶ σωτῆρος Ἰησοῦ Χριστοῦ "into the eternal kingdom of our Lord and Savior Jesus Christ."
> Eph 5:5: οὐκ ἔχει κληρονομίαν ἐν τῇ βασιλείᾳ τοῦ Χριστοῦ καὶ Θεοῦ "has no inheritance in the kingdom of Christ and of God."
> Rev 22:3: ὁ θρόνος τοῦ θεοῦ καὶ τοῦ ἀρνίου "the throne of God and of the Lamb."[21]

Throughout our earliest Christian sources outside the New Testament, from the first through the third centuries, the reign of Jesus Christ is declared eternal and everlasting:

> Justin, *Dial.* 46: καὶ αὐτοῦ ἐστιν ἡ αἰώνιος βασιλεία "and his is the everlasting kingdom."
> Justin, *Dial.* 135: "Christ is the everlasting king."
> Irenaeus, *Epid.* 56 (after citing Isa 9:4–6 LXX): "For thereby it is proclaimed that the Son of God both is to be born and is to be everlasting king."
> Irenaeus, *Haer.* 3.9.2: "He is King, and of his kingdom there will be no end."
> Cf. Justin, *Dial.* 34, 76; Aristides, *Apol.* 15; Clement of Alexandria, *Paed.* 1.5; Tertullian, *Marc.* 4.39; 5.9

One final piece of evidence puts the everlasting continuance of the reign of Christ in Paul's thought beyond doubt. As Wilhelm Thüsing has shown, Paul strikingly expresses the eternal duration of the kingdom of Christ in his letter to the Romans.[22] In Rom 5:17, Paul writes: "For if by the transgression of the one man death reigned [ἐβασίλευσεν] through the one man, much more those who receive the abundance of grace and the gift of righteousness will reign in life through the one man, Jesus Christ

---

20. C. E. Hill, "Christ's Kingdom," 312. J. W. Bailey argues that evidence for this conception may be dated slightly earlier, to the midpoint of the first century; see "The Temporary Messianic Reign in the Literature of Early Judaism," *JBL* 53 (1934): 170–87. However, Bailey's arguments fail to convince.

21. Cf. Matt 16:28; 19:28; 20:21; 25:34; Luke 22:29–30; Eph 1:21–22; 2 Tim 4:1; Heb 1:8–13; Rev 11:15.

22. Thüsing, *Per Christum*, 250–52.

[ἐν ζωῇ βασιλεύσουσιν διὰ τοῦ ἑνὸς Ἰησοῦ Χριστοῦ]." As Thüsing notes: "If Christians, according to Rom 5:17, will reign in life through Christ, then it is therein implicit that they will participate in the kingdom of Christ—and therefore it is also implicit that the reign of Christ will not then cease, but will then first obtain its full glory and dominion."[23] Paul's thought in Rom 5 assumes and requires an everlasting kingdom and reign of Christ. Similarly, Paul's expectation that believers will be glorified together with Christ (Rom 8:17, ἵνα καὶ συνδοξασθῶμεν) assumes not a temporary but an eternal glory of Christ, in which those who belong to Christ will share.[24]

We have seen that in ancient Jewish thought, the reign of the messiah is eternal, and that in the New Testament and early Christian writings, the reign of Jesus Christ is everlasting. Paul's letter to the Romans leaves no doubt that he shared this belief in Christ's eternal reign. First Corinthians 15:24–25 must be read within this Jewish, early Christian, and Pauline historical context. A temporary or limited reign of Jesus is entirely foreign to the New Testament and to early Christian thought, including Paul's thought.[25] As we now explore 1 Cor 15:24–25 in its literary context, we will examine the elements of this passage that lead so many interpreters to claim that it teaches a temporary reign of Christ. We will find that in each case this claim is based on a mistaken exegesis. According to 1 Cor 15:24–25, the consummation of Christ's kingdom at his advent will bring not the end of his reign, but the full realization of the reign of God.

*15:24. Then will be the consummation.* The word τέλος "consummation," like the word τελευτή, can sometimes mean "end" or "cessation."[26] However, its original

---

23. Thüsing, *Per Christum*, 251.
24. Thüsing, *Per Christum*, 251–52.
25. The first figure within ancient Christianity to our knowledge to teach that Christ's reign would have an end was Marcellus of Ancyra in the fourth century AD. Our evidence is clear that the central textual basis for his teaching was 1 Cor 15:24–28 (cf. Cyril of Jerusalem, *Cat.* 15.29–30). Fourth-century figures such as Cyril of Jerusalem, Gregory of Nyssa, and John Chrysostom opposed the teaching of Marcellus, and his exegesis of 1 Cor 15:24–28, as a novelty; see the classic study of Joseph T. Lienhard, "The Exegesis of 1 Cor 15,24–28 from Marcellus of Ancyra to Theodoret of Cyrus," *VC* 37 (1983): 340–59. The reaction to Marcellus's teaching led to the assertion of the eternality of the reign of Christ in several fourth-century creeds, including the First Creed of Antioch (341) and the Creed of Jerusalem (ca. 350), culminating in the celebrated insertion of the clause οὗ τῆς βασιλείας οὐκ ἔσται τέλος ("of whose kingdom there will be no end") into the Nicene-Constantinopolitan Creed (381). Ironically, Marcellus's reading of 1 Cor 15:24–28 as involving a temporary reign of Christ, rejected by the ancient church and within the central Christian creed, has become today the prevailing scholarly reading of this passage. As I show in this chapter, this reading is groundless.
26. BDAG, s.v. "τέλος" (1).

CHAPTER 8

sense denotes the "goal" or "completion" of a process, its "outcome" or "consummation."[27] This is its more common sense in the New Testament (e.g., Rom 6:21–22; Jas 5:11; 1 Pet 1:9), and it is the sense in 1 Cor 15:24 as well.[28] The τέλος here is not the "end," but the "consummation" of the kingdom. The word τέλος is used in this identical sense in the eschatological climax of the epistolary thanksgiving in 1:8.[29] Moreover, the phrase ἕως τέλους in 1:8 matches the identical construction in Dan 7:26–27 LXX, which Paul echoes in 15:24. The epistolary thanksgiving thus foreshadows and requires chapter 15 as its full statement. We find once again that chapter 15 is the culmination of the entire epistle.

What is the temporal relationship between the resurrection of v. 23 and the consummation of v. 24? The conjunction εἶτα "then," when it refers to time, always expresses not coincidence in time but sequence in time.[30] It always "marks a fresh and distinct incident."[31] This would indicate that the consummation of 15:24 follows the resurrection of 15:23 as a distinct event in time. However, the flow of thought within 15:24–25 suggests a different chronological relationship. In vv. 24–25, the τέλος is clearly coincident with Christ's delivering the kingdom to the Father (ὅταν, 15:24b), his abolishing of the powers, and the placement of all enemies under his feet (15:25). The defeat of death as the last of these enemies (15:26) refers to the resurrection, as 15:53–55 confirms.[32] This would indicate that the consummation of v. 24 is not subsequent but coincident in time with the resurrection of v. 23. The most likely explanation of this apparently conflicting evidence is that the τέλος or "consummation" in 15:24 refers to the resurrection *and its subsequent events*. It commences with the resurrection but also includes the events that follow, such as the judgment of the faithful (1 Cor 4:3–5), the judgment of the world (1 Cor 6:2), and the eternal kingdom in which God will be all in all (1 Cor 15:28). To use the language of the Nicene Creed, the τέλος in v. 24 includes not only "the resurrection of the dead," but also "the life of the world to come."

---

27. So Schmidt, *Syn.*, 4:498–99 (§193.2–3): τέλος expresses "die volle Entwicklung oder Reife, die aus dem natürlichen Wachstum des Dinges erfolgt" (4:499 [§193.3]); Cremer, 541–42; BDAG, s.v. "τέλος" (2).

28. Rightly BDAG, s.v. "τέλος" (2); Jeffrey M. Dale, "First Corinthians as an Eschatological Counter to Spiritualizing Tendencies," *Conversations with the Biblical World* 37 (2018): 88. The older argument that τὸ τέλος here is set in contrast with the resurrection of those who belong to Christ in 15:23, denoting the "rest" of the dead who are raised (see e.g., Weiss, 358), is not tenable. For fuller discussion and convincing refutation, see C. E. Hill, "Christ's Kingdom," 308–9.

29. Dale, "Eschatological Counter," 94–95.

30. LSJ, s.v. "εἶτα" (I).

31. MM, s.v. "εἶτα."

32. Cf. C. E. Hill, "Christ's Kingdom," 319.

*when he delivers the kingdom to him who is God and Father.* The language of the kingdom of God, which has occurred previously at important junctures of the letter (4:8, 20; 6:9–10), reaches a climax in chapter 15, with βασιλεία here in 15:24, βασιλεύω in 15:25, and βασιλεία once again in 15:50.[33] This kingdom or reign is here, strikingly, that of Christ, who as the risen Lord now reigns at the right hand of God (15:25; cf. Rom 8:34).[34] The kingdom of God is also the kingdom of Christ (cf. Eph 5:5, ἡ βασιλεία τοῦ Χριστοῦ καὶ θεοῦ).

The conjunction ὅταν "when" identifies the action of this clause, Christ's delivering of the kingdom to the Father, as coincident in time with "the consummation" (τὸ τέλος) of the previous clause. Paul's use of ὅταν with the subjunctive (in contrast with ὅτε and the indicative) marks this time as indefinite, "a future reality whose time is not known."[35] "For you yourselves know well that the day of the Lord will come as a thief in the night" (1 Thess 5:2).

At the consummation, Christ "delivers the kingdom" to God the Father. In the indefinite temporal subjunctive clause ὅταν παραδιδῷ, Paul's use of the present tense focuses attention not on the result of the act but on the act itself.[36] But what does this action of Christ involve? Here we have the first of the two elements in the passage where interpreters believe they find a temporary reign of Christ. The standard scholarly interpretation, simply taken for granted by most expositors, is as follows: Christ now reigns as king instead of the Father, but at the time of the eschaton he will relinquish that kingdom to the Father, who will then reign as king instead of Christ. So Conzelmann: "Christ gives the sovereignty back to God."[37] Similarly, C. K. Barrett speaks of "the transference of the kingdom from Christ to God."[38] But this interpretation, as widespread as it is, is impossible. Moreover, it betrays a basic misunderstanding of Pauline theology and a failure to grasp the powerful theological import of this passage.

First, the conception that the reign of God the Father will begin only at the eschaton is contrary to Pauline theology. In Paul's thought, God even now reigns as king (1 Cor 4:20; cf. Rom 14:17). And the present reign of Christ is a reign at the

---

33. On Paul's teaching regarding the kingdom in chapter 15 as providing the theological and metaphysical grounds for Paul's instructions in chapters 1–14, see Frederick David Carr, "Beginning at the End: The Kingdom of God in 1 Corinthians," *CBQ* 81 (2019): 449–69.

34. Cf. C. E. Hill, "Christ's Kingdom," 313–17.

35. Fee, 833 n. 169.

36. The Byzantine text, joined by a few later Alexandrian witnesses (e.g., 1175 1881 2464) has the aorist subjunctive παραδῷ. However, the present subjunctive παραδιδῷ is strongly supported by our premier witnesses: P[46], Sinaiticus, Alexandrinus, and Claromontanus.

37. Conzelmann, 271.

38. Barrett, 357. Cf. Fee, 836 ("that Christ might turn over the 'rule' to God the Father").

CHAPTER 8

right hand of *God* (15:25, echoing Ps 110:1; cf. Rom 8:34; Eph 1:20–23; Col 3:1). In Paul's conception of the present kingdom of Christ, Christ does not reign apart from God the Father, but the Father reigns in and through the reign of the Son.

Second, the notion that the verb "deliver" here describes Christ's relinquishment or abdication of his kingdom is without foundation. The verb παραδίδωμι means to transmit or deliver, not to lose, abandon, or relinquish. Paul did not relinquish the gospel when he transmitted (παρέδωκα) it to the Corinthians (15:3), nor did the householder in Jesus's parable lose his possessions when he entrusted (παρέδωκεν) them to his slaves (Matt 25:14, 20, 22), nor did the Father lose anything when all things were delivered (παρεδόθη) by him to the Son (Matt 11:27; Luke 10:22). Likewise in 15:24, Christ's deliverance of the kingdom to the Father does not mean that he will cease to reign. As we saw above, in Paul's thought the kingdom of Christ is everlasting (cf. Rom 5:17, ἐν ζωῇ βασιλεύσουσιν διὰ τοῦ ἑνὸς Ἰησοῦ Χριστοῦ).

What, then, is the import of Christ's delivering the kingdom to the Father in 15:24? Strangely, scholars have generally failed to note the striking nature of Paul's language here, and the exalted nature of Christ that it expresses. For here God the Father *receives* the kingdom from the Son. First Corinthians 15:24 is the only verse in the entire Bible in which God is said to *receive* something from a human being! In Paul's theology, to deliver or give something to God is not something that can be said of a mere creature. "Or who has first given [προδίδωμι] to him, that he should repay him?" (Rom 11:35, quoting Job 41:3). The striking language of v. 24 reveals that Jesus is not a mere creature but the divine Son of God, consubstantial with the Father. The closest parallel to 1 Cor 15:24 in the New Testament is Matt 11:27 // Luke 10:22, where the same verb παραδίδωμι is used, but there of the *Father* delivering all things to the *Son*: πάντα μοι παρεδόθη ὑπὸ τοῦ πατρός μου ("all things were delivered to me by my Father"). In Matt 11:27 // Luke 10:22 the Father delivers (παραδίδωμι) all things to the Son; in 1 Cor 15:24 the Son delivers (παραδίδωμι) the kingdom to the Father. We thus find in the New Testament a striking *mutuality* in the relation of Father and Son. This is a conception for which the only adequate language is the language of the Trinity.

This mutuality in the relation of Father and Son is reflected in the way Paul describes God in this verse: ὁ θεὸς καὶ πατήρ ("God and Father"). We find this locution elsewhere in the New Testament, normally in the slightly fuller formula ὁ θεὸς καὶ πατὴρ ἡμῶν: "*our* God and Father" (Gal 1:4; Phil 4:20; 1 Thess 1:3; 3:11, 13). Only occasionally does it occur, as here, with no further qualifier (Eph 5:20; Jas 1:27). In all the instances above, the reference is to believers as the children of God through Christ, and this may be a secondary reference here in v. 24. But the most frequent use of this phrase in the New Testament is in the formula ὁ θεὸς καὶ

## The Eternal Reign of the Father and the Son

πατὴρ τοῦ κυρίου ἡμῶν Ἰησοῦ Χριστοῦ: "the God and Father *of our Lord Jesus Christ*" (Rom 15:6; 2 Cor 1:3; Eph 1:3; Col 1:3; 1 Pet 1:3; cf. 2 Cor 11:31; Eph 1:17; Rev 1:6). The context of 15:24, with its focus on Christ and his work, suggests that here, too, the primary reference is to God as the God and Father of our Lord Jesus Christ. By this description, God is identified as "God of Christ, as creator of his humanity, and Father because he begets the Son."[39] The locution reflects Paul's incarnational Christology: Jesus Christ is the eternal Son of God made flesh. Here, too, we see the mutuality and coequality of Father and Son. For in this way of naming God, as Francis Watson points out, "God's own identity is determined by the relation to Jesus just as Jesus' identity is determined by the relation to God."[40]

Moreover, 15:24 recalls 8:6, the only other occurrence in the epistle (outside the salutation) of the word πατήρ "Father" with reference to God. Here the work of creation is ascribed to "one God, the Father, from whom are all things" and "one Lord, Jesus Christ, through whom are all things." This provides the key to grasping Paul's intention in describing Christ as delivering the kingdom to the Father at its consummation. The mutual relation of Father and Son in the work of *creation* in 8:6 corresponds to the mutual relation of Father and Son at the *consummation* of all things in 15:24. Christ's deliverance of the kingdom to the Father in 1 Cor 15:24 envisions neither the beginning of the Father's reign nor the closure of Christ's reign but rather the consummate revelation of the eternal mystery of Father and Son. The kingdom is "the kingdom of the Son of his love" (Col 1:14), "the kingdom of Christ and of God" (Eph 5:5).

*when he fully abolishes every opposing rule, and every dominion and power.* Paul now discloses another aspect of the kingdom's consummation: the final destruction of all powers that oppose God's reign. Who are these powers? Are they solely human rulers? Or, while including human rulers, are they primarily (as the majority of scholars have held) cosmological powers? The evidence is conclusive in favor of the majority view. The language of "dominions" (ἐξουσίαι) and "powers" (δυνάμεις) occurs frequently in Jewish texts with reference to angelic and supernatural beings.[41] This language is found elsewhere in Paul's letters and in the

---

39. L. Cerfaux, *Christ in the Theology of St. Paul* (New York: Herder & Herder, 1959), 474 (n. 27).

40. Francis Watson, "The Triune Divine Identity: Reflections on Pauline God-Language, in Disagreement with J. D. G. Dunn," *JSNT* 80 (2000): 117.

41. Dan 3:61 LXX, πᾶσαι αἱ δυνάμεις ("all the powers"); 2 Macc 3:24, πᾶσα ἐξουσία ("every dominion"); T. Levi 3.3, αἱ δυνάμεις ("the powers"); 3.8, ἐξουσίαι ("powers"); cf. Isa 24:21–22; 1 En. 61.6, 10; 2 En. 20. Within the LXX, *yhwh ṣabāôt* or "Lord of hosts" is frequently rendered κύριος τῶν δυναμέων ("Lord of the powers"). The situation is different in ancient pagan literature. Here the words ἀρχή and ἐξουσία are used frequently of human rulers but never (prior to the late

CHAPTER 8

New Testament with uncontested reference to spiritual or supernatural beings (Rom 8:38–39; Eph 1:20–21; 3:10; 6:11–12; Col 1:16; 2:10, 15; 1 Pet 3:22). Finally, Paul's inclusion of ὁ θάνατος "death" among these enemies in 15:26 confirms that Paul here has primarily nonhuman, cosmological powers in mind.

Within the Old Testament and Jewish literature, these beings are created by God (Dan 3:61 LXX, πᾶσαι αἱ δυνάμεις αὐτοῦ; 2 Macc 3:24, ὁ τῶν πνευμάτων καὶ πάσης ἐξουσίας δυνάστης). Within Paul's theology, these principalities and powers are created by God's Son (1 Cor 8:6; cf. Col 1:16). These powers comprise the totality of angelic and spiritual beings (T. Levi 3; Eph 3:10; Col 1:16). But here (as in Rom 8:38–39; Eph 6:11–12; Col 2:13–15) these terms denote specifically demonic powers, malevolent spiritual beings opposed to God and hostile to humanity.[42] Thus Paul characterizes them here as God's *enemies* (15:25) and speaks of their *abolition* at Christ's advent (15:24). They are angelic beings fallen from their created goodness and now subservient to Satan (Rom 8:38; 1 Cor 6:3; 2 Cor 12:7; cf. 1 Cor 5:5; 7:5). These beings are identical with those Paul elsewhere in the epistle calls δαιμόνια or "demons," evils spirits who are the spiritual powers lurking behind the false gods of the gentiles (1 Cor 10:19–22; cf. Deut 32:17 LXX; Pss 95:5 LXX; 105:37 LXX; Rev 9:20).[43]

Although drawing in general on ancient Jewish and early Christian terminology for the demonic powers, Paul's language in this verse has its source in a specific Old Testament passage: Dan 7:26–27 LXX.[44] The points of verbal and conceptual contact are striking and unmistakable. Nowhere in all of ancient Greek literature, outside 1 Cor 15:24 and Greek Dan 7:26–27 (both LXX and Theodotion), do we find

---

third century AD) of supernatural powers (see LSJ, s.v. "ἀρχή" [II.4]; "ἐξουσία" [II.2]). Similarly, in non-Jewish literature the word δύναμις is never used of a being, human or nonhuman, who holds power. The closest analogy to such a usage is when δύναμις denotes a military "force" or "army" (LSJ, s.v. "δύναμις" [I.3]). In Jewish texts, by contrast, the use of the language of δύναμις and ἐξουσία with reference to spiritual beings is well documented.

42. Contra Emma Wasserman, "Gentile Gods at the Eschaton: A Reconsideration of Paul's 'Principalities and Powers' in 1 Corinthians 15," *JBL* 136 (2017): 727–46, whose denial of the malevolent nature of these beings within the passage cannot be sustained; rightly Fee, 835 n. 185 ("malevolent, demonic powers"); Garland, 711 ("malignant powers"); Collins, 553 ("hostile to God"); Ellis, 113–15. Moreover, Wasserman's repeated description of these powers as "lesser gods," and the God proclaimed in Paul's gospel as merely "the supreme deity" (742–46) reveals a catastrophic failure to grasp the fully monotheistic character of Paul's theology. On this, see J. Ware, *Paul's Theology*, 7–23.

43. Contra Dale Martin, "When Did Angels Become Demons?" *JBL* 129 (2010): 657–77, who argues that the conception of the δαίμονες and δαιμόνια as fallen angels is a post–New Testament development. Martin vastly underinterprets the New Testament and Pauline evidence.

44. Although it is generally overlooked, a number of interpreters have noted Paul's echo of the Daniel passage here; see Jamieson, "Grammar," 203–4; Ciampa & Rosner, 768–69.

the combination of τέλος, βασιλεία, ἀρχή, and ἐξουσία. Three important exegetical conclusions follow from Paul's echo of the Daniel passage here.

First, Paul clearly identifies the Son of Man of Dan 7 (see especially Dan 7:13–14) with Jesus Christ. Second, the authorities and powers in Dan 7:26–27 are human kingdoms (Dan 7:2–8, 17, 23–25) under the dominion of malevolent spiritual rulers, who war with the beneficent angelic powers Michael and Gabriel (Dan 10:13, 20–21). The word used for these malevolent supernatural rulers in Theodotion's ancient Greek translation of Daniel is ἄρχων (Dan 10:13, 20–21; cf. 1 Cor 15:24, πᾶσαν ἀρχήν). This would suggest that Paul's language of "authority and power" in this verse, as in Daniel, embraces not only demonic forces, but also the human kingdoms through which they rule (cf. Rev 13:2). The inclusion of earthly powers is also suggested by Paul's language of totality (πᾶσαν ἀρχὴν καὶ πᾶσαν ἐξουσίαν καὶ δύναμιν). The dominions and powers of v. 24 thus include both human rulers and cosmological powers, but with primary reference to the demonic powers. Third, the reign of the Son of Man in Dan 7 is emphatically and explicitly an *everlasting* reign (Dan 7:14, 27). This furnishes yet another unmistakable indicator that the reign of Christ in 15:24, which Paul understands as fulfilling the promised reign of the Son of Man of Daniel, is an *eternal* reign and kingdom.

Here, as in the previous clause, Paul's use of ὅταν with the subjunctive indicates a future event whose coming is certain but whose timing is uncertain.[45] The subject of the verb "abolish," as with the verb "deliver" in the previous clause, is Christ.[46] Many interpreters believe that the aorist tense of the verb here expresses priority in time and thus indicates that Christ's subjection of the powers is prior in time to his delivery of the kingdom to the Father.[47] A number of these scholars appear to have been influenced by the entries for ὅταν in BA and BDAG, which claim that in ὅταν clauses the aorist subjunctive precedes the verb of the main clause in time.[48] But this claim is baseless. The aorist in the oblique moods such

---

45. Cf. Fee, 833 n. 169.

46. Rightly Jan Lambrecht, "Paul's Christological Use of Scripture in 1 Cor. 15.20–28," *NTS* 28 (1982): 508–9; Fee, 835; and the vast majority of expositors. Uta Heil argues that the subject is God the Father in "Theo-logische Interpretation von 1Kor 15,23–28," *ZNW* 84 (1993): 33–34. But Christ is the subject (as Heil admits) of the verb preceding (παραδιδῷ, 15:24) and the verb following (βασιλεύειν, 15:25). Heil's claim would thus involve a twofold change of subject from Christ (15:24a), then to God (15:24b), then back to Christ (15:25a), with no grammatical indication of a shift in subject. This is most improbable.

47. So Jan Lambrecht, "Structure and Line of Thought in 1 Cor. 15:23–28," *NovT* 32 (1990): 146, 148–49; U. Heil, "Theo-logische Interpretation," 34; Schrage, 171; Turner, "Messianic Kingdom," 335–36; Wolff, 386–87.

48. See BA, s.v. "ὅταν" (1.b) and BDAG, s.v. "ὅταν" (1.a.β).

CHAPTER 8

as the subjunctive does not indicate time but only aspect.[49] The aorist tense in subjunctive clauses with ὅταν thus does not in itself indicate priority in time (for obvious examples where it does not, see e.g., Matt 5:11; 24:33; Mark 8:38; Luke 6:22, 26; 1 Cor 16:12; Jas 1:2).[50]

What, then, is the force of the aorist tense here? Used with the verb καταργέω "to abolish," the aorist has its "effective" sense, indicating the full accomplishment of the action.[51] Paul's use here of the aorist tense is deliberate, and his point is a crucial one. For 15:24 recalls and completes the thought of an earlier passage in the letter regarding the abolition of the demonic powers. In 2:6 Paul speaks of "the *rulers* of this age who are *being abolished*" (οἱ ἄρχοντες τοῦ αἰῶνος τούτου οἱ καταργούμενοι). These "rulers" (ἄρχοντες) recall the rebellious angelic rulers of Daniel (ἄρχοντες, Theodotion Dan 10:13, 20–21) and are identical with the rulers, authorities, and powers of 15:24. Using the same verb as in 15:24, Paul in 2:6 describes these powers as "being abolished" (καταργέω) by Christ. Paul in 2:6 employs the present tense of the participle, which is thus coincident in time with the present tense verb λαλοῦμεν (2:6, "we speak"), indicating that this victory over the powers is even now underway. We find this concept of Christ's present victory over the demonic powers throughout the New Testament, where a key outcome of the resurrection and ascension of Christ is his exaltation over the rulers and authorities, subordinating them to himself and rendering them powerless (Eph 1:21; Col 2:10, 15; 1 Pet 3:22; cf. Matt 28:18). As Christ's reign has begun with his resurrection (cf. 15:25, δεῖ αὐτὸν βασιλεύειν), so has his subjection of the cosmic powers. "Now is already the time of the sovereignty of Christ, and therewith also of the subjecting of the powers. Believers are still exposed to the latter, but no longer subject to them (Rom 8:34–39)."[52]

But Paul in 2:6 uses the present tense of the participle of καταργέω, indicating an action in progress but not yet fully accomplished. That is because, although it is underway, Christ's abolition of the demonic powers is not yet complete. In 15:24, by contrast, Paul uses the aorist tense of καταργέω with its "effective" sense of completed action, because the second advent of Christ will bring about the final and decisive abolition of these demonic powers (cf. Rom 16:20; Phil 3:21; Rev 12:10). The two linked passages, 2:6 and 15:24, provide a capsule narrative of Christ's vic-

---

49. See Kühner-G., 2.1:182–200 (§389), especially 182, 185–88; Rob., *Gram.*, 848–55; BDR §319; so also (rightly) Fee, 833 n. 171.

50. The supposed priority in time of some aorist subjunctive clauses is only apparent, the result of the "effective" sense of the aorist with verbs that express the idea of the accomplishment or culmination of an action; see Kühner-G., 2.1:187–88 n. 3.

51. Rob., *Gram.*, 850–51; Thiselton, 1233.

52. Conzelmann, 271.

tory over Satan and his demons, one inaugurated through his resurrection from the dead and consummated at his second coming in glory.

*15:25. For he must reign as king.* The explanatory γάρ "for" has reference back to the whole preceding verse. This is evident by the way in which v. 25 picks up both the theme of the kingdom in 15:24a (15:24a, βασιλείαν; cf. 15:25, βασιλεύειν), and that of Christ's subjugation of all opposing powers in 15:24b (15:24b, πᾶσαν ἀρχὴν καὶ πᾶσαν ἐξουσίαν καὶ δύναμιν; cf. 15:25, πάντας τοὺς ἐχθρούς). The reign of Christ as king (βασιλεύειν) here is his present reign at the right hand of God. This is recognized by the great majority of expositors.[53] It is also necessitated by the context. The reign of Christ must culminate in the defeat of all his enemies (15:25). The last of these enemies to be abolished will be death (15:26). But the abolition of death will come about through the resurrection of the dead at Christ's parousia (15:23). Therefore the reign of Christ in 15:25, which will culminate in the resurrection, must refer to the present kingly reign of Christ.[54]

*until he puts all the enemies under his feet.* Paul's language clearly echoes and alludes to Ps 110:1 ("The Lord said to my lord, 'Sit at my right hand, until I make your enemies a footstool for your feet"). There are more quotations and allusions in the New Testament to this verse than to any other verse in the Old Testament. This passage and its conception as a messianic prophecy fulfilled in the person of Jesus was an essential part of the ancient apostolic kerygma.[55] This would indicate that Paul's allusion has the content of this Old Testament passage fully in mind, and that he could count on the Corinthians grasping the allusion.[56]

---

53. E.g. C. E. Hill, "Christ's Kingdom," 311–20; Wolff, 387; Schrage, 170–75; Fitzmyer, 573; Garland, 710–11; Conzelmann, 271; Barrett, 357. A few interpreters mistakenly understand the reign of Christ in 15:25 as an interim messianic kingdom beginning with his parousia; see e.g., Turner, "Messianic Kingdom," 323–42; cf. Godet, 2:362.

54. For the chain of argument, see C. E. Hill, "Christ's Kingdom," 319–20. Turner's argument in response, that there is in Paul's thought "confusion as to the timing of the defeat of death" ("Messianic Kingdom," 340–41), reveals the untenability of his exegesis. The confusion is not Paul's, but Turner's.

55. Matt 22:44 // Mark 12:36 // Luke 20:42–43; Matt 26:64 // Mark 14:62 // Luke 22:69; Acts 2:34; Rom 8:34; Eph 1:20; Col 3:1; Heb 1:3, 13; 8:1; 10:12. On the importance of Ps 110:1 in early Christian thought, see further J. P. Heil, *Rhetorical Role*, 205–6. The widespread use of this passage in the New Testament "suggests a pre-formed, pre-Pauline tradition," as stated by W. Hill, *Paul and the Trinity*, 124 n. 33. The gospels indicate that the source of this tradition was Jesus himself, and this offers the best historical explanation for the widespread, almost universal, use of this passage in ancient Christianity.

56. Rightly J. P. Heil, *Rhetorical Role*, 206–9; W. Hill, *Paul and the Trinity*, 123–25; many oth-

CHAPTER 8

Paul's wording does not follow the LXX precisely. These differences may reflect a different Greek translation or perhaps Paul's own rendering of the Hebrew.[57] However, one change appears to be a deliberate modification. Paul adds the word πάντας "all," which is not present in the MT or LXX. By this means Paul continues the emphasis on the totality of Christ's victory, seen already in v. 24 (πᾶσαν ἀρχὴν καὶ πᾶσαν ἐξουσίαν καὶ δύναμιν). Who is the subject of the verb here, Christ or the Father? In either case, it is the feet of Christ under which all the enemies are subjected. But who puts them there? Christ is the subject of the three preceding personal verbs, and this would suggest that Christ is the subject here as well.[58] However, the intertextual allusion to Ps 110:1 would suggest that the subject is God the Father.[59] A firm decision is difficult. Wesley Hill offers perhaps the most cogent solution of the apparently conflicting evidence. Hill argues that by making Christ the grammatical subject of the verb, the subject of which is God in the scriptural text Paul is intentionally invoking, Paul attributes to Christ the divine function of subduing all enemies, thus underscoring the divinity of the Son and his equality with the Father. The very ambiguity itself is reflective of Paul's Trinitarian theology, in which the will, working, and power of Father, Son, and Holy Spirit is not threefold but one will, one working, and one power.[60]

This clause in 15:25 is the second place in 15:24–25 where expositors imagine they find an end to the reign of Christ. A major cause of the common scholarly view

---

ers. Contra Jan Lambrecht, who argues that Paul here only makes free use of scriptural language and that the content of Ps 110:1 is not decisive for his intent; see Lambrecht, "Christological Use," 505–12; Lambrecht, "Line of Thought," 143–51. Equally unconvincing is the argument of M. de Boer, who suggests that Paul alludes not to Scripture but to a christological tradition or creed familiar to the Corinthians in "Paul's Use of a Resurrection Tradition in 1 Cor 15,20–28," in *The Corinthian Correspondence* (ed. R. Bieringer; BETL 75; Leuven: Peeters, 1996), 639–51. These views are inconsistent with the important place of Ps 110:1 in early Christian thought.

57. In place of the first-person verb and second-person pronouns of the LXX and MT, Paul's pronouns and verbs are in the third person. However, this is not evidence of an alternative translation but is an obvious change necessitated by Paul's grammatical context. But Paul's quote also differs at several additional points from the LXX. Where the LXX reads ἕως ἄν ("until"), Paul has ἄχρι οὗ ("until"). Where the LXX reads ὑποπόδιον τῶν ποδῶν ("footstool of the feet"), Paul has ὑπὸ τοὺς πόδας ("under the feet"). And, in contrast to the LXX, Paul includes no possessive pronoun after ἐχθρούς. The pronoun αὐτοῦ after ἐχθρούς in 1 Cor 15:25 is a late addition (A F G 33) inserted to bring Paul's wording into closer conformity to Ps 110:1 LXX. All these differences suggest an alternative Greek translation of the psalm, perhaps Paul's own.

58. So Lambrecht, "Christological Use," 505–12; Lambrecht, "Line of Thought," 145–51; Fee, 837; Weiss, 359; Dunn, *Theology of Paul*, 249 n. 74.

59. So U. Heil, "Theo-logische Interpretation," 27–35; Barrett, 358; J. P. Heil, *Rhetorical Role*, 207.

60. W. Hill, *Paul and the Trinity*, 125–27.

*The Eternal Reign of the Father and the Son*

that Paul in this passage portrays Christ's kingly reign as temporary is the widespread assumption that, when Paul declares Christ must reign until he puts all his enemies under his feet, the preposition ἄχρι "until" marks a termination point of the kingdom of Christ. Wolfgang Schrage is typical when he asserts that the preposition ἄχρι indicates the *"terminus ad quem der Herrschaft Christi"* ("the end-point of the reign of Christ").[61] The assumption is that the preposition ἄχρι necessarily involves cessation. But this is mistaken. The preposition *can* be used with regard to an action that ceases after that point (e.g., Matt 24:38; Acts 20:11; Gal 4:2). But often this is *not* the case (e.g., Acts 2:29; 23:1; 26:22; Rom 8:22; 1 Cor 4:11; 2 Cor 3:14; Phil 1:5). A further example is Rom 5:13: ἄχρι γὰρ νόμου ἁμαρτία ἦν ἐν κόσμῳ ("for until the law sin was in the world"). Here Paul clearly understands sin to continue in the world after the giving of the law. Similarly, the point of the preposition ἄχρι in 15:25 is hardly that the reign of Christ will cease after that point. The ἄχρι οὗ ("until") does not express the *limit* of Christ's reign, but the *goal* of that reign.

This is evident in the Old Testament allusion on which Paul's thought here is focused. In Ps 110:1 the point of the clause "until I make your enemies a footstool for your feet" is obviously not that the messianic king's reign will end, but that his reign must extend until it subdues all its enemies. The reign of the king in Ps 110 is everlasting: "You are a priest forever, according to the order of Melchizedek" (Ps 110:4). As Murray J. Smith and Ian J. Vaillancourt have shown, the "until" of Ps 110:1 does not envision a cessation of the reign of David's lord but two stages of that reign, first his enthronement among his enemies (Ps 110:1a, 2–3) and then the full consummation of his rule (Ps 110:1b, 4–7): "the inauguration of his cosmic rule is a prelude to his final victory in the world."[62] As Smith and Vaillancourt also show, this understanding of Ps 110 in terms of a two-stage kingdom, first inaugurated and then fully consummated, is universal in early Christian texts, including 1 Cor 15:25.[63]

Paul's point, then, is that the present phase of Christ's reign, in which his enemies are not yet completely subdued, is only temporary. His reign must bring about the defeat of *all* his enemies, including the last enemy, death. *The kingdom of Christ must culminate in the resurrection of the dead.* That is Paul's point in 15:25, which also makes clear how this verse fits within the total argument of the chapter (something that the mistaken assumption that Paul is here declaring an end to Christ's reign utterly fails to do). Paul will now make this point explicit in the verse that follows.

---

61. Schrage, 177.

62. Murray J. Smith and Ian J. Vaillancourt, "Enthroned and Coming to Reign: Jesus' Eschatological Use of Psalm 110:1 in Mark 14:62," *JBL* 141 (2022): 513–31 (quote on 518).

63. Smith and Vaillancourt, "Enthroned," 521–31.

CHAPTER 8

VERSE 26

*The last enemy that is abolished is death.*

As we saw in the introduction to this chapter, 15:24–28 has a concentric structure, which places v. 26 at the heart of the thought of the passage. In addition, Paul's effective use of asyndeton (no grammatical connector between this and the previous clause) adds further force and prominence to Paul's assertion here.[64] The subject of the verb, ὁ θάνατος, through its delay to the end of the clause, is strongly emphatic, putting the focus firmly on death and its destruction. The clause is given further force through Paul's striking use of the futuristic present, which presents the future event of the destruction of death arrestingly and dramatically, with focus on its certainty.[65] The present tense here "effectively establishes the destruction of death as a *fait accompli*."[66] In all these ways, Paul highlights the abolishment of death as the central theme of 15:24–28. We have, in fact, reached the central theme of Paul's resurrection chapter, as its recurrence at the climax of the chapter (15:54–57) confirms. The central theme of 1 Cor 15 is the final triumph of God over death through the resurrection of the dead.

The description of death as the last enemy here in 15:26 includes death among the enemies of Christ mentioned in 15:25. The word ἐχθρός denotes a reciprocal animosity, enmity on both sides (A is hostile to B, and B is hostile to A).[67] It thus here describes death as an enemy who is at enmity with Christ, and with whom Christ is at enmity. Against the background of the ancient world into which the gospel came, the implications of Paul's characterization of death as God's "enemy" are enormous. This was a striking and *new* philosophical claim, which put all of reality into a new light. It distinguishes (in a way the ancient philosophers could not have imagined) between the God-given, good creation and the death and evil that now infect it. And it proclaims an almighty and good creator, who is neither the author of death nor indifferent to it but is its implacable enemy—and its ultimate conqueror.

Verse 26 involves yet another aspect of Paul's teaching in this chapter that excludes the view of Dale Martin that Paul's conception of the resurrection was a compromise with Greco-Roman philosophical expectations of the afterlife as well

---

64. Fee, 838.
65. Schrage, 180–81 n. 817; Robertson & Plummer, 356; Garland, 712. According to A. T. Robertson: "The futuristic present startles and arrests attention. It affirms and not merely predicts. It gives a sense of certainty." (Rob., *Gram.*, 870)
66. Collins, 554.
67. See Schmidt, *Syn.*, 3:497 (§138.1).

as Troels Engberg-Pedersen's claim that Paul's understanding of the resurrection was identical with the Stoic conception of the afterlife of the soul.[68] For the varied forms of afterlife conceived within Greco-Roman philosophical thought are nowhere described as death's *abolishment* or *destruction*. Paul here, by contrast, describes the resurrection as the conquest of death itself. Paul's language is different from the philosophers because his expectation is radically different—the resurrection of the physical body of flesh and bones to everlasting life.

As many interpreters note, Paul, in calling death an "enemy," speaks of death here as a personal being. The great majority conclude that this is merely the rhetorical device of personification.[69] However, Paul's description of death as the "last enemy" to be "abolished" includes death among the cosmological enemies and powers of 15:24–25.[70] As all interpreters recognize, those powers are *personal* beings and powers. Moreover, Paul's description of death as the "last" of these enemies and powers to be vanquished implicitly portrays death as having preeminence among these powers. Wisdom of Solomon 2:24, to which Paul alludes in Rom 5:12, is explicit that death is the work of the devil (Wis 2:24, φθόνῳ δὲ διαβόλου θάνατος εἰσῆλθεν εἰς τὸν κόσμον). The same conception is present in Rom 16:20 (cf. 1 Cor 5:5). Moreover, death as the last ἐχθρός "enemy" in v. 26 may also evoke the ἔχθρα "enmity" between the serpent and the seed of the woman in Gen 3:15.[71] All these factors suggest that Paul here has in mind not only the abolishment of death but also the abolishment of the personal power who brought death into the world: Satan or the devil. The thought and language here are similar to Heb 2:14, which describes the purpose of the incarnation as "that through death he [Christ] might *abolish* the one who has the power of *death*, that is, the devil" (ἵνα διὰ τοῦ θανάτου καταργήσῃ τὸν τὸ κράτος ἔχοντα τοῦ θανάτου, τοῦτ' ἔστιν τὸν διάβολον).

Martinus de Boer argues that Paul's portrayal of the final destruction of death necessarily involves a soteriological universalism, in which every human being must be saved regardless of their response to Christ or to the gospel.[72] But in regard to the destruction of death, Pauline theology knows a crucial qualifica-

---

68. Dale Martin, *The Corinthian Body* (New Haven: Yale University Press, 1995), 104–36; Troels Engberg-Pedersen, *Cosmology and Self in the Apostle Paul: The Material Spirit* (Oxford: Oxford University Press, 2010), 8–38. For further discussion, see the introduction and elsewhere in this commentary.

69. E.g. Schrage, 178–79; Lindemann, 348; Collins, 554; Garland, 712; Hays, 266.

70. The word ἐχθρός refers back to τοὺς ἐχθρούς in 15:25, and καταργεῖται recalls καταργήσῃ in 15:24.

71. I am indebted for this insight to Charles Reed III in personal communication.

72. Martinus de Boer, *The Defeat of Death: Apocalyptic Eschatology in 1 Corinthians 15 and Romans 5* (JSNTSup 22; 1988; repr., London: T&T Clark, 2019), 114–20.

tion. First Corinthians 1:18 contrasts "those who are being saved" and "those who are perishing" (cf. Rom 2:1–11; 1 Cor 11:32; 2 Cor 5:10; 2 Thess 1:5–10). The apostle "knows of an eternal death for the unbelieving."[73] For those who obey the gospel of Christ and are saved, the apostolic message is a fragrance leading "from life to life," that is, from the life bestowed in baptism to the fullness of life at the resurrection (2 Cor 2:15–16). But for those who reject the gospel and perish, the apostolic message is a fragrance leading "from death to death" (2 Cor 2:15–16). If we look at 1 Cor 15:26 and 2 Cor 2:15–16 in concert, Paul's thought and language in these passages are parallel to the book of Revelation, which declares that for the faithful "death will be no more" (Rev 21:4; cf. 1 Cor 15:26) but also speaks of the "second death" in store for the unbelieving (Rev 21:8; cf. 2 Cor 2:15–16).[74] "For Paul, the defeat of death was an essential and climactic part of Christ's cosmological victory, but it did not negate the judgment of all."[75]

The verb καταργεῖται is a "divine passive": only God can raise the dead (Rom 4:17; 2 Cor 1:9). A number of interpreters conclude from this that the agent of this passive verb must not be Christ but must be God the Father.[76] Wolfgang Schrage quotes with approval the dictum of Christoph Burchard that Christ has power to defeat the principalities and powers but not to awaken the dead.[77] But this is a radical misunderstanding of the passage and of Pauline theology. The verb καταργεῖται in 15:26 recalls καταργήσῃ in 15:24, the subject of which is *Christ*. Logic demands that if it is Christ who abolishes "every" power (15:24) and "all" the enemies (15:25), it must be Christ who abolishes the "last" of these enemies. Only a few verses earlier in this chapter, Paul has told the reader that the resurrection of the dead is through Christ (15:21), and that it is in Christ that all will be made alive (15:22). In Paul's thought, it is Christ "who will transform our lowly bodies to be conformed to his glorious body" (Phil 3:21). Thus in 1 Cor 15:26, the understood agent of the divine passive καταργεῖται is Jesus Christ.[78] In this way, Paul once again in this chapter foregrounds Jesus's divine identity as the "one Lord, through whom are all things and we through him" (1 Cor 8:6). He is God, even as the Father is God.

Now in v. 26, for the first time within 15:24–28, it becomes clear why Paul says that the reign of Christ must (δεῖ, 15:25) abolish *every* (πᾶσαν) opposing rule, *every* (πᾶσαν) dominion and power (15:24), and *all* (πάντας) enemies (15:25). The

---

73. Wolff, 388.
74. Cf. Wolff, 388.
75. Andrew Wilson, "The Strongest Argument for Universalism in 1 Corinthians 15:20–28," *JETS* 59 (2016): 812.
76. So U. Heil, "Theo-logische Interpretation," 32; Schrage, 179–80; Lindemann, 348.
77. Schrage, 180 n. 812.
78. Rightly Lambrecht, "Christological Use," 510–11.

reason is that *the reign of Christ must culminate in the abolishing of death through the resurrection of the dead.* The resurrection of the dead must take place, if the kingdom is truly to be the kingdom. And, as Paul will now show in the verses that follow, the resurrection of the dead must take place, if God is to be truly God.

## Verse 27

*For "he has subjected all things under his feet." But when it says that all things have been subjected, it is clear that this excepts the one who subjected all things to him.*

*For "he has subjected all things under his feet."* The causal γάρ "for" indicates that v. 27a provides the grounds for v. 26. The destruction of death (15:26) must take place, because *all* things (πάντα, emphatic by position) have been put under the feet of the risen Christ (15:27a).[79] "All things" includes the last enemy: death. Paul here addresses a truth that the self-professed wise at Corinth who denied the resurrection failed to grasp, for they claimed that "there is no resurrection of the dead" (15:12). In their view, there was at least one power outside the dominion of Christ's kingdom—the power of death. Paul here, by contrast, affirms the totality of Christ's victory and reign. The all-conquering reign of Christ *must* culminate in the resurrection of the dead.

As the great majority of interpreters are agreed, 15:27a is an echo or citation of Ps 8:7.[80] Paul's wording does not follow the LXX precisely, suggesting that he is employing an alternative ancient Greek translation or his own rendering of the Hebrew. The allusion to Ps 8:7 in 15:27 is combined (as we have seen) with an allusion to Dan 7:27 in 15:24 and to Ps 110:1 in 15:25. Strikingly, we find the same combination of allusions to these three passages in Eph 1:20–23 and 1 Pet 3:22 as well as combined allusions to Ps 8:7 and Ps 110:1 in Heb 1:13 and 2:5–9. In each case (Eph 1:20–23; 1 Pet 3:22, and Heb 1:13, 2:5–9), these passages are given, as in 1 Cor 15:24–27, a christological interpretation as fulfilled in Christ. Clearly, we are in touch here with an ancient christological tradition.[81] Given the evidence of its

---

79. Cf. Thüsing, *Per Christum*, 241; Ciampa & Rosner, 774; Wolff, 388.

80. Dissenting are Jan Lambrecht, "Christological Use," 505–12; Lambrecht, "Line of Thought," 143–51; de Boer, "Resurrection Tradition," 639–51.

81. For a detailed examination of the evidence, and convincing arguments for the presence of a catechetical tradition within 1 Cor 15:24–27, see de Boer, "Resurrection Tradition," 641–48. The treatment of de Boer is only lacking in its failure to recognize the role of allusion to Dan 7:27 within this tradition. However, de Boer is mistaken in concluding from the presence of this tradition that Paul is not citing Scripture in 15:24–27 but rather this christological tradition or

CHAPTER 8

widespread diffusion (found in 1 Corinthians, Ephesians, Hebrews, and 1 Peter), this tradition is almost certainly pre-Pauline, apostolic, and most likely not significantly later than the primitive confession preserved in 1 Cor 15:3–7. Within this tradition, Christ's fulfillment of Ps 8:7, through the subjection of all things to himself, is understood as inaugurated at his resurrection (Eph 1:20–23; 1 Pet 3:22; cf. 1 Cor 2:6–8) but only fully consummated at his second coming (1 Cor 15:27; cf. Phil 3:21).

Who is the subject of the verb ὑπέταξεν in 15:27a? The majority of interpreters regard God the Father as the subject.[82] However, a number of interpreters argue that Christ is here the subject.[83] The context of the psalm citation might seem conclusive that the Father is the subject. However, in Paul's allusion to Ps 8:7 in Phil 3:21, Christ is without controversy the subject. A confident decision is difficult. But that the understood subject shifts here to God the Father appears most likely. If so, a comparison of 1 Cor 15:27 and Phil 3:21 provides a window into Paul's thought. For when he affirms in 1 Cor 15:27 that the Father will subject all things, but in Phil 3:21 states that this is the work of the Son, we see that for Paul the will, operation, power, and majesty of Father and Son are not twofold but one and inseparable. When we look at 1 Cor 15:27 and Phil 3:21 in concert, we see that Paul's thought has an undeniably Trinitarian character, for which the only truly adequate language is the church's historic language of the Trinity.

Psalm 8 is a meditation upon Gen 1:26–27, celebrating the exalted role of humankind in implementing God's kingly rule over creation. Paul, and the ancient apostolic tradition that he transmits, understands this divine intention for humanity, vitiated through humanity's fall, to be restored and fulfilled in Christ.[84] He is the ἄνθρωπος of Ps 8:5 because he is the second Adam, the founder of a new, restored humanity.[85] This recalls the focus on Christ as ἄνθρωπος in 15:21–22 (15:21, δι' ἀνθρώπου; 15:22, Ἀδάμ ... Χριστός). In giving Ps 8 a christological interpretation, Paul interprets the ἄνθρωπος of the psalm *individually* as being fulfilled in Jesus, and *collectively* as being fulfilled in the new humanity he brings into being through his saving and redeeming work as the last Adam (cf. 15:45–49). When all things are

---

creed, and that the Corinthians would have been unaware of its scriptural basis. This is highly unlikely given the focus on Scripture and its christological interpretation in Paul's founding instruction at Corinth (1 Cor 15:3–4).

82. U. Heil, "Theo-logische Interpretation," 30–33; Lindeman, 348; Garland, 712–13; Godet, 2:365.
83. Lambrecht, "Christological Use," 510–11; Lambrecht, "Line of Thought," 149–50; Wolff, 389.
84. Matt O'Reilly, *Paul and the Resurrected Body: Social Identity and Ethical Practice* (Atlanta: SBL Press, 2020), 70; Constantine R. Campbell, *Paul and the Hope of Glory: An Exegetical and Theological Study* (Grand Rapids: Zondervan, 2020), 77; Jamieson, "Grammar," 202–4.
85. Cf. Wolff, 389; Robertson & Plummer, 357.

*The Eternal Reign of the Father and the Son*

subjected to Christ at his coming in glory (15:27), those who are united to Christ will share and participate in his victory and rule (cf. 3:21–23; 6:3, 9–10).

The subjection to Christ in 15:27 includes the dethronement and destruction of the inimical powers of 15:24–26. But this subjection to Christ in v. 27 is wider than the placement of all the enemies under Christ's feet in v. 25, embracing not only the hostile powers but "all things" (15:27). Therefore the subjection to Christ in v. 27 must also include a positive sense denoting the right ordering of creation.[86] Through subjection to Christ, all things are "placed in their proper order under the risen Christ, in order for them to be brought to the goal designed for them by the Creator in accord with Psalm 8."[87] Here in v. 27, as in Phil 3:21, Christ's subjection of all things includes his glorious transformation of all things, especially the glorious transformation of his people through the resurrection of the dead.[88] The "subjection" of v. 27 is thus a liberating, salvation-bringing, and life-giving subjection, and at its heart is the resurrection. The two sides of Christ's subjection of all things—the destruction of his enemies and the transformation of the cosmos—are two sides of the same coin, for it is precisely the destruction of the inimical powers that brings about the liberation of creation and the salvation of the people of God.

*But when it says that all things have been subjected.* Who or what is the subject of "says" (εἴπῃ)? A number of interpreters argue that the subject is Christ.[89] However, most interpreters agree that the subject is Scripture.[90] The latter is virtually certain, for the exact phrase Paul uses here (ὅταν with the third-person subjunctive of λέγω) is regularly used in antiquity to cite a passage of literature, especially the Scriptures (so Plato, *Ion* 538c–d [ὅταν λέγῃ Ὅμηρος]; Justin, *Dial.* 114.2–3 [ὅταν λέγῃ]; 138.2 [ὅταν οὖν εἴπῃ]).[91] Paul's use of this expression reveals that v. 27 contains a biblical allusion, which he expected the Corinthians to recognize.[92] The allusion is to Ps 8:7, for the words πάντα ὑποτέτακται ("all things have been sub-

---

86. Thüsing, *Per Christum*, 241–42.
87. J. P. Heil, *Rhetorical Role*, 216.
88. Thüsing, *Per Christum*, 242–43.
89. Lambrecht, "Christological Use," 510; Wolff, 389.
90. So Fitzmyer, 574; Ciampa & Rosner, 774; Lindeman, 348; Collins, 554; Garland, 713.
91. In these passages, as in 1 Cor 15:27, the expression introduces a specific passage. The indefinite temporal subjunctive, which might otherwise appear perplexing when citing a single, definite passage, appears to mean something like "when (on whatever occasion it may be read) it says."
92. A few important witnesses omit the ὅτι after the verb (P[46] B 33), but the majority of manuscripts, including our best witnesses for Paul's letters (ℵ A D), strongly support its inclusion in the text.

CHAPTER 8

jected") refer back to πάντα ὑπέταξεν ("he subjected all things") from the citation of Ps 8:7 earlier in the verse.[93]

*it is clear that this excepts the one who subjected all things to him.* The expression δῆλον ὅτι ("it is clear that") is found frequently in the writings of ancient philosophers. It does not introduce a conclusion of which the writer seeks to persuade his readers but a point of expected agreement between author and audience, often as part of a chain of reasoning.[94] It thus introduces an obvious point, with which Paul expects the Corinthians will immediately agree. That point is that the "all things" subjected to the Son do not include the Father, who subjects them to him. Paul will now build on this point to move to the climactic affirmation of 15:24–28.

## VERSE 28

*And when all things are subjected to him, then the Son himself will subject himself to the one who subjected all things to him, in order that God may be all in all.*

Verse 28, like vv. 24–25, has been a magnet for misinterpretation. A number of interpreters simply assume, without argument, that this verse's description of the submission of the Son to the Father is incompatible with a divine Christology.[95] Other scholars find here, as we saw many do in 15:24–25, an end to the kingdom, mediatorial role, and saving activity of the Son.[96] Even the most capable of scholars often evince a perplexing propensity to forget that this verse belongs to a larger passage (15:24–28), within a larger chapter (chapter 15), within a larger epistle (1 Corinthians). Thus, for example, Richard Hays, in his commentary on the letter, can write that the confession of 1 Cor 8:6 "takes the extraordinarily bold step of identifying 'the Lord Jesus' with 'the Lord' acclaimed in the *Shema*," and ascribes to Christ "both creation and eschatological redemption."[97] But then he can write of 1 Cor 15:28 that "it is impossible to avoid the impression that Paul is operating

---

93. Rightly Schrage, 159; Ciampa & Rosner, 774; Lindemann, 348.
94. Plato, *Euthyphr.* 13a; *Crit.* 47c; *Phaed.* 79b; *Pol.* 285d; *Prot.* 312e; Aristotle, *Eth. eud.* 1248a; *Eth. nic.* 1101b; *Metaph.* 1041b; Theophrastus, *Caus. plant.* 2.13.1; Xenophon, *Mem.* 3.63; 4.2.20; Isocrates, *Antid.* 154, 226; Plutarch, *Fat.* 574d; Epictetus, *Diatr.* 1.6.33; 2.26.1.
95. E.g. Dunn, *Theology of Paul*, 248–49; Meeks, *Christ Is the Question*, 130–32. For further examples, see Jamieson, "Grammar," 189–90.
96. E.g., Fitzmyer, 574.
97. Hays, 140.

*The Eternal Reign of the Father and the Son*

with what would later come to be called a subordinationist Christology."[98] Obviously any such interpretation, which works with this verse entirely outside the context of the larger letter and of Pauline Christology, is worthless. Conversely, as we will see, when 15:28 is read within the context of the larger epistle, Paul's meaning and intent in this powerful verse, and its fully divine and incarnational Christology, become clear.

Verse 28 has a culminating role within 15:24–28. Within the concentric structure of vv. 24–28 (A – v. 24; B – v. 25; C – v. 26; B' – v. 27a, A' – vv. 27b–28), v. 28 corresponds to v. 24. In 15:24 we find the sequence εἶτα ... ὅταν ... ὅταν, and in 15:27b–28 its chiastic reversal: ὅταν ... ὅταν ... τότε. The only two mentions of the word θεός within the passage are found in vv. 24 and 28. The expression ὁ θεὸς καὶ πατήρ in v. 24 corresponds to ὁ υἱός in v. 28. In both v. 24 and v. 28, the incarnate Son of God acts in filial submission to the Father. In 15:28, Paul's thought within 15:24–28 clearly comes full circle and to its climax.

*And when all things are subjected to him.* Gordon Fee is correct: "As what has preceded (vv. 20–22 and 26) makes certain, 'all things' here refers especially to death."[99] At the same time, "all things" embraces all of creation, and includes "those who belong to Christ" (15:23). With the shift from the focus on hostile powers alone in 15:24–26 to "all things" in 15:27–28, the verb ὑποτάσσω, as we have seen, takes on a positive, salvific dimension—the redemption and right ordering of creation under the saving and life-giving rule of Christ.[100]

Regularly in Jewish texts, as Wesley Hill observes, "the sovereignty of God over his enemies and over 'all things' ... distinguishes the one God from all else."[101] Thus, through the description in 15:28 of "all things" (τὰ πάντα) as subject to *Christ*, Paul makes his divine identity and nature clear. The subjection of "all things" (τὰ πάντα) to Christ recalls 8:6, which confesses "one Lord, Jesus Christ, through whom are all things (τὰ πάντα)." In 8:6, all things are created through Christ; in 15:28, all things are subjected to Christ, reaching their goal and fulfillment in him.

*then the Son himself.* It is sometimes suggested that "the Son" (ὁ υἱός) has here a merely covenantal or messianic sense. But this is an inadequate exegesis of this

---

98. Hays, 266.
99. Fee, 841.
100. Thüsing, *Per Christum*, 241–43; J. P. Heil, *Rhetorical Role*, 216.
101. W. Hill, *Paul and the Trinity*, 126. Hill provides a lengthy list of "Jewish texts that employ πάντα to demarcate the sphere of the one God's sovereignty" (126 n. 44).

verse. As many interpreters have recognized, Paul here uses "the Son" in a fully divine sense within a fully divine and incarnational Christology.[102] Several factors make this conclusion inescapable:

(1) Whenever Paul refers elsewhere in his letters to Jesus as "the Son of God" or "his Son," this is always with reference to the eternal Son of God who was made man (e.g., Rom 8:3, "God, sending his own Son in the likeness of sinful flesh"; Gal 4:4, "God sent forth his Son, born of a woman").

(2) First Corinthians in particular evinces throughout a high, divine Christology. The letter is replete with what are commonly called "Christological YHWH texts," that is, passages that reveal Jesus's divine identity by quoting or alluding to passages of the Old Testament about YHWH, and applying them to Jesus.[103] Moreover, we find throughout the letter that the participatory union whereby believers become the temple or dwelling place of *God* (3:16–17; 6:19–20) is their union with *Jesus Christ* (1:9; 6:15–17; 10:14–22; 12:12–17; cf. 1:2; 7:22; 10:17), thus identifying Jesus as God.

(3) Paul here not only calls Jesus the Son of God, but does so in a striking way. He uses this title in its absolute form: ὁ υἱός ("the Son"), without further modifiers, the so-called ὁ υἱός κατ' ἐξοχήν. Found only here in Paul, the designation ὁ υἱός in its unqualified form appears infrequently in the New Testament outside of the Gospel of John, 1 John, and Hebrews. In these texts it is used frequently, reflective of their divine, incarnational Christology. Used in the absolute form without modifiers, ὁ υἱός is the most lofty expression found within the New Testament for Jesus's divine Sonship. Uniquely within the entire New Testament, Paul here heightens the force of this expression through the addition of the intensifier αὐτός "himself," in emphatic position (αὐτὸς ὁ υἱός), making 15:28 arguably the most exalted statement of Jesus's divine Sonship within the entire New Testament.

In light of all these factors, it is clear that αὐτὸς ὁ υἱός ("the Son himself") is used in a divine sense, and within a theological framework in which the identity of the one God includes both Father and Son. The term expresses, as Wesley Hill notes, "Jesus' inclusion in the unique divine identity . . . and his irreducible difference from the one called 'Father.'"[104] As N. T. Wright observes, it is "a way of predicating a relationship which, though differentiated, allows Jesus to be seen *within*, and not

---

102. So W. Hill, *Paul and the Trinity*, 128–33; N. T. Wright, "Adam, Israel, and the Messiah," in *The Climax of the Covenant: Christ and the Law in Pauline Theology* (Minneapolis: Fortress, 1991), 30.

103. E.g. 1:2, echoing Joel 3:5 and Mal 1:11; 1:31, quoting Jer 9:23–24; 2:8, alluding to Ps 24; 2:16, quoting Isa 40:13; 8:6, echoing Deut 6:4; 10:22, alluding to Deut 32:31; 10:26, quoting Ps 24:1; 15:31, echoing Jer 9:23–24 (thus forming an *inclusio* with 1:31 above).

104. W. Hill, *Paul and the Trinity*, 132.

*The Eternal Reign of the Father and the Son*

outside, the Pauline picture of the One God."[105] Paul's reference to Jesus here in 15:28 as "the Son" forms, as we will see in our discussion of the final clause of the passage in 15:28c, part of the Trinitarian framework of the chapter. It is "the Son himself" who is the subject of the clause that now follows.[106]

*will subject himself to the one who subjected all things to him.* The clause that now follows is striking indeed. Verse 28 is unique within the entire New Testament in using the language of "subjection" (ὑποτάσσω) of the Son and in describing the Son as subject to the Father. The ancient Arians and Eunomians pointed to this verse as proof of the Son's less than divine status.[107] Some modern scholars come to a similar conclusion.[108] Many other interpreters assume that this future subjection of the Son means that Christ's role as savior and mediator of humanity will cease. According to Joseph Fitzmyer, "Christ's regnal and salvific role will be at an end."[109] Such a reading of v. 28 is widespread.[110] And in recent years a number of evangelical theologians, preeminently Wayne A. Grudem, have argued that the New Testament teaches an eternal functional subordination of the divine Son to the Father within the relations of the immanent Trinity. Within their argument, 1 Cor 15:28 has played a key role.[111]

However, these are all misinterpretations of the Son's submission to the Father in v. 28. Let us first take the widespread assumption that 15:28 portrays an eschatological picture in which Christ ceases to be mediator and savior. Here the study of

---

105. Wright, "Adam, Israel, and the Messiah," 30.

106. The manuscript witness is divided as to whether an adjunctive καί precedes αὐτὸς ὁ υἱός or should be omitted. The evidence is fairly evenly balanced. However, the number and diversity of important witnesses that support the absence of the conjunction (B D 33 1175 1739) are slightly superior to the key witnesses for its inclusion (ℵ A 81). Moreover, it is easy to explain the insertion of καί by copyists, as a natural adjunct, but not easy to assign a motive for its deletion if it were present originally. The reading without καί is (with some hesitation) to be preferred.

107. On the importance of this verse in antiquity for the Arians and Eunomians, who opposed the doctrine of the divinity of the Son, see the remarks of Hilary, *Trin.* 1.33; 11.8.

108. E.g. Dunn, *Theology of Paul*, 254; James F. McGrath, *The Only True God: Early Christian Monotheism in Its Jewish Context* (Urbana: University of Illinois Press, 2009), 49–50, 53.

109. Fitzmyer, 574.

110. Cf. Potgieter, "Consummation," 216–25; Robertson & Plummer, 358. Thüsing notes that this interpretation of the verse is widely held (*Per Christum*, 251 n. 40).

111. For Grudem's most recent restatement of this position, see Wayne A. Grudem, *Systematic Theology* (2d ed.; Grand Rapids: Zondervan Academic, 2020), 301–18. For an example of the crucial role of 1 Cor 15:24–28 among advocates of this view, see James M. Hamilton, "'That God May Be All in All': The Trinity in 1 Corinthians 15," in *One God in Three Persons: Unity of Essence, Distinction of Persons, Implications for Life* (ed. Bruce A. Ware and John Starke; Wheaton, IL: Crossway, 2015), 95–108; see also Keener, 127.

CHAPTER 8

Wilhelm Thüsing is fundamental. As Thüsing has shown, it is an essential component of Paul's theology that the mediatorial and salvific role of Christ continues for eternity.[112] Within Paul's thought, in the eschaton the faithful will "be clothed with the image of the man from heaven" (1 Cor 15:49) and "be conformed to the image of his Son" (Rom 8:29). This language presupposes that Christ is and remains the only Son and the unique image of God. The faithful share in this image and sonship not independently of him but receiving it *from* him and in *union* with him.[113] Likewise, believers will in eternity be "heirs of God" (Rom 8:17) and "inherit the kingdom of God" (1 Cor 6:9; 15:50) but only as "fellow heirs of Christ" (Rom 8:17, συγκληρονόμοι δὲ Χριστοῦ), that is, heirs through their union with the true heir (Gal 3:16), who is Christ.[114] In the same way, the eternal glorification of believers at the resurrection will be their glorification with *Christ* (Rom 8:17, ἵνα καὶ συνδοξασθῶμεν; cf. Phil 3:21, σύμμορφον τῷ σώματι τῆς δόξης αὐτοῦ). This language presupposes an eternal glory of the Son, which he must have and possess, in order that the faithful may share in it.[115] In all these ways, as Thüsing notes, "the Pauline Christ-picture is predicated on a continuation and fulfillment, and not on a cessation, of his central position."[116] Far from the consummation bringing an end to the Son of God's saving work as mediator, in the Pauline conception the eternal adoption, inheritance, and glorification of the saints are the fruit of their consummated union with Christ. The glorification of those who belong to Christ presupposes (and is unthinkable apart from) the eternal glory and mediatorial work of the Son.

And it is this saving and mediating work of Christ, beginning in time but continuing through all eternity, that provides the context in which his submission to the Father in 15:28 is to be understood. In Pauline theology, "God sent forth his Son, born of a woman . . . that we might receive adoption" (Gal 4:4–5): the purpose of the Son of God becoming human is the salvation and renewal of humanity by participation in the divine life of the Son. One key aspect of the incarnate Son's redemptive work is his human obedience and submission to God as the second Adam, overthrowing the effects of the disobedience of the first Adam (15:21–22, 45–49, 56–57). *Herein we find the key to 1 Cor 15:28.* The language of "subjection" (ὑποτάσσω) in regard to the Son is unique to 1 Cor 15:28. But the conception of the incarnate Son's *obedience* to God in his *human nature* is an important theme in Paul. "For just as through the disobedience of the one human being, the many

---

112. Thüsing, *Per Christum*, 251.
113. Thüsing, *Per Christum*, 247–51.
114. Thüsing, *Per Christum*, 251.
115. Thüsing, *Per Christum*, 119–27, 247–52.
116. Thüsing, *Per Christum*, 251 n. 40: "das paulinische Christusbild ist auf ein Fortdauern bzw. eine Vollendung und nicht auf ein Aufheben seiner zentralen Position angelegt."

were made sinners, so through the *obedience* [ὑπακοή] of the one *human being* [ἄνθρωπος], the many will be made righteous" (Rom 5:19). "And having been found in fashion as a *human being* [ἄνθρωπος], he humbled himself, becoming *obedient* [ὑπήκοος] to the point of death, even death on a cross" (Phil 2:7–8). That this conception of the Son's submission and obedience to God in his human nature is not in conflict with the divinity of the Son and his equality with the Father is shown by the prominence of this theme in John's Gospel, a book whose divine and incarnational Christology is beyond dispute (see e.g., John 1:1–18; 8:28, 49; 10:18; 14:28, 31; 15:10; 20:28).

Herein we see why interpretations that regard v. 28 as incompatible with a divine Christology, or as entailing an eternal subordination of the Son in his divine nature to the Father, go astray. For v. 28 describes the culmination of the second Adam's salvific and redemptive obedience *in his human nature*. The verb ὑποταγήσεται, although passive, has here (as frequently elsewhere in the New Testament) a middle sense: the incarnate Son freely submits himself to God in an act of obedience and love.[117] The Son subjects himself to God not in his divine nature, in which he is equal to God (Phil 2:6), but in his human nature, which he freely assumed in the incarnation (Phil 2:7–11). In so doing, the incarnate Son brings those united to him into the fullness of their adoption (Rom 8:29, συμμόρφους τῆς εἰκόνος τοῦ υἱοῦ αὐτοῦ), their inheritance (Rom 8:17, συγκληρονόμοι δὲ Χριστοῦ), and their glorification (Rom 8:17, ἵνα καὶ συνδοξασθῶμεν).[118] Augustine masterfully sums up the mystery, and Paul's thought in this passage: "Insofar as he is the Son of God, he will with the Father subject us to himself; insofar as he is our high priest, he will with us be subject to him."[119]

---

117. See Larry Richards, "ὑποταγήσεται in 1 Corinthians 15:28b," *AUSS* 38 (2020): 203–6; Wolff, 389; W. Hill, *Paul and the Trinity*, 129 n. 58. For the middle sense of the passive of ὑποτάσσω elsewhere in the New Testament, see Luke 2:51; Rom 8:7; 1 Cor 16:16; Eph 5:21, 24; Jas 4:7.

118. For the submission of 15:28 as involving not the divine nature but the human nature of the Son, and having a redemptive purpose for those in Christ, see Jamieson, "Grammar," 187–207; Thüsing, *Per Christum*, 247–48; Bender, 253–54; and Gary W. Derickson, "Incarnational Explanation for Jesus' Subjection in the Eschaton," in *Looking into the Future: Evangelical Studies in Eschatology* (Grand Rapids: Baker Academic, 2001), 217–32. This understanding of v. 28 (sometimes called the "corporate" or "ecclesial" interpretation) is the dominant patristic interpretation of the passage in antiquity; see, for example, Gregory of Nazianzus, *Or.* 30.4–5; Gregory of Nyssa, *In illud*; Hilary, *Trin.* 11.30–49; Augustine, *Trin.* 1.14–15. The classic study of the patristic exegesis of the passage is Lienhard, "Exegesis"; see also Lewis, *Apocalyptic Message*, 190–209. Following Augustine, this became virtually the universal interpretation of the passage in both the East and the West; see, for example, John of Damascus, *Fid. orth.* 4.18; Aquinas, *ST* I, Q. 42, Art. 4; III, Q. 20, Art. 1.

119. Augustine, *Trin.* 1.20.

CHAPTER 8

Thus, the submission of the Son in 15:28, which so many interpreters have regarded as a christological minus and a diminishment of Christ, is within Paul's theology a soteriological plus—the perfection of those in union with Christ. The uniqueness of the verb ὑποτάσσω in regard to the Son in v. 28 corresponds to the uniqueness of the verb παραδίδωμι with regard to the Father in v. 24. The two verses together reveal the mystery of the incarnation. The Son's bestowal of the kingdom on the Father (15:24), something even the most exalted creature could not do, reveals his divine nature and equality with the Father. Conversely, the Son's submission to the Father (15:28) reveals the perfection of his human nature, by which he brings those who are his own into the fullness of their adoption, inheritance, and glory.

*in order that God may be all in all.* The conjunction ἵνα "in order that" introduces a clause of purpose. It is debated whether the ἵνα clause connects to ὑποτάξαντι and thus expresses a goal of the Father's subjection of all things to the Son, or whether it connects to ὑποταγήσεται and thus expresses the reason for the Son's submission to the Father.[120] The great majority of interpreters take the latter view. However, neither of these alternatives is correct. The referent of the ἵνα is in fact *both* verbs and the entire preceding clause. This is evident from an analysis of the structure of the unit 15:27b–28. Each of the clauses within 15:27b–28 closes with τὰ πάντα, emphatic by final position, a structure that culminates in the final clause with the fuller expression τὰ πάντα ἐν πᾶσιν:

27b   δῆλον ὅτι ἐκτὸς τοῦ ὑποτάξαντος αὐτῷ τὰ πάντα.
28a   ὅταν δὲ ὑποταγῇ αὐτῷ τὰ πάντα,
28b   τότε αὐτὸς ὁ υἱὸς ὑποταγήσεται τῷ ὑποτάξαντι αὐτῷ τὰ πάντα,
28c   ἵνα ᾖ ὁ θεὸς τὰ πάντα ἐν πᾶσιν.

This structural analysis makes clear that, within the flow of thought of 15:27b–28, v. 28b forms a unified whole, and it is v. 28b as a unified whole that is the referent of v. 28c. Furthermore, when we examine v. 28b, we find that this clause depicts both the Father's subjection of all things to the Son and the submission of the Son to the Father. The thought of v. 28c is not, then, as usually supposed, that the submission of the Son brings it about that God is all in all. Rather, God becomes all in all in a twofold way, through (1) the submission of the Son to the Father, and (2) the subjection of all things by the Father to the Son. The focus of v. 28b is on *both* Father and Son. An important conclusion follows. If the focus of v. 28b, which forms the basis of the purpose clause in v. 28c, is both the Son and the Father,

---

120. For the debate, see Schrage, 185–86; Thüsing, *Per Christum*, 239.

*The Eternal Reign of the Father and the Son*

then the God (ὁ θεός) who thereby becomes all in all is not, as often supposed, the Father alone, but both the Father and the Son.

A number of further considerations confirm this conclusion:

1. Each of the three clauses within 15:27b–28b (vv. 27b, 28a, 28b) preceding 15:28c culminate with the subjection of all things *to the Son* (αὐτῷ τὰ πάντα).
2. Within 15:24–28, the word πᾶς occurs ten times, climactically with τὰ πάντα ἐν πᾶσιν in 15:28c. In *all* of the occurrences preceding v. 28c, the "all" are either abolished by *Christ*, put under the feet of *Christ*, or subjected to *Christ* (15:24, 25, 27, 28a–b).
3. In Eph 1:23 we find the identical phrase τὰ πάντα ἐν πᾶσιν, but here it is applied explicitly to the *Son* (τοῦ τὰ πάντα ἐν πᾶσιν πληρουμένου "of the one who fills *all in all*"). Likewise, in Col 3:11 the almost identical expression τὰ πάντα καὶ ἐν πᾶσιν is employed, as it is in 1 Cor 15:28c, as a predicate—but the subject in Col 3:11 is explicitly *Christ* (τὰ πάντα καὶ ἐν πᾶσιν Χριστός). The use in these epistles of identical (or nearly identical) expressions to the one found in 1 Cor 15:28c, but with explicit reference to Christ, is highly significant.
4. First Corinthians 15:28 is, within the larger letter, the complement and completion of the confession regarding Father and Son in 8:6. In this confession, the expression τὰ πάντα occurs twice: first concerning the creation of all things from the Father (8:6, ἐξ οὗ τὰ πάντα), and second, concerning the creation of all things through the Lord Jesus Christ (8:6, δι' οὗ τὰ πάντα). This would indicate that in 15:28, which narrates the final restoration and fulfillment of creation, the God who is "all in all" (τὰ πάντα ἐν πᾶσιν) is the Father and the Son.

All the factors above, taken together, strongly indicate that ὁ θεός in 15:28c does not refer to the Father only but is inclusive of both Father and Son.

But there is more that must be said about the identity of ὁ θεός in 15:28c. For a conception of God that can only be called Trinitarian suffuses 1 Corinthians. Thus, Paul's "God-language" in the epistle is regularly a discourse concerning God, the Lord Jesus, and the Spirit (2:2–5; 12:3). The Corinthians have been washed, sanctified, and justified "in the name of the *Lord* Jesus Christ, and in the *Spirit* of our *God*" (6:11, ἐν τῷ ὀνόματι τοῦ κυρίου Ἰησοῦ Χριστοῦ καὶ ἐν τῷ πνεύματι τοῦ θεοῦ ἡμῶν). The divine and miraculous bestowal of diverse spiritual gifts is the work of one *Spirit* (12:4, πνεῦμα), one *Lord* (12:5, κύριος), and one *God* (12:6, θεός). First Corinthians reveals a theology of God for which the only adequate language is the language of the Trinity.[121]

---

121. For fuller treatment of Paul's Trinitarian theology throughout his letters, see W. Hill, *Paul*

CHAPTER 8

    This Trinitarian theology of the letter, together with Paul's language in the passage of "Father" (15:24) and "Son" (15:28), alerts us to something that expositors have regularly missed. Paul's Trinitarian theology shapes chapter 15 of the letter in particular. For in this chapter, the resurrection is described as the work of the one who is God and Father (ὁ θεὸς καὶ πατήρ, 15:24; cf. θεός, 15:9, 10, 15, 28, 34, 38, 50, 57), as the work of the Son (ὁ υἱός, 15:28; cf. κύριος, 15:31, 57, 58; Χριστός, 15:3, 12, 13, 15, 16, 17, 18, 19, 20, 22, 23, 31, 57), and as the work of the Spirit (15:45, πνεῦμα; cf. 15:44, 46). *The whole of chapter 15 is Trinitarian in the structure of its thought.*

    We already saw that the God who is all in all in 15:28c is inclusive of both the Father and the Son. The Trinitarian shape of Paul's thought throughout the letter, and in particular chapter 15, would strongly suggest that ὁ θεός of 15:28c is inclusive not only of Father and Son but also of Father, Son, and Holy Spirit. A further striking exegetical observation confirms this. The expression τὰ πάντα ἐν πᾶσιν, which occurs in 15:28c, occurs one other time elsewhere in the epistle (12:6). There, the context is *explicitly* Trinitarian, where Paul traces the miraculous power of the gifts to one Spirit (12:4, τὸ αὐτὸ πνεῦμα), one Lord (12:5, ὁ αὐτὸς κύριος), and one God (12:6, ὁ αὐτὸς θεός), who works "all in all" (τὰ πάντα ἐν πᾶσιν). This would indicate that also in 15:28, the God who is all in all is the God who is Father, Son, and Holy Spirit.

    But what does it mean that God becomes "all in all" (τὰ πάντα ἐν πᾶσιν)? In Paul's construction, the expression functions as the predicate complement of the verb εἰμί ("that God may be all in all"). Although it is certain that Paul is using a common expression, its earliest attestation is here in 1 Corinthians (12:6; 15:28).[122] However, a very similar expression, employing the neuter plural πάντα alone (without πᾶσιν) as the predicate complement of the verb εἰμί (expressed or implied), is well attested both before and after Paul.[123] And the full expression πάντα ἐν πᾶσιν is found in a second-century passage (not dependent on Paul) from Athenagoras's *Legatio* (16.1).[124] In all these instances, the subject is a human being (or human beings). The contexts of the passages vary widely from romantic love (Diogenes

---

*and the Trinity*; James P. Ware, *Paul's Theology in Context: Creation, Incarnation, Covenant, and Kingdom* (Grand Rapids: Eerdmans, 2019), 43–91.

    122. The supposed parallels cited by Conzelmann (275, n. 112) are unrelated. The same is true of the saying attributed to the pre-Socratic philosopher Anaxagoras (Dionysius of Halicarnassus, *Rhet.* 9.11; cf. Aristotle, *Phys.* 203a).

    123. Herodotus, *Hist.* 3.157; Demosthenes, *Cor.* 43; Appian, *Bell. civ.* 2.4.25; Lucian, *Abdic.* 21; *Peregr.* 11; Achilles Tatius, *Leuc. Clit.* 5.22.2; Josephus, *A.J.* 19.189; *B.J.* 24.473; Diogenes Laertius, *Vit. phil.* 6.96. For further discussion and examples, see David Fredrickson, "God, Christ, and All Things in 1 Corinthians 15:28," *WW* 18 (1998): 254–63.

    124. The phrase is also found in Dio Chrysostom, *Socr.* 1, but there functioning adverbially.

Laertius, *Vit. phil.* 6.96; Achilles Tatius, *Leuc. Clit.* 5.22.2), to political leadership (Athenagoras, *Leg.* 16.1; Demosthenes, *Cor.* 43; Josephus, *A.J.* 19.189), to personal influence (Josephus, *B.J.* 24.473), to military command (Herodotus, *Hist.* 3.157).[125] But in each case, the predicate πάντα or πάντα ἐν πᾶσιν describes the subject as entirely and completely fulfilling the needs and wishes of another or others, so that nothing else or no one else could possibly be desired.[126] So, for example, Hipparchia would have nothing to do with any of her suitors, because to her Crates was "everything" (Diogenes Laertius, *Vit. phil.* 6.96, ἀλλὰ πάντα ἦν Κράτης αὐτῇ). The perfidious Zopyrus was "everything" to the Babylonians, for they looked to him alone for their safety and defense (Herodotus, *Hist.* 3.157, πάντα δὴ τοῖσι Βαβυλωνίοισι Ζώπυρος). Roman subjects honor their rulers as "all in all," for it is to them that they look to fulfill their needs (Athenagoras, *Leg.* 16,1, ὑμᾶς δὲ πάντα ἐν πᾶσιν ἄγουσι τῇ δόξῃ). To be "all things" (πάντα) or "all things in all" (πάντα ἐν πᾶσιν) is to be, in relation to another or others, all-important, all-sufficing, and all-fulfilling.

In what sense, then, is God "all in all" (τὰ πάντα ἐν πᾶσιν) in 1 Cor 15:28?[127] The wider ancient usage of the term we have traced, with its connotations of love, attachment, and fulfillment of all needs and desires, provides the key to Paul's meaning here.[128] At the same time, in applying it to God, Paul imbues this expression with new dimensions and power. It denotes the fulfillment of all things in God (cf. Rom 11:36, ἐξ αὐτοῦ καὶ δι' αὐτοῦ καὶ εἰς αὐτὸν τὰ πάντα; Col 1:16, τὰ πάντα δι' αὐτοῦ καὶ εἰς αὐτὸν ἔκτισται). It denotes the establishment of the creator God's kingdom and saving rule over the entire cosmos.[129] And it denotes the full revelation

---

125. The instances in Appian, *Bell. civ.* 2.4.25; Lucian, *Abdic.* 21; *Peregr.* 11 are in my view doubtful parallels, as in those passages πάντα occurs as the last in a series and has the sense "everything else besides."

126. Cf. the fuller and illuminating discussion in Fredrickson, "All Things," 257–60.

127. The manuscript evidence for the omission of the article (A B D* 33 81 1739) is stronger than the evidence for its inclusion (ℵ D¹ 1175 1881 Byz). However, in the vast majority of instances of this expression within ancient literature, in both the shorter form πάντα and the fuller form πάντα ἐν πᾶσιν, the word πάντα is anarthrous. Copyists would therefore have a natural tendency, whether deliberate or unintentional, to conform this familiar expression to its more usual form. The article should therefore be retained. The dative plural should be taken, like τὰ πάντα, as neuter (Wolff, 390; Thiselton, 1239; Conzelmann, 275). The addition of ἐν πᾶσιν functions to further emphasize the concept of universality and completeness already present in τὰ πάντα.

128. Rightly Fredrickson, "All Things," 260. The expression, of course, has nothing to do with pantheism or a confusion of creator and cosmos but must be understood within Paul's Jewish context; see Dieter Zeller, "Die Formel εἶναι τὰ πάντα ἐν πᾶσιν (1 Kor 15,28)," *ZNW* 101 (2010): 148–52; Schrage, 186–87; Conzelmann, 275.

129. Contra Fredrickson, "All Things," 254–56, 260–62. This facet of Paul's thought here is recognized by almost all expositors; see e.g., Zeller, "Formel," 152; Wolff, 390.

of the glory and wonder of God, what one might call "the Godness of God." Paul's rhetorical flourish, in climaxing ten instances of the word πᾶς in 15:24–28 with God becoming πάντα ἐν πᾶσιν in 15:28, is almost playful, but it has the weightiest of points: only by Christ's abolishing of "all" opposing powers (15:24), his conquest of "all" enemies (15:25), and the subjection of "all things" to him (15:27–28b), can God become "all in all" (15:28c). Christ must abolish all his enemies, in order that he may bring the universal saving reign of God.

And now we can clearly see how 15:24–28 fits within the chapter as a whole. For if the dead are not raised (15:12–19), the last enemy, death, is not abolished (15:26). And if the last enemy remains an unconquered power alongside God, God cannot be "all in all" (15:28). That is why the kingdom of Christ "must" (15:25, δεῖ) culminate in his conquest of death (15:26). Without the resurrection, God cannot be God. "The one who denies the resurrection of the dead, denies God's power over death; he thereby denies the sure hope, that God in the end will be 'all in all.' And thereby he ultimately denies God himself."[130] And that is why Paul in 15:34 will describe the Corinthian deniers of the resurrection as "without knowledge of God" (ἀγνωσίαν γὰρ θεοῦ τινες ἔχουσιν). Only through the conquest of death, which is the negation of God's good creation (15:21–22, 54–55), can the creator God's kingship over all creation be established.[131] "Only so can God be God in the end as well as in the beginning."[132] Through the resurrection of the dead, God will be all in all. It will be the final triumph of God.

---

130. Andreas Lindemann as quoted in Wolff, 390 n. 234.
131. Cf. Martin Hauger, "Die Deutung der Auferweckung Jesu Christi durch Paulus," in *Die Wirklichkeit der Auferstehung* (ed. Hans-Joachim Eckstein and Michael Welker; Neukirchen-Vluyn: Neukirchener, 2002), 43, 58.
132. Brendan Byrne, "Eschatologies of Resurrection and Destruction: The Biblical Significance of Paul's Dispute with the Corinthians," *DRev* 104 (1986): 296.

CHAPTER 9

## *The Futility of Taking Up the Cross without the Resurrection*

15:29–34

In vv. 29–34 the reader encounters a remarkable shift in style. In contrast with the ornate and sonorous sentences of vv. 20–28, we find here an informal and lively style—short and simple sentences, paratactic syntax, rhetorical questions, imperatives, exclamations, and quotations. These are all features of the *diatribe*, a rhetorical mode widely used by ancient philosophers and moralists to spice up their philosophical discourses. As Abraham J. Malherbe showed in a classic study of the passage, "the language and style of the diatribe are concentrated here to an unusually high degree."[1] Paul's use of four rhetorical questions within the short space of 15:29–32 and his rapid shift from third-person (15:29) to first-person (15:30–32) to second-person verbs (15:33–34) add to the liveliness of the style.

But how do these verses function within the chapter? Interpreters generally regard the passage as a series of *arguments* for the resurrection. And this leads to their second assumption, the conclusion that the passage is a series of *ad hominem* arguments—that is, pragmatic arguments that appeal to the will and emotions but are not logically or philosophically compelling.[2] But this is mistaken. And the mistake lies in the first assumption—the belief that Paul is here presenting arguments for the resurrection. He is doing no such thing. Rather, Paul here demonstrates that, apart from the resurrection, the Christian life of disciple-

---

1. Abraham J. Malherbe, "The Beasts at Ephesus," *JBL* 87 (1968): 72. For Malherbe's discussion of these features, see 72–73.
2. So Schrage, 232–33; Lindemann, 350; Fitzmyer, 577–78; Fee, 842–43.

ship—the bearing of sufferings, privations, and dangers for the sake of Christ—is futile and vain. The passage thus takes up a major theme of the chapter—the vanity and futility of the gospel, kerygma, and faith apart from the hope of the resurrection (15:2, 14, 17, 58). Specifically, 15:29–34 continues and expands upon the thought of 15:12–19. The if-clauses in 15:29 and 15:32 (εἰ ... νεκροὶ οὐκ ἐγείρονται) recall the almost identical clauses in 15:15–16 and thus 15:12–19 as a whole.[3] But 15:29–34 marks an advance on the thought of 15:12–19. There Paul, after arguing that the gospel and faith were in vain apart from the resurrection, concluded in 15:19 with the claim that, apart from the hope of the resurrection, Christ followers are more wretched than all human beings. Why *more* wretched? The reason is something Paul assumed but did not explain in v. 19. Verses 29–34 provide the answer. Authentic discipleship to Christ, as exemplified in Paul and the other apostles, is cruciform, involving dangers, sufferings, privations, and daily death for the sake of Christ (15:30–32). But, if there is no resurrection, these sacrifices are futile and pointless (15:32). Those who bring such afflictions on themselves for the sake of such an illusion are not only wretched, but more wretched than all others. Verses 29–34 thus provide the necessary complement and sequel to 15:12–19, and point ahead to the chapter's concluding exhortation to steadfastness in 15:58.

But the full significance of the passage and its function within the chapter can only be appreciated when we grasp the way in which it brings to a climax a central theme of the whole epistle—Paul's Christlike example of sufferings and self-sacrifice for the sake of the gospel. Throughout the letter, Paul warns the Corinthians against sexual immorality, idolatrous practices, greed, and indifference to the weak as incompatible with a saving union with Christ (5:1–13; 6:1–8, 9–11, 12–20; 8:1–13; 9:24–27; 10:1–22; 11:17–34). As the antidote, he offers himself, his fellow apostles, and his coworkers as living examples of Christ (4:14–21; 9:1–27; 10:31–11:1). He does this most fulsomely in the "hardship catalogue" of 4:9–13. Therefore it is highly significant that there is a striking relationship between 4:9–13 and 15:30–32. These two passages are both hardship catalogues, the only two in the letter. The words πεινῶμεν καὶ διψῶμεν ("we hunger and thirst") in 4:11 contrast with φάγωμεν καὶ πίωμεν ("let us eat and drink") in 15:32. Both catalogues speak of Paul's *hourly* afflictions: ἄχρι τῆς ἄρτι <u>ὥρας</u> ("until the present *hour*") in 4:11 and πᾶσαν <u>ὥραν</u> ("throughout every *hour*") in 15:30. But there is a certain heightening in 15:30, for whereas 4:11 speaks of Paul's hourly *afflictions*, 15:30 speaks of his hourly *dangers*. Finally, Paul's reference to the apostles as ἐπιθανάτιοι ("ones condemned to death") in 4:9 has its only parallels in the letter in 15:31 (καθ' ἡμέραν ἀποθνῄσκω "daily I die") and in Paul's fight with the beasts at Ephesus in 15:32. The two passages thus have

---

3. Cf. Collins, 558; Robertson & Plummer, 362.

*The Futility of Taking Up the Cross without the Resurrection*

an important relationship within the letter. First Corinthians 15:30–32, in drawing out the implications of the earlier catalogue's description of the apostles as "given over to death" (ἐπιθανάτιοι, 4:9), *completes* the hardship catalogue of 4:9–13 and provides the climactic description of Paul's apostolic example within the letter.

We have already seen that Paul in 15:29–34 is not, as so many scholars assume, offering "arguments" for the resurrection but rather is showing that the Christian life of discipleship, with its hardship and sufferings, is vain and futile apart from the resurrection. We can now see that he is doing much more. He is once again, for the final and climactic time within the letter, fleshing out and modeling that life of cruciform discipleship and thereby calling and exhorting the Corinthians to the same commitment of total devotion to Christ. These verses, together with vv. 9–10, 19, 45, 48, and 58, show plainly that 1 Cor 15 is not only doctrinal and didactic but also hortatory and paraenetic. In this chapter, "Paul is not only intent on persuading the recipients to believe in resurrection; he also wants them to adopt certain ethical behaviors."[4] Chapter 15 of 1 Corinthians is not only about doctrine. Rather, in this chapter Paul is also exhorting the Corinthians to discipleship, calling them to conform their present lives to Christ's cross, sufferings, and death, and providing as the model his own apostolic life of suffering for the sake of Christ.[5]

In 15:29–34, as we will see, Paul continues to confront those at Corinth who deny the resurrection head-on, for the "some" (τινες) who are without knowledge of God in 15:34 are clearly identical to the "some" (τινες) of 15:12, who say there is no resurrection. As we have seen, those who deny the resurrection in chapter 15 are identical with the self-professed wise at Corinth, puffed up by their philosophical knowledge, whom Paul opposed in the first four chapters of the letter (1:18–4:21). This fact explains why it is here in 15:29–34 that Paul not only brings to a climax the theme of his apostolic example of the Christlike life (4:9–13) but also, as we will see, brings to a climax other key themes of 1:18–4:21, including boasting in the Lord rather than human wisdom (15:31; cf. 1:26–31; 3:18–23) and the incapacity of the world through its wisdom to know God (15:34; cf. 1:21; 2:6, 8, 11, 14, 16).[6] This fact also explains at least one reason for Paul's choice here of the style of the diatribe,

---

4. Matt O'Reilly, *Paul and the Resurrected Body: Social Identity and Ethical Practice* (ESEC 22; Atlanta: SBL Press, 2020), 93; cf. 72.

5. So, insightfully, Rob A. Fringer, "Dying to Be the Church: 1 Corinthians 15 and Paul's Shocking Revelation about Death and Resurrection," *ERT* 41 (2017): 174–84; cf. G. Walter Hansen, "Resurrection and the Christian Life in Paul's Letters," in *Life in the Face of Death: The Resurrection Message in the New Testament* (ed. Richard N. Longenecker; Grand Rapids: Eerdmans, 1998), 203–24 (see esp. 203–6); Reasoner, on 15:29–34.

6. The way in which 15:29–34 gathers together and completes key themes of the letter provides the decisive evidence against the theory of William O. Walker Jr. that 15:29–34 is a

CHAPTER 9

a stock item of the ancient philosophical repertoire. Paul is here once again, as he did in the logical syllogisms of 15:12–19, meeting the self-professed wise at Corinth on their own ground and beating them at their own game.

VERSE 29

*Since otherwise, what recourse will they have who are baptized for the sake of the dead? If, in fact, the dead are not raised, why are they indeed baptized for their sake?*

Paul begins this section of the letter with reference to a phenomenon well known to the Corinthians but baffling and enigmatic to modern scholars—baptism for or because of the dead. Dozens of different interpretations of this verse have been suggested through the centuries, including a number of new interpretations within recent years. Space precludes a rehearsal of all the various interpretive solutions that have been offered, many of which are quite far-fetched.[7] We can focus here only on the major interpretive options.

Despite the bewildering variety of readings, a few main lines of interpretation may be identified. The majority view, which holds sway over the others, asserts that Paul refers to a practice of vicarious or proxy baptism of the living on behalf of the dead.[8] Scholars often suggest that this proxy baptism was carried out on behalf of those who had newly come to faith but had died prior to receiving baptism.[9] A recent and influential variant on this view is that of Richard E. DeMaris, who imagines a second proxy baptism on behalf of those already baptized as a rite of passage at the time of their deaths.[10]

Three substantive challenges have been offered to the majority view in recent years. According to Michael Hull, within the phrase ὑπὲρ τῶν νεκρῶν the preposition ὑπέρ bears a causal sense, and τῶν νεκρῶν refers to the dead in Christ who will

---

non-Pauline interpolation; see "1 Corinthians 15:29–34 as a Non-Pauline Interpolation," *CBQ* 69 (2007): 84–103.

7. For a fuller discussion, see Joel R. White, "Recent Challenges to the *communis opinio* on 1 Corinthians 15.29," *CurBR* 10 (2012): 379–95.

8. So Fitzmyer, 580; Collins, 556; Schrage, 239–40; Lindemann, 350–51; Schreiner, 317; Fee, 849; Karl Barth, *The Resurrection of the Dead* (trans. H. J. Stenning; 1933; repr., Eugene, OR: Wipf & Stock, 2003), 174–75; and many others. A recent reaffirmation of the majority position is found in Daniel B. Sharp, "Vicarious Baptism for the Dead: 1 Corinthians 15:29," *StBibAnt* 6 (2014): 36–66.

9. E.g., Collins, 556; Fee, 849; Schreiner, 317.

10. Richard E. DeMaris, "Corinthian Religion and Baptism for the Dead (1 Corinthians 15:29): Insights from Archaeology and Anthropology," *JBL* 114 (1995): 661–82. Following DeMaris, in all essentials, is Terri Moore, *The Mysteries, Resurrection, and 1 Corinthians 15: Comparative Methodology and Exegesis* (Lanham, MD: Fortress Academic, 2018), 116–22.

rise. Paul's reference is thus, he argues, to baptism "on account of the dead"—that is, to baptism as an act of faith in the resurrection to come.[11] Hull's view is similar to the common patristic interpretation, which we find, for example, in John Chrysostom. In this interpretation, "the dead" refers to the bodies of all the dead in Christ and especially to one's own now mortal and soon dead body. Thus by "baptism for the sake of the dead" Paul refers to that confession of faith and hope in the resurrection that is part and parcel of every Christian baptism.[12]

Maria Raeder argues that the situation envisaged in 15:29 is the conversion and baptism of the family members and friends of deceased Christians, as motivated by the hope of reunion with them at the resurrection.[13] On this view, the preposition ὑπέρ has a purposive sense; they are baptized for the dead in the sense that their purpose is to be reunited with their deceased loved ones at the resurrection.[14]

Finally, John D. Reaume argues, similarly to Hull, for a causal sense of ὑπέρ in 15:29. But Reaume suggests that those baptized "because of the dead" are individuals brought to conversion and baptism as a result of the testimony and influence of deceased Christians.[15] Reaume points out that "many individuals in the early church were influenced by the testimony of other believers who had recently died or who were martyred."[16] Reaume posits that this is the situation underlying Paul's language of being "baptized because of the dead" in 15:29: individuals brought to faith in Christ through the witness of Christ followers who had later died.

We find, then, four major lines of interpretation regarding the meaning of baptism for or because of the dead in 1 Cor 15:29: (1) vicarious or proxy baptism on behalf of those who died unbaptized (the dominant view); (2) baptism as an act of faith in the resurrection of all in Christ and thus in one's own resurrection (Hull); (3) baptism motivated by the hope of reunion with deceased Christian loved ones at the resurrection (Raeder); and (4) baptism as a result of the testimony and influence while they were living of Christians who had since died (Reaume).[17]

---

11. Michael F. Hull, *Baptism on Account of the Dead (1 Corinthians 15:29): An Act of Faith in the Resurrection* (Atlanta: SBL Press, 2005). Following Hull, with minor differences, are Ciampa & Rosner, 780–86.

12. Chrysostom, *Hom. 1 Cor.* 40.2; cf. 23.3; see also Tertullian, *Marc.* 5.10. Similarly Garland, 716–19; Cremer, 128.

13. Maria Raeder, "Vikariatstaufe in I Cor 15:29?" *ZNW* 46 (1955): 258–60. Raeder's view is followed by Joachim Jeremias, "'Flesh and Blood Cannot Inherit the Kingdom of God' (I Cor. xv. 50)," *NTS* 2 (1956): 155; Thiselton, 1248–49.

14. Raeder, "Vikariatstaufe," 260; Jeremias, "Flesh and Blood," 155.

15. John D. Reaume, "Another Look at 1 Corinthians 15:29, 'Baptized for the Dead,'" *BSac* 152 (1995): 457–75.

16. Reaume, "Another Look," 475.

17. Other recently proposed solutions, which are touched upon below but whose complexity or implausibility prohibits a full summary and discussion here, include: Jerome Murphy-

## CHAPTER 9

In order to assess these various proposed interpretive solutions, we must turn to a detailed exegesis of the verse. Any interpretation of this verse, to be viable, must fit with: (1) the syntax and vocabulary of the verse; (2) the context of 15:29–34; (3) Paul's theology of baptism; and (4) our knowledge of primitive Christianity. Verse 29 poses a unique challenge to the interpreter, and even the most painstaking analysis may not unveil all its obscurities. But I believe a close reading will permit us to judge among the proposed interpretations and to shed further light on this verse.

*Since otherwise, what recourse will they have.* For τί ποιήσουσιν, Robertson and Plummer neatly lay out the options considered by expositors: "either 'what will they have recourse to?' or 'what will they gain?'"[18] The parallel question in 15:32—"what to me is the benefit?"—might seem to suggest the latter meaning.[19] However, the expression τί ποιήσουσιν cannot have this meaning. Throughout ancient Greek literature, clauses with the interrogative τί followed by some form of the verb ποιέω in the future tense always express a state of utter perplexity, despair, and dashed hopes with nowhere to turn (e.g., Isa 10:3 LXX, καὶ τί ποιήσουσιν ἐν τῇ ἡμέρᾳ τῆς ἐπισκοπῆς; Jer 4:30 LXX; 5:31 LXX; Hos 9:5 LXX; Sir 2:14; 1 En. 101.2; Plutarch, *Vit. pud.* 531a). There are no exceptions to this. The question τί ποιήσουσιν thus means "what recourse will they have?" The phrase implies a personal and catastrophic loss for those baptized for the dead's sake, if there is no resurrection of the dead.

*who are baptized for the sake of the dead?* The verb βαπτίζω is used here, as throughout Paul's letters and in particular 1 Corinthians (1:13–17; 10:2; 12:13), to denote the early Christian rite of initiation through water. This excludes the interpretation of DeMaris, which claims that Paul uses the term "baptize" here of an entirely different rite invented by the Corinthians.[20] As we have seen, the word νεκρός, used twice in the verse, is a key term throughout the chapter, where it is always used in its literal sense (15:12 [2×], 13, 15, 16, 20, 21, 29 [2×], 32, 35, 42, 52).[21] The hallmark

---

O'Connor, "'Baptized for the Dead' (1 Cor xv, 29): A Corinthian Slogan," *RB* 88 (1981): 532–43; Joel R. White, "'Baptized on Account of the Dead': The Meaning of 1 Corinthians 15:29 in Its Context," *JBL* 116 (1997): 487–99; James E. Patrick, "Living Rewards for Dead Apostles: 'Baptized for the Dead' in 1 Corinthians 15:29," *NTS* 52 (2006): 71–85.

18. Robertson & Plummer, 359; cf. Schrage, 235.
19. So Garland, 716; Ciampa & Rosner, 780–81; Fitzmyer, 580.
20. DeMaris, "Corinthian Religion," 662–63, 671–77. The proposal of Murphy-O'Connor, "Corinthian Slogan," also founders on this point, among others.
21. This excludes the interpretations of Murphy-O'Connor ("Corinthian Slogan") and White

of several implausible readings, both in the past and more recently, is the interpretation of βαπτίζω, νεκρός, or both words differently from their normal, literal sense. However, each of the four main lines of interpretation sketched above are agreed in understanding these terms in their usual sense.

Where these four interpretations differ markedly is in their understanding of the precise sense of the preposition ὑπέρ that Paul intends here. The majority position (view 1 above) takes this preposition in what is by far its most frequent sense, that of advantage or benefit, thus "for" or "on behalf of."[22] The alternative views discussed above all take ὑπέρ in a causal sense, "because of" or "on account of." This is a less common but nonetheless well-attested meaning of the term. BDAG, for instance, gives as a second meaning of the word, "marker of the moving cause or reason, *because of, for the sake of, for*."[23] The preposition used in this sense expresses the motive, cause, or occasion of the action.[24]

In which sense does Paul use the preposition in 15:29? Here contextual, historical, and theological factors are in my judgment decisive against the majority view. We have no evidence for a practice of proxy baptism in ancient Christianity apart from practices by later heretical groups, such as the Marcionites, which were clearly dependent on 1 Cor 15:29. Nor do we have evidence for analogous rites in the wider pagan world.[25] Moreover, the concept of vicarious baptism is entirely inconsistent with the theology of baptism we find in Paul's letters and especially in 1 Corinthians. Paul has a sacramental and miraculous understanding of baptism as the means through which believers are brought into saving union with Christ (1 Cor 6:9–11; 10:1–4; 12:12–13; cf. Rom 6:1–11; Gal 3:26–28). Within Paul's sacramental theology of baptism, the very idea of a second baptism, undergone as a proxy for another, is unthinkable. That Paul would choose to feature such a practice in 15:29, alongside his own apostolic sufferings in imitation of Christ in 15:30–32, is virtually inconceivable.

Such historical, theological, and contextual considerations in my view exclude the possibility of taking ὑπέρ here in its common sense of advantage or benefit, as expressing a conception of vicarious baptism, and it requires us to take ὑπέρ in its

---

("Meaning"), which depend on reading either one or both occurrences of νεκρός in 15:29 in a nonliteral sense.

22. See BDAG, s.v. "ὑπέρ" (A.1); Robinson, s.v. "ὑπέρ" (1).

23. BDAG, s.v. "ὑπέρ" (A.2); cf. Robinson, s.v. "ὑπέρ" (2); Thayer, s.v. "ὑπέρ" (I.4).

24. We see it used in this sense in John 11:4; Acts 5:41; 9:16; 15:26; 21:13; Rom 1:5; 15:9; 1 Cor 10:30; 2 Cor 12:10; Eph 5:20; Phil 1:29; 2 Thess 1:5; and 3 John 7.

25. See D. Zeller, "Gibt es religionsgeschichtliche Parallelen zur Taufe für die Toten (1 Kor 15,29)?" *ZNW* 98 (2007): 68–76. Cf. White, "Challenges," 384–85; Reaume, "Another Look," 458–59; Fee, 846.

CHAPTER 9

less common but nonetheless well-attested sense as marking motive or cause. But how are we to understand this cause or motive? In Hull's thesis (view 2 above), the motive was the hope of sharing in the coming resurrection to life of all those in Christ. In Paul's theology this is true of every baptism and all the baptized (Rom 6:1–11). However, strikingly, the baptized are here spoken of in the *third person*. Paul is thus evidently not speaking here of all the baptized but of a subset among the faithful, who undergo baptism within a particular context or set of circumstances. The interpretation of Hull, which sees Paul as here describing baptism as it is undergone by every believer, is therefore excluded.

This leaves views 3 and 4. Raeder (view 3 above) argues that the motive was the desire, through conversion to Christ, to be reunited with loved ones in the resurrection. Reaume (view 4 above) contends that the motive or cause for conversion and baptism was the prior testimony of now deceased Christians. Is there a way to decide between these two alternatives? We must continue our exegesis to discover an answer.

*If, in fact, the dead are not raised.* The if-clause here recalls the almost identical clauses in vv. 15 and 16, thus recalling the claim of "some" that there is no resurrection in 15:12.[26] Paul skillfully inserts ὅλως here, which when used after εἰ, as it is here, frequently means "in truth, actually, in fact" (T. Job 31.1; Athanasius, *Inc.* 50.6; *C. Ar.* 2.19.3). The thought here is "if, in fact (as they claim)," and thus is another way in which Paul recalls the claim of 15:12 that there is no resurrection of the dead.

*why are they indeed baptized for their sake?* It is possible that the καί is here adjunctive "also."[27] However, it is more likely intensive, as frequently in questions.[28] The καί adds a certain force to Paul's rhetorical question and implies its unanswerability.

There is an important further key to Paul's argument that has been universally ignored by interpreters. In v. 30, Paul connects the argument there to the previous argument in v. 29 by means of an adjunctive καί before the pronoun ἡμεῖς. Scholars have recognized this but have assumed the καί governs only the pronoun. They have thus assumed that this adjunct signifies merely that Paul in v. 30 is passing on from the example of those baptized for the sake of the dead to his own

---

26. Michael Bachmann, "1Kor 15,12f.: 'Resurrection of the Dead (= Christians)'?" *ZNW* 92 (2001): 297; cf. Collins, 558.
27. So Rob., *Gram.*, 1180.
28. BDR §442.8; Robertson & Plummer, 360.

example and that of his fellow apostles.[29] However, in ancient Greek usage an adjunctive καί before a *nominative* pronoun governs not only that pronoun *but also the following verb*.[30] I know of no exceptions to this rule. The adjunctive καί in 15:30 thus connects not only the pronoun but also the verb to the preceding verse. The verb in 15:30 is κινδυνεύομεν ("we are in danger"), and the clause τί καὶ ἡμεῖς κινδυνεύομεν means "why are we, too, in danger?" This indicates that *those baptized on account of the dead in 15:29, like the apostles in 15:30, also encountered by this very action some form of danger.*

This sheds a wondrous new light on v. 29. In 15:30–32, Paul will present himself (together with his fellow apostles) as a model of radical discipleship, enduring sufferings, afflictions, and dangers out of devotion to Christ, and he will drive home the vanity and futility of these sufferings, if there is no resurrection. We can now see that v. 29 functions in the same way. Those who endanger themselves by their baptism for the sake of the dead are models of costly devotion to Christ, and their example flags up the futility of such costly discipleship, if there is no resurrection.

In what way did those baptized because of the dead endanger themselves by this action? This was clearly well known to Paul and the Corinthians, but we are left with no solid information to go on. What we can know for certain, I believe, stops here. But we might make a leap of disciplined historical imagination in order to offer a suggestion. Even in this early period we know of apostles, leaders, and others put to death for their witness to Christ (Acts 7:54–60; 12:1–2; 22:4; 26:9–10; Rev 2:13). Following Reaume's conjecture that the motive for baptism was the witness of Christ followers now deceased (view 4 above), and adding to this our solid knowledge that the baptized placed themselves at risk by this action, we might surmise that those baptized for the sake of the dead were those who, moved by the courageous witness of martyrs to the point of death, united themselves to the Christian community through confession of faith and baptism in the immediate aftermath of these martyrdoms and at great risk to themselves. Such a phenomenon—conversion motivated by witness of martyrdom—is certainly documented in later periods. According to Tertullian, writing near the close of the second century, it was an experience not uncommon:

> The more we are put to death by you, the more our numbers increase: the blood of Christians is seed.... For who is not deeply moved by the contemplation of such contempt of death, so as to inquire what lies at the heart of it? Who, when he has made this inquiry, does not himself become a disciple? (*Apol.* 50.13–15)

---

29. E.g., Barrett, 364; Ciampa & Rosner, 786.
30. E.g., Matt 6:12; 15:3; Luke 3:14; John 9:40; 11:16; 21:3; 1 Cor 4:8; 2 Cor 1:6; 4:13; Gal 4:3; 1 John 3:16; 4:17; 3 John 12; Basil of Caesarea, *Ep.* 236.4.

CHAPTER 9

We might also surmise that the account of such heroic actions would be passed on by Paul to his converts as well as told and retold in his churches. Paul, then, we may imagine, reminds the Corinthians of these well-known figures here, pointing to them as models of taking up the cross for the sake of Christ and as an illustration of the vanity and futility of such costly discipleship apart from the hope of the resurrection.

## Verse 30

*Why are we also in danger through every hour?*

Paul now adds a third rhetorical question following the first two in 15:29. Who are the "we" of this verse? Some interpreters have suggested that Paul here refers merely to himself.[31] Others have suggested that the "we" refers to all Christians who incur great risks for the sake of the gospel.[32] The answer is provided by the way in which, as we saw in the introduction to 15:29–34, the catalogue of hardships here in 15:30–32 recalls and completes the hardship catalogue of 4:9–13. For that passage dramatically portrayed the sufferings of "we the apostles" (4:9, ἡμᾶς τοὺς ἀποστόλους). The "we" of 15:30 also recalls the apostolic "we" of 15:11, 14, and 15. The "we" of 15:30 are accordingly, as John Chrysostom recognized, "all the apostles together."[33] Paul refers to himself and his fellow apostles.

The adjunctive καί ("we also") links the example of the apostles here to the previous example of those baptized on account of the dead in 15:29. It is universally supposed that καί modifies solely the pronoun ἡμεῖς.[34] But as we saw in our discussion of v. 29, an adjunctive καί in this position with a nominative pronoun always governs both pronoun and verb. The thought is that "we, too, *are in danger.*" This indicates that those baptized for the dead in 15:29, like the apostles in 15:30, encountered by that action some form of danger. (For further discussion, see the commentary on v. 29.)

The dangers and risks undertaken by Paul and his fellow apostles are expressed forcefully in two different ways. First, the present tense of the verb expresses "the continuing and consistent nature of the danger."[35] Second, Paul's reference to each hour—especially through his use of the accusative case, which denotes duration ("through every hour")—expresses the constant and unrelenting character of the

---

31. So Barth, *Resurrection*, 176.
32. So Fitzmyer, 581; Lindemann, 351; Robertson & Plummer, 361.
33. Chrysostom, *Hom. 1 Cor.* 40.3.
34. So Ciampa & Rosner, 786; Barrett, 364.
35. O'Reilly, *Resurrected Body*, 74.

*The Futility of Taking Up the Cross without the Resurrection*

dangers. But if there is no resurrection of the dead, these dangers faced by Paul and the other apostles are in vain and to no purpose.

## Verse 31

*Each day I die, I affirm on oath, by my boasting in you, brothers and sisters, which I have in Christ Jesus our Lord.*

Paul continues the hardship catalogue begun in 15:30, now with the focus on his own apostolic sufferings.

*Each day I die.* Paul here and in v. 32 recalls and expands upon his description of himself and his fellow apostles as "men given over to death" (4:9, ἐπιθανάτιοι) in the hardship catalogue of 4:9–13, of which 15:30–32 (as we saw in the introduction to the passage) provides the climactic rhetorical reiteration. The prepositional phrase καθ' ἡμέραν ("each day"), put first for emphasis, along with the iterative present tense of the verb together stress Paul's daily experience of death for Christ's sake. The thought is very similar to Ps 43:23 LXX, which Paul in Rom 8:36 will also quote directly: ὅτι ἕνεκεν σοῦ θανατούμεθα ὅλην τὴν ἡμέραν ("because for your sake we are put to death through all the day"). The thought and the wording are also strikingly reminiscent of the command of Jesus in Luke 9:23–24 to take up the cross καθ' ἡμέραν ("each day") and lose one's life for his sake.[36] Paul here continues to offer himself as a model of cruciform discipleship to Christ.

*I affirm on oath.* The particle νή with an accusative of oaths is a classical construction, found only here in the New Testament.[37] The oath marker νή is strongly affirmative, meaning "truly, yes!"[38] It is usually followed by the name of a god or goddess, or something of ultimate importance to the speaker.[39] Paul here "swears by that which is dearest to him."[40] The content of Paul's oath is thus carefully chosen to exhort and instruct the Corinthians.

*by my boasting in you, brothers and sisters, which I have in Christ Jesus our Lord.* The possessive adjective that modifies the word "boasting" is equivalent in function

---

36. Ciampa & Rosner, 787.
37. BDR §441.1; Rob., *Gram.*, 487; cf. Reasoner, on 15:31.
38. Rob., *Gram.*, 1150.
39. Ciampa & Rosner, 788; cf. Barrett, 365.
40. Fee, 852.

to an objective genitive (i.e., boasting in you or of you).[41] New Testament scholars often assume this construction is unusual or rare.[42] But this use of the possessive adjective with the force of an objective genitive is in fact, as Kühner and Gerth point out, "very common."[43] Further instances in the New Testament include Luke 22:19; Rom 11:31; 15:4; and 1 Cor 11:24.[44]

The address ἀδελφοί "brothers and sisters," although lacking in many manuscripts (P[46] D F G 1739 1881, most Byzantine texts), is strongly supported in our best witnesses (ℵ A B 33 81) and must be regarded as the original reading. The address thus occurs four times in the chapter (15:1, 31, 50, 58) and twenty times in the letter as a whole. In Paul ἀδελφοί always adds additional emphasis. This address, combined with an oath, lends extraordinary force to the content of Paul's asseveration.

Paul swears by "my boasting in you, brothers and sisters, which I have in Christ Jesus our Lord." Boasting is an important theme in 1 Corinthians, and the language of boasting (καυχάομαι, καύχημα, καύχησις) recurs throughout the letter. The programmatic statement of the theme is in 1:31: "Let the one who boasts, boast in the Lord" (ὁ καυχώμενος ἐν κυρίῳ καυχάσθω). This theme predominates in 1:18–4:21, where the purpose of God's reversal of human wisdom through the gospel is that all boasting may be in the Lord (1:26–31; 3:18–23). Paul models this Christ-centered way of boasting in 9:15–16. Opposed to this is boasting before God (1:29), in human beings (3:21), in one's self (4:7; 13:3), and in liberty for vice (5:6). Paul relates this wrongful boasting closely to the persistent theme of the "self-inflation" (φυσιόω) of some at Corinth (4:6, 18, 19; 5:2; 8:1; 13:4).

This theme of boasting comes to a conclusion within the letter in 15:31. This verse is not only the final occurrence of the language of boasting within the letter, but it is also the only place in the letter outside 1:31 where we find the explicit language of boasting "in the Lord" (1:31, ἐν κυρίῳ; 15:31, ἐν Χριστῷ Ἰησοῦ τῷ κυρίῳ ἡμῶν). Verse 31 of chapter 15 thus forms an *inclusio* with the letter's programmatic statement of this theme in 1:31. Thus 1 Cor 15:31 forms the climactic statement within the letter of the theme of boasting in the Lord, providing further evidence for the unity of the epistle and its intended climax in chapter 15.

How does this verse, then, function within the epistle? Paul here brings to a climax for the Corinthians his Christlike model of boasting only in the Lord (1:31;

---

41. BDR §285 n. 3; Rob., *Gram.*, 685.
42. So Fee, 852 n. 248 ("rare").
43. Kühner-G., 2.1:560 n. 11 (§454).
44. Rob., *Gram.*, 685.

*The Futility of Taking Up the Cross without the Resurrection*

9:15–16; 15:9–10).[45] Paul here implicitly contrasts himself with the boasting in human wisdom and accomplishments (1:29; 3:21; 4:7) and prideful self-inflation (4:6, 18–19; 5:2; 8:1; 13:4) rife among some at Corinth, in particular the self-professed wise whom Paul opposes in the first four chapters of the letter (1:29–3:21; 4:6–7, 18, 19). In this way, Paul continues to offer himself, as he does throughout 15:30–32, as an apostolic example for imitation in his life of pure devotion to Christ.

The *inclusio* formed by 1 Cor 1:31 and 15:31 is also of great theological and christological significance. First Corinthians 1:31 is a quotation of Jer 9:23–24, where in the LXX version κύριος translates the divine name YHWH. Whoever boasts must boast only in YHWH, the God of Israel. In the *inclusio* of 15:31, Paul recalls 1:31 and the boasting alone in the Lord enjoined in Jer 9:23–24 LXX. But here Paul's boasting is "in *Christ Jesus our Lord*" (15:31). Paul thus identifies Jesus as YHWH, the God of Israel. A frequent phenomenon in Paul's epistles is the "christological YHWH texts," that is, passages in which Paul quotes or echoes Old Testament passages about YHWH and understands them as referring to Jesus. The first frame of the *inclusio*, 1 Cor 1:31, is not by itself an explicit christological YHWH text; but in light of the final frame of the *inclusio* in 15:31, it becomes one. The *inclusio* of 1:31 and 15:31 reveals once again Paul's divine and incarnational Christology: Jesus is YHWH, the God of Israel, come in the flesh. This powerful christological affirmation in 15:31 is given extra weight by means of the full christological title "Christ Jesus our Lord." Such a full title (employing "Jesus," "Christ," and "Lord") is found in the letter prior to chapter 15 only in the salutation (1:2–3), the thanksgiving (1:7–9), the body opening (1:10), and at 6:11 and 8:6. But in chapter 15 it occurs twice at key junctures—here in 15:31 and again at the climax of the chapter in 15:57. It is one more way in which we see that chapter 15 forms the deliberate and planned climax of the epistle.

### Verse 32

*If it was for human reasons that I fought with beasts at Ephesus, what to me is the benefit? If the dead are not raised, "Let us eat and drink, for tomorrow we die."*

Paul in this verse continues to set forth his own life as an apostolic model of taking up the cross for the sake of Christ and to show the vanity and futility of such sufferings apart from the hope of the resurrection.

---

45. For this theme elsewhere in Paul's epistles, see Rom 3:27; 4:2; 15:17–18; 2 Cor 10:17; Gal 6:13–14; Phil 3:3.

CHAPTER 9

*If it was for human reasons.* The prepositional phrase κατὰ ἄνθρωπον is "brought forward to the beginning of the protasis for emphasis."[46] This adverbial adjunct denotes generally something done "in a human way" or "from a human standpoint," but its precise nuance varies in Paul depending on the precise point within the context, whether human thinking (Rom 3:5), human origin (Gal 1:11), human way of life (1 Cor 3:3), and so forth. The phrase often has a negative connotation in Paul, being used in implicit contrast with God's ways, presence, or promises (1 Cor 3:3; 9:8; Gal 1:11). This is clearly the case here in 15:32. The precise point within the context is motivation for conduct, as the two previous rhetorical questions using τί "why?" in 15:29–30 show. Abraham J. Malherbe thus expresses the meaning of κατὰ ἄνθρωπον here with precision: "on a merely human level, without a hope of resurrection."[47]

*that I fought with beasts at Ephesus.* Over a century ago, Clayton R. Bowen argued that Paul here refers to an occasion in which he was literally condemned as a criminal to contend, according to the common Roman practice, with wild animals in the arena at Ephesus.[48] However, recent interpreters are virtually unanimous that Paul's statement that he fought with beasts at Ephesus is not meant literally but is a figure of speech referring to struggles with human adversaries.[49] These adversaries have been variously identified. One suggestion is that Paul refers to false teachers whom he opposed in his ministry.[50] Another suggestion is that these opponents were devotees of the huntress goddess Artemis, whose ancient center of worship was at Ephesus.[51] In any case, almost all contemporary interpreters are agreed that Paul's language must be taken metaphorically of human opponents. The fact that it was illegal to condemn a Roman citizen to the beasts, the impossibility that Paul would survive this experience, the absence of any mention of such an event in the book of Acts, and its absence also from Paul's catalogue of hardships in 2 Cor 11:23–29, all render a literal understanding of Paul's statement impossible according to the current consensus.

---

46. Barrett, 365.
47. Malherbe, "Beasts," 80; cf. Schrage, 244–45; Fee, 854.
48. Clayton R. Bowen, "'I Fought with Beasts at Ephesus,'" *JBL* 42 (1923): 59–68. Likewise Godet, 2:393–94.
49. See, for example, Malherbe, "Beasts," 71–72; J. Andrew Doole, "'I Have Fought with Wild Beasts . . . But I Will Stay until Pentecost': What (Else) Can 1 Corinthians Teach Us about Ephesus?" *NovT* 60 (2018): 140–61; Schrage, 242–44; Wolff, 398–99; Fee, 852–53; O'Reilly, *Resurrected Body*, 75–76; Hays, 268; Barth, *Resurrection*, 177; Robertson & Plummer, 362; Sampley, 982–83; Schreiner, 318; Barrett, 366.
50. Malherbe, "Beasts," 79–80.
51. Doole, "Wild Beasts," 147–52.

*The Futility of Taking Up the Cross without the Resurrection*

However, none of these arguments are compelling. Although it was unlawful for Roman citizens to be condemned to combat with the beasts, our evidence is clear that Roman citizens nonetheless could be and were so condemned on various occasions.[52] For instance, in the persecution at Lyons and Vienne in AD 177, Attalus, although a Roman citizen, was condemned to the beasts (Eusebius, *Hist. eccl.* 5.1.44, 50–52). Another instance is the consul Acilius Glabrio's consignment to the beasts during the reign of Domitian (Dio Cassius, *Hist. rom.* 67.14).[53]

The argument that Paul could not have survived such an ordeal gratuitously assumes the impossibility of miraculous divine intervention and is therefore worthless. Moreover, the argument shows no awareness of the unpredictability of wild animals. And in any case, the argument is founded upon a falsehood: instances of individuals surviving combat with beasts in the arena in antiquity, although extremely rare, are documented.[54] The omission of the event from Acts is hardly conclusive, for Acts also omits from its narrative of Paul's career his five scourgings (2 Cor 11:24), two beatings with rods (2 Cor 11:24), three shipwrecks (2 Cor 11:25), his rescue from death by Prisca and Aquila (Rom 16:3–4), and his peril of death in Asia (2 Cor 1:8–11).[55] Moreover, Luke in Acts prefers to highlight the responsible actions of Roman officials toward Christians, and such an egregious violation of Roman law in the treatment of Christians would hardly fit with this agenda. Finally, that Paul would omit reference to this ordeal in the catalogue of hardships in 2 Cor 11:22–33 is readily understandable in light of his previous mention of it here in 1 Cor 15:32 (and possibly in 2 Cor 1:8–11).

These varied arguments, then, for an alleged impossibility of a literal meaning of θηριομαχεῖν in 1 Cor 15:32 are not compelling. We must determine Paul's meaning on the basis of the normal usage of the verb, and the way in which Paul employs it in the context of 1 Cor 15:32. When we do so, the evidence is overwhelming.

The verb θηριομαχεῖν was a technical term for combat with wild animals in the arena.[56] To be sure, the language of wolves, dogs, or wild animals could be used metaphorically to describe cruel taskmasters (Philo, *Mos.* 1.43), false philosophers (Lucian, *Fug.* 19, 23; *Pisc.* 17, 36), or false teachers (Acts 20:29; Phil 3:2; Titus 1:12).[57] However, the specific verb θηριομαχεῖν was never used in connection with such fig-

---

52. For a helpful tally of the evidence, which is substantial, see David J. Williams, *Paul's Metaphors: Their Context and Character* (Peabody, MA: Hendrickson, 1999), 264–65, 281–82 nn. 60–61.
53. For further examples, see Cicero, *Fam.* 10.32.3; Seneca, *Ep.* 99.13.
54. See, for example, Dio Cassius, *Hist. rom.* 67.14. For further discussion and evidence, see Bowen, "Fought with Beasts," 65–66.
55. Cf. Bowen, "Fought with Beasts," 62.
56. Bowen, "Fought with Beasts," 67.
57. Malherbe, "Beasts."

ures. In every instance but one outside 1 Cor 15:32, the verb is used in its literal sense of fighting with beasts at the games. The only instance of a figurative use of the verb is found in Ignatius's letters (Ign. *Rom.* 5.1), where Ignatius uses the term to refer to his struggles with the cruel treatment of his captors. But Ignatius elsewhere uses the verb literally of his own impending consignment to the beasts at Rome (Ign. *Eph.* 1.2; *Trall.* 10). The very real situation of Ignatius's impending fight with the beasts is clearly the setting of Ignatius's figurative use of the verb in *Rom.* 5.1, and the metaphorical sense of the verb there is made evident by the language and context.[58] In 1 Cor 15:32 such contextual factors signaling a metaphorical sense of θηριομαχεῖν are entirely lacking. We can hardly avoid concluding, with Clayton R. Bowen, that "when Paul uses the term without explanation . . . these simple words could not have been understood otherwise than literally by the readers at Corinth."[59]

But it is the context of Paul's statement within the passage that is decisive. The language Paul uses here—that of combat with beasts in the arena—is extraordinary, and unique in his letters. But if Paul here speaks figuratively of struggles with human opponents of his ministry, he is using this extraordinary language to describe a situation he faced on a regular basis, "using a very unusual expression for what was to him a very usual experience."[60] But why, then, did Paul use this exceptional language for such a common and (for him) everyday reality?[61] And why, if Paul is describing a conflict with human opponents, a situation he encountered in almost every city, does he delimit this as taking place specifically "at Ephesus"? The uniqueness of Paul's language here, and his clear reference to a particular incident through the addition of "at Ephesus," must refer to a unique and extraordinary incident that took place in that city. All these factors require a literal meaning of the verb in 15:32.

Moreover, within the context of 15:30–32, where Paul recounts his hourly dangers (15:30) and daily encounters with death (15:31), the fighting with wild beasts in 15:32 must involve, it would seem, some form of life-threatening danger.[62] In fact, the three verbs of 15:30–32 form an ascending "ladder" or "climax" structure: κινδυνεύω ("be in danger"), ἀποθνῄσκω ("die"), θηριομαχέω ("fight with wild beasts").[63] Within this structure, the verb θηριομαχέω is the final and climactic element. It is "the specific and striking illustration of Paul's hourly hazard, of his daily death."[64] But if

58. Bowen, "Fought with Beasts," 66–67.
59. Bowen, "Fought with Beasts," 66.
60. Malberbe, "Beasts," 71.
61. Godet, 2:393.
62. Lindemann, 352.
63. Robertson & Plummer, 362; Wolff, 399.
64. Bowen, "Fought with Beasts," 68.

*The Futility of Taking Up the Cross without the Resurrection*

the verb θηριομαχέω were used here metaphorically to describe mere struggles with human opponents, v. 32 would provide not a fitting climax but a jarring anticlimax. In a passage where Paul is stressing his endurance of deathly perils for the sake of Christ, to move from hourly dangers (15:30) to daily peril of death (15:31) and then to conflicts with heretics or devotees of Artemis hardly makes sense. It does not help to add the proviso, as scholars who take Θηριομαχεῖν figuratively sometimes do, that these heretics or Artemis worshipers must have posed to Paul a mortal peril of some kind.[65] For within the ladder structure of 15:30–32, the verb θηριομαχέω, like the verbs κινδυνεύω and ἀποθνῄσκω, must itself *express* this peril.

The context of 1 Cor 15:30–32 thus demands that Paul's statement be understood in its direct and literal sense. Paul fought with the wild beasts in the arena at Ephesus. And yet he survived the ordeal safe and sound. This reality illumines Paul's language in the hardship catalogue of 4:9–13, which (as we have seen) forms an *inclusio* with 15:30–32, where Paul describes himself and his fellow apostles as "men condemned to death" and "a spectacle to the world, both angels and human beings" (4:9). It furnishes a concrete explanation of why, as Paul reports to the Corinthians, a "great and effective door" of ministry had opened to Paul at Ephesus (16:8–9). And it provides a striking climax to Paul's portrayal within 15:30–32 of his apostolic model of taking up the cross for the sake of Christ.

*what to me is the benefit?* Paul's language of "benefit" (τὸ ὄφελος) continues the theme, so prominent in 15:1–19, of the *vanity* of Christian faith and discipleship apart from the hope of the resurrection (cf. 15:2, 14, 17).[66] Paul's hazard of this gruesome and humiliating death, condemned to the beasts in the arena at Ephesus, provides the crowning illustration of the futility of taking up the cross, if there is no resurrection from the dead. The flip side of this coin is also important. The implication of Paul's rhetorical question is that, since there is a coming resurrection, his devotion to Christ to the point of combat with the beasts is of great benefit. As Andreas Lindemann points out, "the argument in v. 32 implicitly presupposes that the resurrection of the dead also necessarily involves a last judgment."[67]

*if the dead are not raised.* Paul's protasis (εἰ νεκροὶ οὐκ ἐγείρονται) once again takes up and challenges the claim that "the dead are not raised" (15:15, νεκροὶ οὐκ ἐγεί-

---

65. E.g., Doole, "Wild Beasts," 150–52; Lindemann, 352.

66. So, insightfully, Anders Eriksson, "Fear of Eternal Damnation: *Pathos* Appeal in 1 Corinthians 15 and 16," in *Paul and Pathos* (ed. Thomas H. Olbricht and Jerry L. Sumney; SBLSBS 16; Atlanta: Scholars, 2001), 117–19.

67. Lindemann, 353.

ρονται; cf. 15:12, 16).[68] As throughout the chapter, at issue (as we have seen) is the physical, bodily resurrection, as both the substantive νεκροί "corpses" and the verb ἐγείρονται "raised to stand" make clear.

*Let us eat and drink, for tomorrow we die.*" Paul here quotes Isa 22:13. Paul's quote matches with the MT, and also agrees word for word with all known ancient Greek versions (LXX, Theodotion, Symmachus, and Aquila). But the thought expressed here also matches the reasoning of the wicked portrayed in Wis 2:5–7. Most significantly, the thought reflects a well-nigh universal maxim of the ancient pagan world, reflected in numerous ancient Greek and Latin texts.[69] The pagan sentiment is not one of frivolity but reflects a melancholy resignation to the inescapability of death. The contrast here with Paul's theology and example could not be greater. The pagan maxim counsels eating and drinking in view of the inevitability of death. Paul hungers and thirsts (4:11) and dies each day (15:31) to the point of combat with the beasts at Ephesus (15:32) because of the hope of the resurrection from the dead. Paul here himself models for the Corinthians the Pauline theological virtue of hope (cf. 13:7, 13; 15:19; also Rom 5:2–5; 8:24–25; 1 Thess 1:3). In contrast, the pagan maxim Paul quotes sums up the outcome of the teaching of the self-professed wise at Corinth, who deny the resurrection. In 15:33–34, Paul will now directly address the congregation at Corinth about them.

## Verse 33

*Do not be deceived—"evil communications corrupt good morals."*

The command not to be deceived strikes a foreboding tone. As elsewhere in the letter (3:18; 6:9), the command functions to bring home to the Corinthians the utter seriousness of the situation. Nothing less than union with Christ and salvation are at stake. Paul follows this warning with a quotation from the pagan poet Menander—"evil communications corrupt good morals."[70] The attribution to Menander is not fully certain, for the line is also attributed in antiquity to Euripides (*Frag.* 1024).[71] It is widely held that this dictum also circulated as a saying

---

68. Cf. Bachmann, "Resurrection," 297.
69. Cf. *Anth. pal.* 11.56.1–2 (πίνε καὶ εὐφραίνου· τί γὰρ αὔριον ἢ τὸ μέλλον, οὐδεὶς γινώσκει); Petronius, *Satyr.* 34; Strabo, *Geogr.* 14.5.9; Theognis, *Eleg.* 567–570.
70. Probably from the fourth-century BC comedy *Thais*; see BDR §487.1.
71. For full discussion, see John Granger Cook, "1 Cor 15:33: The Status Quaestionis," *NovT* 62 (2020): 375–91; see also Schrage, 247; Lindemann, 353.

*The Futility of Taking Up the Cross without the Resurrection*

of common proverbial wisdom in antiquity, and that therefore it is possible that this proverbial saying was the source of Paul's quotation rather than a play by Menander or Euripides.[72] But this is unlikely. There is in fact no evidence that this line circulated as a popular proverb in antiquity. Whenever it occurs in ancient literature (outside 1 Cor 15:33), it is attributed either to Menander or Euripides. Moreover, the saying is in iambic trimeter.[73] This strongly suggests its origins in a dramatic or poetic context, lending further credence to Menander's *Thais* (or perhaps one of Euripides's plays) as the source of Paul's quotation.[74] The citation of poets and playwrights as part of an argument was a standard practice of Greco-Roman philosophers.[75] Paul employs the technique effectively here. We thus here once again find Paul beating the philosophically minded wise at Corinth at their own philosophical game.

In its surrounding context, the dictum is clearly a warning against the influence of those who deny the resurrection (15:29, 32). According to BDAG, ὁμιλία (its plural form translated as "communications" here) may denote either (1) a "state of close association of persons, *association, social intercourse, company*," or (2) "engagement in talk, either as conversation or as a speech or lecture to a group."[76] The latter meaning is to be preferred (cf. the use of the cognate verb ὁμιλέω of speech in Luke 24:14; Acts 20:11; 24:26).[77] We see here once again Paul's concern with the *teaching* and *speech* of the deniers of the resurrection at Corinth (cf. 15:12, λέγουσιν ἐν ὑμῖν τινες; 15:35, ἐρεῖ τις; 11:19, αἱρέσεις; so also 1:10, τὸ αὐτὸ λέγητε πάντες).

These teachings "corrupt" the church (φθείρουσιν). We find here a clear connection to Paul's earlier warnings in chapters 1–3 against the self-appointed wise at Corinth, where the verb φθείρω is used in the same sense of corrupting the congregation: εἴ τις τὸν ναὸν τοῦ θεοῦ φθείρει, φθερεῖ τοῦτον ὁ θεός (3:17).[78] The "good morals" they corrupt is the Christlike way of the cross that is grounded in the hope of the resurrection and modeled by Paul and the other apostles (15:30–32). Paul may

---

72. So Cook, "1 Cor 15:33"; Fitzmyer, 583; many other commentators.

73. BDR §487 n. 4; Rob., *Gram.*, 422.

74. Paul's quote certainly suggests his knowledge of Menander's play. However, it is going far beyond the evidence to extrapolate, as does Michael Benjamin Cover, from this single quotation to the thesis that the entire epistle (!) is to be read "within the ambit of Greek household situation comedy." See his "The Divine Comedy at Corinth: Paul, Menander and the Rhetoric of Resurrection," *NTS* 64 (2018): 532–50.

75. Cicero, *Tusc.* 2.26; see the discussion in Thomas Kurth, *Senecas Trostschrift an Polybius, Dialog 11: Ein Kommentar* (Stuttgart: Teubner, 1994), 137.

76. BDAG, s.v. "ὁμιλία" (1 and 2).

77. Rightly Schrage, 248; Fee, 856; so also Aquinas, *1 Cor.* 962.

78. Cf. Boris Dunsch, "Menander bei Paulus: Oralität, Performanz und Zituationstechnik im Corpus Paulinum," *JAC* 53 (2010): 15–16.

CHAPTER 9

well enhance his point here with a clever play on words, which would also help to explain Paul's choice of this particular quotation at this point in his exhortation. The word χρηστός "good" is identical in sound, apart from one vowel, to Χριστός. Paul may well intend here a double entendre, in which the ἤθη χρηστά, the "good morals" of Menander's line, are "the ways of Christ," that is, the Christlike way of life modeled by Paul in 15:30–32.[79] We find a similar wordplay in the similarity of sound between χρηστός and Χριστός in Phlm 11, lending further likelihood to its presence here. In any case, we find here again the hortatory character of this chapter, that is, Paul's calling and exhortation of the Corinthians to lives of discipleship to Christ, and we find once again the central and crucial place that the hope of the resurrection has within that life of discipleship. When the self-professed wise at Corinth deny the resurrection, they overturn the entire Christian life.

## Verse 34

*Wake up from your stupor, as is right, and stop sinning; for some have no knowledge of God. I say this to your shame!*

*Wake up from your stupor, as is right, and stop sinning.* The language of wakefulness and sobriety is common in Paul's moral exhortation (cf. 1 Thess 5:6, γρηγορῶμεν καὶ νήφωμεν "let us be watchful and sober-minded"; 5:8, νήφωμεν "let us be sober-minded"). But Paul's choice here of ἐκνήφω ("to sober up from drunkenness or stupor"), which is a *hapax legomenon* in the New Testament, is distinctive, for the verb involves a *change of state* from stupor or drunkenness to sober-mindedness.[80] Paul's choice of this verb, together with the command to cease from sin (μὴ ἁμαρτάνετε), clearly portrays the Corinthians as in a state of stupor and sin and demands a change. The command ἐκνήψατε ("wake up from your stupor") in 15:34 corresponds to the command μὴ πλανᾶσθε ("don't be deceived") in 15:33, and thus identifies this stupor as a form of self-delusion.

What is this sin, stupor, and self-delusion? Two contextual factors make this crystal clear. First, the whole preceding context has been concerned with the denial of the resurrection and the ramifications of this denial (15:29–33). Second, a causal γάρ introducing the succeeding clause (15:34b) provides the grounds or warrant for the command to wake from stupor and stop sinning in the preceding clause (15:34a). In 15:34b we find direct reference to "some" (τινες) who have no knowledge of God. The τινες here are identical with the τινες who deny the res-

---

79. Cf. Dunsch, "Menander bei Paulus," 16–17.
80. See BDAG, s.v. "ἐκνήφω"; Robinson, s.v. "ἐκνήφω."

urrection in 15:12.[81] The spiritual stupor, delusion, and sin, then, to which Paul commands the Corinthians to put a stop is their toleration of the disbelief in the resurrection by the self-professed wise among them.[82]

*for some have no knowledge of God.* Paul's characterization of those who deny the resurrection as without knowledge of God (ἀγνωσία θεοῦ) brings to a climax a key theme of the letter. An important theme of chapters 1–3 of the epistle is that the world through its wisdom cannot know God (1:21; 2:6, 8, 11, 14, 16; 3:1–4, 18–19). By means of this theme, Paul indirectly critiqued the self-styled wise at Corinth, who boasted in their philosophical wisdom. This theme did not recur in chapters 5–14. But now in chapter 15 this theme reaches its culmination, as Paul now says directly of the wise at Corinth who deny the resurrection, in ironic contrast with their self-inflated claims to wisdom and knowledge, that they "have no knowledge of God." We see here once again that the letter reaches its intended culmination in chapter 15, and that Paul's chief concern with the Corinthian wisdom that he deals with in chapters 1–3 is its denial of the resurrection.

Paul's charge of ignorance of God is freighted with theological significance. The wise at Corinth are without knowledge of God because they do not believe in God's power to raise the dead.[83] Faith in the resurrection is faith in God's power as creator (Rom 4:16–25, especially 4:17, 19–21). Conversely, denial of the resurrection is denial of God's power (Matt 22:29 // Mark 12:24, μὴ εἰδότες τὰς γραφὰς μηδὲ τὴν δύναμιν τοῦ θεοῦ). Within the thought of the apostle, at the heart of the pagan world's lack of knowledge of God is its failure to acknowledge his power as creator (Rom 1:18–23, especially 1:20; cf. Wis 13:1, θεοῦ ἀγνωσία).[84] In denying the resurrection, the self-professed wise at Corinth, like the pagan world, refuse to trust in the creator God's power and thus fail to know God. For Paul, to know God is to be in saving union and communion with him (1:9). It is participation in the gift of the Holy Spirit (3:16; 6:19). Those at Corinth who deny the resurrection, by contrast, lack this personal, relational knowledge of God. They are like the pagans around them, "the gentiles who do not know God" (1 Thess 4:5; cf. Gal 4:8; 2 Thess 1:8).

Here the apostle is unyielding. He offers no compromise. Paul does not, as Margaret Mitchell argues, regard the difference between the affirmation of the resurrection and its denial as simply "different views on the resurrection" which

---

81. Rightly Schrage, 250; Wolff, 400; Ciampa & Rosner, 795; Collins, 561; Lindemann, 354; O'Reilly, *Resurrected Body*, 77; Robertson & Plummer, 364; Bender, 255.

82. Fee, 856–57; Schreiner, 518–19; Robertson & Plummer, 364; Schrage, 249.

83. John Chrysostom, *Hom. 1 Cor.* 40.4; so also, rightly, Wolff, 400; O'Reilly, *Resurrected Body*, 77; Schrage, 250.

84. Brendan Byrne, "Eschatologies of Resurrection and Destruction: The Biblical Significance of Paul's Dispute with the Corinthians," *DRev* 104 (1986): 293–94.

CHAPTER 9

call for amicable conciliation and accommodation.[85] Nor does Paul regard the doubt of the resurrection among some at Corinth as a theological difference in need of correction, but not one that calls their essential identity as Christ followers into question.[86] For Paul, the denial of the resurrection is denial of Christ. "It is he [Paul], not the Corinthian doubters, who brings out the fundamental antagonism to its sharpest expression."[87] According to Paul, the promise of resurrection belongs to the very essence of who God is, and therefore hope in the resurrection belongs to the very essence of what it means to know God. Therefore, to deny the resurrection is to be without saving knowledge of God. In the doctrine of the resurrection, "what is involved is the *substance*, the *whole* of the Christian revelation."[88] In Paul's thought, faith in the bodily resurrection is not an addition to faith in God but is faith in God in its true, radical form.[89]

*I say this to your shame!* The πρός in πρὸς ἐντροπήν expresses aim or goal.[90] The word ἐντροπή differs from its synonym αἰσχύνη, in that ἐντροπή implies a resulting change of conduct.[91] Paul wants the Corinthians to be ashamed of this toleration of the denial of God in their midst, to repent, and to take appropriate action. Paul does not spell this out further. We can assume that further guidance would be provided by Stephanus, Fortunatus, and Achaicus (16:15–18) and by Timothy (16:10–11).

In the following verses, Paul will continue the informal and lively "diatribe" style he has used throughout 15:29–34. Nonetheless, the chapter will now take another striking turn in style, tone, and content. For Paul will now engage with an imaginary spokesperson of the self-proclaimed wise at Corinth, addressing their arguments in opposition to the bodily resurrection directly and in great detail (15:35–49). In so doing, Paul will reveal the secret of the resurrection.

---

85. Margaret M. Mitchell, *Paul and the Rhetoric of Reconciliation: An Exegetical Investigation of the Language and Composition of 1 Corinthians* (Louisville: Westminster John Knox, 1991), 176–77.
86. Contra Jeffrey R. Asher, *Polarity and Change in 1 Corinthians 15: A Study of Metaphysics, Rhetoric, and Resurrection* (HUT 42; Tübingen: Mohr Siebeck, 2000), 30–90; followed by Garland, 696.
87. Barth, *Resurrection*, 122.
88. Barth, *Resurrection*, 112.
89. Byrne, "Eschatologies," 288–96.
90. Rob., *Gram.*, 626.
91. Trench, *Syn.*, 69.

CHAPTER 10

## *The Philosophical Challenge to the Resurrection*

15:35

Verse 35 is a key juncture within Paul's resurrection chapter. In this verse, we hear the self-professed wise at Corinth who denied the resurrection speak for themselves. We learn that their objection to the resurrection was a philosophical one, founded upon purported knowledge, reason, and wisdom. This crucial verse not only confirms what the dissenters at Corinth denied but also reveals—for the first time in the chapter—why they did so. Grasping the reason why the wise at Corinth denied the resurrection will wondrously illuminate what Paul affirms in this chapter and will confirm what we find throughout 1 Cor 15—that the resurrection Paul expounds in this chapter is the resurrection of the flesh.

### Verse 35

*But someone will say to the contrary: "How can the dead be raised? And with what kind of body do they return to life?"*

Paul now continues with the lively diatribe style used by the ancient philosophers that he employed in 15:29–34, but here he introduces another feature of that style. He interacts with an imaginary dialogue partner, who raises an objection to the hope of the resurrection affirmed by Paul in 15:12–34.

*But someone will say to the contrary.* The strong adversative ἀλλά marks the beginning of a new section of the chapter: 15:35–49. The use of ἐρεῖ τις to express the fictive interlocutor's objection has close parallels elsewhere in Paul (e.g., Rom 9:19, ἐρεῖς μοι οὖν; 11:19, ἐρεῖς οὖν). Do the questions posed by the imaginary interlocutor merely reflect Paul's judgment as to what questions the Corinthians might ask?[1] Or do they express known objections of the opponents of the resurrection at Corinth?[2] Three factors make the latter far more probable. First, it would be odd if Paul was aware of questions or arguments raised at Corinth but chose to address different questions. But Paul had access to numerous sources (1:11, Chloe's people; 16:15–18, Stephanas, Fortunatus, and Achaicus; 16:12, Apollos), and it is beyond a reasonable doubt he was well informed of the situation at Corinth. Second, the energy, vigor, and length of Paul's response strongly suggest that he is addressing actual arguments, most likely (as Wolff suggests) the "main argument" of the deniers of the resurrection at Corinth.[3] Third, the "someone" (τις) of 15:35, in the context of the wider chapter, is most likely not a mere diatribal device but one among the "some" (τινες) who "say there is no resurrection of the dead" (15:12, πῶς λέγουσιν ἐν ὑμῖν τινες ὅτι ἀνάστασις νεκρῶν οὐκ ἔστιν;) and the "some" (τινες) who "have no knowledge of God" (15:34, ἀγνωσίαν γὰρ θεοῦ τινες ἔχουσιν). As this convergence of evidence suggests, in v. 35 we hear the self-professed wise at Corinth speak for themselves.

*"How can the dead be raised? And with what kind of body do they return to life?"* The great majority of interpreters conclude that the two questions posed are in essence only one question, with the second question merely making the first more precise.[4] However, this view cannot be sustained, as Paul's use of δέ to introduce the second question makes clear. The conjunction δέ is never explicative, as this view would require, but always introduces something new or additional.[5] More-

---

1. So Fitzmyer, 586; Collins, 562–63.
2. So Wolff, 402; Fee, 858, 862–63; Schrage, 270–72; Weiss, 367.
3. Wolff, 402.
4. So Normand Bonneau, "The Logic of Paul's Argument on the Resurrection Body in 1 Cor 15:35–44a," *ScEs* 45 (1993): 79 n. 1; Wolff, 402; Schrage, 279; Fee, 858–59, 862–63; Garland, 727; Hays, 269–70; Thiselton, 1261–62; Weiss, 367; Robertson & Plummer, 368.
5. See Rob., *Gram.*, 1183–86; Kühner-G., 2.2:261–63, 274–75. Cf. in particular: "der Gedanke, der durch δέ an einen vorangehenden Gedanken angereiht wird, drückt etwas Neues und von dem Vorhergehenden Verschiedenes aus" (2.2:274). BDR lists a few instances in which, it is claimed, δέ is used "zur Erklärung oder Steigerung" (§447.1.c), citing Rom 3:22; 9:30; 1 Cor 2:6; and Phil 2:8. But this is mistaken. In each of these cases, the clause introduced by δέ picks up a word from the previous clause in order to express a new thought or consideration concerning that word (e.g., Phil 2:8, μέχρι θανάτου, θανάτου δὲ σταυροῦ). These clauses do not merely explain the term in question but add a new thought. Their explanatory or cumulative force derives from the combination of the repeated term and the new thought about that term signaled by δέ. Such a construction is not found in 1 Cor 15:35.

## The Philosophical Challenge to the Resurrection

over, Paul's response to the questions in 15:36-38 will make not one point but two, as the connective καί in 15:37 reveals. As we will see, 15:36 will respond to the first question, and 15:37-38 will respond to the second. The two questions are related but distinct.[6] The first asks how (πῶς) resurrection can take place; the second inquires regarding the nature or quality (ποῖος) of the resurrected body.

But what kind of questions are these? The interrogative adverb πῶς, which introduces the first question, introduces a genuine question regarding means or mode (i.e., "how [does it come about that]?") in a little less than half of its occurrences in the New Testament. But in a little over half of its occurrences, πῶς introduces a rhetorical question expressing the impossibility of a claim, idea, or action (i.e., "how [is it possible that]?"). This latter function is very common in Paul (e.g., 1 Cor 14:16, πῶς ἐρεῖ τὸ ἀμήν "how will he say the 'amen'?"; cf. Rom 3:6; 6:2; 8:32; 10:14-15; 1 Cor 14:7, 9; 15:12; 2 Cor 3:8; Gal 2:14; 4:9). The interrogative adjective ποῖος, which introduces the second question, can also serve to express impossibility (i.e., "of what kind [can it be that]?"). This usage is less common than with πῶς but is likewise well attested (e.g., Acts 7:49, ποῖον οἶκον οἰκοδομήσετέ μοι "what kind of house will you build for me?"; cf. Luke 6:32-34; 1 Pet 2:20). As the great majority of scholars have recognized, the questions of the interlocutor in 15:35 function in this rhetorical way to deny the possibility of the resurrection.[7]

Several factors within the context show clearly that the questions of the interlocutor in v. 35 are rhetorical questions serving to deny the possibility of the resurrection. The future tense of the verbal form ἐρεῖ ("will say") is important, for it indicates that what the interlocutor says is *in response* to the preceding teaching on the resurrection in 15:12-34. Moreover, the connector at the beginning of 15:35 is not δέ but the strong adversative ἀλλά, indicating that what the fictive interlocutor "will say in response" (ἐρεῖ) is in contrast and *in opposition* (ἀλλά) to Paul's preceding teaching in vv. 12-34. Finally, Paul's characterization of the interlocutor as a "fool" (ἄφρων) in 15:36 shows that the interlocutor's queries in 15:35 are not genuine questions regarding the modality of the resurrection but a rhetorical challenge to the truth of the resurrection itself. It is possible that the questions served as a kind of maxim or slogan of the self-professed wise at Corinth who denied the resurrection, as is perhaps suggested by the alliteration and assonance with which the questions are framed: <u>πῶς ἐγείρονται</u> οἱ νεκροί; <u>ποίῳ</u>

---

6. Rightly Joachim Jeremias, "'Flesh and Blood Cannot Inherit the Kingdom of God' (I Cor. xv. 50)," *NTS* 2 (1956): 151-59; Fitzmyer, 586-87.

7. So Ronald J. Sider, "The Pauline Conception of the Resurrection Body in 1 Corinthians XV.35-54," *NTS* 21 (1975): 429; Lindemann, 356; Ciampa & Rosner, 800; Fee, 862-63; Schreiner, 320; Weiss, 367; Thiselton, 1261-63; Barrett, 369. Contra Schrage, 279; Hays, 269-70.

δὲ σώματι ἔρχονται. In any case, these questions are raised not to seek information but to refute. Like the question posed to Jesus by the Sadducees in Mark 12:23 ("In the resurrection, whose wife shall she be?"), the questions posed by the speaker in 1 Cor 15:35 dismiss the resurrection as impossible and absurd. They are "taunts" that "throw down the gauntlet" regarding the resurrection of the dead.[8]

First Corinthians 15:35 confirms what we have found throughout the chapter concerning *what* the opponents of the resurrection at Corinth denied. We see this in the first question, which challenges how it can be that "the dead are raised" (ἐγείρονται οἱ νεκροί). In our study of the verb ἐγείρω in chapter 3, we saw that the semantics of that verb, when used with reference to the deceased, clearly express the conception of the dead body's return to physical life. As we saw in chapter 6, the substantive νεκρός normally denotes a dead body or corpse, and thus the conjunction of the verb ἐγείρω and the substantive νεκρός unambiguously denotes the physical resurrection of dead bodies from the grave. The language of resurrection within the first question of v. 35, as throughout ancient Greek literature, unambiguously denotes the return to life of the body of flesh and bones.

That the language of resurrection within the first question of v. 35 ("How can the dead be raised?") necessarily entails the revival of the physical body is also evident from its close conjunction with the second question within the same verse: "And with what kind of *body* do they return to life?" The dative σώματι is most likely a dative of accompaniment ("*with* what kind of body"). The verb ἔρχονται, most likely chosen for its assonance with ἐγείρονται in the first question, apparently means to "come forth" or "return to life" from the tomb (cf. John 5:29, ἐκπορεύσονται).[9] We find the verb used in this same sense in 2 Clem. 9.4: καὶ ἐν τῇ σαρκὶ ἐλεύσεσθε ("you will also *return to life* [lit. "come"] in the flesh"). This second question, like the first, would make no sense whatsoever unless it concerned the return to life of the physical body.

In this second question, the word σῶμα "body" makes its first appearance in the chapter. The word σῶμα in Paul, as throughout ancient Greek literature, denotes "a body, as an organized whole made up of parts and members."[10] Like σάρξ "flesh," it denotes the visible, tangible component of the human person, but it does so "differently from σάρξ which expresses rather the *material* of the body."[11] Thus, σῶμα and σάρξ are synonyms, but σάρξ denotes the body from the standpoint of the stuff of which it is composed, whereas σῶμα denotes the body as a composite whole with its varied members. The σῶμα is thus "the organized σάρξ."[12] From the

---

8. Schreiner, 320.
9. Cf. Ellicott, 314.
10. Robinson, s.v. "σῶμα."
11. Robinson, s.v. "σῶμα."
12. Cremer, 537. See also the excellent study of Robert H. Gundry, *Sōma in Biblical Theology: With Emphasis on Pauline Anthropology* (SNTSMS 29; New York: Cambridge University Press,

fact, therefore, that Paul in this chapter affirms the resurrection of the *body*, it necessarily follows that he affirms the resurrection of the *flesh*. Throughout this chapter, the body that Paul affirms will be raised is the body of flesh and bones.

First Corinthians 15:35, then, is helpful in providing further confirmation of *what* Paul affirmed and *what* the opponents of the resurrection at Corinth denied. What Paul affirmed and they denied was the resurrection of the flesh. But this verse is particularly valuable for the precious further insight it provides as to *why* some at Corinth denied the resurrection. They denied the resurrection, as their derisive questions show, because of its seemingly obvious absurdity and impossibility: "How can the dead be raised? And with what kind of body do they return to life?" As we have seen, these two questions, related but distinct, function together as a rhetorical challenge to the resurrection. To see the precise nature of the challenge, let us take each of the questions in turn.

The first question denies the possibility of the resurrection—"*How* can the dead be raised?" Putting this question in historical context illumines it greatly. In Greco-Roman thought, the resurrection of a dead body to life was universally regarded as impossible (Homer, *Il.* 21.55–56; 24.551, 756; Aeschylus, *Eum.* 648; Sophocles, *El.* 940–941; Herodotus, *Hist.* 3.62.3–4). For the philosophically minded, in particular, the very concept of resurrection was thought unreasonable and absurd. What was considered absurd and impossible was that a corpse, once corrupted, decayed, and dissolved in the earth, could be restored to life. Tertullian in his *Apology* quotes an imaginary pagan interlocutor: "'But how,' you say, 'can the decomposed matter of the body be restored to its original condition?'" (*Apol.* 48.5, *Sed quomodo, inquis, dissoluta materia exhiberi potest?*). Similarly, Athenagoras tells us that pagan thinkers, arguing from the body's decomposition and distribution into other bodies, "prove, so they think, that the resurrection is impossible" (*Res.* 4.4, κατασκειάζουσιν, ὡς νομίζουσιν, ἀδύνατον τὴν ἀνάστασιν). This objection to the resurrection, grounded in the empirical fact of the body's dissolution following death, presumably lies behind the first question posed by the Corinthian wise in 1 Cor 15:35.

What, then, of the second question—"And with what kind of body do they return to life?" Normand Bonneau argues that the same philosophical objection we have found latent in the first question (i.e., the argument from the empirical reality of the body's dissolution) lies behind the second question as well: "The second [question] specifies the first, with the sense 'How is resurrection possible or reasonable when clearly the bodies of the dead turn to dust?'"[13] However, the

---

1976). On the untenability of the influential but misguided thesis of Rudolf Bultmann that σῶμα in Paul denotes the person or self, see, in addition to Gundry's classic treatment, Sider, "Resurrection Body," 429–30; Fitzmyer, 587.

13. Bonneau, "Logic," 79 n. 1.

## CHAPTER 10

second question, although most likely including this objection within its scope, would seem to add another argument as well: what kind of body can be made imperishable and immortal when the physical body is *intrinsically* mortal and perishable? Celsus, the Middle Platonic philosopher, in language very similar to the second question in 1 Cor 15:35, brings together both objections:

> For what kind of body, once completely corrupted, is able to return again to its original nature and that very same first formation from which it was dissolved? ... And for the soul, to be sure, the highest divinity might be able to provide an everlasting life. "But corpses," Heraclitus says, "are worse garbage than manure." The flesh, which is full of those things it is not good even to mention, the divinity shall neither wish nor be able to make eternal, contrary to all reason. (Celsus, quoted in Origen, *Cels.* 5.14)

It is instructive to put the questions of the interlocutor in 1 Cor 15:35 side by side with the question of Tertullian's interlocutor and the question of Celsus:

| | |
|---|---|
| But someone will say to the contrary: "How [πῶς] can the dead be raised?" (1 Cor 15:35a) | "But how [*quomodo*]," you say, "can the decomposed matter of the body be restored to its original condition?" (Tertullian, *Apol.* 48.5) |
| "And with what kind of body [ποῖον σῶμα] do they return to life?" (1 Cor 15:35b) | For what kind of body [ποῖον σῶμα], once completely corrupted, is able to return again to its original nature? ... The flesh, which is full of those things it is not good even to mention, the divinity shall neither wish nor be able to make eternal, contrary to all reason. (*Cels.* 5.14) |

The questions in 1 Cor 15:35, then, raise philosophical and rational objections to the resurrection grounded in two claims: (1) the impossibility of the corrupted body's reconstitution; and (2) the impossibility of making the physical body of flesh and bones, which is inherently corruptible, immortal and imperishable. "Resurrection in the flesh appeared a startling, distasteful idea, at odds with everything that passed for wisdom among the educated."[14] We saw in chapter 1 of this commentary that the denial of the resurrection was a teaching embraced by those at Corinth who professed philosophical wisdom, and that they grounded

---

14. Ramsay MacMullen, *Christianizing the Roman Empire, AD 100–400* (New Haven: Yale University Press, 1984), 12.

this teaching in their claim to superior wisdom and knowledge. The philosophical character of the objections raised by the interlocutor's questions in 1 Cor 15:35 is consistent with this philosophical origin of the denial of the resurrection among the self-professed wise at Corinth. However, the philosophical issue was not, as a number of scholars have supposed, a putative "cosmic polarity" forbidding the assumption of an earthly body to the celestial realms of "spirit" or πνεῦμα.[15] This is a figment of scholarly imagination.[16] Such a conception plays no part in the questions raised in v. 35. Rather, the objections raised in v. 35 involve the presumed absurdity of the decomposed body's reintegration, and the supposed impossibility that a human being of flesh could be granted everlasting life in the body.

First Corinthians 15:35, in illumining both *what* the opponents of the resurrection at Corinth denied and *why* they did so, sheds a powerful light on the chapter as a whole. For in the verses that follow, as we will see, Paul will *affirm* what the interlocutor in v. 35 *denies*. Paul will not make concessions to render the doctrine of the resurrection more palatable to the philosophically educated. Rather, he will take the self-avowed "wise" at Corinth head-on. In this chapter, Paul "insists upon an eschatology of resurrection in the face of Corinthian disfavor."[17] To the carefully considered philosophical objections of the educated elite at Corinth concerning the astonishing conception of the miraculous reconstitution of the body from decay and its transformation to an imperishable physical life, Paul will respond, "You fool!" (15:36). Therefore it will not do to contrast Paul's teaching on the resurrection with a supposedly "vulgar Jewish conception of the restoration to life of the old corporeity."[18] It will not do to portray Paul's understanding of the resurrection in 1 Cor 15 as a compromise with the philosophically minded elite at Corinth, and thus as different from the Old Testament and Jewish understanding of resurrection as "a literal resurrection of the very flesh and blood."[19] For it is precisely this doctrine that the imaginary interlocutor in v. 35 derides, and which

---

15. Contra Dale Martin, *The Corinthian Body* (New Haven: Yale University Press, 1995), 114–20; Jeffrey R. Asher, *Polarity and Change in 1 Corinthians 15: A Study of Metaphysics, Rhetoric, and Resurrection* (HUT 42; Tübingen: Mohr Siebeck, 2000), 117–29; Asher, "ΣΠΕΙΡΕΤΑΙ: Paul's Anthropogenic Metaphor in 1 Corinthians 15:42–44," *JBL* 120 (2001): 102–6; Alan G. Padgett, "The Body in Resurrection: Science and Scripture on the 'Spiritual Body,'" *WW* 22 (2002): 155–63; Garland, 725.

16. For the misunderstanding of both 1 Cor 15 and of ancient philosophy upon which this thesis rests, see the commentary on vv. 40–41, 45, and 47.

17. Brendan Byrne, "Eschatologies of Resurrection and Destruction: The Biblical Significance of Paul's Dispute with the Corinthians," *DRev* 104 (1986): 296.

18. Hans Grass, *Ostergeschehen und Osterberichte* (Göttingen: Vandenhoeck & Ruprecht, 1962), 171.

19. Martin, *Body*, 123.

## CHAPTER 10

Paul in vv. 36–58 will defend. The resurrection Paul defends and expounds in 1 Cor 15 is the resurrection of the flesh.

As we have seen, the questions of v. 35 are not sincere questions expecting an answer, but are instead taunts hurled at the doctrine of the resurrection. Yet in the verses that follow Paul will, and not for the first time in this chapter, turn the tables on the self-professed wise at Corinth—for he will respond to their questions. These dismissive jibes, considered by the Corinthian wise as the end of the discussion, Paul will take seriously as questions—and he will answer them. In so doing, Paul will do more than defend the resurrection. In keeping with his apostolic teaching office of revealing mysteries taught by the Spirit (2:6–16), he will provide new revelatory insight into this mystery. Indeed, he will reveal the mystery at the heart of the resurrection.

CHAPTER 11

## Testimonies within Creation to the Glorification of the Flesh

## 15:36-41

Paul's argument that now follows in 15:36-41 "is based on examples drawn from the observation of everyday realities."[1] Here Paul considers seeds, plants, animals, birds, and fish as well as the sun, moon, and stars. Interpreters without exception regard these as "analogies" or "illustrations" of the resurrection.[2] But this is mistaken. Rather, these phenomena are for Paul divinely given testimonies within the present created order to the coming glorification of the flesh. They are God-given signs within creation pointing to the consummation of creation in the mystery of the resurrection. Therefore, although I will in this chapter use the language of "analogy" and "comparison," it will always be with this understanding of these phenomena as divinely given testimonies and signs in mind. Our earliest known commentators on the passage, Clement of Rome and Tertullian, read Paul's comparisons in precisely this way (1 Clem. 24; Tertullian, *Apol.* 48.7-9). For Paul, these natural phenomena are, to be sure, analogies or illustrations of the resurrection—but they are analogies divinely given and intended by the creator. This understanding explains Paul's echoes of the Genesis creation narrative and of the "creation psalms" (Pss 8 and 143) throughout the passage. Each comparison draws

---

1. Normand Bonneau, "The Logic of Paul's Argument on the Resurrection Body in 1 Cor 15:35-44a," *ScEs* 45 (1993): 79. Bonneau provides a list of similar arguments based on everyday realities found elsewhere in Paul's letters (79 n. 3).

2. E.g., Bonneau, "Logic," 79, 83-86; Collins, 563-64; Fitzmyer, 585-86; Schrage, 280-81; Hays, 270-71.

CHAPTER 11

upon a different day or days within the six-day narrative of creation (15:36–38, day three; 15:39, days five and six; 15:40, day two; 15:40–41, day four).[3] These allusions will be unpacked more fully in the discussion of vv. 36–41. But they may be summarized here in the following chart:[4]

| Verses | Creation Aspect | Creation Day | Allusion | Order (Paul vs. Echo) |
|---|---|---|---|---|
| 36–38 | seeds<br>plants<br>trees | Day 3 | Gen 1:11–13 | N/A |
| 39 | humans<br>animals<br>birds<br>fish | Days 5 & 6 | Gen 1:20–31<br>Ps 8 | Reverse<br>Identical |
| 40 | heaven<br>earth | Day 2 | Gen 1:6–8<br>cf. 1:1, 2:1 | Identical |
| 41 | sun<br>moon<br>stars | Day 4 | Gen 1:14–19<br>Ps 148:3 | Identical<br>Identical |

Scholars debate whether 15:36–41 contains one, two, or three comparisons.[5] The debate has its source in the complex interplay of contextual, syntactic, and

---

3. On the echoes of Gen 1 within the passage, see N. T. Wright, *The Resurrection of the Son of God* (vol. 3 of *Christian Origins and the Question of God*; Minneapolis: Fortress, 2003), 341; Ciampa & Rosner, 805.

4. See also the chart in Ciampa & Rosner, 805, to whom I am indebted for some aspects of the chart presented here.

5. Some scholars hold that vv. 36–41 function as one analogy with a single point of comparison. So Constantine R. Campbell, *Paul and the Hope of Glory: An Exegetical and Theological Study* (Grand Rapids: Zondervan, 2020), 179; Ronald J. Sider, "The Pauline Conception of the Resurrection Body in 1 Corinthians XV.35–54," *NTS* 21 (1975): 429–32; Schreiner, 320–21. Other interpreters posit two points of comparison, the first in vv. 36–38 and the second in vv. 39–41. So Bonneau, "Logic," 83–89; Garland, 730–32; Dale Martin, *The Corinthian Body* (New Haven: Yale University Press, 1995), 125–26; Ciampa & Rosner, 807; Barrett, 370–72; Godet, 2:406–9; Robertson & Plummer, 371–72. A third set of interpreters find three analogies, the first in vv. 36–38, the second in v. 39, and the third in vv. 40–41. So G. W. Dawes, "'But If You Can Gain Your Freedom' (1 Corinthians 7:17–24)," *CBQ* 52 (1990): 687–88; Collins, 562–65. For further discussion, see Bonneau, "Logic," 80–86.

rhetorical features within the passage, and it can only be resolved by taking each of these into account. Contextually, vv. 36–41 clearly function as a unity, as is evident from the application in v. 42: οὕτως καὶ ἡ ἀνάστασις τῶν νεκρῶν ("Thus also is the resurrection of the dead"). Syntactically, the passage may plausibly be divided into either three units (15:36–38, 15:39, and 15:40–41) or two units (15:36–38, 15:39–41).[6] Rhetorically, the pericope contains three different types of comparison: botanical (15:36–38), zoological (15:39), and astronomical (15:40–41).[7] Considering these contextual, syntactic, and rhetorical factors together, the upshot would appear to be that we have here three sets of comparisons (15:36–38, 15:39, 15:40–41), each of them closely linked to one another in Paul's mind and functioning together as a unit.

But the key to the passage, as we will see, is to grasp that each one of the three units of the pericope contains not just one but *multiple* points of comparison, all of which will play an important role in the exposition of the resurrection to follow in the chapter. As N. T. Wright notes, in 15:36–41 Paul is "setting up a network of metaphor and simile," which he will then cash out throughout 15:42–58.[8] The closest parallel in antiquity to Paul's analogies in 1 Cor 15:36–41, with their complexity and multiple points of comparison, are the parables of Jesus in the gospels.[9] These

---

6. Verses 37–38 are linked with v. 36 by a connective καί demarcating vv. 36–38 as a single unit. Conversely, the lack of a connector between v. 38 and v. 39 indicates that 15:39 begins a new unit (cf. Bonneau, "Logic," 83–84). Verses 40–41 are introduced by a connective καί. Syntactically, it is possible to take this καί either as introducing a third unit or as continuing the second unit in v. 39 (for the latter view, see Bonneau, "Logic," 83–86). Fee's claim of a chiastic structure in 15:39–41 (783) is not convincing.

7. Cf. Collins, 563–64. Verses 37–38 are thus linked with v. 36 not only by the καί connector but also by the continuation of the botanical metaphor. Verse 39 is distinguished from vv. 36–38 by both asyndeton and the introduction of a new comparative domain (zoological). In vv. 40–41, where syntactically the καί may either mark a new unit or the continuation of v. 39, the rhetorical shift to a new allegorical domain (astronomical) indicates that these verses form a third comparison.

8. Wright, *Resurrection*, 345.

9. As Rodolphe Morissette showed, we do find similar arguments from analogy regarding the resurrection in the later rabbinic literature; see Rodolphe Morissette, "La conditione de ressuscité. 1 Corinthiens 15,34–49: Structure littéraire de la péricope," *Bib* 53 (1972): 208–28. However, the relevance of this material for illumining Paul's thought is questionable, for the texts Morissette cites postdate Paul by many centuries. In any case, what is most striking about Paul's argument is not the similarities but the differences. Paul's comparisons differ from these rabbinic analogies in two important ways. First, whereas the rabbinic analogies have a single point of comparison, Paul's analogies are multilayered and complex, with multiple points of comparison, each of which will play a role in the application in 15:42–58. Second, whereas the rabbinic arguments function to defend the resurrection, usually by an argument *a fortiori*, Paul's

CHAPTER 11

analogies within vv. 36–41 are crucial, for the application of these comparisons will continue throughout 15:42–58 and structure Paul's entire argument. It is by means of these comparisons that Paul will begin to unveil the secret of the resurrection that will form the heart of the chapter.

## VERSE 36

*Fool! What you yourself sow is not made alive unless it dies.*

*Fool!* Paul responds to the taunting questions of the imaginary interlocutor in v. 35 quite sharply: "Fool!" Such epithets in response to misguided questions of a fictive dialogue partner are a regular feature of the lively diatribe style Paul continues to employ here.[10] But more than a rhetorical convention is involved in Paul's use of the term. The term ἄφρων "fool" recalls Paul's discussion of the Corinthian claim to wisdom in chapters 1–4. There Paul portrayed the wisdom of this world as foolishness (1:18–21, 25–29; 3:18–20), because this world's wisdom cannot know God or the things of God (1:21; 2:6–8, 11, 14, 16; 3:1–4). Through the term ἄφρων, Paul takes up this theme of the folly of mere human wisdom and exposes the fatal defect of this wisdom in which some at Corinth boasted—such wisdom excludes the knowledge of God.

The term ἄφρων, although rare elsewhere in the LXX, appears frequently in wisdom books such as Proverbs and Ecclesiastes as well as in the so-called wisdom psalms.[11] In Proverbs, Ecclesiastes, and the book of Psalms, it is the word of choice to denote the "fool" in the biblical sense of one who does not take God into account in his or her thinking or way of life. Paul's epithet may actually echo a particular wisdom psalm—Ps 14:1 (13:1): εἶπεν ἄφρων ἐν καρδίᾳ αὐτοῦ Οὐκ ἔστιν θεός ("The fool has said in his heart: 'There is no God!'"). But in any case, Paul uses the term here in its Old Testament sense of the one who excludes God from his thinking.[12] Of course, it is this biblical, God-centered conception of wisdom and folly that lies behind Paul's treatment of the Corinthian wisdom in chapters 1–4.

---

argument serves (as we will see) not only to confirm the reality of the resurrection but also to teach, providing new revelatory insights into the nature of this mystery.

10. Epictetus uses the address μωρέ "Fool!" in a way very similar to Paul; see, for example, *Diatr.* 3.13.17; 3.22.85; 3.23.17.

11. The word occurs in the LXX only four times outside the wisdom literature, but seventy-six times in Proverbs, thirty in Ecclesiastes, eight in Psalms, five in Job, and eight in the Wisdom of Solomon.

12. Ciampa & Rosner, 800–801; Fee, 863; Fitzmyer, 588; Schrage, 280; Reasoner, on 15:36; Garland, 727.

With the expression ἄφρων, Paul now returns to this theme in a striking way. The interlocutor of v. 35, who speaks for the self-professed wise at Corinth who deny the resurrection, is a fool, for he has failed to reckon with the wisdom and power of the creator God. Like the Sadducees, who likewise rejected the resurrection, the self-professed wise at Corinth "understand neither the Scriptures nor the power of God" (Matt 22:29; Mark 12:24). By denying the resurrection, they reveal that they do not know God (cf. 15:34, ἀγνωσίαν γὰρ θεοῦ τινες ἔχουσιν "for some have no knowledge of God").

Paul's sharp response is thus entirely fitting. "Answer a fool [ἄφρονι] according to his folly, lest he be wise [σοφός] in his own eyes" (Prov 26:5 LXX). Yet, as we will now see, Paul is ready to reason with his interlocutor, appealing to the testimony of creation to bring him to knowledge of the creator.

*What you yourself sow.* Paul continues to address his fictional discussion partner, who represents the self-appointed wise at Corinth. The liveliness of Paul's diatribe style is not fully reproducible in English (σύ, ὃ σπείρεις "You, what you sow"). Its proleptic position places strong emphasis on the σύ "you."[13] In this way, Paul appeals to the interlocutor's own experience of the created world.[14] "Paul tells the sceptics: 'Every time you sow, you supply the answer to your own objection.'"[15] Paul's comparison is well chosen for his ancient readers, for, as Theophrastus in his treatise on horticulture tells us, among the modes of plant genesis, "the most common is that from seed" (κοινοτάτη . . . ἡ ἀπὸ σπέρματος, *Caus. plant.* 4.1.1).

*is not made alive unless it dies.* To fully grasp the power of Paul's comparison, we must blot out a common scholarly mistake. A number of scholars imagine that, in speaking of the death of the seed and describing its blossoming as a return to life, Paul is simply following a common ancient understanding of botanical growth. But as shown in excursus 4 following this chapter, this claim is without foundation. For our ancient sources prior to Paul never speak of the seed as dying or of its growth as a return to life. This understanding of the seed and its growth as a kind of death and resurrection is a new and revolutionary conception. We also find this conception in a saying of Jesus in John 12:24, and Paul may be drawing on this tradition in 1 Cor 15:36. In any case, the conception is unknown in our ancient sources prior to the New Testament. It is a Christian innovation.

---

13. BDR §475 n. 2; Rob., *Gram.*, 423.
14. Lindemann, 356; Fitzmyer, 588; Fee, 863.
15. Sider, "Resurrection Body," 429, citing Robertson & Plummer, 369. Cf. John Chrysostom, *Hom. 1 Cor.* 41.2.

## CHAPTER 11

What does Paul mean when he says that the seed "dies"? Although the language and conception are new, the apostle is referring to a known physical fact. As modern botanists explain, in order for a plant to grow, the coat of its seed must burst and then decay and be dissolved in the soil. Paul's ancient readers were also fully aware of this aspect of botanical growth. John Chrysostom lists four verbs the ancients customarily used of seeds: "it sprouts, and it grows, and it *decays* [σήπεται], and it *is dissolved* [διαλύεται]" (*Hom. 1 Cor.* 41.2). Plutarch writes: "For it is necessary that the seed first be cast into and hidden within the earth, and *undergo decay* [σαπῆναι]" (*Frag.* 11). It is this process, familiar to both ancient and modern botanical study, that Paul is thinking of when he says that the seed "dies."

And yet the very same seed that dies and decays in the earth is given glorious new life. It is "made alive" (ζῳοποιεῖται). "What you sow" is the single subject of both the verb "dies" and the verb "is made alive." We thus see a definite material *continuity* between seed and plant.[16] It is not an *x* that dies and a *y* that is made alive, but the same identical *x* dies and is made alive. And therefore the verb "is made alive" *reverses* the word "dies." What was dead is made alive again. This is the language of *resurrection*. It is the language of the resurrection of the flesh.

Paul's portrayal of planting and growth as a kind of resurrection is not a mere analogy or illustration, as most commentators assume. As we saw in the introduction to this chapter, Paul's comparison draws upon the language of the third day within the Genesis creation narrative (Gen 1:11–13 LXX; see esp. 1:11, 12, σπεῖρον σπέρμα), in order to portray the seed's wondrous transformation into a plant or tree as a divinely given *sign* or *testimony* within the created order pointing toward the coming consummation of creation in the resurrection from the dead. It is a mysterious sign, imprinted into the creation by the creator, now unveiled to the eyes of faith through the resurrection of Christ. This understanding, which reflects the way in which the passage was understood by its earliest readers (1 Clem. 24; Tertullian, *Apol.* 48.7–9), explains why Paul regards the comparison as having not only illustrative but also probative force.

Paul in v. 36 thus directly addresses the first mocking question of the interlocutor in v. 35, "How can the dead be raised?" As we saw in the previous chapter, this question characterized the very idea of resurrection as impossible and absurd. What was considered unreasonable in ancient pagan thought was that a corpse, once decayed and dissolved in the earth, could be restored to life. Through the comparison of the seed in v. 36, Paul provides an answer to this objection. Like the seed, which molders in the ground but springs up to new life, so the bodies of those in Christ, although they perish, decay, and are decomposed in the earth,

---

16. Rightly J. A. Schep, *The Nature of the Resurrection Body* (Grand Rapids: Eerdmans, 1964), 191.

will be given glorious new life. How can this be? The answer is given in the verb ζῳοποιεῖται. This verb is a divine passive, accenting the activity of God.[17] "The 'miracle' of the seed, dying in the ground and bringing forth a new, richer, and more glorious life, is caused by God's almighty power."[18] The resurrection will come about through the incomprehensible power and glory of God (cf. 6:14, ἡμᾶς ἐξεγερεῖ διὰ τῆς δυνάμεως αὐτοῦ "he will raise us up *through his power*").

Paul says the seed is not given life "unless it dies," and a few scholars have accordingly maintained that the point of the comparison is not the resurrection but the necessity of death.[19] But this is a false trail. What would Paul's point be in this case? The once-popular thesis of an overrealized eschatology at Corinth is, as we saw in chapter 6, without foundation. To judge from v. 35, the self-professed wise at Corinth—far from denying the necessity of death— actually based their case against the resurrection on the stark reality of death and the impossibility of its reversal ("How can the dead be raised?"). As C. K. Barrett notes, "Paul is not here using the figure to bring out the necessity of death; rather, the fact of transformation through death and resurrection."[20]

Nonetheless, Paul does not write "What you yourself sow, although it dies, is given life," but instead "What you yourself sow is *not* made alive *unless* it dies" (σύ, ὃ σπείρεις, οὐ ζῳοποιεῖται ἐὰν μὴ ἀποθάνῃ). Putting the matter in this way fits the comparison with the seed aptly, for ancient writers regularly emphasize the necessity that the seed must first be hidden in the earth if it is to bear fruit.[21] But, more importantly, Paul thereby also includes an additional thought regarding the resurrection.[22] The thought is this: just as the goal or telos of the sunflower seed is the sunflower, so the goal of the present body is the risen body conformed to Christ's body. This introduces a key theme, which will be repeated throughout the chapter (15:44b, 46, 49). The seed has a wondrous goal and telos: the flower. Even so, our present bodies do not have their goal in this present mortal life but will find their completion and fulfillment in the resurrection, when the last enemy, death, is defeated (15:26) and all are made alive in Christ (15:22). This follows the pattern

---

17. Fitzmyer, 588. Cf. John Chrysostom, *Hom. 1 Cor.* 41.2.
18. Schep, *Resurrection Body*, 194.
19. The classic exposition of this thesis is Harald Riesenfeld, "Das Bildwort vom Weizenkorn bei Paulus (zu I Cor 15)," in *Studien zum Neuen Testament und zur Patristik* (Berlin: Akademie, 1961), 43–55.
20. Barrett, 370.
21. Plutarch, *Frag.* 11: "For it is *necessary* [δεῖ] that the seed first be cast into and hidden within the earth"; Epictetus, *Diatr.* 4.8.36: "It is *necessary* [δεῖ] that the seed be buried for a time, be hidden."
22. Contra Fee, 864; Garland, 728. Rightly Schrage, 282–83.

of Christ himself, who first died and then was raised (15:3–4). It is the pattern of the whole Christian life, which is a call to "die daily" with Christ (15:30–32, καθ' ἡμέραν ἀποθνῄσκω; cf. 4:9, ὡς ἐπιθανατίους), in order to share in the glory of the resurrection. The call to discipleship, so prominent and explicit elsewhere in the chapter (15:29–34, 48, 58), is thus subtly present here as well.

Like Jesus's parables with their multiple points of comparison, Paul's comparison of the seed "finds several parallels between the life of a seed and the resurrection of the dead."[23] In v. 36 he has already expressed three of them: (1) How can the dead be raised? By God's almighty power, which, as the miracle of the transformation of the seed into the plant shows, can do anything. God's power is limitless. It is able to bring life out of death, corruption, and decay. (2) As there is a material continuity between the seed and its flower, so in the resurrection the same mortal body that dies will be raised to new life. The resurrection is a resurrection of the flesh. (3) The end goal of the present body is the risen body conformed to Christ. More parallels between the growth of the seed and the resurrection are to come in the verses that follow.

## Verses 37–38

*[37] And what you sow, you sow not the body which will be, but an unclothed kernel, if it so happen of wheat, or of some one of the other species. [38] But God gives it a body, just as he willed, and to each of the species of seed its appropriate body.*

The καί that begins v. 37 is not explanatory (καί *explicativum*) but adds an additional thought.[24] Having addressed in v. 36 the first question of v. 35 ("How can the dead be raised?"), Paul here begins his answer to the second question of the interlocutor: "And with what kind of body do they return to life?" (15:35b).[25] Paul's answer to the second question will be much fuller and more developed than his response to the first. The reason for this difference lies in the nature of the two questions. As Godet writes:

> The first question implied an inexplicable mystery, and the answer could only be given by means of a not less mysterious analogous fact. Here it is otherwise,

---

23. Ciampa & Rosner, 801.
24. Contra Lindemann, 357.
25. Rightly Sider, "Resurrection Body," 429; Weiss, 368; Godet, 2:404. So also John Chrysostom, *Hom. 1 Cor.* 41.3.

for the point in question is the nature of the new body, which will result from this unfathomable operation, in contrast to the nature of the present body.[26]

And yet, in the course of answering this second question, Paul will also continue to address the first question in vv. 37-38.

*15:37. And what you sow, you sow not the body which will be.* As he now responds to the second question of the interlocutor regarding what kind of body (σῶμα) will be raised, Paul in 15:37-38 will use the word σῶμα three times (once in v. 37, twice in v. 38). In each of these instances, σῶμα or "body" will denote the plant or tree that results from the seed sown.[27]

This is a masterful use of metaphor that creatively bridges two worlds. Ancient natural philosophers, such as Aristotle, would describe the plant or tree as a "body" or σῶμα. Thus Aristotle remarks that "from one seed one *body* comes, such as from one grain of wheat, one stalk" (*Gen. an.* 728b35-36, ἐξ ἑνὸς σπέρματος ἓν σῶμα γίγνεται, οἷον ἐξ ἑνὸς πυροῦ πυθμήν). He specifically includes plants within the definition of σῶμα (*De an.* 412a11-412b9) and observes that "the seed and the fruit are potentially such a body" (412b26-27, τὸ δὲ σπέρμα καὶ ὁ καρπὸς τὸ δυνάμει τοιονδὶ σῶμα). Paul's comparison is thus not clumsy or slapdash but quite masterfully chosen.

Natural philosophers such as Aristotle also recognized the radical difference between the seed and the resultant tree or plant: "But seed is prior, because from this something else comes" (Aristotle, *Gen. an.* 724b21-22, σπέρμα δὲ τῷ ἐκ τούτου ἄλλο). Paul's οὐ ... ἀλλά construction underscores this radical difference between seed and plant.[28] Paul thus begins to lay out an answer to the second question of the interlocutor by way of this further point of comparison between the resurrection and the growth of seed. Like the seed, the present body will be resurrected to a radically new, transformed existence. In 15:36 the comparison of the seed pointed to the *restoration of life* of the mortal body that will take place when it is raised despite its prior death, decomposition, and decay. Here the comparison points to the *transformation* of the mortal body that will occur in its eschatological resurrection.

*but an unclothed kernel.* The word κόκκος, here translated "kernel," denotes a "seed" with primary reference to its outward shape or form (i.e., "grain," "seed-grain," or

---

26. Godet, 2:404.
27. Paul writes τὸ σῶμα τὸ γενησόμενον ("the body which will be"). The "Western" reading γεννησόμενον (P[46] F G) is clearly secondary.
28. In this construction, "the antithesis is sharp" (Rob., *Gram.*, 1187).

"kernel").²⁹ Paul describes this seed-grain as "naked" or "unclothed" (γυμνός). The lexica and commentators tell us that here Paul is using language that is proper to human bodies but was never used in antiquity with reference to seeds.³⁰ However, this is false. Theophrastus, in his horticultural treatise *De causis plantarum*, expressly uses this language of seeds. In this treatise Theophrastus writes: "But the seed of cereals is unclothed [γυμνά], and especially the seed of wheat and barley" (*Caus. plant.* 4.1.2). Similarly in *Caus. plant.* 4.2.2., the seed of barley is "unclothed" (γυμνός). Theophrastus also uses the term γυμνός of seeds in his work *Historia plantarum* (*Hist. plant.* 8.4.1), even describing certain plants using the adjective γυμνόσπερμος (8.3.4 "having unclothed seed"). Thus we see that, as with the language of σῶμα for the plant "body," Paul's description of the seed as "unclothed" (γυμνός) employs the technical language of ancient horticulture and natural science.³¹ And here again Paul masterfully employs the technique of metaphorical reference (i.e., conceptual blending) to express an important truth about the risen bodies of the faithful, a truth that will form a key theme of the chapter. Like the seed, which is sown as an unclothed kernel, bare and nondescript, but will become a plant or tree, wondrously clothed with trunk or stem, foliage or blossoms, fruit or flowers, so the risen bodies of the saints will "wear" the image of Christ's glorious body (15:49, φορέω [2×]), and "be clothed" with imperishability and immortality (15:53–54, ἐνδύω [4×]). This conception of the present body as now unclothed but clothed in the future resurrection accents, once again, the *transformation* that will take place in the resurrection and the *difference* between the present body and the risen body. But, at the same time, this portrayal of the presently unclothed mortal body as one awaiting being clothed in the resurrection reveals the *continuity* between the present body and the risen body—what is raised to life is the present mortal body, which in the resurrection is clothed with immortality (15:37, 49, 53–54).³²

*if it so happen of wheat, or of some one of the other species.* The combination of εἰ with the optative, as here in the phrase εἰ τύχοι, expresses a mere hypothetical pos-

---

29. See LSJ, s.v. "κόκκος"; BDAG, s.v. "κόκκος"; Robinson, s.v. "κόκκος."

30. See BDAG, s.v. "γυμνός " (1.b); Schrage, 286; Conzelmann, 281 ("For of course this expression does not suit a seed at all"); Ciampa & Rosner, 802; Weiss, 369.

31. Failure to recognize this has led a number of scholars to seek the background of Paul's language in Platonic or Stoic language for the soul or human generation. That these are false trails is shown decisively by John Granger Cook, "A Naked Seed: Platonism, Stoicism, or Agriculture in 1Cor 15,37," *ZNW* 111 (2020): 289–309.

32. Cf. Bernhard Spörlein, *Die Leugnung der Auferstehung: Eine historisch-kritische Untersuchung zu I Kor 15* (Regensburg: Pustet, 1971), 101–2.

sibility.³³ The expression εἰ τύχοι is a "stereotyped phrase."³⁴ As such it approaches an adverbial force, meaning essentially "perhaps." The seed sown may be wheat, or it may be any one of the different varieties of seed. Paul's choice of "wheat" (σῖτος) as his named example is fitting, for the main staple grain of the ancient Mediterranean world was wheat, followed by barley.³⁵ The "other species" Paul mentions might include rye, oats, millet, or the seeds of any number of garden plants and fruit-bearing trees.

Paul's mention here in v. 37 of the various kinds of seeds does not relate to any of the points Paul is making in this verse. Rather, it functions to prepare for the point he will make in v. 38b that God gives "to each of the species of seeds its appropriate body." This is a striking fact, for Paul's careful preparation for this point already in this verse indicates that v. 38b has an extraordinary importance in his exposition of the mystery of the resurrection in this passage. In the commentary on v. 38b below, we will find why this is the case.

*15:38. But God gives it a body, just as he willed.* The bare seed, lifeless and hidden in the earth, becomes a beautiful plant or tree laden with blossoms, leaves, and fruit. This marvelous fact is the work of the creator God. As many scholars have recognized, Paul's addition of "just as he willed" (καθὼς ἠθέλησεν), with its use of the aorist tense, refers to "the order established at creation."³⁶ As Joseph Fitzmyer adds, "Paul is indirectly alluding to the creation account of Gen 1:11–12."³⁷ Paul's use of the present tense δίδωσιν "gives" portrays God's creative work as present and continuous (cf. John 5:17, "My Father is working until now, and I am working") yet in perfect coherence with the order of creation established at the beginning, as seen in the aorist tense ἠθέλησεν ("he willed"). As with the divine passive ζῳοποιεῖται in 15:36, the focus here is on the sovereign will and almighty power of the creator.³⁸

Some interpreters believe Paul's understanding of botanical growth as the work of the creator must involve an inadequate or unscientific conception that

33. Kühner-G., 2.2:477 (§576).
34. Rob., *Gram.*, 1021.
35. Ludwig Alfred Moritz, "Corn," *OCD*, 291.
36. Sider, "Resurrection Body," 432. Similarly Fitzmyer, 589; Wolff, 404; Lindemann, 357; Robertson & Plummer, 370; Godet, 2:405; Garland, 729; Ciampa & Rosner, 803; Fee, 865; Thiselton, 1264–65. Sider persuasively compares the identical phrase in 1 Cor 12:18, where the aorist similarly appears to refer to the arrangement of the members of the human body established at creation. Sider contrasts Paul's use of the aorist in these passages with καθὼς βούλεται in 1 Cor 12:11, where the present tense refers to God's "present bestowal of the gifts" ("Resurrection Body," 432).
37. Fitzmyer, 589; cf. Wolff, 404; Ciampa & Rosner, 803; Garland, 729.
38. Schrage, 287–88.

excludes the organic character and regularity of nature. According to Conzelmann, "it is plain how far Paul is from an organic thought of nature."[39] This is a misunderstanding of Paul's thought. As Sider notes, "Paul's thought excludes a deistic conception of autonomous nature but in no way denies either the regularity of nature or genuine continuity between the seed and the new plant."[40] This is evident in 15:38 in his references to the regular order of nature established at creation (καθὼς ἠθέλησεν) and to the organic relationship between the various species of seed and the plants they produce (καὶ ἑκάστῳ τῶν σπερμάτων ἴδιον σῶμα).

And yet, in Paul's thought, the sole source or cause of this organic logic and regularity of nature is the efficacious will of the creator (15:38, "God *gives* it a body"). Here we come to the heart of Paul's understanding of the seed's growth as a witness to the resurrection. The purpose and effective power evident in the transformation of seed to plant is truly a miraculous fact requiring explanation. Aristotle clearly perceived the purposefulness of nature in the wonder of botanical and biological growth (*Part. an.* 641b) and, more dimly, discerned the source of this purpose in a reality outside nature (*Metaph.* 1072a–1074b; *Phys.* 258b–260a). The apostle, with fuller vision illumined by divine revelation, sees the true explanation of the mystery—the power of an almighty creator God. It is this power of God, evident in the miraculous transformation of seed to plant, that the fool of v. 35 fails to take into account when he denies that the dead can be raised.

But the seed's marvelous growth is more than simply a general witness to God's power. As Paul's language of σῶμα shows, it is a divinely given anticipation of the resurrection within the present created order, for "God gives it a *body*" (ὁ δὲ θεὸς δίδωσιν αὐτῷ σῶμα). Like the seed, the present body will be transformed in the resurrection. The comparison of the seed is important, for it reveals what the chapter will only later make explicit—that the transformation of the body that takes place in the resurrection will be to a state far more glorious. At the same time, the analogy of the seed reveals the *material continuity* between the mortal and risen body. There is an organic continuity between the seed that is sown and the tree or plant that it becomes—for "God gives *it* a body" (ὁ δὲ θεὸς δίδωσιν αὐτῷ σῶμα). Paul's comparison of the seed teaches "substantial continuity . . . *this* body of flesh will be raised."[41] This continuity was already evident in 1 Cor 6:12–20, where the body's future resurrection entails that it should not be used in the present for sexual immorality.[42] This continuity will be evident, as we will see, throughout the

---

39. Conzelmann, 282.
40. Sider, "Resurrection Body," 432.
41. Schep, *Resurrection Body*, 194.
42. Garland, 729.

chapter. Continuity together with glorious transformation—such is the relation of seed to plant and of the present body to the risen body.

*and to each of the species of seed its appropriate body.* Paul here again uses the device of metaphorical reference skillfully for, as we have seen, the ancients could refer to the plant as a "body." Here σπέρμα in the plural denotes "kinds of seed" or "species of seed."[43] Each kind of seed produces a tree, plant, or flower according to its kind (cf. Gen 1:11–13). Aristotle found in this fact yet another proof of the purposive character of nature: "For, indeed, not just anything at random comes from each seed [σπέρματος], but this particular living being from this particular seed" (Aristotle, *Part. an.* 641b26–28). This fact thus enriches Paul's portrayal of botanical growth as a witness to the efficacious will and power of the creator. This fact also underscores the obvious continuity between seed and plant, and thus reinforces the analogy's emphasis on the continuity of the present body and the future risen body.

But Paul has already made these points elsewhere in the analogy. What is Paul's main point here, when he specifically adds the detail that each species of seed is given its own proper body by God? Clearly the point is of extraordinary importance for Paul. This is evident from a remarkable fact. Paul observed in 15:37 that the seed that is sown may be "if it so happen of wheat, or of some one of the other species." This remark, as we saw, did not relate to any of the points Paul made in 15:37, and it appears to have had no other purpose than to prepare for the point he makes here in 15:38b that God gives "to each of the species of seed its appropriate body." Paul's reference, of course, is to the bodies of the faithful, namely, that in the resurrection those who belong to Christ will be given their "appropriate body." What precisely is Paul's point?

Paul's point is this. The present bodies of the faithful, earthen vessels though they are, bear a marvelous treasure (2 Cor 4:7). Their very bodies have been "sealed" (that is, with oil and the sign of the cross at baptism) and given "the first installment of the Spirit" (2 Cor 1:21–22; 5:5; cf. Eph 1:13–14; 4:30).[44] In the Eucharist they "have been made to drink of one Spirit" (1 Cor 12:13). Their bodies are thus

---

43. So BA, s.v. "σπέρμα": "Samenarten" (i.e., "seed-types"); C. Burchard, "1 Korinther 15,39–41," *ZNW* 75 (1984): 237. We find the same sequence found here in vv. 37–38, with κόκκος in reference to a single grain followed by σπέρμα in the plural with reference to the various kinds of seeds, in Mark 4:31.

44. For the practice of sealing with oil at baptism in the Pauline churches, see Wayne A. Meeks, *The First Urban Christians* (2d ed.; New Haven: Yale University Press, 2003), 151. For this practice of baptismal anointing with the sign of the cross in the early church, see Tertullian, *Bapt.* 7–8; *Res.* 8; *Marc.* 1.14; Hippolytus, *Trad. ap.* 21; Cyprian, *Ep.* 70.2.

CHAPTER 11

members of Christ (1 Cor 6:15, τὰ σώματα ὑμῶν μέλη Χριστοῦ ἐστιν). Their bodies are living tabernacles of the Holy Spirit (1 Cor 3:16). "Your *body* is a *temple* of the *Holy Spirit* who indwells you" (1 Cor 6:19, τὸ σῶμα ὑμῶν ναὸς τοῦ ἐν ὑμῖν ἁγίου πνεύματος).[45] But these tabernacles of God in the present time are mortal, perishing, and doomed to death (Rom 8:10, τὸ μὲν σῶμα νεκρὸν διὰ ἁμαρτίαν). The bodies of those united to Christ await a transformation to become bodies appropriate to their identity as members of Christ and temples of the Holy Spirit—glorified and imperishable bodies, to be given at the resurrection. Believers are even now, as bearers of Christ, "the heavenly ones" (15:48); in the resurrection they "will wear the image of the heavenly one" (15:49), when their lowly bodies are transformed to be like Christ's glorious body (Phil 3:21). It is instructive to map Paul's central formulations in Romans regarding the resurrection onto the logic of 1 Cor 15:38b:

| | | |
|---|---|---|
| 1 Cor 15:38b | and to each of the species of seed | its appropriate body |
| Rom 8:11 | But if the Spirit of the one who raised Jesus from the dead dwells in you, | the one who raised Christ from the dead will give life also to your mortal bodies |
| Rom 8:23 | we ourselves who have the first-fruits of the Spirit groan within ourselves, eagerly awaiting | the redemption of our body |

In the resurrection, the present perishable bodies of the faithful will be glorified in order to become fitting everlasting tabernacles of the Holy Spirit, who even now indwells them. In the resurrection, those who are even now bearers of Christ will be given their "appropriate body."

According to 15:36–38, then, the marvel of the seed and its growth, in bringing life out of death and a wondrous transformation, is a divinely given sign within the created order, which points forward to the miracle of the resurrection.

But how can the body of flesh and bones, which is perishable, be raised to an imperishable life? This is the question Paul will address in the next verse.

## Verse 39

*Not all flesh is the same flesh. To the contrary, there is one flesh of human beings, and another flesh of animals, and another flesh of birds, and another of fish.*

---

45. On this key theme within the letter, see Michael K. W. Suh, *Power and Peril: Paul's Use of Temple Discourse in 1 Corinthians* (BZNW 239; Berlin: de Gruyter, 2020).

Paul's comparison takes a new turn from the bodies (σῶμα, three times in 15:37–38) of seeds and plants to the flesh (σάρξ, four times in 15:39) of human beings, animals, birds, and fish. Virtually all expositors understand v. 39 as a mere analogy or illustration. But as we will see, Paul here echoes passages of the Scriptures that celebrate creation. Therefore it would appear that Paul understood the wondrous variety of kinds of flesh among creatures, just as he did the marvel of the seed's transformation into a plant, not as a mere illustration or analogy but as a divinely given testimony or sign, within the present created order, pointing to the resurrection to come.

*All flesh is not the same flesh.* The juxtaposition of σάρξ "flesh" in 15:39 (four times) with σῶμα "body" in 15:37–38 (three times) and 15:40 (twice) shows that here, reflecting the normal usage of Paul's Greek-speaking audience, σάρξ and σῶμα function as interchangeable terms for the human body.[46] Paul similarly uses the two interchangeably in 1 Cor 6:16 (ὁ κολλώμενος τῇ πόρνῃ ἓν σῶμά ἐστιν, ἔσονται γάρ, φησίν, οἱ δύο εἰς σάρκα μίαν). Although frequently synonymous, σάρξ and σῶμα do not within ancient Greek usage have precisely the same meaning. The noun σῶμα denotes a "*body*, as an organized whole made up of parts and members."[47] The σῶμα is thus "the organized σάρξ."[48] The σάρξ, on the other hand, is "der Leib selbst nach seiner Substanz" ("the body itself according to its substance").[49] So also here in 1 Cor 15:39, "σάρξ is here the stuff of which the body consists."[50] The word σάρξ in 15:39, then, expresses the material, stuff, or substance of the bodies of humans, beasts, birds, and fish. But this stuff of the body, although shared in common by each of these creatures (here called collectively πᾶσα σάρξ "all flesh"), differs in each of them in kind or quality. Therefore they are not ἡ αὐτὴ σάρξ ("the same flesh").

*To the contrary, there is one flesh of human beings, and another flesh of animals, and another flesh of birds, and another of fish.* The different kinds of flesh of the four types of creatures are set out in four perfectly balanced clauses of six syllables each.[51] The artistry of the passage is enhanced by Paul's effective use of repetition

---

46. *TLNT* 3:236; cf. Wolff, 404.
47. Robinson, s.v. "σῶμα"; cf. Thayer, s.v. "σάρξ" (2).
48. Cremer, 537.
49. BA, s.v. "σάρξ" (2).
50. Conzelmann, 282.
51. The second member of Paul's fourfold sequence is here translated "animals." In the overwhelming majority of instances, the noun κτῆνος refers specifically to domesticated animals or cattle, and BDAG claims that this is the meaning in force here in v. 39 (BDAG, s.v. "κτῆνος"; cf. BA, s.v. "κτῆνος"). But the word can also have a comprehensive sense denoting animals generally

CHAPTER 11

(ἄλλη, four times) and assonance or parechesis (e.g., κτηνῶν, πτηνῶν).[52] As Paul's comparison of the seed recalled the third day of creation in Gen 1:9–13, so the four kinds of creatures enumerated here recall the fifth and sixth days of creation in Gen 1:20–31, but with the order here being the exact reverse of the order of their creation in Genesis.[53] It is likely that Paul has in mind here not only the creation narrative of Gen 1 but also one of the so-called creation psalms: Psalm 8. To start, Paul has already quoted this psalm only a few verses earlier in the chapter (Ps 8:7 in 15:27). Second, in Ps 8:5, 8–9 LXX we find, in the identical order to Paul, ἄνθρωπος ("human being"), κτήνη ("animals"), πετεινά ("birds"), and ἰχθύες ("fish").

In these Old Testament passages that Paul alludes to here, the created order is pronounced to be "very good" (Gen 1:31), and God is praised for the splendor, variety, and multiplicity of his creation (Ps 8:2–4, 7–10 LXX). This underscores a fact that so many scholars fail to grasp: Paul's thought belongs firmly within this biblical and Jewish context, in which all of creation is intrinsically good, including the physical body.[54] "The earth is the Lord's, and its fullness," as Paul has already instructed the Corinthians in 1 Cor 10:26 (quoting Ps 24:1). Here in v. 39, the "flesh" (σάρξ) of human beings and of the various creatures is an aspect of this good creation.

The goodness of the flesh in Paul's thought, in view of widespread scholarly misunderstanding, requires further elaboration. A recurring motif in Paul's epistles is the contrast between σάρξ and πνεῦμα (e.g., Rom 2:28–29; 7:4–6; 8:3–14; 1 Cor 3:1–4; Gal 3:2–3; 5:16–25; Phil 3:3). In such passages, πνεῦμα has a positive value, and σάρξ has a negative value. Many Pauline scholars regard such passages as obvious evidence that Paul disparaged the body and the material world as intrinsically evil and sinful.[55] But this is a profoundly mistaken understanding of Paul's thought. In the

---

(Gen 6:7 LXX; Deut 4:16–18 LXX; Ps 8:8–9 LXX). The context of v. 39, in which Paul contrasts these creatures with humans, birds, and fish, indicates the word has this comprehensive sense here.

52. BDR §488 n. 7; cf. Lindemann, 357; Conzelmann, 282; Robertson & Plummer, 867; Reasoner, on 15:39.

53. Fee, 867; Fitzmyer, 589; Ciampa & Rosner, 867. David A. Burnett argues that v. 39 alludes not to Gen 1 but to Deut 4:15–19 LXX in "A Neglected Deuteronomic Scriptural Matrix for the Nature of the Resurrection Body in 1 Corinthians 15:39–42?" in *Scripture, Texts, and Tracings in 1 Corinthians* (ed. Linda L. Belleville and B. J. Oropeza; Lanham, MD: Lexington/Fortress, 2019), 187–211. However, the Deuteronomy passage lacks the key term ἄνθρωπος. In addition, v. 39 continues the allusions to Gen 1 begun in the analogy of the seed in vv. 36–38. Deut 4:15–19 LXX lacks any language related to seed, tree, and plant.

54. For fuller discussion, see James P. Ware, *Paul's Theology in Context: Creation, Incarnation, Covenant, and Kingdom* (Grand Rapids: Eerdmans, 2019), 7–23.

55. See, for example, Nikolaus Walter, "Leibliche Auferstehung? Zur Frage der Hellenisierung der Auferweckungshoffnung bei Paulus," in *Paulus, Apostel Jesu Christi: Festschrift für Günter Klein zum 70. Geburtstag* (ed. Michael Trowitzsch; Tübingen: Mohr Siebeck, 1998), 59; Linde-

passages cited, the word πνεῦμα refers to the *Holy Spirit*, and Paul uses σάρξ in a *holistic* way with reference to the whole person, body and soul, bereft of the transforming power of the Spirit of God (e.g., Rom 8:9, "But you are not in the flesh [σαρκὶ], but in the Spirit [πνεύματι], if indeed the Spirit of God dwells in you"). In these passages, σάρξ is Paul's shorthand for human nature alienated from God through the fall. This negative sense of σάρξ in Paul has nothing to do with a disparagement of matter or the body, and everything to do with the broken nature of fallen humanity, which is in need of the gift of the Holy Spirit and restoration of union with God.[56]

But in any case, as all interpreters are agreed, Paul is not using σάρξ in this special theological and negative sense here in 15:39. Here the term, as we have seen, simply denotes the physical substance of the bodies of humans, animals, birds, and fish. As Ceslas Spicq notes, σάρξ in v. 39 is an instance of "the neutral biological meaning, 'flesh' as a synonym of 'body.'"[57] Wolfgang Schrage likewise describes the sense of σάρξ here as not negative but "neutral."[58] And yet, to be precise, even this language of "neutral" is not a wholly adequate way of putting the matter. For, as Paul's allusions in this verse to Gen 1 and Ps 8 ought to remind us, Paul's thought is grounded in the creation theology of the Old Testament. For him, the flesh, as the physical substance of the human body and of the various creatures created by God, is hardly neutral but "very good" (Gen 1:31).

Paul's choice of ἄλλος "another," used four times within the verse, is precise. Unlike its close synonym ἕτερος "another," which generally denotes another of a different class, ἄλλος generally denotes another of the same class.[59] Flesh or σάρξ is common to all the four varieties of creatures, but in each that flesh is of a different quality or kind.[60] The fourfold alliterative repetition of ἄλλη serves to emphasize the variety and diversity of the various kinds of flesh, each befitting the kind of creature to which it belongs.[61]

---

mann, 324–73; Mark D. Given, "Paul and Writing," in *As It Is Written: Studying Paul's Use of Scripture* (ed. Stanley E. Porter and Christopher D. Stanley; SBLSymS 50; Atlanta: Society of Biblical Literature, 2008), 255–56; Peter Lampe, "Paul's Concept of a Spiritual Body," in *Resurrection: Theological and Scientific Assessments* (ed. Ted Peters, Robert John Russell, and Michael Welker; Grand Rapids: Eerdmans, 2002), 103–14; and Hans Grass, *Ostergeschehen und Osterberichte* (Göttingen: Vandenhoeck & Ruprecht, 1962), 146–73.

56. See Ware, *Paul's Theology*, 36–38; David Wenham, *Paul: Follower of Jesus or Founder of Christianity?* (Grand Rapids: Eerdmans, 1995), 230–32; Schep, *Resurrection Body*, 81–106.

57. *TLNT* 3:236.

58. Schrage, 289; Fitzmyer, 589.

59. Schmidt, *Syn.*, 4:559–69 (§198); Rob., *Gram.*, 746–49; Trench, *Syn.*, 357–61.

60. Galen similarly contrasts the different qualities of the flesh (σάρξ) of lions, sheep, and human beings (*Const. art.* 1.255.2–5).

61. Reasoner, on 15:39.

CHAPTER 11

What is the point of this for the resurrection? As Conzelmann notes, "the emphasis on ἄλλος—ἄλλος, 'one—another,' corresponds to that on ἴδιον σῶμα, 'its own particular body.'"[62] Paul thus here continues and expands on the thought of v. 38b. Just as in v. 38b each species of seed received its own appropriate *body*, so too here each kind of creature is given its own appropriate kind of *flesh*. In v. 38b, Paul's point was that just as each kind of seed receives the body appropriate to it, so too Christ followers in the resurrection will be given glorified and imperishable *bodies* befitting their identity as living tabernacles of the Holy Spirit. Here in v. 39, Paul indicates that just as each kind of creature is given its own appropriate kind of flesh, so too at the resurrection those united to Christ will be given glorified and imperishable *flesh* and thus be made fitting everlasting temples for the living God. The interlocutor in 15:35 had asked derisively, "And with what kind of body do they return to life?" on the assumption that flesh is intrinsically and necessarily perishable. But v. 39 reveals that just as God's almighty power can fashion an appropriate kind of flesh for each species of creature, so too in the resurrection God's power will furnish an appropriate kind of flesh for the bearers of Christ—glorified and imperishable flesh. As Schep writes:

> The objectors in Corinth had asked how *this* body of flesh can ever be raised from the dead in a different form and endowed with different characteristics. Paul replies by reminding them that many sorts of fleshly bodies already exist, each having its distinctive structure. Can it then be impossible for God, who created this variety, to change the present body of flesh into a resurrection-body consisting of flesh but nevertheless greatly different from the present body?[63]

The critical importance of 15:39 for Paul's understanding of the resurrection, and its puncturing of popular scholarly pablum, must not be missed. Time and again we are told by interpreters of Paul that his understanding of the resurrection was different from, or less than, the ancient Jewish and Old Testament doctrine of the resurrection of the flesh.[64] But just as Paul's analogy of the seed in 15:36–38 assumes that the risen body will be a *body* (σῶμα, three times in 15:37–38), so Paul's analogy of the various kinds of flesh in 15:39 assumes that the risen body will be composed of *flesh* (σάρξ, four times in 15:39). Paul's comparison of the seed showed that a transformation will take place in the resurrection (15:37–38), and Paul's application of the comparison in his subsequent argument will show that

---

62. Conzelmann, 282.
63. Schep, *Resurrection Body*, 196.
64. E.g. Grass, *Ostergeschehen*, 171; Martin, *Body*, 123; Keener, 131.

the transformation he has in mind is the change from perishability and mortality to immortality and imperishability (15:42–44, 52–54). Verse 39 reveals that this will be a transformation of the *flesh* to glorious imperishability. This flesh of the risen saints will be the same substance as their present bodies but with new and different qualities. In the resurrection, the flesh of the faithful will be *glorified*.

Although many scholars have attempted to do so, there is no getting around v. 39. Its place within Paul's overall argument, as we have shown, is clear. Verse 39 demonstrates that Paul, as the church would do in its historic teaching through the centuries, taught a resurrection of the flesh. Verse 39 also reveals that scholarly interpretations of 1 Cor 15:44, 45, or 50 that read these verses as denying a resurrection of the flesh are without foundation. In particular, it shows that the common interpretation of Paul's dictum in 15:50 ("flesh and blood cannot inherit the kingdom of God") as a denial that the physical flesh shares in resurrection is a naive and uncritical reading, one that fails to read v. 50 within the context of the chapter as a whole. Paul's twin references to σάρξ in vv. 39 and 50 must be read in concert. These two verses make closely related points. Verse 50 affirms that inheritance of the kingdom requires that this present mortal flesh be made immortal and imperishable; v. 39 declares that God's almighty power as creator can and will bring this glorification of the flesh to pass. As v. 39 shows, Paul does not envision the destruction of the flesh but its glorification and transformation to imperishability. "The glory of the risen body will not destroy nature, but will perfect it."[65]

## Verse 40

*Moreover, there are heavenly bodies and earthly bodies. But the glory of the heavenly bodies is of one kind, and that of the earthly bodies is of a different kind.*

Some interpreters regard the conjunction καί that begins v. 40 as indicating that vv. 40–41 involve a mere continuation of the comparison in v. 39.[66] However, the fact that Paul here resumes the language of σῶμα from 15:37–38 and introduces a new conception—the distinction between heavenly and earthly bodies—indicates that 15:40–41 forms a third comparison. Paul now moves, as he continues his threefold comparison, from the botanical (15:36–38) and zoological (15:39) domains to the astrological (15:40–41).

---

65. Aquinas, *ST* Suppl. Q. 85, Art. 1, ad 3.
66. So Bonneau, "Logic," 83–86; Schrage, 290.

CHAPTER 11

*Moreover, there are heavenly bodies and earthly bodies.* By "heavenly bodies" Paul refers to the sidereal heavens—the sun, moon, and stars—as 15:41 will confirm. "Earthly bodies" include the bodies of seeds, plants, trees, humans, animals, birds, and fish, all of which were mentioned in 15:36–39. Just as Paul's previous comparisons of the seed and its growth (vv. 36–38) and of the varied types of creaturely flesh (v. 39) had recalled the third (Gen 1:11–13), fifth (Gen 1:20–23), and sixth (Gen 1:24–31) days of creation, so too here Paul's contrast between heaven and earth recalls the second day of creation, in which the heavens and the earth were divided (Gen 1:6–8). Paul's word order reveals that the focus of the comparison here is on the *heavenly* bodies.[67]

Paul's point here is to introduce the idea of the risen body as a kind of heavenly body. Once again, Paul's use of metaphor or double reference is masterful. In Plato's *Timaeus*, the very phrase "heavenly bodies" (σώματα ἐπουράνια) employed here by Paul is used repeatedly to denote the sun, moon, and stars (Plato, *Tim.* 38c, 38e–39a). Paul's language thus perfectly befits this third field of comparison: the astronomical. But the purpose of Paul's double reference is to open his audience to new truths regarding the risen human body to come. Paul's language of "body" (σῶμα) picks up on the use of this term previously in 15:37–38 and recalls the question of the interlocutor in 15:35, "And with what kind of body [σώματι] do they return to life?" Paul thereby continues his answer to this question of the interlocutor. Paul's answer is that the present body is an earthly body, but it will be raised as a heavenly body. We must explore what this means.

*But the glory of the heavenly bodies is of one kind, and that of the earthly bodies is of a different kind.* Paul now introduces the concept of glory (δόξα), a crucial conception that will reappear four times in 15:41 and again in the all-important

---

67. According to BDAG, these heavenly bodies are here "thought of ... as living beings clothed with light" (BDAG, s.v. "ἐπουράνιος" [1]), and many scholars share this opinion (so Barrett, 371; Schrage, 292; Wolff, 405; Conzelmann, 282). However, this common view, as John Granger Cook has shown, is without foundation; see "1Cor 15,40–41: Paul and the Heavenly Bodies," *ZNW* 113 (2022): 159–79. To be sure, the belief that the sun, moon, and stars were animate, intelligent creatures was widespread in antiquity among the philosophically educated (Cicero, *Rep.* 6.15; Plato, *Tim.* 38c–41b; Aristotle, *Cael.* 292a; Diogenes Laertius, *Vit. phil.* 8.27; Philo, *Plant.* 12; for the Stoics, see *SVF* 1.120, 504; 2.527, 579, 684; Cicero, *Nat. d.* 2.42–43). However, this claim was not universal, for it was rejected by the Epicureans (Epicurus, *Ep. Her.* 76–77; Lucretius, *Nat.* 5.110–145). Moreover, there is no firm evidence for such a conception in ancient Judaism outside Philo, and even he specifically cites ancient philosophy as the source of the doctrine (Philo, *Plant.* 12). Paul's brief treatment in 15:40–41 does not address this ancient controversy one way or the other. As Cook concludes, "Paul does not assume any specific understanding of heavenly bodies in 15,40–41, other than that they are creations of God" ("Heavenly Bodies," 179).

application of the analogy in 15:43. Here and throughout the chapter, Paul will use the word δόξα in that sense exclusive to Jewish and Christian documents in antiquity—to denote not an honor or magnificence bestowed by the estimation of others but an *objective* splendor or majesty inhering in its possessor.[68] Paul contrasts the glory of the heavenly bodies with that of the earthly bodies. Although he contrasts them, Paul in so doing clearly assigns a kind of glory to both. This raises a question. As we have seen, it is the heavenly bodies, not the earthly bodies, that correspond in Paul's analogy to the risen body. In the application of the comparison, Paul will not speak of a glory of the present body, and he will ascribe glory exclusively to the risen body (15:43). Why then does Paul speak here of a glory belonging to earthly bodies as well? This question has generally puzzled commentators.[69]

However, the answer is not difficult to discern. Paul's thought is thoroughly biblical, Jewish, and immersed in the goodness and splendor of creation. Within Israel's Scriptures, the earth, its creatures, and their bodies, as the handiwork of the creator, possess their own peculiar glory and splendor. Isaiah 6:3 in the LXX proclaims: "all the *earth* is filled with his *glory*!" (πλήρης πᾶσα ἡ γῆ τῆς δόξης αὐτοῦ). In Ps 138:14 LXX, the psalmist proclaims of his body formed in the womb: "I was made marvelously [ἐθαυμαστώθην]! Marvelous [θαυμάσια] are your works!" Psalm 103:24 LXX similarly says of all the creation, including the earth and its creatures, "How magnificent [ἐμεγαλύνθη] are your works, Lord!" (cf. Ps 91:6 LXX). Psalm 110:3 LXX acclaims, "His work is majesty and splendor [μεγαλοπρέπεια]." According to Sir 42:17, God firmly founded the creation, in order to "establish the *whole universe* in his *glory*" (στηριχθῆναι ἐν δόξῃ αὐτοῦ τὸ πᾶν).

Nonetheless, Paul sets the glory of the heavenly bodies and that of earthly bodies in stark contrast. Paul's language is chosen with precision. Unlike its close synonym ἄλλος "another," which generally denotes another of the same category or class, ἕτερος "another" generally denotes another of a different class.[70] In 15:39, Paul had used ἄλλος with reference to the flesh shared alike by humans, animals, birds, and fish, each differing in its qualities. Here he uses ἕτερος because he wishes to strongly *contrast* the glory belonging to heavenly bodies with the glory belonging to earthly bodies. The contrast is heightened by Paul's use of the construction ἕτερος μέν . . . ἕτερος δέ. This construction does not simply denote that two entities are distinct ("the one . . . the other") but emphasizes that they are quite *different* (Plato, *Parm.* 129c; *Alc. maj.* 113d; Aristotle, *Mag. mor.* 1211a26–28; Philo,

---

68. Cremer, 206–10; BA, s.v. "δόξα."
69. See, for example, the inconclusive discussion in Schrage, 290–91.
70. Rob., *Gram.*, 746–49; Schmidt, *Syn.*, 4:559–69 (§198); Trench, *Syn.*, 357–61; cf. Godet, 2:408.

CHAPTER 11

*Det.* 49; Sextus Empiricus, *Math.* 7.387). The implication, moreover, is that the glory of the heavenly bodies is not only different but greater, superior, and more splendid. This implication is reinforced by Paul's word order, in which the glory of the heavenly bodies is mentioned first, before that of the earthly bodies. And it will be confirmed in v. 41 by Paul's *sole* focus on the glory of the heavenly bodies. The thought is that the glory of the heavenly bodies is surpassingly greater, of an entirely different class and order, than that of the earthly bodies.

This aspect of Paul's thought here is strongly Jewish. Similarly in Sirach, although the glory of God is reflected in all his creation (Sir 42:16–17), the heavens possess a unique and surpassing glory (42:25–43:12). Within the short space of these verses in Sirach in praise of the heavens, the word δόξα occurs four times (42:25; 43:1, 9, 12). As Sirach acclaims, "The form of heaven gives a manifest vision of *glory*" (43:1, εἶδος οὐρανοῦ ἐν ὁράματι δόξης). The peculiar glory of the sun, moon, and stars is also evident in the so-called creation psalms in the Septuagint. In Ps 18, "the heavens proclaim the *glory* of God" (Ps 18:1, οἱ οὐρανοὶ διηγοῦνται δόξαν θεοῦ). In Ps 8, the psalmist declares, "I will look upon the heavens [τοὺς οὐρανούς], works of your fingers, moon [σελήνην] and stars [ἀστέρας], which you established. What, then, is a human being [ἄνθρωπος]?" (Ps 8:4–5). The distinctive glory of the heavenly bodies is assumed within many passages of the New Testament (Matt 13:43; 17:2; Acts 26:13; Phil 2:15; Rev 1:16, 2:28; 10:1; 12:1; 21:23; 22:5, 16). Paul's comparison likewise assumes this unique superiority of the glory of the heavenly bodies.[71]

But in what way is the glory of the heavenly bodies surpassingly greater? Throughout 15:36–41, Paul appeals to the everyday experience and observation of his interlocutor, and so here too he must be referring to concrete and perceptible realities (cf. Sir 42:25, ὁρῶν δόξαν αὐτοῦ). This glory, then, must denote the luminous splendor, beauty, and magnificence of the heavenly bodies (cf. Deut 4:19 LXX, πάντα τὸν κόσμον τοῦ οὐρανοῦ "all the adornment of heaven"). Within the Jewish world, this luminous splendor of the heavens was celebrated in Scripture (Ps 8:1, 4–5; 19:1; Sir 42:25–43:12). Within the pagan world, it filled the pages of the philosophers and the works of poets and playwrights. For all ancient persons, it was a matter of daily experience.

Within Paul's comparison, the glory of the heavenly bodies portends the glory of the risen bodies of the faithful. The comparison of the seed in vv. 36–38 signified that

---

71. We see Paul's thought here able to function on multiple levels, recognizing a glory in all created bodies, heavenly and earthly, but a superior splendor of the heavenly bodies, in view of which the earthly bodies may be regarded as relatively inglorious or lacking in glory. A parallel is found in 2 Cor 3:7–11, where Paul recognizes a glory belonging to both old and new covenants, but a surpassingly superior glory of the new covenant, in light of which the old covenant may be spoken of as without glory at all—"For, indeed, what has received glory has not received glory, in light of the surpassingly greater glory" (2 Cor 3:10).

*Testimonies within Creation to the Glorification of the Flesh*

in the resurrection the body would be transformed to a state immeasurably more glorious than before. Now in 15:40, Paul's analogy of the heavenly bodies indicates that this transformation will involve the risen body being endued with *heavenly* glory.

Yet the glory of the risen body will also be *different* from the glory of the heavenly bodies. This will be Paul's point in the next verse.

VERSE 41

*There is one glory of the sun, and another glory of the moon, and another glory of the stars. Indeed, one star differs from another star in glory.*

Paul in v. 41 continues his focus on the glory of the heavenly bodies. In this verse, the word "glory" (δόξα) recurs four times. Just as in his previous comparisons he recalled the third day (15:36–38), fifth and sixth days (15:39), and second day (15:40) of creation, so now he recalls the fourth day of creation (Gen 1:14–19).[72] As the allusion to Gen 1 suggests, the sun, moon, and stars do more than simply supply a useful analogy; Paul understands them as a God-given testimony within the created order prophesying and foreshadowing the glory of the resurrection to come.[73] Paul in this verse adds a crucial additional thought that will bring the entire series of comparisons in 15:36–41 to a climactic conclusion.

*There is one glory of the sun, and another glory of the moon, and another glory of the stars.* The sun, moon, and stars are, naturally enough, mentioned together quite commonly in the Old Testament (Gen 1:14–19; Deut 4:19; Pss 136:7–9; 148:3; Jer 8:2; Ep Jer 59; Dan 3:62–63 LXX; Joel 2:10). The word ἀστήρ could be used, as Paul does here, to include both fixed stars and planets.[74] As we have seen is the case throughout 15:36–41, Paul is precise in his use of the synonyms ἄλλος (which means "another" and denotes another of the same class) and ἕτερος (which also means "another" but denotes another of a different class). Paul chooses ἄλλος here, for the sun, moon, and stars each share alike in the unique *heavenly* glory, which Paul distinguished from earthly glory in v. 40. But each of them has a different *kind* of heavenly glory. Paul here again refers to directly observable realities. The

---

72. As most scholars concur, e.g., Collins, 567; Wright, *Resurrection*, 341; Ciampa & Rosner, 805. The claim of Burnett ("Scriptural Matrix," 187–211) that v. 41 alludes not to Gen 1 but to Deut 4:15–19 LXX is not persuasive.
73. Cf. 1 Clem. 24–26; Tertullian, *Apol.* 48.7–9; Minucius Felix, *Oct.* 34.11–12.
74. Robinson, s.v. "ἀστήρ."

CHAPTER 11

book of Sirach in its hymn to creation similarly distinguishes the diverse types of glory belonging to sun (43:2–5), moon (43:6–8), and stars (43:9–10). Through the recurrence of ἄλλη, the repetition of δόξα, and the introduction of each succeeding clause with καί, Paul effectively highlights these diverse kinds of glory.

*Indeed, one star differs from another star in glory.* The γάρ appear to have here an intensifying force, confirming and strengthening Paul's point regarding the diverse kinds of glory among the heavenly bodies: "Why, even one star is different from another star in glory!"[75] The final words of v. 41 (ἐν δόξῃ) effectively prepare for the identical phrase to be used in the application of the analogy in 15:42–44 (15:43, ἐν δόξῃ).

Paul here in 15:41 adds a final and climactic point of comparison in his analogy of the heavenly bodies in 15:40–41. The implication of the distinction between heavenly and earthly bodies in v. 40 was that the risen body will be a body endued with heavenly glory. The implication of the varied kinds of glory in v. 41 is that the risen body will have its own appropriate heavenly glory (cf. v. 38b, "to each of the species of seed its appropriate body"), which is different from that of the celestial bodies. For the analogy of the sun, moon, and stars is, of course, only an analogy. The heavenly glory of the risen bodies of the faithful will be a different and, as we will see, greater kind of heavenly glory.

Before we unpack this greater kind of heavenly glory that will be possessed by the risen bodies of the faithful, we must pause to grasp a crucial point. We see here in 15:40–41, as we saw previously and will see throughout chapter 15, the failure of those readings of 1 Cor 15 that assume Paul here envisions a resurrection body composed of astral or celestial matter, which (on this interpretation) he clumsily proposes as a compromise with ancient philosophical beliefs regarding a hierarchy of matter or "cosmic polarity."[76] For scholars who advocate this interpretation universally assume that Paul mentions the heavenly bodies in 15:40–41 to indicate that the risen body will be composed of celestial matter, the "stuff" constituting the sun, moon,

---

75. For the confirmatory or intensive γάρ, cf. John 9:30; Acts 16:37; 19:35; 1 Cor 11:22; 1 Thess 2:20. For this function of γάρ, see LSJ, s.v. "γάρ" (3.b) ("to confirm or strengthen something said"); Robinson, s.v. "γάρ"; BA, s.v. "γάρ." This usage of the conjunction, which BA calls its "bekräftigend" ("strengthening") function, is unfortunately not included in the entry for γάρ in BDAG.

76. So Martin, *Body*, 117–29; Jeffrey R. Asher, *Polarity and Change in 1 Corinthians 15: A Study of Metaphysics, Rhetoric, and Resurrection* (HUT 42; Tübingen: Mohr Siebeck, 2000), 91–209; Asher, "Anthropogenic Metaphor," 102–6; Troels Engberg-Pedersen, *Cosmology and Self in the Apostle Paul: The Material Spirit* (Oxford: Oxford University Press, 2010), 26–31; Alan G. Padgett, "The Body in Resurrection: Science and Scripture on the 'Spiritual Body,'" *WW* 22 (2002): 157–62; M. David Litwa, *We Are Being Transformed: Deification in Paul's Soteriology* (BZNW 187; Berlin: de Gruyter, 2012), 128–51; Garland, 730–32; Burnett, "Scriptural Matrix," 200–203.

and stars.[77] But this reading utterly fails to grasp the *analogical* nature of 15:40–41. That vv. 36–41 offer a series of analogies and comparisons is clear from Paul's application of the analogies in v. 42: οὕτως ἐστιν ἡ ἀνάστασις τῶν νεκρῶν (*"Thus* is the resurrection of the dead"). The whole point of v. 41 is that just as each of the celestial bodies possesses its own appropriate heavenly glory differing in kind from the others, so too the risen body will have its own form and kind of heavenly glory *different* from that of the sun, moon, and stars. It is this misinterpretation of 15:40–41—the failure to recognize that the sun, moon, and stars function within these verses as an analogy and a comparison—that is at the root of the entire mistaken thesis that Paul envisions a resurrection body composed of astral matter in 1 Cor 15.

The risen body, then, will have its own appropriate heavenly glory, a different kind of glory than that of the sun, moon, and stars. But what kind of heavenly glory is this? Here we come to the heart of Paul's teaching on the resurrection within this astounding chapter.

## The Heavenly Glory of the Risen Body in 15:40–41

The point of Paul's simile of the heavenly bodies becomes clear when we read the language of vv. 40–41 within the context of the chapter as a whole. The word ἐπουράνιος "heavenly" is a key term within 1 Cor 15. Of its nineteen occurrences within the New Testament, five occur within this chapter. Two of these instances occur, as we have seen, in v. 40. Here ἐπουράνιος is used with reference to the spatial, astronomical heavens. Thus Bauer and Aland define the sense in 15:40 as "referring to the heaven, in which the stars dwell."[78] The other three instances of ἐπουράνιος occur in 15:48–49, together with the word οὐρανός "heaven" in 15:47. Clearly, in 15:47–49 we find Paul's application of the analogy in 15:40–41. Here, as all the lexica concur, "heaven" and "heavenly" are used with a *different* sense than in vv. 40–41. Here "heaven" (οὐρανός) denotes the dwelling place of God, and "heavenly" (ἐπουράνιος) is used with reference to heaven as the abode of God's presence. So Bauer and Aland define οὐρανός in 15:47 as "the home of the divine" and ἐπουράνιος in 15:48–49 as "referring to heaven, insofar as it is the dwelling place of God."[79]

---

77. E.g., Martin, *Body*, 125–29; Engberg-Pedersen, *Cosmology and Self*, 27–28; Padgett, "Spiritual Body," 157–61; Burnett, "Scriptural Matrix," 208–9 n. 37.

78. BA, s.v. "ἐπουράνιος" (1.b) ("auf den Himmel bezüglich an dem die Gestirne stehen"). Cf. BDAG, s.v. "ἐπουράνιος" (1): "pertaining to being in the sky or heaven as an astronomical phenomenon."

79. BA, s.v. "οὐρανός" (2) ("als Heimat des Göttlichen") and BA, s.v. "ἐπουράνιος" (1.a) ("auf

CHAPTER 11

Paul's analogy builds upon a crucial conception unique to Christian theology within the ancient world. In ancient pagan thought, the gods were thought to dwell among the sun, moon, and stars within the highest portion of the visible astral heavens (Hesiod, *Op.* 18; Sophocles, *Trach.* 1106; Aristotle, *Cael.* 284a.12–13 [reporting the common view]; Cicero, *Rep.* 6.17; Apuleius, *De deo Socr.* 3). But the first Christians did *not* conceive of God as dwelling in the created sidereal heavens of the sun, moon, and stars. For the early Christians, God is transcendent, not a part of the cosmos or bounded by space or place.[80] When early Christians use the language of "heaven" and "heavenly" for the dwelling place of God, this language does not denote a place but is metaphorical language for God's being and presence (Matt 5:16, 48; 7:21; Luke 1:78; John 6:32–33, 41–42, 50–51, 58; Rom 1:18; 1 Pet 1:12). In Paul's comparison, then, the created glory of the astral heavens (15:40–41) is a metaphor for the uncreated glory of God (15:47–49). The *heavenly* glory within Paul's analogy is thus the *divine* glory. We are now at the core of what Paul is saying in the astronomical analogy of vv. 40–41. To unpack this fully, we must explore the meaning of the language of "glory" (δόξα) within this comparison.

The first occurrences of the word δόξα in 1 Corinthians are found in 2:7–8 (δόξα, twice). The final occurrences of the word within the letter are found in chapter 15 (15:40–41, 43). The connection between 2:7–8 and chapter 15 is yet more striking, for as all interpreters are agreed, 1 Cor 2:7–8 refers to the *eschatological* glory to be given to believers at the resurrection.[81] The word δόξα in this sense of future glory does not recur again in the letter until chapter 15. Moreover, in chapter 15 this use of the word does not simply recur but reaches a true climax, for in chapter 15 the word δόξα with reference to eschatological glory is found *six* times (15:40–41, 43). First Corinthians 2:7–8 thus appears to form an *inclusio* with chapter 15, foreshadowing the discussion of the coming eschatological glory of the faithful within that chapter.[82] We must therefore explore 1 Cor 2:7–8 to grasp the nature of the divine glory Paul has in mind in the analogy of 15:40–41.

---

den Himmel bezüglich, soweit er der Aufenthaltort Gottes . . . ist"). Cf. BDAG, s.v. "οὐρανός" (2); s.v. "ἐπουράνιος" (2).

80. Herm. Mand. 1.1.1; Athenagoras, *Leg.* 8.4.7; Justin, *Dial.* 56, 60, 127; Theophilus of Antioch, *Autol.* 2.3; Clement of Alexandria, *Protr.* 4.50; *Strom.* 5.12.81; 5.38.6; Irenaeus, *Haer.* 2.30.9; Minucius Felix, *Oct.* 18.7–8; 32.1, 7. The closest analogue to this conception within pagan thought in antiquity is Plato's understanding of the highest divinity as dwelling beyond the heavens (*Phaedr.* 247).

81. E.g., Hays, 44; Robertson & Plummer, 38; Schreiner, 81.

82. See Brian Rosner, "Temple and Holiness in 1 Corinthians 15," *TynBul* 42 (1991): 143: "In 2:7–8 the connection of believers' ultimate glorification to their union with Christ (note repetition of δόξα) is a precursor to 1 Corinthians 15."

In 1 Cor 2:7–8, the glory that will be imparted to the faithful (εἰς δόξαν ἡμῶν, 2:7) through the Lord of glory (ὁ κύριος τῆς δόξης), the risen Christ, is nothing less than *the radiant splendor that belongs to God's own nature and being*. This meaning of δόξα has its origins in the Old Testament, where it translates the Hebrew *kābôd* and denotes the radiantly manifested presence of YHWH (Exod 24:16–17; 33:17–23; 40:34–35; 1 Kgs 8:11–13). This sense of δόξα as the majesty and splendor that belongs to God's own being is frequent in the New Testament, especially Paul's letters.[83] The striking thing about Paul's usage is that many of these passages look forward to the *sharing* and *participation* of the faithful in this divine glory at the coming of Christ (Rom 5:2; 8:18, 21, 30; 9:23; 2 Cor 3:18; Phil 3:21; 1 Thess 2:12; 2 Thess 2:14). This is the meaning of δόξα in 1 Cor 2:7–8, where the word denotes "the divine glory that belongs to the crucified and risen Lord (v. 8b) . . . and in which the faithful will one day share in eternal bodily life."[84] First Corinthians 2:7–8 thus expresses "the final goal of salvation, namely, that God's people should share in God's own glory."[85]

The thematic linkage formed by 2:7–8 and chapter 15, as the first and last instances of δόξα in the letter, and the only references within the epistle to eschatological glory, determines the meaning of δόξα in Paul's great resurrection chapter. Here, as in 2:7–8, δόξα denotes *the splendor and majesty that belong to the Son of God's own nature and being*, the radiant manifestation of his presence. This confirms the equation of the *heavenly* glory of 15:40–41 with the *divine* glory that we discovered above in Paul's application of the "heaven" language in 15:47–49. The heavenly glory of 15:40–41, depicted under the analogy of the splendor, beauty, and luminosity of the heavenly bodies, is the radiant splendor of God's own nature, which will be imparted to the *body* in the resurrection, so that the risen bodies of those who belong to Christ will share directly in the splendor and glory of God. It is in this way that the resurrected bodies of the faithful will be heavenly bodies, in that they will be imbued with divine glory. Thus chapter 15, although forming a thematic link with 2:7–8, marks an advance and a climax, for it is here in the letter that we first learn explicitly of this communication of Christ's glorious presence to the *body*. The same conception is expressed strikingly in Phil 3:21: "The Lord Jesus Christ . . . who will transform our lowly bodies to be made like the body of his glory [τῷ σώματι τῆς δόξης αὐτοῦ]."

Paul's use in v. 41 of the imagery of the sun, moon, and stars to depict the glory of God imparted to the bodies of the faithful in the resurrection draws upon a rich

---

83. See Sigurd Grindheim, "A Theology of Glory: Paul's Use of Δόξα Terminology in Romans," *JBL* 136 (2017): 457–62; J. N. D. Kelly, *The Epistles of Peter and of Jude* (London: Black, 1969), 55, 57; Fitzmyer, 176; Cremer, 208–9.

84. Wolff, 55. Cf. Fitzmyer, 176; Conzelmann, 62.

85. Fee, 113.

CHAPTER 11

biblical tradition. In the book of Isaiah, the imagery of the sun and moon is used to depict the glorification of Zion, the divine glory to be given to the people of God (Isa 24:23; 30:26; 60:1–3, 19–20). In Dan 12:3, the splendor of the divine life given to the righteous in the resurrection is portrayed under the imagery of the stars of heaven. And in the New Testament, the sharing of the faithful in God's own glory at the resurrection is frequently depicted with the language and imagery of the sun, moon, and stars (Matt 13:43; Rev 2:28; 21:23; 22:5, 16).

Paul's analogy of the glory of the heavenly bodies in 15:40–41 thus expresses the theme of the impartation of the radiant majesty and splendor belonging to God's own nature to the bodies of the faithful at the resurrection. This is the different and greater heavenly glory to which the differing glory of the sun, moon, and stars in 15:41 bears witness. As in 15:36–39, Paul's command of metaphor or "split reference" within 15:40–41 is complete, for Paul's language of *heavenly bodies* and their *glory* is, as we have seen, language regularly used in antiquity for these astronomical phenomena. But it also richly and appropriately expresses the eschatological hope to which Paul understands these phenomena to bear witness—the *divine glory* imparted to the *bodies* of those who belong to Christ at the resurrection.

We can now see that the widespread view of Paul's analogy of the heavenly bodies in 15:40–41 as betokening an astral resurrection body composed of celestial matter not only fails to grasp the material continuity of the risen body with the present body, set forth in the botanical analogy of 15:36–38, and the flesh and bones nature of the risen body, evident in the zoological analogy of 15:39. It also entirely misses the astounding theological conception at the heart of the astronomical analogy of 15:40–41. For here Paul discloses a conception of resurrection in which the presence and glory of God are imparted not only to the soul but also to the body. In Paul's theology, the resurrection of the body is the full communication of the presence of God. It is the consummation of union with Christ.

## The Testimony of Creation to the Mystery of the Resurrection in 15:36–41

Paul's series of comparisons in 15:36–41 is complex and multivalent. Paul's analogy features three distinct comparisons (15:36–38, 15:39, and 15:40–41), and three domains of comparison—botanical, zoological, and astronomical. Moreover, Paul's comparisons do not function like a modern analogy but like one of Jesus's parables in the gospels, with multiple points of comparison unfolding the mystery of the resurrection. We may summarize these as follows:

1. As the goal or telos of the seed is the plant or flower, so the end goal of the present body is the glorified body of the resurrection (vv. 36, 38).
2. As with the seed and its flower, the same mortal body that dies will be raised to life (vv. 36, 38).
3. Like the miracle of the seed and its growth, the resurrection of the body will take place through the working of God's almighty power (v. 38).
4. As the unclothed seed must be clothed with leaves, flowers, and fruit, so in the resurrection the mortal body will be raised to a transformed and far more glorious state (vv. 37–38).
5. The various kinds of flesh in the created order point forward to the glorified and imperishable flesh of the resurrection (v. 39).
6. As God gives to each seed type its appropriate plant, tree, or flower, and to each of the heavenly bodies its unique glory, so in the resurrection the faithful will receive glorified bodies appropriate to their identity as tabernacles of the Holy Spirit (vv. 38, 40–41).
7. For, in a manner prefigured by the glory of the heavenly bodies, in the resurrection the glory that belongs to God's own nature and being will be communicated not only to the soul but also to the body, resulting in the fullness of union with God (vv. 40–41). This is the great mystery of the resurrection that is at the heart of Paul's threefold analogy in vv. 36–41.

To a degree that scholars have only partially recognized, Paul's use within this passage of metaphor and conceptual blending is nothing less than magnificent. Every single one of the key terms employed by Paul in his comparisons (*sowing*; the plant *body*; the *seed*; the *unclothed* seed; *wheat* as the most common species of seed; *flesh* of animals, birds, and fish; the sun, moon, and stars as heavenly *bodies* with heavenly *glory*) reflect language used for these entities in antiquity and, in several cases, the technical language used within ancient physical science and natural philosophy. And yet, *at the same time*, each of these terms embody a central point in Paul's exposition of the resurrection in the application to follow in 15:42–58. I am unaware of an equally masterful use of extended conceptual metaphor anywhere in ancient literature.

I have called 15:36–41 a series of analogies or comparisons, and in one sense they are. However, Paul's comparisons do not function, as almost all modern interpreters seem to suppose, simply as convenient analogies or illustrations. Rather, Paul finds in the teleology evident in seed and plant growth, the diversity of kinds of creaturely flesh, and the glory of the astronomical bodies divinely given testimonies within the created order signifying that humanity's present mortal life is but a prelude to resurrection and indestructible physical life. *This is a new and revolutionary understanding of the cosmos.* The ancient philosophers saw the botanical process as a process of generation and growth culminating in death and decay (Theophrastus, *Caus. plant.* 5.11.1–5.18.4; Aristotle, *Gen. an.* 731b–732a). But Paul in 1 Cor 15 envisions botanical growth as a process of death and resurrection, which foreshadows the resurrection of the body to come. Likewise, Paul understands the diverse kinds of flesh within the animal world as a mysterious foreshadowing of the glorified and imperishable flesh of the resurrection. And Paul saw the luminous majesty of the sun, moon, and stars as a mystery-laden sign of the body's future share in the radiant splendor of God's own nature and being. At the beginning of Paul's series of comparisons in 1 Cor 15:36–41, the reader lives in one world; by the close of the passage, the reader lives in an entirely different world. It is a new world, suffused with the hope of resurrection and new creation. It is a cosmos whose last word is not death but life. In Paul's great resurrection chapter, we find a new understanding of the natural world illumined by the revelation of its incarnate and risen Lord and transformed by faith, hope, and love (1 Cor 13:13).

EXCURSUS 4

## Two False Trails Regarding Paul's Analogy of the Seed

A common scholarly misconception has impeded a full understanding of the power of Paul's comparison of the seed in 15:36–38. In an influential article, Herbert Braun argued that Paul's portrayal of the seed as not made alive unless it dies reflects a general ancient understanding of a seed and its flowering, in which the seed, before bringing forth its new growth, dies or perishes in the earth.[1] This ancient conception, Braun argued, was "naive" and "biologically erroneous," for it lacked anything like our modern scientific understanding of biological organic growth.[2] The ancients, Braun claimed, did not grasp that the plant or tree was a development from the seed, but instead believed that "the seed, after it is sown, dies."[3] Paul's analogy, according to Braun, assumes this ancient (and erroneous) conception of botanical growth.

Braun's thesis has been widely followed. Citing Braun, Andreas Lindemann tells us that the "presupposition" of Paul's analogy is "the ancient conception of 'death and growth,' according to which the plant does not *develop* from the seed, but the seed 'dies' after its planting in the soil."[4] Hans Conzelmann, also citing Braun, claims that Paul's analogy reflects an understanding of nature "widespread in the ancient world" that conceives the events of nature "as a cycle of death and growth."[5] Christian Wolff likewise assures us (citing Braun) that in his analogy "Paul reflects an understanding of his time in regard to sowing and growth," in

---

1. Herbert Braun, "Das 'Stirb und Werde' in der Antike und im Neuen Testament," in *Gesammelte Studien zum Neuen Testament und seiner Umwelt* (Tübingen: Mohr Siebeck, 1962), 136–58.
2. Braun, "Stirb und Werde," 140–41.
3. Braun, "Stirb und Werde," 143.
4. Lindemann, 356.
5. Conzelmann, 281.

which "the growth of the plant follows upon the decay of the seed."[6] This claim is now commonplace in the literature.[7]

But all of this is nonsense. The growth from seed to plant was not understood in antiquity as a dying and return to life. Nor was the ancient understanding fundamentally different from the modern. The essentials of the modern conception of organic botanical growth—in which the seed contains the embryo of the plant, emits the primary root and first stem, provides nourishment to the emergent root and stem, and thus develops into the plant—are found in the treatises of Aristotle and of his disciple Theophrastus, and were widely known in the ancient world.[8] This knowledge is evident not only in these technical horticultural treatises but also in the universal ancient practice of storing seeds away from moisture, lest they sprout and develop prematurely, the sprout withering due to lack of soil (for this practice, see Theophrastus, *Caus. plant.* 1.7.2).

Braun entirely ignores this evidence from Aristotle and Theophrastus (as do also those scholars who cite him), and he founds his thesis on two (!) ancient passages, one of which he takes out of context, and the other which he misunderstands. First, Braun cites Epictetus, *Diatr.* 4.8.36: "In this way fruit comes to pass: it is necessary that the seed first be buried [κατορυγῆναι] for a time, be hidden [κρυφθῆναι], grow little by little, that it may bear fruit." However, Epictetus does not speak here of the death of the seed but of its hiddenness. The point of Epictetus's comparison in the context is to let one's talents lie hidden and not to seek notoriety prematurely. It has nothing to do with death. Braun then considers a second passage, a fragment from Plutarch, which is the main evidence for his thesis:

> For it is necessary that the seed [τὸ σπέρμα] first be cast down and concealed [κρυφθῆναι] within the soil, and undergo decay [σαπῆναι], and in this way pass on its own inward potential [δύναμιν] to the soil which has concealed it, in order that, from one grain of wheat, or perchance of barley, a multitude may result. For this reason, they say that the seed needs rain and frosty dew at the beginning, pressing down within the seed and releasing the capacities for growth within it [τὰς ἐν αὐτῷ φυσικὰς δυνάμεις]. (Plutarch, *Frag.* 11)

---

6. Wolff, 403.

7. See, for example, C. Burchard, "1 Korinther 15,39–41," *ZNW* 75 (1984): 234; Martinus C. de Boer, *The Defeat of Death: Apocalyptic Eschatology in 1 Corinthians 15 and Romans 5* (JSNTSup 22; 1988; repr., London: T&T Clark, 2019), 130; Schrage, 281–82; Fitzmyer, 588.

8. See Aristotle, *Gen. an.* 731a6–10; 739b35–740a2; 740b6–8; 741b34–37; Theophrastus, *Caus. plant.* 1.7.1–5; 4.3.3–6; 4.7.4–7; *Hist. plant.* 8.2.1–2. Cf. also the full (and quite botanically correct) description of the genesis of plant from seed in Hippocrates, *Nat. puer.* 11.

Braun assumed that Plutarch's statement reflected a "naive" and "biologically erroneous" conception that failed to grasp the plant's organic development from the seed. But this is a misunderstanding of the passage. Plutarch clearly has an organic conception of the growth of the new plant from the seed. The grown plant arises "*from* one grain of wheat, or perchance of barley" (ἐξ ἑνὸς πυροῦ τυχὸν ἢ κριθῆς). The term δύναμις, used twice in the passage by Plutarch, is a technical term within the ancient horticultural literature, referring to the seed's inward potential or capacity for sprouting and growth. We find the natural philosopher Theophrastus using the term in this way in his horticultural treatises (*Caus. plant.* 4.1.3; cf. *Hist. plant.* 8.8.1; 8.11.1). Therefore, when Plutarch speaks of the seed's "inward potential" (δύναμις) being passed on to the soil, he is thinking of the root's emergence from the seed to be nourished henceforth by the soil. Plutarch recognizes, as did all the ancients, that this process necessitated the bursting and decay (σαπῆναι) of the seed. Modern botany is also aware of this process, in which the seed coat bursts, detaches, and decays in the earth.

It is this process, familiar to both ancient and modern botanical study, that Paul is thinking of when he says that the seed "dies." But the conception of this as the *death* of the seed is a Christian innovation. Although familiar with the seed's decay and dissolution, the ancients never refer to this as the death of the seed or to this process as a dying and return to life. But Paul, no doubt also familiar with the plant's organic development from the seed, chooses to describe this process with the language of death and resurrection. What the false trail created by Braun's study has hidden from a generation of biblical scholars is that this language is new. John Chrysostom tells us explicitly that, in speaking of the seed's death and coming to life, Paul is using language "which is not proper to seeds, but to bodies" (*Hom. 1 Cor.* 41.2, ὅπερ οὐ σπερμάτων κυρίως ἐστὶν ἀλλὰ σωμάτων). Paul's description of the process of botanical growth as a death and resurrection is unique. It is a revolutionary way of looking at the natural world and the process of botanical growth. It is founded upon the good news of Jesus's resurrection and sees the mysterious transformation of seed to flower as a divinely given anticipation and foreshadowing within the created order of the bodily resurrection to come.

The second scholarly mistake regarding Paul's analogy of the seed is less common but equally misleading. The claim is occasionally made that the mystery cults of Demeter and Isis utilized the imagery of sowing and harvest to symbolize the resurrection life these mysteries purportedly promised to their initiates. According to David Williams, "the ritual of the Eleusinian mystery had to do with the 'death' and 'rebirth' of wheat . . . into which was interwoven the hope of human immortality."[9] Nicholas Perrin likewise claims that, in the mysteries of Isis and

---

9. David Williams, *Paul's Metaphors: Their Context and Character* (Peabody, MA: Hendrickson, 1999), 39–40. Similarly H. J. Rose, "Demeter," *OCD*, 324.

other mystery cults, "seed imagery was consistently employed to symbolize death and rebirth."[10]

But this claim is also without foundation. To be sure, Demeter, the chief goddess of the Eleusinian mysteries, was the great goddess of grain and harvest (Callimachus, *Hymn Cer.* 1–2, 119–123, 134–138). In the mystery's founding myth, as recounted in the ancient Homeric *Hymn to Demeter* (sixth century BC), the agreement that Persephone spend four months of the year below earth with Hades and eight months above earth with her mother Demeter underlies the annual cycle of sowing and new growth (*Hom. Dem.* 398–403, 441–489).[11] Plutarch's criticism of the notion that such mythic events were the cause of the agricultural cycle confirms that this was the popular understanding (*Is. Os.* 378d–379c). The Stoic mythographers, who allegorized the myths in terms of natural processes, identified Demeter with the fruits of the earth, Persephone with the seed sown in the ground, and the latter's yearly return with new growth and harvest (cf. the remarks of the Stoic Balbus in Cicero, *Nat. d.* 2.66–67; Cornutus, *Nat. d.* 28; Tertullian, *Marc.* 1.13). They likewise interpreted the myth of Isis and Osiris as an allegory of planting, blossoming, and harvest (see Cornutus, *Nat. d.* 28; Tertullian, *Marc.* 1.13; and the criticism in Plutarch, *Is. Os.* 377b–e).

But nowhere in these mysteries do we find any connection whatsoever between the process of botanical growth and the afterlife. Isocrates speaks of Demeter's two great gifts to humanity—the fruits of the earth that support human life and the mysteries, which provide sweeter hopes for the afterlife—but he draws no connection between them (*Paneg.* 28–29). Moreover, the mystery cults did not offer their initiates a hope of resurrection but rather a more blessed afterlife in the realm of the dead.[12] It is difficult to conceive how the seed and its growth might serve as an intelligible symbol for the hope of a more blessed existence of the soul in Hades. Nor do these mysteries depict their divine protagonists as having died

---

10. Nicholas Perrin, "On Raising Osiris in 1 Corinthians 15," *TynBul* 58 (2007): 119–20.

11. Terri Moore argues that "Persephone's cyclic life in Hades and Olympus does not correspond neatly with the harvest, and thus her yearly return does not seem to cause the fertility of the earth." See *The Mysteries, Resurrection, and 1 Corinthians 15: Comparative Methodology and Exegesis* (Lanham, MD: Fortress Academic, 2018), 35. However, the correlation is actually quite precise. Sowing normally took place in late October or early November (Hesiod, *Op.* 383–384, 448–451; Plutarch, *Is. Os.* 378e; Theophrastus, *Hist. plant.* 8.1.2), and the full sprouts appeared at the beginning of spring in late February or early March (Hesiod, *Op.* 561–569). Harvest took place about two months later in early May (Hesiod, *Op.* 383–384). The Homeric *Hymn to Demeter* is explicit that the time of Persephone's annual return to Olympus from her four-month stay with Hades is the beginning of spring (*Hom. Dem.* 401–403). The correspondence with the yearly cycle of sowing and new growth is exact, suggesting that within the hymn Persephone's annual return is the cause of new growth and harvest.

12. For fuller discussion, see excursus 3. See also Moore, *Mysteries*, 29–76.

and been raised to life.[13] In the Eleusinian myth, Persephone does not die but journeys yearly from Olympus to Hades and back (*Hom. Dem.* 360–495). In the Isis myth, Osiris dies and remains permanently in the tomb (Plutarch, *Is. Os.* 358a–b; 359a–d; 364f–365a) and in the underworld, ruling there as the god of the dead (Plutarch, *Is. Os.* 382e–f). In the ancient conception, the correlation of the sown seed with these myths lay in the seed's temporary *concealment* and *reappearance*, corresponding to Demeter's search for and discovery of Persephone (Cornutus, *Nat. d.* 28.42–45; Cicero, *Nat. d.* 2.66–67; *Hom. Dem.* 39–383; cf. 353, σπέρμ' ὑπὸ γῆς κρύπτουσα) and to Isis's search for and discovery of the dismembered body parts of Osiris (Cornutus, *Nat. d.* 28.45–49; Plutarch, *Is. Os.* 357f–358b).

Upon reflection, it is unsurprising that we find in these mysteries no connection between botanical growth and the afterlife. To link sowing with bodily death and the growth of the seed with life after death requires a conception of *bodily resurrection*, which these mysteries did not possess. Such a link is only possible within ancient Judaism or Christianity, in which the hope of resurrection was cherished. Yet we have no evidence for such a link in the Second Temple Judaism of Paul's day.[14]

The understanding, then, of the seed and its growth as a kind of death and resurrection is not found in ancient agricultural thought, in the mystery cults within the pagan world, or within Jewish thought. We find it for the first time in 1 Cor 15. The comparison is, in fact, a new, daring, and revolutionary one. We also find this conception in one other place within the New Testament, in a saying of Jesus in John 12:24. It is likely that Paul is drawing upon this tradition in 1 Cor 15:36.[15] In any case, the conception thereafter becomes common coin in ancient Christianity (1 Clem. 24–26; Tertullian, *Apol.* 48.7–9; Minucius Felix, *Oct.* 34.11–12). This understanding of the growth from seed to plant as a foreshadowing of the resurrection of the dead is unique to the early Christian movement.

---

13. For fuller discussion, see excursus 1.

14. The rabbinic parallels suggested by Braun, "Stirb und Werde," 141–42; Schrage, 281–82; and Wolff, 403 are far-fetched and postdate Paul by several centuries.

15. As suggested by Harald Riesenfeld, "Das Bildwort vom Weizenkorn bei Paulus (zu I Cor 15)," in *Studien zum Neuen Testament und zur Patristik* (Berlin: Akademie, 1961), 52–53; he is followed by Wolff, 403. There are fascinating parallels between the Johannine passage and 1 Cor 15:36–38. As Jeffrey Asher notes: "In John 12:24, the parallels consist of the seed, the death of the seed, and the notion of life being generated from death." See "ΣΠΕΙΡΕΤΑΙ: Paul's Anthropogenic Metaphor in 1 Corinthians 15:42–44," *JBL* 120 (2001): 107.

CHAPTER 12

## *The Glorified Body of the Resurrection*

15:42–44a

Verses 42–44a are a hinge point within the chapter. Here Paul begins his application of the preceding comparisons in 15:36–41 and commences his direct exposition of the resurrection hope in 15:42–58. What the self-professed wise at Corinth denied with their slogan "there is no resurrection of the dead" (ἀνάστασις νεκρῶν οὐκ ἔστιν, 15:12), Paul now unapologetically, one might almost say brazenly, affirms—"so also is the resurrection of the dead" (οὕτως καὶ ἡ ἀνάστασις τῶν νεκρῶν, 15:42). In response to the mocking question of 15:35, "How can the dead be raised?" which utilized the verb ἐγείρω, Paul's answer in 15:42–44a repeats and affirms this same verb four times.

Within this rhetorically powerful chapter, vv. 42–44a (hereafter for convenience vv. 42–44) are a rhetorical highlight. Through an artful, fourfold antithetical pairing of the homonymous verbs σπείρω "sow" and ἐγείρω "raise," Paul unpacks the preceding comparisons of the seed, kinds of flesh, and glory of the heavenly bodies in vv. 36–41, and he sets the present body and the coming glory of the resurrected body in stark contrast. The body is "sown" (σπείρεται) in decay, dishonor, and weakness, as a σῶμα ψυχικόν, but is raised (ἐγείρεται) in incorruption, glory, and power, as a σῶμα πνευματικόν. Although it is hidden in translation, Paul effectively highlights the connection and contrast between the paired verbs through a striking constellation of rhetorical devices. The similar-sounding verb stems σπειρ- and ἐγειρ-, which alternately begin each clause, produce the effect of *anaphora* (similarity of sound at the commencement of a clause). The identical ending of these verbs (-εται) produces *homoioptoton* (similarity of word endings).[1] The assonance created by this combination of anaphora and homoioptoton is quite

---

1. BDR §491 n. 2.

remarkable and is reinforced by Paul's use of *asyndeton* (there are no connectors in 15:42–44).[2] Finally, through the assonance of σῶμα ψυχικόν and σῶμα πνευματικόν, the anaphora of 15:42–43 rises in 15:44 to *symploce* (similarity of sound at both the beginning and the close of a clause).[3] Paul's fulsome use here of rhetorical technique reveals the fallacy of the view that the Corinthian wisdom he opposes in the first four chapters of the letter is rhetorical skill! Rather, as we have seen, the wisdom of the self-professed wise at Corinth was a philosophical wisdom that denied the hope of the resurrection. Paul here in 15:42–44 powerfully counters this false wisdom and, with rhetorical flourish, affirms the resurrection.

## The Significance of Paul's Syntax in Verses 42–44

Strangely, a number of scholars have interpreted 15:42–44 in an opposite sense— as a compromise with the opponents of the resurrection at Corinth and a denial of the physical resurrection of *this* body. For these interpreters, Paul's series of oppositions between the present body and the risen body, with his references to what is sown being $x$ and what is raised being $y$, points to a radical discontinuity between the mortal body and the risen body, which precludes the possibility that Paul conceived of resurrection in straightforward bodily terms.[4]

> Paul reaffirms the resurrection of their *bodies*; but to convince Christians influenced by philosophy, he admits that he himself does not believe in a resurrection of *this* body.[5]

---

2. Rob., *Gram.*, 429.

3. Commentators who recognize at least some features of the rhetorical artistry of 15:42–44 include Collins, 565; Wolff, 406; Weiss, 371; and Fitzmyer, 544.

4. So Dale Martin, *The Corinthian Body* (New Haven: Yale University Press, 1995), 126–30; James D. G. Dunn, "How Are the Dead Raised? With What Body Do They Come? Reflections on 1 Corinthians 15," *SwJT* 45 (2002): 16; Jeffrey R. Asher, *Polarity and Change in 1 Corinthians 15: A Study of Metaphysics, Rhetoric, and Resurrection* (Tübingen: Mohr Siebeck, 2000), 153; Ernst Teichmann, *Die paulinische Vorstellungen von Auferstehung und Gericht und ihre Beziehungen zur jüdischen Apokalyptik* (Freiburg: Mohr, 1896), 48; Troels Engberg-Pedersen, "Complete and Incomplete Transformation in Paul—A Philosophical Reading of Paul on Body and Spirit," in *Metamorphoses: Resurrection, Body and Transformative Practices in Early Christianity* (ed. Turid Karlsen Seim and Jorunn Økland; Berlin: de Gruyter, 2009), 123–46; Engberg-Pedersen, "The Material Spirit: Cosmology and Ethics in Paul," *NTS* 55 (2009): 179–97; and Engberg-Pedersen, *Cosmology and Self in the Apostle Paul: The Material Spirit* (Oxford: Oxford University Press, 2010), 8–38; similarly Wolff, 406; Garland, 731–32.

5. Martin, *Body*, 130.

However, this view involves a misconception of the function of the series of oppositions between the present and risen body in vv. 42–44. This misconception is founded upon a fundamental misunderstanding of ancient Greek syntax. For scholars who take this view assume that Paul's ellipsis of the subject in 15:42–44 permits the conclusion that the paired verbs have *distinct* subjects, so that the subject of the first verb (σπείρεται "is sown") is the present body, but the subject of the second verb (ἐγείρεται "is raised") refers to a new resurrection body distinct from the mortal body.[6] Such a construal of the text, however, is not consistent with ancient Greek usage. Within the conventions of ancient Greek syntax, consecutive verbs, apart from the introduction of a new subject, are understood to have the same subject as the verb preceding (e.g., Matt 6:26; 16:21; Mark 4:32; 1 Cor 13:5–7; 15:3–4).[7] If a change of subject between consecutive verbs occurs, this must normally (for obvious reasons of clarity) be expressed (e.g., Matt 11:5; 13:4–8; 24:40–41; Mark 12:32; Luke 1:11–13; 12:24; Rom 14:4–6). Distinct subjects for the verbs in 15:42–44 would thus require a construction such as ὁ μὲν σπείρεται ... ἄλλο ἐγείρεται ("one [body] is sown ... another [body] is raised").[8] An exception to this rule occurs when the object of a previous verb, or a noun or pronoun within its clause, is taken up as the subject of the verb that follows (e.g., Mark 9:27; Luke 8:29; John 19:31).[9] However, this syntactic feature is not present in the passage under consideration. Other exceptions are rare and are signaled by unmistakable contextual factors (e.g., Matt 14:20; 22:30; Mark 4:27; Heb 4:8; 1 John 5:16). Such factors are lacking in 1 Cor 15:42–44. Moreover, the view that the subject changes between σπείρεται and ἐγείρεται involves the further improbable claim that the subject changes *repeatedly*, without grammatical indication, a total of seven times within the space of verses 42–44. There is simply no precedent for such a phenomenon anywhere in ancient Greek literature.

Some scholars argue that the paired verbs σπείρεται and ἐγείρεται, as "impersonal passives," have no implicit subject but refer merely to the activity of sowing and raising (i.e., "there is a sowing"; "there is a raising").[10] However, this is not possible. Unlike English, German, and other modern languages, there are

---

6. Such an understanding appears to underlie the exegesis of Martin, *Body*, 126–30, and Dunn, "1 Corinthians 15," 10–17.

7. For further discussion of the points that follow, see especially Kühner-G., 2.1:32–36; 2.2:560–71; and Smyth, 259–61. For ease of reference, I will confine the examples given here to the New Testament.

8. Cf. Mark 4:4–8; Luke 23:33; Rom 14:5; 1 Cor 11:21; 12:8–10.

9. Cf. Kühner-G., 2.1:35; 2.2:561.

10. So Barrett, 372; John Gillman, "Transformation in 1 Cor 15,50–53," *ETL* 58 (1982): 327–28; Werner Stenger, "Beobachtungen zur Argumentationsstruktur von 1 Kor 15," *LB* 45 (1979): 100–101.

no true impersonal verbs—that is, finite verbs that lack a subject—in ancient Greek. Those ancient Greek verbs regularly translated into the modern languages as impersonal verbs invariably have an implied subject in their original settings, which is indicated by lexical or contextual factors.[11] So-called "impersonal passives" do not merely express the verbal idea but always have a subject implied within their context.[12]

The conventions of ancient Greek syntax thus demand that the consecutive verbs in 15:42–44 have a subject, and a single subject at that. What, then, is the implied subject of the paired verbs in 1 Cor 15:42–44? It is evident from the following contextual factors that the subject of those verbs is the present, perishable body:

1. In the preceding analogy Paul has identified the seed that is *sown* (ὃ σπείρεις, 15:36; ὃ σπείρεις, 15:37; cf. τῶν σπερμάτων, 15:38) with the present mortal *body* (15:36–38). The obvious implication is that when he uses this same verb (σπείρεται, 15:42–44 [4×]) in the application of the analogy, the subject is the present body.
2. The contrasts in 15:42–44 apply the series of analogies in 15:36–41 (οὕτως καὶ ἡ ἀνάστασις τῶν νεκρῶν, 15:42). These analogies contrast various kinds of *flesh* (15:39) and various kinds of *bodies* (15:37–38, 40–41). Within 15:36–41 the word σῶμα occurs five times. This context indicates that the subject of the contrasts in 15:42–44, in which the analogy is applied, is the human *body* made of *flesh*.
3. In the fourth antithesis in 15:44, the subject of σπείρεται is said to be sown as a σῶμα ψυχικόν. This predicate complement identifies the subject as a *body*, and the following context (15:44b–49) further identifies the σῶμα ψυχικόν as the present mortal body.

All of these factors indicate that the subject of the paired verbs in vv. 42–44 is the present mortal body. This subject, as we have seen, is *one and the same* both

---

11. See Kühner-G., 2.1:36 ("Unpersönliche Verben . . . kennt die griechische Sprache nicht"); Rob., *Gram.*, 391–93 ("The conclusion of the whole matter is that the subject is either expressed or implied by various linguistic devices" [393]). Using a somewhat different nomenclature, Smyth designates a class of "impersonal" and "quasi-impersonal" verbs in ancient Greek, but he points out that in both cases a subject is invariably implied, in the former class by lexical features and in the latter class "derived from the context" (260). The discussion in BDR §129–30 is inadequate.

12. So Rob., *Gram.*, 392: in so-called impersonal passives "the subject is involved in the action of the verb." See also Smyth, 260: in impersonal passives "the subject is merely indicated in the verbal ending" (cf. 396). Thus (to cite one representative example) in 1 Pet 4:6 the implied subject of εὐηγγελίσθη is τὸ εὐαγγέλιον.

for σπείρεται, denoting death and burial, and ἐγείρεται, denoting resurrection. The assonance of these paired verbs, and the rhetorical features we have explored, strongly stress this identity of subject. The importance of this for Paul's understanding of the resurrection event can hardly be overstated. Paul does not describe resurrection as an event in which $x$ (the present body) is sown, but $y$ (a body distinct from the present body) is raised, but rather as an event in which a single $x$ (the present body) is sown a perishable $x$ but raised an imperishable $x$. The same perishable body that is "sown" in mortality and decay (σπείρεται) is thereafter "raised" to imperishable life (ἐγείρεται).[13] Paul's sequence of paired verbs in 1 Cor 15:42–44 indicates that in Paul's thought it is precisely that which perishes—the mortal body—that in the resurrection is given new, imperishable life.

Moreover, the series of contrasts within 15:42–44 between the mortal and risen body do not occur in the *subject* of these sentences but in their *predicates* (verbs and verbal complements). These predicate complements invariably describe a change of *quality* rather than of *substance*, in which what was once perishable, dishonored, weak, and mortal is endowed with imperishability, glory, power, and immortality. Paul's series of oppositions does not describe two different bodies, distinct in substance, but two contrasting modes of existence of the same body, one *prior* to and the other *subsequent* to the resurrection. Many contemporary interpreters assume that the point of Paul's range of contrasts between the present body and the resurrection body is to show that the mortal, perishable body is excluded from participation in final salvation. As we have seen, this claim reflects a misunderstanding of ancient Greek syntax. Paul's point is in fact the opposite: to show how the perishable body, through resurrection, will partake of imperishable life.

### Verse 42

*So also is the resurrection of the dead. The body is sown in corruption, it is raised in incorruptibility.*

*So also.* Frequently elsewhere we find οὕτως καί ("so also") introducing the application of a comparison or analogy (Matt 23:38; 24:33; Mark 13:29; Luke 21:31; 1 Cor 2:11;

---

13. Cf. Ronald Sider, "The Pauline Conception of the Resurrection Body in 1 Corinthians XV.35–54," *NTS* 21 (1975): 435; Andrew Johnson, "Turning the World Upside Down in 1 Corinthians 15: Epistemology, the Resurrected Body and the New Creation," *EvQ* 75 (2003): 298; Bernhard Spörlein, *Die Leugnung der Auferstehung: Eine historisch-kritische Untersuchung zu I Kor 15* (Regensburg: Pustet, 1971), 117; Fee, 867–68; Ciampa & Rosner, 81.

14:12; Gal 4:3; Eph 5:24; 2 Tim 3:8; Jas 1:11; 2:17, 26). This would indicate that here also this conjunctive phrase begins the application of Paul's comparisons in 15:36–41. Moreover, Paul's *single* use of οὕτως καί, which follows all the comparisons, reveals that Paul thinks of these comparisons, as diverse as they are, as constituting a unity.[14] Elsewhere we find οὕτως καί following a single analogy with multiple points of comparison (1 Cor 12:12; Heb 5:5) or following two analogies with a single point of comparison (1 Cor 14:9; Jas 3:5). But here in 15:42 we find οὕτως καί introducing an application of multiple analogies with (as we have seen) multiple points of comparison. The closest analogy to Paul's usage here is the use of οὕτως καί within Jesus's parables with their multiple figures, scenes, and points of comparison (Matt 18:35; Luke 17:10). As the phrase οὕτως καί signals, Paul will now commence to apply and unpack the complex of comparisons within 15:36–41.

*is the resurrection of the dead.* The phrase "the resurrection of the dead" (ἡ ἀνάστασις τῶν νεκρῶν) is, of course, crucial. For, as we saw in our study of this expression in the commentary on 15:12–19, it denotes unambiguously the hope of *the return of the dead body to physical life*.[15] This expression in itself reveals the baseless character of those interpretations of 1 Cor 15 that portray Paul as affirming something less than a resurrection of the flesh. To the contrary, Paul's language expressly affirms it.

Paul's use of this expression here packs a powerful rhetorical punch. For "the resurrection of the dead" (ἡ ἀνάστασις τῶν νεκρῶν) here in 15:42 explicitly reverses and repudiates the slogan of the self-proclaimed wise at Corinth in 15:12, "there is no resurrection of the dead" (ἀνάστασις νεκρῶν οὐκ ἔστιν). Paul employs the expression ἀνάστασις νεκρῶν or ἡ ἀνάστασις τῶν νεκρῶν four times in the chapter. He employs it the first two times in vv. 12–13 to describe the denial of the resurrection by some at Corinth, and then the final two times in v. 21 and v. 42 to reaffirm the resurrection in the face of the Corinthians' denial. As the final occurrence of this crucial expression, at a nodal point within the chapter, 15:42 has a conclusive and climactic force. This force is heightened by Paul's use, for the first time in the chapter, of the articular form of the expression, synonymous with but weightier than its anarthrous form. This climactic reaffirmation of "the resurrection of the dead" is important for our understanding of the chapter. Far from seeking to appease or compromise with those at Corinth who denied the resurrection, Paul has arranged the instances of [ἡ] ἀνάστασις [τῶν] νεκρῶν within the chapter so as to powerfully

---

14. Cf. Thiselton, 1271; Schrage, 294.
15. See the full discussion in chapter 6.

CHAPTER 12

and triumphantly *affirm* what some at Corinth *denied*—the resurrection of *this* body of flesh and bones to everlasting embodied life.

*The body is sown in corruption.* The verb σπείρεται ("is sown") recalls the threefold use of σπείρεις ("you sow") in 15:36–37, showing that Paul is here directly applying the comparison of the seed in 15:36–38.[16] As Matt O'Reilly notes, "The importance of the sowing metaphor is now on full display."[17] Befitting the application to "the resurrection of the dead," what is sown is here (in the application) no longer the seed (as in the comparison) but the human body. Paul has carefully prepared the ground for this application through the repeated use, as already exhibited in the preceding comparisons, of σῶμα "body" (15:37, 38 [2×], 40 [2×]) and σάρξ "flesh" (15:39 [4×]). The threefold use of σπείρω "sow," in the analogy of the seed (15:36, 37 [2×]), where it refers to the burial of the seed in the earth, determines the meaning of σπείρω here. The sowing of the body thus denotes the body's death and burial.[18]

Two alternative interpretations of the meaning of the verb σπείρω here have been offered. First, many interpreters have suggested that the verb here denotes mortal human life from birth to death, the present time of mortal human existence.[19] Second, Jeffrey Asher argues that the verb here functions as an "anthropogenic metaphor" referring to the creation of Adam.[20] A number of scholars have followed Asher's thesis.[21] However, neither of these suggested interpretations is viable.

(1) First, the very nature of the verb Paul employs rules out the view that it is a general reference to present mortal life. Such a reference to an ongoing state of being would require a stative verb or a verb denoting ongoing activity. But the verb σπείρω denotes not a state or ongoing activity but an action that is performed or accomplished: the seed is buried in the earth. Paul's choice of verb is not consistent with the reading of σπείρεται as denoting the ongoing state of mortal existence.

(2) The specific context of the verb σπείρω in v. 42 is the preceding comparison of the seed in vv. 36–38, where Paul uses σπείρω three times to denote the burial of

---

16. Cf. Bonneau, "Logic," 87; Lindemann, 359.

17. Matt O'Reilly, *Paul and the Resurrected Body: Social Identity and Ethical Practice* (ESEC 22; Atlanta: SBL Press, 2020), 82.

18. Correctly, Weiss, 371; Robertson & Plummer, 372; J. A. Schep, *The Nature of the Resurrection Body: A Study of the Biblical Data* (Grand Rapids: Eerdmans, 1964), 199. So also Aquinas, *1 Cor.* 980.

19. So Schrage, 294 ("die gegenwärtige Zeit irdischer Leiblichkeit"); Lindemann, 359; Godet, 2:410–12; Fee, 868; Ciampa & Rosner, 811.

20. Jeffrey R. Asher, "ΣΠΕΙΡΕΤΑΙ: Paul's Anthropogenic Metaphor in 1 Corinthians 15:42–44," *JBL* 120 (2001): 101–22.

21. E.g., Wolff, 406; Garland, 732–33.

the seed in the ground (15:36–37) and specifically states that the seed "dies" (15:36). This fixes the meaning of the verb in 15:42 as denoting death and burial, thus ruling out both alternative interpretations. Asher has seen this clearly, and so, to maintain his view, he is driven to deny that 15:36–38 is an analogy of the resurrection at all, and to deny that there is any connection whatsoever between the verb σπείρω in 15:42 and the three occurrences of this same verb in 15:36–37![22] Such desperate expedients only underscore the untenability of this interpretation.

(3) Paul's introduction to the language of sowing and resurrection in 15:42–44, οὕτως καὶ ἡ ἀνάστασις τῶν νεκρῶν ("so also is the resurrection of *the dead*"), shows that he is thinking of the dead body or corpse, not humanity's original condition or living mortal existence.

(4) Finally, Paul's description of the body as sown in corruption or decay (ἐν φθορᾷ) emphatically rules out a reference to Adam's original creation, for in Paul's theology human death and decay entered the world not through creation but through the fall (15:21–22, 56; cf. Rom 5:12–21). But it also rules out the view that the verb here refers to present mortal life. For it is through death that the body is corrupted. The body that is sown in decomposition or decay can therefore only be the corpse that is laid in the grave.

The main argument of those who deny that σπείρεται in 15:42–44 denotes the body's death and burial is that the last three predicate complements of the verb in vv. 43–44 ("in dishonor"; "in weakness"; "a body of the soul") conflict with such a meaning of the verb.[23] But as we will see in our discussion of vv. 43–44 below, this is not the case.

Here the noun φθορά denotes the physical corruption or decay that ensues upon death and burial. Like our terms "corruption," "decomposition," or "disintegration," the word φθορά, as J. H. H. Schmidt notes, "is the general term for the destruction of a thing, especially where this arises from causes intrinsic to the thing itself."[24] Paul here comes to what we have seen was the main objection to the resurrection by the self-defined philosophically wise at Corinth, as expressed in the mocking questions of the interlocutor in 15:35—the empirical fact of the body's dissolution following death. For the ancient philosophers, it was considered absurd and impossible that a corpse, once corrupted and decayed in the earth, could be restored to life. As the philosopher and great opponent of Christianity, Celsus, asked in derision, "But what kind of body [ποῖον σῶμα; cf. 1 Cor 15:35,

---

22. Asher, "Anthropogenic Metaphor," 104–9.
23. E.g., Garland, 732–33; Godet, 2:410–11; Wolff, 406.
24. Schmidt, *Syn.*, 4:86 (§158.3): "φθορά aber ist der allgemeine Ausdruck für die Vernichtung eines Dinges, besonders wo diese aus innerhalb des Dinges liegenden Ursachen hervorgeht."

ποίῳ δὲ σώματι], once completely corrupted, is able to return again to its original nature?"[25] In the focus of v. 42 on the physical decay of the corpse buried in the earth, which was the main argument of the Corinthian wise against the resurrection, we have here yet another indication that with v. 42 we have reached a nodal point of the chapter. Paul will now begin to unfold an answer to this chief objection of the wise at Corinth to the resurrection, an answer that will reach a stunning climax in v. 44.

*it is raised in incorruptibility.* Paul begins here the rhetorically powerful use of anaphora and homoioptoton, as discussed in the introduction to this chapter, through the complex assonance of the paired verbs σπείρεται and ἐγείρεται. The verb ἐγείρω, as we saw in chapter 3 of this commentary, conveys unambiguously the conception of the physical restoration to life of the corpse laid in the tomb. That is why the interlocutor in 15:35 had asked in derision, "How can the dead be *raised*?" (πῶς ἐγείρονται οἱ νεκροί;). In the preceding clause in v. 42, οὕτως ἡ ἀνάστασις τῶν νεκρῶν, Paul's words τῶν νεκρῶν had taken up the words οἱ νεκροί of the interlocutor's question in v. 35 (πῶς ἐγείρονται οἱ νεκροί;). So here Paul's verb ἐγείρεται recalls the verb ἐγείρονται from the same objection (πῶς ἐγείρονται οἱ νεκροί;). Paul's response to the interlocutor (and thus to the wise at Corinth) here is anything but compromising. What the interlocutor in v. 35 *denied*, Paul here emphatically *affirms*—the bodily resurrection.

The body that was buried in decay is in the resurrection restored to life in freedom from decay (ἐν ἀφθαρσίᾳ). In Paul's focus here on the imperishability of the risen body, in contrast with the perishability of the present body, we have reached a major theme of the chapter. This theme was foreshadowed in 9:25 in the contrast between the corruptible (φθαρτός) and the incorruptible (ἄφθαρτος) wreath of victory. It was latent in the comparison of the seed and its contrast between the seed corrupted in the earth (15:36–37) and the wondrous new growth that God causes to spring from it (15:38). This theme will reach a massive climactic crescendo in 15:50–54, where, in the space of five verses, φθορά, ἀφθαρσία, and their cognates will occur *seven* times. What the ancient philosophers, and the wise at Corinth, could see only as foolishness and a contradiction in terms, Paul here boldly proclaims—the human body of flesh and bones made incorruptible and imperishable. Moreover, the word ἀφθαρσία, in its biblical usage, bears rich, full overtones of not only *endless* life but also *fullness* of life (Rom 2:7; 1 Cor 9:25; 2 Tim 2:10; cf. Mart. Pol. 14.2).[26]

---

25. Celsus, quoted in Origen, *Cels.* 5.14.
26. Thiselton, 1271–72; Barrett, 372; cf. Aquinas, *1 Cor.* 980.

## Verse 43

*It is sown in dishonor, it is raised in glory. It is sown in weakness, it is raised in power.*

*It is sown in dishonor.* As in the previous clause, the implicit subject is the body, and the verb σπείρεται ("it is sown") refers to the death and burial of the body. Used here of the physical body, the term ἀτιμία "dishonor," does not refer, as it normally does, to the subjective estimation of a person(s) by others but instead denotes an objective state or condition of the body buried in the ground—its lowliness, indignity, and degradation.[27] Although this language may also apply to the mortal body, in its fragility and infirmity, the primary referent (as we have seen the verb σπείρεται requires) is to the death and burial of the body. Some scholars have argued that the language of dishonor is not appropriate to a deceased body, and that therefore Paul's reference must be to the mortal but living body.[28] But this is mistaken. The indignity, dishonor, degradation, and disgrace of the corpse buried in the earth were proverbial in antiquity. The poet Theognis of Megara writes of his own future death and burial: "lifeless below the earth will I lie, like a mute stone" (*Eleg.* 1.567–570). In a well-known saying, the philosopher Heraclitus writes: "For corpses are more fit to be cast out than manure" (*Frag.* 96, νέκυες γὰρ κοπρίων ἐκβλητότεροι). Writing of the superiority of living creatures to inanimate objects, Plutarch also reveals in passing his own attitude, and the attitude he assumes his ancient readers hold, regarding the dishonor attaching to the buried body: "But whatever things have not shared in life, nor by their nature are able to share in it, have a more dishonorable portion even than corpses [ἀτιμοτέραν ἔχει νεκρῶν μοῖρον]" (*Is. Os.* 382b). It is striking that Plutarch uses the adjective ἄτιμος, cognate to the noun ἀτιμία used by Paul, to describe the corpse. The body, lifeless and in the process of corruption, is buried in a state of degradation and dishonor.

*it is raised in glory.* In v. 43 we find the final occurrence of the word δόξα within the chapter and within the letter as a whole. Paul has carefully prepared the ground for this climactic occurrence of the word in both the chapter and the larger letter. Within the letter, the first two instances of the word δόξα occur in 2:7–8, where it refers (as all expositors concur) to the *eschatological* glory to be bestowed on

---

27. Cf. Robinson, s.v. "ἀτιμία" on the use of the word here: "'absence of honor' i.e. *vileness, meanness* sc. of condition 1 Cor 15,43." For ἀτιμία used elsewhere to denote an objective condition, see Rom 1:26; 9:21; 2 Tim 2:20.

28. Thus Asher, "Anthropogenic Metaphor," 110; Schrage, 296–97; Garland, 732.

CHAPTER 12

the faithful.[29] In 2:7, "our glory" (εἰς δόξαν ἡμῶν), through its linkage to "the Lord of glory" (ὁ κύριος τῆς δόξης) in 2:8, denotes "the divine glory that belongs to the crucified and risen Lord . . . and in which the faithful will one day share in eternal bodily life."[30] Through this glory, believers will "share in God's own glory."[31] The final occurrence of the word δόξα in the letter is in 15:43. First Corinthians 2:7–8 and 15:43 thus form an intratextual thematic frame, linking the last occurrence of δόξα in 15:43 to its first occurrence in 2:7–8, thereby determining the meaning of δόξα here in 15:43. As in 2:7–8, δόξα here refers to the Son of God's own glory, in which the faithful will one day share through their union with him.[32] However, 15:43 marks an advance upon 2:7–8, for in 15:43 it is explicit that this divine glory will be given to the risen *body*.

Paul has also carefully prepared for the use of δόξα here by the preceding analogy of the heavenly bodies in 15:40–41. There the word δόξα occurs no less than *five* times, and the final words of the comparison in v. 41, ἐν δόξῃ, provide a direct link to the identical phrase in v. 43. This comparison in 15:40–41, in which the celestial *bodies* possess a *heavenly* glory, determines the meaning of δόξα in 15:43 as denoting the heavenly glory of God bestowed upon the body at the resurrection.

Whether, then, we trace the context of δόξα in 15:43 within the letter as a whole, in which 2:7–8 and 15:43 form an *inclusio* linking the δόξα of 15:43 to the communication of Christ's own glory in 2:7–8, or we trace that context within the chapter, where the preceding analogy of the heavenly bodies in 15:40–41 identifies the glory of 15:43 with the glory of God communicated to the bodies of the faithful in the resurrection, the results are the same. The glory in which the body is raised in 15:43 is thus *the radiant splendor that belongs to God's own nature and being*. This meaning of δόξα, which is a usage found only within the biblical and Jewish context, appears frequently in the New Testament, especially in Paul's letters (Rom 5:2; 8:18, 21, 30; 9:23; 2 Cor 3:18; Phil 3:21; 1 Thess 2:12; 2 Thess 2:14).[33] The origin of this usage is in the LXX, where δόξα frequently translates the Hebrew *kābôd* and denotes the radiant splendor of the presence of the Lord (Exod 24:16–17; 33:17–23; 40:34–35; 1 Kgs 8:11–13).

---

29. E.g., Robertson & Plummer, 38; Schreiner, 81; Hays, 44.

30. Wolff, 55.

31. Fee, 113. Cf. Wolff, 55 ("a share in God's own glory"); Fitzmyer, 176; Conzelmann, 62.

32. See Brian Rosner, "Temple and Holiness in 1 Corinthians 15," *TynBul* 42 (1991): 143: "In 2:7–8 the connection of believers' ultimate glorification to their union with Christ (note repetition of δόξα) is a precursor to 1 Corinthians 15."

33. On the importance of this meaning of δόξα in Paul, see Fitzmyer, 176; Sigurd Grindheim, "A Theology of Glory: Paul's Use of Δόξα Terminology in Romans," *JBL* 136 (2017): 457–62; Cremer, 208–9.

## The Glorified Body of the Resurrection

In Phil 3:21, Paul writes of "the Lord Jesus Christ . . . who will transform our lowly bodies to be made like the body of his glory [τῷ σώματι τῆς δόξης αὐτοῦ]." In that passage, where we find δόξα used in this sense of the divine glory, we also find two important connections to the thought in 1 Corinthians. First, we find in Phil 3:21, as we did in 1 Cor 2:7–8, that this glory possessed by God alone, the expression of God's very being, is the glory of *Christ*. We see here again the incarnational and Trinitarian nature of Paul's thought. The glory of God is the glory of Christ. Second, in Phil 3:21 this glory, the splendor and majesty that belongs to God's own nature, is in the resurrection imparted to the *body*. So also here in 1 Cor 15:43, the divine splendor that belongs to the Son of God's own being, the radiant manifestation of his presence, will be bestowed in the resurrection upon the *bodies* of the faithful. The body will be "raised in glory" (15:43) because the glory and presence of the Son of God, which now dwells within the bodies of the faithful but in an anticipatory way, will be given in the resurrection in its fullness—enlivening, transforming, and suffusing those very bodies themselves. The risen body will share directly in the splendor and glory of God. The resurrection will be the fullness of the presence of Christ, imparted not only to the soul but also to the body. It will be the believer's union with Christ brought to consummation.

*It is sown in weakness.* The verb *is sown*, as we have seen, refers to the death and burial of the corpse. Some have argued that *is sown* cannot here refer to burial, since the modifier *in weakness* denotes diminished capacity, not the total incapacity of a corpse.[34] However, ἀσθένεια "weakness" is the negation of the noun σθενός "strength, power," and its basic sense is "powerlessness."[35] It serves as the regular antonym of δύναμις "power."[36] As such it has a "wholly general" meaning that can range from diminished capacity to absolute incapacity.[37] As with ἀτιμία "dishonor" in the preceding clause, ἀσθένεια might also aptly fit the living mortal body in its infirmity and debility, but this weakness and incapacity is most starkly evident when the body is laid lifeless in the earth. But for those united to Christ, this will be reversed.

*it is raised in power.* The power of God is a major theme within 1 Corinthians. At the opening of the body of the letter, Paul declares: "For the word of the cross is to

---

34. So Asher, "Anthropogenic Metaphor," 110; Schrage, 296–97; Garland, 732.
35. See Frisk, 2:698–99; cf. Cremer, 526.
36. As frequently seen in classical (e.g., Isocrates, *Archid.* 58), Jewish (e.g., Josephus, *B.J.* 6.328), and early Christian (e.g., 2 Cor 12:9; 13:4) sources.
37. Schmidt, *Syn.*, 4:692–93 (§148).

CHAPTER 12

those who are perishing foolishness, but to us who are being saved it is the power of God" (1:18). The theme of the gospel of Christ as the power or δύναμις of God pervades the first four chapters of the epistle (1:18, 24–25; 2:4–5; 4:19–20). In 6:14 we learn that the resurrection will be the final triumph of God's power (ἡμᾶς ἐξεγερεῖ διὰ τῆς δυνάμεως αὐτοῦ). First Corinthians 15:43 brings this theme of the power of God, with its final fulfillment in the resurrection, to its climax.

The power in which the body is raised in 15:43 is thus the power *of God* (cf. 1:18, 24–25; 2:4–5; 4:19–20; 5:4; 6:14). We have already seen that δόξα in this verse denotes the manifest splendor of God's own nature. And whenever in the New Testament that δόξα and δύναμις are used together, as they are here, δύναμις is related closely to God's own nature and being (Matt 24:30; Mark 13:26; Luke 21:27; Rev 15:8; 19:1). Moreover, the Holy Spirit and δύναμις are closely associated throughout the New Testament (Luke 1:17, 35; 24:49; Acts 1:8; 10:38; Rom 1:4; 15:13, 19; Eph 3:16; 1 Thess 1:5; 2 Tim 1:7). This is a key equation in Paul's thought, as we see in 1 Cor 2:4, where Paul characterizes the kerygma as a demonstration "of Spirit and power" (πνεῦμα καὶ δύναμις).

The power Paul thinks of here in v. 43, then, is the power of God and of the Spirit. Moreover, as the modal modifier ἐν δυνάμει indicates, Paul thinks of this power of the Holy Spirit not merely as operating *upon* the body (as διὰ τῆς δυνάμεως might imply) but as imparted and communicated *to* the body. The risen body will participate in the Spirit and power of God (cf. 2:4–5).[38] The thought here prepares the way for the climactic asseveration that now follows in v. 44a.

## Verse 44a

*It is sown a body of the soul, it is raised a body of the Spirit.*

*It is sown a body of the soul.* As in 15:42–43, the implied subject of the verb continues to be the human body, which is once again described as "sown." And as in the previous three uses of the verb "sow" in 15:42–43, here too the "sowing" of the body refers to its death and burial in the earth. And as in 15:42–43, this verb denoting burial is once again modified by a following predicate, in order to denote a quality of the body that lies in the grave.

But a crucial shift of syntax occurs here in v. 44. In the three previous clauses in vv. 42–43, the predicate was expressed with a prepositional phrase denoting a quality or condition of the corpse buried in the earth (corruption, dishonor,

---

38. Cf. Weiss, 371; Schrage, 297; Lindemann, 359.

powerlessness). But here in v. 44 the predicate is a predicate nominative, denoting the body itself and a quality inhering in the body itself, that is, what *kind* of body it is. And the kind of body this is, as expressed in v. 44, is clearly the *cause* of the conditions of decay, dishonor, and powerlessness expressed in vv. 42–43.

Paul describes the body that is buried as ψυχικός, an adjective derived from the noun ψυχή "soul."[39] The adjective thus denotes someone or something *related to, fit for, or determined by the soul.* It means "of the soul or life, spiritual, opposed to σωματικός [bodily]."[40] This adjective is thus used in ancient texts, without exception, with reference to the properties or activities of the soul.[41] Both etymology and universal ancient usage, then, demonstrate that the adjective ψυχικός refers to the soul.[42] This is recognized by the vast majority of interpreters.[43] Modifying σῶμα as here, the adjective describes the body as a body *of the soul*, that is, a body enlivened, fit for, or determined by the soul.

Recognizing that the adjective ψυχικός describes the body as animated by the soul, some interpreters have questioned whether the sowing of the body can refer here to the body's death and burial, since in death the soul is separated from the body.[44] But as we have seen, the context of 15:36–44 requires this meaning of σπείρω. And the problem these scholars raise is apparent rather than real. The noun σῶμα can certainly refer to a dead body.[45] The adjective here describes the *kind* of body mortal human beings have, from the moment of conception to

---

39. Frisk, 2:1141.

40. LSJ, s.v. "ψυχικός."

41. E.g., 4 Macc. 1.32; Aristotle, *Eth. nic.* 1117b28–1118a2; Epictetus, *Diatr.* 3.7.5–7; Philo, *Leg.* 1.97; Plutarch, *Plac. philos.* 1.8.

42. It is therefore astonishing to find BDAG, departing from Bauer-Aland, define this adjective as "physical" and σῶμα ψυχικόν in 1 Cor 15:44 as a "physical body" (BDAG, s.v. "ψυχικός" [2]; contrast BA, s.v. "ψυχικός" [2]). The same mistranslation is found in the NRSV. Such a rendering of ψυχικός has no warrant whatsoever in our ancient sources. In fact, so far is ψυχικός from denoting the bodily or the physical that it is regularly *contrasted* with the word σωματικός or "bodily" (Aristotle, *Eth. nic.* 1101b34–35; 1117b28–1118a2; Diogenes Laertius, *Vit. phil.* 7.106; Polybius, *Hist.* 6.5.7; 4 Macc. 1.32; Philo, *Mut.* 33; *Abr.* 219). After all, the adjective ψυχικός refers to the ψυχή, which all the ancients (whatever their views regarding the materiality or nonmateriality of the soul) understood to be invisible, intangible, and impalpable.

43. So Wolff, 407–8; Ciampa & Rosner, 817–18; Collins, 567; Thiselton, 1275–81; Barrett, 372; Schreiner, 322; Hays, 272; Fee, 869–70; O'Reilly, *Resurrected Body*, 83–86; John Granger Cook, "Philo's *Quaestiones in Genesin* and Paul's σῶμα πνευματικόν," in *Alexandria: Hub of the Ancient World* (ed. Benjamin Schliesser, Jan Rüggemeier, Thomas J. Kraus, and Jörg Frey; Tübingen: Mohr Siebeck, 2021), 303–21; Volker Rabens, *The Holy Spirit and Ethics in Paul: Transformation and Empowering for Religious-Ethical Life* (WUNT 2.283; Tübingen: Mohr Siebeck, 2010), 94–96.

44. See Asher, "Anthropogenic Metaphor," 110; Wolff, 406; Garland, 732–33; Godet, 2:410–11.

45. See Frisk, 2:842; LSJ, s.v. "σῶμα"; MM, s.v. "σῶμα"; BDAG, s.v. "σῶμα."

the close of life in death. Indeed, the description of the body laid in the grave as a body whose vital force is the soul pinpoints with precision the existential dilemma of human beings who bear such a body—the impermanent and transitory nature of the life it provides. Is there an answer to this curse of death under which the body lies? Paul provides the answer in the very next clause.

*it is raised a body of the Spirit.* In order to explore Paul's answer fruitfully, we must first set aside a common but radically mistaken scholarly reading of this passage.

*The Mistaken Exegesis of σῶμα πνευματικόν as a "Body Composed of Spirit"*

It is a common assumption in some scholarly quarters that the σῶμα πνευματικόν in 1 Cor 15:44 refers to a body composed of "spirit-matter" or corporeal *pneuma*, an ethereal body composed of "spirit," distinct from the body of flesh laid in the tomb.[46] The consequences of this erroneous reading are massive, for it not only frontally conflicts with Paul's understanding of the resurrection (expressed throughout chapter 15) as a resurrection of the flesh but also entirely misses the crucial point he is making here in v. 44, which is central to the whole chapter. So let us first dispose of this mistaken reading, so that we may then explore what Paul is really saying in v. 44. The following considerations are decisive that σῶμα πνευματικόν here does not refer to a body composed of material spirit or pneumatic matter:

(1) There is no evidence in Paul's letters that the notion of "spirit-matter" had any place in his thought, and such a notion has no connections to Paul's thought elsewhere.[47]

(2) The notion that verse 44 introduces the concept of a new body, distinct in substance from the body sown in death, misunderstands the structure of Paul's syntax in this verse. The σῶμα ψυχικόν and σῶμα πνευματικόν do not function, as

---

46. E.g. Martin, *Body*, 117, 120, 126; Engberg-Pedersen, *Cosmology and Self*, 26–34; Asher, *Polarity and Change*, 153–68, esp. 153–54 (n. 17); Dunn, "1 Corinthians 15," 11–18; Bruce Chilton, *Resurrection Logic: How Jesus' First Followers Believed God Raised Him from the Dead* (Waco: Baylor University Press, 2019), 70–77; M. David Litwa, *We Are Being Transformed: Deification in Paul's Soteriology* (BZNW 187; Berlin: de Gruyter, 2012), 119–71; Matthias Klinghardt, "Himmlische Körper: Hintergrund und argumentative Funktion von 1Kor 15,40f," *ZNW* 106 (2015): 216–44; so earlier Teichmann, *Auferstehung*, 48–53; Otto Pfleiderer, *Paulinism: A Contribution to the History of Primitive Christian Theology* (vol. 1, *Exposition of Paul's Doctrine*; trans. E. Peters; London: Williams & Norgate, 1877), 128, 131–32, 250.

47. O'Reilly, *Resurrected Body*, 84.

sometimes assumed, as the subject of the verbs in 15:44.[48] As shown above, the implied grammatical subject of the verbs in verse 44 is the mortal, fleshly body that is sown in decay (σπείρεται) but thereafter raised to immortal life (ἐγείρεται). The terms σῶμα ψυχικόν and σῶμα πνευματικόν function *predicatively* ("It is sown as a σῶμα ψυχικόν, it is raised as a σῶμα πνευματικόν"), and thus describe two contrasting *modes of existence* of this same body, one prior to the resurrection and the other following the resurrection.

(3) The understanding of the σῶμα πνευματικόν as involving a "body composed of *pneuma*," distinct in substance from the fleshly body, entirely ignores the actual lexical meaning and usage, within Paul and within the wider ancient world, of the key terms in question. This view is thus routinely bedeviled by the gratuitous assumption that the contrast Paul draws in 15:44 is that of *flesh* and *spirit*. Paula Fredriksen, for example, understands Paul to assert that "the Christian's fleshly body, whether living or dead, will be transformed, like Christ's, into a spiritual body."[49] But as we have seen, the adjective that Paul here contrasts with πνευματικός is not σάρκινος (cognate with σάρξ), referring to the *flesh*, but ψυχικός (cognate with ψυχή), referring to the *soul*. Modifying σῶμα with reference to the present body, that adjective describes this present body as a *body of the soul*, determined in its life and activity by the soul. The adjective ψυχικός has nothing to do with the body's composition but denotes the source of the mortal body's life and activity.

(4) The meaning of the paired adjective ψυχικός in 15:44 is extremely significant, for it reveals that the exegesis of the σῶμα πνευματικόν as an ethereal body composed of spirit matter involves a fundamental misunderstanding of the passage. For if σῶμα πνευματικόν in this context describes the composition of the future body, as a body composed only of spirit, its correlate σῶμα ψυχικόν would perforce describe the composition of the present body as a body *composed only of soul*. Paul would then be asserting the absence of flesh and bones not only from the risen body but also from the present mortal body as well! The impossibility that ψυχικός here refers to the body's composition rules out the notion that its correlated adjective πνευματικός refers to the body's composition. Contrasted with ψυχικός, the adjective πνευματικός must similarly refer to the source of the body's life and activity.

---

48. For this misconception, see e.g., J. Gillmann, "Transformation in 1 Cor 15,50–53," *ETL* 58 (1982): 327–28; Stenger, "Argumentationsstruktur," 117; Collins, 567.

49. Paula Fredriksen, "Vile Bodies: Paul and Augustine on the Resurrection of the Flesh," in *Biblical Hermeneutics in Historical Perspective* (ed. Mark S. Burrows and Paul Rorem; Grand Rapids: Eerdmans, 1991), 81.

We will see further evidence against the interpretation of the σῶμα πνευματικόν as a body of spirit matter in the course of our exposition of the term that follows.

*The Meaning of σῶμα πνευματκόν in Verse 44*

Having avoided this disastrous detour from Paul's thought, we are now in a position to grasp what Paul is really saying here. We saw that the previous clause ("it is sown a body of the soul") marked an important shift in syntax, in which Paul used a predicate nominative to identify the *kind* of body that is buried in corruption, dishonor, and powerlessness. Now in this clause Paul contrasts this with the very different quality and kind of body that will be raised in incorruptibility, glory, and power. With 15:44, Paul's argument has clearly reached a climactic point.[50] "This is the nub of his argument."[51] The interlocutor asked in v. 35, "And with what kind of body do the dead return to life?" Paul now, in this clause, answers this question in the most stunning way.

Paul's answer is this. The body when it is buried is a σῶμα ψυχικόν, but this same body when it is raised will be a σῶμα πνευματκόν. As the adjective ψυχικός is derived from the noun ψυχή, so the adjective πνευματικός is derived from the noun πνεῦμα.[52] Paul is using new language here. The phrase σῶμα ψυχικόν, the expression σῶμα πνευματικόν, the drawing of a *contrast* between the adjectives ψυχικός and πνευματικός, the implicit contrast between ψυχή and πνεῦμα—all are unique to ancient Christianity and are found nowhere prior to 1 Corinthians.[53] The

---

50. Rightly Fitzmyer, 595; Collins, 567.
51. Hays, 272.
52. Frisk, 2:566.
53. The only distant analogy in antiquity of this contrast of ψυχή and πνεῦμα witnessed in Paul and early Christianity is found in Philo's distinction between the ψυχή and the πνεῦμα θεῖον, a somewhat baffling and complex entity that Philo apparently understood as an intermediary angelic being (Philo, *Spec.* 4.49; *Virt.* 217; *Gig.* 28). On this conception in Philo, see John R. Levison, "The Prophetic Spirit as an Angel according to Philo," *HTR* 88 (1995): 189–207; Levison, "Inspiration and the Divine Spirit in the Writings of Philo Judaeus," *JSJ* 26 (1995): 271–323, esp. 274–80. Many scholars engage in a "mirror reading" of Paul's language, maintaining that Paul, in using the terms ψυχικός and πνευματικός, is employing (and at the same time opposing!) language originally used by the Corinthians; see e.g., Timothy A. Brookins, *Rediscovering the Wisdom of the Corinthians: Paul, Stoicism, and Spiritual Hierarchy* (Grand Rapids: Eerdmans, 2024), 117–27, 210–18; Birger Pearson, *The Pneumatikos-Psychikos Terminology in 1 Corinthians: A Study in the Theology of the Corinthian Opponents of Paul and Its Relation to Gnosticism* (SBLDS 12; Missoula, MT: Scholars, 1973), 27–43; Christopher M. Tuckett, "The Corinthians Who Say 'There Is No Resurrection of the Dead' (1 Cor 15,12)," in *The Corinthian Correspondence* (ed. R. Bieringer;

uniqueness of Paul's language in 15:44, and the solemn way in which he introduces it, suggest that Paul understands his language here as fulfilling, in a most powerful way, his apostolic function of speaking "in words taught by the Spirit" (1 Cor 2:13). Through the expression σῶμα πνευματικόν, the apostle reveals the mysteries of God (1 Cor 2:7; 4:1) in words given by God (1 Cor 2:13).

Interpreters have generally failed to notice the startling thing about Paul's new language here. Among the classical writers, philosophers, and Philo, the adjective ψυχικός always bears the most positive connotations of excellence and superiority, referring as it does to the powers of the ψυχή or soul (e.g., Aristotle, *Eth. nic.* 1099a7–12; Diogenes Laertius, *Vit. phil.* 7.106; Philo, *Leg.* 2.59; 3.146; *Migr.* 92). But here in 1 Cor 15:44, the σῶμα ψυχικόν is clearly lesser than and inferior to the σῶμα πνευματικόν with which it is contrasted. A lesser and deprecatory sense is given to the adjective ψυχικός, and thus to the soul or ψυχή. This is something unknown outside the New Testament and does not appear prior to Paul.[54] Why is the σῶμα ψυχικόν or "body of the soul" portrayed as lesser and inadequate? What greater gift could the body receive than the soul, the source of life, thought, and being? The answer is simple but staggering in its implications: that greater gift is the Spirit of God. As the majority of recent interpreters have recognized, the σῶμα πνευματικόν is a body *of the Spirit*. It is a body "animated by the Spirit of God."[55] It is "a physical human body that has been enlivened, transformed, and is continually characterized by the Spirit."[56] It is a body "energized by the Spirit of the living God."[57]

Paul has carefully prepared the way for this language of "the body of the Spirit" throughout the letter. The contrasted pair of ψυχικός and πνευματικός was crucially foreshadowed in 1 Cor 2:14–15, where ὁ ψυχικὸς ἄνθρωπος was contrasted

---

Leuven: Leuven University Press, 1996), 254; Martinus de Boer, *The Defeat of Death: Apocalyptic Eschatology in 1 Corinthians 15 and Romans 5* (JSNTSup 22; 1988; repr., London: T&T Clark, 2019), 98–103; Andrew Lincoln, *Paradise Now and Not Yet: Studies in the Role of the Heavenly Dimension in Paul's Thought with Special Reference to His Eschatology* (SNTSMS 43; Cambridge: Cambridge University Press, 1981), 40–42. However, there is no persuasive evidence that supports this speculative hypothesis, and as we will see, there is positive evidence that contradicts it. The language is Paul's.

54. On this contrast between the classical and early Christian usage of the term, see Trench, *Syn.*, 267–70.

55. Barrett, 372.

56. O'Reilly, *Resurrected Body*, 86.

57. Collins, 567. See also Wolff, 407 ("durch und durch vom göttlichen Geist herrschter Leib"); Ciampa & Rosner, 817 ("fully animated by God's Spirit"); Schreiner, 322 ("empowered and animated by the Holy Spirit"); Lincoln, *Paradise*, 42 ("dominated by the Spirit"); Rabens, *Holy Spirit and Ethics*, 96 ("transformed, animated and enlivened by God's Spirit"); Fee, 869–70.

CHAPTER 12

with ὁ πνευματικὸς [ἄνθρωπος]. In this passage the contrast is clearly not between a person composed of flesh and blood and a person composed of spirit matter or corporeal *pneuma*! Rather, ὁ ψυχικὸς ἄνθρωπος is the person who possesses only the natural life of the soul (ψυχή) and is bereft of the Holy Spirit, in contrast with ὁ πνευματικὸς [ἄνθρωπος], the person possessing and transformed by the Spirit of God (τὸ πνεῦμα τοῦ θεοῦ, 2:11-12). This contrasting pair is not found again in the letter until 15:44. But the adjective πνευματικός plays an important role throughout the letter, where it is used without exception with reference to persons or things given, enlivened, energized, or characterized by the Spirit of God (2:13; 3:1; 9:11; 10:3-4; 12:1; 14:1, 37). The final four uses of the adjective πνευματικός within the letter occur in 15:44-46. It is in 15:44-46 that the contrasting adjectives ψυχικός and πνευματικός also recur three times, the first time they have appeared together in the letter since 2:14-15. First Corinthians 15:44-46 thus clearly forms an *inclusio* with 2:14-15 and a climactic application of the πνευματικός terminology employed by Paul throughout the epistle with reference to the Holy Spirit. Paul has thus prepared the way throughout the letter for the revelation of the body of the Spirit in 15:44.

The use of the adjective ψυχικός as a term in contrast to the person and work of the *Holy Spirit* is the uniform meaning of this word throughout the New Testament. In Jas 3:15, the adjective is used to describe human wisdom apart from the Spirit (cf. Jas 3:13-18). In Jude 19, ψυχικοί persons are expressly defined as πνεῦμα μὴ ἔχοντες ("not having the Spirit"). This conforms with Paul's contrast of ψυχικός and πνευματικός in 1 Cor 2:14-15, where (as we have seen) πνευματικός refers to the person and activity of the Holy Spirit.[58] When Paul uses these same terms in 1 Cor 15:44 regarding the body, it is clear that Paul's contrast is between the present body animated only by the *soul*, and therefore mortal and corruptible, and the risen body that will also be energized and infused with the *Holy Spirit*, and will thus be transformed to be glorious and imperishable. This confirms, once again, that the σῶμα πνευματικόν of 1 Cor 15:44 denotes not a body composed of celestial spirit matter (a conception entirely unknown within the New Testament), but the risen body of flesh and bones, whose vital principle will be the Spirit of the living God.

Paul's thought throughout 15:42-44 has been leading toward the disclosure of the body of the Spirit in v. 44. As we saw, the *glory* in which the body is raised in v. 43a is the manifest splendor of God's presence and being, which will suffuse

---

58. The use of this terminology in the New Testament outside Paul's letters is decisive evidence against the common scholarly notion, mentioned above (note 53) that Paul drew his contrasting use of ψυχικός and πνευματικός from the Corinthians. See e.g., Brookins, *Wisdom of the Corinthians*, 117-27, 210-18. If so, we could not explain its presence elsewhere in the New Testament.

the physical body, and the *power* in which it will be raised in v. 43b denotes the transforming power and presence of the Holy Spirit. This train of thought reaches its climax in v. 44 in the expression "body of *the Spirit*," which denotes the body's direct participation in the life, glory, and power of the Spirit of God.

All this requires further unpacking. For we have now come to the heart of Paul's teaching in 1 Cor 15.

### The σῶμα πνευματικόν as the Full Gift of the Holy Spirit

If, within 1 Corinthians, we count not only instances of the word πνεῦμα when denoting the Holy Spirit (28×) but also occurrences of the word πνευματικός, which always refers to the Holy Spirit (12×), references to the Holy Spirit occur with greater frequency in 1 Corinthians than in any other Pauline letter. The gift of the Holy Spirit and his indwelling of the faithful—always a central theme in Paul—has an especially prominent place in this epistle (2:12; 3:16–17; 6:11, 17, 19; 12:3, 13). The related theme of the bodies of believers as living tabernacles or temples of the Holy Spirit (3:16–17; 6:19–20) also plays an important role in this letter.[59] "Or do you not know that your body [σῶμα] is a temple of the Holy Spirit who is in you [τοῦ ἐν ὑμῖν ἁγίου πνεύματος]?" (6:19). Through the gift of the Holy Spirit, believers even now are no longer ψυχικοί, persons of the soul alone, bereft of the Holy Spirit's presence and power (2:14), but they are πνευματικοί, persons of the Spirit, temples of the living God (2:15; cf. 3:1; 14:37).

This theme of the faithful as temples of the Holy Spirit receives its crown in 1 Cor 15:44. In 2:14–15, Paul had used the adjective πνευματικός to describe Christ followers as *persons* indwelt by the Holy Spirit. Now in 15:44, he uses the adjective πνευματικός of the risen body, in order to describe the gift of the Holy Spirit given to the *body*. In 6:19, Paul had spoken of the body (σῶμα) as a temple of the indwelling Holy Spirit (ναὸς τοῦ ἐν ὑμῖν ἁγίου πνεύματος). But this passage was but a foreshadowing of the σῶμα πνευματικόν of 15:44, where the body itself partakes of the gift of the Spirit.[60] In the resurrection, the Spirit who now dwells *in* the body will be given *to* the body. This gift of the Holy Spirit to the body will be the consummation of union with God.

Some scholars believe that because Paul contrasts the σῶμα ψυχικόν and the σῶμα πνευματικόν, he must then be envisioning the risen body as without a soul. This

---

59. On the importance of the temple theme in 1 Corinthians, see Rosner, "Temple and Holiness," 137–45.

60. Cf. O'Reilly, *Resurrected Body*, 105: Paul's language in 6:19 "may anticipate the language of σῶμα πνευματικόν in 15:44."

CHAPTER 12

is mistaken. In 2:14–15, Paul contrasts the person of the Spirit (ὁ πνευματικός, 2:15) with the person of the soul (ὁ ψυχικὸς ἄνθρωπος, 2:14), but this hardly means that the person of the Spirit ceases to have a soul. Rather, ὁ πνευματικός is the person indwelt, both body and soul, by the Holy Spirit. So also the risen life of the σῶμα πνευματικόν does not exclude but rather includes and enhances the soul. That the resurrection comprehends both body and soul is a universal assumption within early Christian literature (see John 12:25; Acts 2:25–31; 1 Clem. 49.6; cf. John 10:17–18). We find this conception of the resurrection as the work of the Spirit, granting incorruptible life to both body and soul, succinctly expressed in Mart. Pol. 14.2, where the aged martyr Polycarp gives thanks to God that he has been counted worthy to share in the cup of his Christ, leading "to the resurrection of eternal life, of both soul and body, in the incorruptibility of the Holy Spirit" (εἰς ἀνάστασιν ζωῆς αἰωνίου ψυχῆς τε καὶ σώματος ἐν ἀφθαρσίᾳ πνεύματος ἁγίου).

The language of "the body of the Spirit" is unique to 1 Corinthians. But the conception it expresses, that the resurrection involves the full gift of the Spirit given to the body, is found elsewhere in Paul. It is strikingly expressed in Romans 8:23:

> And not only this, but also we ourselves, who have the firstfruits of the Spirit, we also groan in ourselves, awaiting our adoption, the redemption of our body.

In regard to the phrase ἡ ἀπαρχὴ τοῦ πνεύματος ("the firstfruits of the Spirit"), many interpreters regard the genitive τοῦ πνεύματος as epexegetical (i.e., "the firstfruits that is the Spirit"), in which case the present (and presumably complete) gift of the Spirit is the firstfruits, in that it anticipates the bodily resurrection to come. However, ἀπαρχή is never used in the LXX with an epexegetical genitive. The use of ἀπαρχή with a partitive genitive, on the other hand, is very frequent.[61] Moreover, in the New Testament, whenever ἀπαρχή is accompanied by a genitive, that genitive is always partitive (Rom 16:5; 1 Cor 15:20; 16:15; Jas 1:18). The evidence is thus overwhelming that the genitive in the expression ἡ ἀπαρχὴ τοῦ πνεύματος is a partitive genitive. The sense of the expression in Rom 8:23 is thus that the present gift of the Holy Spirit is partial and preparatory, anticipating the full gift of the Spirit to be given at the bodily resurrection, "the redemption of our body." This is confirmed by the related theme of adoption (υἱοθεσία) in Rom 8:12–25, in which the adoption as God's children that takes place in baptism through the Holy Spirit (ἐλάβετε πνεῦμα υἱοθεσίας, 8:15; cf. 8:14, υἱοὶ θεοῦ; 8:16, τέκνα θεοῦ; 8:17, τέκνα) is bestowed in its fullness only at the resurrection (8:23, υἱοθεσίαν ἀπεκδεχόμενοι;

---

61. See Exod 22:29; 23:19; Lev 23:10; Num 15:20, 21; 18:12; Deut 18:4; 26:2, 10; 1 Kgdms 10:4; 2 Chr 31:5; Neh 10:37, 39; Jdt 11:13; Ps 77:51; 104:36; Sir 7:31; 32:8; 45:20; Ezek 44:30.

cf. 8:19, οἱ υἱοὶ τοῦ θεοῦ; 8:21, τὰ τέκνα τοῦ θεοῦ). The "firstfruits of the Spirit," then, refers to the present gift of the Spirit as anticipatory of the full gift of the Spirit to be given to the body at the resurrection, which will thus be "the redemption of our body."[62]

Elsewhere Paul speaks of ὁ ἀρραβὼν τοῦ πνεύματος ("the down payment of the Spirit"), given with the anointing and sealing with the sign of the cross at baptism (2 Cor 1:22; 5:5).[63] The most important treatment of the term ἀρραβών in modern scholarship is that of Barnabas Ahern, who shows convincingly that this word was used in antiquity with the twofold sense of pledge and partial payment. It is a "first installment pledge," a "part-payment pledge."[64] Much like ἡ ἀπαρχὴ τοῦ πνεύματος ("the firstfruits of the Spirit") in Rom 8:23, the expression ὁ ἀρραβὼν τοῦ πνεύματος ("the downpayment of the Spirit") in 2 Cor 1:22 and 5:5 thus stresses that the present indwelling of the Holy Spirit, given in baptism, is only a foretaste of the fullness of union with God to come (cf. Irenaeus, *Haer.* 5.8.1–2). As in Rom 8:23, this fullness of the Spirit is to be given at the resurrection (2 Cor 5:1–5). What is implicit in 2 Cor 1:22 and 2 Cor 5:5, and is explicit in Rom 8:23, is strikingly conveyed by Paul's expression σῶμα πνευματικόν in 1 Cor 15:44—that the fullness of union with God bestowed at the resurrection will involve the Holy Spirit being given directly *to* the body. The body will be glorified through its direct participation in the Spirit of God.

> Such great life and incorruptibility this flesh is able to receive, when the Holy Spirit has been united to it. Nor is anyone able to fully tell or express the things which the Lord has prepared for his chosen ones. (2 Clem. 14.5)

Having explored the meaning and implications of the "body of the Spirit" in 15:44—as the physical body's participation in the fullness of the presence of God—note how far we have traveled from the notion of the σῶμα πνευματικόν as a body composed of insubstantial spirit matter! The assumption of that interpretation is that the resurrection is in Paul's theology a minus, a diminution and a subtraction, and not a plus. But the body of the Spirit in 1 Cor 15:44 is not a minus

---

62. Cf. Wolff, 407; Ciampa & Rosner, 818.

63. For the practice of anointing at baptism in Paul's churches, see Wayne A. Meeks, *The First Urban Christians* (2d ed.; New Haven: Yale University Press, 2003), 151. For this practice of anointing with the sign of the cross at baptism in the ancient church, see Tertullian, *Bapt.* 7–8; *Res.* 8; *Marc.* 1.14; Hippolytus, *Trad. ap.* 21; Cyprian, *Ep.* 70.2.

64. Barnabas Ahern, "The Indwelling Spirit, Pledge of Our Inheritance (Eph 1:14)," *CBQ* 9 (1947): 179–89. See also Kurt Erlemann, "Der Geist als ἀρραβών (2 Kor 5,5) im Kontext der paulinischen Eschatologie," *ZNW* 83 (1992): 202–23.

but most emphatically a plus. It is not the loss of the physical body of flesh. It is the physical body of flesh endued with the full life of the Holy Spirit. The σῶμα πνευματικόν in Paul is not about what God takes away from the body; it is about what he bestows upon it: his own radiant presence and glory, experienced not only by the soul but also by the physical body. Therefore it is the completion and perfection of that relationship and union with God begun in baptism, preserved through faith, and increased and strengthened through the life of discipleship. It is the consummation of union with God.

In the resurrection, the body will no longer derive its life, character, and being from the soul alone, but will do so directly from the Spirit of God, endowing the body with incorruptibility and immortality. The physical body will be endowed with the full life of the Holy Spirit. We find little exploration among contemporary theologians of the varied implications of this staggering reality for the life of the body. But it is a topic of interest among classical theologians such as Irenaeus, Augustine, and Aquinas. The fullest exploration is found in St. Thomas. According to Thomas, in the risen life of the redeemed, "the divine glory given to the soul will overflow into the body" (*ST* Suppl., Q. 85, Art. 1). As with any gift or transfer, the gift of the Holy Spirit to the body will not be received according to the mode of the giver (i.e., God) but according to the mode or manner of the recipient (i.e., the body). The body's response to this influx of the divine presence will therefore be a *bodily* and *sensory* one (Q. 85, Art. 1). Therefore the body's sensory modes, as well as the sensations and physical pleasures attending the body's activity, agility, and repose, will not only be in use but greatly enhanced (Q. 82, Art. 4). Moreover, the different parts of the body will respond in differing modes and ways appropriate to each (Q. 85, Art. 1, ad 4). The risen life of the body will also experience the awakening of new and hitherto unimagined sensations and physical pleasures as the body responds, on the sensory level, in its own appropriate modes to the inflow of the Holy Spirit (Q. 82, Art. 4). In all these ways, "the divine glory given to the resurrected body will not destroy nature but will perfect it" (Q. 85, Art. 1, ad 3). As Irenaeus expressed it, "The fruit of the work of the Spirit is the salvation of the flesh" (*Haer.* 5.12.4).

CHAPTER 13

# *The Bestowal of the Holy Spirit by the Risen Son of God*

15:44b–49

First Corinthians 15:44b–49 is widely considered one of the most difficult passages in the entire New Testament. Heavily debated and notoriously controversial, it has been the subject of much study—and much speculation. Considerable effort has been devoted to what has proven to be a futile search for a prior source for Paul's presentation in this passage of Christ as the last Adam. Claims of a Gnostic background, once popular, are now almost universally rejected.[1] In recent decades many scholars have sought the background of the passage in supposed "creation traditions" within Alexandrian Judaism (for which Philo's doctrine of the "two human beings" is our only evidence) that were, as the scenario goes, taken up by the Corinthians and opposed by Paul.[2] However, as a number of scholars have pointed out, the conceptions of the two Adams in Philo and Paul are drastically different, and this Philonic background fails to illumine the passage.[3] Others have

---

1. For this hypothesis, see Conzelmann, 284–86.

2. See, for example, Birger Pearson, *The Pneumatikos-Psychikos Terminology in 1 Corinthians: A Study in the Theology of the Corinthian Opponents of Paul and Its Relation to Gnosticism* (SBLDS 12; Missoula, MT: Scholars, 1973); Gregory E. Sterling, "'Wisdom among the Perfect:' Creation Traditions in Alexandrian Judaism and Corinthian Christianity," *NovT* 37 (1995): 355–84; Felipe de Jesús Legarreta-Castillo, *The Figure of Adam in Romans 5 and 1 Corinthians 15: The New Creation and Its Ethical and Social Reconfiguration* (Minneapolis: Fortress, 2014), 135–49; Stefan Nordgaard, "Paul's Appropriation of Philo's Theory of 'Two Men' in 1 Corinthians 15.45–49," *NTS* 57 (2011): 348–65. Nordgaard differs from the others cited in claiming that Paul does not oppose Philo's theory but enlists it in support of his own teaching.

3. See Stephen Hultgren, "The Origin of Paul's Doctrine of the Two Adams in 1 Corinthians 15.45–49," *JSNT* 25 (2003): 343–70; Sigurd Grindheim, "Wisdom for the Perfect: Paul's Challenge to the Corinthian Church (1 Corinthians 2:6–16)," *JBL* 121 (2002): 702–4.

CHAPTER 13

sought the source of Paul's thought in supposed parallels within rabbinic literature dating centuries after the time of Paul.[4] Still others explain Paul's portrayal of Christ as the second Adam, prefigured in the first Adam of Gen 2:7, as the outworking of Paul's reading of specific Old Testament texts, such as Gen 5:3 or Ezek 37.[5] All these attempts to find a Jewish source for Paul's thought in this passage flounder on one simple fact: the conception of a last Adam, undoing the fall of the first Adam and uniting humanity to God, came into the world with the Christian gospel and was previously unknown in the world into which that gospel came.

Because of its description of the risen Lord as a πνεῦμα ζῳοποιοῦν or "a Spirit who is life-giving" (15:45), this passage is often understood to assert that through his resurrection Jesus has become a "spirit being," with a body composed of spirit substance rather than flesh and bones. The verse is thus often considered a major "prooftext" of the view (which has been previously pilloried in these pages) that Paul in this chapter envisions resurrection, including the resurrection of Christ, in terms of a fleshless body composed of "corporeal spirit."[6] This description of Christ in 15:45, wrested from its context, is also the main source for the theologically misguided "Spirit-Christology" advocated by James D. G. Dunn.[7] Such readings, as we will see, not only introduce foreign, un-Pauline, and even anti-Pauline ideas into the passage but, in so doing, conceal the vital and rich treasures of Christology and soteriology found within this powerful passage.

Verses 44b–49 are a commentary on and expansion of 15:20–23, as the repetition of key terms and concepts from that earlier passage reveals (e.g., ἄνθρω-

---

4. So Hultgren, "Two Adams," 359–70; Menahem Kister, "'First Adam' and 'Second Adam' in 1 Cor 15:45–49 in the Light of Midrashic Exegesis and Hebrew Usage," in *The New Testament and Rabbinic Literature* (ed. Reimund Bieringer et al.; JSJSup 136; Leiden: Brill, 2010), 351–65.

5. Bernardin Schneider, "The Corporate Meaning and Background of 1 Cor 15,45b—'Ο ΕΣΧΑΤΟΣ ΑΔΑΜ ΕΙΣ ΠΝΕΥΜΑ ΖΩΙΟΠΟΙΟΥΝ," *CBQ* 29 (1967): 144–61 (the claimed source is Ezek 37:1–14); Benjamin J. Gladd, "The Last Adam as the 'Life-Giving Spirit' Revisited: A Possible Old Testament Background of One of Paul's Most Perplexing Phrases," *WTJ* 71 (2009): 297–309 (the claimed source is Gen 5:3); Jason Maston, "Anthropological Crisis and Solution in the *Hodayot* and 1 Corinthians 15," *NTS* 62 (2016): 533–48 (the claimed source is Ezek 37).

6. So, among many examples, Daniel A. Smith, "Seeing a Pneuma(tic Body): The Apologetic Interests of Luke 24:36–43," *CBQ* 72 (2010): 766–68; Troels Engberg-Pedersen, *Cosmology and Self in the Apostle Paul: The Material Spirit* (Oxford: Oxford University Press, 2010), 30–34; Bruce Chilton, *Resurrection Logic: How Jesus' First Followers Believed God Raised Him from the Dead* (Waco: Baylor University Press, 2019), 72–75; M. David Litwa, *We Are Being Transformed: Deification in Paul's Soteriology* (BZNW 187; Berlin: de Gruyter, 2012), 127–51.

7. James D. G. Dunn, "1 Corinthians 15:45—Last Adam, Life-Giving Spirit," in *Christ and Spirit in the New Testament* (ed. Barnabas Lindars and Stephen S. Smalley; Cambridge: Cambridge University Press, 1973), 127–41.

πος, 15:21 [2×], 45, 47 [2×]; Ἀδάμ, 15:22, 45 [2×]; ζωοποιέω, 15:22, 45). Verses 20–23 asserted that all who belong to Christ will be made alive in Christ, the second Adam. Verses 44b–49 deepen the thought of vv. 20–23, revealing *how* this can take place. The passage thus provides the chapter's full response to the question of the interlocutor in 15:35: "How can the dead be raised?" Paul's answer, centered upon the person of Jesus Christ, will constitute the very theological heart of this great chapter. First Corinthians 15:44b–49 deserves to be ranked with the other great christological statements in Paul's letters, such as Phil 2:5–11. In it we find the letter's deepest revelation of Christology and thus of the very being and mystery of God. As such, Paul's answer will embrace the whole economy of salvation, the sacraments, and all of Christian life.

## Verse 44b

*If there is a body of the soul, there is also a body of the Spirit.*

As we saw in the previous chapter, the "body of the soul" is the present mortal body, and the "body of the Spirit" is the risen body of flesh fully united to the Spirit of God. Paul's assertion ἔστιν καὶ πνευματικόν ("*there is* a body of the Spirit") offers a fitting contrast and rejoinder to the claim of the Corinthian wise, ἀνάστασις νεκρῶν οὐκ ἔστιν ("*there is no* resurrection of the dead").[8] Verse 44b is cast in the form of a necessary inference: if *a*, then *b*. What is the basis of this necessity? It is hardly the abstract philosophical notion, as Jeffrey Asher proposes, that "one opposite presupposes the existence of its counterpart."[9] More plausibly, a number of interpreters contend that the necessity in v. 44b is grounded in what follows in vv. 45–49.[10] However, Paul will not introduce the Scripture quote in 15:45 with

---

8. The twofold repetition of ἔστιν and the position of these verbs add force to Paul's assertion. However, the accent on these normally enclitic forms in v. 44b does not, as interpreters sometimes suppose, supply additional force. The accented form ἔστιν is normal after εἰ (as in the first instance in v. 44b) and at the beginning of a clause (as in the second instance in v. 44b). See Rob., *Gram.*, 234. Our oldest manuscripts of 1 Corinthians lack accents.

9. So Jeffrey R. Asher, *Polarity and Change in 1 Corinthians 15: A Study of Metaphysics, Rhetoric, and Resurrection* (Tübingen: Mohr Siebeck, 2000), 113; he is followed by Garland, 734. Asher and Garland see this necessity as grounded in a "cosmic, locative polarity" requiring the replacement of the fleshly body with "a body made of pneumatic stuff" (see Asher, *Polarity*, 110–17; Garland, 734–37). On the key misapprehension involved in this conception, see the commentary on 15:47 below.

10. So Leonhard Goppelt, *Typos: The Typological Interpretation of the Old Testament in the New* (trans. Donald E. Madvig; Grand Rapids: Eerdmans, 1982), 134; Schrage, 302; Lindemann, 360.

the words "for thus it has been written" (οὕτως γὰρ γέγραπται), indicating that v. 45 provides the ground for v. 44b, but with the words οὕτως καὶ γέγραπται ("thus *also* it has been written"), indicating that v. 45 provides further corroboration to grounds already given. It is more likely, then, that the inference and necessity expressed in v. 44b are grounded in Paul's whole *preceding* argument. It was implicit in 15:20, in the affirmation of Christ as the firstfruits of the resurrection, and in 15:22, "For just as in Adam all die, so also in Christ all will be made alive." In 15:36–41, the teleology evident in all nature reveals that the present mortal body is, within God's grand design, the forerunner of the glorified body. Indeed, the necessity of the "body of the Spirit" is implicit in the very conception of "the body of the Spirit" itself, introduced in 15:44a. For, as we saw in the preceding chapter, this conception understands the present indwelling of the Spirit, bestowed on the faithful in baptism, as the "firstfruits" (Rom 8:23) or "part-payment" (2 Cor 1:22) of the full gift of the Spirit to be imparted to the physical body in the resurrection. The flow of Paul's thought can be seen by a comparison of v. 44b with the structure and thought of Rom 8:11:

| 1 Cor 15:44b | If there is a body of the soul, | there is also a body of the Spirit. |
|---|---|---|
| Rom 8:11 | But if the Spirit of the One who raised Jesus from the dead dwells in you, | the One who raised Christ from the dead will give life also to your mortal bodies, through his Spirit who dwells within you. |

The present gift of the Spirit has a goal, a telos, a necessary outcome—the full gift of the Spirit imparted to the body in the resurrection. Paul's point here was hardly an abstract one for the Corinthians, for, as he will remind them in his second letter, this is the very teleology that was expressed at their baptism into Christ in the anointing and sealing of their own bodies with the sign of the cross and "the part-payment pledge of the Spirit" (2 Cor 1:22; 5:5).[11]

In all these ways, Paul has provided the grounds for his assertion, "If there is a body of the soul, there is also a body of the Spirit." Now, in the verses that follow, Paul will further deepen and ground this assertion. He will do so through a further exposition of the economy of salvation, the fullest and richest in the chapter.

---

11. For the primitive Christian practice of anointing and sealing the newly baptized with the sign of the cross, see the commentary on 15:44a in the previous chapter.

## Verse 45

*Thus also it has been written: the first human being, Adam, became a soul who was living; the last Adam became a Spirit who is life-giving.*

*Thus also it has been written.* We now have the third of four direct citations of Scripture within the chapter (15:3, 4, 45, 54). As Andreas Lindemann notes, Paul's formula of Scripture citation here is "wholly unusual."[12] In fact, in its use of οὕτως καί before γέγραπται, it is unique. Elsewhere the adverb οὕτως when used with γέγραπται indicates the agreement of the passage cited with a preceding statement or teaching (Matt 2:5; Luke 24:46). Therefore, here the οὕτως marks the Scripture quotation as agreeing with the preceding affirmation in 15:44b: "if there is a body of the soul, there is also a body of the Spirit." But here γέγραπται is also preceded by καί, indicating that the Scripture cited is not the whole basis for the truth affirmed in v. 44b but provides further corroboration. Paul does not say, "For thus it has been written" (cf. Matt 2:5) but "thus *also* it has been written." As we saw in the commentary on v. 44b, Paul has already grounded the truth of v. 44b in Christ's identity as the firstfruits of the resurrection (15:20–22), in the teleology divinely inscribed into all of nature (15:36–41), and in the very conception of "the body of the Spirit" itself (15:44a), which is the outcome of the full gift of the Spirit, of which the firstfruits of the Spirit bestowed in baptism is a guarantee (Rom 8:23; 2 Cor 1:22; 5:5). What follows will confirm and deepen the affirmation of v. 44b: "if there is a body of the soul, there is also a body of the Spirit."

*the first human being, Adam, became a soul who was living.* Paul quotes only the last clause of Gen 2:7, but as will become clear, he has the whole verse in mind. Paul makes two additions to the text of Gen 2:7 LXX, πρῶτος "first," and probably Ἀδάμ "Adam," although the latter is also found in the ancient Greek versions of Symmachus and Theodotion, and so may have been in Paul's text as well.[13] We have seen that 15:44b–49 as a whole is a commentary and expansion on 15:20–23. Paul's focus in v. 45 is on vv. 21–22, as his echoes of these verses show (ἄνθρωπος, v. 21; Ἀδάμ, v. 22; ζῳοποιέω, v. 22). Paul now advances and deepens his teaching in 15:21–22 in light of the new element of "the body of the soul" introduced in 15:44. As in 15:22 the origin of death was traced to Adam, so here the origin of the mortal and perishable "body of the soul" (σῶμα ψυχικόν) is traced to the first man, Adam, who "became

---

12. Lindemann, 360.
13. Cf. Collins, 570.

a soul [ψυχήν] who was living." The adjectival participle ζῶσα "living," modifying ψυχή "soul," denotes the physical life of Adam.[14] But if Adam was created as "a soul that was living" (ζάω), how did he bring death (θάνατος, 15:21) on all humanity?

The answer is that Paul in this chapter presupposes a reading of the Genesis narrative in which Adam and Eve were created with bodies free by divine grace from death (Rom 5:12; cf. Gen 2:17; 3:2–3) but not in possession of an indestructible immortality (cf. Gen 3:19). They were capable through the free decision of union with God of being elevated to a state of everlasting life (2 Cor 11:2–3; cf. Gen 2:9; 3:22). They were also capable, through disobedience, of forfeiting this gift and undergoing the judgment of death (1 Cor 15:21–22; cf. Gen 3:19, 22). Adam's body possessed no incorruptibility or immortality in its own nature, but only enjoyed immortality by the gift of God. In choosing sin and death (1 Cor 15:56; cf. Gen 3:1–24), Adam was given over to corruption (Rom 5:12; cf. Gen 3:19) and brought the curse of death on all humanity: "in Adam all die" (1 Cor 15:21–22). All human beings therefore receive from Adam a body like his (Rom 5:14–17; cf. Gen 5:3), possessing only the mortal and corruptible life of the soul or ψυχή. All human beings have, like Adam, a σῶμα ψυχικόν or "body of the soul" (1 Cor 15:44).[15]

The human dilemma, then, within Paul's theology is therefore not only moral but also physical. Human beings, through Adam's fall, are not only sinful and alienated from God. They also possess bodies in the image of Adam, having only the corruptible life of the soul, that are incapable of everlasting life. But the dilemma is *not* the body's physicality. This is precisely where so many contemporary interpreters go astray. The dilemma is that the ψυχή or soul can only provide to the body a being and life that is transitory, perishable, and corruptible. The dilemma is not what the body *has* or *is* but rather what it *lacks*—incorruptibility and immortality. Far from denigrating the body, the very nature of the human dilemma within Paul's theology assumes the created goodness of the physical body, and that the body or the flesh is an integral component of the human being (cf. Gen 1:26–27).

Paul has now, in one half-verse (15:45a), dramatically taken his hearers back to the beginning of creation. He does so because "to view Christ in the right context it is necessary to go back to the creation of man."[16] This is so because, as Paul will now show, the work of Christ is nothing less than the renewal of the creation and of humanity.[17]

---

14. See BA, s.v. "ζάω" (1.a); BDAG, s.v. "ζάω" (1.a); Cremer, 270; cf. Schmidt, *Syn.*, 4:40–53.
15. See the subtle exposition of these aspects of Paul's reading of the Genesis narrative in Irenaeus, *Haer.* 5.12.2–3; Augustine, *Civ.* 13.23–24.
16. Barrett, 373.
17. Cf. Matt O'Reilly, *Paul and the Resurrected Body: Social Identity and Ethical Practice*

*the last Adam became a Spirit who is life-giving.* Paul's quotation of Scripture concluded with the previous clause in 15:45a.[18] However, the clause that now follows in 15:45b is closely integrated with that quotation, assuming its main verb ἐγένετο, repeating the prepositional construction with εἰς, and providing a match for each of its nouns and adjectives. But each matching element in this second clause involves a heightening and completion of the corresponding element in the first. In this way, Paul expresses the conception that the first Adam was a prophetic type, anticipation, and foreshadowing, and that the last Adam, Christ, is the completion and fulfillment (cf. Rom 5:14, Ἀδάμ ὅς ἐστιν τύπος τοῦ μέλλοντος). The description of Jesus as "the *last* Adam" asserts more than mere numerical or temporal order; he is the *goal* of creation begun with the first Adam.[19]

How, then, is the creation begun in Adam brought to fulfillment in Christ? This is explained by the final two words of the clause, postponed until the end of the sentence for emphasis.[20] In contrast with the first Adam, who became "a soul who was living," the last Adam became "a Spirit who is life-giving." What does this mean? The answer will bring us into the heart of Pauline Christology. To unpack this, we must first eliminate a common but erroneous misinterpretation.

## *A Common Misinterpretation of πνεῦμα in 15:45*

Those scholars who interpret resurrection in 1 Cor 15 as involving a body composed of corporeal spirit substance hold that πνεῦμα in v. 45 describes Christ as having been changed into a spirit being, that is, a personal, intelligent being now without flesh and bones. Upon close examination, we find that these scholars interpret 15:45 in a way that oscillates vaguely between an understanding of πνεῦμα as (1) Jesus's disembodied soul; (2) the supposed "stuff" of the astral heavens (a usage, it is claimed, that was common among the philosophers, in particular the Stoics); and (3) a spirit being composed of spirit matter. So, for example, according to Daniel A. Smith, in Christ's resurrection "the spirit is raised" (here πνεῦμα is interpreted as Jesus's disembodied soul).[21] Christ's physical body, Smith

---

(ESEC 22; Atlanta: SBL Press, 2020), 88; N. T. Wright, *The Resurrection of the Son of God* (vol. 3 of *Christian Origins and the Question of God*; Minneapolis: Fortress, 2003), 355.

18. Cf. Ellicott, 319.

19. C. Burchard, "1 Korinther 15,39–41," *ZNW* 75 (1984): 244–45; cf. Wolff, 409; Lindemann, 361; Godet, 2:421.

20. Scott Brodeur, *The Holy Spirit's Agency in the Resurrection of the Dead: An Exegetico-Theological Study of 1 Corinthians 15,44b–49 and Romans 8,9–13* (TGST 14; Rome: Gregorian University Press, 2004), 106.

21. Smith, "Pneuma(tic Body)," 768.

claims, could not survive death, but his disembodied soul or spirit could, because "according to popular philosophy human/terrestrial and divine/celestial beings shared πνεῦμα in common" (here πνεῦμα is understood as both Jesus's soul and the "stuff" of the heavenly bodies).[22] But this, according to Smith, involved a further change, for "Paul has in mind a divine transformation of flesh and blood into πνεῦμα . . . presumably with no remainder" (here πνεῦμα is interpreted as a being composed of spirit).[23] In this way, claims Smith, πνεῦμα in v. 45 describes Jesus as having become, through his resurrection, a fleshless spirit being. Similarly, according to Troels Engberg-Pedersen, "when he [Paul] said that the last 'Adam' (Christ) became 'life-producing pneuma', what he meant is that Christ became the kind of heavenly 'stuff' called pneuma" (here πνεῦμα is interpreted as the matter of the celestial realm).[24] But this, claims Engberg-Pedersen, was simply the resolution of Christ's whole being "into an immortal being consisting only of the one 'uppermost' element," the soul or spirit (here Engberg-Pedersen understands πνεῦμα as Jesus's disembodied soul).[25] The result, according to Engberg-Pedersen, is that "the resurrected Christ is a pneumatic being" (i.e., a spirit being).[26] Similar interpretations of πνεῦμα in v. 45 as identifying Christ as a fleshless "spirit being" are legion.[27]

However, this reading of 1 Cor 15:45 is impossible, for *none* of the three senses of πνεῦμα that this reading claims (rather vaguely and confusedly) to find are possible within the context of this verse. That πνεῦμα here refers to the last Adam's disembodied human soul is excluded, for πνεῦμα in 15:45b is explicitly set in *contrast* to ψυχή "soul" in 15:45a ("the first human being, Adam, became a soul who was living"). The interpretation of πνεῦμα as heavenly "stuff" is also impossible, for *no* ancient text, philosophical or otherwise, identifies πνεῦμα with the celestial sphere. The repeated claim of a number of New Testament scholars that the Stoics used πνεῦμα to denote the material of the heavenly bodies reflects a basic misunderstanding of Stoic philosophy. For the Stoics confined the πνεῦμα, composed of air and fire, to the earth and to the airy heavens below the moon, and they denied that it extended to the astral heavens (*SVF* 1.159, 533–34; 2.310, 416, 441–42, 473, 814, 817, 1105; Diogenes Laertius, *Vit. phil.* 7.156).[28] That πνεῦμα describes Christ

22. Smith, "Pneuma(tic Body)," 767.
23. Smith, "Pneuma(tic Body)," 767.
24. Engberg-Pedersen, *Cosmology and Self*, 30.
25. Engberg-Pedersen, *Cosmology and Self*, 32–34.
26. Engberg-Pedersen, *Cosmology and Self*, 57.
27. E.g., Dale Martin, *The Corinthian Body* (New Haven: Yale University Press, 1995), 132; Chilton, *Resurrection Logic*, 72–75; Asher, *Polarity and Change*, 154; Litwa, *Deification*, 127–51.
28. See further on this point in the commentary on v. 47 below.

as a "spirit being" composed of spirit matter is also impossible in the context of v. 45. For here the last Adam as a πνεῦμα ζῳοποιοῦν is parallel to the first Adam as a ψυχὴ ζῶσα. Clearly ψυχή in v. 45a does not refer to the substance of the first Adam's *body*. Verse 45a hardly describes Adam as a "soul being," with a body composed of "soul"! In the same way, v. 45b can hardly refer to Christ as a "spirit being," with a body composed of "spirit." J. A. Schep observes: "Since it is obvious that 'soul' does not denote the substance of Adam's body, it follows that 'spirit' cannot possibly denote the substance of Christ's glorified body."[29] Indeed, just as 15:45a assumes the first Adam's body of flesh and bones (cf. Gen 2:23), so 15:45b assumes the last Adam's body of flesh and bones. The parallel is, in fact, senseless, unless the last Adam, just as the first Adam, has a flesh and bones body.

*The Meaning of πνεῦμα in Verse 45*

We have seen that πνεῦμα in v. 45 denotes neither Jesus's disembodied soul nor the "stuff" of the celestial heavens. Nor can it refer to Christ as a disincarnate "spirit being." This leaves, by process of elimination, only one possible sense of πνεῦμα in 1 Cor 15:45. It is the sense that predominates in the New Testament and early Christian literature—πνεῦμα as denoting the Spirit of God. This is, indeed, the understanding of our earliest interpreters of this passage (Irenaeus, *Haer*. 5.12.2; Tertullian, *Res*. 53; *Carn. Chr*. 17; Cyril of Alexandria, *Quod un*. 772d–773a; John Chrysostom, *Hom. 1 Cor*. 41). It is also the interpretation of the great majority of modern expositors.[30] Several factors confirm that this is indeed the meaning of the word in 15:45:

(1) Verse 45 provides a further exposition of the pair ψυχικός and πνευματικός, which were used in v. 44. We have already seen that within this pair πνευματικός is used with reference to the Holy Spirit.[31] It follows that πνεῦμα in v. 45 must also refer to the Holy Spirit.

(2) There is a striking *contrast* between ψυχή and πνεῦμα, found nowhere in pagan literature, that appears for the first time in antiquity within the New Testa-

---

29. J. A. Schep, *The Nature of the Resurrection Body: A Study of the Biblical Data* (Grand Rapids: Eerdmans, 1964), 174.

30. E.g., François Altermath, *Du corps psychique au corps spirituel: Interprétation de 1 Cor. 15,35–49 par les auteurs chrétiens des quatre premiers siècles* (BGBE 18; Tübingen: Mohr Siebeck, 1977), 41; Brodeur, *Holy Spirit's Agency*, 120–22; Schneider, "Corporate Meaning," 153–56; Richard B. Gaffin, "'Life-Giving Spirit': Probing the Center of Paul's Pneumatology," *JETS* 41 (1998): 573–89. As Gaffin notes, "across a broad front a substantial majority of commentators and other interpreters who address the issue recognize a reference to the Holy Spirit in v. 45" (579).

31. See the commentary on v. 44a in the previous chapter.

ment (1 Cor 2:14–15; 15:45; Jude 19). Everywhere within the New Testament outside of this passage, this contrast of ψυχή and πνεῦμα contrasts the human *soul* and the *Holy Spirit*. In Jude 19, the author defines persons of *soul* (ψυχικοί) as "not having the *Spirit*" (πνεῦμα μὴ ἔχοντες). Likewise, and crucially, earlier in 1 Corinthians (2:14), Paul affirms that "a person of the *soul* [ψυχικὸς ἄνθρωπος] does not welcome the things of *the Spirit of God*" (τὸ πνεῦμα τοῦ θεοῦ; cf. 2:15, ὁ πνευματικός). Thus in 15:45, πνεῦμα contrasted with ψυχή must refer to the Spirit of God.

(3) Finally, the Spirit is described in v. 45 as "life-giving" or "life-creating" (ζῳοποιέω). Throughout the New Testament, the power to give life is an exclusively *divine* prerogative and attribute, and the verb ζῳοποιέω is used exclusively of the activity of *God* (e.g., John 5:21; Rom 4:17; 8:11). Moreover, the power to give life, and the verb ζῳοποιέω, are especially associated with the *Holy Spirit* (2 Cor 3:6, τὸ δὲ πνεῦμα ζῳοποιεῖ; Rom 8:10, τὸ δὲ πνεῦμα ζωή; John 6:63, τὸ πνεῦμά ἐστιν τὸ ζῳοποιοῦν). Paul's use of πνεῦμα in 15:45 with the modifier ζῳοποιοῦν thus puts the matter beyond doubt that the reference here is to the Holy Spirit, the Spirit of God.

The πνεῦμα ζῳοποιοῦν of v. 45, then, is the Spirit of God, the Holy Spirit. But this immediately raises a pressing question. Does Paul not, then, here identify Christ and the Spirit? Indeed, it is on the basis of this very verse that James D. G. Dunn, rightly seeing that πνεῦμα here denotes the Spirit of God, has proposed that Paul's letters evince a "Spirit-Christology" identifying Christ and the Spirit.[32] I believe Dunn's proposed "Spirit-Christology," which effaces the ontological distinction between Christ and the Spirit, is misguided, theologically confused, and radically un-Pauline. Reacting to Dunn's mistaken proposal, other scholars have denied that 1 Cor 15:45 is relevant for Christology at all![33] This is understandable, but it is an obvious case of overreaction. It is also untenable, for Christ is the direct subject of Paul's assertions in 15:45. Indeed, as we will see, 1 Cor 15:44b–49 offers one of the richest statements of Christology in all of Paul's letters.

Let us unpack this dense and powerful theological affirmation of the apostle, by doing what scholars in general have hitherto strangely failed to do: place this passage in the context of Paul's teaching regarding the Holy Spirit throughout the first letter to the Corinthians. The Holy Spirit enters chapter 15 explicitly for the first time here in 15:44–46 (πνεῦμα, 15:45; πνευματικός, 15:44, 46). However,

32. Dunn, "Life-Giving Spirit," 127–42; Dunn, *The Theology of Paul the Apostle* (Grand Rapids: Eerdmans, 1998), 261–65.

33. So Fee: "the concern is *not* Christological" (871). Likewise Brodeur writes that v. 45 contains no "Christological pronouncement of any kind" (*Spirit's Agency*, 119). So also N. T. Wright, who states the verse is "not christological but anthropological" in his essay "Monotheism, Christology and Ethics: 1 Corinthians 8," in *The Climax of the Covenant: Christ and the Law in Pauline Theology* (Minneapolis: Fortress, 1991), 130–32.

the Holy Spirit is a very prominent theme in the letter as a whole. Indeed, if one takes into account not only instances of the noun πνεῦμα but also of the adjective πνευματικός, references to the Holy Spirit are more frequent in 1 Corinthians than in any other Pauline letter. This focus on the Spirit reflects, as we will now see, the Trinitarian character of Paul's thought within the epistle.

### The Trinitarian Structure of Paul's Thought in 1 Cor 15

Throughout his letters, Paul's theology has a profoundly Trinitarian structure.[34] The Trinitarian framework of Paul's thought is especially prominent in 1 Corinthians. Throughout this letter, Paul's language about God is shaped and structured as a discourse concerning God, the Lord Jesus Christ, and the Holy Spirit (6:11, ἐν τῷ ὀνόματι τοῦ κυρίου Ἰησοῦ Χριστοῦ καὶ ἐν τῷ πνεύματι τοῦ θεοῦ ἡμῶν; 12:4–6, τὸ δὲ αὐτὸ πνεῦμα ... ὁ αὐτὸς κύριος ... ὁ δὲ αὐτὸς θεός; cf. 2:2–5; 12:3). This Trinitarian structure of Paul's thought, evident throughout 1 Corinthians, reaches its climax in chapter 15. Paul clearly understands the resurrection to be the work of the one creator God. But as chapter 15 unfolds, the resurrection is identified not only as the work of God (ὁ θεός, vv. 9–10, 15, 28, 38, 57; θεός, vv. 10, 34, 50), but also as the work of Christ (Χριστός, vv. 12–13, 16–20, 23, 31, 57; ὁ Χριστός, vv. 15, 22–23) and as the work of the Holy Spirit (πνεῦμα, v. 45; πνευματικός, vv. 44, 46). Moreover, within this chapter God is further identified as Father (ὁ θεὸς καὶ πατήρ, v. 24) and Jesus as the Son (ὁ υἱός, v. 28), and the Son is closely related to the Holy Spirit (πνεῦμα, v. 45). Paul normally prefers such combinations as God, Christ, and Spirit (Rom 15:18–19; 1 Cor 2:2–5; Phil 3:3); or God, Son, and Spirit (Rom 8:3–4; Gal 4:4–6); or God, Lord, and Spirit (2 Cor 13:13[14]; 1 Thess 1:4–6). The precise combination of Father, Son, and Spirit is rare in his letters (cf. Gal 4:6, τὸ πνεῦμα τοῦ υἱοῦ αὐτοῦ εἰς τὰς καρδίας ὑμῶν κρᾶζον ἀββα ὁ πατήρ). But we find Father (15:24), Son (15:28), and Spirit (15:45) here in 1 Cor 15. In addition, in chapter 15 the Son is further described as Lord (ὁ κύριος, vv. 31, 57, 58). The juxtaposition of "God" (vv. 9–10, 15, 28, 34, 38, 50, 57) and "Lord" (vv. 31, 57–58) within the chapter recalls 8:6 ("one *God*, from whom are all things, and we for him, and one *Lord*, Jesus Christ, through whom are all things, and we through him"). The echo of this passage in chapter 15 is significant, for 1 Cor 8:6 echoes Israel's central confession, the Shema of Deut 6:4, in order to

---

34. On the Trinitarian structure of Paul's thought, see further Wesley Hill, *Paul and the Trinity: Persons, Relations, and the Pauline Letters* (Grand Rapids: Eerdmans, 2015); Gordon D. Fee, *Pauline Christology: An Exegetical Theological Study* (Peabody, MA: Hendrickson, 2007), esp. 481–593; James P. Ware, *Paul's Theology in Context: Creation, Incarnation, Covenant, and Kingdom* (Grand Rapids: Eerdmans, 2019), 79–91.

bestow on Jesus the divine Name.[35] The combination within chapter 15 of "God" (15:9–10, 15, 28, 34, 38, 50, 57), "Lord" (15:31, 57–58), and "Spirit" (15:45; cf. 15:44, 46) also recalls the ad hoc Trinitarian baptismal formulation of 6:11 (ἐν τῷ ὀνόματι τοῦ κυρίου Ἰησοῦ Χριστοῦ καὶ ἐν τῷ πνεύματι τοῦ θεοῦ ἡμῶν) and the Trinitarian formulation in 12:4–6 (12:4, τὸ δὲ αὐτὸ πνεῦμα; 12:5, ὁ αὐτὸς κύριος; 12:6, ὁ δὲ αὐτὸς θεός).

Some scholars will respond to the exegetical arguments offered here not with opposing arguments but with the well-worn claim that a Trinitarian exegesis of Paul merely imposes later dogmatic formulations upon the apostle. Such a charge is without foundation. Of course, the church's later developed Trinitarian terminology and categories are not present in 1 Cor 15 or elsewhere in Paul's epistles. But Paul expresses a theology here of which those categories are the logical outworking. Paul's letters exert a "pressure" upon the interpreter that compels a Trinitarian interpretation.[36] The whole of chapter 15 is Trinitarian in the structure of its thought and brings the Trinitarian theology of the epistle as a whole to a climax.

### Paul's Apparent Identification of Christ and the Spirit in Verse 45

But in v. 45 Paul appears to *identify* Christ with the Holy Spirit. Does this not demand Dunn's nonincarnational and non-Trinitarian "Spirit-Christology"? How does this fit with Paul's Trinitarian theology throughout the letter, which we have seen comes to its climax with this chapter? The first thing we must see is a striking but often overlooked fact: this close correlation of Christ and the Spirit is an important theme and emphasis of Paul throughout the letter. In 2:15–16 we learn that ὁ πνευματικός ("the person *of the Spirit*") is defined as one who has ὁ νοῦς τοῦ Χριστοῦ ("the mind *of Christ*"). In 6:17, the one joined to *Christ* becomes one *Spirit* (ἓν πνεῦμα) with him. The Eucharist, which is described in 10:16 as a sharing in the body and blood of *Christ*, is described in 10:3–4 as "food of the *Spirit*" (πνευματικὸν βρῶμα) and "drink of the *Spirit*" (πνευματικὸν πόμα). In 10:4 Paul explains regarding "the rock of the *Spirit*" that followed the Israelites (πνευματικὴ ἀκολουθοῦσα πέτρα): "the rock was *Christ*" (ἡ πέτρα δὲ ἦν ὁ Χριστός). In 12:13, where Paul conjoins baptism and the Eucharist, he describes the Corinthians as, through the Eucharist, being "given to drink of one *Spirit*" (ἓν πνεῦμα; cf. 6:17). Paul also elsewhere in his letters closely correlates Christ and the Holy Spirit (Rom 8:9–10; 2 Cor 3:3, 17–18). But this close correlation (or even seeming identification) is, we have seen, an especially prominent theme in 1 Corinthians. But this close correlation cannot,

---

35. Cf. W. Hill, *Paul and the Trinity*, 112–20; Wright, *Resurrection*, 571; Ware, *Paul's Theology*, 51–53.

36. See C. Kavin Rowe, "Biblical Pressure and Trinitarian Hermeneutics," *ProEccl* 11 (2002): 295–312.

in fact, be simple identification, for Paul elsewhere in 1 Corinthians, as we saw earlier, clearly distinguishes the Spirit from the Son (2:2–5; 6:11; 12:3). He does so in his other letters as well (2 Cor 11:4; 13:13[14]; Gal 3:5). What is the explanation of this apparently conflicting evidence?

*The Trinitarian Solution to the Dilemma*

The answer to the apparent dilemma is found in Paul's Trinitarian theology itself. For the answer is that in Paul's theology the Holy Spirit is "the Spirit *of his Son*" (Gal 4:6, τὸ πνεῦμα τοῦ υἱοῦ αὐτοῦ). The Spirit of God is "the Spirit *of Christ*" (Rom 8:9, πνεῦμα Χριστοῦ). The Holy Spirit is "the Spirit *of Jesus Christ*" (Phil 1:19, τὸ πνεῦμα Ἰησοῦ Χριστοῦ; cf. Acts 16:7). In Paul's thought, the Holy Spirit is the Spirit not only of the Father (Rom 8:11) but also of the Son (Rom 8:9; Gal 4:6; Phil 1:19). Even as the eternal Son has his source in the eternal Father, so the Son is the font and source of the Holy Spirit within the eternal mystery of the triune God. Ancient interpreters of Paul sought to express this aspect of Pauline theology using various images. Tertullian described the triune God as ever-flowing waters—the Father the spring, the Son the pool flowing from the spring, and the Spirit the stream flowing from the pool (*Prax.* 8). Using yet another image to express the mystery, Tertullian pictured the Father as the sun, the Son as its rays, and the Holy Spirit as the light shed from the rays (*Prax.* 8). Gregory of Nyssa pictured the Trinity as an eternal fire, the flame of the Son kindled from the flame of the Father, and the flame of the Holy Spirit kindled from the flame of the Son (*Spir.* 6). But the favored language of the early church fathers, drawn from the Gospel of John, spoke of the Spirit eternally *proceeding* from the Father and the Son (Ambrose, *Spir.* 1.11.120; Epiphanius, *Ancor.* 8, 71, 73, 75) or from the Father through the Son (Gregory of Nyssa, *Quod non* 10; John of Damascus, *Fid. orth.* 1.12). Many ancient writers use both formulas interchangeably (Tertullian, *Prax.* 4, 8; Cyril of Alexandria, *Thes.* 34; *Ador.* 1; Hilary, *Trin.* 2.29; 12.55–57).

This crucial Pauline theological conception, that the Holy Spirit is the Son's own Spirit and has his source in the Son, integrates the apparently conflicting evidence in Paul's letters in a striking way. It illumines why in 1 Corinthians Paul in some passages unmistakably distinguishes the Son from the Spirit (2:2–5; 6:11; 12:3), while in other passages he seems to identify the Son and the Spirit (2:15–16; 6:17; 10:3–4; 12:13). It explains why Paul can throughout the letter use the expressions "in Christ" (1:2, 4, 30; 3:1; 4:10, 15, 17; 15:18–19, 22, 31; 16:24), "in the Lord" (1:31; 4:17; 7:22, 39; 9:1–2; 11:11; 15:58; 16:19 ), and "in the Spirit" (6:11; 12:3, 9, 13; 14:16) *interchangeably*. Paul can do so because the Holy Spirit is the Spirit of God's Son.[37]

---

37. Following Paul, other early Christian writings also use the language of the Spirit with reference to both Father and Son but, like Paul, do so within an incarnational and Trinitarian

This also explains 1 Cor 15:45. Paul here speaks of the Son (cf. 15:28) as the Spirit. He can do so not because the Son is the Holy Spirit, but because the Holy Spirit is the Spirit of God's Son. The Spirit is the Son's own Spirit, belonging to him, proceeding from him, and consubstantial with him. The Spirit of which Paul speaks is "the Spirit of God's Son" (Gal 4:6), "the Spirit of Christ" (Rom 8:9), "the Spirit of Jesus Christ" (Phil 1:19). Far from pointing to Dunn's confused and misguided "Spirit-Christology," v. 45 is only comprehensible within Paul's divine Christology and Trinitarian theology.

*How Christ Became a Spirit Who Is Life-Giving*

The verbal construction ἐγένετο ... εἰς ("became"), expressed in the first clause (15:45a) and implicit in the second (15:45b), is in the aorist tense, pointing to a past event at a particular point in time. As virtually all ancient and modern interpreters are agreed, this event, in the context of this great resurrection chapter, is the resurrection of Jesus Christ from the dead (cf. 15:3–8, 11, 12–17, 20–23).[38] Through his resurrection, Christ "became a Spirit who is life-giving."

This brings us to the heart of what Paul is saying in this passage. But it also brings us to a statement that many interpreters have found perplexing. Granted that Paul is here (as we have shown) referring to the Holy Spirit, what can Paul possibly mean when he describes Christ as *becoming*, through his resurrection, *a* Spirit who is life-giving? The word πνεῦμα is predicate and anarthrous (i.e., it lacks a definite article), and it is thus in this context rightly translated with an indefinite article in English: "*a* Spirit." If Paul is referring to the Holy Spirit, why does he not use the definite article? Further, the aorist tense verb ἐγένετο clearly indicates a *change of state* that took place in the resurrection, which was not true prior to the resurrection but became true through the resurrection. How is this appropriate language with reference to the eternal Spirit of God? Many interpreters find Paul's expression baffling and unintelligible.

---

framework recognizing the distinction between Father, Son, and Holy Spirit. See, for example, 2 Clem. 9.5; Irenaeus, *Haer.* 2.30.8; 5.1.3; *Epid.* 71; Tertullian, *Apol.* 21.10–14; 23.12; Tatian, *Or. Graec.* 7.1; Hippolytus, *Noet.* 4. Cf. Anthony Briggman, "Spirit-Christology in Irenaeus: A Closer Look," *VC* 66 (2012): 1–19. According to Augustine, it is of the nature of the Trinity that the noun *spiritus* can be used of all three persons, but is the proper name only of the third (Augustine, *Trin.* 5.11; *Tract. Ev. Jo.* 99.7).

38. E.g., Gaffin, "Life-Giving Spirit," 578; Altermath, *Du corps psychique*, 41; Brodeur, *Holy Spirit's Agency*, 116–18; Peter Jones, "Paul Confronts Paganism in the Church: A Case Study of First Corinthians 15:45," *JETS* 49 (2006): 734. Among ancient interpreters, see Irenaeus, *Haer.* 5.12.3; Cyril of Alexandria, *Quod un.* 772d–773a.

These perplexities disappear, and Paul's meaning is evident, when we read Paul's words in their context. Let us first review what we have already seen. In the context of v. 45, the description of the last Adam in v. 45b as "a Spirit who is life-giving" is parallel to the description of the first Adam in v. 45a as "a soul who was living." Verse 45a is a quotation of Gen 2:7. It does not refer to Adam as a being whose body was composed of soul (which would be absurd). Rather, it denotes Adam as *a flesh and bones human being whose bodily life was determined by his human soul*. The parallel expression, then, for the last Adam as "a Spirit who is life-giving" cannot refer to Christ as a being whose body is composed of "spirit." Rather, as we saw, it refers to the risen Christ as *a flesh and bones human being whose bodily life is determined by the Holy Spirit*. Verse 45 thus functions to further elucidate the two kinds of *bodies* in v. 44b, the body of the soul and the body of the Spirit.

Now let us consider Paul's anarthrous and indefinite reference to Christ ("a Spirit who is life-giving") in light of this context. In v. 45a, the description of the first Adam as ψυχὴ ζῶσα is also anarthrous and indefinite ("*a* soul who was living"). The reason is obvious: Adam is one, particular, individual human being. *So also is Christ*. However impenetrable may be the mystery, it is of the very essence of the incarnation that the Son of God became incarnate as one, particular, individual human being, Jesus of Nazareth. Just as the expression "a soul who was living" in v. 45a refers to the whole embodied person of Adam as a particular human being, so the parallel expression "a Spirit who is life-giving" in v. 45b must refer to the whole embodied person of Christ as a particular human being. Once we grasp this, the difficulties with Paul's anarthrous, indefinite construction in v. 45b disappear. *Of course* the last Adam, just like the first Adam, is *a* human being!

What, then, of Paul's language of "becoming" in v. 45? What does Paul mean when he states that the last Adam through his resurrection "*became* a Spirit who is life-giving"? Here once again the key is to read Paul's affirmation within the context of the verse. Verse 45 tells the entire story of creation and redemption, the economy of salvation "ordained before the ages for our glory" (2:8), in miniature. It does so through a contrast of the first and last Adams. Through its aorist verb ἐγένετο "became," v. 45 focuses in laser-like fashion on the flesh and bones bodies of the two Adams, on the moment when those bodies were brought to life, and on the nature of that life. In 15:45 the bodies of the first and last Adam each undergo a change whereby they are *vivified* but in contrasting ways. In the case of the first Adam, the change took place at his *creation*. At that creation, life was given to Adam's previously lifeless body. He became thereby "a soul who was living," that is, a flesh and bones human being whose bodily life was given and determined by his human soul. But this was a perishable and mortal life. Through Adam's

CHAPTER 13

forfeiture, through sin, of the divine life offered him, all Adam's progeny share in corruptible and mortal bodies subject to death (15:21–22, 56; cf. Rom 5:12–21; 8:10). In the case of the last Adam, the change took place at his *resurrection*. In his incarnation, the Son of God assumed a mortal body (Rom 8:3), and in his passion and crucifixion he freely submitted that body to suffering and death (Phil 2:7–8). But in the resurrection, life was given to Christ's previously dead and lifeless body. Through his resurrection from the dead, the body of the last Adam was endowed with a new kind of life, imperishable and indestructible, given by the very Spirit of God (cf. Rom 1:4; 1 Tim 3:16; 1 Pet 3:18). He thereby "became a Spirit who is life-giving," that is, a flesh and bones human being whose bodily life was given and determined by the Holy Spirit. At the creation, the body of Adam was vivified with a *destructible* life; in the resurrection, the body of Christ was vivified and glorified with an *indestructible* life. Through the resurrection, the body of Christ, which once was a σῶμα ψυχικόν ("a body of the soul"), became a σῶμα πνευματικόν ("a body of the Spirit"). "The last Adam begins by realizing *in Himself* the perfect state."[39] As the eternal Son of the Father, the source together with him of the Holy Spirit, the Son of God in his divine nature always possessed this life. But through his resurrection, the Holy Spirit now suffuses and energizes his physical human body with imperishable life.

In this way, the risen Christ is the model, in his own person, of "the body of the Spirit" (v. 44) that will be given to the faithful at the resurrection, when they are "conformed to the body of his glory" (Phil 3:21). But he is more than the model. He is absolutely unique, because he is the divine Son of God. The life of the Holy Spirit that infuses his risen body is his own divine life. The Holy Spirit that raised to life and now enlivens the flesh of the Son of God is his own Spirit, proceeding from him and consubstantial with him. That is why Paul describes him in this unique way, which can be said of no mere creature: "a Spirit who is life-giving." Just as Paul can denote the first Adam "a soul who was living," not because the soul is identical with him but because the soul is his own and belongs to him, so Paul designates the last Adam "a Spirit who is life-giving," not because Christ and the Spirit are identical but because the Holy Spirit is his own Spirit and proceeds from him. Verse 45 thus brings to a climax what we have seen is a striking feature of the letter: Paul's repeated references to Christ as the Spirit (2:15–16; 6:17; 10:3–4; 12:13). Here as throughout the letter, Paul refers to Christ as the Spirit, not because the Son and the Holy Spirit are identical, but because the Holy Spirit is the Spirit of God's Son.

And because the Holy Spirit who endows the physical body of the risen Son of God with imperishable life is the Son's own Spirit, the risen Son of God can

---

39. Godet, 2:421.

bestow this life of the Spirit of God on all those united to him by faith. The risen Christ is thus "a Spirit *who is life-giving*" (πνεῦμα ζῳοποιοῦν, the adjective ζῳοποιοῦν emphatic by final position). Through his own resurrection, Christ is the "firstfruits" (ἀπαρχή) of this new life (15:20). He is not only the model but also the cause of the resurrection of the dead. For through the resurrection of his physical human body, he now bestows the Holy Spirit. "Because I live, you shall live also" (John 14:19). He is both the risen Lord and the bestower of this resurrection life on those united to him: "the Lord is for the body" (6:13). We can now grasp Paul's full meaning in affirming that "the last Adam became a life-giving Spirit": *the Son of God, by endowing his own body with imperishable life through his resurrection from the dead, now bestows his Holy Spirit to grant this same imperishable life to all who belong to him.*

Paul has thus, in v. 45, deepened, enriched, and illumined v. 22: "For just as in Adam all die, so in Christ all will be made alive." Verse 22 affirms that all in Christ will be made alive but does not explain how. Verse 45 supplies the answer. They will be made alive by the Spirit of God's Son. But the Holy Spirit and its lifecreating power could only be given through the resurrection of the Son of God's physical human body. Thus v. 45 also fully explains v. 21: "For since death came through a human being, the resurrection of the dead also came through a human being." Moreover, v. 21 involves a mystery that only v. 45 resolves. Within Pauline theology, it is only God who gives life (Rom 4:17) and raises the dead (2 Cor 1:9). How then can it be that "the resurrection of the dead also came *through a human being*"? Verse 45 provides the key that unlocks the mystery. The human being through whom it came is God in the flesh. By conquering death through his divine power in his own human body, he now imparts his own Holy Spirit, whose power will raise the bodies of all those united to him to imperishable life.

The original work of creation and the work of the eschatological new creation are related as type and antitype. The type, the original creation of Adam (v. 45a), was preparatory, anticipating its fulfillment in the greater and perfecting work of the antitype, the re-creation of humanity in Christ (v. 45b). In the original creation, the human body was endowed with a living soul, which can furnish only a destructible life. In the consummation of the eschatological work of the new creation, the human body will be endowed with the very Spirit of the creator God, and given immortal and imperishable life. In the gift, through the resurrection, of the σῶμα πνευματικόν or "body of the Spirit," humanity will be elevated above even its pre-fall state of beatitude, and the original creation of humankind will reach its divinely intended goal.[40]

---

40. Cf. Altermath, *Du corps psychique*, 41; Burchard, "1 Korinther 15,39–41," 245–47.

CHAPTER 13

There is a wonderful and striking symmetry of great theological importance in 1 Cor 15:45. In Paul's divine Christology, all things were created through the Son (8:6, δι' οὗ τὰ πάντα καὶ ἡμεῖς δι' αὐτοῦ). Paul therefore thinks of the Son as active in *both* halves of v. 45. He is the creator who first fashioned human nature, forming Adam from the dust, breathing into his nostrils the breath of life, and making him to become a living soul (15:45a; cf. Gen 2:7). He now comes as the last Adam to renew and restore the human nature he first fashioned (15:45b). The same one who made human nature in the beginning is the one through whom human nature is renewed.[41]

But there is a striking difference between the Son's work in creation and his work of new creation. The creator could only bring about the eschatological new humanity, of which the first Adam was a type, by himself becoming the antitype, the last Adam. The original creation of humanity required no incarnation, but the renewal of humanity required the incarnation, the cross, and the resurrection. This is the deepest reason why in Paul's thought it was necessary that "the resurrection of the dead came through a human being" (15:21). "In the Incarnation creation is fulfilled by God's including himself in it."[42]

### How the Risen Christ Communicates His Life-Giving Spirit

But precisely *how* does the risen Christ convey the Holy Spirit? It is significant that in v. 45 the participle ζῳοποιοῦν ("life-giving") is in the *present* tense.[43] The participle ζῳοποιοῦν describes a continual action coincident in time with its associated verb ἐγένετο, and thus denotes an ongoing reality brought about through the resurrection of Christ. This indicates that although the fullness of this life is yet future (cf. the future ζῳοποιηθήσονται in 15:22), Christ already bestows this life now. This coheres with the whole treatment of the economy of salvation we will discover in 15:46–49, which will move from the present heavenly gift (15:46–48) to its consummation at the resurrection (15:49). It also coheres with Paul's portrayal of the present bodies of the Corinthians as temples of the Holy Spirit (3:16–17; 6:19; cf. 2:12, 15; 6:11; 12:3). Christ, then, conveys his Spirit to the faithful even now. How does Paul understand Christ to mediate the Holy Spirit even now to the Corinthians?

We find the answer in 1 Cor 10:1–4. In this passage, Paul refers to a πνευματικὸν βρῶμα ("food of the Spirit") and πνευματικὸν πόμα ("drink of the Spirit").[44] This

---

41. Cf. Clement of Alexandria, *Protr.* 1.7.

42. Søren Kierkegaard, *Journals and Papers* (trans. Howard V. Hong and Edna H. Hong; Bloomington: Indiana University Press, 1970) 2:1391.

43. Wolff, 410.

44. Paul's language has no prior parallels in ancient Greek literature. John Granger Cook claims that we find an expression similar or identical to Paul's πνευματικὸν βρῶμα in Philo,

passage thus has close connections to the σῶμα πνευματικόν of 15:44 not only via the adjective πνευματικός but also through the close assonance of the nouns βρῶμα (10:3), πόμα (10:4), and σῶμα (15:44). As most interpreters are agreed, the baptism of the wilderness generation in the Red Sea, and their partaking of food and drink of the Spirit, are seen here by Paul as types or foreshadowings of the Corinthians' participation in baptism and in the Eucharist.[45] Paul's reference to baptism in 10:1–2 recalls his description of baptism as a washing "in the Spirit of our God" in 6:11. And in his reference in 10:3–4 to the eucharistic bread and cup as πνευματικός, Paul portrays the Eucharist as bestowing the Holy Spirit. In the fact that Paul describes the rock in the wilderness as πνευματικός, and at the same time identifies it with Christ (10:4, ἡ πέτρα δὲ ἦν ὁ Χριστός), we find in 10:3–4 the same close correlation of Christ and the Spirit we have encountered in 15:45. In 12:13a Paul tells the Corinthians, "in one Spirit we were all baptized into one body," and in 12:13b he tells them, "we were all given to drink of one Spirit." In light of the explicit reference to baptism in 12:13a, the language of being given to drink of one Spirit in 12:13b is almost certainly a reference to the Eucharist. Here again in 12:13, as in 10:1–4, baptism and the Eucharist are portrayed as a participation in the Holy Spirit. Elsewhere in the letter the Eucharist is described as a participation in the body and blood of Christ (10:16–17; 11:23–29). We thus see here once more the same close correlation of the Holy Spirit and Christ so strikingly present in 15:45.

In all these passages we find baptism and the Lord's Supper, which is a partaking of the body and blood of Christ, portrayed as a participation in the Holy Spirit. The Eucharist is a "food of the Spirit" (10:3) and a "drink of the Spirit" (10:4). We have thus found the means whereby, in Paul's understanding, Christ gives his life-creating Holy Spirit to the Corinthians. It is through their baptism into Christ and their participation in the body and blood of Christ in the Eucharist. The flesh of Christ, as the flesh of the divine Son of God, now suffused through his resurrection with the imperishable life of his own Spirit, is itself life-giving

---

*QG* 4.102; see his "Philo's *Quaestiones in Genesin* and Paul's σῶμα πνευματικόν," in *Alexandria: Hub of the Hellenistic World* (ed. Benjamin Schliesser, Jan Rüggemeier, Thomas J. Kraus, and Jörg Frey; Tübingen: Mohr Siebeck, 2021), 303–21. Cf. also his article, "Philo's *Quaestiones et solutiones in Genesin* 4.102 and 1 Cor 10:3: The πνευματικὸν βρῶμα," *NovT* 59 (2017): 384–89. However, this is highly unlikely. Cook's thesis is based on the Armenian version of *QG* 4.102, and it is most likely that the Christian translator has been influenced by Paul's formulation in 1 Corinthians.

45. Cf. Richard Hays, *Echoes of Scripture in the Letters of Paul* (New Haven: Yale University Press, 1989), 95; Fitzmyer, 382; Keener, 84; Collins, 365 ("The allusion to the Eucharist is easily recognized"); *pace* Linda L. Belleville, "Paul's Christological Use of the Exodus-Wilderness Rock Tradition in 1 Corinthians 10:4," in *Scripture, Texts, and Tracings in 1 Corinthians* (ed. Linda L. Belleville and B. J. Oropeza; Lanham, MD: Lexington/Fortress, 2019), 133.

CHAPTER 13

and bestows life on all who partake of it. Through the waters of baptism and this real union with Christ in the Eucharist, the Corinthians become sharers in his own risen life, the life of the Holy Spirit, a participation that will culminate in the resurrection of their bodies. Through this union they are empowered to take up the cross in suffering on behalf of Christ (15:30–32). It is this union that is in Paul's mind when he writes in 1 Cor 15:22 that "*in Christ* all will be made alive" (ἐν Χριστῷ πάντες ζῳοποιηθήσονται).

## Verse 46

*However, the body of the Spirit is not first, but the body of the soul, then the body of the Spirit.*

We saw in v. 45 that Christ is even now the life giver through the glorification of his human body in his resurrection on the third day, and he bestows his own Holy Spirit on those who believe through the washing of baptism and his life-giving flesh given in the Lord's Supper. But Paul in v. 46 now explains for his hearers why this does not entail an immediate bodily resurrection for those in Christ. Through his twofold use here in v. 46 of πνευματικός, Paul concludes the striking cluster of πνεῦμα language in 15:44–46 (15:44, πνευματικός [2×]; 15:45, πνεῦμα; 15:46, πνευματικός [2×]), which brings to a climax the focus on the Holy Spirit that is such a striking aspect of this letter. Paul's use of neuter articles indicates that we must understand the adjectives as modifying an implicit σῶμα.[46] Paul thus continues the contrast of the body of the soul and the body of the Spirit introduced in 15:44.

The "body of the soul" is the body the Corinthians now have, which has been given only a corruptible life by the soul and, through Adam's transgression, is subject to death and decay (15:21–22, 56). This was the kind of body that the Son of God, although himself free from the original sin of Adam (2 Cor 5:21), freely assumed in the incarnation (Rom 8:3). Through his resurrection he now has a "body of the Spirit," because his physical body of flesh and bones is now suffused with the imperishable divine life of the Holy Spirit. By means of his glorified flesh he now imparts his own Holy Spirit to all who believe. But he wears this glorified body by way of anticipation, as "the firstfruits of those who sleep" (15:20). The resurrection of all those in Christ is yet to come. That is the whole point of v. 46.

In accenting that the resurrection is not a present but a future reality, Paul is here reinforcing a point he has made repeatedly in the chapter. It was evident

---

46. Barrett, 373–74. So Irenaeus, *Haer.* 5.12.2; Tertullian, *Res.* 52–53; *Marc.* 5.10.

in the comparisons of 15:36–41, pointing to the present mortal body as the forerunner, within the divine design, of the glorified body. It was implicit in 15:22 in the contrast between the *present* tense "in Adam all die" (ἀποθνῄσκουσιν) and the *future* tense "in Christ all will be made alive" (ζῳοποιηθήσονται). It was also implicit in Paul's description of death as the "last" enemy to be conquered (15:26). And Paul has already expressed this thought directly in 15:23: "But each in his own order: Christ the firstfruits, then [ἔπειτα] those who belong to Christ, at his coming."

The point of v. 46, then, is that the resurrection of the faithful must await Christ's coming in glory. Why should this be so? The answer involves the whole economy of salvation, moving from present life in Christ to the glory that is to come. Paul will now unpack this economy of salvation in vv. 47–49.

## Verse 47

*The first human being was from the earth, of the dust; the second human being is from heaven.*

In 15:47–49 Paul continues the focus of 15:45 on Gen 2:7 and the two Adams and even expands this focus. However, a shift of vocabulary takes place from the language of soul and Spirit in 15:44–46 to the language of earth and heaven in 15:47–49.[47] Paul in this way now applies the analogy of the heavenly bodies introduced in 15:40–41. But he does so in order to deepen and complete his teaching in 15:44–46 regarding the body of the Spirit.

*The first human being was from the earth, of the dust.* Paul here continues the allusion to Gen 2:7. But he now also draws Gen 3:19 into the picture. For Paul's description of the first human being as ἐκ γῆς, χοϊκός ("from the earth, of the dust") is a composite echo of Gen 2:7 LXX (χοῦν ἀπὸ τῆς γῆς) and Gen 3:19 LXX (τὴν γῆν, ἐξ ἧς).[48] We see here once again the Jewish character of Paul's thought, for within the ancient Jewish context Gen 2:7 and Gen 3:19 are frequently brought together (Eccl 12:7; Ps 146:4; Sir 17:1; Wis 15:8; 1QH xii, 26–27), and Gen 3:19 "plays an important part in the formulation of biblical anthropology."[49] This verse, and

---

47. Ciampa & Rosner, 821–22.

48. Paul's adjective χοϊκός may also allude to Gen 3:19, for the Hebrew text of Gen 3:19 employs *'āpār* "dust," twice, although in Gen 3:19 (unlike 2:7) the LXX translator renders it as γῆ. Paul may be thinking of the Hebrew of Gen 3:19 or using an alternative Greek text, which rendered *'āpār* in this verse as χοῦς.

49. Harry Sysling, *Teḥiyyat ha-Metim: The Resurrection of the Dead in the Palestinian Tar-*

in particular its final words, "You are dust, and to dust you shall return," is frequently echoed in ancient Jewish literature "to illustrate the transitoriness and futility of human existence."[50] We see the verse echoed in this way in Eccl 3:20, in Job 10:9 and 34:14–15, and in Pss 90:3 and 104:29. By drawing in Gen 3:19 alongside Gen 2:7, Paul here accents, even more sharply than in 15:45, the human dilemma of transitoriness, mortality, and death. Through this composite echo of Gen 2:7 and 3:19, Paul encapsulates the entire narrative of Gen 2–3, recalling not only Adam's creation but also his fall.

In the expression ἐκ γῆς, the preposition ἐκ denotes origin—the first human was of earthly origin. In what sense does Paul use γῆ here? To denote the *soil*, that is, the *ground*? Or to denote the *earth* as opposed to *heaven*? The contrast in 15:47b (ἐξ οὐρανοῦ) makes it evident that Paul here is thinking of the earth in contrast with heaven.[51] The first human being's origin was earth, not heaven. The word χοϊκός is formed from the word χοῦς "dust" by means of the adjective ending -ικος. The word is not found prior to Paul and may well be a Pauline neologism.[52] Scott Brodeur points out how ancient philosophers were fond of forming new words with the -ικος termination.[53] We may thus have here one more instance of Paul beating the philosophically inclined, self-professed wise at Corinth at their own game.

What is the meaning of the adjective here? A number of scholars, and the standard New Testament lexica, assume that it is "a word describing physical composition."[54] But adjectives with the -ικος termination seldom if ever denote composition.[55] Rather, such -ικος adjectives denote a quality characteristic of, belonging to, or proper to the related noun stem. For instance, βασιλικός never means "made of a βασιλεύς," but it instead describes something or someone as belonging to or proper to a king (i.e., "royal"). The adjective χοϊκός thus describes the first human being as belonging to, or proper to, the dust. The focus of the word here is on Adam's *earthly origin*. This is confirmed by (1) the parallelism with ἐκ γῆς ("*from* the earth"); (2) its apparent synonymous equivalence to ἐπίγειος ("earthly") in the earlier analogy in 15:40; and ( 3) the contrast in the parallel clause in 15:47

---

*gums of the Pentateuch and Parallel Traditions in Classical Rabbinic Literature* (Tübingen: Mohr Siebeck, 1996), 71–77.

50. Sysling, *Teḥiyyat ha-Metim*, 71.
51. *Pace* Brodeur, *Holy Spirit's Agency*, 127–28.
52. So Brodeur, *Holy Spirit's Agency*, 128–30.
53. Brodeur, *Holy Spirit's Agency*, 98–99, 130.
54. Wright, *Resurrection*, 345. So also Ciampa & Rosner, 806; BA, s.v. "χοϊκός" ("aus Erde [χοῦς] bestehend, irdisch"); BDAG, s.v. "χοϊκός" ("made of earth/dust").
55. BDR §113.2; Rob., *Gram.*, 158–59; Brodeur, *Holy Spirit's Agency*, 128–30.

with ἐξ οὐρανοῦ ("from heaven"). The adjective χοϊκός with ἄνθρωπος thus describes a human being whose origin is the dust (Gen 2:7), and who has been condemned because of sin to return to the dust (Gen 3:19). The adjective retells the whole story of creation and the fall: how Adam and Eve were created with a body that was mortal and perishable (Gen 2:7; 1 Cor 15:45), a σῶμα ψυχικόν (1 Cor 15:44, 46), and yet they were able to live forever through their free decision of communion with God (Gen 2:9, 17; 3:2–3, 22; so Rom 5:12), and how, through their forsaking of communion with God, human bodily death entered into the creation (Gen 3:19; Rom 5:12–14; 1 Cor 15:21–22, 26, 56).

It is crucial to grasp that the human plight, as the apostle describes it here, is not conceived as a plus requiring subtraction. That is, Paul does not, as Plato does, consider the physical body as problematic or needing to be discarded or shed, so that the human being may partake of life. Rather, the human dilemma is conceived as a minus requiring addition. The problem is that the human being is exclusively earthly, lacking the divine imperishable life. We will find the solution to this human plight in the very next clause.

*the second human being is from heaven.* There is no conjunction between the two contrasting clauses of v. 47: Paul employs the rhetorical device of asyndeton to sharpen and highlight the contrast between them.[56] This contrast concerns the *origin* of the two human beings. The origin of the first Adam is earth (ἐκ γῆς); the origin of the second Adam is heaven (ἐξ οὐρανοῦ). Paul now begins to apply and unpack the comparison of the earthly and heavenly bodies of vv. 40–41, and this application will continue through v. 49.

But how does Paul apply the comparison of 15:40–41 here? In what way is the second Adam's origin "from heaven"? We have frequently discussed in this commentary the mistaken thesis that Paul in this chapter envisions a resurrection body composed not of flesh but of ethereal *pneuma*. For the authors that take this view, vv. 47–49 constitute the major "prooftext" of this thesis. Paul's language here of "heaven" and "earth," according to these scholars, plainly expresses the conception of a dichotomous cosmology or "cosmic polarity" involving an understanding of salvation as ascent to dwell among the heavenly stars and planets, which requires the body's change from earthly flesh and bones to a heavenly pneumatic substance in order to dwell among these astral bodies.[57] On this view, the second

---

56. Reasoner, on 15:47.
57. So Martin, *Body*, 126–32; Asher, *Polarity and Change*, 110–17; Asher, "Anthropogenic Metaphor," 102–6; Engberg-Pedersen, *Cosmology and Self*, 26–31; Alan G. Padgett, "The Body in Resurrection: Science and Scripture on the 'Spiritual Body,'" *WW* 22 (2002): 160–61; Litwa, *Deification*,

Adam is described in 15:47 as "from heaven" because at his resurrection his body was changed from an earthly body of flesh into a body of the same substance as his human spirit or *pneuma*, and thus to a body of heavenly, ethereal, pneumatic material fitted to ascend among the heavenly stars and planets, which are composed of the same material of *pneuma*.[58] Thus Padgett tells us that the phrase ἐξ οὐρανοῦ "does not indicate that Jesus was *from* heaven" but that he "is 'of heaven' in the sense that he is made of the very stuff of the heavens."[59]

We have repeatedly seen the failure of this thesis of a resurrection body of corporeal *pneuma* to provide a plausible exegesis of passage after passage within this chapter. Does it provide a plausible exegesis of Paul's description of Christ as "from heaven" in 15:47? No, it does not. The interpretation fails on several counts:

(1) This interpretation is founded on the assumption that the ancients believed that the heavenly realm, and its stars and planets, was composed of pneumatic substance. However, this is simply false. All ancient philosophers, despite the diverse ways in which they used and understood the term πνεῦμα, assigned πνεῦμα exclusively to the sublunary and terrestrial realm. For the Stoics, the heavenly bodies are composed not of *pneuma* but of the divine fire (*SVF* 1.115–16; 2.118, 527, 555, 642, 668; Diogenes Laertius, *Vit. phil.* 7.137; Cicero, *Nat. d.* 2.42–43). The πνεῦμα, by contrast, is composed of air and fire (*SVF* 2.310, 442, 1100).[60] Therefore it belongs to the sublunary, earthly realm of earth, water, and air, and it can have no place in the heavenly realm, which consists solely of fire or ether (Diogenes Laertius, *Vit. phil.* 7.137, 155; *SVF* 2.527). For this reason the Stoics identified the πνεῦμα with the world-soul, not in its celestial mode but only as the form this divine crafting fire takes within the sublunary and terrestrial realms (*SVF* 1.159, 533–34; 2.416, 473). For this same reason, in Stoic teaching the human πνεῦμα, likewise composed of air and fire (*SVF* 2.786–87, 841), can ascend only as high as the moon, the terminus of the region of air (*SVF* 2.814, 817, 1105; cf. Tertullian, *An.* 54–55). The entire conception of a heavenly realm composed of πνεῦμα, on which this interpretation depends, is founded upon a misunderstanding of ancient Stoic philosophical thought.[61] No philosophical text in antiquity imagines that the heavenly bodies

---

152–71. In all this, these authors insist, Paul was merely following, as Padgett puts it, "the science of his day" ("Science and Scripture," 161).

58. See, e.g., Martin, *Body*, 126, 132, 276 n. 82. Cf. Brodeur, *Holy Spirit's Agency*, 133–34, 147–55.

59. Padgett, "Science and Scripture," 161.

60. See M. Lapidge, "Stoic Cosmology," in *The Stoics* (ed. J. M. Rist; Berkeley: University of California, 1978), 169–78.

61. Cf. John Granger Cook, "1 Cor 15,40–41: Paul and the Heavenly Bodies," *ZNW* 113 (2022): 162–64, 173–74. Engberg-Pedersen, who claims that "it is a distinctly Stoic idea that 'heavenly' bodies are also 'pneumatic' ones" (*Cosmology and Self*, 28), admits in a footnote to this same

are composed of *pneuma* or envisions the human *pneuma* ascending there. This is fatal for the thesis that the point of v. 47 is to affirm that Christ's body is composed of astral *pneuma*.

(2) As virtually all interpreters are agreed, Paul in 15:47–49 applies the analogy of the heavenly bodies in 15:40–41. But on the interpretation of 15:47 as referring to a putative astral body of Christ, 15:40–41 is not an analogy at all but a straightforward, literal description of the substance of Christ's risen body. But the placement of vv. 40–41 with the other analogies in vv. 36–41, and Paul's overt indication that vv. 36–41 are a series of analogies or comparisons (15:42, "*thus* also is the resurrection of the dead"), demonstrate that 15:40–41 *is* in fact a comparison and analogical. We thus find another fatal miscalculation in the view that 1 Cor 15:47 refers to the composition of Jesus's body from celestial material: the failure to account for the analogical character of 15:36–41.

(3) Paul declares that Christ is "from heaven" in v. 47. The view we are considering interprets the words "from heaven" as denoting the composition of Jesus's risen body as one supposedly composed of celestial *pneuma*.[62] But the prepositional phrase ἐξ οὐρανοῦ does not denote composition but *origin*. It does not mean that the second Adam is *composed of* heaven, but that he is *from* heaven.

The reasons given above rule out not only the interpretation of "from heaven" in v. 47 as a reference to the composition of Jesus's body, but the entire thesis that Paul in 1 Cor 15 envisions a resurrection body composed of ethereal *pneuma*.

What does Paul mean, then, when he describes the second human being as "from heaven"? Some scholars understand v. 47 as a reference to Christ's resurrection.[63] But it is difficult to see how the description of Christ as "from heaven" could be a reference to his resurrection on the third day. Other scholars suggest that Paul refers in v. 47 to the session of Christ in heaven at the right hand of God.[64] Still others suggest that Paul here refers to the second coming of Christ from heaven.[65] However, Christ's sitting at God's right hand, and his coming again in glory,

---

sentence: "I have been unable to find the term itself 'pneumatic' employed in Stoic sources in direct connection with the heavenly bodies" (217 n. 76). The reason such language cannot be found in Stoic texts is that such a notion is contrary to Stoic thought. Our Stoic sources not only do not use the term but positively and explicitly exclude the conception that the heavenly bodies are composed of *pneuma*.

62. Martin, *Body*, 126, 132, 276 n. 82; Padgett, "Science and Scripture," 161; Brodeur, *Holy Spirit's Agency*, 133–34, 147–53.

63. E.g., Burchard, "1 Korinther 15.39–41," 246; Schrage, 309–10; Fee, 876–78; O'Reilly, *Resurrected Body*, 89.

64. Gaffin, "Life-Giving Spirit," 578; Fitzmyer, 599; Schreiner, 323.

65. Barrett, 375–76; Robertson & Plummer, 374; Garland, 736–37; Godet, 2:428–29; Wright, *Resurrection*, 355.

are the *climax* of the narrative about Christ, the last Adam (1 Cor 1:7–8; 15:23–28; Phil 2:9–11; 3:20–21; 1 Thess 4:13–18). But 15:47 focuses on the *origin* of the second Adam. As the first clause of v. 47 answered the question "Where did the first Adam come from?" so the second clause answers the question "Where did the second Adam come from?" For the answer, we must go to the *beginning* of Paul's narrative about Christ. The story of Christ in Paul does not begin with his resurrection, ascension, or second coming. It begins with the incarnation of the Son of God in human flesh: "But when the fullness of time had come, God sent forth his Son, born of a woman" (Gal 4:4). It is this beginning and origin to which Paul refers in 15:47: the second human being is "from heaven" (ἐξ οὐρανοῦ) because he is the incarnate Son of God.[66] Paul elsewhere speaks of Christ in his incarnation as coming from heaven (Rom 10:6), as does Luke's Gospel (1:78–79). This language is common in early Christian writings (cf. Clement of Alexandria, *Protr.* 11.86, αὐτὸς ἦκεν ὡς ἡμᾶς οὐρανόθεν ὁ λόγος ["the Word himself came to us from heaven"]; 2 Clem. 20.5; Tatian, *Or. Graec.* 7.1). This language is especially prominent in John's Gospel (John 3:13, 31; 6:32–33, 38, 41–42, 50–51, 58; cf. 6:62; 8:23). We find here another of the striking correspondences between John's theological language and that of Paul. That 1 Cor 15:47 refers to the Son of God coming from heaven in the incarnation is the well-nigh universal understanding of ancient interpreters.[67]

Here we find the word "heaven" used in a nonspatial and metaphorical sense to denote the dwelling place of God. This was an ancient Jewish and early Christian usage of the word unknown in the wider polytheistic world. The conception that God, as the transcendent creator, is not bounded by space but is his own place is implicit in ancient Judaism (1 Kgs 8:27; 2 Chr 2:6; Pss 8:1; 57:5, 11; 108:4–5; 113:4–6; 148:13; T. Levi 3.4) and is explicit in early Christian texts.[68] The use of the word "heaven" in this nonspatial sense to denote the dwelling and presence of God pervades the New Testament.[69] Heaven is the throne of God (Matt 5:34). God is enthroned "in heaven" (Rev 4:2). God the Father is, in Jesus's teaching, "my Father in the heavens" (Matt 10:32–33; 12:50; 16:17; 18:19), "your Father in the heavens"

---

66. Among modern interpreters who recognize that 15:47 asserts the divine identity of the incarnate Lord, see Altermath, *Du corps psychique*, 45; Goppelt, *Typos*, 134; Schep, *Resurrection Body*, 177; cf. Aquinas, *1 Cor.* 995.

67. E.g., Tertullian, *Res.* 49, 53; *Carn. Chr.* 8; Gregory of Nazianzus, *Ep.* 101; Hilary, *Trin.* 10.17; Methodius, *Res.* 1.13; Cyril of Alexandria, *Quod un.* 723c–d; 725b–c; 771c–d; Augustine, *Civ.* 13.23; *Faust.* 2.4.

68. E.g., Herm. Mand. 1.1.1; Justin, *Dial.* 56; 60.2; 127; Athenagoras, *Leg.* 8; Theophilus of Antioch, *Autol.* 2.3; Irenaeus, *Haer.* 2.30.9; Clement of Alexandria, *Strom.* 5.12.81; 5.38.6; Minucius Felix, *Oct.* 18.7–8; 32.1.

69. See BDAG, s.v. "οὐρανός" (2): "the dwelling place (or throne) of God."

(Matt 5:16, 45; 6:1, 9; 7:11; 18:14; Mark 11:25), and "your heavenly Father" (Matt 5:48; 6:14, 26, 32; 18:35; 23:9). The Holy Spirit is given "from heaven" (John 1:32; 1 Pet 1:12; cf. Luke 11:13). The Son through his incarnation is "from heaven" (John 3:13, 31; 6:32–33, 41–42, 50–51, 58; cf. Luke 1:78; John 8:23). It is this last usage, in which the Son through his incarnation is said to be "from heaven," that we find in 1 Cor 15:47. Paul can say that the second human being is "from heaven," not because his human nature is from heaven but in view of the single subjectivity and unity of the person of the divine Son of God, who in the incarnation assumed a human nature (cf. John 3:13, ὁ ἐκ τοῦ οὐρανοῦ καταβάς, ὁ υἱὸς τοῦ ἀνθρώπου).

The analogy of the astral heaven in 15:40–41 thus finds its application in 15:47 in the use of the word "heaven" to denote the dwelling and presence of God. This coheres with our earlier discovery that the analogy of the celestial *glory* of 15:40–41 has its application in that glory which is the radiant manifestation of God's own being and presence. Paul now in v. 47 further deepens and enriches v. 45. How can the last Adam, by rising from the dead, bestow the life-giving Spirit of God as his very own Spirit (v. 45)? He can do so, v. 47 explains, because he is the divine Son of God in human flesh (cf. Rom 1:3–4; 8:3–4; 9:5; 1 Cor 8:6). As Augustine put it: "He came from heaven, that he might be clothed with a body of earthly mortality, that he might clothe that body with heavenly immortality" (*Civ.* 13.23).

Verse 47 thus fully resolves the mystery of v. 21: how can the resurrection of the dead, the God of Israel's promised conquest of death, come about through a mere *human being* (15:21, καὶ δι' ἀνθρώπου ἀνάστασις νεκρῶν)? Verse 47 resolves the mystery, for it reveals that this human being is from heaven. This human being is the God of Israel in the flesh (15:47, ὁ δεύτερος ἄνθρωπος ἐξ οὐρανοῦ). This second Adam is the one Lord and creator (8:6), through whom the first Adam was created. Through his resurrection, he brings his own divine intention for humanity to fulfillment in his own person. "In the Incarnation creation is fulfilled by God's including himself in it."[70]

## Verse 48

*As is the nature of the one of dust, so is the nature of those who are of the dust, and as is the nature of the one of heaven, so is the nature of those who are of heaven.*

Paul in 15:44b–47 has retold the story of the incarnation, death, and resurrection of the Son of God. Paul will now in 15:48–49 complete the narrative of the econ-

---

70. Kierkegaard, *Journals and Papers*, 2:1391.

omy of salvation, describing the present renewal of the Holy Spirit wrought by Christ (15:48), and the future resurrection that is its telos and goal (15:49). Verse 48 focuses on this present renewal.[71]

The pronoun οἷος "is qualitative, and not a mere relative."[72] Similarly, its correlated pronoun τοιοῦτοι "is the demonstrative of quality."[73] These pronouns of quality call attention to a contrast in *nature* of the two kinds of humanity paralleled here. "Those who are of the dust" (οἱ χοϊκοί) are fallen humanity, who are "in Adam" (15:22, ἐν τῷ Ἀδάμ). Adam's nature (οἷος) is by birth their nature (τοιοῦτοι): possessing only the corruptible life given by the soul (15:45, ψυχὴ ζῶσα, echoing Gen 2:7), bereft of the life of God through sin (15:56), and therefore condemned to return to the dust (15:47a, echoing Gen 3:19). The one in Adam is a ψυχικὸς ἄνθρωπος (2:14), without the Spirit of God (2:15–16; cf. Jude 19). Such were the Corinthians prior to conversion and baptism (1:26–31; 6:9–11; 12:1–3; 15:1–2), and such are all who do not call on the name of Christ (1:1–2, 18–31; 2:14; 5:12–13; 9:19–23; 16:22).

"Those who are of heaven" (οἱ ἐπουράνιοι) are those who are "in Christ" (15:22, ἐν τῷ Χριστῷ). They are "those who belong to Christ" (15:23, οἱ τοῦ Χριστοῦ). In calling believers "heavenly" Paul is referring to the present life of those in Christ. We see here once again the failure of that exegesis that reads Paul's references to "heaven" in vv. 40–41 and 47–49 as denoting the celestial spirit matter of which the risen body is allegedly composed. For the Corinthians to whom Paul writes in v. 48 do not have bodies composed of astral pneumatic matter! The difference between

---

71. A number of interpreters take v. 48 as referring to the future resurrection (e.g., Wolff, 411; Barrett, 377; Ciampa & Rosner, 823). But such a reading is impossible for the following reasons. (1) In cases of ellipsis of the verbal copula, as seen here, the omitted verb is in the present tense. Instances of the ellipsis of the future tense are extremely rare and are always indicated by unmistakable contextual features (see Kühner-G., 2.1:41 n. 2; BDR §127–28; Rob., *Gram.*, 395). (2) Verse 48 continues the verbal ellipsis from 15:47, where (beyond controversy) the omitted verb is in the present tense. (3) The connective καί that begins v. 49 shows that the thought of that verse, which takes up the resurrection, is not coordinate with v. 48 but additional. The καί reveals that Paul's thought moves from present life in Christ in v. 48 to the future resurrection in v. 49. (4) Finally, the participle ζωοποιοῦν in 15:45 is present tense, thus denoting an ongoing activity brought about by the resurrection of Christ, and setting up the treatment of the entire economy of salvation moving from present salvation in 15:48 to future resurrection in 15:49. All these factors are decisive that the omitted verb in 15:48 is present tense, and that this verse refers to present life in Christ. Ancient interpreters are unanimous that v. 48 concerns present life in Christ (see Irenaeus, *Haer.* 5.9.3; Tertullian, *Marc.* 5.10; *Carn. Chr.* 8; Cyril of Alexandria, *Quod un.* 725b; Ambrose, *Spir.* 1.66).

72. Rob., *Gram.*, 731.

73. Rob., *Gram.*, 710.

*The Bestowal of the Holy Spirit by the Risen Son of God*

them and their unbelieving neighbors is not the composition of their bodies. In what way, then, are believers in Christ "heavenly" or "of heaven"?

The context of v. 48 is vv. 45–47. Jesus Christ is "from heaven" (15:47), the divine Son of God, his eternal divine nature united in the incarnation to his assumed human nature (Rom 1:3–4; 8:3–4; 9:5, Gal 4:4–6; Phil 2:5–11). As the Son of God (1 Cor 15:28), he is the source of the Holy Spirit, who belongs to him and is consubstantial with him (6:17; 10:1–4; 12:4–6, 13). Through his death and resurrection he now bestows his life-giving Spirit (15:45, πνεῦμα ζωοποιοῦν) on those united to him by faith and baptism (6:11; 12:13). In contrast with the one in Adam, ὁ ψυχικὸς ἄνθρωπος (2:14), possessing only the life of the soul (15:45a), the one in Christ is thus ὁ πνευματικός (2:15; 3:1), possessing the Spirit of God. Those united to Christ are living tabernacles of the Holy Spirit (3:16–17). Their bodies are a temple of the Holy Spirit (6:19; cf. 2:12; 12:3–11, 13). They are "of heaven" because they share in the Son of God's divine nature through the indwelling of his Holy Spirit.[74]

First Corinthians 15:48 is the only place in the New Testament where those who share in the Holy Spirit are called "heavenly" (ἐπουράνιος). But there are analogous usages elsewhere. Hebrews 6:14 refers to the Holy Spirit as "the heavenly gift" (ἡ δωρεὰ ἡ ἐπουράνιος). In 1 Peter, the faithful have received "the Holy Spirit sent from heaven" (1 Pet 1:12). In Luke 24:49, the Holy Spirit whom the disciples are to receive is described as "power from heaven" (ἐξ ὕψους δύναμις). Elsewhere in 1 Corinthians, Paul's preferred adjective for the presence and working of the Spirit of God is πνευματικός (2:13, 15; 3:1; 10:2, 4; 12:1; 14:1, 37; 15:44, 46). But here in 15:48–49 Paul uses ἐπουράνιος three times as he continues to apply the comparison of the heavenly bodies in 15:40–41. The astral heaven of the analogy in vv. 40–41 is, in the application of vv. 47–49, the divine nature, the presence and being of God. Christ is "from heaven" (15:47) and "the one who is from heaven" (15:48) because he is the divine Son of God; the Corinthians are "those who are of heaven" (15:48) because they are united to Christ by the indwelling of the Holy Spirit. This conception of the sharing of the faithful in Christ's heavenly nature has perhaps its closest parallel in John 17:14: "They are not from the world, just as I am not from the world." But the closest parallel in the New Testament to 15:48 as a whole is John 3:6: "That which is born of the flesh is flesh, and that which is born of the Spirit is spirit." In both John 3:6 and 1 Cor 15:48, being "flesh" (John 3:6) or "of the dust" (1 Cor 15:48) is not a plus requiring subtraction, the shedding of the flesh and bones body, but a lack requiring endowment—the gift of the Spirit of God.

---

74. This is the regular interpretation of 15:48 among ancient interpreters; see Irenaeus, *Haer.* 5.9.3; Tertullian, *Carn. Chr.* 8; Cyril, *Quod un.* 725b; Ambrose, *Spir.* 1.66.

"Those who are of heaven" have the Spirit of Christ; "those who are of the dust" lack the Spirit and the life it bestows.

This language and conception of the faithful as sharing in Christ's *heavenly* nature are present at one other place within the epistle. We have seen in our discussion of v. 45 that believers become "one Spirit" (ἓν πνεῦμα, 6:17) with Christ, and thus πνευματικοί, bearers of his Spirit (2:15; 3:1), by partaking of the "food of the Spirit" (10:3, πνευματικὸν βρῶμα) and the "drink of the Spirit" (10:4, πνευματικὸν πόμα), that is, the eucharistic body and blood of Christ (10:16–17; 11:17–34). It is in 10:1–4 that we also find a conception of this "food of the Spirit" as *heavenly* food. For in this passage Paul portrays the Eucharist as foreshadowed in the manna in the wilderness (10:3, πάντες τὸ αὐτὸ πνευματικὸν βρῶμα ἔφαγον). And in the Old Testament, the manna is described as bread *from heaven* (Exod 16:4 LXX, ἄρτους ἐκ τοῦ οὐρανοῦ; Ps 77:24 LXX, ἄρτον οὐρανοῦ ἔδωκεν αὐτοῖς). The fact that Paul connects τὸ πνευματικὸν βρῶμα of the Eucharist in 10:3 with the Corinthians' identity as πνευματικοί (2:15; 3:1), sharers in the Holy Spirit, suggests that Paul connects the heavenly associations of the manna, and thus of the Eucharist, with the Corinthians' heavenly identity in 15:48. Through this ἄρτος οὐρανοῦ, "bread of heaven" (Ps 77:24 LXX), the Corinthians are even now οἱ ἐπουράνιοι, "those who are of heaven."

## Verse 49

*And just as we wore the image of the one who is of the dust, we will also wear the image of the one who is of heaven.*

The καί that introduces v. 49 reveals that this verse contains a new thought, beyond and in addition to the thought of v. 48. The anaphora (repetition) of both the verb ("to wear") and its direct object ("the image") effectively highlights the *contrast* between the man of dust, Adam, and the man of heaven, Christ.[75] The key to this contrast lies in the twice-repeated verb and object: to "wear the image."

What does it mean to "wear the image"? The verb φορέω is the frequentative of φέρω ("bear, carry") and thus means "*to bear about with or on oneself, to wear.*"[76] The verb is thus used of something *worn* externally, "most commonly of clothes, armor, and the like."[77] Our closest parallel in antiquity to Paul's language of wearing an *image* (εἰκών) is found in reference to the wearing (φορέω) of an image

---

75. Reasoner, on 15:49.
76. Robinson, s.v. "φορέω."
77. LSJ, s.v. "φορέω" (2).

(εἰκών) on signet rings (Plutarch, *Sull.* 3.4 [φορεῖν εἰκόνα]; *Quaest. conv.* 672c [εἰκόνα ... ἐφόρει]; Aristotle, *Frag.* 5.30.197 [θεῶν τε εἰκόνας ἐν δακτυλίοις μὴ φορεῖν]). These parallels confirm that Paul's language denotes what is bodily and external. But Paul's language is also unique, for Paul employs the word "image" (εἰκών) not with reference to something worn upon the body but to the body itself.[78] The image (εἰκών) that is worn (φορέω) is thus the physical, external body. Paul's use of φορέω "wear" here recalls his use of clothing imagery to denote resurrection in 15:37 and foreshadows the climactic image of resurrection as clothing in 15:53–54.

So then, Paul's language in 15:49 is the language of resurrection and of the body. Paul contrasts here the present body, which is in the image of Adam, with the future risen body, which will be in the image of Christ. We now see the new thought implicit in the καί at the beginning of the verse. Verse 48 concerned the transformation wrought by the man from heaven (15:47) in present life in Christ; v. 49 concerns the fullness of this transformation that will take place at the resurrection. "He will transform our lowly bodies to be made like his glorious body" (Phil 3:21).[79]

Paul here brings to a climax his application of the comparison of the heavenly bodies in 15:40–41. As we saw in 15:47–48, the glory of the astral heaven of 15:40–41 is a metaphor for the divine glory. Therefore, in affirming that the faithful will "wear the image of the one who is of heaven" (15:49), Paul indicates that their very bodies will participate in the glory of the Son of God. Those who belong to Christ will have glorified bodies like Christ's glorified body. The body that is "the image of the one from heaven" (15:49) and "the body of the Spirit" (15:44, 46) are one and the same, for the Holy Spirit that will be given in its fullness to the body at the resurrection is the Spirit of the Son (15:45).

Paul also carefully connects his portrayal of the resurrection in 15:49 to his

---

78. To be sure, the imagery of clothing as a metaphor for embodiment is frequent in antiquity (cf. Plutarch, *Cons. ux.* 10; Aristotle, *De an.* 407b20–23). It is Paul's use of the word εἰκών in this connection that is unique.

79. The great majority of manuscripts and our best witnesses read the aorist subjunctive φορέσωμεν ("let us wear") rather than the future indicative φορέσομεν ("we will wear"). The future indicative is supported only by B, I, 6, 630, 1881, and a few other manuscripts and versions. Normally such preponderance of external evidence is to be followed. However, the confusion of o and ω is the most common form of orthographical error in the New Testament and is thus a special case (see Rob., *Gram.*, 200–201; Ciampa & Rosner, 824 n. 310). Important patristic witnesses support the future indicative (Methodius, *Res.* 2.5; Cyril of Alexandria, *Quod un.* 723c). The decisive factor is the context and diction of v. 49. Here Paul's language of "wearing" the image denotes, as we have seen, a bodily and physical reality and thus involves not moral likeness to Christ in the present but physical conformity to Christ in the resurrection. The language of 15:49, and its context within the chapter, decisively favors the future indicative.

portrayal of present life in Christ in 15:48, through his studied use of the word εἰκών or "image." In Pauline theology, the Son is the eternal, uncreated image of the Father, co-sharing with the Father in the divine nature and being (2 Cor 4:4–6; Col 1:15; cf. Rom 8:29).[80] The first Adam was made in the likeness of this image (Gen 1:26–27; 5:1; 1 Cor 11:7). This divine image, given in creation but marred in the fall, is now in the process of being restored and renewed in Christ. This involves a moral transformation, in which believers, even now, are being remade in the image of the Son (2 Cor 3:17–18; 4:4–6; Eph 2:14–18; 4:20–24; Col 3:9–11).[81] But this process has a goal not only of moral conformity but also of physical conformity to the image of the Son in the resurrection (εἰκών, Rom 8:29; 2 Cor 3:18).[82] In light of this rich and multifaceted theological meaning of the word εἰκών in Paul's thought, his use of this word in v. 49 portrays this physical likeness to Christ's risen body at the resurrection as the culmination of a process of moral conformity to the Son already at work in the lives of believers now through the power of the Holy Spirit. Paul's careful choice of the word εἰκών thus ties v. 49 closely to the depiction of present life in Christ in v. 48. The physical conformity to Christ at the resurrection is the culmination of a process begun in baptism and lived out in a life of cruciform discipleship to Christ. Verse 49 thus carries a hortatory undertone, an implicit exhortation to sanctification and discipleship.

## Verses 44b–49 in the Thought of the Chapter

We are now in a position to see how, in depicting the future resurrection as the culmination of likeness to the Son through the work of his Spirit, vv. 44b–49 marvelously correspond with and deepen Paul's teaching throughout the chapter. Paul here unpacks his assertion in 15:22 that it is "in Christ" that all will be made alive, and the necessity of taking up the cross in discipleship to Christ, which he so urgently expresses in 15:30–32. For, as Paul explains here, the present life in Christ, which brings about moral conformity to Christ, is the necessary prelude to the physical conformity to Christ that will be bestowed at the resurrection. Moreover, we find in 15:44b–49 that Paul's analogy of the heavenly bodies in 15:40–41 finds its application not only in the resurrection but also in a larger narrative begin-

---

80. On this Pauline conception of the Son as the consubstantial image of the Father elsewhere in early Christian thought, see Barn. 5.5; Irenaeus, *Haer.* 4.20.1; Tertullian, *Res.* 6; Hilary, *Trin.* 7.37; Basil, *Spir.* 18.45; Augustine, *Trin.* 12.6.6.

81. Robert Scholla, "Into the Image of God: Pauline Eschatology and the Transformation of Believers," *Greg* 78 (1997): 33–54.

82. Scholla, "Image of God," 47–54.

ning with the incarnation of the divine Son of God (15:47), continuing with the present sharing of his divine life through the gift of the Holy Spirit (15:45, 48), and culminating in the body's full participation in the divine life of the Son and of his Spirit at the resurrection (15:49). Finally, the link that Paul forges here in 15:49 between the believer's moral conformity to the image of Christ now and their physical conformity to Christ at the resurrection reminds us that the risen "body of the Spirit," which Paul expounds here in 15:44b–49, is but the culmination and outworking of the gift of the Holy Spirit given to the faithful in the present through their participation in the food and drink of the Spirit (10:3–4, 16–17; 12:13), whereby they become even now living tabernacles of the Spirit of God (3:16–17; 6:19).

We saw above that Paul in 15:47–49, through his description of the first Adam as ἐκ γῆς (15:47) and χοϊκός (15:47, 48, 49), echoes not only Gen 2:7 and the creation of Adam from the dust but also Gen 3:19 and his sentence of return to the dust. We have also seen the frequent connection of Gen 2:7 and 3:19 in ancient Jewish thought and the importance of these two texts in Jewish anthropology. It is within its Jewish context that we can see the striking and unique character of Paul's thought here. For the biblical hope of resurrection, in light of Gen 3:19, involves a mystery. The resurrection promised by YHWH in the later strata of the Old Testament clearly overturns and cancels out the sentence of return to the dust in Gen 3:19. But the Old Testament nowhere explains how this can come about or be so. The mystery is compounded by the fact that the two most central passages expressing the hope of resurrection in the Old Testament, Isa 26:19 and Dan 12:2, both allude to Gen 3:19![83] But neither text explains how it is possible for the decree of Gen 3:19 to be reversed through resurrection. In rabbinic Judaism the answer is located in the soul-life breathed into Adam at his creation (Gen 2:7), which is understood as the source of the coming reversal of death in the resurrection.[84] But this is illogical, for Gen 3:19 itself locates the necessity of human mortality in the very nature of human beings as created from the dust (Gen 2:7). The sentence of death in Gen 3:19, far from finding its reversal in Gen 2:7, would seem to follow ineluctably from it.

Here we see the striking and unique character of Paul's Christian thought. For Paul, in this great resurrection chapter, resolves the mystery. The answer is the incarnation of the Son of God, who unites God and humanity (15:47) and, through his death and resurrection, bestows his own life-giving Holy Spirit (15:45, 48), a gift that will culminate in the communication of the Holy Spirit to the physical body in the resurrection (15:44, 46, 49). The incarnation brought something utterly

---

83. See Sysling, *Teḥiyyat ha-Metim*, 72–73.
84. Genesis Rabbah 14:7; b. Sanhedrin 91a. See Sysling, *Teḥiyyat ha-Metim*, 67–90.

## CHAPTER 13

new into the world: the heavenly, divine, imperishable life of God. Through the communication of this divine life in baptism and the eucharistic table (15:45; cf. 10:3–4, 16–21), those united to Christ by faith are given to share in the Son of God's imperishable, divine life. The divine Son of God, entering into his own creation as the last Adam, thus becomes the exemplar and founder of a new humanity, one imbued with the life of his own Holy Spirit (15:45, 48–49). And in this way human beings, created with only mortal bodily life, are enabled to share in resurrection to everlasting bodily life. "He came from heaven, that he might be clothed with a body of earthly mortality, that he might clothe that body with heavenly immortality" (Augustine, *Civ.* 13.23).

CHAPTER 14

*The Mystery of the Glorification of the Flesh*

15:50–53

In the previous section, which in many ways is the theological heart of the chapter, Paul unveiled the mystery of the source of the resurrection life to be bestowed at Christ's second coming. Its source, Paul revealed, is the Son of God, who through his incarnation brings his own divine and heavenly life into the world (15:47), and through his death and resurrection bestows his own life-giving Holy Spirit (15:45, 48) and brings this gift to its culmination in the full endowment of his Spirit and his imperishable life to the physical body in the resurrection (15:44b, 46, 49). The image of Christ, implanted now in the faithful by their union with Christ through baptism and the Eucharist, will be worn also by their physical bodies, when their bodies are transformed in the resurrection to be like Christ's glorious body (15:49). Now, in 15:50–53, Paul will explore the necessity of this glorious transformation to come. In so doing, Paul will, in his revelatory capacity as an apostle, reveal to the Corinthians a mystery regarding the resurrection (15:51). Paul will then unfold this mystery in one of the most lyrical and sublime depictions of the resurrection within Paul's epistles (15:52–53).

It is all the more ironic, then, that this passage is also perhaps the most abused and misused passage in all of Paul's letters. The focus of this misuse is v. 50: "And this I say, brothers and sisters, that flesh and blood is not able to inherit the kingdom of God, nor does corruption inherit incorruptibility." In book after book and article after article within the scholarly literature, this verse is invoked (usually without exegesis or argument) as absolute, unquestioned proof that, in Paul's understanding, the risen body of Christ and the bodies of those who belong to Christ in the resurrection to come cannot be physical, palpable, and material like our present bodies, that is, bodies of flesh and bone, but must be bodies without

CHAPTER 14

flesh, composed of some kind of ethereal spiritual substance. So, for instance, Paula Fredriksen writes that Christ arose "in a spiritual body, Paul insists, and definitely *not* in a body of flesh and blood (1 Cor 15:44, 50)."[1] Bruce Chilton tells us that, in light of v. 50, "a survival of flesh or soul would contradict Paul's resurrection science."[2] This verse is a widely used "prooftext" that Paul, unlike the gospels, did not affirm that Jesus rose in the flesh and did not believe in a coming resurrection of the flesh. When this claim is made, one normally looks in vain for exposition of the passage, attention to its context, or consideration of the verse within Paul's larger theology. Many scholars apparently feel they "just know" that this must be the meaning of this verse. However, as we will see, this is a woefully mistaken exegesis of this passage that not only misconstrues the nature of the resurrection in Paul but also entirely misses the profound theological mystery at the heart of 1 Cor 15:50–53. Our task in this chapter is to explore what Paul really said in this passage.

We begin with its structure, which as we will see is crucial for its interpretation. First Corinthians 15:50–53 is a very carefully structured unit.[3] As Rodolphe Morissette has shown, the passage is arranged in a concentric A B A' pattern, with v. 50 (A) and v. 53 (A') framing vv. 51–52 (B).[4] Moreover, as Morissette also shows, the central subunit within this structure, 15:51–52, evinces an internal chiastic structure of its own.[5] John Gillman follows Morissette's proposed structure, at the same time suggesting a modification of the internal chiasm in 15:51–52 as proposed by Morissette.[6] The chart below follows Morissette's proposed structure, together with Gillman's suggested modification.[7] I would also suggest an internal chiasm spanning v. 50 (A) and v. 53 (A'). In the outline below, the key

---

1. Paula Fredriksen, *Paul: The Pagans' Apostle* (New Haven: Yale University Press, 2017), 4.
2. Bruce D. Chilton, *Resurrection Logic: How Jesus' First Followers Believed God Raised Him from the Dead* (Waco: Baylor University Press, 2019), 76.
3. See Rodolphe Morissette, "La chair et le sang ne peuvent hériter du Règne de Dieu (I Cor., XV, 50)," *ScEs* 26 (1974): 41–43; John Gillman, "Transformation in 1 Cor 15.50–53," *ETL* 58 (1982): 309–22. For further discussion of the literary and rhetorical structure of the passage, see Duane F. Watson, "Paul's Rhetorical Strategy in 1 Corinthians 15," in *Rhetoric and the New Testament* (ed. Stanley E. Porter and Thomas H. Olbricht; JSNTSup 90; Sheffield: JSOT, 1993), 247; Michael Bünker, *Briefformular und rhetorische Disposition im 1 Korintherbrief* (Göttingen: Vandenhoeck & Ruprecht, 1983), 71–72; and Margaret M. Mitchell, *Paul and the Rhetoric of Reconciliation: An Exegetical Investigation of the Language and Composition of 1 Corinthians* (Louisville: Westminster John Knox, 1991), 290.
4. Morissette, "La chair et le sang," 42–43.
5. Morissette, "La chair et le sang," 43.
6. Gillman, "Transformation," 314–22.
7. Gillman's structural analysis is also followed by Jeffrey R. Asher, *Polarity and Change in*

linking features within the passage are put in italics. Verses 50–53 appear to have the following structure:

A  (50) And this I say, brothers and sisters, that
   a  *flesh and blood* is not able to inherit the kingdom of God,
   b  nor does *corruption* inherit incorruptibility.
B  (51–52) Behold, a mystery to you I tell!
   c  We will not all sleep, but we will all *be changed*;
   d  in a moment of time, in the blink of an eye, at the last *trumpet*.
   d'  For the *trumpet* will sound,
   c'  and the dead will be raised incorruptible, and we will *be changed*.
A' (53) For it is necessary that
   b'  *this corruptible body* be clothed with incorruptibility,
   a'  and *this mortal body* be clothed with immortality.

As Gillman points out, v. 50 and v. 53 correspond closely to one another. Both state a general principle, each employing synonymous parallelism, and each using present tense, third-person singular main verbs.[8] Verse 50 states the principle negatively, whereas v. 53 states it positively: οὐ δύναται ("is not able") in v. 50 corresponds to δεῖ ("it is necessary") in v. 53.[9] The middle portion, 15:51–52, contrasts with 15:50 and 15:53 in its use of future tense, first-person plural verbs, its distinction between the living and the dead, and its introduction of the concept of transformation.[10] There is a progression of thought from A (15:50) to A' (15:53), through the mystery revealed in B (15:51–52).[11] Within this progression of thought within 15:50–53, v. 50 presents the *plight* (οὐ δύναται), to which v. 53, in light of the mystery unveiled in vv. 51–52, provides the *solution* (δεῖ).

A grasp of the structure of 15:50–53 is crucial for its interpretation. For, as the structure of the passage reveals, vv. 50 and 53 are intimately related and mutually interpret one another. We cannot grasp the nature of the plight in v. 50 outside the context of the solution to the plight in v. 53. The problem with much scholarly interpretation of 1 Cor 15:50 is that many interpreters have sought to do just that. The result has been a widespread scholarly interpretation of v. 50 that is diametrically opposed to Paul's own meaning. As we now examine the plight of 15:50,

---

*1 Corinthians 15: A Study of Metaphysics, Rhetoric, and Resurrection* (Tübingen: Mohr Siebeck, 2000), 164–65 n. 42.

  8. Gillman, "Transformation," 320–21.
  9. Gillman, "Transformation," 320–21.
  10. Gillman, "Transformation," 321–22.
  11. Morissette, "La chair et le sang," 43; Gillman, "Transformation," 322.

## CHAPTER 14

within the context of Paul's carefully structured argument in 15:50–53, we will seek to uncover the true nature of that plight, its resolution through the mystery disclosed in 15:51–52, and its solution in 15:53.

## Verse 50

*And this I say, brothers and sisters, that flesh and blood is not able to inherit the kingdom of God, nor does corruption inherit incorruptibility.*

*And this I say, brothers and sisters.* A few scholars have argued that 15:50 belongs with the previous unit, 15:44b–49, and that 15:51 begins the new unit.[12] However, Paul's address τοῦτο δέ φημι, ἀδελφοί tells emphatically against this. For in the only other instance in Paul's letters (1 Cor 7:29, τοῦτο δέ φημι, ἀδελφοί), and in the analogous instance τί οὖν φημι in 1 Cor 10:19, this address functions to open rather than to close a unit of thought. It builds on the previous argument but also advances that argument with a new consideration.[13] That 15:50 introduces a new stage in the argument also coheres with the concentric structure of 15:50–53, in which (as we have seen) 15:53 provides the solution to the dilemma of 15:50.

We see, then, that the address τοῦτο δέ φημι, ἀδελφοί, as the great majority of interpreters have recognized, here "signals the beginning of a new textual unit" designed to "reiterate and amplify" what has already been said.[14] The expression τοῦτο δέ φημι, as a marker of emphasis, also adds additional weight to what follows.[15] Similarly, the addition of the vocative ἀδελφοί, the third of four instances in the chapter (15:1, 31, 50, 58), calls attention to the importance of what is about to be said. The thought introduced in vv. 50–53 involves the transformation that will take place in eschatological resurrection. To be sure, this marvelous change from φθορά "corruption" to ἀφθαρσία "incorruptibility" was foreshadowed in 9:24–26, depicted in the comparisons of 15:36–41, and set forth as an explicit and central motif in 15:42–49, especially 15:42 ("the body is sown in corruption, it is raised in incorruptibility"). What is new, however, in 15:50 is Paul's emphatic statement of

---

12. E.g., James D. G. Dunn, "How Are the Dead Raised? With What Body Do They Come? Reflections on 1 Corinthians 15," *SwJT* 45 (2002): 10–13.

13. Similarly λέγω δὲ τοῦτο in 1 Cor 1:12, τοῦτο δὲ λέγω in Gal 3:17, and λέγω δέ in Gal 4:1; 5:16.

14. Matt O'Reilly, *Paul and the Resurrected Body: Social Identity and Ethical Practice* (ESEC 22; Atlanta: SBL Press, 2020), 92; cf. Joachim Jeremias, "Flesh and Blood Cannot Inherit the Kingdom of God (1 Cor. XV.50)," *NTS* 2 (1956): 154–55; Fee, 887–88; Fitzmyer, 602–3.

15. Constantine R. Campbell, *Paul and the Hope of Glory: An Exegetical and Theological Study* (Grand Rapids: Zondervan Academic, 2020), 219; Ciampa & Rosner, 828; Schreiner, 323.

*The Mystery of the Glorification of the Flesh*

something implicit throughout the chapter but here made explicit for the first time: the *necessity* of this transformation.

*that flesh and blood is not able to inherit the kingdom of God.* Scholars routinely cite 1 Cor 15:50 as obvious evidence for Paul's exclusion of all that is fleshly and palpably material from eschatological salvation. Adela Yarbro Collins, for instance, writes: "The remark in verse 50, 'flesh and blood cannot inherit the kingdom of God, nor does the perishable inherit the imperishable,' implies that the resurrection 'body' is not material in the same way that the earthly body is."[16] Dale Martin asserts: "Paul himself believes that the resurrected body will not be composed of flesh (see v. 50)."[17] Similarly, Troels Engberg-Pedersen reasons: "But since flesh and blood cannot inherit the kingdom of God (see 15:50), this body of flesh and blood must also necessarily be changed away from (being made up of) flesh and blood."[18] For many scholars, it seems self-evident that the problem addressed in v. 50 is the body's palpable, physical nature, with the implicit solution being the replacement of the present body of flesh with a body composed of a spiritual pneumatic substance. Verse 50 is a commonly used "prooftext" that Paul, in contrast to the gospels and historic Christian teaching, neither believed that Jesus rose in the flesh nor in a future resurrection of the flesh. This understanding of resurrection in Paul seeks support, as we have seen, in other passages in the chapter as well (e.g., 15:44–45). But v. 50 is its holy grail. The astute reader of this commentary already knows how impossible such an interpretation of this verse is in the context of the rest of the chapter. But what, then, is Paul's point in this verse? We must explore the meaning of the crucial expression "flesh and blood" (σὰρξ καὶ αἷμα), and the reason why Paul asserts the impossibility of flesh and blood inheriting the kingdom of God.

---

16. Adela Yarbro Collins, "The Empty Tomb in the Gospel According to Mark," in *Hermes and Athena: Biblical Exegesis and Philosophical Theology* (ed. Eleonore Stump and Thomas P. Flint; Notre Dame: University of Notre Dame Press, 1993), 113.

17. Dale Martin, *The Corinthian Body* (New Haven: Yale University Press, 1995), 126.

18. Troels Engberg-Pedersen, "Complete and Incomplete Transformation in Paul—A Philosophical Reading of Paul on Body and Spirit," in *Metamorphoses: Resurrection, Body and Transformative Practices in Early Christianity* (ed. Turid Karlsen Seim and Jorunn Økland; Berlin: de Gruyter, 2009), 128; cf. also Engberg-Pedersen, *Cosmology and Self in the Apostle Paul: The Material Spirit* (Oxford: Oxford University Press, 2010), 32. See in the same vein Ernst Teichmann, *Die paulinische Vorstellungen von Auferstehung und Gericht und ihre Beziehungen zur jüdischen Apokalyptik* (Freiburg: Mohr, 1896), 51; Ellicott, 323; Paula Fredriksen, "Vile Bodies: Paul and Augustine on the Resurrection of the Flesh," in *Biblical Hermeneutics in Historical Perspective* (ed. Mark S. Burrows and Paul Rorem; Grand Rapids: Eerdmans, 1991), 81–82; Keener, 131.

CHAPTER 14

*Suggested Meanings of* σὰρξ καὶ αἷμα *in v. 50*

In view of its widespread use as a "prooftext" in scholarly discussion of Pauline theology, the scholarly literature devoted to 1 Cor 15:50 and to the expression σὰρξ καὶ αἷμα is surprisingly sparse, confined to a handful of articles, cursory discussions in the commentaries, and a few brief treatments in specialized studies.[19] All interpreters are agreed that σὰρξ καὶ αἷμα in v. 50 denotes some kind of lack or deficiency. But there are different views as to the meaning of this expression in v. 50, and the precise kind of lack or deficiency it denotes:

(1) The common but erroneous view discussed above assumes that σὰρξ καὶ αἷμα describes physical substances—the "stuff" of the human body. So Dale Martin: "Flesh and blood constitute ... part of the body. ... its corruptible and corrupting aspects."[20] On this interpretation, the deficiency that prohibits the entry of "flesh and blood" into the kingdom is the *coarse physicality* of these substances. Thus Paul J. Achtemeier understands v. 50 to say that "God is Spirit, and flesh and blood cannot survive in the presence of God"—hence the need (on this view) for the loss and destruction of the body of flesh and blood.[21]

The other scholarly interpretations of σὰρξ καὶ αἷμα in v. 50 reject the view that this expression denotes separate material substances of the body. They hold, by contrast, that the phrase constitutes a single unit or grammatical entity and refers to the whole embodied person. But they differ as to the aspect of the human person under consideration.

(2) Rodolphe Morissette argues for an ethical interpretation, in which "flesh and blood" refers to *sinful* humanity—the whole human person, whose lack or deficiency is the *proneness to evil*. According to Morissette, the phrase refers to "l'homme pécheur" ("man as sinner").[22]

---

19. See Jeremias, "Flesh and Blood," 151–52 (extremely brief discussion); Morissette, "La chair et le sang," 46–51, 55–57 (fullest treatment anywhere); Gillman, "Transformation," 318–19 (slightly fuller treatment than Jeremias); Andy Johnson, "On Removing a Trump Card: Flesh and Blood and the Reign of God," *BBR* 13 (2003): 175–92, esp. 180–82 (most full discussion in English); J. A. Schep, *The Nature of the Resurrection Body: A Study of the Biblical Data* (Grand Rapids: Eerdmans, 1964), 201–5; and Ronald Sider, "The Pauline Conception of the Resurrection Body in 1 Corinthians XV.35-54," *NTS* 21 (1975): 435–37.

20. Martin, *Body*, 128. For this interpretation, see also the scholars and studies enumerated in notes 16 and 18 above. See also Lindemann, 365 (considers the most likely view); Robertson & Plummer, 375; Gillman, "Transformation," 318–19, 332–33 (with reservations).

21. Paul J. Achtemeier, "The Continuing Quest for Coherence in St. Paul: An Experiment in Thought," in *Theology and Ethics in Paul and His Interpreters* (ed. Eugene H. Lovering Jr. and Jerry L. Sumney; Nashville: Abingdon, 1996), 138.

22. Morissette, "La chair et le sang," 50. Similarly Thiselton, 1291–92. This interpretation is found in many patristic writers; see e.g., Irenaeus, *Haer.* 5.9–10.

(3) Other interpreters claim that the chief connotation of the term is creaturely distance from God. On this view, the expression "flesh and blood" signifies *creaturely* humanity, the whole human being in his or her *contrast with God*. Thus, according to Andy Johnson, the phrase "has the rhetorical function of distinguishing what is merely human from what is divine."[23] Likewise Joachim Jeremias states that "it denotes the natural man as a frail creature in opposition to God."[24]

(4) The majority of scholars take a fourth view. On this interpretation, "flesh and blood" denotes *mortal* humanity—the whole embodied human being, with focus on his or her *corruptibility*. In this view, the deficiency or lack in view is humanity's perishability and mortality. So N. T. Wright: "'flesh and blood'" is a way of referring to ordinary, corruptible, decaying human existence ... subject to decay and death."[25] A number of scholars find a twofold force of the expression, in which σὰρξ καὶ αἷμα signifies both *creaturely* and *mortal* humanity—the whole physically embodied human being, with focus on human *corruptibility* and *contrast with God*. Thus, according to J. A. Schep, the expression refers to "the whole man ... as a frail and perishable creature, in contrast to the eternal and almighty God."[26] Likewise, for Christoph Burchard, "flesh and blood" denotes "den Menschen als vergängliches Wesen im Gegensatz zu seinem Schöpfer" ("the human person as a perishable being in contrast to his creator").[27]

We find, then, four proposed interpretations of the expression σὰρξ καὶ αἷμα in 1 Cor 15:50. The first (1) is an outlier in identifying "flesh and blood" in v. 50 with separate physical substances of the body and seeing the lack or deficiency in view as their tangible physicality. The other proposed interpretations all regard σὰρξ καὶ αἷμα as denoting the whole embodied person, but differ as to the lack or deficiency in view, whether that deficiency is (2) human sinfulness; (3) human creatureliness; or (4) human mortality. A number of interpreters regard the incapacity in view as both human mortality and human creatureliness.

Which of these interpretations fits the ancient meaning of σὰρξ καὶ αἷμα? We must examine the usage of this crucial phrase in antiquity.

---

23. Johnson, "Trump Card," 182.
24. Jeremias, "Flesh and Blood," 152.
25. N. T. Wright, *The Resurrection of the Son of God* (vol. 3 of *Christian Origins and the Question of God*; Minneapolis: Fortress, 2003), 359. So also Ben F. Meyer, "Did Paul's View of the Resurrection of the Dead Undergo Development?" *TS* 47 (1986): 381; Bernhard Spörlein, *Die Leugnung der Auferstehung: Eine historisch-kritische Untersuchung zu I Kor 15* (Regensburg: Pustet, 1971), 119–20; O'Reilly, *Resurrected Body*, 92; Hays, 274–75. Although the ethical interpretation (view 2 above) is perhaps the majority view among patristic authors, this interpretation is also found among them; cf. Theodoret, *Comm. 1 Cor.* 368: Σάρκα καὶ αἷμα τὴν θνητὴν φύσιν καλεῖ ("Paul calls our mortal nature 'flesh and blood'").
26. Schep, *Resurrection Body*, 202.
27. Christoph Burchard, "1 Korinther 15,39–41," *ZNW* 75 (1984): 249.

## CHAPTER 14

*The Usage of σὰρξ καὶ αἷμα in Antiquity outside 1 Corinthians 15:50*

There is limited use of this expression in antiquity. Jeremias and Johnson discuss only four occurrences of this phrase outside 1 Corinthians: Sir 14:17–18 and 17:30–32, Matt 16:17, and Gal 1:16. Johnson claims that: "Besides 1 Cor 15:50, there are only four other instances of the use of this exact idiom, σὰρξ καὶ αἷμα, in Greek literature prior to and including the first century."[28] However, the term also occurs in the Greek text of 1 En. 15.4 and, if we include a text that may date to the first century and most probably not later than AD 150, T. Ab. 13.7 as well. We must examine each of these.

Expounding upon the inescapability of death, Sir 14:18 affirms: "Like flourishing foliage on a thick tree, which drops some and puts forth others, so is the generation of flesh and blood [σαρκὸς καὶ αἵματος]; one dies, and another is born." Here σὰρξ καὶ αἷμα clearly refers to the whole person and has the mortal, perishable nature of humankind in view. Similarly, in Sir 17:30b–32 we read:

> For a son of man is not immortal. [31] What is more luminous than the sun? Even this fails; and flesh and blood [σὰρξ καὶ αἷμα] will ponder worthless thoughts. [32] He [God] numbers the host of the highest heaven; and all human beings are but dust and ashes.

The synonyms of the expression in Sir 17:30 (υἱὸς ἀνθρώπου) and 17:32 (ἄνθρωποι), and its use with a singular verb in 17:31, reveal that here again σὰρξ καὶ αἷμα is a single conception used with reference to the whole person. As in Sir 14:18, the emphasis is again on embodied humanity's mortal, corruptible nature (17:30, οὐκ ἀθάνατος "not immortal"; 17: 32, γῆ καὶ σποδός "dust and ashes"). The precise nature of the "worthless thoughts" (πονηρόν) that flesh and blood ponders in 17:31 is disputed. In any case, "flesh and blood" is set in contrast here not with God but with angels (17:32, δύναμιν ὕψους οὐρανοῦ "the host of the highest heaven").

In 1 En. 15.1–7, Enoch is divinely instructed to announce judgment upon angels who fell through sexual relations with human women. These angels "lusted, even as they [i.e., humans] do, after flesh and blood [σάρκα καὶ αἷμα], who die and perish" (1 En. 15.4). Here the masculine pronoun οἵτινες (15.4), and the synonymous terms οἱ ἄνθρωποι "human beings" in 15.2 and υἱοὶ τῆς γῆς "sons of the earth" in 15.3, show that by σὰρξ καὶ αἷμα whole persons are meant. In this text, "flesh and blood" clearly denotes embodied human beings in their mortality and corruptibility (15.4, οἵτινες ἀποθνῄσκουσιν καὶ ἀπόλλυνται "who *die* and *perish*"). They are

---

28. Johnson, "Trump Card," 180.

strongly contrasted with the angels, who are immortal (15.4, πνεύματα ζῶντα αἰώνια "spirits who live eternally"; cf. 15.6).

In Gal 1:16 ("I did not immediately consult with flesh and blood"), the context makes clear that σὰρξ καὶ αἷμα is a single entity and refers to the whole person— for only a person, not bodily substances, can be consulted. Here σὰρξ καὶ αἷμα refers to the human being (cf. ἄνθρωπος, 1:1, 11, 12) in contrast with God (ὁ θεός, 1:15–16). Similarly in Matt 16:17 ("flesh and blood did not reveal this to you, but my Father in the heavens"), σὰρξ καὶ αἷμα denotes a single entity, the whole embodied person. For the verb of which σὰρξ καὶ αἷμα is the subject is in the singular, and only persons, not bodily substances, can reveal something to someone. Here the expression sets human beings in contrast with "my Father in the heavens" (16:17, ὁ πατήρ μου ὁ ἐν τοῖς οὐρανοῖς). In T. Ab. 13.7 (Rec. B), Abraham says to the angel, "For I am altogether unworthy to draw near to you, for you are a high spirit [ὑπηλὸν πνεῦμα], but I am flesh and blood [σὰρξ καὶ αἷμα], and for this reason I am not able [οὐ δύναμαι] to bear your glory." In this passage, σὰρξ καὶ αἷμα refers to Abraham as a whole person and denotes his incapacity (οὐ δύναμαι) and inferiority in comparison with the glory of the angels.

What may we conclude from this study of the usage of the expression σὰρξ καὶ αἷμα in antiquity? First, in all these texts, as in 1 Cor 15:50, σὰρξ καὶ αἷμα is always used negatively, describing humanity as lacking or deficient in some way. Second, it is a *Jewish* idiom; all of its occurrences are in Jewish or early Christian texts.[29] This by itself excludes the interpretation (view one) that the deficiency in view in this term is embodied physicality, for in none of these Jewish texts surveyed is physical embodiment viewed in a negative light or as problematic. Third, in the instances in which the phrase is the grammatical subject, it has a singular verb, and in every instance "flesh and blood" is endowed with personal qualities, such as birth, thought, knowledge, consultation, and revelation. Thus, in this Jewish idiom, the two nouns form a *single* conception, denoting not substances of the body but the *whole embodied human person*.[30] We find our evidence here once again rules out view one, according to which this expression denotes individual substances of the body.

Fourth and finally, our texts describe the lack or deficiency inherent in the term as having two aspects, (1) human mortality or corruptibility (Sir 14:18; 17:31; 1 En. 15.4) and (2) humanity's inferiority to God (Matt 16:17; Gal 1:16) and to the angels (Sir 17:31;

---

29. Cf. Jeremias: it is a "Semitic word-pair" ("Flesh and Blood," 152); Johnson: "a Jewish idiom" ("Trump Card," 180); Fitzmyer, 603.

30. Cf. BDAG, s.v. "σάρξ" (3.a); Jeremias, "Flesh and Blood," 151–52; Schep, *Resurrection Body*, 201; Johnson, "Trump Card," 180; Wolff, 414.

1 En. 15.4; T. Ab. 13.7). Here again our evidence is not consistent with the claim that the deficiency in view is the body's material and physical nature (view one). Our texts also provide little or no support to the "ethical" interpretation that the incapacity involved is human sinfulness (view two). On the other hand, we find clear and abundant evidence to support view four, the interpretation of σάρξ καὶ αἷμα as denoting humanity in its perishability and mortality (Sir 14:18; 17:32; 1 En. 15.4). The consistent focus in our texts on human mortality reveals that view three, the interpretation of σάρξ καὶ αἷμα as denoting solely creaturely humanity, is inadequate. But from the fact that in some of our texts "flesh and blood" contrasts with God, one might conclude that our evidence supports the view of those scholars who see this idiom as denoting both mortal and creaturely humanity. But this conclusion would be overhasty, as this view requires modification. For our texts, as we have seen, not only contrast "flesh and blood" with God (Matt 16:17; Gal 1:16) but also with the angels (Sir 17:31; 1 En. 15.4; T. Ab. 13.7).[31] This indicates that the focus of the idiom is not on human creatureliness (for angels and human beings are both alike creatures) but on that which distinguishes human beings from both God and the angels—human mortality, frailty, weakness, and corruptibility. Therefore, σάρξ καὶ αἷμα would seem to denote *mortal* humanity—the whole embodied human being, with the deficiency in view being human *mortality*, which is *in contrast with God and the angels*.

We therefore see that the deficiency denoted by the expression "flesh and blood" is not, as so many scholars assume, human *physicality* (i.e., humanity's coarse material nature), but human *perishability*. To be sure, the expression σάρξ καὶ αἷμα refers to the whole human being, embodied in flesh and blood, and it is in their physical embodiment that humans are mortal and perishable. But the negative and deficient aspect of humanity expressed by this Jewish idiom is not physical embodiment per se, but instead human embodiment's liability to corruption and decay. In contrast with God and his angels, who are ever living and immortal, human beings are mortal and corruptible.

The force of the idiom σάρξ καὶ αἷμα "flesh and blood" is further clarified by its contrast in antiquity with the expression σάρξ καὶ ὀστέα "flesh and bones." We find σάρξ καὶ ὀστέα and related expressions, in both Jewish and Hellenistic contexts, used with reference to the physical, bodily aspect of human beings (Luke 24:39; Job 2:5 LXX; Homer, *Od.* 11.219; Aristotle, *Cael.* 278a33; 300b29; *Metaph.* 1034a6–7) or to whole human beings in their physical, bodily aspect (LXX Gen 2:23; 29:14; Judg 9:2; 2 Kgdms 5:1; 19:13–14; 1 Chr 11:1; cf. Ezek 37:1–14). Within the

---

31. So, rightly, BDAG, s.v. "σάρξ" (3.a): "a *human being* in contrast to God and other transcendent beings." Cf. Cremer, 854: "what man is in his nature as distinct from God and all other non-terrestrial beings."

*The Mystery of the Glorification of the Flesh*

Jewish context and the Bible, this idiom is always used *positively*, never negatively (e.g., Judg 9:2 LXX; 2 Kgdms 5:1 LXX). For example, the risen Jesus says to the disciples in Luke's Gospel, "Touch me and see, because a spirit does not have flesh and bones [σάρκα καὶ ὀστέα] as you see that I have" (Luke 24:39). By contrast, the expression σὰρξ καὶ αἷμα, as we have seen, always bears a *negative* connotation of lack or deficiency, denoting human beings in their liability to corruption and decay in contrast with God and his heavenly hosts. It is highly significant, then, that Paul in 1 Cor 15:50 chooses the term "flesh and blood" and not the term "flesh and bones." For in Paul's Jewish context, "flesh and bones" is a positive term that denotes human beings in their *physicality*; "flesh and blood" is a negative expression that denotes human beings in their *mortality*. In light of the usage of σὰρξ καὶ αἷμα in antiquity, the plight or deficiency envisioned by this term is emphatically *not* humanity's embodiment in flesh but the fleshly body's bondage to corruption.

*The Meaning of σὰρξ καὶ αἷμα in Verse 50*

As we turn to v. 50, we find that the usage of σὰρξ καὶ αἷμα in this verse reflects the usage of this idiom we have traced throughout antiquity. First, the word pair expresses a *single* conception, as evident from Paul's use of a *singular* verb (δύναται).[32] The idiom here thus cannot refer to individual bodily substances (as commonly supposed) but must denote the *whole embodied human being*. Second, that the expression denotes the whole person is also clear from the fact that σὰρξ καὶ αἷμα is the subject of κληρονομῆσαι "to inherit"—and only persons can inherit. Paul is not referring to physical substances but to the whole physically embodied person. Third, we also find here expressed, as in the other texts we examined, the *deficiency* or *incapacity* of the human being (οὐ δύναται). What is this deficiency or incapacity? In our study of the usage of σὰρξ καὶ αἷμα in antiquity, we found that term regularly denoted human persons in their mortality and corruptibility. We find this clearly the case here in v. 50 as well. The key lies in the structure of the passage (see the diagram and discussion in the introduction to the present chapter). The following considerations are decisive that the plight envisioned in v. 50 is not human *physicality*, but human *mortality*:

(1) As the majority of scholars have recognized, v. 50 employs synonymous parallelism, stating the same thought in two different ways.[33] Within this paral-

---

32. Virtually all expositors are agreed that the singular δύναται (supported by ℵ and B along with Clement and Origen) is the original reading, and that the plural δύνανται (supported by A C D and Irenaeus) reflects a change by later copyists.

33. See Gillman, "Transformation," 316; Wolff, 414; Ciampa & Rosner, 828; Collins, 579; Fee,

lelism, σάρξ καὶ αἷμα is synonymous with φθορά "corruption." The parallelism may be illustrated thus:

a *flesh and blood* is not able to inherit the kingdom of God
b nor does *corruption* inherit incorruptibility.

Paul's synonymous parallelism in 15:50 identifies σάρξ καὶ αἷμα in 15:50a with φθορά in 15:50b. The structure of the verse therefore indicates that "flesh and blood" denotes human beings in their mortality and corruptibility. The plight envisioned is thus not humanity's physical nature but the *corruptibility* of that physical nature.

(2) Moreover, within the unit 15:50–53, as we have seen, 15:50 and 15:53 are parallel to one another, and form a chiastic structure:

(50) A *flesh and blood* is not able to inherit the kingdom of God,
     B nor does *corruption* inherit incorruptibility;
(53)    B' *this corruptible body* must be clothed with incorruptibility,
   A' and *this mortal body* be clothed with immortality.

In this chiastic structure, σάρξ καὶ αἷμα in 15:50 corresponds to τὸ θνητὸν τοῦτο ("this mortal body") in 15:53. This shows once again that σάρξ καὶ αἷμα in 15:50 refers to humanity in its mortal nature. The deficiency in view is thus not human physicality but instead human mortality and impermanence.

(3) In the overall structure of Paul's argument in 15:50–53, as we have seen, 15:50 states the plight (οὐ δύναται) to which 15:53 provides the solution (δεῖ). Solution corresponds to plight, and the solution to the dilemma of 15:50 is not the annihilation of the body, but that "this corruptible body be clothed with incorruptibility, and this mortal body be clothed with immortality" (15:53). The human plight envisioned in v. 50 is, consequently, not human embodiment and physicality but physical humanity's bondage to corruption and decay. In the flow of Paul's argument in vv. 50–53, "flesh and blood" does not express a *plus* (physical embodiment) that requires a subtraction (the sloughing off of the body), but a *minus* (the mortality of embodied humanity) that requires an addition (the divine gift of incorruptibility and immortality). The insufficiency envisioned is not the possession of a *body*; it is having a *mortal* body. "Flesh and blood" in v. 50, then, does not refer to humanity's

---

883–84; Fitzmyer, 603. A few scholars follow Joachim Jeremias in regarding the parallelism as synthetic, referring to the living and the dead respectively ("Flesh and Blood," 151–52); so Sider, "Resurrection Body," 436; Meyer, "Development," 379; Johnson, "Trump Card," 185–86; Barrett, 379.

material makeup, the substance of flesh, but rather refers to the mortal nature of fleshly humanity in its perishability and bondage to decay.

(4) Another crucial contextual factor, generally ignored by expositors, confirms these findings. Within chapter 15, v. 50 picks up and completes the thought of v. 39. In v. 39, we recall, Paul's statement that "not all flesh is the same flesh" (οὐ πᾶσα σὰρξ ἡ αὐτὴ σάρξ) contrasted the present corruptible flesh with the incorruptible flesh to be given in the resurrection. Verse 39 argues that the creator's power to fashion an appropriate kind of flesh for each type of creature reveals his power, in the resurrection, to transform the present perishable flesh into immortal, glorified flesh. Verse 39 shows that just as Paul's argument in 1 Cor 15 clearly affirms the resurrection of the *body*, it just as clearly affirms the resurrection of the *flesh*.[34] Verses 39 and 50 are closely tied together as the only two references to σάρξ within the chapter (v. 39, σάρξ [4×]; v. 50, σάρξ καὶ αἷμα). The two verses are mutually interpretive and must be read in concert. In v. 50, the expression σάρξ καὶ αἷμα corresponds to the present corruptible σάρξ of v. 39. The implication of v. 39 is that this present perishable flesh is inadequate to inherit the kingdom, and this is made explicit in v. 50. Both v. 39 and v. 50 affirm the glorification of the flesh, but v. 39 focuses on the creator's *power* to bring about this glorification, whereas v. 50 affirms the *necessity* of this glorification. Clearly, in light of v. 39, v. 50 does not express the necessity of the flesh's destruction but rather the necessity of its transformation to incorruptibility in the resurrection.

To sum up our study of σάρξ καὶ αἷμα thus far: our findings regarding the ancient usage of this word pair outside 1 Cor 15, and in its context within 1 Cor 15:50–53, emphatically rule out the view, accepted uncritically and unreflectively by so many scholars, that the human predicament Paul identifies in v. 50 is human physicality, the possession of bodies of flesh and bone. In its ancient usage, and in the context of 1 Cor 15, σάρξ καὶ αἷμα denotes *mortal* humanity—the whole embodied person in his or her *mortality* and *in contrast with God and his heavenly hosts*. The deficiency or incapacity that prohibits flesh and blood from inheriting the kingdom is not bodily physicality, but bodily mortality and perishability.

But there is more that must be said about the function of this key term in the context of v. 50.

*"Flesh and Blood" and Inheritance of the Kingdom*

Mortal human beings, Paul declares in v. 50, are not able to inherit the kingdom of God. Paul's use of present tense verbs in 15:50 (δύναται, κληρονομεῖ) indicates

---

34. For fuller discussion, see the commentary on v. 39.

that here a general law or principle is being stated.[35] The reference to inheriting God's kingdom recalls the twofold reference to inheriting the kingdom of God in 6:9–10 and the description of that kingdom in 15:24–25. Paul is speaking of the consummation of the kingdom at the second coming of Christ. The general law Paul states is the incapacity (οὐ δύναται) of humanity in its present mortal state to inherit the eschatological kingdom. Hence the necessity of the change from corruption to immortality, which Paul will vividly describe in 15:51–53.

Paul's use of the verb κληρονομέω "inherit," is theologically significant. Inheritance implies a *filial* relationship, that is, adoption as God's children. It is the *children* of God who are the *heirs* of God's kingdom (Rom 8:17, εἰ δὲ τέκνα, καὶ κληρονόμοι; Gal 4:7, εἰ δὲ υἱός, καὶ κληρονόμος διὰ θεοῦ). In Romans, it is the full gift of the Spirit of God's Son, of which believers now have only the firstfruits (Rom 8:23a; cf. 8:9, 15), which brings about "our adoption, the redemption of our body" (Rom 8:23b). In that letter, the resurrection is the full adoption as children of God (Rom 8:23) in conformity with the image of God's Son (Rom 8:29).

The thought here in 1 Cor 15:50 is the same. Inheritance requires the fullness of adoption. Although they are even now temples of the Holy Spirit (3:16; 6:19), the faithful, if they are to inherit God's kingdom, must through the full gift of the Spirit of God's Son (15:44–45) receive physical conformity to the likeness of God's Son in the resurrection (15:49; cf. Phil 3:21). Paul in 2 Thess 2:14 calls this "obtaining the glory [δόξης] of our Lord Jesus Christ." In 2 Thess 2:14, δόξα "glory" refers to the full radiant manifestation of the presence of the Lord that will be communicated to the body in the resurrection. Full adoption is bodily glorification. The necessity of this glorification for entering the kingdom is reflected in Paul's collocation of "kingdom" and "glory" in 1 Thess 2:12, where he speaks of God calling the Thessalonians "into his own *kingdom* and *glory*" (εἰς τὴν ἑαυτοῦ βασιλείαν καὶ δόξαν). The *necessity* of this bodily glorification for entrance into the kingdom of God is Paul's precise point in 1 Cor 15:50.

Here again we see the aptness of Paul's choice of the idiom σὰρξ καὶ αἷμα in v. 50. For, as we saw, that word pair elsewhere describes mortal humanity in its distance from the life of *God* (Matt 16:17; Gal 1:16). That contrast or distance is reflected in Paul's choice of word order, in which σὰρξ καὶ αἷμα ("flesh and blood") and βασιλεία θεοῦ ("kingdom of God") are juxtaposed, thus contrasting "flesh and blood" and "God" (ὅτι σὰρξ καὶ αἷμα βασιλείαν θεοῦ κληρονομῆσαι οὐ δύναται). The idiom σὰρξ καὶ αἷμα is therefore the *converse* of the full adoption as God's children in the resurrection. It is thus the fitting term to express the *necessity* of this adoption through the glorification of the flesh.

---

35. Gillman, "Transformation," 312; Lindemann, 365.

## The Mystery of the Glorification of the Flesh

There is another factor that further illumines Paul's specific choice of the idiom σὰρξ καὶ αἷμα in v. 50. For this idiom, as we have seen, frequently contrasts human beings in their mortality with the imperishable *angels* (Sir 17:31; 1 En. 15.4; T. Ab. 13.7). In Jesus's teaching in the gospels, and elsewhere in ancient Christian literature, we find the conception that, in becoming immortal and imperishable through the glorification of their bodies in the resurrection, the faithful thereby become equal or even superior to the angels (Luke 20:34–36; Mark 12:25; Matt 22:30; Herm. Vis. 2.2.7; 9.25.2; 9.27.2; Mart. Pol. 2.3; Irenaeus, *Haer.* 5.35.1; Mart. Ascen. Isa. 8.14–15; cf. 2 Bar. 51.5–12). Strikingly, we also find within 1 Corinthians passages that clearly reflect the equality or superiority of the risen saints to the angels (6:3, "Do you not know that we will judge angels?") or may imply this (4:9; 13:1). Paul's use here of the idiom σὰρξ καὶ αἷμα, which contrasts human beings with the angels, and which thus points to the necessity of the coming transformation to imperishability whereby the saints become equal to the angels (15:51–53), fits well within this framework.

In Jesus's teaching in the canonical gospels, we find a threefold conception in regard to the resurrection. Those who rise from the dead (1) are made immortal; (2) become children of God; and (3) are equal to the angels:

> For they are *unable to die* any longer, for they are *equal to the angels*, and are *children of God*, being children of the resurrection. (Luke 20:36)

The idiom σὰρξ καὶ αἷμα, in denoting *mortal* humanity in its *contrast with God and the angels*, perfectly expresses the present *converse* of this future threefold inheritance of immortality, full adoption as God's children, and equality to the angels that will take place through the glorification of the flesh in the resurrection to come. It thus most fitly points to the *necessity* of the mysterious transformation that will bring this about (15:51–53).

*nor does corruption inherit incorruptibility.* As we have seen, v. 50 states a general principle, the two halves of the verse united by synonymous parallelism. Paul now provides the second half, synonymous in meaning with the first, of the general law or principle he states in v. 50. The noun φθορά denotes not merely the destruction of something (as does ἀπώλεια), but the corruption of its essential nature proceeding from causes intrinsic to the subject itself.[36] Since it is the subject of κληρονομέω "inherit," and only persons can be inheritors, this abstract noun functions as the abstract for the concrete, referring to human beings. It refers here,

---

36. Schmidt, *Syn.*, 4:86–91 (§158.3–6).

## CHAPTER 14

like its synonymous parallel σὰρξ καὶ αἷμα, to *corruptible* human beings, both (as Paul will make clear in vv. 51–52) the living and the dead. Paul can apply the term φθορά "corruption," as he does here, not only to the dead but also to the living, for the living are in the process of corruption.[37] The use of the abstract substantive φθορά with reference to human beings may sound odd—until we remember the analogous use of "dust" in Gen 3:19 ("You are dust" ), the passage echoed by Paul in the immediately preceding verses (15:47–49). We find the analogous use of "dust and ashes" with reference to human beings in many other passages of the Old Testament (e.g., Gen 18:27 LXX, ἐγὼ δέ εἰμι γῆ καὶ σποδός "But I am dust and ashes"; Sir 17:32, οἱ ἄνθρωποι πάντες γῆ καὶ σποδός "All human beings are dust and ashes"; cf. Job 42:6 LXX). Precisely as with φθορά in 15:50, the designation "dust and ashes" in these LXX passages is applied not only to the dead but also prospectively to the living, as those doomed to become but dust and ashes.

Within the parallelism of v. 50, the word ἡ ἀφθαρσία "incorruptibility" is in synonymous relation to βασιλεία θεοῦ ("kingdom of God") earlier in the verse, and it therefore refers to the kingdom of God, describing it as incorruptible. In the book of Daniel, the kingdom of God is described as incorruptible (Dan 2:44 LXX, καὶ οὐ φθαρήσεται "and it shall not be corrupted"; 7:14, ἥτις οὐ μὴ φθαρῇ "which shall surely never be corrupted"). In Romans, the inheritance of the saints is the whole renewed creation, which will be set free from its bondage to φθορά (Rom 8:17–21; cf. 1 Pet 1:4, κληρονομία ἄφθαρτος). The abstract substantive ἡ ἀφθαρσία in 15:50 thus refers to the renewed creation, which will be made incorruptible. In order to inherit the renewed creation, which is imperishable, the bodies of the saints must likewise be made incorruptible. This theme of the change from corruption to incorruption, foreshadowed in 9:24–26, was first struck in the chapter in v. 42—σπείρεται ἐν φθορᾷ, ἐγείρεται ἐν ἀφθαρσίᾳ ("the body is sown in corruption, it is raised in incorruptibility"). There the focus was on the *reality* of this coming change; here in v. 50 the focus is on its *necessity*. This theme of the change from corruption to imperishability, and its necessity, will dominate the verses that follow (15:51–53).

Let us step back, as we close our discussion of 15:50, to survey the larger picture. The common scholarly misuse of this verse not only drastically misconstrues the physical, flesh-and-bones nature of the resurrection in Paul's thought. It also entirely misses the deepest theological dimension of Paul's understanding of the resurrection. On this common misreading of v. 50, what Paul calls the "resurrection" requires a diminishment of humanity, the loss of the physical body. On this

---

37. Cf. 2 Cor 4:16, ὁ ἔξω ἡμῶν ἄνθρωπος φθείρεται "our outer person is in the process of being corrupted"; Eph 4:22, τὸν παλαιὸν ἄνθρωπον τὸν φθειρόμενον "our old person who is in the process of being corrupted."

reading, the body of flesh and bones is an impediment that must be discarded or, as Dale Martin puts it, "shed . . . like so much detritus," if human beings are to enter everlasting life.[38] Such an understanding would befit a body-self dualism, such as we find in Plato, but within Paul's Jewish and biblical understanding of the person as a composite being of soul and body, it is truly an oxymoron. According to what Paul really says in v. 50, the impediment to everlasting life is not the body's physicality but the physical body's perishability and mortality. But the Son of God's incarnation, death, and resurrection brought something entirely new into the world: the divine and imperishable life of God. What is necessary, says Paul in v. 50, is the full gift of the Son's incorruptible divine life, given to the physical body in the resurrection (15:22, 42–49, 51–54). In this way, human beings will be given to share, even in their bodies, in the very being and life of God. First Corinthians 15:50 is not about the present body's destruction but instead its transformation, enhancement, and glorification. In the resurrection, the humanity of those united to Christ will be granted to share in the Son of God's divine nature, not only in the soul but also in the body. It will be the consummation of union with Christ. "Enter into the joy of your Lord" (Matt 25:21). In excluding from the kingdom mortality and bodily death, this verse proclaims a kingdom in which the flesh, too, shares in everlasting life, through its participation in the radiant presence and imperishable life of the divine Son of God.

VERSE 51

*Behold, a mystery to you I tell! We will not all sleep, but we will all be changed;*

*Behold, a mystery to you I tell!* The particle ἰδού, which occurs only here within the letter, adds force and vigor to Paul's pronouncement. The stress, as the word order shows, is on μυστήριον "mystery." Paul uses μυστήριον here in the Jewish sense of a secret or enigma once concealed but now revealed by God—but which, since it is divine, nonetheless retains a certain mysterious, wondrous character.[39]

38. Martin, *Body*, 128.
39. Raymond Brown, *The Semitic Background of the Term "Mystery" in the New Testament* (Philadelphia: Fortress, 1968); Birger Pearson, "Mystery and Secrecy in Paul," in *Mystery and Secrecy in the Nag Hammadi Collection and Other Ancient Literature: Ideas and Practices* (ed. C. H. Bull, L. I. Lied, and J. D. Turner; Leiden: Brill, 2012), 287–302; Richard N. Longenecker, "Is There Development in Paul's Resurrection Thought?" in *Life in the Face of Death: The Resurrection Message of the New Testament* (ed. Richard N. Longenecker; Grand Rapids: Eerdmans, 1998), 189; Fee, 885; Schreiner, 324.

## CHAPTER 14

In 2:6–16 Paul described his teaching for the mature in Christ as the wisdom of God hidden in a mystery (2:6–7), and in 4:1 he described himself and his fellow apostles as stewards of the mysteries of God. By opening his exposition of the resurrection in chapter 15 with the word γνωρίζω (15:1)—a term used in the LXX, especially in Daniel, to introduce divine revelation—Paul announced his intention to enact, throughout this chapter, this apostolic function of expounding the divine mysteries. He now brings this unfolding of divine mysteries in chapter 15 to a climax through the further unveiling of a particular mystery, one not fully known to the Corinthians previously, in 15:51–52.[40] This mystery is thus a part of the hidden wisdom Paul discussed in 2:6–9. And yet this revelation is not an esoteric doctrine different from the message of the crucified and risen Christ; it is a further unfolding of the good news of the resurrection that Paul proclaimed to the Corinthians from the very first (15:1–11). "The concept of the hidden does not lead in the NT to esotericism. It leads to world mission."[41]

*We will not all sleep.* Sleep is a frequent metaphor for death in the New Testament (Matt 9:24; 27:52; Mark 5:39; Luke 8:52; John 11:11; Acts 7:60; 13:36; 1 Cor 7:39; 11:30; 15:6, 18, 20; 1 Thess 4:13–15; 5:10; 2 Pet 3:4). It is used of the body, without motion and without consciousness in death. In its portrayal of physical death as only a temporary sleep, it forms part of the New Testament's vocabulary of bodily resurrection.[42] Paul here shifts the placement of the negative οὐ (hyperbaton); according to normal Greek word order, the clause would mean "none of us will sleep."[43] Some ancient copyists (ℵ C D 33 1739) sought to alleviate the difficulty by shifting the negation to the following clause (i.e., "we will all sleep, but we will not all be changed"). Codex Claromontanus (D) also changed κοιμηθησόμεθα ("we will sleep") to ἀναστησόμεθα ("we will rise"). But the original reading, as modern textual critics are agreed, is preserved in B, in D², and in the Byzantine textual tradition.[44] Paul's use of the rhetorical device of hyperbaton in this clause is apparently for the sake of parallelism with the following clause.[45] Through this shift in word order, the two clauses match closely, effectively bringing out the contrast between οὐ "not" in the first clause and δέ "but" in the second, and the contrast between the verbs "sleep" and "change." Earlier in the chapter, Paul proclaimed the risen Christ

---

40. Cf. Markus Bockmuehl, *Revelation and Mystery in Ancient Judaism and Pauline Christianity* (WUNT 2.36; Tübingen: Mohr Siebeck, 1990), 172–73.
41. Pearson, "Mystery," 301, citing Rudolf Meyer.
42. For much fuller discussion, see the commentary on v. 18.
43. BDR §477 n. 2; Rob., *Gram.*, 423.
44. Cf. Schrage, 370.
45. BDR §433 n. 3; Robertson & Plummer, 376.

*The Mystery of the Glorification of the Flesh*

as "the firstfruits of those who sleep" (15:20). Paul's statement here that "we will not all sleep" is not a contradiction of v. 20 but a qualification. Nor is this a new revelation, for it is entirely congruent with the ancient apostolic and pre-Pauline confession of the coming of Christ to judge "the living and the dead" (cf. Acts 10:42; Rom 14:9; 2 Tim 4:1; 1 Pet 4:5). What Paul here provides is a deepened revelation of this mystery, with focus on the following clause.

*but we will all be changed.* The "we" implicit in the verb here (different from the ἡμεῖς in 15:52) includes all who are in Christ, both the living and the dead.[46] Paul's language of "change" is significant, and it has not been fully appreciated by those scholars who imagine that resurrection in Paul involves the abandonment or destruction of the present body of flesh and blood. For *x* to *change*, *x* must *continue to exist*. The language of "change" implies the continued existence of that which is changed; its quality is altered, but the subject of the change remains the same. Paul's language of "change" makes no sense unless the resurrection of which he is speaking is a resurrection of the flesh.[47]

---

46. Rightly Schrage, 372 n. 1856; Wolff, 415; and most expositors.

47. Perhaps not surprisingly, among the proponents of an ethereal resurrection body in Paul, it is the philosophically trained Troels Engberg-Pedersen who has grasped most perceptively the challenge that Paul's language of "change" presents to this interpretation. By way of solution, Engberg-Pedersen proposes that Paul here invokes the specialized Aristotelian concept of *substantive change*; see Engberg-Pedersen, *Cosmology and Self*, 32; cf. 220–21 n. 84. This technical philosophical conception involves a unique kind of "change" whereby someone or something passes into or out of existence, comes into being or ceases to be, or undergoes a simultaneous process of destruction and generation that produces an entirely new entity; see Aristotle, *Cat.* 15a13–15b16; *Phys.* 224a21–225a19; *Gen. corr.* 317a32–320a8. This conception of "substantive change" contrasts with Aristotle's notion of *qualitative change* (ἀλλοίωσις), which reflects the general nonphilosophical use of the vocabulary of "change" in antiquity. In qualitative change, the substance or essence of an entity remains intact, but the entity changes in its qualities, properties, or mode of existence (see Aristotle, *Phys.* 244b1–245a12; *Cael.* 270a13–35; *Cat.* 15a13–15b16; *Metaph.* 1042a32–1042b8). Engberg-Pedersen proposes that Paul uses "change" in the specialized sense of substantive change, to denote the "passing-away" of the body composed of flesh and the "coming-to-be" of the body composed of *pneuma* in Engberg-Pedersen, "Transformation," 128. This interpretation is not convincing. The verb Paul uses for "change" (ἀλλάσσω) is unrelated to Aristotle's vocabulary for substantive change, but closely related to Aristotle's term for qualitative change (ἀλλοιόω). Moreover, the common signification of "change" in antiquity, in agreement with the philosophical concept of qualitative change, implies the continued existence of the substance that is changed. Engberg-Pedersen's claim that Paul uses "change" in a technical sense of Aristotelian philosophy that is contrary to the normal meaning of the term, with no indication that he is doing so, is most improbable and has the air of an ad hoc expedient. Finally, Paul in the following verses will explicitly define this change as a change in quality—from corruption to incorruption, and from mortality to immortality (15:52–53).

CHAPTER 14

The mysterious change of which Paul speaks, as the rest of the chapter has shown, is the glorification of the flesh through the body's participation in the Son of God's divine nature, and thus in his imperishable life. It is the change from corruptibility to incorruptibility (cf. 15:42, σπείρεται ἐν φθορᾷ, ἐγείρεται ἐν ἀφθαρσίᾳ). The source of this change is expressed in Paul's choice of the passive voice, which, as many scholars have recognized, is a so-called divine passive, in which the implicit agent of the action is God (cf. 6:14).[48] More precisely, the one who will effect this ineffable change is the Lord Jesus Christ, "who will transform [μετασχηματίσει] our lowly bodies, to be conformed to the body of his glory, by the power through which he is able also to subject to himself all things" (Phil 3:21).[49] Here, as throughout vv. 51–52, the use of the "divine passive" with Christ as the understood agent powerfully underscores Paul's divine and incarnational Christology.[50] Not only is Christ the one who will effect this change or transformation, but as we have learned in 15:49, it is his image into which the faithful will be transformed (cf. 2 Cor 3:18, τὴν αὐτὴν εἰκόνα μεταμορφούμεθα ἀπὸ δόξης εἰς δόξαν). This change will bring about the full gift of the Holy Spirit to the physical body (15:44, σῶμα πνευματικόν). It will enable the human body to share in the divine life of God (15:45). And it will be the completion of the process of moral conformity to the image of the Son, through complete physical conformity to the body of Christ in its glory and incorruptibility (15:49).

## Verse 52

*in a moment of time, in the blink of an eye, at the last trumpet. For the trumpet will sound, and the dead will be raised incorruptible, and we will be changed.*

The change will be sudden, immediate, and instantaneous, taking place at the second coming of Christ.

*in a moment of time, in the blink of an eye.* Employing a word denoting anything indivisible, and here referring to an indivisible unit of time, the expression ἐν ἀτόμῳ indicates "in a moment of time" (cf. Aristotle, *Phys.* 236a6, ἐν ἀτόμῳ; Symmachus Isa 54:8, ἐν ἀτόμῳ ὀργῆς). The noun ῥιπή signifies any type of rapid movement,

---

48. So Wolff, 415; Fitzmyer, 604.
49. Cf. Schrage, 371 n. 1851; Gillman, "Transformation," 323; Fitzmyer, 604.
50. For further discussion of Paul's divine Christology within 1 Cor 15, see especially chapters 8 and 13 of this commentary.

such as the "cast" of a stone or the "rush" of wind.[51] In this case it refers to the quick movement of the eye, a usage not found in ancient literature prior to Paul (but cf. T. Ab. 4.5 [Rec. A], ἐν ῥιπῇ ὀφθαλμοῦ). Interpreters sometimes think of the "glance" or "twinkling" of an eye, but Gregory of Nyssa and John Chrysostom are surely correct when they inform us that the expression refers to the "blink" of the eyelids.[52] By means of these expressions, Paul highlights the sudden and instantaneous nature of the change.

*at the last trumpet. For the trumpet will sound.* As we saw earlier, 15:50–53 forms a concentric structure (A 15:50; B 15:51–52; A' 15:53). The central unit (B 15:51–52) forms a chiasm, in the heart of which is Paul's twofold reference to the last trumpet:

A  We will not all sleep, but we will all *be changed*;
B  in a moment of time, in the blink of an eye, at the last *trumpet.*
B'  For the *trumpet* will sound,
A'  and the dead will be raised incorruptible, and we will *be changed.*

Here the noun σάλπιγξ "trumpet" refers to the sound or blast of the trumpet.[53] The preposition ἐν is temporal, denoting the time when the trumpet sounds.[54]

The source of Paul's reference to an eschatological trumpet is almost certainly the saying of Jesus preserved in Matt 24:31.[55] In this logion of the Lord, the sound of "a great trumpet" is the summons or signal for the ingathering of God's people at the advent of the Son of Man (Matt 24:31, ἐπισυνάξουσιν τοὺς ἐκλεκτοὺς αὐτοῦ). Jesus's saying in turn echoes Isa 27:13, where a "great trumpet" is the signal for the ingathering of Israel in the time of the new exodus.[56] This logion of Jesus provides the clue to the function of the trumpet in 1 Cor 15:52. In v. 52, as in Matt 24:31, the sound of the trumpet functions to summon or signal the gathering together of the people of God, both the living and the dead, to Christ at his return.[57]

---

51. See LSJ, s.v. "ῥιπή"; BDAG, s.v. "ῥιπή."
52. Gregory of Nyssa, *In sanctum pascha* 9.52: ῥιπὴ δὲ ὀφθαλμοῦ ἐπίμυσις βλεφάρων ἐστί; John Chrysostom, *Hom. 1 Cor.* 42.3.
53. See BDAG, s.v. "σάλπιγξ" (2).
54. Rob., *Gram.*, 587.
55. See David Wenham, *Paul: Follower of Jesus or Founder of Christianity?* (Grand Rapids: Eerdmans, 1995), 331–32.
56. On the trumpet as the signal for Israel's ingathering in the Old Testament, see James A. Borland, "The Meaning and Identification of God's Eschatological Trumpets," in *Looking into the Future: Evangelical Studies in Eschatology* (ed. David W. Baker; Grand Rapids: Baker Academic, 2001), 67.
57. Cf. Aquinas, *1 Cor.* 1008.

## CHAPTER 14

The concept of the ingathering of the people of God implicit in Paul's mention of the trumpet relates to two important aspects of the resurrection. The first aspect is the *theocentric* nature of this hope as the culmination of union with God: this ingathering is ingathering to *Christ* (cf. 1 Thess 4:16–17).[58] The second aspect is the *social* dimension of the resurrection as the joyous and triumphant union and gathering of God's people (cf. 15:51, πάντες δὲ ἀλλαγησόμεθα "*we* will *all* be changed").

Paul's characterization of the trumpet as "the *last* trumpet" (ἡ ἐσχάτη σάλπιγξ) picks up Paul's earlier description of death as "the *last* enemy" (15:26, ὁ ἔσχατος ἐχθρός). For the union of the faithful with the Son of God and with one another is only possible through the defeat of God's enemy: death. The last trumpet will thus herald the moment of God's final triumph—the triumph over death. This victory of God over death will be Paul's focus in the words that follow, as the chapter now begins to swell to its grand conclusion.

*and the dead will be raised incorruptible.* As we saw in the commentary on v. 4, the verb ἐγείρω, when used with reference to the dead, unambiguously denotes the return of the dead body to physical life. The substantive νεκρός, translated here as "the dead," differs from the English term in regularly denoting the dead in their *bodily* aspect, being most nearly equivalent to our "corpse."[59] The conjunction of verb and substantive here (οἱ νεκροὶ ἐγερθήσονται) renders the normal sense of νεκρός as "corpse" noncancelable, and the whole phrase thus denotes, emphatically and without ambiguity, the return to life of the dead in their bodies of flesh and bones. The expression here recalls its several prior occurrences in the chapter: νεκροὶ οὐκ ἐγείρονται in 15:15–16, 29, and 32, and πῶς ἐγείρονται οἱ νεκροί in 15:35. In each of these previous instances, the expression had reference to what some at Corinth denied: νεκροὶ οὐκ ἐγείρονται ("the dead are *not* raised"). Now, in this final and climactic use of this crucial expression within the chapter, Paul triumphantly and climactically *affirms* what the self-professed wise at Corinth *denied*: οἱ νεκροὶ ἐγερθήσονται ("the dead will be raised"). Paul has so structured the chapter, which begins with the denial of the resurrection (15:15, νεκροὶ οὐκ ἐγείρονται "the dead are not raised"), that it concludes with a powerful reaffirmation of the resurrection (15:52, οἱ νεκροὶ ἐγερθήσονται "the dead will be raised"). This belies the claim that Paul in this chapter offers a compromise to those at Corinth who denied

---

58. As Joseph Fitzmyer points out, a trumpet also served to herald the theophany of God at Mount Sinai (Exod 19:13, 16, 19; 20:18). See Fitzmyer, 605; cf. Reasoner, on 15:52.

59. See Schmidt, *Syn.*, 4:54; and cf. Matt 11:5; 23:27; Luke 7:14–15; 24:5; Heb 11:35. For full discussion, see chapter 6.

*The Mystery of the Glorification of the Flesh*

the resurrection. Paul does not give an inch. What they deny, he reaffirms with a flourish of trumpets. The passive verb is, of course, a "divine passive": the agent is Christ (15:21, 45; cf. Phil 3:21). Once again, we see Paul's divine and incarnational Christology on full display. The power of Christ overcomes the human dilemma of v. 50 that "corruption" (ἡ φθορά) cannot inherit the incorruptible kingdom, for the dead will be raised "incorruptible" (ἄφθαρτοι).

*and we will be changed.* The "we" are those alive at the time of the parousia in distinction from the dead. We thus find in v. 52 the "living and the dead" of the ancient apostolic confessional formulas (Acts 10:42; Rom 14:9; 2 Tim 4:1; 1 Pet 4:5). Through his use of the first-person plural pronoun, Paul includes himself and his Corinthian readers among those still living at the time of Christ's advent. However, in 6:14, through the same device, he includes both himself and his Corinthian readers among those who are dead and will be raised at Christ's coming. Paul clearly wishes to foster among the Corinthians an imminent expectation of the Lord's return (1:7–9), but he does not claim to know the day or the hour.

As in the previous clause, the verb is a "divine passive," and the agent of the action is Christ (cf. Phil 3:21, ὃς μετασχηματίσει).[60] The change the living undergo is the change from corruptibility to incorruptibility (cf. 15:53–54). The means of this change, as we have seen, is the glorification of the body through its full participation in the Spirit of Christ (15:42–49). Paul will now elaborate on this change.

VERSE 53

*For it is necessary that this corruptible body be clothed with incorruptibility, and this mortal body be clothed with immortality.*

Within the concentric structure of 15:50–53, as we have seen, v. 53 corresponds to v. 50. Both verses (in contrast with the future tense, first-person plural verbs of 15:51–52) employ present tense, third-person singular verbs to state a general principle involving corruptibility (15:50, ἡ φθορά; 15:53, τὸ φθαρτὸν τοῦτο) and incorruptibility (15:50, τὴν ἀφθαρσίαν; 15:53, ἀφθαρσίαν).[61] Taken together, the subjects of the paired clauses within these two corresponding verses form a chiasm: (A) "flesh and blood" (B) "corruption" (B') "this corruptible body" (A') "this mortal body." Within this structure, "flesh and blood" (15:50, σὰρξ καὶ αἷμα) corresponds to "this

---

60. Cf. Wolff, 416.
61. Cf. Gillman, "Transformation," 320–22; Robertson & Plummer, 377.

CHAPTER 14

mortal body" (15:53, τὸ θνητὸν τοῦτο). This correspondence within the chiasm underscores the fact that the incapacity or insufficiency denoted by "flesh and blood" in 15:50, as we have seen, is not human physicality and coarse materiality but human mortality. Verse 50 states a *negative* principle, a dilemma—the impossibility (οὐ δύναται) of corruptible human beings inheriting the incorruptible kingdom. Verse 53 states a *positive* principle, which builds on the revelation of the mystery in vv. 51–52, and is the *solution* to the dilemma of v. 50—the necessity (δεῖ) of the *change* from corruptibility to incorruptibility, from mortality to immortality.

Within v. 53, the neuter adjectives φθαρτόν and θνητόν assume an implicit σῶμα.[62] The subject that clothes itself with imperishability is thus "this perishable body" (τὸ φθαρτὸν τοῦτο) and "this mortal body" (τὸ θνητὸν τοῦτο). The repeated τοῦτο "this" is extremely significant. To be sure, it is not necessarily the case, as some interpreters aver, that we must think of Paul pointing to his own mortal body as he writes.[63] However, Paul is certainly referring to the present mortal bodies of himself and his readers. The force of the syntax is not really contested, but its far-reaching implications for Paul's understanding of the resurrection have not been sufficiently recognized. For v. 53 forms a striking counterpoint to Dale Martin's assertion that Paul "does not believe in a resurrection of *this* body."[64] For in 15:53 the subject that undergoes transformation is precisely "*this* corruptible body" (τὸ φθαρτὸν <u>τοῦτο</u>) and "*this* mortal body" (τὸ θνητὸν <u>τοῦτο</u>). It is *this* present mortal body that is raised to life and made incorruptible and immortal. "The subject persists throughout the radical change."[65] Mortal flesh, far from being excluded from this divine, saving transformation, is the subject of that transformation.

*For it is necessary that this corruptible body be clothed with incorruptibility.* Already in 15:42 we learned of the marvelous change from φθορά "corruption" to ἀφθαρσία "incorruptibility." In 15:50, the focus was on the impossibility of corruptible human beings (ἡ φθορά) inheriting the kingdom apart from this change. In 15:53 the focus is again on the necessity of this change but now as a glorious coming reality, the divine solution to the human plight of 15:50. The theme of the *incorruptibility* of the resurrected body, foreshadowed in 9:24–26 and first struck within the chapter in 15:42, reaches a climax in 15:50–54 with the profusion of the language of incorruptibility and imperishability in these verses. The words φθορά, ἀφθαρσία, and their cognates occur *seven* times within the space of 15:50–54. In describing

---

62. Fitzmyer, 605; Fee, 888; Barrett, 382.
63. E.g., Fitzmyer, 605; Robertson & Plummer, 377; cf. Ellicott, 326.
64. Martin, *Body*, 130.
65. Sider, "Resurrection Body," 438; cf. Spörlein, *Leugnung*, 44.

the present perishable and mortal body as "clothed" with incorruptibility and immortality at the resurrection, Paul here brings to a climax the clothing imagery he has used throughout the chapter (15:37, γυμνὸς κόκκος "unclothed seed"; 15:49, φορέω "wear" [2×]; 15:53–54, ἐνδύω "clothe" [4×]). The clothing imagery reveals in yet another way that Paul does not understand resurrection, as so many scholars seem to think, as a minus, the removal or destruction of the present body of flesh and bones. One can hardly "clothe" that which no longer exists! The "clothing" of the mortal body necessitates its revival, enhancement, and enrichment. Resurrection in Paul's thought is not a minus but a plus. It is, as Caroline Walker Bynum describes the historic Christian doctrine of the resurrection, "the "enhancement of what is, not metamorphosis into what is not."[66]

*and this mortal body be clothed with immortality*. To the profusion of instances of ἀφθαρσία "incorruptibility" and its cognates in 15:50–53 are now added, in the final clause of 15:53 and for the first time within the letter, the words θνητός and ἀθανασία, terms cognate with θάνατος "death." In this way, the apostle prepares the way for the climactic description of the final conquest of death in 15:54–57.

"This mortal body" (τὸ θνητὸν τοῦτο) in 15:53 corresponds within the chiastic structure of 15:50 and 15:53 to the "flesh and blood" (σὰρξ καὶ αἷμα) of 15:50—mortal, perishable flesh. But when clothed with immortality at the resurrection, it will be the new and different kind of flesh that Paul contemplates in the comparison of the various kinds of flesh in 15:39 (σάρξ [4×]). It will no longer be mortal and corruptible flesh, but glorified flesh—the flesh clothed with the heavenly glory, the image of the Son, the radiant presence of God, and the full gift of the Holy Spirit (15:40–42, 43, 44, 49), and thus with incorruptibility and immortality. "The fruit of the work of the Spirit is the salvation of the flesh" (Irenaeus, *Haer.* 5.12.4).

---

66. Caroline Walker Bynum, *The Resurrection of the Body in Western Christianity, 200–1336* (New York: Columbia University Press, 1999), 8.

CHAPTER 15

## *The Resurrection of the Body as the Final Triumph of God*

15:54–58

As the very climax of his exposition of the resurrection in chapter 15, Paul now contemplates the resurrection as the abolition of death and the final victory and triumph of God. The restatement of 15:53 in 15:54a provides a seamless link to the previous section (15:50–53).[1] The closing word of this restatement, ἀθανασία "deathlessness," prepares in turn for the portrayal of the conquest of death in 15:54b–57. Verses 54b–57 form a skillfully structured unit. I propose that these verses exhibit a chiastic structure by means of the key words νῖκος "victory" and κέντρον "sting," linked together as a chiasm in the order νῖκος – κέντρον – κέντρον – νῖκος.[2] The structure, I suggest, is as follows:

(54a)   And when this corruptible body is clothed with incorruptibility, and this mortal body is clothed with immortality, then will come to pass the word that has been written:

(54b–55a)   A   "Death has been swallowed up in *victory*!" "Where, O death, is your *victory*?"

---

1. Rodolphe Morissette, "La chair et le sang ne peuvent hériter du Règne de Dieu (I Cor., XV, 50)," *ScEs* 26 (1974): 44; John Gillman, "Transformation in 1 Cor 15.50–53," *ETL* 58 (1982): 320.

2. Gillman proposes a similar but somewhat different structure: A (v. 54); B (vv. 55–56); A' (v. 57) ("Transformation," 320–22). The main difference is that I see vv. 55–56 as segmented through the twofold occurrence of κέντρον, thus making the structure chiastic rather than merely concentric.

| | | |
|---|---|---|
| (55b) | B | "Where, O death, is your *sting*?" |
| (56) | B' | Now the *sting* of death is sin, and the power of sin is the law. |
| (57) | A' | But thanks be to God, who gives us the *victory* through our Lord Jesus Christ! |

As we will see, the breadth and sweep of the theological sequence of thought within these brief verses is stunning, as the passage moves from the resurrection of the body (15:54a), to the resurrection as the conquest of death (15:54b–55), to the defeat of sin that is death's power (15:56), to boasting in the power, wisdom, and goodness of God, who bestows this victory over sin and over death (15:57). This in turn prepares the way for the final exhortation of the chapter in 15:58: the call to take up the cross in labor for Christ. The theological depth and grandeur of this final portion of the chapter render it unsurpassed and among the most sublime passages within the New Testament.

## Verse 54

*And when this corruptible body is clothed with incorruptibility, and this mortal body is clothed with immortality, then will come to pass the word that has been written: "Death has been swallowed up in victory!"*

*And when this corruptible body is clothed with incorruptibility.* Paul here continues his exposition of the great change that was the subject of 15:50–53—the glorification of the flesh. Paul restates v. 53 not as a general principle (15:53, δεῖ "it is necessary") but now as looking ahead in expectation to the fulfillment (15:54, ὅταν "when"). One feature of the indefinite temporal subjunctive clause that Paul employs here, which is impossible to bring out in English, is that the timing of the event or act in view is left indefinite or undetermined.[3] It is another way in which Paul expresses the impossibility of knowing the day or the hour when these things will take place.[4] As in v. 53, the subject of this coming change is "this corruptible body." "This corruptible body" is the perishable body of flesh. It is thus the body of flesh that is the subject of this change. Verse 54 thus shows once more that this transformation does not do away with the flesh but transforms and glorifies it. The change is the transformation from corruptibility to incorruptibility. The language and concept of incorruptibility (ἀφθαρσία and its cognates), introduced

---

3. Rob., *Gram.*, 970–74.
4. For further discussion, see the commentary on v. 52 above.

CHAPTER 15

in the chapter in 15:42, and so predominant throughout 15:50–53, finds its final and climactic occurrence in the chapter here.

*and this mortal body is clothed with immortality.* Paul continues his restatement of v. 53 in the mode of expectation. But this is not mere redundancy. The reprisal of v. 53 in v. 54 has a lyrical, hymnic quality that invites and draws the reader into contemplation of these mysteries. Perhaps the best commentary on the spirit of Paul's repetition here is given by Clement of Alexandria at the close of his *Protrepticus*, where he gives the reason for that treatise's repetition and length: περὶ γάρ τοι τῆς παῦλον οὐδαμῇ οὐδαμῶς ἐχούσης ζωῆς οὐκ ἐθέλουσιν οὐδ' οἱ λόγοι παύσασθαι ποτε ἱεροφαντοῦντες ("For, in truth, concerning that life which can in no way and in no manner ever cease, even the words themselves are unwilling ever to cease inviting all to its mysteries"). This clause in 15:54, together with its matching clause in 15:53b, introduces (for the first time in the letter) the words θνητός "subject to death" and ἀθανασία "deathlessness." In this way, Paul deftly prepares the way for the climactic theme of the victory over death that now follows.

*then will come to pass the word that has been written.* This is Paul's final explicit quotation of Scripture in the chapter and in the letter. The expression ὁ λόγος ὁ γεγραμμένος ("the word that has been written") is unique in Paul, providing a solemn and ornate introduction to the passage. Here λόγος refers, of course, to the passage Paul is about to cite, but it may also recall Paul's use of the word λόγος to describe the good news of the resurrection in 15:2 (cf. 1:18; 2:4). Paul's reference to the scriptural λόγος here may also imply a contrast with the λόγος of human wisdom espoused by the self-proclaimed wise at Corinth (1:17; 2:1; 4:19–20).

*"Death has been swallowed up in victory!"* Paul quotes Isa 25:8, but the quotation does not follow the MT exactly and is very different from the LXX. But his quotation agrees word for word with Theodotion Isaiah (a Greek translation of Hebrew Isaiah by Theodotion in the late second century AD), suggesting that Paul is here using a Greek translation of Isaiah in agreement with the "proto-Theodotionic" or "*Kaige*-Theodotion" revision of the LXX (first century BC) first isolated by Dominique Barthélemy.[5]

Paul's quotation is from Isa 25:6–9, an oracle envisioning the coming of YHWH to Mount Zion, the holy city of Jerusalem, to redeem all nations. The Hebrew of the oracle in the MT reads:

---

5. Dominique Barthélemy, *Les devanciers d'Aquila* (VTSup 10; Leiden: Brill, 1963). For further discussion of "proto-Theodotion," see Karen H. Jobes and Moisés Silva, *Invitation to the Septuagint* (Grand Rapids: Baker Academic, 2000), 41–42, 284–86.

And on this mountain the Lord of hosts will prepare for all the peoples a feast of rich foods, a feast of aged wines, of choicest rich foods, of finest aged wines. And he will swallow up on this mountain the burial cloth that covers all the peoples, the mourning veil that veils all the nations—he will swallow up death forever! And the Lord YHWH will wipe away the tears from all faces, and will remove the reproach of his people from all the earth, for YHWH has spoken. And it will be said in that day, "Behold, here is our God! We put our hope in him, and he has saved us. Here is YHWH! We put our hope in him; let us rejoice and be glad in his salvation." (Isa 25:6–9)

Astonishingly, this Isaian oracle foretells that YHWH, in the time of his coming kingdom and reign, would reveal himself as the one true God by doing what only the one true creator God could do—"he will swallow up death forever!" (Isa 25:8). As Richard Hays points out, Paul's quotation of Isaiah's prophetic announcement of the conquest of death is in striking agreement with the focus and content of the Isaian passage and evokes the whole rich context and imagery of the oracle.[6] In evoking this Isaianic vision, Paul makes clear that the resurrection will not only destroy death but also bring about a new world order in which evil will be vanquished, and suffering and sorrow will be no more. Through the resurrection, the covenant's ancient promise of *life* to the people of God (Deut 30:15–20; 32:47; Ezek 18; Amos 5:4–7; Zech 14:8) will come to pass in an unimagined fullness. In Isaiah's oracle, in both the MT ("he will swallow up death forever") and the proto-Theodotionic version ("death has been swallowed up in victory"), the conquest of death is the triumphal work of YHWH, Israel's God. Paul's quotation of Isa 25:8 in its proto-Theodotionic version is even more emphatic than the MT in explicitly identifying this abolition of death as the triumph or *victory* of God (15:54, κατεπόθη ὁ θάνατος εἰς νῖκος).

First Corinthians 15:54b is a culminating point of the chapter. Used only occasionally elsewhere in the letter, the words θάνατος (prior to chapter 15 only 3:22; 11:26; but then 15:21, 26, 54, 55, 56) and ἀποθνῄσκω (prior to chapter 15 only 8:11; 9:15; but then 15:3, 22, 31, 32, 36) pervade chapter 15. The recurring focus of Paul's use of this vocabulary throughout the chapter is the *reversal* of death through the resurrection from the dead (15:21–22, 26, 36). This theme now culminates with the victory over death in 15:54b. The announcement here recalls, parallels, and completes the earlier mention of the destruction of death in 15:26:

15:26 καταργεῖται ὁ θάνατος
15:54 κατεπόθη ὁ θάνατος

6. Hays, 275–76.

This conception of the conquest of death is absolutely unique in antiquity. In the ancient pagan, polytheistic world into which Paul's gospel came, death was believed to be an eternal and unchangeable reality of the cosmic order, unalterable even by the gods. Although a variety of beliefs existed regarding soul survival, heavenly afterlife, and reincarnation, neither the common person nor the philosophers believed that a human being, once dead, might live again. All were agreed on the impossibility of resurrection—the return from bodily death to an everlasting embodied life. As Apollo explained in the *Eumenides*, "for death alone my father Zeus has no divine enchantment" (Aeschylus, *Eum.* 649). Both the gods of ancient polytheistic worship and the philosophical deities of Plato, Epicurus, and the Stoics were considered powerless before the invincible power of death.[7] Paul in 1 Cor 15:54b proclaims a different kind of God, a different promise, and a different hope—the final triumph of God over death itself.

There is a deep, essential connection between the defeat of death here in 15:54b and the unveiling of the "how" of the resurrection as the outworking of the full gift of the Spirit of God's Son in 15:44–49. For in Paul's thought the contrast or opposite of death is the *Holy Spirit*. Thus Paul in 2 Corinthians contrasts "the ministry of *death*" (2 Cor 3:7, ἡ διακονία τοῦ θανάτου) with "the ministry of *the Spirit* (2 Cor 3:8, ἡ διακονία τοῦ πνεύματος). And Paul can say not only "the Spirit gives life" (2 Cor 3:6, τὸ δὲ πνεῦμα ζῳοποιεῖ; cf. Rom 8:2, 6), but even "The Spirit is life" (Rom 8:10, τὸ δὲ πνεῦμα ζωή). The result of the full gift of the Spirit of God (15:44–49) can be nothing less than the destruction of death (15:54b).

## Verse 55

*"Where, O death, is your victory? Where, O death, is your sting?"*

The theme of the conquest of death now continues with a second quotation of Scripture. Paul quotes Hos 13:14, although his wording does not agree exactly with the MT, the LXX, or any known ancient Greek version.[8] Paul's quotation is skillful, for the word "victory" in the Hosea citation links to the word "victory" in the Isaiah quotation in v. 54b. Paul will continue this rhetorical pattern throughout

---

7. E.g., Homer, *Od.* 3.229–238; *Il.* 16.433; Cicero, *Div.* 2.25; Lucretius, *Nat.* 1–3; Plato, *Tim.* 41a–42e, 69c–73d; Epictetus, *Diatr.* 1.1.10–12; Seneca, *Prov.* 6.5–8.

8. On the relationship of Paul's quotation to MT Hosea, LXX Hosea, and other ancient versions, see Łukasz Popko, "Why Paul Was Not Wrong in Quoting Hosea 13:14," *BibAn* 9 (2019): 493–512.

## The Resurrection of the Body as the Final Triumph of God

vv. 55–56, to form an artful *gradatio* (a rhetorical device in which the last word of each clause is taken up in the next). Scholars dispute whether Hos 13:14 in its immediate context offers a divine promise of hope (as Paul clearly reads the passage) or a threat of destruction.[9] But in either case, Paul is rightly reading Hos 13:14 in light of that book's larger message, which prophetically envisions the ultimate triumph of God's saving purposes for Israel and the whole world (Hos 1:7, 10–11; 2:14–23; 3:3–5; 11:8–11; 14:1–8).[10]

In Hos 13:14 these words are spoken by YHWH, and God may be understood as the speaker here in 1 Cor 15:56. But it is more likely that Paul speaks here on behalf of the people of God. Paul sings a derisive taunt song, in the words of Hosea, against death. It is possible that Paul speaks here from the vantage point of the future, as one raised from the dead, when death has been abolished. But more likely Paul speaks from the vantage point of the present and from the standpoint of faith and hope, for death has already been conquered, and the final victory over death assured, by the resurrection of Christ.[11]

The word κέντρον can denote either a "sting," such as is inflicted by scorpions or locusts, or a "goad," such as is used to urge on oxen or other animals.[12] Paul almost certainly uses the word here in the sense of "sting," with reference to death's power to harm and destroy. Death is thus here portrayed as "an inimical, suprahuman, and cosmic power."[13] We are reminded of Paul's portrayal of death in 15:26 as the "last enemy" (ἔσχατος ἐχθρός). Yet Paul can mock and taunt death, for in the resurrection it will be swallowed up in triumph, its power to destroy abolished forever.

It is worth noting that 1 Cor 15:54b–55 reveals, once again and from yet another angle, the palpable, physical, and fleshly nature of the resurrection in Paul. For Paul's robust language of the defeat and annihilation of death hardly fits with popular and scholarly notions of "resurrection" in Paul as an ethereal afterlife, without flesh and blood, as an airy and intangible spirit form. Only a resurrection of the physical and fleshly body—the whole human being—makes sense of Paul's description of the resurrection here as the final destruction and defeat of death.

Verse 55 continues the triumphant, lyrical, and hymnic tone begun in v. 54. It is truly hymnic not only in tone but also in content, for Paul's mocking and triumphal song is a boasting and glorying in *God*, the vanquisher of death. Paul's

---

9. For discussion, see Schrage, 364–65.
10. Rightly Hays, 276; Schreiner, 325.
11. Hays, 276.
12. Robinson, s.v. "κέντρον"; cf. Schrage, 380–81.
13. Martinus C. de Boer, *The Defeat of Death: Apocalyptic Eschatology in 1 Corinthians 15 and Romans 5* (JSNTSup 22; 1988; repr., London: T&T Clark, 2019), 184.

thought moves here from contemplation of the resurrection of the body (v. 54a), to contemplation of the resurrection as the conquest of death (v. 54b), to praise of the power, goodness, and glory of the God who gives this victory (v. 55). We find a similar movement of thought in 15:20–28, in Rom 8:18–39, and in 2 Cor 5:1–5. This movement of thought is therefore clearly a core element of Paul's theology and of his worship of God. This praise of the glory and majesty of God, the "Godness" of God, will reach its climax in v. 57. But Paul must first reveal more concerning the depth and profundity of God's victory in v. 56.

## Verse 56

*Now the sting of death is sin, and the power of sin is the law.*

Verse 56 links to v. 55 to continue the skillful *gradatio* (where the last word of a clause is picked up in the succeeding clause) begun in v. 54. In Paul's *gradatio*, νῖκος "victory" links v. 55a back to v. 54, κέντρον "sting" links v. 56 back to v. 55b, and ἁμαρτία "sin" links v. 56b back to v. 56a. Paul's sparse syntax in v. 56, without linking verbs, identifies the two statements in v. 56 as axioms or principles, such as often expressed by the ancient philosophers.[14] It is one more feature within the philosophical style of the chapter whereby Paul outdoes the boastful self-professed wise at Corinth within their own philosophical arena. But these axioms, although in philosophical form, do not express the philosophical wisdom of the world, but instead make known the divinely revealed mysteries of "the word of the cross" (1:18).

Scholars generally find Paul's insertion of these axioms at this point in the chapter perplexing and problematic. "This bit of Pauline theology," says Joseph Fitzmyer, "is awkward in its context."[15] After the stirring portrayal of the conquest of death in vv. 54b–55, the verse seems to many to be out of place and anticlimactic, appearing to have little or no connection to the previous thought of the chapter or to the thought of the letter as a whole.[16] For these reasons, a number of scholars in the past, and more recently F. W. Horn, have declared the verse a non-Pauline gloss.[17] However, the consensus of contemporary scholarship affirms

---

14. Chris Alex Vlachos, "Law, Sin, and Death: An Edenic Triad? An Examination with Reference to 1 Corinthians 15:56," *JETS* 47 (2004): 279–80.

15. Fitzmyer, 607.

16. So Frank Thielman, *Paul and the Law: A Contextual Approach* (Downers Grove, IL: IVP Academic, 1994), 107; Vlachos, "Edenic Triad," 277–78; Fee, 805.

17. F. W. Horn, "1 Kor 15,56—Ein exegetischer Stachel," *ZNW* 82 (1991): 88–105.

the authenticity of the verse. Indeed, not only the Pauline authorship of this verse but also the character of this verse as a classic expression of Pauline theology can hardly be doubted.[18] But what interpreters have found difficult is the function of this verse within the argument of the chapter. In the words of Harm W. Hollander and J. Holleman, "Why did Paul insert these words in an argument on the resurrection of believers in which sin has hardly figured and law not at all?"[19] But in fact, as we will see, v. 56 is closely tied to the thought of the chapter, and deepens and enriches that thought, revealing a further dimension of the victory of God over death of which Paul boasts in 15:54–57.

*Now the sting of death is sin.* The δέ indicates that 15:56 will now provide a further deepening of the thought in 15:54–55. The "sting" of death does not refer to adventitious aspects of death, such as psychological distress, but to that which gives death its power to kill and destroy. What gives death its power over humanity, Paul asserts, is sin.

Despite frequent claims to the contrary, this axiom is not disconnected from the rest of the chapter but picks up and completes a theme that has already figured prominently within it. In 15:21–22 we find a key theme of the chapter—the entrance of death into the world through Adam. From Rom 5:12–21 it is clear that in Paul's thought this takes place through Adam's sin (Rom 5:12, "through one human being sin entered into the world, and through sin, death"; cf. Rom 5:15, 17, 21). This is presupposed in the abbreviated formulations of 1 Cor 15:21–22.[20] It is now made explicit in 15:56. But if sin is the cause of death, then the conquest of death requires nothing less than the defeat of sin. This reveals another dimension of God's victory: the conquest of sin. This brings us back to Paul's summary of the apostolic kerygma at the beginning of the chapter: "Christ died for our sins" (15:3, Χριστὸς ἀπέθανεν ὑπὲρ τῶν ἁμαρτιῶν ἡμῶν). And if we reverse Paul's counterfactual in 15:17, we see that those in Christ are no longer in their sins (15:17, ἐν ταῖς ἁμαρτίαις ὑμῶν). The cross of Christ is the saving power of God, because it brings deliverance

---

18. Contra Harm W. Hollander and J. Holleman, who, although acknowledging Paul's authorship of the verse, trace the thought of this verse to widespread conceptions regarding sin, law, and death within the Hellenistic world, unrelated to Paul's teachings elsewhere in his epistles regarding death, sin, and the law; see "The Relationship of Death, Sin, and Law in 1 Cor 15:56," *NovT* 35 (1993): 270–91. They are followed by Collins, 582–83. However, this thesis is far-fetched and has been rightly rejected by the great majority of interpreters.

19. Hollander and Holleman, "Death, Sin, and Law," 272.

20. Rightly Thomas Söding, "'Die Kraft der Sünde ist das Gesetz' (1Kor 15,56): Anmerkungen zum Hintergrund und zur Pointe einer gesetzeskritischen Sentenz des Apostels Paulus," *ZNW* 83 (1992): 78–80; cf. Vlachos, "Edenic Triad," 290–91.

from the condemnation and power of sin, which leads to death. It is a dimension of God's victory over death that is already a reality in the present. Paul will now deepen this point in the axiom that follows.

*and the power of sin is the law.* We have here in abbreviated form what Paul draws out much more fully in Rom 7 and 2 Cor 3—the role of the law within the reign of sin. The law to which Paul refers is the law of God, given at Sinai to Israel through Moses (Rom 5:13–14, 20–21; Gal 3:17) but also known in its essentials inwardly by the gentiles (Rom 1:32; 2:1; 7:5; possibly 2:14–16). The law is the "power" of sin in the sense that it is the catalyst of sin, revealing sin (Rom 7:13), giving sin its power to condemn (Rom 3:20; 7:7; 2 Cor 3:9), and making sin alive and effective in the human heart (Rom 7:5, 8–11).[21] Sin receives its power through the law. Victory over sin and death therefore necessarily requires victory over the law as well.

As we have seen, scholars generally consider Paul's insertion of axioms regarding death, sin, and the law in v. 56 as without connection to the prior themes of the chapter and the letter. We have already seen that this is mistaken in the case of the first axiom regarding death as the product of sin. And also this second axiom, regarding sin and the law, brings to a head a theme that has run as a subtle undercurrent throughout the epistle. In the first chapter, the incapacity of the law to save is implicit in Paul's contrast of the saving power of the gospel not only with pagan philosophical wisdom but also with "the scribe" (1:20, γραμματεύς) and with "the Jews" who demand signs and do not believe in Jesus (1:22–23).[22] Likewise in chapter 7, the law's lack of power to save is implicit in Paul's axiom that "circumcision is nothing, and uncircumcision is nothing" (7:18–19). And Paul's brief discussion of the law in 9:20–21 portrays those united to Christ as set free from the power and dominion of the law. The important connection between this last passage and 15:56 requires further discussion.

In 1 Cor 9:20, Jewish persons outside of Christ, in contrast with Paul as a Jewish Christ follower, are portrayed as ὑπὸ νόμον. This is essentially a Pauline expression, found only once in all ancient literature prior to Paul's letters.[23] The expression is frequent in Paul and an important part of Paul's theological vocabulary (Rom 6:14–15; 1 Cor 9:20; Gal 3:23; 4:4–5, 21; 5:18). The phrase does not simply refer to being under the law's jurisdiction, as has been commonly supposed. For in the analo-

---

21. Cf. Vlachos, "Edenic Triad," 283–85. According to Vlachos, in 15:56 "ὁ νόμος is likely being portrayed here in a *catalytic* role, that is, the law is defined as the dynamo *that sets in motion the power of sin*" (284).

22. See Söding, "Kraft," 83.

23. Ps.-Plato, *Def.* 415c3. We also find ὑπὸ τοὺς νόμους, but even this only twice, in Aristotle, *Pol.* 1270a and Demosthenes, *Timocr.* 131.

gous construction in Paul, ὑφ' ἁμαρτίαν, the preposition ὑπό denotes being "under the dominion" of sin (Rom 3:9; 7:14; Gal 3:22). Similarly, then, the expression ὑπὸ νόμον denotes being under the *dominion* of the law (e.g., Rom 6:14, ἁμαρτία γὰρ ὑμῶν οὐ κυριεύσει· οὐ γάρ ἐστε ὑπὸ νόμον "for sin will not have *dominion* over you, for you are not *under the law*"). Thus already in 9:20, through the expression ὑπὸ νόμον, the law is implicitly portrayed as a *power*.[24]

In 15:56, the law is explicitly presented as a power (δύναμις). Here we find a δύναμις not wielded by God that is wielded against humanity. Moreover, sin (ἁμαρτία) is presented as a purposive being using this power to bring forth death (cf. Rom 7:8, 11, 13). It thus becomes clear that Paul here contemplates, behind the nexus of law, sin, and death in 15:56, the work of the powers and authorities (πᾶσαν ἐξουσίαν καὶ δύναμιν) of 15:24: Satan and the demonic powers. These beings use the holy law of God (Rom 7:12), exploiting the weakness of human nature (Rom 8:3), to bring about sin (Rom 7:8–11, 13) and God's righteous judgment of death (Rom 1:32; 7:13; 8:6). In the hands of fallen human beings enslaved to the satanic powers, the law—although "holy and righteous and good" (Rom 7:12)—becomes "the law of sin and death" (Rom 8:2). That is why the conquest of death celebrated in 15:54b–57 could not come to pass through an act of divine *power* alone, for it required humanity's liberation from its willing enslavement to the demonic powers at work through sin and the law (cf. Rom 8:38–39). It required "the wisdom of God concealed in a mystery" (1 Cor 2:7), the crucifixion of "the Lord of glory" (2:8), to free humanity from the power of Satan and sin. This is a present victory, not only a future one, and thus the celebration of it here involves yet another implicit exhortation and call to discipleship within the chapter (cf. 15:29–34, 48, 58).

So far from being an awkward intrusion into the passage, as so many scholars suppose, v. 56 addresses and unlocks a major mystery within the Scriptures. We have already seen that, in the creation account of Genesis, Adam and Eve were created with bodies that were free from death but did not have unalterable possession of eternal life. Everlasting life was a gift to be bestowed in consequence of their free decision to remain in covenantal union with God (Gen 2:9, 17; 3:2–3, 19, 22; cf. Rom 5:12; 2 Cor 11:2–3). The account is explicit that, once Adam and Eve had sinned, they were kept from partaking of the tree of life, lest they live forever (Gen 3:22–24). Why? The theological conception is profound. Everlasting life given to the bodies of human beings in a state of separation from God would mean everlasting death. The promise of resurrection in the Old Testament (Isa 25:6–9; 26:19; Dan 12:2) thus involved an impenetrable mystery. Such a reversal of the curse of death of Genesis 3 required a twofold redemptive work of God, not only

---

24. Söding, "Kraft," 81 n. 26 ("Der Nomos ist bereits in 1 Kor 9,20 als Macht vorgestellt").

CHAPTER 15

the conquest of physical death but also triumph over sin, and the restoration of human beings to covenantal union with God. How could this come about? It is the unveiling of this mystery in "the word of the cross" (1:18) that is at the heart of Paul's doxological praise of God in vv. 56–57. Through his cross and resurrection, the crucified and risen "Lord of glory" (2:8) frees those who believe from their sins (15:3, 17) and bestows on them his Holy Spirit (15:45, 48), becoming even now their "wisdom from God, righteousness, sanctification, and redemption" (1:31). And at his coming (15:23), he will complete this union by the gift of the Holy Spirit to their bodies (15:44, 49). Thus will come about the reversal of the curse of death of Genesis through the gift of everlasting embodied life (15:42–44, 50–54). This is the twofold triumph, the twofold victory of Christ, over sin and over death that Paul celebrates in this passage.

VERSE 57

*But thanks be to God, who gives us the victory through our Lord Jesus Christ!*

The poetic and hymnic character of the passage, and its triumphal and celebratory tone, now reaches a high point, as Paul's thought within the chapter now comes to a striking climax.[25] Paul's thought had earlier moved from reflection upon the resurrection as the gift of imperishability and immortality to the body (15:52–54a), to contemplation of the resurrection as God's conquest and defeat of death (15:54b–55). Paul's thought then explored the deepest dimensions of that victory—redemption from the law, from sin, and from the power of Satan and his demons (15:56). Now in 15:57, Paul's thought moves to its climax, as he contemplates how this victory reveals the greatness, splendor, majesty, and glory of God. By crushing death, and the power of sin and Satan that lurked behind it, this God reveals that he is truly the one true God. The resurrection reveals "the Godness of God." This movement of thought—from the resurrection, to the conquest of death, to the triumph over Satan, to the greatness of God—is also found elsewhere in Paul and appears to be a core element of his thinking (e.g., Rom 8:38–39; 1 Cor 15:20–28; 2 Cor 5:1–5). For Paul, those who deny the resurrection can have no knowledge of God (1 Cor 15:34). For the resurrection, and it alone, reveals that God is truly God.

---

25. On the passage's hymnic character, see Schrage, 361. Robertson speaks of "the perfection of poetic form in the noble prose" of this passage (Rob., *Gram.*, 1200).

*But thanks be to God.* The word χάρις here denotes "thanksgiving" (cf. Rom 6:17; 7:25; 1 Cor 10:30; 2 Cor 2:14; 8:16; 9:15; 1 Tim 1:12; 2 Tim 1:3). But in keeping with its predominant use in Paul with reference to the "grace" of God, the word χάρις when denoting thanksgiving in Paul always denotes thanksgiving in response to God's unfathomable grace and mercy to the sinful and unworthy. It is thus the fitting word for thanksgiving in response to the victory of God contemplated here, which is not only a victory over death but also a victory over sin and the enslaving power of sin. The phrase χάρις τῷ θεῷ ("thanks be to God") is found in Rom 6:17 and 7:25 as well as 2 Cor 8:16 and 9:15. But only here and in 2 Cor 2:14 do we find the word order τῷ δὲ θεῷ χάρις ("to God be thanks"). Paul's syntax here puts the emphasis firmly on God.

Paul's thanksgiving brings to completion two key themes within the letter. Boasting in God is an important conception within Paul's theology (Rom 5:1–11; 15:16–19; 2 Cor 1:12–14; 10:12–18; Gal 6:11–16; Phil 3:3). A prominent theme within 1 Corinthians is that of boasting in the Lord. The purpose of God's reversal and abolition of human wisdom through the gospel is that all boasting may be in the Lord (1:26–31; 3:18–23). Within the letter, the programmatic statement of boasting "in the Lord" (ἐν κυρίῳ) in 1:31 forms an *inclusio* with the final statement of boasting "in the Lord Jesus Christ" (ἐν Χριστῷ Ἰησοῦ τῷ κυρίῳ ἡμῶν) in 15:31. But now in 15:54b–57 Paul brings this theme of boasting in the Lord to a marvelous climax within the letter by doing so *performatively*. First Corinthians 15:54b–57 is boasting in God in action (cf. Rom 8:31–39).

The second key theme of the letter that vv. 54b–57 bring to a climax is that of the power of God. In the first chapters of the letter, the salvific incapacity of human wisdom and of the law is set in contrast to the word of the cross as the *power of God* (1:18, δύναμις θεοῦ; 1:24, θεοῦ δύναμιν; 2:5, ἐν δυνάμει θεοῦ). Here, too, in vv. 56–57 Paul contrasts the *power* of sin and the law (15:56, ἡ δύναμις τῆς ἁμαρτίας ὁ νόμος) with *God* and his saving victory (15:57, τῷ δὲ θεῷ χάρις).[26] Thus here in chapter 15 we find the final development of Paul's theme of the gospel as the power of God (1:18, 24; 2:5).

*who gives us the victory.* Paul now caps the theme of the resurrection as the triumph of God over death, which he began in 15:54b. However, there has been a progression of thought within 15:54b–57. For in v. 56 we learn that Christ's triumph over death involves also his triumph over Satan, the law, and sin. Therefore, when in v. 57 we now return to the νῖκος of God, first announced in 15:54, it is with a deepened knowledge of the nature of this victory and of its surpassing greatness. The victory

---

26. Cf. Söding, "Kraft," 83.

CHAPTER 15

over death is a comprehensive victory over the law, sin, and Satan.[27] The present tense participle is thus not a prospective present tense, referring merely to "God's future gift of victory."[28] Rather, the tense is present, because the fruits of Christ's victory are already experienced by the faithful even now, as they await the future culmination of that victory when death, the last enemy, is abolished (15:26).[29] Even now, their consciences are set free from the accusation of the law (15:56b; cf. 9:20, μὴ ὢν αὐτὸς ὑπὸ νόμον); they are liberated from the power of sin (15:56a) and filled with the holiness that the law requires through the power of the Holy Spirit (15:45, 48; cf. 9:21, ἔννομος Χριστοῦ). The law could not "give life" (Gal 3:21, εἰ γὰρ ἐδόθη νόμος ὁ δυνάμενος ζῳοποιῆσαι). But through his incarnation, death, and resurrection, the Son of God even now bestows his "life-giving" Holy Spirit (15:45, πνεῦμα ζῳοποιοῦν; cf. 15:48). And at his parousia he will bestow the Holy Spirit in fullness, so that all those in Christ "will be given life" in their physical bodies (15:22, ἐν τῷ Χριστῷ πάντες ζῳοποιηθήσονται). The victory of God on which the apostle meditates here is thus all-embracing, moving from the present triumph of the faithful over sin and Satan to the culminating victory of the resurrection.

*through our Lord Jesus Christ!* We have throughout this commentary traced the way in which the Trinitarian structure of Paul's thought marks the entire chapter. Strikingly, in this climactic ascription of praise to God for his incomparable majesty and glory, Paul's divine and incarnational Christology, and his Trinitarian theology, are once again on full display: "Thanks be to *God*, who gives us the victory through our *Lord* Jesus Christ!" (15:57). Paul's language here recalls the central monotheistic confession of the Old Testament: Deut 6:4 LXX. This crucial Old Testament passage employs both the divine title "God" and the divine Name "the Lord" to affirm that the God of Israel is the only God: "Hear, O Israel, the Lord our God is one Lord!" Paul's ascription here of the divine title ("God") to the Father, and the divine Name ("Lord") to the Son (a practice that is a constant feature of his letters, e.g., Rom 5:1; 8:39; 15:6; 1 Cor 1:9; 6:11, 13–14; 2 Cor 13:13[14]; 1 Thess 3:11–13) identifies the "one God, one Lord" of Israel's central confession as God the Father and the Lord Jesus Christ. Paul's divine and incarnational Christology is strikingly evident. As he now celebrates "the Godness of God," the God whom he celebrates is the God made known in and as the incarnate Lord, Jesus Christ. The God whom Paul worships is Father, Son, and Holy Spirit.

In keeping with the deepened sense of the resurrection victory brought to light in the course of 15:54b–57, the διά clause here is comprehensive, including Christ's

---

27. Wolff, 418–19; cf. Godet, 2:447–48; Hays, 277; Fee, 892.
28. *Pace* Collins, 583.
29. Cf. Wolff, 419.

past saving acts, his living presence and power among his people in the present, and his raising to life of those who belong to him at his advent.[30] The διά clause here recalls 15:21: δι' ἀνθρώπου ἀνάστασις νεκρῶν ("*through* a human being came the resurrection of the dead"). The full title used here, "our Lord Jesus Christ," recalls the way in which Paul has now, through this chapter, illumined how it can be that the divine work of resurrection should come to pass "through a human being." For, as Paul has now shown, this human being is the divine Son of God (15:28), incarnate from heaven (15:47).

Together with the present participle διδόντι "gives," the full reference to "our Lord Jesus Christ" contrasts existence under the power of the law, sin, and death (15:56) with the new, heavenly life in Christ (15:45), which the faithful possess even now (15:48) and will possess in its fullness in the resurrection (15:49).[31] The victory over the law, sin, and death, in which Paul now exalts at this climax of the chapter, is nothing other than the *good news* that Paul set out to *make known* more fully to the Corinthians at the very beginning of the chapter (15:1, γνωρίζω δὲ ὑμῖν, ἀδελφοί, τὸ εὐαγγέλιον).[32] The chapter has now come full circle. In 15:1, Paul's statement "And I make known to you, brothers and sisters, the gospel" implied, as we saw, that Paul would in this chapter expound the same gospel he brought long ago to the Corinthians, but in such a way as to deepen and enrich their understanding of the apostolic message. That he has now done, and in spades.

## Verse 58

*So then, my beloved brothers and sisters, be steadfast, immovable, abounding in the work of the Lord always, knowing that your labor is not in vain in the Lord.*

Verse 58 brings chapter 15 to a conclusion. This final verse forms an *inclusio* with vv. 1–2 that frames the entire chapter. The central themes of vv. 1–2—*knowledge* of the gospel, *standing firm* in it, and *vanity*—all recur at the conclusion of the chapter here in v. 58:

| | |
|---|---|
| And I *make known* to you, *brothers and sisters*, the gospel ... in which you stand ... if you *hold it fast* ... unless you believed *in vain*. (15:1–2) | So then, my beloved *brothers and sisters*, be *steadfast, immovable* ... *knowing* that your labor is not *in vain* in the Lord. (15:58) |

---

30. Cf. Wolff, 419.
31. Söding, "Kraft," 82.
32. Wolff, 419 (following Schniewind).

But v. 58 also has a larger function. As we saw in chapter 1, chapter 15 brings to a close the main body of the epistle and is the culmination and climax of the entire letter. Therefore v. 58 also serves as the conclusion to the main body of the letter. Befitting its role as the conclusion to both the chapter and the body of the letter, v. 58, as we will see, deftly summarizes both the key themes of the chapter and the central themes of the letter as a whole.

*So then, my beloved brothers and sisters, be steadfast, immovable.* When used at the beginning of a sentence with an indicative or an imperative, as it is here, the inferential conjunction ὥστε ("therefore, so then") is highly emphatic.[33] As used here, the conjunction does not refer merely to the immediately preceding verses but to the chapter as a whole.[34] Paul is now drawing the entire chapter to its conclusion. The address ἀδελφοί ("brothers and sisters") occurs here for the fourth and final time in the chapter (15:1, 31, 50, 58). This address is common in 1 Corinthians, and elsewhere in Paul's epistles. But the fuller address we find here, ἀδελφοί μου ἀγαπητοί ("my beloved brothers and sisters"), is highly unusual for him (elsewhere in Paul only in Phil 4:1).[35] As Raymond F. Collins observes: "The exceptional character of this formula of direct address indicates that the exhortation provides a conclusion not only for the pericope and the chapter but also for the entire letter."[36] We see here again the culminating role of chapter 15 within the epistle.

The adjective ἑδραῖος "steadfast" is derived from the noun ἕδρα, which denotes a dwelling place, base, or established abode.[37] The root idea of the adjective is thus to be established in a fixed and unalterable dwelling place.[38] It is thus nicely complemented by ἀμετακίνητος, related to μετακινέω ("to move from one place to another") and meaning "immovable."[39] The two adjectives together strongly accent the idea of remaining firmly and fixedly in place. This is not a generic exhortation to general steadfastness but has in mind the false teaching addressed throughout the chapter—the false wisdom of the self-professed wise at Corinth who oppose the resurrection. The Corinthians must not be led away to this false teaching but must remain firmly grounded in Christ, not moved away from the

---

33. Robinson, s.v. "ὥστε" (3).
34. *Pace* Ellicott, 328. Rightly Schreiner, 326.
35. Schrage, 384; Lindemann, 371; Fee, 893 n. 410; Robertson & Plummer, 379.
36. Collins, 583.
37. Frisk, 1:443.
38. So BDAG, s.v. "ἑδραῖος": "pertaining to being firmly or solidly in place, *firm, steadfast.*" Cf. Frisk, 1:443: "mit festem Wohnsitz, fest."
39. So LSJ, s.v. "ἀμετακίνητος ": "*not to be moved from place to place, immovable.*"

hope of the resurrection.[40] The exhortation to steadfastness in the faith at the close of the chapter here in 15:58 recalls and repeats the appeal to stand firm in the gospel that opened the chapter in 15:1–2.[41]

*abounding in the work of the Lord always.* The previous clause repeated and reinforced the counsel of 15:1–2 to hold fast to the gospel; this clause now goes beyond this to exhort the Corinthians to active labor for Christ. This clause of the exhortation is made more winsome by a pleasing assonance, with the "p" sound occurring at the beginning of its opening and closing words (περισσεύοντες ... πάντοτε). Interpreters take different views regarding the nature and scope of "the work of the Lord" to which Paul here urges the Corinthians. The word ἔργον and its cognates are frequently used by Paul with reference to the work of spreading the gospel (Rom 16:3, 21; 1 Cor 9:1; 16:9–10; 2 Cor 11:13; Gal 2:8; Phil 1:22; 4:3; 1 Thess 3:2). For this reason some scholars conclude that Paul is speaking here of the work of mission, that is, winning unbelievers to the faith.[42] Other interpreters, by contrast, find here a general reference to any kind of activity undertaken for the Lord.[43] The key to the question, in my view, is the way in which Paul's language here calls his readers back to 3:5–15, the only other place in the letter where ἔργον "work" and κόπος "labor" occur together (3:8, 13–15; cf. 3:9). There Paul and Apollos are "coworkers of God" (3:9, θεοῦ γάρ ἐσμεν συνεργοί) and the Corinthians continue this work (3:10–15, ἔργον in 3:13 [2×], 14, 15).[44] Not only Paul who plants but also Apollos who waters engage in this activity (συνεργοί, 3:9). Likewise the household of Stephanas, who minister to the believers at Corinth (16:15, διακονίαν τοῖς ἁγίοις) also participate in this labor (16:16, παντὶ τῷ συνεργοῦντι καὶ κοπιῶντι). Paul's exhortation here thus embraces every kind of Christian work. But Paul's use here of the language of τὸ ἔργον τοῦ κυρίου ("the work of the Lord"), with its strongly missional overtones, places all this activity within the larger framework of the church's mission to "hold forth the word of life" (Phil 2:16). The church is missionary by its very nature.[45] Paul's choice of language here functions to reinforce this missional perspective and outlook.

---

40. Garland, 747; Fee, 893; Ellicott, 328–29; Lindemann, 372; cf. Aquinas, *1 Cor.* 1023.

41. H. H. Drake Williams, "Encouragement to Persevere: An Exposition of 1 Corinthians 15:58," *ERT* 32 (2008): 76; Lindemann, 372; Fee, 893; Garland, 747.

42. So Constantine R. Campbell, *Paul and the Hope of Glory: An Exegetical and Theological Study* (Grand Rapids: Zondervan Academic, 2020), 185, 440–41; Fee, 893; Collins, 583–84.

43. So Ciampa & Rosner, 838; Keener, 135; Garland, 747; Williams, "Encouragement to Persevere," 77–79.

44. Cf. Collins, 584.

45. On the missional nature of the church in Paul's theology, see James P. Ware, *Paul*

The genitive τοῦ κυρίου is a genitive of possession; it is the Lord's work, who assigns the labor to each person, and to whom an accounting will be due.[46] Moreover, in Paul's theology this work is in reality the activity of Christ, at work in the faithful through the power of his Holy Spirit.[47] Therefore, there may also be an undertone of the subjective genitive in the apostle's mind—it is the work that *God* does through his people (cf. 3:9, θεοῦ γάρ ἐσμεν συνεργοί; see also Rom 14:20, μὴ ... κατάλυε τὸ ἔργον τοῦ θεοῦ; 15:18; Phil 1:6; 2:12–13; 1 Thess 3:2).

*knowing that your labor is not in vain in the Lord.* This concluding clause, emphatic by its final position in the verse, receives additional emphasis through Paul's striking use of assonance: εἰδότες ὅτι ὁ κόπος ὑμῶν οὐκ ἔστιν κενὸς ἐν κυρίῳ. The language of knowledge and wisdom that has dominated the letter, especially chapters 1–4 (see 1:17–31; 2:1–16; 3:10–23; 4:9–13, 18–20), has its final and climactic occurrence with the participle εἰδότες "knowing" in v. 58. This participle εἰδότες is causal, supplying the motive not only for the preceding clause but also for the exhortation of the whole preceding verse.[48] The motive is the knowledge of the resurrection set forth in chapter 15.[49] This is the true knowledge that punctures the false wisdom of the self-professed wise at Corinth, who deny the hope of the resurrection, and who thus lack knowledge of God (15:34). Paul's final use here within the letter of the language of knowledge and wisdom, so prominent in the epistle, thus packs a wallop.

Like ἔργον in the previous clause, the evangelistic connotation of the noun κόπος (cf. John 4:38; 1 Cor 3:8; 2 Cor 10:15; 1 Thess 3:5) accents the missional purpose of all Christian work. But unlike ἔργον, the word κόπος "labor" highlights the burdensome, laborious nature of this work.[50] As Ceslas Spicq notes, the very word itself thus involves an exhortation: "There is no Christian life, no apostolic ministry, without rough, persevering labor."[51] The wording here recalls Paul's model of abundant labor by God's grace in 15:10 (περισσότερον ... ἐκοπίασα; cf. 15:58, περισσεύοντες ... ὁ κόπος ὑμῶν). It also recalls Paul's vivid description of his apostolic

---

*and the Mission of the Church: Philippians in Ancient Jewish Contex*t (Grand Rapids: Baker Academic, 2011).

46. Weiss, 380. Cf. Campbell, *Hope of Glory*, 185: "Christian service conducted for the cause and purposes of the Lord."

47. See Ware, *Mission of the Church*, 237–92.

48. Ciampa & Rosner, 838.

49. Schrage, 386 n. 1936.

50. *TLNT* 2:322–29; Schmidt, *Syn.*, 2:618 (§85.4); Trench, *Syn.*, 377–78; LSJ, s.v. "κόπος"; BDAG, s.v. "κόπος" ("to engage in activity that is burdensome, *work, labor, toil* ").

51. *TLNT* 2:329.

sufferings in 15:30–32.[52] In v. 58, the exhortation to follow Christ in the narrow way of discipleship, so prominent throughout the chapter (15:10, 19, 29–34, 48, 49), reaches its conclusion and climax.

A major theme of chapter 15 is that, apart from the resurrection hope, the gospel and faith are "in vain" (15:2, 14, 17, 58). Verse 58, as we have seen, thus forms an *inclusio* with v. 2, where this theme is first introduced, and brings this theme within the chapter to its climax. In this way, v. 58 also brings to a climax the whole body of the epistle for, as we saw, this theme was foreshadowed in the opening of the body of the letter in 1:17 (ἵνα μὴ κενωθῇ ὁ σταυρὸς τοῦ Χριστοῦ "in order that the cross of Christ not be made vain"). Verse 58 brings this theme to a powerful culmination by reversing the counterfactuals of 1:17 and 15:2, 14, 17: because of the sure hope of the resurrection, labor in the Lord is not in vain. The promise of eschatological reward for labor in the Lord's vineyard recalls 3:8, 10–15.[53] Here "in vain" is an effective litotes or rhetorical understatement, betokening a reward that is rich and full beyond measure.[54] This litotes is especially powerful, coming as it does at the conclusion of this chapter, with its mind-bending exposition of the resurrection as the body's participation in the very glory and presence of God.

But there is yet another reason why Paul knows that labor in the Lord is not in vain. Paul's language of "labor" and "vanity" alludes to Isa 49:4. Beneath Paul's shorthand allusion, like the tip of an iceberg, lies a rich theological reading of the book of Isaiah. This requires unpacking.

Isaian scholars Willem A. M. Beuken, Brevard Childs, and Joseph Blenkinsopp have argued persuasively for a crucial movement of thought within Isa 40–66 from an individual "Servant" in chapters 40–53 to a plurality of "servants" in chapters 54–66. The figure of the Servant of YHWH is unique to Isaiah 40–55. Integral to the development of the figure of the Servant within these chapters are four "Servant Songs" (42:1–9; 49:1–6; 50:4–11; 52:13–53:12), discrete poetic units that nonetheless function seamlessly within the larger literary context of chapters 40–55.[55] Corresponding to the individual identity of the Servant that emerges within these chapters, the term "servant" is always employed, from chapter 40 to the close of the fourth song, in the singular (42:1, 19; 43:10; 44:1–2, 21, 26; 45:4; 48:20; 49:3, 5–7; 50:10; 52:13; 53:11).[56] However, at the climax of the fourth song, the

---

52. Cf. Reasoner, on 15:58; Fee, 893.
53. Williams, "Encouragement to Persevere," 80.
54. Ciampa & Rosner, 838.
55. On the function of the Servant Songs within the literary framework of Isaiah 40–55, see W. A. M. Beuken, *Jesaja* (4 vols.; POuT; Nijkerk: Callenbach, 1979–1989), 2A:106–33; 2B:11–30, 183–241.
56. W. A. M. Beuken, "The Main Theme of Trito-Isaiah: 'The Servants of YHWH,'" *JSOT* 47 (1990): 67.

Servant is promised a seed or offspring (53:10).[57] This seed or offspring promised to the Servant, the faithful remnant redeemed by him, are then identified as "the servants of YHWH" in Isa 54:17.[58] Hereafter in the book of Isaiah the term "servant" occurs only in the plural (56:6; 63:17; 65:8–9, 13–15; 66:14), with reference to these followers of the Servant. They are the servants of the Servant.

Recent studies have shown that this interplay between the Servant and his servants within Isaiah is clearly recognized and undergirds a specific theological reading of the book in several New Testament texts, including Paul's letters.[59] In this ancient Christian exegetical tradition, Jesus Christ fulfills the prophetic promise of the Servant, and those united to Christ by faith are the servants of the Servant. This theological reading of the book of Isaiah underlies Paul's allusion here. In Paul's conception, it is the union of believers with the risen Christ through the gift of his Holy Spirit that empowers Christ followers to imitate him, as servant followers of the Servant. In Isaiah, just as the Servant of Isaiah did not "labor in vain" (Isa 49:4 LXX, κενῶς ἐκοπίασα), so also the servants of the Servant "will not labor in vain" (Isa 65:23 LXX, οὐ κοπιάσουσιν εἰς κενόν). Thus Paul knows that those who are in Christ, who are the servants of the Servant envisioned in Isaiah, will not labor in vain. We have already traced the various ways in which 1 Cor 15:58 forms an *inclusio* with the opening verses of the chapter, and here we find one more. For in 15:3 we saw that Christ is portrayed within the apostolic formula as fulfilling the promise of Isaiah's Servant, and here in 15:58 we find that those united to Christ are portrayed as fulfilling the promise of Isaiah's servants of the Servant.

Coming at the close of the verse, the expression "in the Lord" (ἐν κυρίῳ) expresses the truth of the union of the faithful with Christ. The words ἐν κυρίῳ are especially emphatic by their final position.[60] That Paul's exposition of the resurrection in this chapter should conclude with these words is quite fitting, for we have discovered that a major theme of 1 Cor 15 is the union of believers with

---

57. Beuken, "Servants of YHWH," 67–68.

58. Beuken, "Servants of YHWH," 67–68; Joseph Blenkinsopp, "The Servant and the Servants in Isaiah and the Formation of the Book," in *Writing and Reading the Scroll of Isaiah: Studies of An Interpretive Tradition* (ed. Craig C. Broyles and Craig A. Evans; Leiden: Brill, 1997), 1:157–58.

59. See, for example, Michael A. Lyons, "Psalm 22 and the 'Servants' of Isaiah 54; 56–66," *CBQ* 77 (2015): 640–56; Mark Gignilliat, *Paul and Isaiah's Servants: Paul's Theological Reading of Isaiah 40–66 in 2 Corinthians 5:14–6:10* (LNTS 330; London: T&T Clark, 2007); Holly Beers, *The Followers of Jesus as the 'Servant': Luke's Model from Isaiah for the Disciples in Luke-Acts* (LNTS 535; London: Bloomsbury T&T Clark, 2015); and James P. Ware, "The Servants of the Servant in Isaiah and Philippians," in *Isaiah's Servants in Early Judaism and Christianity: The Isaian Servant and the Exegetical Formation of Community Identity* (ed. Michael A. Lyons and Jacob Stromberg; WUNT 2.554; Tübingen: Mohr Siebeck, 2021), 255–71.

60. Lindemann, 372.

## The Resurrection of the Body as the Final Triumph of God

Christ. Through this union they are even now endowed with the very Spirit of God (15:45, 48), empowering them to follow the apostolic example of sacrificial service to Christ (15:10, 30–32). And the reason why Paul can here affirm that this labor is not in vain is that this life-giving union with Christ does not exclude but includes the body. That is Paul's point in this final clause of the chapter.

Paul's confidence expressed here that union with Christ must culminate in the resurrection brings to a climax a theme we have seen throughout 1 Cor 15. Thus the apostle's indignant rejection of the suggestion, inherent in the rejection of the hope of the resurrection, that those who have died "in Christ" (ἐν Χριστῷ) have perished (15:18). Thus his repudiation of the notion that the faithful have hope "in Christ" (ἐν Χριστῷ) for this life only (15:19). For "in Christ" (ἐν τῷ Χριστῷ) all the faithful will be made alive (15:22). The final outcome of their life-giving union with Christ will be the resurrection, when the body itself will be glorified, endowed with the presence and glory of the Spirit of God's Son (15:44, 46), and made like Christ's glorified body (15:49). It belongs to the very heart of the mystery of the resurrection in Paul's thought, that it is the consummation of that union with Christ begun in baptism, and preserved through faith and its fruits in the life of cruciform discipleship to Christ. It is thus fitting, in this final exhortation of the chapter, that Paul recalls to the minds of his hearers their identity "in the Lord." It is in the power of this present union with Christ, and in the sure and certain hope of its consummation at the resurrection, that Paul calls his readers to live. For, as Paul has shown throughout chapter 15, the Christian moral life is impossible apart from the hope of the resurrection. Christian faith in its true, radical form is trust in the staggering promise of the resurrection of the body. Christian faith is trust in the final triumph of God.

## *Acknowledgments*

I wish to thank the following persons who graciously took time from their own scholarly work to read all or parts of the manuscript and make helpful comments: Ernst Wendland, Mark Reasoner, Ron Mercer, Jeffrey A. Gibbs, Timothy A. Brookins, and Glen Thompson. I am grateful to the Rev. Thomas Fast for providing feedback on each chapter as it was completed, for our enriching discussions of 1 Cor 15, and for his prayers on behalf of this project. I am also grateful to Trevor Thompson, acquisitions editor at Eerdmans, for his support of this book from its inception, and to Laurel Draper and Blake Jurgens for their excellent editorial work and many improvements to the book. Above all, I wish to thank my beloved wife, Jan, who read through the first draft of the entire commentary and made many fruitful suggestions. I am also thankful for her overflowing love and encouragement through the many years of labor on this book. I could not have written it without her. To Jan this book is dedicated.

*James P. Ware*
*Evansville, Indiana*
*March 31, 2024*
*Easter Sunday of the Resurrection of the Lord*

# Index of Authors

Achtemeier, Paul J., 7n20, 372
Ackerman, David A., 12–13, 14n21, 16n31, 56n3
Ahern, Barnabas, 331
Allison, Dale C., Jr., 6n16, 68n11, 82, 83n62, 88, 89n85, 92n91, 95n96, 118n36, 118–20, 145–48, 149–51, 152, 165
Altermath, François, 3n2, 341n30, 346n38, 349n40, 358n66
Aquinas, Thomas, 136, 152, 159n19, 170n51, 174, 176n67, 186n100, 186n102, 194, 197n20, 203, 239n118, 263n77, 293n65, 316n18, 318n26, 332, 358n66, 387n57, 407n40
Asher, Jeffrey R., 5, 165n35, 187, 266n86, 273n15, 298n76, 309n15, 311n4, 316–17, 319n28, 321n34, 323n44, 324n46, 335, 340n27, 355n57, 368–69n7

Bachmann, Michael, 167, 169nn47–48, 172–74, 252n26, 262n68
Bailey, J. W., 216n20
Bailey, Kenneth E., 14–15, 20n20, 25n53, 45n121
Baird, William, 33, 36n99
Barclay, John M. G., 82n56, 109, 114n22
Barrett, C. K., 24n52, 30n30, 77n36, 79n45, 107n2, 124n3, 127n17, 151n31, 194n9, 214, 219, 225n53, 226n59, 253n29, 254n34, 255n39, 258n46, 258n49, 269n7, 276n5, 281, 294n67, 312n10, 318n26, 323n43, 327n55, 338n16, 352n46, 357n65, 360n71, 378n33, 390n62
Barth, Karl, 14, 16, 55, 57n12, 60n20, 65n41, 107, 151, 187n107, 248n8, 254n31, 258n49, 266nn87–88
Barthélemy, Dominique, 394n5
Bauckham, Richard, 70n14, 72n22, 73n24, 120n47
Baur, F. C., 32, 36–37
Becker, Jürgen, 6n16, 70n15, 92n90, 110n15, 114n22, 117n27, 117n29, 119–20, 121n51, 132n31
BeDuhn, Jason David, 198n23
Beers, Holly, 140n47, 410n59
Bell, Richard H., 70n14, 72n17
Belleville, Linda L., 19n44, 22n49, 23n50, 24n51, 26n57, 51n130, 56n4, 57n7, 351n45
Bender, Kimlyn, 128n24, 239n118, 265n81
Bergeron, Joseph W., 117n33
Beuken, W. A. M., 409, 410nn57–58
Bird, Michael F., 181n88
Bishop, Eric F. F., 117n31
Bjerkelund, Carl J., 16n32, 26, 27, 31, 154
Blenkinsopp, Joseph, 409, 410n58
Bockmuehl, Markus, 44, 45n121, 384n40
Boer, Martinus C. de, 11, 12n4, 15, 24nn63–64, 26, 36n100, 51n130, 55n2, 157n8, 159n20, 160n21, 197n21, 200n27, 226n56, 229, 231nn80–81, 306n7, 327n53, 397n13
Bolt, Peter G., 208n10, 209n11
Bonneau, Normand, 268n4, 271, 275nn1–2, 276n5, 277n6, 293n66, 316n16
Borg, Marcus J., 6n16, 81–82, 88, 89n83, 132n31
Borland, James A., 387n56

# INDEX OF AUTHORS

Bostock, D. Gerald, 207n7
Bowen, Clayton R., 258, 259nn54–56, 260
Braun, Herbert, 205nn1–3, 305–7, 309n14
Bremmer, Jan N., 103n18
Briggman, Anthony, 346n37
Brodeur, Scott, 339n20, 341n30, 342n33, 346n38, 354, 356n58, 357n62
Brookins, Timothy, 33n90, 34n94, 35n98, 37–39, 157n8, 326n53, 328n58
Brown, Paul J., 98n1, 156, 160
Brown, Raymond, 117n33, 383n39
Bruce, F. F., 127n117
Bryan, Christopher, 68n12, 94n93, 96n101, 144n1
Bucher, Theodor G., 166n36, 167–68, 170n52, 172, 176, 178, 179nn81–82, 183n95
Bultmann, Rudolf, 6, 89, 271n12
Bünker, Michael, 212n4, 368n3
Burchard, Christoph, 230, 287n43, 306n7, 339n19, 349n40, 357n63, 373
Burgess, Jonathan S., 99
Burnett, David A., 290n53, 297n72, 298n76, 299n97
Bynum, Caroline Walker, 4n7, 391
Byrne, Brendan, 244n132, 265n84, 266n89, 273n17

Calvin, John, 136n40
Campbell, Constantine, 174n63, 181n88, 193n8, 232n84, 276n5, 370n14, 407n42, 408n46
Carr, Frederick David, 16n31, 219n33
Cerfaux, L., 221n39
Chadwick, Henry, 3n3
Childs, Brevard, 409
Chilton, Bruce, 5n14, 7n20, 70n14, 72nn17–19, 82n56, 145n9, 165n35, 324n46, 334n6, 340n27, 368
Ciampa, Roy E., 13–14, 15, 20, 34n92, 37n105, 62n30, 73n25, 75n30, 81n55, 96n98, 107n3, 114n23, 117n28, 119n43, 122n52, 127n13, 137n41, 141n58, 193n7, 194n9, 201n29, 203n37, 213n6, 222n44, 231n79, 233n90, 234n93, 249n11, 250n19, 253n29, 254n34, 255n36, 255n39, 265n81, 269n7, 276n3, 276n5, 278n12, 282n23, 284n30, 285nn36–37, 290n53, 297n72, 314n13, 316n19, 323n43, 327n57, 331n62, 353n47, 354n54, 360n71, 363n79, 370n15, 377n33, 407n43, 408n48, 409n54
Classen, Carl Joachim, 17
Claudel, Gërard, 109n10
Collins, Raymond F., 9n24, 61n23, 62n30, 67n8, 73n25, 108n7, 122n52, 123n1, 128n24, 140n51, 157n7, 160n22, 168–69, 172n58, 181n89, 194n9, 214n10, 222n42, 228n66, 229n69, 233n90, 246n3, 248nn8–9, 252n56, 265n81, 268n1, 275n2, 276n5, 277n7, 297n72, 311n3, 323n43, 325n48, 326n50, 327n57, 337n13, 351n45, 377n33, 399n18, 404n28, 406, 407n42, 407n44
Conzelmann, Hans, 15n29, 57, 66n1, 66n3, 67n4, 70n15, 72n20, 76n35, 79n44, 81n52, 94n94, 169n47, 174n63, 178n77, 181n87, 185n98, 201n29, 214n10, 219, 224n52, 225n53, 242n122, 243nn127–28, 284n30, 286, 289n50, 290n52, 292, 294n67, 301n84, 305, 320n31, 333n1
Cook, John Granger, 83n62, 100n9, 101–2, 103, 104n25, 112n18, 144n1, 262n71, 263n72, 284n31, 294n67, 323n43, 350, 365n61
Coppins, Wayne, 56n4, 57n8, 58n15, 64n38
Cover, Michael Benjamin, 263n74
Cremer, Hermann, 58n16, 60n22, 124n5, 178n76, 180n85, 218n27, 249n12, 270n12, 289n48, 295n68, 301n83, 320n33, 321n35, 338n14, 376n31
Croon, Johan, 206n5
Crossan, John Dominic, 145n9
Crouzel, Henri, 3n3
Cullmann, Oscar, 147n16

Dahl, M. E., 3n2, 4n8, 5n12, 15n27
Dahl, Nils, 15n27
Dale, M. E., 190n1, 218nn28–29
Davis, Stephen T., 108n8, 110nn15–16
Dawes, G. W., 276n5
DeMaris, Richard E., 248, 250
Dempster, Stephen, 96n101
Derickson, Gary W., 239n118
Doole, J. Andrew, 258n49, 258n51, 261n65
Doty, William G., 16n35, 19n43, 22n49, 24n51, 26n57
Downing, F. Gerald, 38n111

## Index of Authors

Dunn, James D. G., 6n14, 8, 212n3, 214, 226n58, 234n95, 237n108, 311n4, 312n6, 324n46, 334, 342, 344, 346, 370n12
Dunsch, Boris, 263n78, 264n79
Dykstra, William, 174n63, 175n65, 190n2

Eadie, John, 75n31
Eckstein, Hans-Joachim, 69, 108n5, 108n7, 115, 116n25
Eijk, A. H. C. van, 83n62, 84n64
Ellicott, Charles J., 88n81, 136n40, 140n53, 270n9, 339n18, 371n18, 390n63, 406n34, 407n40
Ellis, E. Earle, 5n13, 17n38, 25n55, 222n42
Endsjø, Dag Øistein, 7, 98–102
Engberg-Pedersen, Troels, 5, 81–82, 88, 165, 229, 298n76, 299n77, 311n4, 324n46, 334n6, 340, 355n57, 356–57n61, 371, 385n47
Eriksson, Anders, 56n3, 72n22
Erlemann, Kurt, 331n64
Evans, Christopher F., 70n15, 94n94, 95n95, 114n22, 135n38
Evans, Craig A., 80, 91

Farmer, William, 78n39
Farnell, L. R., 100n8, 102n16
Fee, Gordon, 19n44, 24n52, 25n55, 34n92, 35n96, 61n25, 63n36, 73n23, 73n25, 76n32, 78, 81n55, 88n78, 94n93, 95n97, 96n99, 96n101, 107n2, 114n23, 117n32, 119n43, 122n52, 127, 151n31, 169n46, 174n63, 194n9, 219n35, 219n38, 222n42, 223nn45–46, 224n49, 226n58, 228n64, 235, 245n2, 248nn8–9, 251n25, 255n40, 256n42, 258n47, 258n49, 263n77, 265n82, 268n2, 268n4, 269n7, 278n12, 279n14, 281n12, 285n36, 290n53, 301n85, 314n13, 316n19, 320n31, 323n43, 327n57, 342n33, 343n34, 357n63, 370n14, 377–78n33, 383n39, 390n62, 398n16, 404n27, 406n35, 407nn40–42, 409n52
Fergusson, David, 14n18, 14n23, 75n28, 261n66
Finkenzeller, Josef, 84n62, 84n64
Fitzmyer, Joseph, 9, 12n11, 17, 24n52, 25n55, 33n88, 34n94, 44n116, 44n120, 51n130, 52n136, 56nn4–5, 58, 61n25, 76, 81n55, 88n78, 96n98, 108n8, 123n1, 140n52, 176n70,

185n98, 191n3, 194n9, 199n25, 201n29, 213, 225n53, 233n90, 234n96, 237, 245n2, 248n8, 250n19, 254n32, 263n72, 268n1, 269n6, 271n12, 275n2, 278n12, 279n14, 281n17, 285, 290n53, 291n58, 301nn83–84, 306n7, 311n2, 320n31, 320n33, 326n50, 351n45, 357n64, 370n14, 375n29, 378n33, 386nn48–49, 388n58, 390nn62–63, 398
Frazer, James George, 102–3
Fredericks, Daniel C., 74n26
Frederickson, David, 242n123, 243n126, 243nn128–29
Fredriksen, Paula, 5n14, 7, 58n15, 61n25, 62n30, 72n21, 73n23, 73n25, 75n30, 76n32, 165n35, 325, 368, 371n18
Fringer, Rob A., 57n6, 58n17, 247n5
Frisk, Hjalmar, 57n11, 58n13, 62n33, 84n64, 163n30, 180n84, 182n92, 183n96, 193n5, 321n35, 323n39, 323n45, 326n52, 406nn37–38

Gaffin, Richard B., 341n30, 346n38, 357n64
Gant, Peter, 82n56, 145n9
Garland, David E., 35n96, 61n23, 67n8, 73n25, 75n29, 77n37, 88n78, 94n93, 96n99, 96n101, 107n3, 108n8, 116n25, 117n32, 119nn44–45, 124n3, 124n6, 127, 128n24, 187n104, 197n19, 201n29, 213n5, 222n42, 225n53, 228n65, 229n69, 232n82, 233n90, 249n12, 250n19, 266n86, 268n4, 273n15, 276n5, 278n12, 281n22, 285nn36–37, 286n42, 298n76, 311n4, 316n21, 317n23, 319n28, 321n34, 323n44, 335n9, 357n65, 407nn40–41, 407n43
Gerhardsson, Birger, 66n1, 68, 94n93
Gerth, Bernhard, 53n137, 62n31, 75n31, 88n81, 124n8, 133n34, 172n56, 224nn49–50, 256, 268n5, 285n33, 312n7, 312n9, 313n11, 360n71
Gieniusz, Andrzej, 107n2, 108nn6–8, 110n15, 117n33, 127n20, 128n22
Gignilliat, Mark S., 140n47, 410n59
Gillman, John, 312n10, 325n48, 368–69, 372nn19–20, 377n33, 380n35, 386n49, 389n61, 392nn1–2
Gilmour, S. MacLean, 117n30
Given, Mark D., 291n55
Gladd, Benjamin J., 334n5

# INDEX OF AUTHORS

Godet, Frédéric, 24n52, 58n15, 60n21, 61n25, 75, 117nn28–29, 117n31, 119n43, 128n24, 140n49, 141n59, 201nn28–30, 214n10, 225n53, 232n82, 258n48, 260n61, 276n5, 282–83, 285n36, 295n70, 316n19, 317n23, 323n44, 339n19, 348n39, 357n65, 404n27
Goppelt, Leonhard, 335n10, 358n66
Graham, Daryn, 11n1
Grass, Hans, 6n14, 6n16, 89n83, 92n90, 109n13, 118n35, 144–46, 148, 165, 273n18, 291n55, 292n64
Green, Celia, 118n34
Grindheim, Sigurd, 37n105, 43–44n116, 301n83, 320n33, 333n3
Grudem, Wayne, 8, 9n23, 237
Gundry, Robert H., 270n12

Habermas, Gary R., 117n33, 148n20
Hall, David R., 34
Hamilton, James M., 9n23, 237n111
Hansen, G. Walter, 247n5
Harriman, K. R., 157n8, 158n12, 160–61
Hauger, Martin, 124n6, 244n131
Hays, Richard, 5, 12n10, 16, 63, 66n1, 88n82, 107n3, 119n43, 124n6, 129n25, 168n44, 187n105, 201n29, 202n34, 229n69, 234, 235n98, 258n49, 268n4, 269n7, 275n2, 300n81, 320n29, 323n43, 326n51, 351n45, 373n25, 395, 397nn10–11, 404n27
Head, Peter M., 19n44
Heil, John Paul, 212n4, 225nn55–56, 226n59, 235n100
Heil, Uta, 223nn46–47, 226n59, 230n76, 232n82, 233n87
Hengel, Martin, 5, 82–83, 141, 143–44n1
Henriksen, Jan-Olav, 81n54, 83n62, 89n85, 92n90, 94n93, 107n5, 108n7, 111n17, 135n38
Hill, C. E., 9n24, 212n2, 212n4, 214, 216n20, 218n28, 218n32, 218n34, 225nn53–54
Hill, Wesley, 9n24, 212n2, 212n4, 213, 214, 225nn55–56, 226, 235–36, 239n117, 241–42n121, 343n34, 344n35
Hoffmann, P., 145n9
Hollander, Harm W., 126n11, 128n24, 399
Holleman, Joost, 6n16, 82n56, 86–87, 109n13, 118n35, 194n11, 399

Horn, F. W., 398
Horsley, Richard, 37n104
Hull, Michael F., 248–49, 252
Hultgren, Stephen, 333n3, 334n4
Hurd, John Coolidge, 26n62, 160n22

Jamieson, R. B., 9n24, 214n13, 222n44, 232n84, 234n95, 238n118
Jeremias, Joachim, 72, 76, 78n39, 249nn13–14, 269n6, 370n14, 372n19, 373, 374, 375nn29–30, 378n33
Jobes, Karen H., 394n5
Johnson, Andrew, 5n13, 194n11, 314n13, 372n19, 373, 374, 375nn29–30, 378n33
Jones, Peter R., 123n2, 124n3, 124n6, 127n13, 346n38
Jordaan, G. J. C., 214n15

Käsemann, Ernst, 7
Kató, Szabolcs-Ferencz, 194n12, 196n16
Kearney, Peter J., 118
Keener, Craig, 7n20, 9n23, 114n23, 237n111, 292n64, 351n45, 371n18, 407n43
Kelly, J. N. D., 67n9, 301n83
Kendall, Daniel, 88n80
Kierkegaard, Søren, 350n42, 359n70
Kister, Menahem, 200n26, 334n4
Klappert, Berthold, 72
Klauck, H.-J., 17n35
Klinghardt, Matthias, 324n46
Kloppenborg, John, 66nn1–4, 67n5, 68n10, 70n16, 72n22, 73n24, 96n100
Kneale, Martha, 167n38
Koch, Dieterich-Alex, 113n21
Kotansky, Roy D., 109n13, 118n35
Kreitzer, L. Joseph, 214n11
Kremer, J., 83n62, 84n64, 85n68, 86n69
Kühner, Raphael, 53n137, 62n31, 75n31, 88n81, 124n8, 133n34, 172n56, 224nn49–50, 256, 268n5, 285n33, 312n7, 312n9, 313n11, 360n71
Kurth, Thomas, 263n75

Lake, Kirsopp, 144
Lambrecht, Jan, 57n12, 72n22, 75n28, 107n3, 119n43, 156n3, 156n5, 158n18, 159n20, 160n21, 167–68, 169n47, 170nn51–52, 172, 174n63, 176n67, 176n69, 179nn81–82, 212n4,

*Index of Authors*

223nn46–47, 226n56, 226n58, 230n76, 231n80, 232n83, 233n89
Lampe, Peter, 6n14, 6n16, 82n56, 291n55
Lang, Friedrich, 111n17, 134n36
Lapidge, M., 356n60
Legarreta-Castillo, Felipe de Jesús, 55n2, 106n18, 333n2
Lehmann, Karl, 67nn6–7, 92n90, 94n94, 96n101
Lehtipuu, Outi, 3n3
Lessing, Gotthold Ephraim, 149–50, 151, 152
Levison, John R., 326n53
Lewis, Scott M., 160n22, 211n1, 239n118
Lienhard, Joseph T., 217n25, 239n118
Lietzmann, Hans, 55
Lightfoot, J. B., 57
Lincoln, Andrew T., 157n7, 327n53, 327n57
Lindemann, Andreas, 6n14, 6n16, 63n36, 76n32, 81n52, 87, 89n83, 96n99, 96n101, 107n2, 109n13, 118n35, 119n45, 132n31, 137n41, 138n44, 141n55, 151n31, 191n3, 197n19, 200n27, 214n10, 229n69, 230n76, 234n93, 244n130, 245n2, 248n8, 254n32, 260n62, 261, 262n71, 265n81, 269n7, 279n14, 282n24, 285n36, 290n52, 305, 316n16, 316n19, 322n38, 335n10, 337, 339n19, 372n20, 380n35, 406n35, 407nn40–41, 410n60
Litfin, Duane, 15n27, 26n64, 37n105
Litwa, M. David, 298n76, 324n46, 334n6, 340n27, 355–56n57
Longenecker, Richard N., 383n39
Lüdemann, Gerd, 66n1, 87
Lührmann, Dieter, 42n114, 45n121, 48n126
Lütgert, W., 37n102
Lyons, Michael A., 139–40n47, 410n59

MacGregor, Kirk R., 70n14
MacMullen, Ramsay, 210n12, 272n14
Malcolm, Matthew R., 51n130, 157n7
Malherbe, Abraham J., 16–17n35, 182n90, 245, 258, 259n57, 260n60
Martin, Dale, 5, 7, 17, 33n90, 37n105, 157n8, 160n24, 165, 222n43, 228, 229n68, 273n15, 273n19, 276n5, 292n64, 298n76, 299n77, 311nn4–5, 312n6, 324n46, 340n27, 355n57, 356n58, 357n62, 371, 372, 383, 390

Martini, Jeromey, 197n19
Maston, Jason, 334n5
McCreery, Charles, 118n34
McGrath, James F., 8n22, 237n108
McIver, Robert K., 146n14
Meeks, Wayne, 212n3, 214–15, 234n35, 287n44, 331n63
Merklein, Helmut, 11–12n3
Metzger, Bruce M., 96n98, 175n66
Meyer, Ben F., 5n13, 373n25, 378n33
Milinovich, Timothy, 14–15, 56–57n6
Mitchell, Margaret M., 12–13, 15–16, 17n37, 20n46, 21n48, 24, 26, 27–30, 33n87, 33–34n91, 187, 212n4, 265, 266n85, 368n3
Mitchell, Matthew W., 125n10, 126n11, 128n21, 129n25
Moore, Terri, 103n18, 103n22, 248n10, 308nn11–12
Morissette, Rodolphe, 201, 277n9, 368–69, 372, 392n1
Moritz, Ludwig Alfred, 285n35
Moule, C. F. D., 171
Murphy-O'Connor, Jerome, 11n2, 70n15, 250nn20–21
Murray, John, 88n80

Nasrallah, Laura Salah, 161n26
Nickelsburg, George W. E., 128n23
Nilsson, Nils, 206n5
Nordgaard, Stefan, 332n2

O'Collins, Gerald, 88n80, 113n19
O'Connell, Jake H., 118n34, 144n1
O'Donnell, Brooke, 88n80
Oepke, A., 83n62, 86n69
O'Reilly, Matt, 12n10, 26n58, 48, 156n2, 156n4, 157n11, 158, 232n84, 247n4, 254n35, 258n49, 265n81, 265n83, 316, 323n43, 324n47, 327n56, 329n60, 338n17, 357n63, 370n14, 373n25

Padgett, Alan G., 273n15, 298n76, 299n77, 355n57, 356, 357n62
Pagels, Elaine E., 3n3
Park, Janghoon, 197n21
Pascuzzi, Maria, 33n86
Patrick, James E., 250n17

# INDEX OF AUTHORS

Paulsen, Henning, 52
Paulus, H. E. G., 144
Pearson, Birger, 33, 37, 44n116, 326n53, 333n2, 383n39, 384n41
Perrin, Nicholas, 103n23, 207n8, 307–8
Peterson, Jeffrey, 68, 79, 81n51, 116–17
Pfleiderer, Otto, 4–5n11, 324n46
Pickup, Martin, 95n97
Pitts, Andrew W., 17, 18n42
Plummer, Alfred, 34n94, 73n23, 75n29, 79, 113n20, 117n28, 117n31, 119n43, 124n4, 137n41, 139n46, 140n49, 140n53, 141n59, 174n63, 202n34, 213n6, 228n65, 232n85, 237n110, 246n3, 250, 252n28, 254n32, 258n49, 260n63, 265nn81–82, 268n4, 276n5, 279n15, 285n36, 290n52, 300n81, 316n18, 320n29, 357n65, 372n20, 384n45, 389n61, 390n63, 406n35
Pogoloff, Stephen M., 15n29, 27, 33n86, 37n105, 37n107, 52n133
Poirier, John C., 95n97
Popko, Łukasz, 396n8
Porter, Stanley, 72n18
Potgieter, Pieter, 214, 237n110
Prince, Deborah Thompson, 101n13
Proctor, Mark A., 168n42, 172n58, 178n80, 181n88, 185n98

Rabens, Volker, 323n43, 327n57
Radl, Walter, 57n11, 57n13
Raeder, Maria, 249, 252
Rashkow, Ilona, 126n10
Reasoner, Mark, 64n38, 247n5, 255n37, 278n12, 290n52, 291n61, 355n56, 362n75, 388n58, 409n52
Reaume, John D., 249, 251n25, 252, 253
Redman, Judith C., 146n14
Reimarus, Hermann Samuel, 144
Richards, Larry, 239n117
Riesenfeld, Harald, 281n19, 309n15
Ring, George C., 103n22, 207n8
Robertson, Archibald, 34n94, 73n23, 75n29, 79, 113n20, 117n28, 117n31, 119n43, 124n4, 137n41, 139n46, 140n49, 140n53, 141n59, 174n63, 202n34, 213n6, 228n65, 232n85, 237n110, 246n3, 250, 252n28, 254n32, 258n49, 260n63, 265nn81–82, 268n5, 276n5, 279n15, 285n36, 290n52, 300n81, 316n18, 320n29, 357n65, 372n20, 384n45, 389n61, 390n63, 406n35
Robertson, A. T., 53n37, 61nn24–26, 62n29, 63n37, 88n81, 116n26, 118n40, 135n39, 140n48, 141n54, 182n93, 198, 224n49, 224n51, 228n65, 252n27, 255n37–38, 256n41, 256n44, 263n73, 266n90, 268n5, 279n13, 283n28, 285n34, 291n59, 295n70, 311n2, 313nn11–12, 335n8, 354n55, 360nn71–73, 363n79, 384n43, 387n54, 393n3, 402n25
Robinson, Edward, 52n134, 59n19, 61n24, 62n31, 62n33, 74n26, 127n13, 186n101, 251nn22–23, 264n80, 270nn10–11, 284n29, 289n47, 297n74, 298n75, 319n27, 362n76, 397n12, 406n33
Robinson, James M., 6n16, 89n83, 132n31
Rose, H. J., 204n1, 206n5, 307n9
Rosner, Brian S., 13–14, 15, 20, 34n92, 37n105, 62n30, 73n25, 75n30, 81n55, 96n98, 107n3, 114n23, 117n28, 119n43, 122n52, 127n13, 137n41, 141n58, 193n7, 194n9, 201n29, 203n37, 213n6, 222n44, 231n79, 233n90, 234n93, 249n11, 250n19, 253n29, 254n34, 255n36, 255n39, 265n81, 269n7, 276nn3–5, 278n12, 282n23, 284n30, 285nn36–37, 290n53, 297n72, 300n82, 314n13, 316n19, 320n32, 323n43, 327n57, 329n59, 331n62, 353n47, 354n54, 360n71, 363n79, 370n15, 377n33, 407n43, 408n48, 409n54
Rowe, C. Kavin, 344n36

Sampley, J. Paul, 160n22, 174n63, 258n49
Sandelin, Karl-Gustav, 213n6
Sanders, E. P., 145n9
Sandnes, Karl Olav, 81n54, 83n62, 89n85, 92n90, 94n93, 107n5, 108n7, 111n17, 135n38
Saw, Insawn, 12n10, 56n3
Schaefer, Markus, 127, 129
Schep, J. A., 96n98, 110n16, 135n37, 157n8, 280n16, 281n18, 286n41, 291n56, 292, 316n18, 341, 358n56, 372n19, 373, 375n30
Schlier, Heinrich, 66n1
Schmidt, J. H. H., 57n11, 110n14, 124n5, 163n32, 182n92, 183n97, 193n5, 218n27, 228n67, 291n59, 295n70, 317, 321n37, 338n14, 381n36, 388n59, 408n50

## Index of Authors

Schmithals, Walter, 32–33, 37
Schmitt, Joseph, 67n7
Schneider, Bernadin, 334n5, 341n30
Schoeps, H. J., 127n17
Scholla, Robert, 364nn81–82
Schrage, Wolfgang, 9n24, 14n21, 62n30, 67n4, 67n6, 70n15, 72n21, 73nn23–25, 78n39, 88n78, 92n90, 94n94, 96n101, 111n17, 117n29, 119n43, 120n49, 124nn3–4, 124n6, 127n14, 128n24, 129n25, 137n41, 139nn45–46, 202, 214n10, 223n47, 225n53, 227, 228n65, 229n69, 230, 234n93, 240n120, 243n148, 245n2, 248n8, 250n18, 258n47, 258n49, 262n71, 263n77, 265nn81–83, 268n2, 268n4, 269n7, 275n2, 278n12, 281n22, 284n30, 285n38, 291, 293n66, 294n67, 295n69, 306n7, 309n14, 315n14, 316n19, 319n28, 321n34, 322n48, 335n10, 357n63, 384n44, 385n46, 386n49, 397n9, 397n12, 402n25, 406n35, 408n49
Schreiner, Thomas R., 9n24, 17, 24n52, 25n55, 33n88, 78n39, 107nn3–4, 117n31, 119n43, 124n6, 129n25, 157n8, 168n44, 194n9, 197n19, 201n32, 214n10, 248nn8–9, 258n49, 265n82, 269n7, 270n8, 276n5, 300n80, 320n29, 323n43, 327n57, 357n64, 370n15, 383n39, 397n10, 406n34
Schubert, P., 22n49
Scott, James M., 127n16
Sharp, Daniel B., 248n8
Sider, Ronald, 5n13, 81n54, 94n93, 110n16, 134n36, 269n7, 276n5, 279n12, 279n15, 282n25, 285n36, 286, 314n13, 372n19, 378n33, 390n65
Silva, Moisés, 394n5
Simon, Marcel, 51–52n133
Sleeper, C. Freedman, 117n30
Smith, Daniel A., 5n14, 6n16, 82n56, 87n74, 109n13, 118n35, 132n31, 133, 145n9, 165n35, 334n6, 339–40
Smith, Jonathan Z., 103n18
Smith, Morton S., 103n18
Smith, Murray J., 227
Söding, Thomas, 399n20, 400n22, 401n24, 403n26, 405n31
Spicq, Celas, 62, 291, 408

Spörlein, Bernhard, 5n13, 84n64, 284n32, 314n13, 373n25, 390n65
Stenger, Werner, 56n3, 176n67, 179n82, 312n10, 325n48
Sterling, Gregory E., 333n2
Strauss, David Friedrich, 144
Strawbridge, Jennifer R., 1n1
Strüder, Christof W., 34n91
Suh, Michael K., 288n48
Sumney, Jerry, 6n14
Sysling, Harry, 353n49, 354n50, 365nn83–84
Szymik, Stefan, 156n3, 158n17, 160n24

Talbert, Charles H., 98, 101nn13–14
Tannehill, Robert C., 79n42
Teichmann, Ernst, 4–5, 8, 165, 311n4, 324n46, 371n18
Thayer, Joseph Henry, 62n33, 116n26, 118n40, 124n7, 128n24, 141n57, 171, 251n23, 289n47
Thielman, Frank, 398n16
Thiessen, Jacob, 194n12, 195n13
Thiselton, Anthony C., 5n13, 13, 14n21, 16n31, 37n105, 37n107, 52n136, 61n23, 63, 67n8, 114n23, 117n29, 117n31, 119n43, 122n52, 129n25, 138, 141n59, 157n7, 181n88, 200n26, 224n51, 243n127, 249n13, 268n4, 269n7, 285n36, 315n14, 318n26, 323n43, 372n22
Thomasen, Einar, 87
Thüsing, Wilhelm, 213n6, 216–17, 231n79, 233n86, 233n88, 235n100, 237n110, 238, 239n118, 240n120
Toit, A. B. du, 88, 144n1
Tomlin, G., 38n111
Trench, R. C., 266n91, 291n59, 295n70, 327n54, 408n50
Tuckett, Christopher M., 156n7, 158, 326n53
Turner, Seth, 212n2, 214n11, 223n47, 225nn53–54
Twelftree, Graham H., 148n20

Vaillancourt, Ian J., 227
Vlachos, Chris Alex, 398n14, 398n16, 399n20, 400n21
Vorster, J. N., 141, 158, 170, 187n106
Vos, Johan, 156n3, 156n5, 158n18, 167–68, 170nn51–52, 172, 176n67, 176n69, 177, 178, 179n82, 183n95

# INDEX OF AUTHORS

Walker, William O., Jr., 247n6
Walter, Nikolaus, 5–6n14, 6n16, 290n55
Walton, Francis R., 204n2, 207n9, 221
Ware, James P., 73n24, 83n63, 89n85, 106n1, 140n47, 198n23, 222n42, 242n121, 290n54, 291n56, 343n34, 344n35, 407–8n45, 408n47, 410n59
Wasserman, Emma, 222n42
Watson, Duane F., 56n3, 212n4, 368n3
Watson, Francis, 221n40
Webber, Randall C., 70n15
Wedderburn, A. J. M., 157nn9–10, 158n12
Wegener, Mark, 16n30, 56n3
Weiss, Johannes, 57n12, 61n25, 109n13, 119n43, 141n57, 168n40, 171n53, 172n58, 194n9, 214n10, 218n28, 226n58, 268n2, 268n4, 269n7, 282n25, 284n30, 311n3, 316n18, 322n38, 408n46
Welborn, Laurence L., 27, 28, 30n78, 32n82, 37n106
Wells, Bruce, 196n17
Wenham, David, 291n56, 387n55
Wheelwright, Philip, 206n6
White, Joel, 194n12, 248n7, 250n17, 250–51n20, 251n25
White, John L., 16n35
Wiles, Gordon P., 14n22, 16n32
Williams, David J., 50n128, 126n11, 195n15, 259n52, 307

Williams, H. H. Drake, 407n41, 407n43, 409n53
Wilson, Andrew, 230n75
Wilson, Jack H., 157n9, 159n20, 160
Winter, Bruce, 33n86, 37n105
Witetschek, Stephan, 147n16
Wolff, Christian, 20, 22, 23n50, 25nn52–53, 25n55, 44n120, 58n14, 62n30, 66n3, 67n4, 70n15, 72n21, 76n33, 78n39, 81nn53–54, 88n78, 92n90, 94n93, 97n102, 108nn5–8, 110n16, 116n25, 117nn29–30, 118n39, 119n43, 124n6, 134n36, 140n50, 169n45, 174n63, 181n87, 191n3, 194n9, 198n24, 201n29, 223n47, 225n53, 230nn73–74, 231n79, 232n83, 232n85, 233n89, 239n117, 243n127, 243n129, 244n130, 258n49, 260n63, 265n81, 265n83, 268, 285nn36–37, 289n46, 294n67, 301n84, 305, 306n6, 309nn14–15, 311nn3–4, 316n21, 317n23, 320nn30–31, 323nn43–44, 327n57, 331n62, 339n19, 350n43, 360n71, 375n30, 377n33, 385n46, 386n48, 389n50, 404n27, 404n29, 405n30, 405n32
Wright, N. T., 5, 81n55, 82–83, 95n96, 132n31, 134n36, 143n1, 147n16, 148, 150, 236, 237n105, 276n3, 277, 297n72, 339n17, 342n33, 344n35, 354n54, 357n65, 373

Yarbro Collins, Adela, 6n16, 82, 132n31, 144–46, 148, 371

Zeller, Dieter, 37n104, 243nn128–29, 251n25

## Index of Subjects

Abraham, 80, 96, 108, 375
Achilles, 99, 165, 205, 209
Acts of the Apostles, 2, 3, 51, 89–91, 92, 96, 106, 109, 111–15, 117, 122, 130, 132, 133–37, 145
Adam, 174, 190–91, 196–97, 198–202, 316–17, 334, 336, 337–38, 341, 347–48, 350, 352–53, 354–55, 360–61, 362–64, 365, 399, 401; second, 232, 238–39, 333–35, 339–41, 347–50, 355–59, 366
Adonis, 104. *See also* dying and rising gods
advent of Christ. *See* second coming
Aeschylus, 162, 166, 205, 209, 396
Aetius, 102
all in all (τὰ πάντα ἐν πᾶσιν), 213, 218, 240–44
anaphora, 310, 311, 318, 362. *See also* rhetorical device
angels, 95, 108, 198n23, 222n43, 261, 374–76, 381
Anselm, 78
Apollo, 103, 162, 166, 205, 209, 396
Apollonius of Tyana, 101–2
Apollos, 32–35, 37, 268, 407
apostolic commission, 36, 40, 49, 75, 112–13, 115–16, 121, 137
apostolic formula, 1, 7, 66–97, 105–53, 170–71, 181, 204, 410
apostolic testimony, 24–25, 59, 66, 73, 74, 105–7, 131–37, 139, 141, 147, 150–51, 171, 177–79, 187, 191. *See also* resurrection: testimony to
apostolic work. *See* labor

Arianism, 212, 237
Aristeas of Proconnesus, 101
Aristotle, 29, 166–67, 208, 283, 286, 287, 306, 385n47
Artemis, 258, 261
ascension, 113, 114, 117, 122, 130, 131–33, 136–37, 224, 358
asyndeton, 63, 228, 277n7, 311, 355. *See also* rhetorical device
Athena, 205
Athenagoras, 166, 242, 271
atonement, 77–79, 80, 181, 399–400; in the Old Testament, 79–80, 96–97
Attis, 104. *See also* dying and rising gods
Augustine, 4, 17, 239, 332, 346n37, 359

baptism, 10, 22, 23, 36, 76, 81, 113, 151, 202, 230, 251–52, 287, 330–32, 336, 337, 344, 351–52, 360–61, 364, 366, 367, 411; for the dead, 1, 10, 157–58, 173, 248–53
Barnabas, 122
beasts, fighting with, 1, 10, 187, 246, 257, 258–62
boasting, 13, 25, 35, 38, 42–43, 140, 167, 247, 255–57, 265, 278, 393, 397, 398–99, 403
bodily resurrection, 2–4, 5, 6–8, 10, 48, 64, 86–88, 104, 110–11, 115, 120, 122, 132, 134–37, 144–46, 156–58, 162, 163–65, 182, 185–86, 191, 193, 198, 200, 209–10, 213, 262, 266, 267, 270–72, 280–82, 284–86, 292–93, 307, 309, 310–32, 352, 365–66, 379, 384, 390, 397–98,

423

# INDEX OF SUBJECTS

411. *See also* burial (θάπτω); empty tomb; flesh, resurrection of the; non-fleshly resurrection, claim of; resurrection; risen body

burial (θάπτω), 68, 80–81, 89–91, 92–93, 97, 99, 151, 163, 190, 314, 316–17, 319, 321, 322–23. *See also* empty tomb

Cadmus, 100, 205
calling, 22, 23, 247, 264
Castor, 99, 100
Celsus, 166, 272, 317–18
Cephas. *See* Peter
Chloe, 30, 32, 34n91, 268
Christ (Χριστός), 76–77, 191, 211, 264
Christology, 1, 8–9, 185, 212, 214, 221, 230, 231–32, 234–37, 239–40, 257, 321, 335, 339, 341–52, 386, 389, 404; and the Old Testament, 79–80, 227, 236, 257, 334, 362. *See also* coequality of the Father and the Son; incarnation; "Spirit-Christology," of James D. G. Dunn; subordination of the Son; Trinity
Christ party, 32–33
church of God, 22–23, 137–38
Cicero, 38, 101, 207, 208
Clement of Alexandria, 394
Clement of Rome, 3–4, 275
Cleomedes, 101
coequality of the Father and the Son, 9, 220–21, 226, 232, 239–40. *See also* subordination of the Son; Trinity
collection for the saints, 19–20, 121
consummation of the kingdom (τέλος), 23, 45, 217–19, 221, 227, 232, 238, 302, 336, 349, 380, 411. *See also* reign of Christ; second coming
Corinthians, First Letter to the: body closing, 18–20, 406; body opening, 18, 19, 25–41, 49, 54, 55, 65, 154–55, 175, 257; chief concern of, 26, 27–32, 34, 40, 41, 46, 54, 154–55, 161, 169–70, 263, 265, 270; letter closing, 18–19; salutation, 18, 22–23, 53, 221, 257; structure of, 15–16, 18–25, 53–54, 246–47; thanksgiving, 18, 22–25, 26, 32, 41, 53, 55, 65, 155, 179, 218, 257; unity of, 11–16, 24, 41–54

corruptibility (φθαρτός), 50, 115, 272, 282, 314, 316–17, 318, 319, 322, 326, 328, 338, 348, 352, 360, 367, 369, 370, 372–80, 381–82, 385n47, 386, 389–91, 392, 393; moral, 39, 45–46, 47, 263–64. *See also* incorruptibility (ἄφθαρτος)
cosmic powers, 190, 221, 223, 224, 229, 230, 233, 397, 401; in the Old Testament, 222
covenant, 80, 235, 296n71, 395, 401–2
creation, 190, 197, 221, 275–76, 289–91, 295, 333, 338–39, 353–55, 364, 401; and resurrection, 280, 285, 288, 289–90, 294, 297, 302–4, 336, 365
cross, 46–47, 64, 77–78, 80, 87, 93, 135, 181, 191, 203, 239, 247, 254, 255, 257, 261, 263, 350, 352, 364, 393, 399, 409; sign of, 287, 331, 336; word (λόγος) of, 30, 39–40, 43, 77, 151, 321–22, 398, 402, 403
cruciform discipleship, 10, 32, 40, 46–47, 54, 186–87, 203, 246–47, 255, 364, 411

David, 76, 80, 215, 227
day of the Lord, 22, 24, 219. *See also* second coming
death (θάνατος), 120, 181–82, 193, 196–98, 201, 222, 229–30, 354, 338, 395–96, 399–400, 401; conquest of, 8, 43, 50, 79, 87–88, 121, 164, 174, 180, 192, 194, 199, 211, 213, 225, 227, 228–31, 244, 388, 392–93, 394–98, 402–4
Demeter, 206, 208, 209, 307–9. *See also* mysteries
demonic powers, 79, 190, 211, 213, 223–25, 401, 402; in the Old Testament, 222–23
diatribe, 245, 247–48, 266, 267, 278, 279
Diogenes Laertius, 51n132, 102
Dionysius of Halicarnassus, 102
Dionysus, 103–4, 206, 208
discipleship. *See* cruciform discipleship; sanctification
disclosure (γνωρίζω) formula, 36, 45, 56, 57–58, 59, 75, 154, 384, 405
division. *See* factionalism
Domitian, 259
dualism, 157, 158–59, 383
dying and rising gods, 102–4

Easter, 1, 86, 122, 123, 144–46, 174

# Index of Subjects

Elysium, 98, 99–100, 204–5, 207, 209
Empedocles, 101
empty tomb, 6, 7, 69, 87, 89–91, 94–95, 114, 132, 144–46, 148
Ephesus, 1, 10, 11, 187, 246, 257–58, 260–61, 262
Epictetus, 119, 278n10, 306
Epicureanism, 51, 159, 208, 294n67, 396
epistolary analysis, 16–54, 57, 161n26, 179, 218
epistolary situation, 17–18, 161n26
Essenes, 51
Eucharist, 20, 21, 50–51, 53, 68, 76, 79, 151, 287, 344, 351–52, 362, 366, 367
*Eumenides*. See Aeschylus
Euripides, 262–63
Ezekiel, 29

factionalism, 12, 13, 15, 18, 20–21, 26–35, 40, 50–53, 154, 158, 169–70
faith (πίστις), 10, 39, 41–42, 46, 50–53, 60, 61, 63–65, 107, 139, 140, 149–53, 155, 159–60, 175–77, 180–81, 183–84, 185, 186–87, 246, 248–49, 253, 261, 265–66, 280, 304, 332, 349, 361, 366, 397, 407, 409–11
fall, 190, 196–98, 232, 291, 317, 334, 338, 348, 349, 354–55, 364, 399
First Corinthians. See Corinthians, First Letter to the
firstfruits (ἀπαρχή), 121, 164, 174, 180, 192–96, 198, 202–3, 288, 330–31, 336, 337, 349, 352–53, 380, 385; Feast of, 97, 194–96
flesh (σάρξ), 270, 289, 290–93, 316, 325, 338, 379; and blood (αἷμα), 7, 293, 328, 340, 367, 371–81, 382, 385–86, 389–90, 391, 397; and bones, 376–77; resurrection of the, 3–7, 90–91, 164–65, 267, 270–71, 273–74, 280–82, 292–93, 303–4, 315, 324, 379–86, 391, 393. *See also* glorification of the flesh
*Folgetext*, 41, 47, 48, 53

glorification of the flesh, 275, 288–93, 303–4, 331, 352, 363, 377–81, 386, 389, 391, 393–94, 411
glory (δόξα), 44–45, 48, 79, 87, 132, 135–36, 185, 186, 213, 217, 225, 233, 238, 240, 244, 281–82, 310, 314, 319–21, 326, 328–29, 332, 347, 353, 358–59, 375, 380, 391, 398, 404, 409, 411; body of, 194, 210, 299–303, 321, 348, 386; of heavenly bodies, 293, 294–99, 363; Lord of, 44, 301, 320, 401–2
Gnosticism, 3–4, 37, 83n61, 212, 333
Good Friday, 1, 123
gospel: foolishness of, 15, 53, 140, 271–73, 318; made vain (κενός, μάταιος), 15, 39–40, 46, 53–54, 139, 155, 175–76, 180, 245–66, 409–10; Paul's, 13, 15, 24–25, 26, 30, 36–37, 41–43, 47, 57, 59–65, 74–75, 137, 141, 161, 169, 179, 198, 201, 209, 222n42, 396, 405, 407
grace (χάρις), 60, 138–39, 140, 152–53, 197, 201, 216, 338, 403, 408
*gradatio*, 397, 398. *See also* rhetorical device
Gregory of Nyssa, 217n25, 345, 387

Hades, 103, 204, 207, 308–9
hardship catalogue, 1, 46–47, 246–47, 254, 255, 261
heaven (οὐρανός), 6, 82, 86–87, 93, 136, 145, 194n11, 199, 238, 296, 299–301, 355, 358–59, 360–63, 366, 405
heavenly bodies, 293–99, 301–2, 303, 310, 320, 340, 353, 355–57, 361, 363, 364
Helen, 205
Heracles, 100–101, 206
Heraclitus, 272, 319
Herodotus, 100, 165
heroes, 98–102, 104, 110, 160, 205, 207–8, 209
Hesiod, 99, 204–5, 207
Hipparchia, 243
Hippocrates, 125
Holy Spirit, 9, 10, 45, 48, 78, 129–30, 182, 199, 202–3, 242, 265, 287–88, 291–92, 322, 327–32, 333–66, 367, 380, 386, 391, 396, 402, 404, 408, 410. *See also* life-giving (ζῳοποιέω); spiritual (πνευματικός)
Homer, 99, 186, 204–5, 206–7, 209, 308
homoioptoton, 310, 318. *See also* rhetorical device
Hyginus, 100
hyperbaton, 384. *See also* rhetorical device
Hyperboreans, 205–6

idolatry, 13, 20–21
Ignatius, 260

## INDEX OF SUBJECTS

ignorance (ἀγνωσία), 31, 42, 46, 58, 244, 265, 268, 279, 408
image (εἰκών), 362–64
incarnation, 76–77, 182, 198–99, 229, 345n37, 347–50, 352, 358–59, 361, 365–66, 367, 383; and Paul's Christology, 8–9, 185, 212, 214, 221, 235–36, 238–39, 257, 321, 386, 389, 404
*inclusio*, 41, 43, 45, 47, 56–58, 64, 75, 137, 140, 236n103, 256–57, 261, 300, 320, 328, 403, 405, 409, 410
incorruptibility (ἄφθαρτος), 50, 60–61, 98, 310, 314, 318, 326, 330–32, 338, 367, 369, 370, 378–79, 381–83, 385n47, 386, 387, 388–91, 392, 393. *See also* corruptibility (φθαρτός)
inheriting the kingdom, 7, 238, 293, 367, 371, 377–79, 380–83, 389
Ino, 99, 100
Irenaeus, 332
Isis, 103, 208, 307–9
Isocrates, 308

James (brother of Jesus), 50, 67, 70–72, 75, 105–7, 112–13, 121–22, 123–24, 131, 133, 137, 147–48
James (son of Zebedee), 106
Jeremiah, 29, 80
Jerome, 3n5
Jerusalem, 72, 80, 113–14, 117, 121, 123, 136–37, 147–48, 394
John, Gospel of, 2–3, 7, 82, 92–93, 97, 111, 112, 113, 114, 115, 122, 130, 144–45, 148, 239, 358
John Chrysostom, 34–35, 65, 217n25, 249, 254, 280, 307, 387
Josephus, 29, 51, 148
Judaizers, 36–37

kerygma (κήρυγμα), 6, 15, 41–42, 62, 68, 76, 81, 90, 93, 140, 145, 155, 169, 170–71, 175–77, 180–81, 183–84, 186, 189, 192, 225, 246, 322, 399
knowledge, 22, 23, 25, 38, 42, 57–58, 64, 79, 131, 161, 165, 267, 273, 408; of God, 42, 45–46, 152, 244, 247, 264–66, 268, 278–79, 402, 408; of the gospel, 57–58, 68, 72–73, 405. *See also* speech; wisdom (σοφία)

labor, 39, 49–50, 57–58, 138–40, 151, 393, 405, 407–11

Last Supper, 68, 151
law of Moses, 78, 80, 181, 227, 393, 398, 400–402, 403–4, 405
life-giving (ζῳοποιέω), 7, 202, 233, 235, 334, 339, 342, 346–52, 359, 361, 365, 367, 404, 411
litotes, 409. *See also* rhetorical device
logical forms, 166–89. *See also modus ponens*; *modus tollens*; *reductio ad absurdum*; *sorites*
Lord's Supper. *See* Eucharist
Lucian, 38, 101
Luke, Gospel of, 2–3, 7, 82, 89–91, 92–93, 95, 97, 109, 111–15, 117, 122, 130, 132, 133–36, 144–45, 148, 358

Marcionites, 251
Mark, Gospel of, 3, 7, 82, 92–93, 97, 111, 113, 122, 144–45, 148
martyrdom, 106–7, 148, 249, 253, 330
Mary Magdalene. *See* women at the tomb
Matthew, Gospel of, 3, 7, 82, 92–93, 97, 111–14, 122, 144–45, 148
Menander, 262–64
Menelaus, 99, 100, 205
metempsychosis. *See* reincarnation
Methodius, 3n5
mirror reading, 18, 30, 326n53
Mithras, 104. *See also* dying and rising gods
*modus ponens*, 166–67, 170, 189
*modus tollens*, 166–67, 172, 175, 178, 189
mysteries, 76, 102–4, 199, 221, 239–40, 274, 280, 282, 345, 347, 349, 359, 365, 367–70, 381, 383–84, 385, 386, 390, 394, 398, 401–2; of God, 43–45, 58–59, 327, 335, 383–84; of the resurrection, 275, 285–86, 302–4, 411
mystery cults, 160, 206–7, 208, 209, 307–9

Neopythagoreans, 208
non-fleshly resurrection, claim of, 3, 4–8, 9, 81–82, 86–88, 91, 109, 131–37, 144, 156–57, 209–10, 212, 311–12, 324–26, 334, 355–57, 360, 382–83. *See also* bodily resurrection; resurrection
nymphs, 205–6

Ophites, 3, 83n61. *See also* Gnosticism
Origen, 3, 4
Orphism, 206–7, 209

426

*Index of Subjects*

Osiris, 103–4, 207–8, 308–9
Ovid, 100, 101

*parakalō* (παρακαλῶ) clause, 26, 30–32, 154
parousia. *See* second coming
Passover, 68, 79, 97, 195–96
Peleus, 99, 100, 205, 209
Pentecost, 117n30, 121, 130, 195
Peregrinus, 101
Persephone, 104, 206, 208, 308–9. *See also* dying and rising gods; mystery cults
Peter, 32–34, 37, 49–50, 67, 68, 70–72, 75, 105–7, 112–15, 116, 121, 123–24, 131, 133, 135, 137, 147–48
Pharisees, 51
Philo of Alexandria, 37, 38, 108, 195, 294n67, 326n53, 327, 333, 350n44
philosophy, 37–39, 160–61, 166–68, 208–9, 228–29, 247–48, 263, 271–73, 294n67, 303, 311, 318, 340, 385n47
Philostratus, 99, 100, 101–2
physical resurrection. *See* bodily resurrection
Pindar, 206–7
Plato, 29, 102, 159, 206–7, 208, 209, 284n31, 294, 300n80, 355, 383, 396
Platonism, 208
Plutarch, 28n72, 103, 205, 280, 306–7, 308, 319
Polycarp, 330
polysyllogism. *See* sorites
power (δύναμις), 265, 281, 307, 321–22, 361, 401, 403
Pythagoras, 102, 206, 207

*reductio ad absurdum*, 166, 176, 178, 179, 180, 183, 184, 188
reign of Christ, 211–45
reign of the messiah, 215–16, 217
reincarnation, 206, 207, 208, 396
resurrection: as clothing, 284, 363, 366, 367, 389–91, 393–94; of the dead, 3–4, 48, 60, 65, 90–91, 156, 161–66, 168–75, 179–80, 184, 186, 190–91, 198–99, 200–202, 209, 213, 231, 233, 244, 271, 302–4, 314, 315–17, 352–53, 379, 383, 392–411; denial of, 25, 30–32, 40, 41, 42, 46–47, 54, 63–64, 142, 154–87, 192, 194, 245–47, 252, 261–62, 264–66, 267–74, 279, 310–11, 315–16, 388, 402; doctrine of, 1, 4, 7, 9, 13, 14, 32, 43, 44, 49, 65, 104, 180, 229–30, 261, 274, 364–66, 380, 384, 405, 411; of the flesh, 3–7, 90–91, 164–65, 267, 270–71, 273–74, 280–82, 292–93, 303–4, 315, 324, 379–86, 391, 393; in Greco-Roman thought, 98–104, 165–66, 204–10, 271; of Jesus, 1, 2–3, 6–7, 24–25, 49, 66–69, 72–73, 81, 87, 93–95, 97, 98, 109, 120, 132, 143–53, 160, 191–96, 346, 349, 357, 367–68; in Jewish tradition, 82–83, 162, 164, 365; language about (ἐγείρω, κεῖμαι, ὀφθῆναι, ἀνάστασις, ἀλλάσσω), 81–88, 107–12, 115–16, 118, 120, 123, 129, 132–33, 134–35, 146, 161–64, 173–74, 178, 181–82, 192–93, 318, 384, 385–86, 388, 389; necessity of, 52, 336, 367, 371, 379, 380–81, 390; in the Old Testament, 2, 95–97, 199, 204, 273, 292, 365, 382, 401; testimony to, 24–25, 49–50, 66–67, 72, 75–76, 105–12, 115–16, 119–20, 124, 130, 131–37, 141, 159, 171, 177–79, 275–304. *See also* bodily resurrection; mysteries: of the resurrection; non-fleshly resurrection, claim of
Rhadamanthys, 100, 205
rhetorical criticism, 12, 14, 17, 19–20, 21, 26, 27, 48–49, 53, 55–56, 63–64, 141, 194n11, 244, 245, 269, 277, 278, 310–11, 314, 315, 373, 396–97
rhetorical device, 33–34, 229, 278, 310–11, 318, 355, 384, 397, 409. *See also* anaphora; asyndeton; *gradatio*; homoioptoton; hyperbaton; litotes; rhetorical questions
rhetorical questions, 245–55, 258, 261, 268–74
rhetorical skill. *See* speech
risen body, 281–82, 284, 286–87, 292–93, 294–95, 296–97, 298–302, 311–12, 314, 318, 320–22, 324–32, 335, 360, 363–64, 367, 380–81. *See also* spiritual (πνευματικός)
Romulus, 101
rulers (ἄρχοντες), 44, 221, 223–24

Sadducees, 51, 270, 279
salvation, 3n5, 24, 60–61, 62, 64, 76, 77, 94, 96–97, 159, 176, 183–84, 185–86, 200–201, 206, 233, 238, 262, 301, 314, 332, 355, 371, 391, 395; economy of, 335–36, 347, 350, 353–64; history, 44, 45, 52, 129–31, 174, 180, 191
sanctification, 13–14, 15, 22–23, 32, 78, 151, 364, 402. *See also* cruciform discipleship

## INDEX OF SUBJECTS

Satan, 211, 222, 225, 229, 401, 402, 403–4
schism. *See* factionalism
second coming, 1, 24, 43–44, 183, 185, 190, 191, 203, 211, 213–14, 217, 222, 224–25, 232, 357–58, 367, 380, 386–88, 389, 399, 404–5. *See also* day of the Lord; reign of Christ
Second Council of Constantinople, 3
seeds, 10, 60, 275–76, 279–89, 292, 294, 296–97, 303, 305–9, 310, 313, 316–17, 318, 410
Seneca, 38
Servant Songs, 78, 79, 139, 409–10
Severian of Gabala, 125
Sextus Empiricus, 38, 51n132
sexual immorality, 13, 20–21, 48, 246, 286
Socrates, 119, 207
Son of Man, 215, 223, 374, 387
Soranus, 125–26
*sorites*, 166–67, 171, 175–76, 188
soul, 101, 104, 156–59, 185–86, 206–7, 208, 209–10, 229, 308, 323; annihilation of, 156, 158–59
soul animated (ψυχικός), 45, 310–11, 313, 317, 322–28, 329–30, 335–38, 339–42, 347–48, 352, 355, 360–61. *See also* spiritual (πνευματικός)
speech, 22, 23, 25, 26, 27, 29–30, 35–37, 39–40, 64, 263. *See also* knowledge; wisdom (σοφία)
"Spirit-Christology," of James D. G. Dunn, 8, 334, 342, 344, 346. *See also* Christology
spiritual (πνευματικός), 45, 48, 310, 324–32, 335–36, 337, 341–43, 344, 347–49, 350–51, 352, 353, 361–62, 363, 365, 386. *See also* Holy Spirit; life-giving (ζωοποιέω); soul animated (ψυχικός)
spiritual gifts, 20–23, 25, 241
Stoicism, 38, 51, 101–2, 166–67, 172, 208, 229, 284n31, 308, 339, 340, 356, 396
Strabo, 29, 206
subordination of the Son, 8–9, 212, 219, 234–35, 237–41. *See also* coequality of the Father and the Son; Trinity
suffering, 61, 156, 159, 173, 186–87, 203, 246–47, 251, 253, 254, 255, 257, 348, 352, 395, 409
suffering Servant. *See* Servant Songs

Tertullian, 253, 271–72, 275, 345
Theognis, 319
Theophrastus, 279, 284, 306–7
third day, 7, 68, 71, 91–97, 107, 114, 143, 144, 146, 150–51, 195, 352, 357
Trinity, 9, 212, 214, 220, 226, 232, 237, 241–42, 321, 343–46, 404. *See also* coequality of the Father and the Son; incarnation; subordination of the Son
twelve disciples, the Twelve, 2, 69, 70, 72, 75, 105–7, 111, 113–15, 116, 121–22, 124, 129, 131–33, 135–37, 147
typology, 79, 80, 97, 196, 199, 339, 349, 351, 362

union with Christ, 22, 23, 24, 182–84, 200–203, 236, 238, 240, 246, 251, 262, 300n82, 302, 320–21, 349, 352, 367, 383, 410–11
union with God, 10, 78, 197–98, 291, 303, 329, 331–32, 338, 355, 388, 401–2
untimely birth (ἔκτρωμα), 1, 10, 124–31

Valentinians, 3, 83n61. *See also* Gnosticism
vanity, 30, 39–40, 53, 57–58, 62–65, 77, 139, 149, 151, 156, 175–76, 180–81, 186–87, 246, 253–55, 257, 261, 405, 408–11
victory (νῖκος), 50, 121, 174, 211, 213, 224, 226–27, 230, 231, 233, 318, 388, 392–405

wisdom (σοφία), 36–38; Corinthian, 23, 27, 35–40, 41, 42, 45–47, 54, 55, 58, 154–55, 161, 167, 177, 180, 184, 231, 247–48, 263, 265, 267–68, 278–79, 281, 310–11, 317–18, 406, 408; God's, 36, 42, 43–45, 59, 384, 401; human, 10, 15, 26, 30, 39–40, 41–43, 46, 47, 53–54, 140, 155, 169, 175, 247, 256–57, 278, 328, 394, 398, 403. *See also* knowledge; speech
women at the tomb, 95, 106, 113

Xenophon, 29

Zeus, 100, 101, 186, 205, 206, 396
Zopyrus, 243

# Index of Scripture and Other Ancient Texts

**OLD TESTAMENT**

**Genesis**
| | |
|---|---|
| 1 | 290n53, 291, 297 |
| 1:1 | 276 |
| 1:6–8 | 276, 294 |
| 1:9–13 | 290 |
| 1:11–12 | 285 |
| 1:11–13 | 276, 280, 287, 294 |
| 1:14–19 | 276, 297 |
| 1:20–23 | 294 |
| 1:20–31 | 276, 290 |
| 1:24–31 | 294 |
| 1:26–27 | 232, 338, 364 |
| 1:31 | 290–91 |
| 2–3 | 196, 354 |
| 2:1 | 276 |
| 2:7 | 334, 337, 347, 350, 353–55, 360, 365 |
| 2:9 | 197, 338, 355, 401 |
| 2:17 | 196–97, 338, 355, 401 |
| 2:23 | 341, 376 |
| 3 | 401 |
| 3:1–24 | 338 |
| 3:2–3 | 197, 338, 355, 401 |
| 3:15 | 229 |
| 3:19 | 196–97, 338, 353–55, 360, 365, 382, 401 |
| 3:22 | 197, 338, 355, 401 |
| 3:22–24 | 401 |
| 5:1 | 364 |
| 5:3 | 334, 338 |
| 6:7 | 289–90n51 |
| 12:7 | 108 |
| 17:1 | 108n7 |
| 18:1 | 108n7 |
| 18:27 | 382 |
| 22:4 | 96 |
| 22:16 | 80 |
| 23:4 | 163 |
| 23:6 | 163 |
| 23:8 | 163 |
| 23:11 | 163 |
| 23:13 | 163 |
| 23:15 | 163 |
| 26:2 | 108n7 |
| 26:24 | 108n7 |
| 29:14 | 376 |
| 31:13 | 108n7 |
| 33:2 | 74 |
| 35:1 | 108n7 |
| 35:9 | 108n7 |
| 38:25 | 61n24 |
| 41:4 | 84n64 |
| 42:18 | 96 |
| 46:29 | 110 |
| 48:3 | 108n7 |

**Exodus**
| | |
|---|---|
| 3:2 | 108n7 |
| 5:8 | 84n66 |
| 12 | 79 |
| 16:4 | 362 |
| 16:10 | 108n7 |
| 19:11 | 96 |
| 19:13 | 388n58 |
| 19:16 | 96, 388n58 |
| 19:19 | 388n58 |
| 20:18 | 388n58 |
| 22:29 | 330n29 |
| 23:5 | 85 |
| 23:16 | 195 |
| 23:19 | 193, 330n29 |
| 24:16–17 | 301, 320 |
| 30:14 | 116 |
| 33:17–23 | 301, 320 |
| 34:22 | 195 |
| 40:34–35 | 301, 320 |

**Leviticus**
| | |
|---|---|
| 2:12 | 193 |
| 5:7 | 80 |
| 9:2 | 80 |
| 9:23 | 108n7 |
| 16:3 | 80 |
| 16:5 | 80 |
| 21:17 | 61n24 |
| 22:12 | 193 |
| 23:9–14 | 97, 194–95 |
| 23:10 | 195, 330n61 |

429

## INDEX OF SCRIPTURE AND OTHER ANCIENT TEXTS

| | |
|---|---|
| 23:14 | 193 |
| 23:15–21 | 195 |
| 23:19–24 | 196 |
| 23:24 | 195 |
| 26:11–12 | 182 |
| 27:7 | 116 |

**Numbers**

| | |
|---|---|
| 4:3 | 116n26 |
| 8:8 | 8 |
| 12:12 | 125 |
| 14:10 | 108n7, 109n11 |
| 14:22 | 109n11 |
| 15:17–21 | 193 |
| 15:20 | 330n61 |
| 15:21 | 330n61 |
| 16:19 | 108n7 |
| 18:11–13 | 193 |
| 18:12 | 330n61 |
| 20:6 | 108n7 |
| 28:26 | 195 |

**Deuteronomy**

| | |
|---|---|
| 4:15–19 | 290n53, 297n72 |
| 4:16–18 | 289–90n51 |
| 4:19 | 296–97 |
| 6:4 | 236, 343, 404 |
| 10:22 | 236 |
| 10:26 | 236n103 |
| 18:4 | 193, 330 |
| 26:1–11 | 193 |
| 26:2 | 330 |
| 29:17 | 61n24 |
| 30:15–20 | 395 |
| 32:17 | 222 |
| 32:29 | 199 |
| 32:31 | 236n103 |
| 32:47 | 395 |

**Judges**

| | |
|---|---|
| 2:16 | 60, 84n65 |
| 3:9 | 84n65 |
| 6:12 | 108 |
| 6:14 | 60 |
| 9:2 | 376–77 |

**1 Samuel**

| | |
|---|---|
| 2:6 | 199 |

**2 Samuel**

| | |
|---|---|
| 7:13 | 215 |
| 7:16 | 215 |

**1 Kingdoms (LXX)**

| | |
|---|---|
| 2:8 | 85 |
| 5:3 | 85 |
| 9:22 | 73 |
| 10:1 | 60 |
| 10:4 | 330n61 |

**2 Kingdoms (LXX)**

| | |
|---|---|
| 5:1 | 376–77 |
| 12:17 | 84n66, 85 |
| 19:13–14 | 376 |

**1 Kings**

| | |
|---|---|
| 8:11–13 | 301, 320 |
| 8:27 | 358 |

**2 Kings**

| | |
|---|---|
| 2:17 | 97 |
| 5:7 | 199 |
| 20:1–11 | 97 |

**3 Kingdoms (LXX)**

| | |
|---|---|
| 3:5 | 108n7 |
| 9:2 | 108n7 |
| 11:9 | 108n7 |
| 18:2 | 110 |
| 21:9 | 74 |

**4 Kingdoms (LXX)**

| | |
|---|---|
| 18:5 | 185 |

**1 Chronicles**

| | |
|---|---|
| 11:1 | 376 |
| 15:15 | 79 |

**2 Chronicles**

| | |
|---|---|
| 1:7 | 108n7 |

| | |
|---|---|
| 2:6 | 358 |
| 3:1 | 108n7 |
| 7:12 | 108n7 |
| 30:5 | 79 |
| 31:5 | 330n61 |

**Nehemiah**

| | |
|---|---|
| 10:37 | 330n61 |
| 10:39 | 330n61 |

**Esther**

| | |
|---|---|
| 5:1 | 97 |

**Job**

| | |
|---|---|
| 2:5 | 375 |
| 3:16 | 125–26 |
| 10:9 | 354 |
| 19:25–27 | 82 |
| 20:18 | 180 |
| 34:14–15 | 354 |
| 41:3 | 220 |
| 42:6 | 382 |
| 42:17 | 82, 162 |

**Psalms**

| | |
|---|---|
| 1:5 | 3 |
| 2 | 76 |
| 2:7 | 96 |
| 8 | 232–33, 275–76, 290–91, 296 |
| 8:1 | 296, 358 |
| 8:2–4 | 290 |
| 8:4–5 | 296 |
| 8:5 | 232, 290 |
| 8:7 | 231–34, 290 |
| 8:7–10 | 290 |
| 8:8–9 | 290 |
| 14:1 | 278 |
| 16:8–11 | 96 |
| 16:10 | 95n97 |
| 18 | 296 |
| 18:1 | 196 |
| 19:1 | 296 |
| 24 | 236 |
| 24:1 | 236, 290 |

## Index of Scripture and Other Ancient Texts

| | | | | | |
|---|---|---|---|---|---|
| 32:21 | 185 | **Proverbs** | | 40:5 | 108n7 |
| 33:6 | 60 | 6:9 | 84n64 | 40:13 | 236 |
| 35:7 | 185 | 10:12 | 84n65 | 42:1 | 409 |
| 39:7 | 80 | 15:1 | 84n65 | 42:1–9 | 409 |
| 42:23 | 255 | 26:5 | 279 | 43:10 | 409 |
| 57:5 | 358 | | | 43:25 | 80n48 |
| 57:9 | 125 | **Ecclesiastes** | | 44:1–2 | 409 |
| 57:11 | 358 | 1:2 | 180 | 44:21 | 409 |
| 58:9 | 125 | 1:14 | 180 | 44:22–23 | 80, 181 |
| 68:20 | 199 | 2:1 | 180 | 44:26 | 409 |
| 72:5–7 | 215n19 | 2:11 | 180 | 45:4 | 409 |
| 72:17 | 215n19 | 2:15 | 180 | 48:20 | 409 |
| 77:24 | 362 | 2:17 | 180 | 49:1–6 | 409 |
| 77:51 | 330 | 2:19 | 180 | 49:3 | 409 |
| 89:4 | 215n19 | 2:23 | 180 | 49:4 | 139, 409–10 |
| 89:29 | 215n19 | 2:26 | 180 | 49:5–7 | 409 |
| 89:36–37 | 215n19 | 3:19 | 180 | 49:6 | 96 |
| 90:3 | 354 | 3:20 | 354 | 50:4–11 | 409 |
| 91:6 | 295 | 4:10 | 84–85 | 50:10 | 409 |
| 95:5 | 222 | 6:3 | 125–26 | 52:13 | 96, 409 |
| 103:24 | 295 | 12:7 | 353 | 52:13–53:12 | 78–79, 409 |
| 104:29 | 354 | | | 53:5 | 78 |
| 104:36 | 330 | **Isaiah** | | 53:10 | 139, 410 |
| 105:8 | 60 | 4:4 | 80 | 53:11 | 96, 409 |
| 105:10 | 60 | 4:4–5 | 80n48, 181 | 53:12 | 78 |
| 105:21 | 60 | 6:3 | 295 | 54–66 | 409 |
| 105:37 | 222 | 8:23–9:6 | 76 | 54:8 | 386 |
| 108:4–5 | 358 | 9:4–6 | 216 | 54:8–10 | 80n48 |
| 110 | 227 | 9:7 | 215 | 54:17 | 410 |
| 110:1 | 215, 220, 225–27, 231 | 10:3 | 250 | 55:3 | 80n48, 96 |
| 110:3 | 295 | 11:1–10 | 76 | 56–66 | 139 |
| 110:4 | 227 | 14:9 | 85 | 56:6 | 410 |
| 110:4–7 | 227 | 22:13 | 262 | 56:6–7 | 182 |
| 112:7 | 85 | 24:21–22 | 221n41 | 59:15–21 | 80n48 |
| 113:4–6 | 358 | 24:23 | 302 | 60:1–3 | 302 |
| 118:22 | 96 | 25:6–9 | 204, 394–95, 401 | 60:19–20 | 302 |
| 126:2 | 63n35, 84n66, 85 | 25:8 | 394–95 | 63:17 | 410 |
| 130:7–8 | 80, 181 | 26:19 | 82, 162–63, 204, 365, 401 | 65:8–9 | 410 |
| 130:8 | 80 | | | 65:13–15 | 410 |
| 132:12 | 215n19 | 27:13 | 387 | 65:23 | 410 |
| 136:7–9 | 297 | 30:7 | 180 | 66:14 | 410 |
| 138:14 | 295 | 30:26 | 302 | | |
| 143 | 275 | 40–53 | 409 | **Jeremiah** | |
| 146:4 | 353 | 40–55 | 409 | 3:16–17 | 182 |
| 148:3 | 276, 297 | 40–66 | 409 | 4:30 | 250 |
| 148:13 | 358 | | | | |

| | | | | | |
|---|---|---|---|---|---|
| 5:31 | 250 | 1:10–11 | 397 | **Judith** | |
| 6:29 | 63n35 | 2:14–23 | 80n48, 181, 397 | 10:23 | 85 |
| 8:2 | 297 | 3:3–5 | 397 | 11:13 | 330n61 |
| 9:23–24 | 236n103, 257 | 6:1–2 | 97 | | |
| 28:12 | 84n66 | 6:1–3 | 96n101 | **Wisdom of Solomon** | |
| 31:31–34 | 80 | 6:2 | 96–97 | 2:5–7 | 262 |
| 33:8 | 80n48, 181 | 9:5 | 250 | 2:24 | 229 |
| 33:17 | 215 | 11:8–11 | 397 | 13:1 | 265 |
| 50:20 | 80n48, 181 | 12:2 | 180 | 15:8 | 353 |
| | | 13:13 | 127 | | |
| **Ezekiel** | | 13:14 | 396–97 | **Sirach** | |
| 18 | 395 | 14:1–8 | 397 | 2:14 | 250 |
| 36:22–38 | 80n48, 181 | | | 7:31 | 330n61 |
| 37 | 334 | **Joel** | | 14:17–18 | 374 |
| 37:1–14 | 334n5, 376 | 2:10 | 297 | 14:18 | 374–76 |
| 37:24–25 | 215 | 3:5 | 236n103 | 17:1 | 353 |
| 37:27–28 | 182 | | | 17:30–32 | 374 |
| 40–48 | 182 | **Amos** | | 17:31 | 374–76, 381 |
| 44:30 | 330 | 5:4–7 | 395 | 17:32 | 376, 382 |
| | | 9:7–15 | 76 | 32:8 | 330n61 |
| **Daniel** | | | | 42:16–17 | 296 |
| 2:44 | 382 | **Jonah** | | 42:17 | 295 |
| 3:61 | 221n41, 222 | 1:17 | 97 | 42:25 | 296 |
| 3:62–63 | 297 | | | 42:25–43:12 | 296 |
| 7 | 223 | **Micah** | | 43:2–5 | 298 |
| 7:2–8 | 223 | 5:1–5 | 76 | 43:6–8 | 298 |
| 7:13–14 | 223 | | | 43:9–10 | 298 |
| 7:14 | 215, 223, 382 | **Zechariah** | | 45:20 | 330n61 |
| 7:17 | 223 | 9:9–10 | 76 | 49:13 | 85n66 |
| 7:23–25 | 223 | 13:1 | 80, 181 | | |
| 7:26–27 | 218, 222–23 | 14:8 | 395 | **Epistle of Jeremiah** | |
| 7:27 | 223, 231 | | | 59 | 297 |
| 10:10 | 85 | **Malachi** | | | |
| 10:13 | 223–24 | 1:11 | 236n103 | **2 Maccabees** | |
| 10:20–21 | 223–24 | 1:31 | 236n103 | 2:8 | 108n7 |
| 11:25 | 85n65 | | | 3:24 | 221n41, 222 |
| 12:2 | 162, 182n91, 204, 365, 401 | **DEUTEROCANONICAL BOOKS** | | 7 | 82, 204 |
| 12:2–3 | 82 | | | 7:9 | 162 |
| 12:3 | 302 | | | 7:14 | 162 |
| 12:7 | 199 | **Tobit** | | 12:43 | 162 |
| 12:13 | 162 | 2:8 | 163 | 12:44 | 162 |
| | | 6:18 | 84n66 | 12:44–45 | 120, 193 |
| **Hosea** | | 12:22 | 108 | 12:45 | 182 |
| 1:7 | 397 | | | | |

## Index of Scripture and Other Ancient Texts

1 Esdras
1:23     84n65
5:44     85n66

## Pseudepigrapha

2 Baruch
29     215
51.5–12     381
73–74     215

1 Enoch
15.1–7     374
15.3     374
15.4     374–76, 381
61.6     221n41
61.10     221n41
92.3     120, 182, 193
101.2     250
103.4     83n61

2 Enoch
20     221n41

4 Ezra
7.26–30     215
13.39–50     215

Joseph and Aseneth
20.7     199–200

Jubilees
23.30–31     83n61

4 Maccabees
1:32     323nn41–42

Martyrdom and Ascension of Isaiah
8.14–15     381

Psalms of Solomon
17.4     215

Sibylline Oracles
3.290     85n66
4.137     84n65
4.179–192     82

Testament of Abraham
4.5     387
13.7     374–77, 381

Testament of Benjamin
10.8–9     74

Testament of Job
31.1     252

Testament of Levi
3     222
3.3     221n41
3.4     358
3.8     221n41
18.2     84n65

## Dead Sea Scrolls

1QH (Thanksgiving Hymns)
xii, 26–27     353

4Q521 (Messianic Apocalypse)
5     199
7     199

4Q530 (Book of Giants)
2 ii 3–22     127n16

## Ancient Jewish Writers

Josephus

Antiquitates judaicae
3.250–251     195
3.251     193, 195
3.252     195
10.107     29
16.369     29n74
17.35     29n75
18.288     51
18.293     51
18.375     28n73
18.378     28n73
19.189     242–43
20.199     51
20.200     148

Bellum judaicum
6.328     321n36
24.473     242n123, 243

Vita
10     51
12     51
191     51
197     51

Philo

De Abrahamo
219n42     323

De agricultura
122     85

De confusione linguarum
133     85n66

De congressu eruditionis gratia
79     38

De ebrietate
156     85

De gigantibus
28     326n53

De Iosepho
126     84

De migratione Abrahami
92     327
122     85

De mutatione nominum
33     323n42
56     85

433

INDEX OF SCRIPTURE AND OTHER ANCIENT TEXTS

| *De plantatione* | |
|---|---|
| 12 | 294n67 |
| 151 | 51 |

| *De posteritate Caini* | |
|---|---|
| 54 | 85n66 |
| 149 | 85 |

| *De somniis* | |
|---|---|
| 1.174 | 84 |

| *De specialibus legibus* | |
|---|---|
| 2.162 | 195 |
| 2.162–171 | 195 |
| 2.162–175 | 195 |
| 2.170–180 | 193 |
| 2.171 | 195 |
| 2.175 | 195 |
| 2.175–186 | 195 |
| 2.176 | 193 |
| 3.73 | 29 |
| 4.49 | 326n53 |

| *De virtutibus* | |
|---|---|
| 217 | 326n53 |

| *De vita Mosis* | |
|---|---|
| 1.43 | 259 |

| *Legum allegoriae* | |
|---|---|
| 1.97 | 323n41 |
| 2.59 | 327 |
| 3.146 | 327 |

| *Quod deterius potiori insidari soleat* | |
|---|---|
| 49 | 294–95 |

## NEW TESTAMENT

**Matthew**

| | |
|---|---|
| 1:24 | 84n63 |
| 2:5 | 337 |
| 2:13–14 | 85n67 |
| 2:20–21 | 85n67 |
| 5:1–2 | 119 |
| 5:11 | 224 |
| 5:16 | 30, 359 |
| 5:22 | 63 |
| 5:34 | 358 |
| 5:45 | 359 |
| 5:48 | 300, 359 |
| 6:1 | 359 |
| 6:9 | 359 |
| 6:12 | 253n30 |
| 6:14 | 359 |
| 6:26 | 312359 |
| 6:32 | 359 |
| 7:11 | 359 |
| 7:21 | 30 |
| 7:28–29 | 119 |
| 8:8 | 138 |
| 8:15 | 85 |
| 8:22 | 163 |
| 8:25 | 60, 183 |
| 8:25–26 | 84n63 |
| 8:26 | 85n67 |
| 8:39 | 60, 183 |
| 9:5–7 | 85 |
| 9:9 | 162 |
| 9:24 | 182n91, 384 |
| 10:2 | 112 |
| 10:8 | 163 |
| 10:32–33 | 358 |
| 11:5 | 163, 312, 388n59 |
| 11:11 | 84n65 |
| 11:27 | 220 |
| 12:11 | 85 |
| 12:38–40 | 97 |
| 12:40 | 92–93 |
| 12:50 | 358 |
| 13:4–8 | 312 |
| 13:12 | 119 |
| 13:24–36 | 119 |
| 13:43 | 296, 302 |
| 14:2 | 86n72 |
| 14:13–23 | 119 |
| 14:20 | 312 |
| 15:3 | 253n30 |
| 16:4 | 97 |
| 16:16–19 | 112 |
| 16:17 | 358, 374–76, 380 |
| 16:18 | 112 |
| 16:21 | 92–93, 312 |
| 16:25 | 60, 183 |
| 16:28 | 216n21 |
| 17:1 | 112 |
| 17:2 | 296 |
| 17:7 | 85 |
| 17:9 | 86n72 |
| 17:23 | 92–93 |
| 18:14 | 359 |
| 18:19 | 358 |
| 18:35 | 315, 359 |
| 19:28 | 216n21 |
| 20:19 | 92–93 |
| 20:21 | 216n21 |
| 20:23 | 44n117 |
| 20:28 | 78 |
| 21:7 | 116n26 |
| 22:29 | 265, 279 |
| 22:30 | 163n34, 164, 312, 381 |
| 22:44 | 225 |
| 23:9 | 359 |
| 23:27 | 388n59 |
| 23:38 | 314 |
| 24:7 | 84n65 |
| 24:11 | 84n65 |
| 24:30 | 322 |
| 24:31 | 387 |
| 24:33 | 224, 314 |
| 24:38 | 227 |
| 24:40–41 | 312 |
| 25:14 | 220 |
| 25:20 | 220 |
| 25:21 | 383 |
| 25:22 | 220 |
| 25:31–46 | 201 |
| 25:34 | 44n117, 216n21 |
| 26:16–20 | 116–17 |
| 26:37 | 112 |
| 26:46 | 84n66, 85 |
| 26:61 | 92–93 |
| 26:64 | 225 |
| 27:36 | 92 |
| 27:40 | 92–93 |
| 27:52 | 49, 120, 182, 193, 384 |
| 27:57–61 | 80 |
| 27:62 | 97 |
| 27:63 | 92 |

434

| Reference | Pages | Reference | Pages | Reference | Pages |
|---|---|---|---|---|---|
| 27:63–64 | 92 | 13:10 | 52 | 8:15 | 62 |
| 27:64 | 86n72, 92 | 13:26 | 322 | 8:29 | 312 |
| 28 | 91 | 13:29 | 314 | 8:51 | 112 |
| 28:1 | 92–93, 97 | 14:5 | 116n26 | 8:52 | 182n91, 384 |
| 28:2 | 116n26 | 14:33 | 112 | 9:7 | 86n72 |
| 28:7 | 86n72, 135 | 14:36 | 61n24 | 9:22 | 92–93 |
| 28:8–20 | 114, 122, 130 | 14:42 | 85 | 9:23–24 | 255 |
| 28:9 | 108n9 | 14:57 | 162 | 9:24 | 60, 183 |
| 28:9–10 | 113 | 14:58 | 92 | 9:28 | 112 |
| 28:10 | 135 | 14:62 | 225n55 | 9:31 | 109n11 |
| 28:16–20 | 114 | 15:29 | 92 | 9:32 | 109n11 |
| 28:17 | 135 | 15:42 | 97 | 9:60 | 163 |
| 28:18 | 224 | 15:42–47 | 80 | 10:22 | 220 |
|  |  | 16 | 91 | 11:7–8 | 162 |
| **Mark** |  | 16:1 | 97 | 11:8 | 84–85 |
| 1:31 | 85 | 16:2 | 92–93, 97 | 11:13 | 359 |
| 2:9 | 85 | 16:7 | 113, 135 | 11:27–28 | 119 |
| 2:11–12 | 85 |  |  | 11:29–30 | 97 |
| 3:3 | 85 | **Luke** |  | 12:24 | 312 |
| 3:16 | 112 | 1:2 | 66n4, 73, 115 | 13:12 | 92 |
| 4:1–2 | 119 | 1:11 | 108, 109n11 | 13:32 | 92 |
| 4:4–8 | 312n8 | 1:11–13 | 312 | 16:25 | 184 |
| 4:27 | 312 | 1:12 | 109n11 | 17:8 | 61n24 |
| 4:31 | 287n43 | 1:17 | 322 | 17:10 | 315 |
| 4:32 | 312 | 1:33 | 216 | 18:33 | 92–93 |
| 5:37 | 112 | 1:35 | 322 | 20:34–36 | 381 |
| 5:39 | 182n91, 384 | 1:69 | 84 | 20:35 | 163n34, 164 |
| 6:14 | 86n72 | 1:78 | 300, 359 | 20:36 | 381 |
| 8:31 | 52, 92–93 | 1:78–79 | 358 | 20:42–43 | 225 |
| 8:35 | 60, 183 | 2:51 | 239n117 | 21:15–19 | 112 |
| 8:38 | 224 | 3:14 | 253n30 | 21:27 | 322 |
| 9:2 | 112 | 4:16 | 162 | 21:31 | 314 |
| 9:27 | 85, 162, 312 | 4:18–19 | 171 | 22:19 | 256 |
| 9:31 | 92–93 | 5:23–24 | 85 | 22:29–30 | 215n21 |
| 10:34 | 92–93 | 6:8 | 162 | 22:31–32 | 112 |
| 10:45 | 78 | 6:9 | 60, 183 | 22:43 | 108 |
| 10:49 | 85 | 6:14 | 112 | 22:45 | 162 |
| 11:25 | 359 | 6:17–20 | 119 | 22:47–23:23 | 97 |
| 12:20–22 | 124 | 6:22 | 224 | 22:69 | 225 |
| 12:23 | 270 | 6:26 | 224 | 23:33 | 312n8 |
| 12:24 | 265, 279 | 6:32 | 269 | 23:50–56 | 80 |
| 12:25 | 381 | 7:1 | 119 | 23:54 | 97 |
| 12:32 | 312 | 7:6 | 138 | 23:56 | 97 |
| 12:36 | 225 | 7:14–15 | 163, 388n59 | 24 | 69, 89, 91–92, 114, 122 |
| 13:7 | 52 | 7:22 | 163 | 24:1 | 92–93, 97, 113 |
|  |  |  |  | 24:1–8 | 114 |

# INDEX OF SCRIPTURE AND OTHER ANCIENT TEXTS

| | | | | | |
|---|---|---|---|---|---|
| 24:1–11 | 69 | 4:38 | 408 | 17:14 | 361 |
| 24:1–12 | 2, 89 | 4:39 | 178 | 17:26 | 58 |
| 24:1–53 | 117 | 5:8 | 85 | 18:28 | 97 |
| 24:5 | 163, 388n59 | 5:17 | 285 | 19:14 | 97 |
| 24:7 | 92, 95 | 5:21 | 199–200, 342 | 19:31 | 97, 312 |
| 24:7–8 | 93 | 5:24–29 | 3, 201 | 19:35 | 178 |
| 24:8 | 95 | 5:29 | 270 | 19:38–42 | 80 |
| 24:13–15 | 113 | 6:32–33 | 300, 358–59 | 19:42 | 97 |
| 24:14 | 263 | 6:38 | 358 | 20–21 | 91 |
| 24:19–43 | 133 | 6:39–40 | 3 | 20:1 | 92–93, 97 |
| 24:21 | 92–93, 114 | 6:41–42 | 300, 358–59 | 20:11–18 | 113 |
| 24:23–24 | 2, 89 | 6:44 | 3 | 20:11–29 | 114, 122, 130 |
| 24:33–40 | 69 | 6:50–51 | 300, 358–59 | 20:17 | 130 |
| 24:33–43 | 113, 115 | 6:58 | 300, 358–59 | 20:18 | 135 |
| 24:34 | 68–69, 109, 113–15, | 6:54 | 3 | 20:19 | 92–93, 97, 108n9 |
| | 133n33, 135 | 6:62 | 358 | 20:19–23 | 114, 116 |
| 24:36 | 108n9 | 6:63 | 342 | 20:20 | 135 |
| 24:36–43 | 114 | 7:2–9 | 121 | 20:22 | 130 |
| 24:39 | 2, 69, 109, 135, 377 | 7:39 | 130 | 20:24 | 108n19, 114 |
| 24:39–43 | 122, 130, 136 | 7:52 | 82n65 | 20:24–29 | 3, 114 |
| 24:41–43 | 69 | 8:23 | 358–59 | 20:26 | 108n9 |
| 24:44–49 | 116 | 8:28 | 239 | 20:27 | 135 |
| 24:46 | 92–94, 98, 337 | 8:49 | 239 | 20:28 | 239 |
| 24:48 | 111–12, 115 | 9:30 | 298 | 20:29 | 135 |
| 24:48–49 | 130 | 9:40 | 253n30 | 21:1 | 108n9 |
| 24:49 | 130, 322, 361 | 10:17–18 | 330 | 21:1–23 | 130 |
| | | 10:18 | 239 | 21:3 | 253n30 |
| **John** | | 11:4 | 251n24 | 21:13 | 108n9 |
| 1:1–18 | 239 | 11:11 | 120, 182, 193, 384 | 21:14 | 86n72, 178 |
| 1:2 | 112 | 11:16 | 253n30 | 21:15–23 | 116 |
| 1:12–13 | 130 | 11:29 | 85 | 21:22–23 | 119 |
| 1:14 | 203 | 11:31 | 162 | 21:24 | 115 |
| 1:32 | 359 | 12:1 | 86n72, 163 | | |
| 1:41–42 | 112 | 12:9 | 86n72, 163 | **Acts** | |
| 1:42 | 112 | 12:17 | 86n72, 163, 178 | 1 | 114 |
| 2:19 | 92 | 12:24 | 279, 309 | 1:1–3 | 122 |
| 2:19–20 | 85, 92–93 | 12:25 | 330 | 1:1–11 | 117 |
| 2:20 | 92 | 13:4 | 85 | 1:2 | 113 |
| 2:22 | 86n72 | 14:2 | 44n117 | 1:3 | 108n9 |
| 3:3–8 | 130 | 14:15–26 | 130 | 1:3–4 | 3, 114, 122, 130, 133, |
| 3:6 | 361 | 14:19 | 249 | | 136 |
| 3:11 | 178 | 14:28 | 239 | 1:3–8 | 116 |
| 3:13 | 358–59 | 14:31 | 85, 239 | 1:4 | 130n30 |
| 3:31 | 116n26, 358–59 | 15:10 | 239 | 1:4–5 | 130 |
| 4:25 | 76 | 15:26–27 | 130 | 1:5 | 130 |
| | | 16:12–15 | 130 | | |

436

## Index of Scripture and Other Ancient Texts

| | | | | | |
|---|---|---|---|---|---|
| 1:7–8 | 130 | 9:1–9 | 133 | 13:34–37 | 3, 96 |
| 1:8 | 111–12, 115, 322 | 9:3–4 | 136 | 13:36 | 182, 193, 384 |
| 1:13 | 112 | 9:3–8 | 136 | 13:46 | 130 |
| 1:14 | 121 | 9:4–7 | 136 | 13:48 | 130 |
| 1:15 | 130n29 | 9:5–6 | 136 | 14:4 | 122, 135 |
| 1:15–26 | 112 | 9:7 | 135 | 14:10 | 162 |
| 1:21–22 | 111, 113, 122, 130, 137 | 9:8 | 85 | 14:14 | 135 |
| 1:21–26 | 113, 122 | 9:8–9 | 135–36 | 14:15 | 180 |
| 1:22 | 112, 115 | 9:12 | 136 | 14:41 | 122 |
| 2 | 117n30 | 9:16 | 251n24 | 15 | 137 |
| 2:1–4 | 130 | 9:17 | 109, 133n33, 136 | 15:1–35 | 106 |
| 2:14 | 113 | 9:17–18 | 135–36 | 15:4–31 | 121 |
| 2:14–41 | 112 | 9:26 | 162 | 15:5 | 51 |
| 2:24–42 | 96 | 9:27 | 109, 133n33, 135 | 15:6–21 | 112 |
| 2:25–31 | 3, 330 | 9:30 | 130n29 | 15:13 | 121 |
| 2:29 | 227 | 9:32–42 | 112 | 15:26 | 251n24 |
| 2:32 | 112, 115 | 9:34 | 162 | 16:6–10 | 11n1 |
| 2:34 | 225n55 | 9:41 | 162 | 16:7 | 345 |
| 2:38 | 130 | 10–12 | 112 | 16:9–10 | 110 |
| 3:1–4:31 | 112 | 10:23 | 130n29 | 16:37 | 298n75 |
| 3:6–7 | 85 | 10:26 | 84n66, 85 | 17:25 | 184 |
| 3:7 | 84n66 | 10:37–42 | 113, 122, 130 | 17:30–31 | 201 |
| 3:13 | 96 | 10:38 | 322 | 17:31 | 90 |
| 3:15 | 86n72, 112, 115 | 10:39–42 | 137 | 17:32 | 163n34 |
| 3:18 | 96 | 10:40 | 92, 94 | 19 | 11n1 |
| 3:21 | 96 | 10:40–41 | 114 | 19:1–7 | 130 |
| 3:24 | 96 | 10:40–42 | 3, 116, 122, 130, 133, 136 | 19:35 | 298n75 |
| 4:1–2 | 3 | | | 20:11 | 227, 263 |
| 4:2 | 164 | 10:41 | 112, 115 | 20:29 | 259 |
| 4:10 | 86n72 | 10:42 | 385, 389 | 21:13 | 251n24 |
| 4:10–11 | 96 | 10:43 | 96 | 21:18 | 121 |
| 4:13 | 112 | 10:44–47 | 130 | 22:3–11 | 133 |
| 4:33 | 24–25 | 11:15–18 | 130 | 22:4 | 253 |
| 5:1–42 | 112 | 11:18 | 130 | 22:5 | 178 |
| 5:17 | 51 | 12:1–2 | 253 | 22:6–7 | 136 |
| 5:20 | 130 | 12:2 | 106 | 22:6–11 | 136 |
| 5:32 | 112, 115 | 12:3–4 | 97 | 22:7–10 | 136 |
| 5:41 | 251n24 | 12:7 | 84n64 | 22:8 | 136 |
| 6:3 | 130n29 | 12:17 | 106, 121, 130n29 | 22:9 | 135 |
| 7:26 | 110 | 13:22 | 84n65 | 22:10 | 136 |
| 7:49 | 269 | 13:26–37 | 89 | 22:11 | 136 |
| 7:54–60 | 253 | 13:30–31 | 111, 114–15, 137 | 22:11–13 | 135 |
| 7:60 | 49, 182, 193, 384 | 13:30–33 | 96 | 22:13 | 136 |
| 8:14–17 | 130 | 13:31 | 86n72, 112–13, 115, 122, 130, 133, 136 | 22:14–15 | 135 |
| 8:14–25 | 112 | | | 22:15 | 112 |
| 8:33 | 184 | 13:34 | 96 | 23:1 | 227 |

437

INDEX OF SCRIPTURE AND OTHER ANCIENT TEXTS

| | | | | | |
|---|---|---|---|---|---|
| 23:6 | 163n34, 164 | 2:28–29 | 290 | 6:9–10 | 87 |
| 23:7–10 | 3 | 3:4 | 152 | 6:11 | 182n94 |
| 24:5 | 51 | 3:5 | 258 | 6:14 | 401 |
| 24:14 | 51 | 3:6 | 269 | 6:14–15 | 400 |
| 24:14–15 | 3 | 3:9 | 401 | 6:17 | 66n4, 73, 403 |
| 24:15 | 201 | 3:20 | 400 | 6:17–18 | 181 |
| 24:21 | 163n34, 164 | 3:22 | 268n5 | 6:20–21 | 197 |
| 24:26 | 263 | 3:24–26 | 78 | 6:21–22 | 218 |
| 25:23 | 163n34, 164 | 3:27 | 257n45 | 6:23 | 182n94 |
| 26:5 | 51 | 4:2 | 257n45 | 7 | 400 |
| 26:6–8 | 3 | 4:6–8 | 181 | 7:4 | 86n72, 202–3 |
| 26:8 | 199 | 4:16–25 | 265 | 7:4–6 | 290 |
| 26:9–10 | 253 | 4:17 | 199–200, 230, 265, 342, 349 | 7:5 | 400 |
| 26:9–23 | 133 | | | 7:7 | 400 |
| 26:12–18 | 136 | 4:19–21 | 265 | 7:8 | 401 |
| 26:13 | 296 | 4:24 | 86n72, 169n46 | 7:8–11 | 400–401 |
| 26:13–14 | 136 | 4:24–25 | 67, 90 | 7:11 | 401 |
| 26:14 | 135 | 4:25 | 77–78, 181n88 | 7:12 | 401 |
| 26:14–15 | 136 | 5:1 | 404 | 7:13 | 400–401 |
| 26:15–18 | 136 | 5:1–5 | 185 | 7:14 | 401 |
| 26:16 | 112, 133n33, 162 | 5:1–11 | 185, 403 | 7:25 | 403 |
| 26:22 | 227 | 5:2 | 44n120, 60, 185, 301, 320 | 8:2 | 396, 401 |
| 26:22–23 | 3, 96 | 5:2–5 | 262 | 8:3 | 77, 80, 198, 236, 348, 352, 401 |
| 26:23 | 193n6 | 5:8 | 77 | | |
| 26:30 | 162 | 5:12 | 196–97, 200, 229, 338, 355, 399, 401 | 8:3–4 | 77, 181–82, 343, 359, 361 |
| 28:22 | 51 | | | | |
| | | 5:12–14 | 355 | 8:3–14 | 29 |
| **Romans** | | 5:12–21 | 196, 317, 348, 399 | 8:6 | 396, 401 |
| 1:1 | 43n115 | 5:13 | 227 | 8:7 | 239n117 |
| 1:2 | 79 | 5:13–14 | 40 | 8:9 | 202–3, 291, 345–46, 380 |
| 1:3–4 | 67, 76–77, 90, 359, 361 | 5:14 | 339 | 8:9–10 | 344 |
| | | 5:14–17 | 338 | 8:10 | 288, 342, 348, 396 |
| 1:4 | 151, 163n34, 198, 322, 348 | 5:15 | 399 | 8:11 | 86n72, 169n46, 200, 288, 336, 342, 345 |
| 1:5 | 139, 251m24 | 5:15–19 | 197 | | |
| 1:9 | 159, 186 | 5:17 | 201, 216–17, 220, 399 | 8:12–25 | 330 |
| 1:15 | 43n115 | 5:19 | 200, 239 | 8:14 | 330 |
| 1:18 | 300 | 5:20–21 | 400 | 8:14–16 | 130 |
| 1:18–23 | 265 | 5:21 | 399 | 8:15 | 330, 380 |
| 1:26 | 319n27 | 6:1–11 | 251–52 | 8:16 | 330 |
| 1:32 | 400–401 | 6:2 | 269 | 8:17 | 217, 238–39, 330, 380 |
| 2:1 | 400 | 6:3 | 182n94 | 8:17–21 | 382 |
| 2:1–11 | 230 | 6:3–4 | 81 | 8:18 | 44n120, 186, 301, 320 |
| 2:4–5 | 152 | 6:3–6 | 181 | 8:18–25 | 185 |
| 2:7 | 318 | 6:4 | 81, 86n72, 88, 169n46, 182n94 | 8:18–39 | 398 |
| 2:14–16 | 400 | | | 8:19 | 330 |
| | | 6:9 | 86n72, 87–88, 192 | 8:21 | 44n120, 301, 320, 330 |

438

## Index of Scripture and Other Ancient Texts

| | | | | | |
|---|---|---|---|---|---|
| 8:22 | 227 | 15:9 | 251n24 | 1:10–11 | 18, 51 |
| 8:23 | 288, 330–31, 336–37, 380 | 15:13 | 185, 322 | 1:10–12 | 26 |
| | | 15:15 | 139 | 1:10–17 | 18–19, 25–27, 40–41, 54–55, 65 |
| 8:24 | 185 | 15:16–19 | 403 | | |
| 8:24–25 | 185, 262 | 15:17–18 | 257n45 | 1:10–4:21 | 20, 54, 161 |
| 8:29 | 238–39, 364, 380 | 15:18 | 408 | 1:10–16:14 | 18 |
| 8:30 | 44n120, 301 | 15:18–19 | 343 | 1:11 | 21, 30–32, 50, 268 |
| 8:31–39 | 403 | 15:19 | 322 | 1:11–16 | 35 |
| 8:32 | 78, 80, 269 | 16:3 | 407 | 1:11–17 | 26 |
| 8:34 | 90, 219–20, 225n55 | 16:3–4 | 259 | 1:12 | 32–33, 106, 147n16 |
| 8:34–39 | 224 | 16:5 | 330 | 1:12–19 | 176 |
| 8:36 | 255 | 16:11 | 182n94 | 1:12–4:5 | 34 |
| 8:38 | 184, 222 | 16:17 | 74 | 1:13 | 77 |
| 8:38–39 | 222, 401–2 | 16:20 | 224, 229 | 1:13–16 | 36 |
| 8:39 | 182n94, 404 | 16:21 | 407 | 1:13–17 | 74, 151, 250 |
| 9:5 | 77, 359, 361 | | | 1:13–15:13 | 19 |
| 9:19 | 267 | **1 Corinthians** | | 1:16 | 19n43 |
| 9:21 | 319n27 | 1–3 | 31, 39, 263, 265 | 1:17 | 26, 35–36, 39–40, 46, 49, 64–65, 68, 106, 131, 137, 139, 151, 155, 175, 394, 409 |
| 9:23 | 44n120, 301, 320 | 1–4 | 12–13, 15, 23–24, 26–27, 28n72, 33, 35–36, 39–41, 53–55, 58, 175, 278 | | |
| 9:30 | 268n5 | | | | |
| 10:2 | 178 | | | 1:17–18 | 25, 40, 64–65, 77 |
| 10:6 | 358 | 1–14 | 10, 41, 49, 155 | 1:17–31 | 18, 408 |
| 10:8–10 | 90 | 1:1 | 106, 131 | 1:18 | 19, 30, 39–41, 50, 60–61, 64–65, 68, 77, 151, 183, 201, 322, 394, 402–3 |
| 10:9 | 86n72, 169n46 | 1:1–2 | 68, 360 | | |
| 10:14–15 | 269 | 1:1–3 | 18, 53 | | |
| 10:15 | 171 | 1:1–9 | 18, 23–24 | | |
| 11:19 | 267 | 1:2 | 22–23, 138, 151–52, 182n94, 236, 345 | 1:18–19 | 41 |
| 11:20 | 60 | | | 1:18–21 | 41–42, 278 |
| 11:31 | 256 | | | 1:18–31 | 43–44, 107, 360 |
| 11:35 | 220 | 1:2–3 | 257 | 1:18–2:5 | 41–43, 140, 155, 169, 175 |
| 11:36 | 243 | 1:4 | 345 | | |
| 12:3 | 139 | 1:4–9 | 18, 32, 41, 53, 55, 65 | 1:18–2:16 | 23, 58 |
| 12:5 | 182n94 | 1:5 | 22–23, 25 | 1:18–4:21 | 10, 20–23, 26, 41–42, 45, 47, 54, 154–55, 247, 256 |
| 12:12 | 185 | 1:5–7 | 25 | | |
| 13:4 | 63 | 1:6 | 24–25, 31n80, 74, 111, 150, 155, 179 | | |
| 13:11 | 84n64 | | | 1:18–15:57 | 12 |
| 14:4–6 | 312 | 1:7 | 22, 25 | 1:18–15:58 | 18, 20, 26 |
| 14:5 | 312 | 1:7–8 | 203, 358 | 1:21 | 41–42, 140, 155, 169, 175, 247, 265, 278 |
| 14:8 | 203 | 1:7–9 | 23–24, 183, 257, 389 | | |
| 14:9 | 68, 385, 389 | 1:8 | 218 | 1:22–23 | 400 |
| 14:10–12 | 201 | 1:8–15:58 | 20 | 1:23 | 38, 42, 68, 135, 140, 151, 155, 199 |
| 14:14 | 182n94 | 1:9 | 22–23, 77, 152, 182, 236, 404 | | |
| 14:17 | 219 | | | 1:24 | 23, 169, 403 |
| 14:20 | 408 | 1:10 | 12, 18, 26–32, 39, 50, 154–55, 169, 257, 263 | 1:24–25 | 322 |
| 15:4 | 256 | | | 1:25–29 | 278 |
| 15:6 | 221, 404 | | | | |

439

# INDEX OF SCRIPTURE AND OTHER ANCIENT TEXTS

| | | | | | |
|---|---|---|---|---|---|
| 1:26 | 23 | 3:1–2 | 25, 74 | 4:9 | 47, 49, 105, 247, 254–55, 261, 381 |
| 1:26–31 | 42, 74, 247, 256, 360, 403 | 3:1–4 | 26, 43, 130, 265, 278, 290 | 4:9–13 | 46–47, 246–47, 254–55, 261, 408 |
| 1:29 | 256–57 | 3:1–10 | 36 | 4:9–16 | 54, 186 |
| 1:29–3:21 | 257 | 3:3 | 31, 258 | 4:9–17 | 40 |
| 1:30 | 23, 151–52, 345 | 3:5–9 | 34–35 | 4:10 | 90, 345 |
| 1:30–31 | 152 | 3:5–11 | 25 | 4:11 | 227, 246, 262 |
| 1:31 | 42–43, 256–57, 345, 402–3 | 3:5–15 | 407 | 4:14–15 | 23, 74 |
| | | 3:8 | 49, 408–9 | 4:14–21 | 246 |
| 2:1 | 25n54, 41, 43, 394 | 3:9 | 407 | 4:15 | 36, 130, 345 |
| 2:1–5 | 25, 74, 151 | 3:10 | 74, 139 | 4:17 | 22, 30, 151, 345 |
| 2:1–16 | 408 | 3:10 15 | 409 | 4:18 | 256–57 |
| 2:2 | 31n80, 135 | 3:10–16 | 45 | 4:18–19 | 42, 257 |
| 2:2–5 | 241, 343, 345 | 3:10–18 | 34 | 4:18–20 | 26, 30, 47, 54, 408 |
| 2:4 | 41, 61, 155, 175, 322, 394 | 3:10–23 | 408 | 4:18–21 | 40 |
| 2:4–5 | 35, 41–42, 140, 322 | 3:13 | 407 | 4:19 | 256–57 |
| 2:5 | 41, 155, 175, 403 | 3:13–15 | 90 | 4:19–20 | 23, 35, 322, 394 |
| 2:6 | 42–44, 224, 247, 265, 268n5 | 3:14 | 407 | 4:20 | 219 |
| | | 3:14–15 | 183 | 5–7 | 13, 20–23 |
| 2:6–8 | 44n119, 45, 232, 278 | 3:15 | 407 | 5–14 | 31, 42, 47–48, 55, 155, 265 |
| 2:6–9 | 384 | 3:16 | 31n80, 265, 288, 380 | | |
| 2:6–16 | 42–45, 58–59, 274, 384 | 3:16–17 | 182, 201, 236, 329, 350, 361 | 5:15 | 12, 15 |
| | | | | 5:16 | 24, 26 |
| 2:7 | 43–45, 320, 327, 401 | 3:17 | 23, 35 | 5:1 | 21, 31n80 |
| 2:7–8 | 300–301, 319–21 | 3:17–19 | 46 | 5:1–13 | 20–21, 246 |
| 2:8 | 42–43, 45, 247, 265, 301, 320, 401–2 | 3:17–20 | 45–46 | 5:2 | 42, 256–57 |
| | | 3:18 | 26, 31, 35, 262 | 5:4 | 322 |
| 2:9 | 43 | 3:18–19 | 265 | 5:4–5 | 201 |
| 2:11 | 42, 159, 186, 247, 265, 278, 314 | 3:18–20 | 42, 58, 278, 408 | 5:5 | 183, 203, 222, 229 |
| | | 3:18–23 | 23, 42, 247, 256, 403 | 5:6 | 42, 70, 256 |
| 2:11–12 | 328 | 3:20 | 39, 46, 139, 155, 180 | 5:6–8 | 195–96 |
| 2:12 | 43, 329, 350, 361 | 3:21 | 26, 256–57 | 5:7 | 68, 77, 79, 151, 195 |
| 2:13 | 45, 327–28, 361 | 3:21–23 | 35, 233 | 5:7–8 | 79 |
| 2:13–15 | 45 | 3:22 | 106, 147n16, 184, 395 | 5:9–13 | 186 |
| 2:14 | 42, 247, 265, 278, 329, 342, 360–61 | 3:23 | 203 | 5:13 | 201 |
| | | 4–14 | 39 | 6:1–8 | 246 |
| 2:14–15 | 45, 327–30, 342 | 4:1 | 43, 45, 58, 327 | 6:1–11 | 20–21, 251 |
| 2:14–16 | 43, 152 | 4:1–5 | 34 | 6:2 | 31n80, 218 |
| 2:15 | 36, 329, 342, 350, 361–62 | 4:2 | 43 | 6:3 | 53, 222, 233, 381 |
| | | 4:3–5 | 218 | 6:4 | 151 |
| 2:15–16 | 344–45, 348 | 4:5 | 183, 203 | 6:5 | 31n80 |
| 2:16 | 42, 247, 265, 278 | 4:6 | 33–34, 42, 256–57 | 6:9 | 238, 262 |
| 2:22–32 | 90 | 4:6–7 | 257 | 6:9–10 | 219, 233, 380 |
| 2:25–31 | 90 | 4:6–8 | 47, 54 | 6:9–11 | 152, 186, 201, 246, 251, 360 |
| 3:1 | 43, 45, 328–29, 345, 361–62 | 4:7 | 35, 40, 42, 256–57 | | |
| | | 4:8 | 157, 219 | | |

440

*Index of Scripture and Other Ancient Texts*

| | | | | | |
|---|---|---|---|---|---|
| 6:11 | 23, 30n79, 74, 76, 151, 241, 257, 329, 343, 345, 350–51, 361, 404 | | 111, 124n6, 131, 134, 178–79, 407 | 10:33 | 201 |
| | | | | 10:36–41 | 90 |
| | | 9:1–2 | 36, 106, 345 | 11–14 | 21 |
| 6:12–20 | 20–21, 32, 48, 246, 286 | 9:1–5 | 50 | 11:2 | 62, 74 |
| | | 9:1–27 | 246 | 11:2–16 | 20–21 |
| 6:13 | 38 | 9:5 | 49–50, 75, 105–6, 121, 147n16 | 11:2–14:40 | 13, 20–23 |
| 6:13–14 | 48–49, 404 | | | 11:3 | 57 |
| 6:14 | 48n125, 151, 164, 281, 322, 386, 389 | 9:6 | 122 | 11:7 | 364 |
| | | 9:8 | 258 | 11:11 | 345 |
| 6:15 | 288 | 9:11 | 328 | 11:13 | 31n80 |
| 6:15–17 | 236 | 9:12 | 150 | 11:16 | 22 |
| 6:16 | 289 | 9:12–23 | 36 | 11:17 | 53 |
| 6:17 | 329, 344–45, 348, 361–62 | 9:15 | 395 | 11:17–34 | 20–21, 151, 246, 362 |
| | | 9:15–16 | 42, 256–57 | 11:18 | 31, 50–52 |
| 6:18 | 202 | 9:19–23 | 360 | 11:18–19 | 52–53 |
| 6:19 | 31n80, 48, 203, 265, 329, 350, 361, 365, 380 | 9:20 | 400–401, 404 | 11:19 | 31, 51–52, 263 |
| | | 9:20–21 | 400 | 11:20 | 53 |
| 6:19–20 | 182, 236, 329 | 9:22 | 30n79 | 11:20–32 | 53 |
| 7 | 20 | 9:22–27 | 201 | 11:21 | 312n8 |
| 7:1 | 21 | 9:24–26 | 382, 390 | 11:21–22 | 51 |
| 7:1–40 | 21 | 9:24–27 | 186, 246 | 11:22 | 22–23, 138 |
| 7:5 | 222 | 9:24–10:22 | 152 | 11:23 | 59, 66n4, 68, 74–75, 151 |
| 7:10–11 | 68, 76, 150 | 9:25 | 50, 318 | | |
| 7:14 | 23 | 9:27 | 52, 155 | 11:23–25 | 67–68, 79, 151, 195 |
| 7:15 | 23 | 10:1 | 57 | | |
| 7:16 | 201 | 10:1–2 | 351 | 11:23–26 | 76 |
| 7:17 | 22 | 10:1–4 | 53, 74, 76, 151, 351, 361–62 | 11:23–29 | 351 |
| 7:17–18 | 23 | | | 11:24 | 77, 256 |
| 7:18–19 | 400 | 10:1–13 | 186 | 11:26 | 203, 395 |
| 7:20–22 | 23 | 10:1–22 | 246 | 11:30 | 31n80, 49, 182, 384 |
| 7:22 | 182n94, 236, 345 | 10:2 | 45, 250, 361 | 11:32 | 201, 230 |
| 7:24 | 23 | 10:3 | 351, 362 | 11:33–34 | 51 |
| 7:29 | 370 | 10:3–4 | 328, 344–45, 348, 351, 365–66 | 12:1 | 21, 45, 57, 328, 361 |
| 7:29–31 | 53, 203 | | | 12:1–3 | 360 |
| 7:34 | 23 | 10:4 | 45, 351, 361–62 | 12:1–14:40 | 20–21 |
| 7:39 | 49, 182, 345, 384 | 10:7–9 | 30n79 | 12:2–3 | 74 |
| 8:1 | 21, 42, 256–57 | 10:12 | 60 | 12:3 | 57, 59n18, 152, 241, 329, 343, 345, 350 |
| 8:1–11 | 13, 20–23 | 10:14–22 | 236 | | |
| 8:1–13 | 23, 246 | 10:16–17 | 68, 151, 351, 362, 365 | 12:3–11 | 361 |
| 8:6 | 53, 67, 77, 198n23, 221–22, 230, 234–35, 241, 257, 343, 350, 359 | 10:16–21 | 366 | 12:4 | 23, 241–42, 344 |
| | | 10:17 | 236 | 12:4–6 | 343–44, 361 |
| | | 10:19 | 370 | 12:5 | 242, 344 |
| | | 10:19–22 | 222 | 12:6 | 241–42, 344 |
| 8:7 | 30n79 | 10:30 | 241n24 | 12:8–10 | 312n8 |
| 8:11 | 77, 201, 395 | 10:31–11:1 | 246 | 12:9 | 23 |
| 9:1 | 49–50, 68, 109, | 10:32 | 22, 138 | 12:11 | 285n36 |

441

## INDEX OF SCRIPTURE AND OTHER ANCIENT TEXTS

| | | | | | |
|---|---|---|---|---|---|
| 12:12 | 315 | | 181, 183, 186, 246, 261, | 15:7–8 | 97 |
| 12:12–13 | 251 | | 394, 409 | 15:8 | 1, 10, 69–71, 105, 109, |
| 12:12–17 | 236 | 15:2–3 | 188 | | 123–24, 126–27, 129, |
| 12:13 | 130, 151, 250, 287, 329, | 15:3 | 59–60, 66, 68–71, 74–75, | | 131–35, 137, 140, 178 |
| | 344–45, 348, 351, 361, | | 77, 79, 88, 95–96, 110, | 15:8–9 | 36 |
| | 365 | | 121–23, 138, 151, 171, | 15:8–10 | 49 |
| 12:18 | 285n36 | | 181, 188, 199, 220, 242, | 15:9 | 22–23, 68, 123, 137–39, |
| 12:28 | 23 | | 337, 395, 399, 402, | | 151, 242 |
| 12:28–29 | 106 | | 410 | 15:9–10 | 69, 131, 141, 247, 257, |
| 12:30–31 | 23 | 15:3–4 | 81, 86, 94, 110, 115, | | 343–44 |
| 13:1 | 381 | | 192, 232, 282, 312 | 15:9–11 | 105, 123, 137 |
| 13:2 | 43 | 15:3–5 | 66–67, 69–70, 76, 110 | 15:10 | 78, 138, 152–53, |
| 13:3 | 42, 256 | 15:3–7 | 66–72, 76, 89, 91, 105, | | 175–76, 242, 343, |
| 13:4 | 42, 256–57 | | 115, 129, 147–48, 195 | | 408–11 |
| 13:5–7 | 312 | 15:3–8 | 1, 6–7, 10, 25, 69, 105, | 15:11 | 36, 41–42, 63, 66–67, |
| 13:7 | 185, 262 | | 123, 134, 143, 146, | | 69, 72, 75, 140–41, |
| 13:8–13 | 53, 183, 203 | | 148–49, 151, 181, 192, | | 150, 152–53, 160, |
| 13:13 | 155, 185, 262, 304 | | 195, 204, 346 | | 168–71, 175, 177, 179, |
| 13:34–37 | 90 | 15:3–11 | 40, 56, 58, 72, 170, | | 188, 254, 346 |
| 14:1 | 45, 328, 361 | | 172, 188 | 15:11–12 | 41 |
| 14:5 | 62n32 | 15:3–52 | 20 | 15:12 | 30–32, 40, 53, 58, 76, |
| 14:7 | 269 | 15:4 | 68, 80, 83, 91–96, | | 111, 154–55, 158, 160, |
| 14:9 | 269, 315 | | 107, 110, 114, 119, 134, | | 162, 164, 166, 169–72, |
| 14:12 | 315 | | 150–51, 168–69, 174, | | 177, 187–88, 192, 231, |
| 14:16 | 269 | | 192, 194–95, 204, 337 | | 242, 247, 250, 252, |
| 14:25 | 31n80 | 15:4–28 | 1, 8–9, 56, 190, 203, | | 262–63, 265, 268–69, |
| 14:33 | 22–23 | | 211 | | 310, 315 |
| 14:36 | 74 | 15:5 | 70–71, 105–6, 110–12, | 15:12–13 | 161, 163–64, 174, 184, |
| 14:37 | 45, 328–29, 361 | | 115, 121, 133, 178–79 | | 315, 343, 360 |
| 15:1 | 36, 45, 56–64, 66, 150, | 15:5–7 | 70–72, 75, 122, 126, | 15:12–17 | 173, 346 |
| | 152, 154, 160, 256, | | 129, 131–32, 141, 171, | 15:12–19 | 25, 55, 63, 141, |
| | 370, 384, 405–6 | | 179 | | 154–55, 158–59, |
| 15:1–2 | 19, 25, 30, 36, 56–59, | 15:5–8 | 50, 68, 91, 105–7, | | 166–70, 174–75, 177, |
| | 63–65, 69, 73–74, 77, | | 109–11, 116, 124, 129, | | 183–84, 187–88, |
| | 140, 177, 180, 188, 360, | | 131, 133–34, 139, | | 190–92, 194, 244, 246, |
| | 405, 407 | | 147, 151–53, 159, 171, | | 248, 315 |
| 15:1–9 | 41 | | 177–79, 188 | 15:12–21 | 172–74 |
| 15:1–11 | 36, 47, 55–56, 58–59, | 15:5–11 | 50 | 15:12–34 | 265, 269 |
| | 67, 69, 140–42, 154, | 15:6 | 25, 30n79, 49, 69–70, | 15:12–58 | 47, 58, 154 |
| | 159–60, 168, 170, 175, | | 76, 105–6, 111, 115–16, | 15:13 | 19n45, 76, 162, 166, |
| | 179, 181, 188, 384 | | 118–20, 122, 124, 133, | | 168–69, 172–76, |
| 15:1–19 | 42 | | 147, 171, 178–79, 182, | | 179–80, 188, 191–92, |
| 15:1–58 | 41, 55, 57 | | 193, 384 | | 242, 250 |
| 15:2 | 39–42, 46, 60–64, 73, | 15:6–7 | 70, 116, 122 | 15:13–15 | 166, 176, 179 |
| | 107, 139, 141, 152, 175, | 15:7 | 70–71, 105, 111, 121, 124, | 15:14 | 39–41, 46, 62–63, 111, |
| | | | 133, 147, 178–79 | | 139–40, 149, 152, 155, |

## Index of Scripture and Other Ancient Texts

| | | | | | |
|---|---|---|---|---|---|
| | 166, 168, 171, 172n56, 175–78, 180, 186, 188, 246, 254, 261, 409 | | 190–91, 202, 211, 213, 334, 337, 346 | 15:27 | 212, 231–33, 240–41 |
| | | 15:20–26 | 79 | 15:27–28 | 8, 212, 235, 240–41 |
| 15:14–15 | 175–76, 180–81, 187 | 15:20–28 | 1, 55, 245, 398, 402 | 15:28 | 190, 199, 211–13, 218, 234–44, 242, 343–44, 346, 361, 405 |
| 15:14–33 | 19n45 | 15:21 | 162, 164, 169, 173–74, 191, 194, 197–200, 230, 232, 250, 315, 335, 337–38, 349–50, 359, 389, 395, 405 | 15:29 | 1, 10, 157–58, 162–64, 169, 173–74, 245–46, 248–54, 263, 388, 401 |
| 15:15 | 25, 42, 68, 76, 79, 88, 111, 115, 150, 152, 155, 162, 166, 169, 171, 172n56, 173–74, 177–79, 186–88, 242, 250, 252, 254, 261, 343–44, 388 | | | 15:29–30 | 258 |
| | | 15:21–22 | 174, 190–91, 200, 232, 238, 244, 317, 337–38, 348, 352, 355, 395, 399 | 15:29–32 | 156, 245 |
| | | | | 15:29–33 | 264 |
| 15:15–16 | 163–64, 174, 184, 246, 388 | | | 15:29–34 | 1, 55–56, 61, 63, 159, 186–87, 245–47, 250, 254, 265, 282, 409 |
| 15:16 | 76, 168–69, 172n56, 173–74, 179–80, 184, 188, 191–92, 242, 250, 252, 262 | 15:22 | 76, 79, 174, 183, 191, 194, 200–202, 230, 242, 281, 335–37, 345, 349–50, 353, 360, 383, 395, 404 | | |
| | | | | 15:30 | 47, 246, 252–55, 260–61 |
| 15:16–17 | 166, 179 | | | 15:30–31 | 138 |
| 15:16–19 | 179n82 | 15:22–23 | 190, 343, 364 | 15:30–32 | 32, 46–47, 54, 78, 159, 245–47, 251, 253–55, 257, 260–61, 263–64, 282, 351, 364, 409, 411 |
| 15:16–20 | 343 | 15:22–58 | 172–74 | | |
| 15:17 | 39–40, 46, 62–63, 76, 138–39, 152, 155, 166, 168, 172n56, 175, 180–81, 187–88, 242, 246, 261, 399, 402, 409 | 15:23 | 76, 183, 190–91, 193, 201–3, 218, 225, 235, 242, 343, 358, 360, 402 | | |
| | | | | 15:30–34 | 40 |
| | | 15:23–26 | 124 | 15:31 | 43, 47, 76, 140, 242, 246–47, 255–57, 260–62, 343–45, 370, 395, 403, 406 |
| | | 15:23–28 | 203 | | |
| 15:17–18 | 186, 191 | 15:24 | 44, 190, 211–13, 217–18, 220–26, 230–31, 235, 240–43, 401 | | |
| 15:18 | 42, 49, 76, 79, 120–21, 156, 166, 173, 181–84, 188, 193, 242, 384, 411 | | | 15:32 | 1, 10, 11n1, 156, 162–64, 169, 173–74, 246, 250, 257, 259–63, 388, 395 |
| | | 15:24–25 | 79, 213–15, 217–18, 226, 229, 234, 380 | | |
| 15:18–19 | 173, 201, 345 | | | | |
| 15:19 | 32, 40, 54, 61, 76, 156, 158, 166, 172n56, 173, 179, 184–85, 188, 191, 242, 246–47, 262, 409, 411 | 15:24–26 | 233, 235 | 15:32–34 | 32, 47, 54 |
| | | 15:24–27 | 190, 231 | 15:33 | 31n81, 263–64 |
| | | 15:24–28 | 212, 217n25, 228, 230, 234–35, 237n111, 241, 244 | 15:33–34 | 46, 158, 160, 245, 262 |
| 15:20 | 49, 61, 76, 86, 120–21, 151, 162, 169, 174, 182, 190–93, 195–96, 202, 242, 250, 330, 336, 349, 352, 384–85 | | | 15:34 | 31, 42, 58, 152, 242, 244, 247, 264, 268, 279, 343–44, 402, 408 |
| | | 15:25 | 52, 212, 219–20, 222, 223n46, 224–28, 230–31, 233, 241, 244 | | |
| | | | | 15:35 | 31, 56, 162, 166, 169, 173–74, 250, 263, 267–74, 278–82, 286, 292, 304, 310, 317–18, 335, 388 |
| 15:20–21 | 173 | 15:26 | 194, 198, 212–13, 218, 225, 228, 230–31, 235, 244, 281, 353, 355, 388, 395, 397, 404 | | |
| 15:20–22 | 235, 337 | | | | |
| 15:20–23 | 56, 174–75 | | | 15:35–49 | 55, 265, 265 |

443

| | | | | | |
|---|---|---|---|---|---|
| 15:36 | 269, 273, 277n6, 278–80, 282–84, 303, 309, 313, 316–17, 395 | 15:42–58 | 277–78, 303, 310 | | 380, 386, 391, 402, 405, 409, 411 |
| 15:43 | 45, 295, 300, 319–22, 328–29, 391 | 15:50 | 7, 50, 219, 238, 242, 256, 293, 343–44, 368–75, 377–83, 387, 389–91, 406 |
| 15:36–37 | 316–18 | 15:43–44 | 317 | | |
| 15:36–38 | 10, 269, 274, 276–77, 288, 292–94, 296–97, 302, 305, 313, 316–17 | 15:44 | 7, 45, 242, 281, 293, 311, 318, 322, 323n42, 324–29, 331, 335–38, 341–44, 348, 351–52, 361, 363, 367–68, 370, 386, 391, 402, 411 | 15:50–53 | 56, 367–70, 378–79, 387, 389, 391–94 |
| 15:36–39 | 302 | | | 15:50–54 | 318, 390, 402 |
| 15:36–41 | 56, 275–78, 296–97, 299, 302–4, 310, 313, 315, 336–37, 353, 357, 370 | | | 15:50–58 | 55 |
| | | 15:44–45 | 371, 380 | 15:51 | 45, 49, 59, 120–21, 182, 193, 367, 370, 383 |
| | | 15:44–46 | 328, 342, 352–53 | | |
| | | 15:44–47 | 359 | 15:51–52 | 1, 45, 368–70, 382, 384, 386–87, 389–90 |
| 15:36–44 | 323 | 15:44–49 | 1, 8–9, 56, 199, 313, 333–35, 337, 342, 364–65, 396 | | |
| 15:37 | 282–85, 287, 316, 363, 391 | | | 15:51–53 | 380–82 |
| 15:37–38 | 269, 277n6, 282–83, 289, 292–94, 302–3, 309n15, 313 | 15:45 | 7, 78, 138, 194, 197, 199–200, 202, 242, 247, 273n16, 293, 334–44, 346–47, 349–55, 359–63, 365–67, 386, 389, 402, 404–5, 411 | 15:51–54 | 174, 383 |
| | | | | 15:52 | 61, 162, 164, 169, 173–74, 250, 385, 387–89, 393 |
| 15:38 | 283, 285–88, 292, 298, 303, 316, 318, 343–44 | | | 15:52–53 | 367 |
| 15:39 | 276–77, 288–89, 290n53, 291–93, 295, 297, 302–3, 313, 316, 379, 391 | | | 10:52–54 | 402 |
| | | 15:45–47 | 361 | 15:52–57 | 79 |
| | | 15:45–49 | 61, 79, 183, 197, 232, 238, 335 | 15:53 | 52, 368–70, 378, 387, 390–94 |
| 15:39–41 | 277 | 15:46 | 45, 48, 242, 281, 342–44, 352–53, 361, 363, 367, 411 | 15:53–54 | 50, 61, 284, 363, 389, 391 |
| 15:40 | 276, 289, 293, 297, 299, 301, 316, 354–55 | | | 15:53–55 | 218 |
| 15:40–41 | 45, 273n16, 276–77, 293, 294n67, 298–300, 302–3, 313, 320, 353, 357, 359–61, 363–64 | 15:46–49 | 350 | 15:53–57 | 20 |
| | | 15:47 | 197, 199, 273, 299, 335, 340n28, 354–59, 361, 363, 365, 367, 405 | 15:54 | 293, 337, 392–98, 401 |
| | | | | 15:54–55 | 244, 392–93, 397–99, 402 |
| | | | | 15:54–57 | 43, 50, 194, 213, 391–92, 399, 403–4 |
| 15:40–42 | 391 | 15:47–48 | 78, 363 | 15:54–58 | 1, 20, 56, 392 |
| 15:41 | 276, 294, 297–99, 301–2, 320 | 15:47–49 | 299–300, 353, 355, 357, 360–61, 365, 382 | 15:55 | 393, 395, 397–98 |
| | | | | 15:55–56 | 392n1, 397 |
| 15:42 | 50, 162, 163n34, 164, 169, 173–74, 250, 310, 313, 315, 317–18, 357, 370, 382, 386, 390, 394, 402 | 15:48 | 78, 138, 202, 247, 282, 288, 359–65, 367, 401–2, 404–5, 409 | 15:56 | 197, 199, 317, 338, 348, 352, 355, 360, 393, 395, 397–403, 405 |
| | | | | 15:56–57 | 138, 228, 238, 402–3 |
| 15:42–43 | 311, 322–23 | 15:48–49 | 61, 299, 359, 361, 366 | 15:57 | 76, 183, 242, 257, 343–44, 360, 392n1, 393, 402–4 |
| 15:42–44 | 56, 61, 293, 298, 310–14, 317, 328 | 15:49 | 194, 201, 238, 281, 284, 288, 350, 355, 360, 363–65, 367, | | |
| 15:42–49 | 79, 370, 383, 389 | | | | |

## Index of Scripture and Other Ancient Texts

| | | | | | | | |
|---|---|---|---|---|---|---|---|
| 15:57–58 | 343–44 | 3:5–6 | 139 | 12:1 | 111 |
| 15:58 | 19–20, 32, 39–40, | 3:6 | 342, 396 | 12:1–7 | 124, 134 |
| | 46, 54, 57–58, 61, 63, | 3:7 | 396 | 12:7 | 222 |
| | 139, 151, 175–76, 183, | 3:7–11 | 296n71 | 12:9 | 321n36 |
| | 246–47, 256, 282, | 3:8 | 269, 396 | 12:10 | 251n24 |
| | 343, 345, 348, 370, | 3:9 | 400 | 12:21 | 152 |
| | 393, 405–410 | 3:10 | 296n71 | 13:4 | 87, 321n36 |
| 16 | 15 | 3:14 | 227 | 13:5 | 182 |
| 16:1 | 21 | 3:17–18 | 344, 364 | 13:13 | 345, 343, 404 |
| 16:1–4 | 19–20, 121 | 3:18 | 44n120, 301, 320, 364, | | |
| 16:1–14 | 18–19 | | 386 | **Galatians** | |
| 16:1–27 | 19n45 | 4:4–6 | 364 | 1:1 | 75, 86, 169n46, 375 |
| 16:2 | 68 | 4:7 | 287 | 1:4 | 68, 77, 181, 220 |
| 16:3–4 | 147 | 4:13 | 253n30 | 1:8–9 | 74 |
| 16:4 | 19 | 4:14 | 182n94 | 1:9 | 59, 67n4, 74 |
| 16:8–9 | 11, 261 | 4:16 | 382n37 | 1:11 | 57, 59, 258, 375 |
| 16:10–11 | 265 | 4:17 | 186 | 1:11–12 | 75 |
| 16:12 | 35, 224, 268 | 5:1–5 | 159, 331, 398, 402 | 1:12 | 60, 75, 375 |
| 16:13 | 155, 349 | 5:5 | 287, 331, 337–38 | 1:13 | 138 |
| 16:15 | 330, 407 | 5:6–8 | 159 | 1:15 | 130 |
| 16:15–18 | 19, 21, 266, 268 | 5:10 | 201, 230 | 1:15–16 | 75–76, 128, 375 |
| 16:15–24 | 18–19 | 5:14 | 198 | 1:15–18 | 195 |
| 16:16 | 239n117, 407 | 5:21 | 78, 182n94, 352 | 1:16 | 131, 374–76, 380 |
| 16:19 | 345 | 6:1 | 176 | 1:17 | 71 |
| 16:19–20 | 18–19 | 6:16 | 182, 199 | 1:18–19 | 72, 75–76, 106, 121, |
| 16:21–22 | 18–19 | 6:16–18 | 130 | | 137, 147 |
| 16:22 | 360 | 7:9–10 | 152 | 1:19 | 121–22, 147 |
| 16:23–24 | 18–19 | 8:1 | 57 | 1:23 | 138 |
| 16:24 | 345 | 8:3 | 178 | 2:1–10 | 75, 121, 137, 195 |
| | | 8:9 | 182 | 2:2 | 76, 139, 176 |
| **2 Corinthians** | | 8:16 | 403 | 2:6–9 | 106 |
| 1:3 | 221 | 9:15 | 403 | 2:7–9 | 76 |
| 1:6 | 253n30 | 10:7 | 203 | 2:8 | 407 |
| 1:8–11 | 11n1, 259 | 10:12–18 | 403 | 2:9 | 121, 137, 139, 147 |
| 1:9 | 199, 230, 349 | 10:15 | 408 | 2:13 | 121 |
| 1:12–14 | 403 | 10:17 | 182n94, 257 | 2:14 | 169, 269 |
| 1:21–22 | 287 | 11:2–3 | 197, 338, 401 | 2:19–20 | 182 |
| 1:22 | 331, 336–37 | 11:4 | 345 | 3:2–3 | 290 |
| 1:24 | 60 | 11:7 | 59 | 3:4 | 63 |
| 2:5–7 | 33 | 11:13 | 407 | 3:5 | 345 |
| 2:14 | 403 | 11:13–15 | 34 | 3:10–14 | 198 |
| 2:15–16 | 230 | 11:22–23 | 259 | 3:13 | 78 |
| 3 | 400 | 11:23–29 | 258 | 3:16 | 238 |
| 3:3 | 199, 344 | 11:24 | 259 | 3:17 | 370n13, 400 |
| 3:5 | 139 | 11:25 | 259 | 3:17–19 | 202 |
| | | 11:31 | 221 | | |

445

| | | | | | |
|---|---|---|---|---|---|
| 3:21 | 404 | 3:7 | 139 | 3:7–11 | 24n51, 159 |
| 3:21–22 | 197 | 3:8 | 137 | 3:8 | 182n94 |
| 3:22 | 401 | 3:10 | 222 | 3:11 | 86n72, 163n34, 201 |
| 3:23 | 400 | 3:14–19 | 43n115 | 3:19–20 | 60, 183 |
| 3:26 | 182n94 | 3:16 | 44n120, 322 | 3:20–21 | 24n51, 159, 358 |
| 3:26–27 | 130 | 4:11–16 | 43n115 | 3:21 | 34, 87, 194, 224, 230, |
| 3:26–28 | 251 | 4:20–24 | 364 | | 232–33, 238, 288, 301, |
| 3:27 | 182 | 4:22 | 382n37 | | 320–21, 348, 363, 380, |
| 3:29 | 203 | 4:30 | 287 | | 386, 389 |
| 4:1 | 370n13 | 5:5 | 216, 219, 221 | 4:1 | 182n94, 406 |
| 4:2 | 227 | 5:14 | 86n72 | 4:3 | 407 |
| 4:3 | 253n30, 315 | 5:20 | 220, 251 | 4:4 | 182n94 |
| 4:4 | 236, 358 | 5:21 | 239n117 | 4:9 | 59, 67n4, 74 |
| 4:4–5 | 238, 400 | 5:24 | 239n117, 315 | 4:19 | 182n94 |
| 4:4–6 | 77, 182, 198, 343, 361 | 6:11–12 | 222 | 4:20 | 220 |
| 4:6 | 130, 343, 345–46 | | | 4:21 | 182n94 |
| 4:7 | 380 | **Philippians** | | | |
| 4:8 | 265 | 1:1 | 182n94 | **Colossians** | |
| 4:9 | 269 | 1:5 | 227 | 1:3 | 221 |
| 4:11 | 63, 139 | 1:6 | 408 | 1:11 | 44n120 |
| 4:15 | 178 | 1:10–11 | 24n51 | 1:14 | 221 |
| 4:21 | 400 | 1:13 | 182n94 | 1:15 | 364 |
| 5:5 | 185 | 1:14 | 182n94 | 1:16 | 222, 243 |
| 5:5–6 | 185 | 1:19 | 345–46 | 1:18 | 193n6 |
| 5:10 | 33, 182n94 | 1:20 | 184 | 1:27 | 44n120 |
| 5:16 | 370n13 | 1:22 | 407 | 1:28–2:3 | 43n115 |
| 5:16–25 | 290 | 1:23 | 159 | 1:29 | 139 |
| 5:18 | 400 | 1:25 | 119 | 2:10 | 222, 224 |
| 5:20 | 52n122 | 1:26 | 182n94 | 2:12 | 81, 86n72 |
| 5:24 | 202 | 1:28 | 60, 183 | 2:13–15 | 222 |
| 5:24–25 | 202–3 | 1:29 | 251 | 2:15 | 222, 224 |
| 6:11–16 | 403 | 2:5–11 | 77, 335, 361 | 2:18 | 63 |
| 6:13–14 | 182 | 2:6 | 239 | 3:1 | 220, 225n55 |
| | | 2:7–8 | 239, 348 | 3:9–11 | 364 |
| **Ephesians** | | 2:7–11 | 239 | 3:11 | 241 |
| 1:3 | 221 | 2:8 | 268n5 | 4:13 | 178 |
| 1:13–14 | 287 | 2:9–11 | 358 | | |
| 1:15–23 | 43n115 | 2:12–13 | 408 | **1 Thessalonians** | |
| 1:17 | 221 | 2:13 | 140 | 1:2–10 | 185 |
| 1:20 | 86n72, 225n55 | 2:15 | 296 | 1:3 | 185, 220, 262 |
| 1:20–21 | 222 | 2:16 | 139, 176, 407 | 1:4–6 | 343 |
| 1:20–23 | 220, 231–32 | 2:19 | 182n94 | 1:5 | 322 |
| 1:21 | 224 | 2:24 | 182n94 | 1:9 | 199 |
| 1:21–22 | 216n21 | 2:29 | 182n94 | 1:9–10 | 67 |
| 1:23 | 241 | 3:2 | 259 | 1:10 | 24n51, 86n72, 169n46 |
| 2:14–18 | 364 | 3:3 | 257n45, 290, 343, 403 | 2:1 | 139, 176 |
| 3:2 | 139 | 3:6 | 138 | | |

## Index of Scripture and Other Ancient Texts

| | | | | | |
|---|---|---|---|---|---|
| 2:12 | 44n120, 301, 320, 380 | 2:17–18 | 157 | 3:15 | 328 |
| 2:13 | 59, 67n4, 74 | 2:20 | 319n27 | 4:7 | 239n117 |
| 2:20 | 298n75 | 3:8 | 315 | 4:12 | 60, 183 |
| 3:2 | 407–8 | 4:1 | 216n21, 385, 389 | 4:14 | 184 |
| 3:5 | 139, 176, 408 | | | 5:11 | 218 |
| 3:11 | 220 | **Titus** | | 5:15 | 84n66, 85 |
| 3:11–13 | 24n51, 404 | 1:12 | 259 | | |
| 3:13 | 220 | 3:9 | 180 | **1 Peter** | |
| 4:1 | 74 | 3:10 | 52n122 | 1:3 | 221 |
| 4:5 | 265 | | | 1:4 | 382 |
| 4:13–15 | 120, 182, 193, 384 | **Philemon** | | 1:8 | 44n120 |
| 4:13–18 | 49, 185, 358 | 6 | 182n94 | 1:9 | 218 |
| 4:13–5:11 | 24n51 | 10 | 130 | 1:12 | 300, 359, 361 |
| 4:14 | 90n86 | 11 | 264 | 1:18 | 180 |
| 4:16–17 | 388 | | | 1:21 | 86n72 |
| 5:2 | 219 | **Hebrews** | | 1:23–25 | 60 |
| 5:6 | 264 | 1:3 | 225n55 | 2:20 | 269 |
| 5:8 | 185 | 1:8–13 | 216n21 | 2:24 | 78 |
| 5:8–10 | 185 | 1:13 | 225n55, 231 | 3:18 | 348 |
| 5:10 | 77, 182n91, 384 | 2:5–9 | 231 | 3:18–22 | 90n86 |
| 5:21 | 62 | 2:14 | 229 | 3:19 | 171 |
| 5:23 | 159, 186 | 3:6 | 62 | 3:22 | 222, 224, 231–32 |
| | | 3:14 | 62 | 4:5 | 385, 389 |
| **2 Thessalonians** | | 4:8 | 312 | 4:6 | 313n12 |
| 1:5 | 251n24 | 5:5 | 315 | 4:13–14 | 44n120 |
| 1:5–10 | 230 | 5:11–6:3 | 43n115 | 5:10 | 44n120 |
| 1:7–10 | 24n51 | 6:2 | 163n34, 164 | | |
| 1:8 | 265 | 7:3 | 184 | **2 Peter** | |
| 2:1–12 | 24n51 | 7:25–28 | 181n88 | 1:11 | 216 |
| 2:14 | 44, 320, 380 | 8:1 | 225n55 | 2:1 | 51 |
| 2:15 | 66n4, 73–74, 301 | 10:12 | 225n55 | 3:4 | 49, 182, 193, 384 |
| 3:6 | 60, 67n4, 74 | 10:23 | 62 | | |
| | | 11:16 | 44n117 | **1 John** | |
| **1 Timothy** | | 11:19 | 86n72 | 1:1–4 | 111 |
| 1:12 | 403 | 11:35 | 388n59 | 1:2 | 112, 115, 178 |
| 1:27 | 61n24 | | | 1:10 | 152 |
| 3:16 | 348 | **James** | | 2:24 | 74 |
| 5:19 | 62n32 | 1:2 | 224 | 3:1 | 130 |
| 6:13 | 199 | 1:11 | 315 | 3:9–10 | 130 |
| | | 1:18 | 330 | 3:16 | 253n30 |
| **2 Timothy** | | 1:26 | 180 | 4:17 | 253n30 |
| 1:3 | 403 | 1:27 | 220 | 5:1–2 | 130 |
| 1:7 | 322 | 2:17 | 315 | 5:4 | 130 |
| 1:10 | 60–61 | 2:26 | 315 | 5:10 | 152 |
| 2:8 | 86 | 3:5 | 315 | 5:16 | 312 |
| 2:10 | 318 | 3:13–18 | 328 | 5:18 | 130 |

447

# INDEX OF SCRIPTURE AND OTHER ANCIENT TEXTS

3 John
7 251n24
12 253n30

Jude
3 66n44, 73–74
19 328, 342, 360

Revelation
1:5 193n6
1:6 221, 296
2:13 253
2:28 296, 302
3:17 186
4:2 358
5:2 171
9:20 222
10:1 296
11:1 84n66
11:15 216n21
12:1 296
12:10 224
13:2 223
15:8 322
19:1 322
21:4 230
21:8 230
21:14 113
21:23 296, 302
22:3 216
22:5 296, 302
22:16 296, 302

## RABBINIC TEXTS

b. Sanhedrin
91a 365n84

Genesis Rabbah
14:7 365n84

m. Berakot
5:2 199

## APOSTOLIC FATHERS

1 Clement
5–6 106, 148
24 275, 280
24–26 4n6, 297n73, 309
34 44
49.6 330
59.4 85

2 Clement
9.4 270
9.5 346n37
14.5 331
20.5 358

Shepherd of Hermas
Mandates
1.1.1 300n80, 358n68

Similitudes
9.23.5 52

Visions
1.4.1 85
2.1.3 85
2.2.7 381
3.2.4 85
9.25.2 381
9.27.2 381

## EARLY CHRISTIAN TEXTS

Ambrose
De Spiritu Sancto
1.11.120 345
1.66 360n71, 361n74

Epistulae
41.7 78n41

Athanasius
De incarnatione
6–9 78
50.6 252

Orationes contra Arianos
2.19.3 252
2.55 78

Athenagoras
De resurrectione
4.4 166, 271

Legatio pro Christianis
8 358n68
8.4.7 300n80
16.1 242–43

Augustine
Contra Faustum Manichaeum
2.4 358n67

De civitate Dei
13.23 358n67, 359, 366
13.23–24 338n15
20.20 4n6
22.4 101
22.21–24 4n6

De doctrina christiana
4.11 17
4.11–12 17
4.15 17

De Trinitate
1.14–15 239n118
1.20 239n119
5.11 346n27
12.6.6 364n80
14.18 78n41
16.21 78n41

In Evangelium Johannis tractatus
99.7 346n27

448

# Index of Scripture and Other Ancient Texts

**Basil of Caesarea**

*De Spiritu Sancto*
18.45     364n80

*Epistulae*
236.4     253n30

**Clement of Alexandria**

*Paedagogus*
1.5     216

*Protrepticus*
1.7     350n41
4.50     300n80
11.86     358

*Stromateis*
5.12.81     300n80, 358n68
5.38.6     300n80, 358n68

**Constitutiones apostolorum**
7.41     4n9, 90n87, 91n88

**Cyprian**

*De catholicae ecclesiae unitate*
4     112

*De lapsis*
17     78

*Epistulae*
33.1     112
43.5     112
70.2     287n44, 331n63

**Cyril of Alexandria**

*De adoratione*
1     345

*Quod unus sit Christus*
723c     363n79
723c–d     358n67
725b     360n71, 361n74
725b–c     358n67
771c–d     358n67
772d–773     341, 346n38

*Thesaurus*
34     345

**Cyril of Jerusalem**

*Catecheses*
13.33     78n41
15.29–30     217n25

**Didascalia Apostolorum**
23     52n135

**Epiphanius**

*Ancoratus*
8     345
71     345
73     345
75     345

**Epistle of Barnabas**
5.5     364n80

**Epistle to Diognetus**
5     78n41

**Eusebius**

*Demonstratio evangelica*
4.12     78n41

*Historia ecclesiastica*
2.25.6–7     148n17
2.25.8     147n16, 148n17
5.1.44     259
5.1.50–52     259

**Gregory of Nazianzus**

*Epistulae*
101     358n67

*Orationes*
30.4–5     239

**Gregory of Nyssa**

*De anima et resurrectione*
1898–1923     3n5

*De Spiritu Sancto*
6     345

*In sanctum pascha*
9.52     387n52
251–270     3n5

*Quod non sint tres dei*
10     345

**Gregory the Great**

*Moralia in Job*
17.30.46     78n41

**Hilary**

*De Trinitate*
1.33     237n107
2.29     345
7.37     364n80
10.17     358n67
11.8     237n107
11.30–49     239n118
12.55–57     345

**Hippolytus**

*Contra haeresin Noeti*
4     346n37

*Traditio apostolica*
21     287n44, 331n63

**Ignatius**

*To the Ephesians*
1.2     260
6.2     51

## INDEX OF SCRIPTURE AND OTHER ANCIENT TEXTS

*To the Romans*
4.3      106, 148n17
5.1      260

*To the Smyrnaeans*
1.1–2      90n86

*To the Trallians*
6.1      51
9      90n86
10      260

### Irenaeus

*Adversus haereses*
1.10.1      90n86
1.30.13      3, 83n61
2.30.8      345–46n37
2.30.9      300n80, 358n68
3.1–3      148n17
3.3.2      106
3.4.2      90n86
3.9.2      216
3.16.6      90n86
4.20.1      364
5.1.3      345–46n37
5.7–14      4n6
5.8.1–2      331
5.9.3      360n71, 361n74
5.9–10      372
5.12.2      341, 352n46
5.12.2–3      338
5.12.3      346n38
5.12.4      332, 391
5.35.1      381

*Epideixis*
56      216
71      346n37

### Jerome

*Adversus Joannem Hierosolymitanum liber*
25–36      3n5

*Adversus Jovianum libri II*
1.26      112

*Commentariorum in Isaiam libri XVIII*
14.53.5      78n41

*Epistulae*
108.23–24      4n6

### John Chrysostom

*Homiliae in epistulam i ad Corinthios*
3.1      34n95
12.1      34–35n97
23.3      249n12
38.2      60n20, 65n40
40.2      249n12
40.3      254n33
40.4      265n83
41      341
41.2      279n15, 280, 281n17, 307
41.3      282n25
42.3      387n52

### John of Damascus

*De fide orthodoxa*
1.12      345
4.18      239n118

### Justin Martyr

*Apologia i*
20      29n77
21.1      90n86
31.7      90n86
42.4      90n86
46.5      90n86

*Dialogus cum Tryphone*
34      216
35.3      51, 52n135
46      216
52.2      84n65
56      300, 358n68
60      300
60.2      358n68
63.1      90n86
76      216
85.2      90n86
95      78n41
114.2–3      233
127      300, 358n68
132.1      90n86
135      216
138.2      233

### Martyrdom of Polycarp
2      44
2.3      381
14.2      318, 330

### Methodius

*De resurrectione*
1.13      358n67
1.13–14      4n6
2–3      3n5
2.5      363n79

### Minucius Felix

*Octavius*
18.7–8      300n80, 358n68
32.1      300n80, 358n68
32.7      300n80
34.11–12      297n73, 309

### Olympiodorus

*Commentarii in Job*
44      126

### Origen

*Commentarium in evangelium Matthaei*
17.29–30      3

*Contra Celsum*
3.12      51
5.14      166, 272, 318n25
5.18–23      3
8.48–49      166

## Index of Scripture and Other Ancient Texts

*De principiis*

| | |
|---|---|
| 2.10–11 | 3 |

*Homiliae in Exodum*

| | |
|---|---|
| 5.4 | 112 |

*Selecta in Psalmos*

| | |
|---|---|
| 11.384 | 3 |

### Pseudo-Clementines

*Homilies*

| | |
|---|---|
| 16.4.3 | 29n75 |
| 16.21.4 | 52n135 |

### Rufinus

*Commentarius in symbolum apostolorum*

| | |
|---|---|
| 41–47 | 4n6 |
| 42–45 | 3n5 |

### Severian of Gabala

*Fragmenta in epistulam i ad Corinthios*

| | |
|---|---|
| 272 | 125 |

### Tatian

*Oratio ad Graecos*

| | |
|---|---|
| 7.1 | 346n37, 358 |

### Tertullian

*Adversus Marcionem*

| | |
|---|---|
| 1.13 | 308 |
| 1.14 | 287n44, 331n63 |
| 4.5 | 148n17 |
| 4.39 | 216 |
| 5.9 | 216 |
| 5.10 | 249n11, 352n46, 360n71 |

*Adversus Praxean*

| | |
|---|---|
| 2 | 90n86 |
| 4 | 345 |
| 8 | 345 |

*Apologeticus*

| | |
|---|---|
| 21.10–14 | 346n37 |
| 23.12 | 346n37 |
| 48.5 | 271 |
| 48.7–9 | 275, 280, 297, 309 |
| 50.13–15 | 253 |

*De anima*

| | |
|---|---|
| 54–55 | 356 |

*De baptismo*

| | |
|---|---|
| 7–8 | 287n44, 331n63 |

*De carne Christi*

| | |
|---|---|
| 8 | 358n67, 360n71, 361n74 |
| 17 | 341 |

*De monogamia*

| | |
|---|---|
| 8 | 112 |

*De praescriptione haereticorum*

| | |
|---|---|
| 5 | 52n134 |
| 13 | 90n86 |
| 36 | 148n17 |

*De pudicitia*

| | |
|---|---|
| 21 | 112 |

*De resurrectione carnis*

| | |
|---|---|
| 6 | 364n80 |
| 8 | 287n44, 331n63 |
| 48.5 | 272 |
| 48–57 | 4n6, 44 |
| 49 | 358n67 |
| 52–53 | 352n46 |
| 53 | 341, 358n67 |

*De virginibus velandis*

| | |
|---|---|
| 1 | 90n86 |

### Theodoret

*Interpretatio epistulae i ad Corinthios*

| | |
|---|---|
| 368 | 373 |

### Theophilus of Antioch

*Ad Autolycum*

| | |
|---|---|
| 1.10 | 74 |
| 1.14 | 44 |
| 2.3 | 300n80, 358n68 |
| 2.6–7 | 74 |
| 2.10 | 74 |

### Zosimus of Panopolis

*Cheirokmeta*

| | |
|---|---|
| 2.203 | 125–26 |

## GNOSTIC TEXTS

### Gospel of Philip

| | |
|---|---|
| 56.26–57.22 | 3, 83n61 |

## GRECO-ROMAN LITERATURE

### Achilles Tatius

*Leucippe et Clitophon*

| | |
|---|---|
| 5.22.2 | 242n123, 243 |

### Aeschines

*In Timarchum*

| | |
|---|---|
| 4 | 74 |

### Aeschylus

*Choephori*

| | |
|---|---|
| 373 | 205 |

*Eumenides*

| | |
|---|---|
| 647–649 | 197n22 |
| 648 | 162, 166, 209, 271 |
| 649 | 396 |

### Anthologia palatina

| | |
|---|---|
| 11.56.1–2 | 262n69 |

451

## INDEX OF SCRIPTURE AND OTHER ANCIENT TEXTS

**Antiphon**

*De choreuta*
7      29n74

**Appian**

*Bella civilia*
2.4.25      242–43
4.12.97      28
5.1.2      51
5.8.7      51

**Apuleius**

*De deo Socratico*
3      300

*Metamorphoses*
11      208

**Aretaeus**

*De causis et signis diuturnorum morborum*
     126n12

**Aristophanes**

*Ecclesiazusae*
71      84n65

*Lysistrata*
18      84n64
306      84n65

*Nubes*
9      84n64

*Ranae*
154–164      206
455–459      206

**Aristotle**

*Categoriae*
15a13–15b16      385n47

*De anima*
407b–408b      208

407b20–23      363
409a31      29
412a11–412b9      283
412b26–27      283
415b      208
430a      208

*De caelo*
2.92a      294
270a13–35      385
278a33      376
284a.12–13      300
300b29      376

*De generatione animalium*
724b21–22      283
728b35–36      283
731a6–10      306n8
731b–732a      304
739b35–740a2      306n8
740b6–8      306n8
741b34–37      306n8
773b      125–26

*De generatione et corruptione*
317a32–320a8      385n47

*De partibus animalium*
641b      286
641b26–28      287

*Ethica eudemia*
1248a      234n94

*Ethica nicomachea*
116b      84n65
1099a7–12      327
1101b      234n94
1101b34–35      323n42
1117b28–1118a2      323nn41–42

*Fragmenta*
5.30.197      363

*Magna moralia*
1211a26–28      295

*Metaphysica*
1034a6–7      376

1041b      234n94
1042a32–1042b8      385n47
1072a–1074b      286

*Oeconomica*
13.45a      84n64, 85n67

*Physica*
203a      242
224a21–225a19      385n47
236a6      386
244b1–245a12      385n47
258b–260a      286

*Politica*
1270a      400n23

**Bacchylides**

*Epinicia*
3.23–62      205n4

**Callimachus**

*Epigrammata*
11.1–2      182n90

*Hymnus in Cererem*
1–2      308
119–123      308
134–138      308

**Catullus**

*Carmina*
5.5–6      182n90

**Cicero**

*De divinatione*
2.25      197n22, 209n11, 396n7

*De finibus*
1.3      38

*De legibus*
1.3–5      101, 112, 134

*De natura deorum*
2.42–43      294n67, 356

452

## Index of Scripture and Other Ancient Texts

| | | | | | |
|---|---|---|---|---|---|
| 2.62 | 101 | **Dio Chrysostom** | | **Epictetus** | |
| 2.66–67 | 308–9 | *De regno iv* | | *Diatribai* | |
| *De officiis* | | 135 | 29n75 | 1.1.10–12 | 197n22, 209n11, 396n7 |
| 2.43 | 38n112 | *De Socrate* | | 1.4.21 | 63n35 |
| *De republica* | | 1 | 242n124 | 1.5.6 | 84n63 |
| 2.17–20 | 101 | *De tumultu* | | 1.6.33 | 234n94 |
| 3.32 | 101 | 2 | 62n32 | 2.19.20 | 51 |
| 6.9–29 | 208 | | | 2.23.3–4 | 63n35 |
| 6.15 | 294 | **Diodorus Siculus** | | 2.26.1 | 234 |
| 6.17 | 300 | *Bibliotheca historica* | | 3.7.5–7 | 323n41 |
| *Epistulae ad familiares* | | 2.29 | 51 | 3.13.17 | 278n10 |
| 10.32.3 | 259n52 | 4.38.5 | 100 | 3.22.85 | 278n10 |
| 89.4 | 38 | 6.96 | 242n123, 243 | 3.23.17 | 278n10 |
| *Tusculanae disputationes* | | 7.44–45 | 167n47 | 3.23.19 | 119 |
| 1.1 | 38 | 7.65–83 | 167n47 | 3.23.35 | 119 |
| 1.13 | 208 | 7.106 | 323n42, 327 | 3.24.112 | 63n35 |
| 1.24–76 | 208 | 7.137 | 356 | 4.1.47 | 84n63 |
| 1.38–39 | 207 | 7.151 | 102 | 4.3.3 | 63n35 |
| 1.77 | 208 | 7.155 | 356 | 4.8.36 | 281n21, 306 |
| 2.26 | 263n75 | 7.156 | 340 | 4.11.27 | 63n35 |
| 4.26 | 38n112 | 7.156–157 | 208 | *Enchiridion* | |
| 5.9 | 38 | 8.1–23 | 206 | 20 | 74 |
| | | 8.27 | 294n67 | **Euripides** | |
| **Cornutus** | | 10.29.1 | 84n64 | *Alcestis* | |
| *De natura deorum* | | | | 127 | 162 |
| 28 | 308 | **Diogenes Laertius** | | 155 | 77–78n38 |
| 28.42–45 | 309 | *Vitae philosophorum* | | 282 | 77–78n38 |
| 28.45–49 | 309 | 1.120 | 51n132 | 284 | 77–78n38 |
| | | 8.67–69 | 101 | 340 | 77–78n38 |
| **Demosthenes** | | | | 461 | 77–78n38 |
| *De corona* | | **Dionysius of Halicarnassus** | | 524 | 77–78n38 |
| 43 | 242n123, 243 | *Antiquitates romanae* | | 682 | 77–78n38 |
| *In Timocratem* | | 1.67.3 | 29n75 | 690 | 77–78n38 |
| 131 | 400n23 | 4.70.4 | 28n73 | 701 | 77–78n38 |
| | | 6.13.4 | 119 | 716 | 77–78n38 |
| | | 7.72.13 | 192 | 956 | 77–78n38 |
| **Dio Cassius** | | *Ars rhetorica* | | 1006–1163 | 206 |
| *Historiae romanae* | | 8.12 | 29n77 | *Andromache* | |
| 67.14 | 259n54 | 9.6 | 29n77 | 1254–1262 | 100, 205 |
| 77.18.4 | 101 | 9.11 | 242n122 | 1259–1262 | 99, 205 |
| | | | | *Bacchae* | |
| | | | | 1330–1339 | 100, 205 |

453

INDEX OF SCRIPTURE AND OTHER ANCIENT TEXTS

*Fragmenta*
| | |
|---|---|
| 1024 | 262 |

*Hecuba*
| | |
|---|---|
| 34–44 | 99 |

*Helena*
| | |
|---|---|
| 1666–1669 | 100, 205 |

*Iphigenia taurica*
| | |
|---|---|
| 435–438 | 99, 205 |

**Eustathius**

*Commentarii ad Homeri Iliadem*
| | |
|---|---|
| 4.298 | 126 |

**Galen**

*De constitutione artis medicae*
| | |
|---|---|
| 1.255.2–5 | 291n60 |

**Herodotus**

*Historiae*
| | |
|---|---|
| 2.81 | 206 |
| 3.62.3–4 | 162, 271 |
| 3.157 | 242n123, 243 |
| 4.9.1 | 84n64 |
| 4.15.2 | 101 |
| 4.15.3 | 101 |
| 4.32–36 | 206 |
| 6.69 | 101n12 |
| 7.49.6 | 84n65 |
| 8.69 | 73 |
| 8.94 | 73 |
| 9.86 | 73 |

**Hesiod**

*Opera et dies*
| | |
|---|---|
| 18 | 300 |
| 108–120 | 205 |
| 156–173 | 204 |
| 167 | 204 |
| 383–384 | 308n11 |
| 561–569 | 308n11 |

*Theogonia*
| | |
|---|---|
| 666 | 84n65 |

**Hesychius**

*Lexicon*
| | |
|---|---|
| ε 1770 | 125n9, 126 |

**Hippocrates**

*De morbis mulierum*
| | |
|---|---|
| 1.64 | 126n12 |
| 2.1 | 126n12 |
| 2.13 | 126n12 |

*De natura muliebri*
| | |
|---|---|
| 1.63 | 126n12 |
| 2 | 125 |

*De natura pueri*
| | |
|---|---|
| 11 | 306n8 |

*De octimestri*
| | |
|---|---|
| 1–13 | 126 |
| 9 | 125 |

*Praenotiones coacae*
| | |
|---|---|
| 532 | 125 |

**Homer**

*Ilias*
| | |
|---|---|
| 2.440 | 84n65 |
| 4.352 | 84n65 |
| 5.208 | 84n65 |
| 5.413 | 84n64 |
| 9.424 | 74 |
| 11.241 | 182n90 |
| 15.643 | 73 |
| 16.433 | 197n22, 209n11, 397n7 |
| 17.446–447 | 186 |
| 21.55–56 | 162, 271 |
| 24.344 | 84n64 |
| 24.551 | 162, 165, 271 |
| 24.756 | 162, 271 |

*Odyssea*
| | |
|---|---|
| 3.229–238 | 197n22, 396n7 |
| 3.236–237 | 205 |
| 4.561–569 | 100, 204–5 |
| 4.563–565 | 100, 205 |
| 5.333–338 | 100 |
| 5.48 | 84n64 |
| 8.180 | 73 |
| 11.147 | 163n32 |
| 11.219 | 376 |
| 11.298–304 | 100 |
| 15.46 | 84n64 |
| 24.164 | 84n65 |

**Homeric Hymns**

*Hymn to Aphrodite*
| | |
|---|---|
| 256–272 | 205 |
| 259 | 205 |

*Hymn to Demeter*
| | |
|---|---|
| 39–383 | 309 |
| 223–262 | 209 |
| 360–495 | 309 |
| 398–403 | 308 |
| 401–403 | 308n11 |
| 441–489 | 308 |
| 470–482 | 206 |

*Hymn to Dionysus*
| | |
|---|---|
| 29 | 205n4 |

**Hyginus**

*Fabulae*
| | |
|---|---|
| 2 | 100 |
| 4 | 100 |
| 36 | 100 |
| 51 | 206 |
| 80 | 100 |
| 102 | 100 |
| 224 | 100 |

**Isocrates**

*Antidosis*
| | |
|---|---|
| 154 | 29n74 |
| 226 | 29n74 |

## Index of Scripture and Other Ancient Texts

*Archidamus*
| | |
|---|---|
| 37 | 28n73 |
| 58 | 321n36 |

*Epistulae*
| | |
|---|---|
| 7.13 | 29n74 |

*Evagoras*
| | |
|---|---|
| 27 | 29n74 |
| 53 | 28n73 |

*Helenae encomium*
| | |
|---|---|
| 39.4 | 29n74 |

*Nicocles*
| | |
|---|---|
| 50 | 29n74 |

*Panegyricus*
| | |
|---|---|
| 28–29 | 308 |

*Philippus*
| | |
|---|---|
| 122 | 28n73 |

*Plataicus*
| | |
|---|---|
| 32 | 28n73 |

## Leontius

*Contra Nestorianos*
| | |
|---|---|
| 3.1605 | 126n12 |

## Lucian

*Abdicatus*
| | |
|---|---|
| 21 | 242n123, 243n125 |

*Anacharsis*
| | |
|---|---|
| 25 | 63n35 |
| 38 | 63n35 |

*De luctu*
| | |
|---|---|
| 19 | 62n32 |

*De morte Peregrini*
| | |
|---|---|
| 11 | 242n123, 243n125 |
| 36–42 | 101 |

*Dialogi meretricii*
| | |
|---|---|
| 1.2 | 62n32 |

*Dialogi mortuorum*
| | |
|---|---|
| 11.4 | 62n32 |

*Fugitivi*
| | |
|---|---|
| 19 | 259 |
| 23 | 259 |

*Hermotimus*
| | |
|---|---|
| 7 | 101 |

*Philopseudes*
| | |
|---|---|
| 17 | 62n32 |

*Piscator*
| | |
|---|---|
| 6 | 62n32 |

*Pro imaginibus*
| | |
|---|---|
| 23 | 62n32 |
| 28 | 62n32 |

*Rhetorum praeceptor*
| | |
|---|---|
| 3 | 38 |
| 4 | 38 |
| 6 | 38 |
| 6–7 | 38 |
| 9–10 | 38 |
| 11–15 | 38 |
| 14 | 38 |
| 16 | 38 |
| 23–24 | 38 |
| 24–25 | 38 |
| 26 | 38 |

*Tyrannicida*
| | |
|---|---|
| 12–13 | 62n32 |

## Lucretius

*De rerum natura*
| | |
|---|---|
| 1–3 | 197n22, 209n11, 396n7 |
| 3.417–829 | 208 |
| 5.110–145 | 294n67 |

## Lysias

*Contra Simonem*
| | |
|---|---|
| 21 | 29n74 |

*De caede Eratosthenis*
| | |
|---|---|
| 36 | 29n74 |

| | |
|---|---|
| 47 | 29n74 |

*Epitaphius*
| | |
|---|---|
| 67 | 28n73 |

*In Eratosthenem*
| | |
|---|---|
| 58 | 28n73 |

*Orationes*
| | |
|---|---|
| 25.3 | 28n73 |
| 25.15 | 28n73 |
| 25.21 | 28n73 |
| 25.29 | 28n73 |
| 26.18 | 28n73 |

## Megasthenes

*Fragmenta*
| | |
|---|---|
| 30 | 29n77 |

## Ovid

*Metamorphoses*
| | |
|---|---|
| 8.741–779 | 205 |
| 9.251–272 | 101 |

## Pausanias

*Graeciae descriptio*
| | |
|---|---|
| 1.42.7 | 100 |
| 3.13.1 | 100 |
| 3.16.6 | 101n12 |
| 3.19.9–10 | 100 |
| 6.9.6–8 | 101 |

## Petronius

*Satyricon*
| | |
|---|---|
| 34 | 262n69 |

## Philodemus

*De morte*
| | |
|---|---|
| 1 | 208 |
| 19 | 208 |
| 20 | 208 |
| 26 | 208 |
| 28–32 | 208 |

## INDEX OF SCRIPTURE AND OTHER ANCIENT TEXTS

**Philostratus**

*Heroicus*
| | |
|---|---|
| 2.9–11 | 103n22 |
| 7.3 | 102, 103n22 |
| 8–22 | 208 |
| 18.1–2 | 102, 110 |
| 20.4–21.1 | 102 |
| 21.1 | 110 |
| 28.1 | 100 |
| 33.47 | 102 |
| 43.3 | 102 |
| 52–57 | 208 |
| 52.3–54.1 | 99 |
| 53.10 | 99, 209 |
| 58.2 | 103n22 |

*Vita Apollonii*
| | |
|---|---|
| 5.42 | 101 |
| 8.31 | 101 |

**Pindar**

*Isthmionikai*
| | |
|---|---|
| 8.54–67 | 99 |

*Nemeonikai*
| | |
|---|---|
| 4.49–50 | 99, 205 |
| 10.55–90 | 100 |

*Olympionikai*
| | |
|---|---|
| 2.28–30 | 100 |
| 2.55–80 | 207 |
| 2.70–71 | 207 |
| 2.71–76 | 100, 205 |
| 2.78 | 100, 205 |
| 2.78–80 | 99, 205 |

*Pythionikai*
| | |
|---|---|
| 2.73–74 | 100, 205 |
| 3.100–103 | 99 |
| 10.29–49 | 205 |

**Plato**

*Alcibiades major*
| | |
|---|---|
| 113d | 295 |

*Apologia*
| | |
|---|---|
| 17a1–18a6 | 119 |
| 20d4–21a8 | 119 |
| 30a | 84n65 |
| 30a7–30d5 | 119 |
| 31a | 84n64 |
| 33c7–34b5 | 119 |
| 35e1–36b2 | 119 |
| 37e3–38b9 | 119 |
| 39e1–42a5 | 119 |

*Crito*
| | |
|---|---|
| 47c | 234n94 |

*Euthyphro*
| | |
|---|---|
| 13a | 234n94 |

*Gorgias*
| | |
|---|---|
| 449c2 | 29n77 |

*Leges*
| | |
|---|---|
| 828d | 207 |

*Parmenides*
| | |
|---|---|
| 129c | 295 |

*Phaedo*
| | |
|---|---|
| 66 | 207 |
| 79b | 234n94 |
| 80a–84b | 207 |

*Phaedrus*
| | |
|---|---|
| 245c–249d | 207 |
| 247 | 207, 300n80 |
| 248a–249d | 207 |
| 250 | 207 |

*Politicus*
| | |
|---|---|
| 285d | 234n94 |

*Protagoras*
| | |
|---|---|
| 312e | 234n94 |

*Respublica*
| | |
|---|---|
| 440c | 84n65 |
| 522c | 74 |
| 600d | 206 |

*Theaetetus*
| | |
|---|---|
| 178b | 29 |

*Timaeus*
| | |
|---|---|
| 38c | 294 |
| 38e–39a | 294 |
| 41a–42e | 197n22, 209n11, 396n7 |
| 41a–43a | 207 |
| 41c–42d | 207 |
| 44a–c | 207 |
| 46a | 84 |
| 69c–d | 207 |
| 69c–73d | 197n22, 209n11, 396n7 |
| 81d–e | 207 |
| 90a–d | 207 |
| 90–92 | 207 |

**Pliny**

*Naturalis historia*
| | |
|---|---|
| 35.51 | 100 |

**Plutarch**

*Cato Minor*
| | |
|---|---|
| 62.3 | 29n74 |

*Consolatio ad uxorem*
| | |
|---|---|
| 10 | 103–4n25, 208, 363n78 |

*De defectu oraculorum*
| | |
|---|---|
| 2.415c–416c | 205 |
| 417b–c | 208 |

*De facie in orbe lunae*
| | |
|---|---|
| 38–30 | 208 |

*De fato*
| | |
|---|---|
| 574o | 234n94 |

*De genio Socratis*
| | |
|---|---|
| 21–22 | 208 |

*De Iside et Osiride*
| | |
|---|---|
| 357a–b | 209 |
| 357f–358b | 309 |

## Index of Scripture and Other Ancient Texts

| | | | | | |
|---|---|---|---|---|---|
| 358a–b | 103, 309 | 1.106 | 206 | **Sophocles** | |
| 359a–d | 103, 309 | 2.113 | 205n4 | *Elektra* | |
| 364f–365a | 103–4, 309 | 2.120 | 205n4 | 927 | 162 |
| 365a | 104 | 2.160 | 100 | 940–941 | 271 |
| 377b | 103n22, 104 | 3.137 | 100 | | |
| 377b–e | 308n11 | 3.171 | 209 | *Trachiniae* | |
| 378d–379c | 308 | *Epitome* | | 1106 | 300 |
| 382a–f | 103 | 5.5 | 99 | | |
| 382b | 319 | 6.30 | 100, 205 | **Soranus** | |
| 382e–f | 309 | | | *Gynaecia* | |
| **Demosthenes** | | **Pseudo-Hippocrates** | | 1.44 | 125 |
| 9.6 | 62n32 | *Epistulae* | | 1.52 | 125 |
| | | 27.130–131 | 110 | 3.17 | 125 |
| *De placita philosophorum* | | | | 3.26 | 126 |
| 1.8 | 323 | **Pseudo-Plato** | | 3.40 | 126 |
| | | | | 3.47 | 125–26 |
| *De vitioso pudore* | | *Definitiones* | | 4.1–13 | 128 |
| 531a | 250 | 415c3 | 400n23 | | |
| *Pompeius* | | | | **Strabo** | |
| 36.4 | 85n67 | **Seneca** | | *Geographica* | |
| *Quaestionum convivialum* | | *Ad Marciam de consolatione* | | 12.8.7 | 29n77 |
| 672c | 363 | 24–26 | 208 | 14.5.9 | 262n69 |
| | | | | 15.1.57 | 29n77, 206 |
| *Romulus* | | *Ad Polybium de consolatione* | | 15.3.7–8 | 29 |
| 28.5–6 | 101 | 9.3 | 208 | | |
| | | 9.8 | 208 | **Theognis** | |
| *Sulla* | | | | | |
| 3.4 | 363 | *De providentia* | | *Elegiae* | |
| | | 6.5–8 | 197n22, 209n11, | 1.567–570 | 262n69, 319 |
| *Vitae decem oratorum* | | | 396n7 | | |
| 846e | 29n74 | | | **Theophrastus** | |
| | | *Epistulae morales* | | | |
| **Polybius** | | 99.13 | 259n53 | *De causis plantarum* | |
| *Historiae* | | 102.21 | 208 | 1.7.1–5 | 306n8 |
| 2.62.4 | 28n73 | 102.28–29 | 208 | 1.7.2 | 306 |
| 5.104.1 | 28n73 | | | 2.13.1 | 234n94 |
| 6.5.7 | 323n42 | **Sextus Empiricus** | | 4.1.1 | 279 |
| 38.10.8 | 28n73 | *Adversus mathematicos* | | 4.1.2 | 284 |
| | | 7.387 | 296 | 4.1.3 | 307 |
| **Pseudo-Apollodorus** | | 9.13 | 38 | 4.2.2 | 284 |
| *Bibliotheca* | | | | 4.3.3–6 | 306n8 |
| 1.15 | 206 | *Pyrrhoniae hypotyposes* | | 4.7.4–7 | 306n8 |
| 1.27 | 205n4 | 1.16 | 51n132 | 5.11.1–5.18.4 | 34 |
| 1.31 | 209 | 1.17 | 51n132 | | |

INDEX OF SCRIPTURE AND OTHER ANCIENT TEXTS

*Historia plantarum*

| | |
|---|---|
| 8.1.1–3 | 306n8 |
| 8.1.2 | 308n11 |
| 8.3.4 | 284 |
| 8.4.1 | 284 |
| 8.8.1 | 307 |
| 8.11.1 | 307 |

**Thucydides**

*Historiae*

| | |
|---|---|
| 1.113.2 | 28n73 |
| 2.74 | 53n137 |
| 2.75 | 53n137 |
| 3.70.6 | 28n73 |
| 4.20 | 29n76 |
| 5.31.6 | 28n73 |
| 5.46.4 | 28n73 |

**Vergil**

*Aeneid*

| | |
|---|---|
| 6.730–751 | 208 |

**Xenophon**

*Cynegeticus*

| | |
|---|---|
| 1.6 | 162 |

*Cyropaedia*

| | |
|---|---|
| 2.1.4 | 29 |

*Memorabilia*

| | |
|---|---|
| 3.63 | 234n94 |
| 4.2.20 | 234n94 |

*Oeconomicus*

| | |
|---|---|
| 5.4 | 85n67 |